JOURNEYS TO THE BANDSTAND

THIRTY JAZZ LIVES IN VANCOUVER

CHRIS WONG

FriesenPress

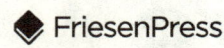

One Printers Way
Altona, MB R0G 0B0
Canada

www.friesenpress.com

Copyright © 2024 by Chris Wong
First Edition — 2024

All rights reserved.

No part of this publication may be reproduced in any form, or by any means, electronic or mechanical, including photocopying, recording, or any information browsing, storage, or retrieval system, without permission in writing from FriesenPress.

Front cover photos by Bill Boyle (John Dawe), Jesse Cahill (Jodi Proznick), Chris Cameron (Ornette Coleman), Vincent Lim (Natasha D'Agostino, Bruno Hubert), Franz Lindner (Charles Mingus), Mark Miller (Ross Taggart), Steve Mynett (Hugh Fraser, Ron Small, Dr. Lonnie Smith, Amanda Tosoff, Brad Turner, Cory Weeds), and unknown photographers (Jim Kilburn, Dave Quarin).
Back cover photo by Franz Lindner (Ernestine Anderson).
Author photo by Amanda Palmer.

Edited by David Ferman.

ISBN
978-1-03-916161-0 (Hardcover)
978-1-03-916160-3 (Paperback)
978-1-03-916162-7 (eBook)

1. MUSIC, GENRES & STYLES, JAZZ

Distributed to the trade by The Ingram Book Company

CONTENTS

Foreword by Nou Dadoun — vii
Acknowledgements — xi
The Individual Path in Jazz: Preface and Introduction — xv
In Time: Selected Chronology — 1
1 / Living the Jazz Life: John Dawe — 9
2 / The Electrical Guitarist and his Only Son: Jim and Rick Kilburn — 24
3 / The Man with the Plastic Saxophone: Ornette Coleman — 43
4 / Far Out: Al Neil — 54
5 / Father and Son: Barry and Dylan Cramer — 79
6 / Mind of Mingus: Charles Mingus — 98
7 / Fisherman's Jazz: Dave Quarin — 120
8 / The Road from Avonlea to the Cellar: Bobby Hales — 154
9 / Total Honesty: PJ Perry — 167
10 / Jazz Dreamer: Carol Fox — 181
11 / The Voice: Ron Small — 189
12 / Deep Connection: Bob Murphy — 212
13 / Let Your Voice Be Heard: Hugh Fraser — 233
14 / Thankfully: Ross Taggart — 269

15 / Here Now: Brad Turner	294
16 / Life of Bruno: Bruno Hubert	320
17 / How My Heart Sings: Kate Hammett-Vaughan	343
18 / Hardest Working Man in Jazz Business: Cory Weeds Part 1: How to Succeed as a Jazz Club Owner	361
18 / Hardest Working Man in Jazz Business: Cory Weeds Part 2: Fin de l'Affaire, Living the Jazz Dream	389
19 / The Doctor and the Ambassador: Dr. Lonnie Smith and Seleno Clarke	425
20 / Big G: George Coleman	439
21 / The Rhythm Section: Tilden Webb, Jodi Proznick, and Jesse Cahill	449
22 / Keeping It Real: Roy McCurdy	470
23 / Sense and Sensibility: Amanda Tosoff	481
24 / Love Walked In: Mike Allen	494
25 / Endings Rarely Are: Natasha D'Agostino	507
It Takes a Community—and Visionary Individuals—to Raise a Jazz Scene: Coda	527
Selected Discography	529
Bibliography	536
Notes	540
Index	577
About the Author	605

FOREWORD

MUSIC IS ONE of the ephemeral arts. As Eric Dolphy said quite famously, "When you hear music, after it's over, it's gone in the air, you can never capture it again." Ironically, that utterance survives in a recording captured at one of his last concerts, but the intent is clear. For music that is constructed through improvisation like jazz, it exists in the moment—a product of its setting, the skill and life experiences of the players involved, the communication, and the flashes of inspiration that produce great art.

Jazz is a performance art; recordings are just shadows on the wall left behind when the moment has passed. Those recordings, those shadows, can provide signposts for where the music has been and, for students of the music and for its active practitioners, where it can go in the future.

The flashes of inspiration and the communication are truly ephemeral—no technology or recording device will ever catch those—but the settings and the players are important elements of how the music is created.

It is accepted wisdom that jazz was born in early twentieth century New Orleans as a combination of ragtime, African percussion, European chamber music, marching bands, and the blues—a true mongrel music! The jazz diaspora of the following decades spread across the continent and around the world, adopted and modified by each community where it took root. Some of these scenes developed regional and distinct styles, like the swing of Kansas City, bebop incubated in the jam sessions of New York, the creative music of the Association for the Advancement of Creative Musicians (AACM) in Chicago, South African jazz, British free jazz, and Asian Improv movements.

Historically, most writing about jazz has focused on biographies, the life stories of figures and practitioners who have been essential to the evolution of the art form. A number of authors have chosen to focus on particular communities, such as Ted Gioia in *West Coast Jazz*, Mark Miller in numerous books exploring the Canadian jazz scene, Kevin Whitehead in *New Dutch Swing*, Milton Krieger with *The Less Subdued Excitement* on the Bellingham and Whatcom County scene, Mark Stryker with *Jazz from Detroit*, and many more.

Another approach has been examining the development of jazz in specific communities by way of oral histories, where people *who were there* tell their personal stories so that from them, readers can construct their own understanding of the narratives involved. These include classic works like *Hear Me Talkin' to Ya: The Story of Jazz as Told by the Men [and Women] Who Made It*, assembled by Nat Shapiro and Nat Hentoff, and *Central Avenue Sounds: Jazz in Los Angeles*, produced by the UCLA Oral History Project.

In many ways, this volume—*Journeys to the Bandstand: Thirty Jazz Lives in Vancouver*, by Chris Wong—is an amalgam of these different approaches in its exploration of jazz in Vancouver. At the book's core are biographical portraits of figures, both local and visiting players, who have had an impact on the community's development. Wong has developed these portraits through numerous interviews that allow many of these individual artists to tell their stories from their own viewpoints and experiences. As well, the author has added his own impressions in the interviews, events, and experiences in which he personally participated, through a conversational style that is very effective in providing a window into the community.

Along the way we see patterns that are played out in the history of many jazz communities. Jazz lovers who put their passions and efforts into establishing places to play, both informal like the Wailhouse, and commercial like the two Cellars, and the financial, cultural, and sometimes legal forces that work against them. Figures from one generation that pass their passions and influences across generations, like Al Neil, the Kilburns, the Perrys, and the Cramers. Musicians practicing their craft and enriching the cultural life of the city. The wider international jazz scene and players from outside the community who develop relationships with people in it, like Ornette Coleman, Don Cherry, Charles Mingus, Wes Montgomery, George

Coleman, Dr. Lonnie Smith, Roy McCurdy, Joey DeFrancesco, and others. The (trials and) successes of jazz heroes like John Dawe and Cory Weeds, the contributions of jazz angels who help make things happen without fanfare or recognition, and the tragic loss of those gone too soon, like Ross Taggart, Bob Murphy, Hugh Fraser, and Natasha D'Agostino. I've been immersed in this scene for over forty years, and the fascinating stories in this book helped me connect many dots in many meaningful ways.

Above all, these are human stories about people for whom jazz is life. Dive in and celebrate!

Nou Dadoun
Host of A-Trane on Vancouver Co-op Radio (CFRO, 100.5 FM) since 1986, contributor to Vancouver's jazz scene since 1979

ACKNOWLEDGEMENTS

LIKE THE MUSICIANS featured in this book, I'm fortunate to be part of a remarkable community that has supported me in countless ways. I am deeply grateful for the support from many people that has empowered me to research, write, and publish *Journeys to the Bandstand*.

Thank you to librarians and archivists at the City of Vancouver Archives, Vancouver Public Library, BC Archives, Simon Fraser University Library Special Collections and Rare Books, Western Front, Sylvan Lake & District Archives, and York University Libraries: Clara Thomas Archives & Special Collections for your assistance.

Big thanks to Peter Stigings for instilling a love of music in me.

Thanks to individuals who, in my early days of researching the book, helped me delineate a path: Cory Weeds, Nou Dadoun, Milton Krieger, Gary Cristall, Missy Jena, and Andrea Damiani.

Thank you to Alan Davies for enabling me to see the space that housed the original Cellar jazz club before it was demolished.

My thanks to Jane Gowan and Michael de Courcy for providing access to interviews you conducted with Al Neil.

Thanks to Peter and F. for publishing an early version of the chapter on George Coleman in *Absintheminded* magazine.

Thank you to the photographers who contributed great images that appear in the book: Hank Bull, Jesse Cahill, Chris Cameron, Kathy Campbell, Judy Chee, Bill Coon, Pier-Alexandre Gagné, Greg Hansen, Vincent Lim, Franz Lindner, Mark Miller, Steve Mynett, Graham Ord, Neil Taylor, and Cory Weeds. Thanks to Kathy Campbell, James Carney, Anna and Rocco

Journeys to the Bandstand

D'Agostino, David Ferman, Marian Jago, Rick Kilburn, Walley Lightbody, Barbara Lindner Coates, Tamina Lindner, Christina Lust, Kevin Mooney, Marcus Mosley, Dave Quarin, Jalen Saip, and Cory Weeds for helping me obtain photos. Thank you, Amanda Palmer, for the wonderful author photo.

Enormous thanks to the many musicians who helped immensely with *Journeys to the Bandstand*, and without whom, this book wouldn't exist. Special thanks to Julie Brown, Bill Clark, John Dawe, Lorae Farrell, Hugh Fraser, Kate Hammett-Vaughan, Bruno Hubert, Rick Kilburn, John Korsrud, Roy McCurdy, Sharon Minemoto, Dave Quarin, Campbell Ryga, Gregg Simpson, Brad Turner, Gavin Walker, Jan Walters, and Cory Weeds.

Thank you to Mark Miller for your inspiration and wisdom.

An army of volunteers kindly helped me transcribe interviews I conducted for this book. Thank you, Susan Addario, Michael Baker, Hannah Barath, Anna Bekirova, David Ferman, Mike Lightstone, Julianna Perkins, and Sarah Wong. Special thanks to Dave Ronald for going far beyond the call of transcription duty.

Thank you to Jocelyne Hamel of Reframe Insight for your insightful coaching that helped me get to where I was going.

Thanks to Glenny Sipacio, Camila Ramos Bravo, and Jacky Chui for your encouragement.

Thank you to Tim Reinert (Infidels Jazz), Ian Shaw, Guy MacPherson, Brian Nation, and Mike Lightstone for your support.

Thank you to Rocco and Anna D'Agostino for your faith in me.

Many thanks to FriesenPress. Special thanks to Lee-Ann Jaworski, Rebecca Reid, and Marc Brick.

Thank you to those who read the manuscript, spotted changes that were needed, and offered helpful suggestions: Maria Chu, Nou Dadoun, and Brian Fraser. Thanks also to Nou for the pithy Foreword and to Will Chernoff of *Rhythm Changes* for your support.

Big thanks to David Ferman for your outstanding work as the editor and photo coordinator of *Journeys to the Bandstand*, our Monday morning calls that fueled me, and always having my back. Thank you Patricia Ferman for giving me a starting point.

Massive thanks to Dave Ronald for your many meaningful contributions and positivity that helped me in countless ways.

Acknowledgements

My heartfelt thanks to Joan Mariacher, Cory Weeds, Larry Donaldson, Susan Munro, and Pat Lewis for your very generous and patient support of this book.

Thank you to Miles Wong, Sarah Wong, Elysse Cloma, and Liv Barath for your support and artistic creativity that inspired me as I researched and wrote about the artists in this book.

Thank you to my parents George and Helen Wong and family for all that you have done for me.

Thank you to my wife Maria Chu for your unwavering belief and support. I love you.

I dedicate *Journeys to the Bandstand* to Bob Smith, Joan Mariacher, Hugh Fraser, and Natasha D'Agostino—men and women from different generations who embodied and expressed a deep passion for jazz with an inspiring life force. I also dedicate this book to George and Helen Wong, bold and resourceful improvisers in life and my greatest influences.

Chris Wong
Vancouver
October 2023

THE INDIVIDUAL PATH IN JAZZ: PREFACE AND INTRODUCTION

BOB SMITH WAS, for once, at a loss for words. The dean of Vancouver jazz writers and broadcasters needed a moment.

It happened one night in the late 1970s, when the highly respected *Vancouver Sun* jazz critic and decades-long host of CBC Radio's *Hot Air* program was holding court in a North Vancouver high school classroom. He was teaching a jazz appreciation class that involved sharing great tunes from his vast collection, giving an overview of jazz history, and taking questions from the adult students. Given Smith's endless jazz knowledge and his engaging repartee, it was the kind of thing he could easily deliver.

At one point when he asked if there were any questions, there was an awkward silence. A woman in the class, Patricia Ferman, decided to fill the void by asking what she thought was an innocuous question: "How do I know if I'm listening to good or bad jazz?" Smith looked right at her and said absolutely nothing.

She asked herself if it was a dumb question. Smith didn't say anything during the rest of the class to assuage Ferman's fears. But at the end of the next session the following week, he quietly handed her two flawlessly typed pages with seven paragraphs. The first paragraph said there are no absolutes in jazz and, therefore, no single best way of performing a song; each musical moment offers meaning.[1]

The sixth and seventh paragraphs were key. Here the author argued that no music depends on the individual player as much as jazz, which calls for individuality in the way a musician interprets a melody, improvises, and expresses emotion. It went on to say that jazz players shouldn't sound like each other—that one's musical voice should be distinctively personal. The author wrote that the history of jazz could likely be told through the lens of how the individual sound has developed, changed, and expanded over time.[2]

Smith didn't indicate who wrote the mini-treatise on jazz. For many years Ferman thought Smith had composed it himself. Decades before Google existed, she couldn't know that the passages were taken verbatim from the introduction to *The Jazz Tradition*, a pithy and important book by jazz critic Martin Williams, published in 1970. Giving Ferman the excerpt was Smith's way of responding to her question with his answer: individual expression is at the heart of compelling jazz.

More than half a century after Williams wrote about the significance of the individual in jazz, his central sentiment still holds true—the individual voice remains vital in jazz. What the excerpt didn't say is that committing to collaboration and developing a close rapport with fellow musicians are also crucial to jazz ensembles. Williams said as much in the very next paragraph that Smith didn't include in the missive to Ferman. Jazz at its most striking demands consummate group interplay.[3] That interplay goes beyond the bandstand when a jazz scene functions as a supportive and nurturing community.

That said, each musician takes an individual path in jazz. It's often a serpentine route, with countless challenges that emerge along the way: absorbing the art form's history; learning technique; understanding how to express the soul of your chosen instrument(s); and discovering how to transcend the well-worn with unique expression. On top of all that are the life issues that jazz musicians, like anyone else, must contend with: money worries, physical and mental health setbacks, addictions, racism, sexism, the disappointment of failure and rejection, and other challenges. Invariably, musicians' experience with these personal trials impacts the music.

Each individual path forms a complex and fascinating passage—the journey to the bandstand.

• • •

About a decade after Ferman met Smith, I spent half a day with the man himself, who ended *Hot Air* every week by saying, "God bless jazz fans everywhere." With his wife Deedee behind the wheel, we drove around Vancouver looking at the former locations of classic Vancouver jazz venues: the original Cellar, Flat Five, the Riverqueen, Espresso Coffee House, and other fabled joints that Smith had haunted on an almost nightly basis. The entire time we were together, Smith passionately talked about these places that he knew so well. Our afternoon drive was for a story I planned to write as a cub reporter at the *Vancouver Sun* about the long-gone jazz clubs that lived on only in memory, including the characterful local and visiting musicians who played in them, as well as their proprietors and patrons. As I sat transfixed in the back seat, Smith was an erudite tour guide to vanished places and to the vigorous jazz that energized them.

I never wrote the piece. But even more than thirty years later, I vividly remembered my remarkable encounter with Smith. Meeting him and reading his compelling work reinforced the importance of documenting jazz history in Vancouver. My dilemma was figuring out how to approach that history—either by recounting the whole saga of the city's tremendous jazz scene from the 1950s to now, or focusing on specific human stories from different eras. Gradually, inexorably, I opted for the latter. Like Martin Williams and Bob Smith, I gravitated to individual musicians because their musical and personal passages have been so compelling.

The criteria for deciding who to include in this book were open-ended. Suffice it to say that each person resonated with me, as musicians and humans. Those who inspired me to do a deep dive into their lives were mostly Vancouver musicians and some American players who had memorable musical experiences in this city. A number of them played at Vancouver's original Cellar jazz club and at another Cellar that existed years later under the ownership of Cory Weeds. A few weren't musicians at all, but they contributed to the scene in other ways. While many have received international recognition of their artistry, others are obscure and forgotten footnotes in local jazz history. All have meaningful stories, shared in narratives based primarily on oral history. There are scores of other exceptional musicians who I could have also focused on, and while circumstances didn't make that happen, their stories are important and will hopefully be told.

What I didn't know: I would become full-on, hopelessly obsessed with finding out every arcane detail about the artists gathered in these pages, whether they are living or long gone. Those myriad facts are puzzle pieces that—even though some pieces are missing—form portraits of extraordinary people with a hunger for jazz and other artforms, a determination to overcome struggles, and a deep joy for creating profound expression.

. . .

How to read this book: I positioned the chapters so they're approximately in chronological order, according to when the artists were active—from the 1940s to now. While you can read the chapters sequentially, feel free to read them out of order. The chapters are interconnected, but very much freestanding.

If memory serves: As I learned while interviewing people for this book, memory is malleable. Some things people said as fact turned out, after further research, to be somewhat or completely incorrect. It's understandable, given that many years had passed since the events I asked them about. I fact-checked as much as possible. In some cases, grey areas remained and the absolute truth remained elusive, so I went with the best version of the truth.

About the title: *Journeys to the Bandstand* came to mind as the perfect way to encapsulate this book. Then there was unease about whether saying someone is on a "journey" has become a cliché. While it has to some extent, I decided to stick with the title. One of the definitions of "journey"—a passage from one place to another—exactly describes what the artists in this book truly have been on.

IN TIME:
SELECTED CHRONOLOGY

THIS CHRONOLOGY HIGHLIGHTS major events in *Journeys to the Bandstand* and also delineates key milestones in Vancouver's jazz history.

October 9, 1946: Hilker Attractions presents Norman Granz' Jazz at the Philharmonic, featuring Roy Eldridge, Coleman Hawkins, Illinois Jacquet, Helen Humes, Trummy Young, Buck Clayton, and others at the Strand Theatre, 600 West Georgia Street.

February 23, 1954: As part of the Festival of Modern American Jazz, the Stan Kenton Orchestra, featuring soloists including Charlie Parker and Dizzy Gillespie, performs at Georgia Auditorium, 1805 West Georgia Street.

April 1956: The original Cellar jazz club[1], 2514 Watson Street, opens.

May 1957: Art Pepper performs at the original Cellar with the Al Neil Trio. At one point Chris Gage replaces Neil and sits in.

October 25–November 3, 1957: Ornette Coleman performs with Don Cherry, Don Friedman, Ben Tucker, and Billy Higgins at the original Cellar and University of BC Auditorium.

May 25–27, 1958: The inaugural Vancouver New Jazz Society Festival takes place at Georgia Auditorium.

November 1958: The Harold Land Quartet, with Elmo Hope, Scott LaFaro, and Lenny McBrowne, performs at the original Cellar. Barry Cramer introduces the band. In 2007, Lone Hill Jazz releases a bootleg recording of the performances: *Jazz at the Cellar 1958*.

February 17, 1959: Kenneth Patchen records at the CBC Vancouver studios with the Alan Neil Quartet, including Dale Hillary, Lionel Chambers, and Bill Boyle. Later that year, Folkways Records releases the recording: *Kenneth Patchen Reads with Jazz in Canada*.

July 24–August 2, 1959: Art Pepper performs at the original Cellar with Chris Gage, Stan "Cuddles" Johnson, and Jimmy Wightman.

1959: Isy and Richard Walters open Isy's Supper Club, 1136 West Georgia Street.

January 1961: The original Cellar, the Scene (1306 Wharf Street, Victoria), and UBC's Jazzsoc present Charles Mingus, with Charles McPherson, Lonnie Hillyer, and Dannie Richmond.

January 12 and March 28, 1961: "Mind of Mingus," produced by James Carney and partially filmed at the original Cellar, airs on CBC-TV Vancouver and CBC-TV's *Quest*.

March–April 1961: Wes Montgomery, Buddy Montgomery, Monk Montgomery, and Paul Humphrey perform at the original Cellar. Fantasy Records and Milestone Records release live tracks recorded at the club: *The Montgomery Brothers in Canada* (1961) and *Groove Brothers* (1979 and 1998).

1963: The Flatted Fifth, later renamed the Flat Five, 3623 West Broadway Street, opens. The Blue Horn opens in the same space in 1965 and closes in 1966.

1964: The original Cellar closes.

November 18, 1964: The Marco Polo supper club, 90 East Pender Street, opens.

December 15, 1965: The Al Neil Trio, including Richard Anstey and Gregg Simpson, performs in a studio at 2951 West 4th Avenue. Blue Minor Records releases a recording of the performance: *Retrospective 1965-1968* (2001).

1966: The Sound Gallery, 2951 West 4th Avenue, opens.

1966: Motion Studio, 1236 Seymour Street, opens.

July 29–31, 1966: The Trips Festival takes place at PNE Garden Auditorium.

May 12, 1968: Carol Fox opens Jazz Alley, 2514 Watson Street, later renamed the Alley.

1968: The Riverqueen, 1043 Davie Street, opens.

November 5, 1969: Vancouver police arrest Ron and Shirley Small and all involved with the theatrical production of "The Beard" at the Riverqueen for unlawfully presenting an obscene performance.

1970: The Riverqueen closes.

1970: The Alley closes.

1970: Ron and Shirley Small open the Old Cellar, 2514 Watson Street.

September 28–October 3, 1970: Herbie Hancock, with Eddie Henderson, Julian Priester, Bennie Maupin, Buster Williams, and Billy Hart, perform at the Old Cellar.

1970: Ornette Coleman, with Dewey Redman, Charlie Haden, and Ed Blackwell, perform at the Old Cellar.

Journeys to the Bandstand

1972: The Old Cellar closes.

1975: Vancouver Jazz Society (led by Brian Nation) launches.

March 9–12, 1977: Vancouver Jazz Society presents Lee Konitz and Warne Marsh, with Bob Murphy, Torben Oxbol, and George Ursan, at Vancouver Jazz Society Auditorium, 2611 West 4th Avenue.

June 1, 1980: Vancouver Ensemble of Jazz Improvisation (VEJI) performs the group's first concert at Western Front, 303 East 8th Avenue.

August 19–25, 1985: The inaugural and only Pacific Jazz & Blues Festival takes place. Kate Hammett-Vaughan opens the festival.

June 23–29, 1986: The inaugural du Maurier International Jazz Festival takes place.

July 3, 1987: The Hugh Fraser Quintet wins the Concours de Jazz Alcan at Festival International de Jazz de Montréal and opens for Dave Brubeck at Place des Arts.

August 31, 1996: Alma Street Café, 2505 Alma Street, concludes more than a decade of offering live jazz.

December 20, 1996: A fire destroys the Glass Slipper, 2714 Prince Edward Street.

October 27, 1999: C.W. Productions (Cory Weeds) presents Eric Alexander, with Ross Taggart, André Lachance, and Dave Robbins, at Cellar Jazz Café, 3611 West Broadway Street. Peter Bernstein, Paul Gill, and Joe Farnsworth sit in.

January 14–15, 2000: The Brad Turner Quartet, featuring Seamus Blake and including Bruno Hubert, André Lachance, and Dylan van der Schyff, performs at Cellar Jazz Café. Later that year, Maximum Jazz releases a self-titled recording of the performances.

August 8, 2000: Cory Weeds' Cellar Jazz Club[2], 3611 West Broadway Street, opens with the Mike Allen Trio, including Darren Radtke and Julian MacDonough.

June 1–2, 2001: The Ross Taggart Quartet, with Mike Rud, Bob Murphy, and Bernie Arai, performs at the Cellar. For its first release, in 2001, Cellar Live puts out a recording of the performances: *Thankfully*.

September 2001: Maximum Jazz releases *Maximum Jazz Presents Live at the Cellar*, a compilation of eight tracks recorded live at the Cellar.

September 19, 2001: Joe Lovano and the Brad Turner Quartet, including Bruno Hubert, André Lachance, and Dylan van der Schyff, perform at Capilano College Performing Arts Theatre.

January 13–14, 2002: The Bruno Hubert Trio, with André Lachance and Brad Turner, performs at the Cellar. In 2002, Cellar Live releases a recording of the performances: *Get Out of Town*.

July 26–27, 2002: Charles McPherson, with Ross Taggart, Jodi Proznick, and Blaine Wikjord, perform at the Cellar. In 2002, Cellar Live releases a recording of the performances: *Live at the Cellar*.

September 5–6, 2003: Dr. Lonnie Smith, with Crash—Cory Weeds, Jerry Cook, Dave Sikula, Mark Humeniuk, and Bernie Arai—perform at the Cellar, marking the club's third anniversary. The following year, Cellar Live releases a recording of the September 6 performance: *The Doctor Is In*.

December 11–12, 2004: David "Fathead" Newman with the Tilden Webb Trio, including Jodi Proznick and Jesse Cahill, perform at the Cellar. The following year, Cellar Live releases a recording of the performances: *Cellar Groove*.

September 22–23, 2006: George Coleman and Eric Alexander—with Ross Taggart, Jodi Proznick, and Jesse Cahill—perform at the Cellar, marking the jazz club's sixth anniversary.

January 9–10, 2010: Cory Weeds, Joey DeFrancesco, Chris Davis, and Byron Landham perform at the Cellar. Later that year, Cellar Live releases a recording of the performances: *The Many Deeds of Cory Weeds*.

2012: *Bruno's Blues*, starring Bruno Hubert, briefly plays in a few cinemas in Vancouver, Toronto, and Montreal.

February 24–25, 2012: Peter Bernstein performs with the Tilden Webb Trio, including Jodi Proznick and Jesse Cahill, at the Cellar. In 2013, Cellar Live releases a recording of the performances: *Peter Bernstein with the Tilden Webb Trio*.

January 4–5, 2013: Seleno Clarke performs at the Cellar with Cory Weeds, Ian Hendrickson-Smith, Dave Sikula, and Julian MacDonough. It's the last time Clarke performed in Vancouver before passing away December 28, 2017.

April 5–7, 2013: George Coleman performs with Miles Black, Jodi Proznick, and Jesse Cahill at the Cellar, as a tribute to Ross Taggart, who passed away January 9, 2013.

September 26–29, 2013: Cory Weeds, with Harold Mabern, John Webber, and Joe Farnsworth, perform at the Cellar, marking the jazz club's thirteenth anniversary. In 2014, Cellar Live releases a recording of the group made at Baker Studios in Victoria: *As of Now*.

Mid-November 2013: Cory Weeds announces his Cellar jazz club will close at the end of February 2014.

February 26, 2014: The Cellar presents its final night before closing.

March 2014: The building that housed the original Cellar is demolished.

October 8, 2015: Frankie's Jazz Club, 755 Beatty Street, opens with the Cory Weeds Quintet featuring David Hazeltine and including Chris Davis, Ken Lister, and Jesse Cahill.

October 29, 2015: A Celebration of Life for Bob Murphy, who passed away October 22, 2015, takes place at Unitarian Church of Vancouver.

December 4–5, 2015: Dr. Lonnie Smith performs with the Jill Townsend Big Band at Orpheum Annex. It's the last time Smith performed in Vancouver before passing away September 28, 2021.

November 5, 2016: A Celebration of Life for Bobby Hales, who passed away October 15, 2016, takes place at First Memorial Burkeview Chapel in Port Coquitlam.

January 26, 2019: A Celebration of Life for Natasha D'Agostino, who passed away January 6, 2019, takes place at the BlueShore Financial Centre for the Performing Arts in North Vancouver.

May 26, 2019: A Celebration of Life for Ron Small, who passed away November 3, 2018, takes place at False Creek Community Centre.

June 23, 2019: At Pyatt Hall, Hugh Fraser performs for the final time with VEJI.

October 25–27, 2019: At Frankie's Jazz Club, Hugh Fraser performs for the final time with the Hugh Fraser Quintet.

December 1, 2019: Cory Weeds' inaugural Shadbolt Jazz Walk festival takes place at the Shadbolt Centre for the Arts in Burnaby.

October 17, 2021: A Celebration of Life for Hugh Fraser, who passed away June 17, 2020, takes place at the Vogue Theatre.

February 11–13, 2022: Cory Weeds' second jazz festival at the Shadbolt Centre for the Arts, Jazz @ The Bolt, takes place.

February 13, 2022: As part of Jazz @ The Bolt, the Ostara Project—co-led by Jodi Proznick and Amanda Tosoff—makes its debut performance and the next day records a self-titled album that Cellar Music releases that year.

February 4–5, 2023: The third Jazz @ The Bolt festival takes place at the Shadbolt Centre for the Arts, programmed by Cory Weeds and Tim Reinert (Infidels Jazz).

1 / LIVING THE JAZZ LIFE: JOHN DAWE

IF YOU ASSEMBLED a group of jazz aficionados with deep knowledge about the history of jazz in Vancouver and gave them a specific task—name the city's greatest jazz trumpeters since the 1950s—the following names could figure prominently in the exercise: Carse Sneddon, Stew Barnett, Arnie Chycoski, Bobby Hales, Blaine Tringham, Donnie Clark, Brad Turner, Bill Clark, Alan Matheson, Vince Mai, Chris Davis, and JP Carter. Add one more to the list: John Dawe.

It's an audacious inclusion. Here's why: There's hardly any surviving documentation of his musicality; the only audio evidence of his trumpet playing that I know of is a wonky recording of a quintet session; the best available recordings of Dawe captured him on baritone horn and valve trombone, not trumpet; he was a less-than-stellar sight reader, which meant he was not close to being a first-call trumpeter; Dawe rarely led bands; he wasn't a composer; and Dawe essentially gave up playing music in his thirties. Not exactly bona fides for jazz trumpet immortality.

None of those things matters. Dawe still unequivocally belongs on the list. Great musicians who played with or listened to Dawe wax passionate about his innate quality as a jazz multi-instrumentalist in the late fifties and parts of the sixties. Those few recordings, even with him on other horns, confirm his merit—not in a technical sense, but in his instinct for the music. Dawe had an affecting tone, and he played with emotional soul. Plus, for a period in his life, he fully embodied what it meant to be a round-the-clock jazz musician and raffish character in Vancouver. Dawe has a unique place in the local scene's colourful past and an underdog story that needs to be told.

• • •

In early 2013 I stumbled upon a blog that, at the time, illuminated a previously obscure chapter in Vancouver's jazz history. The Original Cellar Jazz Club blog tells an extraordinary story, in words and photos, about a musician-run jazz club that existed in Vancouver from 1956 to early 1964. The Cellar was both incubator and showcase for the city's bebop scene. The more I read, the more my fascination with the club grew. Written in a loose, hipster-casual style with liberal use of ellipses, the blog tells of a great jazz club unique to Vancouver and perhaps all of Canada. A club that played host to Charles Mingus, Ornette Coleman, Art Pepper, Barney Kessel, and many other visiting and local jazz musicians. About trumpeter Don Cherry and his Jazz Messiahs, the blog had this to say: "....... this group knocked us all on our asses.....wow!!"[1] About vibraphonist and quintet leader Bob Frogge: "He was the funniest, grooviest and most laid-back cat you'd ever meet....... and he was totally insane (in a very groovy way).... I don't know what planet he was from, but it wasn't in this galaxy, or the next ...."[2] The cool daddy-o writing and reminiscing on the blog? One John Dawe.

• • •

July 17, 2013. I'm in Richmond, the city immediately south of Vancouver and the Fraser River. I've arrived at the hulking, seventies era apartment building with brutalist design where Dawe lives. I pass through several sets of doors in a long hallway before I reach his door. Dawe greets me warmly, and as I enter his apartment my eyes struggle to take in all the bric-a-brac accumulated by an octogenarian. We sit, and as he lights the first of many cigarettes, I ask if I can start the interview. He smiles and says enthusiastically with his gravelly voice, "Shoot, man!"

John David Daw was born March 7, 1931, in Victoria, BC, to Dr. William Daw and Mable Fowles. Dr. Daw died seven years later, and after the onset of war, the family split up. Both his brothers entered the military, and his two sisters went separate ways.[3] That left mother Mable with John, and they moved to Vancouver when he was about twelve. Maybe it was an early sign that John would take his own path in life, but it was around this time that he became the only one in his family to resurrect the "e" in Dawe.[4] A diminutive of David, Dawe means "lucky" and "beloved," and in many ways he ended up being both.

Dawe started playing trumpet at about fourteen, when he discovered jazz on the radio. "It just caught my ear," he said. "You hear something one day that really grabs you, and from there you go. I never really got my ears going until I heard Bird and Dizzy. And they just woke me up like something you wouldn't believe."[5] After completing grade ten at Kitsilano Secondary School, Dawe dropped out at sixteen and proceeded to move from "one dumb job to another," mainly at department stores, including Spencer's and Woodward's.[6] He also kept playing trumpet, teaching himself the instrument's fundamentals, despite the best efforts of his mom. "My mother grabbed the horn one day and took it away from me. She thought it was a bad influence, and it was."[7]

Dawe would not be deterred, however, and he got the horn back after six months and resumed his jazz self-education. By the late 1940s, Dawe was playing in a big band led by alto saxophonist Bob Berglund that played arrangements of modern jazz tunes from Stan Kenton's repertoire and other charts. That band didn't play bebop, but Dawe and several of the musicians in the ensemble developed a shared passion for the dynamic and complex style that Charlie Parker, Dizzy Gillespie, Bud Powell, Max Roach, Thelonious Monk, and other greats pioneered in the forties. Dawe and his friends would rent halls on Sunday afternoons for two dollars and jam, just playing for themselves.

In the early 1950s, Dawe played in big bands that performed swinging dance music in venues around town—places like the Alma Academy at Broadway and Alma, on the same block where the Flat Five, Cory Weeds' Cellar, and other music venues would open years later. In a classic photo of the fifteen-piece Ken Hole Big Band taken at the Alma Academy, that's skinny John Dawe at the far left of the four-man trumpet section. Dawe and at least six other musicians in the photo—all looking sharp in suits and ties—would go on to play important roles at Vancouver's original Cellar jazz club.

Ken Hole Big Band. Back row (left to right): George Burgess, Bill Trussell, Bud Trussell, Tony Clitheroe, Bill Shiner, John Dawe, Arnold Emery, Arnie Chycoski, and James Carney. Middle row: Ken Hole. Front row: Gordy Brown, Charles Hendricks, Jim Johnson, Jim Peters, and Walley Lightbody. Alma Academy, circa mid-1950s. Photographer unknown. Courtesy Ken Hole.

In 1955, Dawe followed the lead of his drummer friend Bill Boyle and spent some time in Toronto. They were both impressed with the jazz scene in TO, and in particular with one of the city's first after-hours jazz clubs: the House of Hambourg. Run by pianist and promoter Clement Hambourg and his wife Ruth from 1948 to 1963, the House of Hambourg hosted all-night jam sessions frequented by Toronto musicians and visiting stars like Dave Brubeck.

Meanwhile, back home, Ken Hole, Jim Johnson, Al Neil, James Carney, and other friends of Dawe created their own jam space in Richmond, which was mostly farmland at the time. They could play as late and loud as they wanted at the Wailhouse. Dawe missed the whole Wailhouse scene because of his Toronto sojourn, but he returned to Vancouver at a pivotal time in 1956. Inspired by what he saw in Toronto, Dawe "started putting the bug" in the ear of Hole—an entrepreneur and bassist—about finding a place where they could play.[8] Hole proceeded to discover a basement on Watson Street that would become the Cellar.

Dawe was part of a core group of musicians and artists who hammered, sawed, did electrical work, painted, created and procured artwork for the walls, and whatever else it took for the Cellar to open its doors in April 1956. Or, as Dawe described the genesis of the club in the Original Cellar Jazz Club blog: "The original Cellar club was something just short of a miracle!!...... we took a bare-assed concrete basement and turned it into what later became one of the most important jazz clubs on the west coast........"[9]

Dawe toiled at the main Vancouver post office in the daytime and early evening. He lived for the wee small hours—especially on weekends—when live jazz and friendship flourished at the Cellar. At the club, musicians organized themselves into two main groups: one led by pianist Al Neil—also a post office employee—and another led by guitarist Jim Kilburn. Dawe played in Neil's quintet, usually alongside Johnson on tenor sax, bassist Tony Clitheroe, and Boyle on drums. While both ensembles had leaders, they were run cooperatively. The groups mainly played at the Cellar on weekends, but some like Dawe would go to the club throughout the week to practice and hang out. The Cellar was not just their place to play; it was their clubhouse.

John Dawe's Cellar Musicians and Artists Society Charter Member card.

When Dawe wasn't at the Cellar, he lived the jazz life at home. For a number of years, he lived at "Bebop House," a shared house at Manitoba and 10th, a short walk from the Cellar. Dawe had the upstairs front bedroom and at various times his close friend Terry Hill, as well as Johnson, Chycoski, PJ Perry, Jerry Fuller, and others were roommates. According to Hill, who played bass, partying wasn't prevalent at Bebop House. "Not party-party, not nutty," said Hill. "Just a place where a bunch of musicians hung out, and it was just lovely. It was a memory maker, you know."[10]

Dawe described the level of musicianship among the local players at the Cellar as "uneven" but "constantly improving all the time." He explained: "We kind of knew what we could do and stuck at those sorts of levels. But we moved along. Six, seven years later it was totally different down there. We had all accelerated musically."[11]

Kilburn flat-out called Dawe a "great trumpet player."[12] A CBC Radio session Dawe did with the Al Neil Quintet in 1957, which someone made a lo-fi home recording of, didn't verify that greatness. But it confirmed that at this stage in his development, Dawe had a fluency on his horn and with the music. On standards including "Jordu," "Parisian Thoroughfare," "Tune Up," "Take the 'A' Train," and "Room 608," his trumpet playing is solid, but not spectacular. What stands out is his instinctive understanding of hard bop, which comes across in his comfortable delivery of the melodies and simple but appealing solos. His ability to be right in the hard bop pocket was impressive given that it was still an emerging style. Dawe was learning the idiom in real time. He didn't have the luxury of absorbing decades of recordings over months and years like players of later generations. Dawe truly played in the moment.

On two other scratchy home recordings of CBC *Jazz Workshop* radio broadcasts that also aired in the fifties, Dawe shines. One is with Neil's quintet, the other is with a sextet led by saxophonist Dave Quarin. Dawe plays valve trombone on seven tunes broadcast with Neil's group and baritone horn on the five-song session with Quarin. "By the way, this *Jazz Workshop* is also the first time that a baritone horn has been used in Vancouver as a jazz instrument, or that's what Dave Quarin believes," announcer Ray Nichol said before the sextet went into "Penny Packer." Dawe's playing on the tune again exhibits his hard bop capability. He navigates the tricky, note-heavy melody in unison with Quarin and with the right vibrant feel; on his solo, Dawe builds energetic lines with well-timed inflections.

In 1959, when eighteen-year-old Wilmer (Bill) Fawcett—then a budding jazz guitarist—started hanging out at the Cellar, he got to know musicians like Dawe. "John was always a very personable guy with a great sense of humour," said Fawcett, who went on to become an accomplished classical double bassist. Dawe was also "the epitome of what a jazz cat looked like."[13] There's a great group photo of Cellar musicians that captures Dawe's look: lean, subtly slicked back hair with a side part, suit and tie, and a big smile on his face.

Living the Jazz Life

Jerry Fuller (drums), John Dawe (trumpet), and Jim Johnson (tenor saxophone), the original Cellar, circa 1959. Photo by Don Cumming, courtesy James Carney.

By mid-1959, another group had formed at the Cellar, with younger, talented musicians, including saxophonist PJ Perry, multi-instrumentalist Don Thompson, drummer Jerry Fuller, bassist Tony Clitheroe, and Dawe. Perry led the group for two-and-a-half years. "We read each other's minds musically," said Dawe. "We were right together musically. It's like the gears were

15

meshing. I'm going to stick my neck out and say that was probably the best group north of San Francisco. We played so well together."[14]

Dawe introduced Perry to some of the tunes that became part of the group's repertoire, including "Sippin' At Bells" by Miles Davis and "Donna Lee" (which was attributed to Charlie Parker but also claimed by Davis). Dawe made an impact on Perry. "John Dawe was not what you would call a fantastic technician on the trumpet in terms of range and lead trumpet playing," said Perry. "But what John could do that nobody else could do was make music on the trumpet and touch people emotionally, which he did with me. It was always a real treat for me to play jazz melodies on tenor in unison with John Dawe because he knew how to phrase the tunes. It was always very special."[15]

I was curious about what other trumpeters who frequented the Cellar thought of Dawe because they were the ones who listened with the most knowledge about jazz trumpet technique and expression. "Johnny Dawe was a very good jazz trumpet player, and he could certainly hold his own," said John Frederickson, a trumpeter who led small and large ensembles. "He was doing Clifford Brown stuff from just having heard the records. He could play it, and it's damn difficult."[16]

Another trumpeter who often played at the Cellar, Ed Roop, did a radio session with Dawe led by pianist Fred Massey. Roop observed at the session, and numerous times at the Cellar, that Dawe played in a heartfelt and engaging way. Roop stopped short of calling Dawe a great player, but he lauded his fellow trumpeter's work ethic and authenticity: "I think he worked hard at it and did what he did and what he felt like doing, and that's what any player should do. Play what feels good."[17]

Trumpet isn't one of the three instruments Don Thompson has mastered, but he's more capable than most of hearing when someone is a difference maker on the horn. "John Dawe was brilliant," said Thompson, who played piano in Perry's quintet. "I really wish I had some recordings of him playing the trumpet. All I have is one of him playing valve trombone. But he was amazing, and all the downtowners agreed. They couldn't believe what he could play on trumpet. He was a fantastic musician."[18]

John Dawe (trumpet) and Harold Krause (piano), the original Cellar, circa 1959. Photo by Bill Boyle, courtesy James Carney and Marian Jago.

Downtowners were A-list musicians who got the plum gigs at downtown Vancouver supper clubs like the Cave and Isy's, on CBC-TV and Radio, and in recording studios. Some have said that certain downtowners looked down on the musicians who mainly just played in the Cellar. But Dawe earned their respect. Bobby Hales, who played trumpet in both the downtown and Cellar scenes, confirmed that. Hales remembered being impressed by Neil's quintet that included Dawe. "They were the closest thing to being a jazz group in Vancouver," said Hales. "They had all the current jazz tunes down, they rehearsed a lot, and they always sounded good. John Dawe was a great bebop player."[19]

Dawe occasionally subbed for Hales at downtown gigs, but there was a gulf between many Cellar dwellers and the downtowners in terms of reading ability and chops. "To play downtown, you had to have chops all the time," said Hales. "These guys didn't have a lot of chops, but they had a lot of soul. The downtowners were more polished and more correct, whereas John Dawe and the guys were more free-form. They [downtowners] played jazz from the outside in rather than from the inside out. [Translation: downtowners played with their audiences in mind, while musicians like Dawe played from the heart.] There were some nights they [regular Cellar players] played their asses off, and the next night they sounded like amateur hour. So how they felt had a factor in how they played."[20]

Hales said listening to and playing music at the Cellar opened his ears. "It was just good to hear because the downtowners never played that way. So to me it was always fresh and new to think, 'Oh, listen to that. There's something.' They had a different feel to me. It was jazzier than what we played downtown."[21]

The jazz Eden that Hales cherished couldn't, however, sustain itself. As other jazz venues opened and musicians like Perry, Thompson, and Fuller kept improving, they were offered more lucrative opportunities than the low-paying Cellar gigs. By late 1962, it was hard to put a high-level group together that was willing to play at the club, whose crowds were dwindling. "It [the Cellar] destroyed itself by becoming too good," said Dawe.[22]

In November 1962, Dawe performed in Calgary and Edmonton with strong players, including saxophonist Dale Hillary, Thompson, Wilmer Fawcett, and drummer Terry Hawkeye. After the Alberta gigs, which included a weekend engagement at Edmonton's Yardbird Suite, the musicians (except Fawcett, who was living in Edmonton) were supposed to return to Vancouver. That's when what Dawe described as a "kidnapping" occurred. He realized something was up after getting in a huge Oldsmobile with Hillary and Hawkeye, who was at the wheel. "I'm noticing we're going out of town. We're starting to head out to a freeway somewhere. I thought, 'Aren't we going to pick Don up?' Hillary says, 'Terry and I had a talk last night and we're not going to take him, we're going to go east, we're not going back to Vancouver. All news to me. I didn't know what these two bastards had cooked up." So they left Thompson stranded in Edmonton. "It was a rotten thing to do, but I had no control. That's why I say I was abducted." The new plan was to pick up gigs on the way to Toronto, where they would play more. What they hadn't counted on was driving into a blizzard, running so low on money that they had enough for gas but not for food, and gigs being in short supply. They made it to Toronto, but Dawe had a miserable time on the "dastardly" trip.[23]

Back in Vancouver, where Dawe returned in early 1963, the Cellar was struggling. At a personal level, the passion for playing jazz and being part of the scene had lost its hold on Dawe. He had a new and urgent desire for steady and secure income. "It [jazz] was really important at the time. We thought it was. But after about five or six years most of us had had enough of it. Some of us quit playing entirely, like myself, and others kept playing what gigs they could find."[24]

I found it hard to imagine that he could just walk away. But that's exactly what he did. "I was thirty-two-years-old with no education to speak of," he said. "I had to get a job because I could see the light. I wasn't going to make a living the rest of my life off music. I cared about my playing enough that I couldn't work a day gig and practice at the same time to keep my playing up. I wanted to get out of it totally."[25] Dawe also developed muscular problems that impeded his ability to physically play trumpet.[26]

I kept asking Dawe about his momentous decision to quit, probing his rationale to see if there were other factors at play. He doubled down. "I was glad to get away from music. I'd had it with all the problems." Dawe cited "working with dope fiends" and "working bad gigs" as examples of the challenges. "I mean if I'd been a marvellous studio trumpet player, I would have said, I'll stick with it." But Dawe wasn't that. In the end, it wasn't a hard choice. "I made up my mind, and it was a good decision."[27]

Breaking away so completely from the only way of life he knew meant the loss of a big part of his essence. To the self-aware Dawe, it also meant salvation.

• • •

After the Cellar closed, while Neil, Perry, and other Cellar mainstays continued their music careers, Dawe landed a full-time job in the kitchen at Vancouver General Hospital (VGH), which he stayed at for twenty-six years.[28] Oddly, it was here where our lives converged. As we talked about this post-Cellar period, it dawned on me that he got this non-musical gig around the same time my father George became a cook at the hospital. Incredibly, it turned out that they worked alongside each other for years. When Dawe suddenly handed me a photo of my dad making soup at VGH, I was shocked and elated. Somehow, circumstances brought me together with my father's work friend—a jazz musician no less—whose existence was completely unknown to me.

John Dawe, Richmond, January 25, 2014. Photo by Chris Wong.

Dawe didn't have children, as one thing that remained unchanged was his status as a committed bachelor. "I've done a lot of dumb things, but that [staying single] was the smartest thing I ever did because I'm not that type. I just can't do it. I've got to have freedom. I could never get a chick I could talk to about music. That's the only thing I'm interested in."[29] When we met, he still conveyed that singlemindedness. Dawe never stopped listening to and reading about jazz. At one point, he even tried playing jazz again in the place that meant the most to him.

In 1968, Carol Fox opened a jazz club in the same space that housed the original Cellar. As he had done with the first club, Dawe was among the local musicians who helped Fox prepare the space that re-opened as Jazz Alley. Something also inspired him to pick up his trumpet for the first time in years and play some gigs there. To his mind, they didn't go well. Others didn't hear it that way.

When Tom Keenlyside was in grade twelve, he would sneak out of his family's house late at night to go to jazz hot spots, where he would listen and sit in on trumpet. At Jazz Alley and the Espresso Coffee House, he encountered Dawe performing with musicians such as drummer Rocky Weems. "It was magic," recalled Keenlyside about Dawe and Weems' playing. "It was like nectar. I couldn't get enough of these guys playing because it was so, so soulful."[30]

He described Dawe as a "fabulous trumpet player, in the style of Jack Sheldon,"[31] who was an underrated American jazz trumpeter. Keenlyside was especially struck by Dawe's beautiful tone. "It was not that real edgy trumpet sound. It was really mellow and had a huge cushion of air around it. I just thought it was magic. It was just so incredibly romantic and poetic." Keenlyside went as far as equating the effect of Dawe's sound to the impact of sublime alto saxophonist Paul Desmond's lyrical playing.[32] "To actually express yourself, it's a way harder act than just playing a bunch of really flashy licks," said Keenlyside about Dawe's approach. "It's very fragile, that kind of expression a guy like John Dawe could do. He filled the horn with pathos when he played."[33]

The quality of Dawe's playing, however, was inversely proportional to the amount he drank. "Sometimes he would be so drunk, he would sort of be a cartoon representation of a beatnik. It was really sad to see," said Keenlyside.[34]

Musicians I've interviewed drank excessively or used drugs at times in their lives, including Dawe, who dabbled in heroin but stopped using cold turkey when he got spooked by its effects. This was part of their human condition, which diminished but didn't nullify their artistry. Keenlyside heard that not long after Dawe's finite return to playing, "He quit drinking and completely sobered up and never touched a drop for the rest of his life, as far as I know."[35] Dawe also developed a passion for playing tennis, which kept him fit.

There was something else at play. Keenlyside, who would become one of Vancouver's top jazz and commercial musicians on tenor sax, flute, and other woodwinds, was perceptive beyond his years, and he discovered a startling reality: Dawe and playing music wasn't a healthy combination.

"Sometimes music, although it comes from the heart, is not the best medicine for everybody," said Keenlyside. "And I've met many people in my career, in my life, who are fabulous musicians, but there's something about the art of creating, the act of creating music, that takes people down a path, a dark path. John realized that early, and so he gave up. He gave up playing. He didn't give up his love of music—you can't do that—but he gave up playing and it probably saved his life because he was a tortured soul back then.

"If you caught him early enough [during a gig], you'd hear the most beautiful music coming out of the guy's horn. It was fantastic. I mean he was awesome. But, if you caught him too late, which I did a number of times, sometimes he would end up under the table. Literally under the table, and kind of very dark, kind of dismissive of jazz and music."[36]

Keenlyside's analysis raised so many questions. What engendered Dawe's dark side? Was Dawe upfront with me about his reasons for abandoning music? Did frustrations that accrued during his playing days really kill his desire to perform jazz, or as Keenlyside posited, was making music fundamentally detrimental for him? My guess is that he was transparent about his reasons for quitting. I also think there was truth to what Keenlyside outlined, and it was also tougher for Dawe to leave the jazz life—the only life he knew—than he let on.

Still, when looking back at his career and life choices, Dawe said he wouldn't change a thing. "No regrets at all, man. It was great. It was really fun. And it was really good when it [the Cellar] closed," he said, unironically. "I felt it saved my life when it closed. I could let that go and get on to surviving."[37] I noticed that he intentionally said "surviving," and not "living." That was a sad sentiment, but I don't think Dawe lived a sad life. While he didn't have wealth or recognition, Dawe had a sanguine outlook and was comfortable with himself.

• • •

March 9, 2018. I'm on the phone with Dawe two days after his eighty-seventh birthday, celebrated in East Vancouver's German-Canadian Care Home where he now lives. Some serious health scares have led to his move here. But he still has the same spirit and sense of humour. Dawe tells me that he quit smoking three months ago. "But it didn't help [with his ailments]," he says with his familiar laugh.[38]

I tell him I'm still working on my book about Vancouver jazz musicians, almost five years after I first interviewed him. Dawe has forgotten all about the book, but he encourages me, saying it will be better in the end after all the extra time I've spent on it.

I also ask him if he's excited about another book that's coming out: *Live at the Cellar: Vancouver's iconic jazz club and the Canadian co-operative jazz scene in the 1950s and '60s* by Marian Jago. Dawe, who's quoted extensively in the book, is happy that the Cellar story is being told beyond his blog. Back when I first met Dawe, my plan was to write a history of the two Cellars—the original Cellar and Cory Weeds' Cellar. I realized a few years into it that a chronological narrative about the two Cellars wasn't the story I was meant to tell. Personal stories about individual musicians from different eras resonated with me much more. Spending time with Dawe, perhaps more than anybody, led to this epiphany.

Before saying goodbye, I tell him that I might drop by sometime to visit. "Do that, man," says Dawe. "That would be a gas, man."[39] I regret never making that visit. John Dawe passed away December 12, 2018. His obituary said that while in the care home, he told family, "It's time to let this cat go!" Dawe excelled at just letting go. As per his request, there was no funeral service.[40] And there were no newspaper articles paying tribute to him. Dawe simply exited life's bandstand, with his way cool lingo and boundless zest for jazz, still fully and sweetly intact.

2 / THE ELECTRICAL GUITARIST AND HIS ONLY SON: JIM AND RICK KILBURN

I'M SITTING WITH Jim Kilburn in his Qualicum Beach home, but we're also time travelling through two portals to a key place in his life. The first portal goes through a weathered, two-ring, loose leaf science notebook. On the notebook's cover there's an illustration of a totem pole and written in red: "JAMES KILBURN ... 811 FRANCIS RD ... RICHMOND BC." Nestled inside are page after page of homemade sheet music with just chord symbols—no melodies—set down in India ink. More than fifty years before this sunny day in August 2013, the guitarist carefully wrote out the music to jazz standards such as "Lover Man," "Round Midnight," and "All Blues." The notation still looks resolutely bold, like it was penned yesterday.

While I leaf through the vintage DIY fake book and gaze enraptured at the songs that meant so much to him, Jim breaks my spell. "I'll show you something," he says in his soft-spoken voice. We go to another room, where Jim opens a guitar case to reveal portal number two: a pristine 1952 Gibson Les Paul—one of the first one hundred made of the famous electric guitar. It's the one he played with a tender style at Vancouver's original Cellar jazz club in the late 1950s and early 1960s. I have to hold the rare and beautiful instrument to get closer to what it was like for him to make music at the pioneering club. The guitar, which has a solid mahogany body and maple top, is heavy but comforting to cradle. Just by touching it, and seeing the sanguine expression on Jim's face, I can clearly imagine the exhilaration he felt when playing the instrument in the Cellar.

Jim Kilburn, Qualicum Beach, August 13, 2013. Photo by Chris Wong.

Jim's son Rick Kilburn knows all about these talismanic artifacts. He grew up with them as everyday household items. As a child and adolescent, he met elite musicians like Wes Montgomery, who visited the Kilburn home during Cellar engagements. Rick sometimes got to hear music at the Cellar, falling asleep in the club to the sounds of swinging bebop and hard bop. Invariably, like his dad, Rick became passionate about jazz. That passion took him all the way to Carnegie Hall, where he played bass with Dave Brubeck and his band, including Paul Desmond. Despite reaching lofty heights in the jazz world, at times Rick struggled with confidence and felt his bass playing wasn't good enough. But he didn't question his instinct for the music. Rick has an intuitive feel for jazz—a direct inheritance from Jim's idyllic Cellar days, and the close bond between father and son.

• • •

Jim was born October 3, 1927, in Winnipeg, and lived in Pointe du Bois, about 150 kilometres east of the Manitoba capital. His father Miles Kilburn—who played guitar—left his wife and son when Jim was only one, and that was the last they saw of him. His mother Louise Kilburn—who played piano—moved with her only child to Vancouver when Jim was two. They eventually settled in Steveston, a fishing and farming community in Richmond, across the Fraser River from Vancouver.

Music grabbed hold of Jim when, as a teenager, he "went nuts" after hearing Charlie Christian on record for the first time.[1] It's no wonder why. During his short life, Christian redefined jazz as played on the electric guitar through his extraordinary comping, inventive riffs and licks, and fluent solos that swung like crazy and foreshadowed bebop. The master guitarist did this as a sideman with the Benny Goodman Sextet and Orchestra, never recording as a leader. Jim was inspired to salvage a "junk guitar" and learn solos by Christian,[2] who died of tuberculosis at twenty-five in 1942.

In the late 1940s and early 1950s, Jim regularly played with pianist and vibraphonist Dave Wright, bassist Jim Thomas, drummer Danny Crooks, and vocalist Austin Gibson. They occasionally played gigs, with the objective of having fun. Making money as a musician wasn't important to Jim because, starting in 1951, he had steady work as an electrician with the City of Vancouver that eventually led to him becoming an electrical technician. Jim had a strong work ethic and sharp mind that enabled him to succeed in his career. That said, jazz inspired him, and he took every opportunity to listen to and play the burgeoning art form. This was the stable and creative environment Rick was born into, on April 2, 1951.

A pivotal motivational experience for Jim was seeing and hearing Charlie Parker and Dizzy Gillespie play in Vancouver. While Jim was fuzzy on the date, it was very likely February 23, 1954. That night Bird and Dizzy performed in two shows at the Georgia Auditorium, which stood at the corner of Georgia and Denman until it was demolished in 1959 and replaced with a parking lot. The concert was billed as the Festival of Modern American Jazz, featuring an incredible line-up of Stan Kenton and his orchestra, Parker, Gillespie, Erroll Garner, Lee Konitz, June Christy, and Cándido.[3] Jim was thrilled to hear Parker and the others play. "Shivers went up and down my spine," he said. "I just couldn't believe it. I fell in love with it."[4]

The Electrical Guitarist and his Only Son

In the following day's *Vancouver Sun*, there was a huge photo of Gillespie playing his trumpet during one of the shows. It zoomed in on his trademark puffy cheeks. "King of the be-boppers, trumpet man Ol' Diz Gillespie, was the big hit of Stan Kenton's jazz concert at Georgia Auditorium Tuesday night," read the photo caption. "Dizzy doesn't just blow the trumpet in his intricate arrangements; he "fires" it like a musical machine gun."[5]

Vancouver Sun, February 13, 1954.

As far as I know, no recording of the Georgia Auditorium jazz extravaganza has ever publicly emerged. But two nights after the Vancouver performances, the same artists performed at Portland's Civic Auditorium, and someone recorded at least part of the show. Tracks from the recording turned up on various releases and can be found after a few keystrokes in Spotify and YouTube. They include three tunes Gillespie robustly played on as a featured soloist with the Kenton orchestra, and three songs featuring Parker: "Night and Day," "My Funny Valentine," and "Cherokee." I listened to them to hear what Jim heard. By that point in his life, Parker was a long way from his peak form; after years of hard living, his tone had degraded. But he was still a formidable improviser, expressing advanced harmonic ideas in his note choices at breakneck speed, which dazzled Jim.

After the Vancouver shows, which drew several thousand people but still lost the promoters $2,000 according to a *Vancouver Sun* review,[6] Jim got to meet Parker. He was a friendly jazz God. "A lot nicer than Mingus," Jim said, referring to tempestuous bassist Charles Mingus, who held court at the Cellar about seven years later.[7] Parker died in March 1955, just over a year after Jim heard him, at thirty-four.

The same year that Parker passed, Jim was one of the musicians who started playing at a jam space known as the Wailhouse in Richmond. In 1956, he and the same players co-founded the Cellar on Watson Street in Vancouver. Alongside architect John Grinnell, artist Harry Webb, and pianist Al Neil, Jim played a key role in transforming an unfinished basement into a hip jazz club. Naturally, he did much of the electrical work and carpentry, building several versions of the bandstand over the years.

On that bandstand, Jim emerged as one of the leaders of the Cellar's top bands of local musicians that played on weekends. At various times, Jim's band included Jim Johnson or Bill Holmes on tenor sax, bassist Tony Clitheroe, Bill Boyle or Chuck Logan on drums, Harvey Adams on bassoon, Doreen Williams on vocals, and others. Jim also played in a group with American vibraphonist Bob Frogge, who by all accounts was an uninhibited character.

Jim was in the enviable position of being virtually the only local guitarist who played at the Cellar. The only other Vancouver guitarist he remembered playing there was his friend Ray Norris, who was a jazz and country musician often heard on CBC Radio and TV with his quintet and other groups. Norris taught at the Western Conservatory of Music on Seymour Street, along with another guitarist Felix Smalley, who was Kilburn's teacher.[8] Norris was also in demand for gigs downtown and likely didn't perform much at the Cellar before moving to Toronto, where the forty-two-year-old died in 1958 after an accidental three-storey fall from an apartment window.[9] So Jim was essentially it at the Cellar as far as locals on electric guitar.

I'm curious about what Jim sounded like at the Cellar. While there are no available recordings of his playing in the club, Jim gave me five tracks he played on with a sextet led by saxophonist Dave Quarin, including John Dawe on the euphonium-like baritone horn, Tony Clitheroe, pianist Harold Krause, and drummer Al Cleland. They were recorded in 1957 for broadcast on *Jazz Workshop*, a CBC Radio show produced in Vancouver. Jim soloed on four of the tunes, and his playing confirmed his innate quality as a jazz guitarist. With the Charlie Christian influence coming through, Kilburn crafted crisp melodic lines with well-placed and appealing inflections.

Jim Kilburn. Photographer unknown. Courtesy Dave Quarin.

Don Thompson, the sublime pianist, vibraphonist, and bassist who played at the Cellar, said "Jim Kilburn was great. He was a beautiful guitar player."[10] Jim used the word "amateur" to describe himself and other locals who played at the Cellar,[11] but Thompson said that wasn't the case with Jim and other key players at the club. "They were stellar, triple-A musicians," said Thompson.[12]

Regardless of Jim's humble self-regard, other guitarists admired him. Wilmer (Bill) Fawcett was a student at Como Lake High School in Coquitlam and a beginner rock guitarist when he attended a game-changing jazz performance at the school. It featured Cellar regulars, including Jim. "This group with Jim Kilburn, it just knocked me out," said Fawcett. "I went up to him and got my courage up and asked him if he was giving guitar lessons. He said, 'Not really,' but he [also] said, 'If you are interested, let's get together.'"[13]

What followed were weekly lessons at Jim's house. They often entailed just listening to records by guitarists Wes Montgomery, Jim Hall, Tal Farlow, and others that Jim felt Fawcett should hear. "It just attracted me so much what he [Jim] was doing on guitar compared to what I was used to listening to," said Fawcett.[14] The respect was mutual. "That kid played wonderfully," said Jim about the teenaged Fawcett,[15] who cherished listening to music at the Cellar and playing at the Black Spot jazz coffeehouse on Dunbar Street. Fawcett became an accomplished classical bassist with the Vancouver Symphony Orchestra and other orchestras and ensembles.

Meanwhile, Jim took on a leadership role at the club, which was cooperatively run by musicians. He was elected president of the Cellar's board in early 1958, after fellow founders Ken Hole and Walley Lightbody left the club due to differences with other members over the Cellar's musical and business directions.

Aside from helping to build the Cellar's interior and its musical reputation, Jim also designed and constructed—mostly by himself—the family house on Francis Road in Richmond where he lived with his wife Joyce (who helped out at the Cellar and assisted in building the house) and Rick. The house became a sort of Cellar satellite, where jam sessions and socializing took place. Among the visitors was Howard Roberts, the fine guitarist who played at the Cellar. Roberts wrote instructional guitar books, which influenced Jim to also write a book on playing guitar that was never published.

Jim and Joyce Kilburn. Photographer unknown. Courtesy Rick Kilburn.

One unforgettable houseguest was Elmo Hope, the immensely original but terribly messed-up pianist and composer who played legendary sets with the great tenor saxophonist Harold Land at the Cellar in November 1958. Hope was a heroin addict, and one time he locked himself in the Kilburns' bathroom and overdosed. "We finally got him out by ripping out the bathroom's outside window and crawling in and unlocking the door," wrote Jim in a short, unpublished history of the Cellar he put together.[16] That wasn't the end of the story. Rick, who was at his grandparents' place that night, had a bunk bed. "We tossed Elmo in the lower bunk hoping he'd sober up. A couple of horny little buggers wanted to have a little bit of sex. So they climbed in the upper bunk."[17] The top bunk gave way and "Elmo wound up wearing a 4x8 sheet of plywood plus a couple of semi-nude bodies."[18] The incident had a coda: "Fortunately, no one was injured, and it seemed to wake Elmo from his torpor. He suddenly decided that he was the conductor of the New York Philharmonic and proceeded to group everyone into categories (strings, horns, etc.) and conduct them with his arms and a variety of facial expressions."[19] Hope died of heart failure at forty-three, nine years after he played at the Cellar.

Also in the band that played at the Cellar with Land and Hope was the brilliant young bassist Scott LaFaro. Jim took Rick to the club one afternoon during the group's Cellar run, and LaFaro was there practicing. Rick soaked in LaFaro's unique double bass sound and was captivated. "It just impressed me, so much," said Rick. "How could it not? The guy had an energy about him. So I believe I told Dad at the time, that's what I wanted to do."[20]

While gentle Jim never pushed his son to become a musician, growing up as a jazz kid greatly influenced Rick. "I really didn't have a choice as to whether or not I was going to be a musician," he said. "It was obvious with the environment I grew up in, which was all-pervasive as far as music and jazz music went, that there was only one way for me to go."[21] As for LaFaro, he would go on to play with pianist Bill Evans and drummer Paul Motian in a trio that made transcendent, landmark jazz. It was heartbreaking when, less than three years after playing at the Cellar, LaFaro died in a car crash. He was just twenty-five.

Jim also wrote in his Cellar history about how prominent jazz musicians playing big shows in Vancouver, such as Stan Getz, would drop in the club after midnight and jam until as late as five a.m. One night Jim saw Getz "smash his tenor sax repeatedly against the concrete wall adjacent to the bandstand (for no apparent reason)." Another night, "Oscar Peterson and Herb Ellis dropped in, and Herb sat in with the group using my guitar (which never sounded better)."[22]

Of all the titans that played at the Cellar, guitarist Wes Montgomery was especially important to Jim. Like Christian, Montgomery was a genius on the fretboard. Wes' brothers Monk and Buddy performed at the Cellar in 1957 with the Mastersounds. Then the Montgomery Brothers, including Wes, played at the club in 1960 and 1961. During the latter engagement, a recording was made in front of a small audience with Wes, Buddy on vibes, Monk on bass, and Paul Humphrey on drums. Eight tracks from the recording came out on various releases, including one that had "massive crowd reaction" that was dubbed in, according to liner notes by the celebrated jazz producer Orrin Keepnews.[23] Then Keepnews produced *Groove Brothers*, which combined two previous releases—*The Montgomery Brothers* and *The Montgomery Brothers in Canada*—and eliminated the fake applause.[24] The tracks on *Groove Brothers* recorded at the Cellar sound immaculate, like they were recorded in a studio and not in a basement jazz club. The music shimmers with gorgeous colours and textures. Jim was drawn to Wes' robust technique and bravura soloing style, which the Cellar recording crisply captured. "My jaw dropped every time I heard him."[25]

The guitarists became friends and jammed at the Kilburn home. During one living room session, Wes and Jim heard a sound. "He and I peeked around the corner, and there was Rick plunking on an old violin [that only had one string]," said Jim. "We burst out in laughter."[26] Young Rick wasn't amused. "I was playing along with them with this violin, plucking on it, randomly playing notes but being involved in the feeling of the whole thing even though I was around the corner," he said. "And then all of a sudden they weren't playing anymore, and I was still playing, and they were peeking around the corner laughing, so that was embarrassing."[27] Rick ran off, crying, but the embarrassment didn't deter him from wanting to play music like the grownups.

Tears aside, the memory of Montgomery in their house spoke to the connection between Wes and Jim. "Wes really had a lot of respect for Dad," said Rick. "Looking back at it, I couldn't believe that he could actually sit there with Wes Montgomery and play guitar with him, but Wes viewed him as an equal. It makes sense because Dad was absolutely a very talented jazz guitar player."[28] The guitarists kept in touch before Wes died at forty-five, which was a huge loss to the jazz world.

Jim's underrated musicality came across during a high-profile show at Seattle World's Fair on May 23, 1962. Bandleader, trombonist, and composer/arranger Dave Robbins recruited Jim to be in a twenty-nine-piece jazz orchestra that played at the Fair. Many of Vancouver's top jazz musicians—including Chris Gage, Fraser MacPherson, Bobby Hales, Ray Sikora, Paul Ruhland, and Eleanor Collins—were in the orchestra led by Robbins. It played very modern, large-ensemble jazz, intricately arranged with ample room for improvisation, in the inventive style of Gil Evans. An unreleased recording of the entire Seattle show, which was nationally broadcast on CBC Radio, includes the orchestra's exhilarating version of Evans' "La Nevada." Jim can be heard throughout the tune, with distinctive strumming and picking at the beginning and a patiently constructed solo later that leaves no doubt about his ability as an improviser.

Journeys to the Bandstand

Wes (electric guitar) and Monk (bass) Montgomery, the original Cellar. Photographer unknown. Courtesy Dave Quarin.

At that time the Cellar was still an important jazz venue, but it had entered a period of slow decay. Jim kept playing there in the club's final months, and he occasionally did gigs elsewhere, like at the Flatted Fifth (later renamed the Flat Five) that supplanted the Cellar. "Guitarist Jim Kilburn has a strong sense of rhythm and tends to drop his notes directly on top of the beat," wrote a *Province* reviewer about his playing at the Flatted Fifth.[29] By the time the Cellar shut down in early 1964, Jim's name had disappeared from gig notices in Vancouver newspapers. As if someone yanked the power cord, he simply stopped performing. Like fellow Cellar player John Dawe, Jim chose the practical utility of the working man's regular paycheque over the unreliable nature of life as a musician. It was a double loss: Jim never got the opportunity to further polish his sound or enjoy the acclaim that should have come his way, and too few jazz fans discovered his talents. But music didn't define Jim and wasn't intrinsic to his self-esteem. He was a well-rounded individual who enjoyed his job, pursued a passion for fly fishing, developed a knack for writing and cartooning, and embraced being a family man.

All of this came across as I sat with him and chatted in his Qualicum Beach home, which was another house that Jim built. I asked him many questions about the Cellar, life after the jazz club, and his life story. Jim responded with short answers that, for the most part, weren't quoteworthy. Initially I questioned whether his succinct style would enable the portraiture through words I had in mind for him. Then I realized, this was the essence of Jim. While he excelled at his pursuits, Jim's way of being was self-effacing. I learned a lot about the fine art of staying grounded just by being in his presence.

· · ·

Jim's retirement from Vancouver's jazz scene didn't mean he stopped playing and mentoring. Tom Keenlyside was in grade nine when he met Rick, who, after first playing piano and guitar, chose to play bass. Rick invited Keenlyside to jam with the Kilburns, and making music together became a regular ritual. "We would play tunes all night, with Rick, Jim, and me [on flute and trumpet], and we did that a lot," said Keenlyside, who went on to have a long career in music, primarily as a tenor saxophonist and flutist. "It was an unbelievable learning experience because Jim was a really, really fine guitar player. And Rick and I were both learning our instruments, so he was extremely helpful."[30] When the teenagers started working as musicians, Jim would often drive them to the gigs.

During the late-night jam sessions that continued the tradition of music-making in the Kilburn home, Jim didn't talk much about the Cellar, recalled Keenlyside. But when the club came up in conversation, it was apparent that "he was very proud of being deeply involved" with the Cellar, said Keenlyside.[31] As Rick's musicianship grew and significant opportunities came his way, Jim was also proud of his son. Not in a boastful way, but in Jim's quiet style.

Teenaged Rick played music with his dad every day after Jim came home from work. Rick was nineteen when he joined Chilliwack as the rock band's electric bassist. It was a brief dalliance away from jazz. Rick felt a strong desire to study jazz double bass, which he did with Dave Young in Edmonton before attending the Berklee College of Music in Boston for two semesters.

Moving to the US afforded Rick musical opportunities his father never had. By 1974, Rick was living in New York City and playing with Dave Brubeck, Paul Desmond, and Brubeck's sons in various configurations. Another renowned artist who regularly hired Rick was Chet Baker. It was a heady feeling to be performing and touring with jazz stars in fabled clubs, at Carnegie Hall and other large theatres, and as part of major festivals at a young age. Did Rick feel like he had made it? "I might have thought that but, in retrospect, I have to go back and wonder, why the heck did they hire me? I think I know the answer to that. It was just the feel that I brought to the music because I couldn't help but bring a feel from my upbringing."[32]

Rick also worked with the inimitable singer and pianist Mose Allison for seven years. "It was fantastic," said Rick about his time with Allison, who combined blues, jazz, and offbeat humour. "Talk about a unique player and having your own voice in jazz."[33] Just as it was when he played with the Brubecks and Desmond at Vancouver's Queen Elizabeth Theatre, Rick triumphantly returned home to perform with Allison at the Sheraton Landmark Jazz Bar, Café New York, and at other Vancouver venues.

When not touring, in NYC Rick accompanied Jimmy Rowles at Bradley's, Joanne Brackeen and other pianists at Surf Maid, and played many other fulfilling gigs. It was also an era when the city's artists lived cheaply in large, abandoned, formerly industrial lofts located in faded areas before they gentrified. At one point, Rick was paying $225 a month to live in an 1,100 square foot loft that had a close-up view of the Empire State Building. Elite

The Electrical Guitarist and his Only Son

Two Generations of Brubeck. Back row (left to right): Dan Brubeck, Darius Brubeck, and Dave Brubeck. Front row: Rick Kilburn, Jerry Bergonzi, and Perry Robinson. 1975. Photographer unknown. Courtesy Rick Kilburn.

Dave Brubeck and Rick Kilburn, Orpheum Theatre, June 29, 2002. Photo by Ross Taggart, courtesy Rick Kilburn.

37

jazz musicians like Michael Brecker, Steve Grossman, Gerry Mulligan, Jerry Bergonzi (who lived in the same building), and Desmond came to the loft to play with Rick and others.

In January 1980, *The New Yorker* published a profile of bassist Michael Moore. Whitney Balliett, the weekly magazine's venerated jazz critic, wrote the piece. Like all of Balliett's literary jazz criticism, it was an incredibly insightful article, filled with micro-detail that caught his perceptive eyes and ears. Balliett devoted a large chunk of the profile to describing a lesson that Moore gave Rick. In one very long paragraph and a bunch of smaller ones, Balliett captured the complex process of an experienced teacher imparting essential knowledge to a keen student—ranging from how to effectively hold and bow the bass, to how to make harmonic decisions when soloing. Balliett observed that Rick was relaxed and watched with rapt attention when Moore demonstrated a technique or harmonic ideas. After the lesson was over and Rick left, Moore talked to Balliett about how promising he believed the young bassist was.[34] To have Moore—a tremendous musician who had performed with many top-flight players—say something like that to one of the world's greatest jazz critics in the hallowed pages of *The New Yorker* was like being anointed.

Back home, Vancouver's equivalent to Balliett—jazz writer and broadcaster Bob Smith—noticed the focus on Rick in *The New Yorker*. In his *Vancouver Sun* column, Smith highlighted what Balliett wrote. Smith also talked to Jim, who recounted Rick's musical growth. "One thing I'm glad I told him out front, although I had to sit on him to keep at it, was to develop his ear," Jim told Smith.[35] Years later, Rick told me that his dad had "an incredible ear."[36] So Rick respected and absorbed his father's wisdom.

It's interesting to speculate on where Rick would have gone in music if he had stayed on this path. But around the time Rick was in New York, the city was on the verge of bankruptcy. Although the fiscal crisis eventually eased, economic decline in the metropolis led to less disposable income, which meant fewer gigs. "My confidence wasn't very high at the time either, and there were some things going on personally that I needed to deal with," said Rick.[37] Despite the prominent gigs and high praise he received, Rick honestly felt that he was still "learning how to play" during his New York City period.[38] So after a decade in NYC, he knew it was time to leave.

At thirty-three, Rick temporarily moved in with his parents, a world away from New York in slow moving Qualicum Beach on Vancouver Island. While it took time and reflection for Rick to adjust to the culture shock, he made the transition to his next phase. The student became a teacher, at Malaspina College, Vancouver Community College, and the Banff Centre for the Arts. Rick also became an ace producer and engineer, contributing to myriad albums in his own recording studios and elsewhere.

Rick Kilburn, 2019. Photographer unknown. Courtesy Rick Kilburn.

And he kept playing. On cruise ships and close to home. In 1997, I saw him and drummer John Nolan provide strong accompaniment to Mose Allison at a Vancouver show. It was an odd concert due to the buttoned-down venue—the downtown Law Courts Inn. While the setting wasn't the historic Village Vanguard (which Rick played in during his NYC period), his professional approach and low-key, bluesy sturdiness helped Rick overcome the environment.

In 2020, Rick received well-earned recognition with the release of a ten-and-a-half-minute documentary, *In the Zone: Rick Kilburn*. Directed by Kerilie McDowall, the eloquent and award-winning short includes a scene from 2008 where Rick, Jim, and pianist Ron Hadley perform "It Might Have Been in Spring," It's an original by Rick based on "It Might as Well Be Spring." During the tune, Rick—who closes his eyes and seems to hold his upright bass extra close to himself as if he's embracing it—crafts a long solo that embodies the documentary's title. Drawing from his years of experience and the in-the-moment joy of performing with his dad and Hadley, Rick achieves a rare flow state in his improvisation that's exquisite.

When I asked Rick face-to-face if he had enjoyed his life in music, the Kilburn humility was front and centre. "Well, I have to say yes," he said. "There have been struggles, of course, but that's music. That's being an artist. And my main struggle—I'm still struggling with it—I'm still trying to get good [as a bass player]. I don't know if I'm going to achieve that in this lifetime." He also expressed immense appreciation for his jazz upbringing—the influence of his dad, the original Cellar, and other musicians who played there—that inspired his remarkable odyssey in music. "There is a string through everything, right to the present time."[39]

• • •

At the Old School House Arts Centre, in a gorgeous classical revival building in Qualicum Beach that's more than a century old, Jim sits down and gets comfortable. He performed here many times over the course of about fourteen years, so the guitarist feels at home. Jim is holding a different electric guitar from the one he showed me that morning. This one's a sleek black Fender Telecaster, and he uses it to play "When Sunny Gets Blue," "C Jam Blues," "Angel Eyes," and other standards with Hadley and bass clarinetist Liam Hockley. Jim, who has a bandage on his forehead due to a recent tumble, struggles with some of the melodies and misses notes here and there. After the performance for an audience of eleven, he apologizes to me for his playing. "You heard the worst of me. It's not like it used to be."[40] I assure Jim he played well, and I mean it. I don't care about the mistakes because the feel and spirit are inherently still there.

At one point in 2015, Jim put his beloved guitars away in their cases for the last time. "It just started going away," said Rick about Jim's ability to play like he used to. Jim was diagnosed with dementia years before I met him, and while his condition stayed mild for a long time, "it's not getting better," explained Rick in 2019.[41] Four years earlier, on Boxing Day 2015, Jim's wife Joyce passed away. They were married sixty-seven years.[42] Rick had been a caregiver for his mom, and after her passing, he moved back into the Qualicum Beach house to be Jim's primary caregiver. After years of being a close, mutually supportive family, with swinging jazz as their soundtrack, Rick wanted to be there for his dad.

Jim Kilburn (guitar), Ron Hadley (piano), and Rick Kilburn (bass), Old School House Arts Centre, Qualicum Beach. Photo by Clifford Anderson, courtesy Rick Kilburn.

Jim passed away in his home on the morning of November 13, 2021. He was ninety-four. "I am still trying to wrap my head around this incredible loss to not only myself, but also to everybody who knew Dad," wrote Rick on Facebook. "He was larger than life in a quiet, understated way and to my way of thinking, he occupied the upper echelon of humanity, while still being very much human."[43]

When I consider what has stood out for me the most about the Kilburns, my mind turns to fly fishing. Jim was as impassioned about fly fishing as he was about playing jazz. He co-founded the Totem Flyfishers club (along with Rick and others) in 1968, and a collection of his essays on fly fishing for trout and salmon in BC was published in a book: *The Compleat Kilburn*. On a day after one of trumpeter Don Cherry's late-night gigs at the Cellar in the late fifties, Jim took him fly fishing on the Vedder River in Chilliwack. "Jim fished while Cherry played his pocket trumpet," wrote Rick. "A soldier from the nearby Army camp meandered by and asked what they were doing. It was explained to him that Jim was fishing and Don Cherry, with his trumpet, was mesmerizing and calling the fish into Jim so that he could catch them. They had a good laugh over that."[44]

Jim introduced the deep pleasures of the sport to Rick, Tom Keenlyside, and others. There are close parallels between fly fishing and playing jazz. Both involve acquiring knowledge, patiently practicing technique, adapting on the fly, and being dedicated to a craft. All of which are perfect descriptors of the authentic and enduring approaches to life and music that Jim took and Rick continues to take. It's unequivocally the Kilburn way.

3 / THE MAN WITH THE PLASTIC SAXOPHONE: ORNETTE COLEMAN

ORNETTE COLEMAN WAS a jazz giant who didn't look the part. Small in physical stature, soft-spoken, and gentle, Coleman played a white Grafton alto saxophone—made from acrylic plastic—that looked like a toy. Yet when he was on the bandstand at Vancouver's original Cellar jazz club in 1957, the assertive sounds coming out of his horn sparked debate—involving both awe and negativity—among musicians and others in the club who witnessed what would be historic gigs.

It's unlikely those in attendance could have predicted that Coleman would go on to revolutionize jazz. But it was clear his music wasn't the bebop and hard bop heard most nights inside the club's walls. There was something else going on with Coleman's harmonic concept and emerging sound that those who didn't tune out, and instead listened with open ears, could hear. Something new, exciting, and disruptive.

The seeds for Coleman's Cellar performances, and his musical breakthroughs that happened shortly after, were planted in Los Angeles during the early and mid-1950s. After moving there from his hometown of Fort Worth, Texas, Coleman—like any young jazz musician—pursued playing opportunities. But that's where his similarities with others ended. His plastic sax had a harsh tone, which Coleman made the most of. He also played melodies and soloed with a discordance that turned off people who heard him. When Coleman tried to sit in at LA clubs such as the Lighthouse, the California

Club, and the Jazz Cellar, club owners and musicians were antagonistic and contemptuous.[1] Unable to find work as a musician, he took on jobs like operating an elevator at Bullock's department store. Coleman wasn't enthusiastic about the gig; he would sometimes park elevators and read books on music theory and harmony.[2]

Then there were the musicians who liked what they heard from Coleman, including Sonny Rollins. Around the time Rollins was in LA performing with the Max Roach Quintet and recording his classic *Way Out West* album for Contemporary Records, the iconic tenor saxophonist met Coleman. The two saxophonists—both born in 1930—practiced on the beach together, and Rollins said years later that he admired Coleman for his adventurous free spirit and courage.[3] Another supporter was young trumpeter Don Cherry, who found his bearings in LA's thriving Central Avenue jazz scene. Clifford Brown informally mentored Cherry, which represented the kind of acceptance from the jazz establishment that eluded Coleman. Cherry was scared when he first met Coleman, who had Christlike long hair and a beard and wore an overcoat in hot weather.[4] But Cherry and Coleman forged a bond and became close, longtime allies.

Cherry was the catalyst for Coleman, after being scorned in LA, getting an opportunity in Vancouver. Ken Hole, the first manager of Vancouver's Cellar, booked Cherry to perform at the club in 1956 with the Jazz Messiahs: alto saxophonist George Newman, bassist Don Payne, and drummer Billy Higgins. Cherry played at the Cellar a second time in August 1957 with the Jazz Messiahs. *Down Beat*, North America's top jazz magazine, took note of the gigs in its "strictly ad lib" column published in the September 1957 issue: "Members of trumpeter Don Cherry's neo-bop quartet returned from their two weeks in Vancouver's Cellar flipping over the Musicians & Artists club there."[5] (The club was registered under the BC *Societies Act* as the Cellar Musicians and Artists Society.)

Cherry had an affinity for the Cellar and Vancouver, so it was inevitable that he would be booked again. But the third time he would play with someone who was unknown in Vancouver and in most jazz scenes at the time: Ornette Coleman. How the booking came about is a bit murky. Ken Hole said that he booked Coleman, Cherry, and the other musicians. Dave Quarin, who would succeed Hole as manager of the club in early 1958, said it was a conversation he had with Cherry about Coleman that was key to the Cellar booking the saxophonist. Cherry told Quarin: there's this saxophonist operating elevators in LA who you need to hear.

Word spread about the band that was booked for the Cellar October 25 to November 3, 1957. Pianist Al Neil said a palpable buzz preceded the gigs. "Word of mouth was that this weird group was coming up," said Neil, who summed up the advance scouting report this way: "If you think bebop is over the top, wait 'til you hear this!"[6]

The band consisted of Cherry, pianist Don Friedman, bassist Ben Tucker, and Higgins. They were billed as the Los Angeles Jazz All-Stars, which was a misnomer, but it had a ring to it. What made the engagement historically noteworthy was that it marked Coleman's professional debut as the leader of a jazz band.

Ben Tucker (bass), Ornette Coleman (alto saxophone), and Billy Higgins (drums), the original Cellar, October–November 1957. Photographer unknown. Courtesy James Carney.

By the time I learned about Coleman's performances at the Cellar, only two members of the band were still alive: Coleman and Friedman. I wanted some insights about Coleman's time at the club and in Vancouver, so short of contacting Coleman, who wasn't doing interviews in the twilight of his life, I emailed Friedman in 2014. It took him just one hour to reply: "I do have some memories of playing there with Ornette and Don Cherry," he wrote.[7]

On the phone from his home in New York, Friedman wasted no time retrieving fifty-seven-year-old memories of Vancouver, the Cellar, and the leading players in the band he performed with at the club. "What I remember very distinctly about the gig is that we were living in some sort of rooming house," said Friedman, who was twenty-two at the time. "Don [Cherry] and Ornette were staying upstairs from where I was, and I used to hear them practicing up there during the daytime. I don't know if Don couldn't read [music], I think he could read, it's just how Ornette wrote the charts; they weren't very clear. So, Ornette would just play them over and over again until Don had them memorized. That's how he taught Don all the heads [melodies]."[8]

Friedman's memory of Coleman's shortcomings in music notation matches a recollection from Dave Quarin. At one point during Coleman's stay in Vancouver for the Cellar shows, he wrote a tune at Quarin's house. "I even put the bar lines in for Ornette on that number," Quarin told Jim Banham of the *Province*. "Ornette had a lot of music in his head, but he had trouble writing it down."[9] Quarin also asked Coleman if he thought about anything when playing. "He said to me, 'I hear violins.'"[10]

Friedman remembered that "Invisible" was among the tunes Coleman taught Cherry. That would be the lead track on *Something Else!!!!*, Coleman's 1958 debut recording on Contemporary Records. Another was "Lonely Woman," which would open Coleman's third recording that came out in 1959—*The Shape of Jazz to Come*—and become arguably his best-known and most-loved composition.

Don Friedman (piano), Ben Tucker (bass), Billy Higgins (drums), Don Cherry (trumpet), and Ornette Coleman (alto saxophone), the original Cellar, October–November 1957. Photographer unknown. Courtesy James Carney.

Many local jazz musicians went to Coleman's Cellar gigs, and their reactions reflected the differences of opinion about the saxophonist. "I was not very excited about him," said tenor saxophonist Jim Johnson. "It was quite amazing to hear what he was doing, sort of making it up as he goes along. It was like freedom. I guess it was the beginning of freedom [in jazz]. He was capable of making long lyrical statements and running them together, but I didn't care much for Ornette."[11]

Trumpeter John Dawe recalled that the tunes Coleman wrote and played at the time were "conventional," compared with the full-on free jazz that he would eventually play. "Ornette was a little more under control at that time," said Dawe. "He was a lot more melodic than he was a couple years later." But Dawe said Coleman was still "shocking" to hear. "We didn't know what was happening when we heard Ornette. He was hard to take. That wasn't ordinary jazz."[12]

Al Neil was the most unconventional musician in the Cellar crowd, so Coleman and the group's approach personally resonated. "I was just ecstatic because I always had a tendency to think a little bit more abstract than the beboppers, but I hadn't really formulated any way to do that [play abstract music] yet," said Neil. "So, it was really exciting to me to see that these guys could do it [play in a different way] with such elegance and fluidity, and it seemed to make sense. They weren't consciously trying to just make a complete break [from more traditional jazz]. It still went along in 4/4 mode, and as far as I was concerned, it still swung. It was lyrical."[13] Neil noted that while the Cellar gigs were never mentioned in highlights of Coleman's career, they were momentous for the fledgling scene based at the jazz club.[14]

As for Friedman, he was a big fan of Coleman's playing, even if he found accompanying the altoist a challenge. "I loved it. I always loved his playing. He had this beautiful sound, this bluesy feeling, this great rhythmic feeling. It was just hard to play with him because he didn't play on changes exactly. Even if we tried to play a tune, like "All the Things You Are," he wouldn't follow the changes. He just played whatever he felt like playing.

"I personally believe that the reason why he didn't use piano [pianists] for almost his whole career was because as long as he didn't have a chord instrument, he could play whatever he wanted. A chord instrument in some ways forces a person—a saxophone player, a trumpet player—to adhere to what the piano player is doing. And Ornette couldn't do that; he didn't know how to do that."

Knowing that about Coleman, Friedman had to adapt his piano playing. "I didn't pay any attention to the written part of the music. When they played the melodies, I would mostly just lay out and let them play the tune because the chords didn't make much sense. When Ornette would start improvising, I would hear—I had very good ears—where he was in relation to the keys he was playing in, and I would just try to find chords that sounded something like what he was playing."[15]

Ken Hole found the sax player's music "a little far out. He did some weird things with the saxophone, but he did them very well." Hole recalled how appreciative Coleman was about getting booked to play at the Cellar. "At the end of the gig, he put his arms around me and gave me a big hug. He said 'Ken, you're the first person that's ever hired me to play [a jazz gig as a leader], ever.' And he said, 'I really want to thank you. No matter where I am or what I'm doing, if you need me to play a gig, I'll come and do it for nothing for you.' That was Ornette Coleman."[16]

Ornette Coleman (alto saxophone), Ben Tucker (bass), and Billy Higgins (drums), the original Cellar, October–November 1957. Photographer unknown. Courtesy Walley Lightbody.

The University of British Columbia's jazz club, Jazzsoc, also presented Coleman and the group November 1, 1957, in a noon-hour concert at the UBC Auditorium. In a review of the concert published in UBC's student newspaper, *The Ubyssey*, Roger Purves noted some of the tunes the band played: "The Ambassador from Greenland" (written by Cherry), "Embraceable You," and "Blackbird," which may have been "Bye Bye Blackbird." Purves wrote that "Arnette Coleman" played solos that consisted of "overextended lines utilizing every register of the instrument in a noisily pyrotechnical manner. Moreover, individual notes within the lines lacked definition to the extent that their contribution to the line was quite lost." His parting shot: Coleman's solos were "fortunately" short.[17] The fusty review foreshadowed what would come from critics: close-minded dismissals of his music.

• • •

After the Cellar gigs, Coleman went back to LA, where he put in more time developing his sound, improvisation approach, and composition style. Cherry stayed in Vancouver for a few months until Coleman wrote with news that the saxophonist had secured his first record date. Cherry returned to LA and played on Coleman's *Something Else!!!!* In the late fifties, that album—along with *Tomorrow Is the Question!* and *The Shape of Jazz to Come*—put the jazz world on notice that Coleman was a completely original artist who wouldn't be constrained by traditional harmony and song structure.

Then, in November 1959, Coleman and his quartet—including Cherry, bassist Charlie Haden, and Higgins—began a legendary residency at the Five Spot Café in New York City that set off a furor in the music world. Miles Davis and Max Roach were among the jazz masters who listened to Coleman at the Five Spot, and they didn't like what they heard. Roach went as far as expressing his anger about what Coleman was doing to jazz by allegedly punching him in the mouth backstage. As it turned out, Friedman was playing "intermission piano" at the Five Spot at one point during the residency, which was extended from two to ten weeks. So Friedman experienced Coleman's epochal performances up close. From that point on, regardless of the continued opposition, Coleman could no longer be shunned or hemmed in. His place in history as a pioneer of avant-garde jazz was assured.

Gradually, more musicians and critics celebrated Coleman. The Cellar had a role in enabling one influential voice, *Down Beat* west coast editor John Tynan, to discover Coleman. As Tynan recounted in a *Down Beat* feature, Don Payne called Tynan shortly after Cherry, James Clay, Payne, and

Higgins played as the Jazz Messiahs at the Cellar in August 1957. As Tynan recalled, "He [Payne] told me about the job in Vancouver and said, 'Look, we made some tapes up there. I'd like you to hear them because I really think you'll dig the charts. Some of them are Ornette Coleman's and, John, they're just too much.' That, I believe, was the first time I had heard the name Ornette Coleman."[18]

Tynan went to Payne's apartment in Hollywood to hear the Cellar recording. "What I heard that afternoon in 1957 convinced me that in Coleman jazz had birthed an important *writer*. I had yet to hear him play."[19] Tynan's first experience hearing Coleman perform live was at the Jazz Cellar in Hollywood. At that Cellar, Coleman "blasted loose with the fiercest, weirdest, most abandoned utterance I had heard in over 15 years of listening to jazz. It was almost literally stunning," wrote Tynan. "Here was an originality never before experienced in jazz."[20]

The divisive nature of Coleman's atonal sound resulted in dramatic vicissitudes in the critical appraisal of his career. He inspired polar opposite reactions among critics—even within the minds of individual critics. Less than two years after Tynan wrote so glowingly of Coleman in *Down Beat*, he did an about-face and trashed the *Free Jazz* album Coleman recorded in December 1960 with a double quartet including Cherry, Eric Dolphy, Freddie Hubbard, and other prominent players. The music consisted of almost forty minutes of dissonant and unrestrained improv recorded in a single take, with no overdubs added. In his three-paragraph *Down Beat* review that awarded the album "no stars," Tynan wrote that "these eight nihilists were collected together in one studio at one time and with one common cause: to destroy the music that gave them birth."[21] *Down Beat* ran Tynan's critique alongside another, longer review of the album that gave it five stars.[22]

Cherry, who played with Coleman for so long and was also a free jazz innovator, became a major voice on the trumpet. In a 1963 feature on Cherry written by LeRoi Jones for *Down Beat*, there's a reference to a gig Cherry played with Coleman in "Vancouver, Washington." Jones quoted Cherry as saying, "It was Ornette's first jazz gig [as a leader], and he was really beautiful."[23] Something got lost in translation. In a letter published in *Down Beat* in 1964, jazz broadcaster and writer Bob Smith pointed out that the gig was at the Cellar in Vancouver, BC, Canada. "As a matter of fact, at least two of their sets were broadcast live on station CFUN in our town, and I had the pleasure of emceeing," wrote Smith.[24]

It's long been rumoured that those broadcasts still exist somewhere as recordings, but they've never surfaced. If these aural Holy Grails are ever found, then listeners will get a rare chance to hear Coleman just before he shook up the jazz world. But after all this time, it's highly unlikely any audio artifacts will be found. The sound of Ornette Coleman in late 1957 will live on only in the hazy memories of those who were there and in the vivid imaginations of the rest of us.

• • •

In September 1970, Coleman played sax, trumpet, and violin in the same basement space that housed the original Cellar. By then it was known as the Old Cellar, and his astonishing band included tenor saxophonist Dewey Redman, bassist Charlie Haden, and drummer Ed Blackwell. These were Coleman's first shows in Vancouver since the performances at the original Cellar in 1957. While more than a dozen years had passed, the sounds spilling out of Coleman's horn were as enthralling—and as contentious—as ever.

At this point, Coleman still played a plastic sax and also a metal one. Smith noticed that Coleman only played a metal alto at the Old Cellar. So he asked the man why. "That current favourite horn of mine [the plastic one] was damaged on the way out here," Coleman quietly explained. "I really miss it. I don't feel right on this one." For Smith, this possibly explained why Coleman's tone "sounded a shade sweeter, less strident" than it did twelve years earlier. Regardless of any differences in Coleman's sound, Smith was unequivocal about the fiery music he heard. "After 12 years, Coleman's lamp is still burning brightly in these eyes."[25]

John Orysik and Ken Pickering were teenagers when they saw Coleman at the Old Cellar. "I remember being thrilled by the solos and the spirit in the music," said Orysik, who with Pickering and Robert Kerr would years later co-found the Coastal Jazz & Blues Society and Vancouver's annual jazz festival. "I remember the contours and the emotional heft that the music had, and it was thrilling to hear what they were doing because it was so interesting melodically with Ornette and the way the rhythms were being played within the music. It was just so cool to hear a new syntax and vocabulary that Ornette was bringing to the music at that time."[26]

Vancouver pianist, organist, and music educator Bob Murphy was in the band that opened for Coleman at the Old Cellar over multiple evenings. "Every night the place would be fairly full, and they would start a set, and about ten minutes later a good ten, fifteen, twenty percent of the audience would run for the door," said Murphy. "The rest of them got a thrill ride. And on their most intense sets, I can remember them clearing a good third of the audience out, and then everybody else would just be inching closer and closer to the stage as the night went on." Opening for Coleman and hearing him up close in a small venue was an "astounding experience," added Murphy. "That was like getting it injected right into your core."[27]

Alan Sharpe, guitarist with a Vancouver band called Sunship Ensemble, made a cassette recording of Coleman playing at the Old Cellar.[28] About forty-eight years later, an eleven minute and nineteen second snippet of the audio relic arrived in my inbox. Even though it has horrendous sound quality, I can hear that during a more than six-minute solo, Coleman played vigorously, with absorbing harmonic ideas, his highly recognizable and engaging sound, and a relentless momentum.

Coleman played in Vancouver four more times. One of the performances was on June 25, 1986, at the New York Theatre, at the time a scruffy seventy-three-year-old venue where promoters often booked rock, metal, and punk bands. That year Coastal Jazz & Blues transformed its one-year-old local jazz festival into a huge international event, with headliners including Miles Davis, Wynton Marsalis, and Coleman performing on alto sax and trumpet with his Prime Time band: two guitarists, two bassists, and two drummers (including his son Denardo). A *Vancouver Sun* review of Coleman's show described the music as a "busy wall of sound . . . Everything blurred together, like sounds on a noisy freeway."[29] I didn't hear it that way. For me, each complex element had clarity, coalescing into a mesmerizing sonic gale.

A friend had a photo pass that allowed him to go backstage at the New York Theatre, so I tagged along. We suddenly came face-to-face with Coleman, who was alone in a small dressing room with the door open. No words were exchanged, but Coleman—wearing a beautiful blazer with an intriguing pattern on it—very subtly flashed a smile for us and the camera.

The once ridiculed little man was now an esteemed genius, who exuded soft elegance and humility. It was an indelible moment.

Ornette Coleman, New York Theatre, June 25, 1986. Photo by Chris Cameron.

In the years that followed, he received a MacArthur Fellowship, Pulitzer Prize, Grammy Lifetime Achievement Award, and other top honours. At his final performance in June 2014, Coleman— wearing a purple pinstripe suit—played on two tunes before sitting with his alto sax in his lap as Laurie Anderson, John Zorn, Patti Smith, Joe Lovano, and many other greats played in his honour. Almost exactly a year after that tribute concert in Brooklyn, Coleman died of a heart attack at eighty-five. The Coleman lamp finally went out after an incandescent musical life.

4 / FAR OUT: AL NEIL

WORLD WAR II veteran. Bebop pianist and co-founder of Vancouver's original Cellar jazz club. Heroin addict. Autobiographical author. Avant-garde pianist and visual artist. Outsider. Master of mixed media collage. Hermit. Shaman. Survivor. Civic hero.

Al Neil was all of those things, according to the well-documented narrative and mythology of his extraordinary life. I wanted to go beyond the public record and learn more about Neil's essence by talking to the man himself. So I requested an interview in summer 2013. This required going through his longtime partner, artist Carole Itter. After pleading my case, Itter passed on my request to Neil, and then politely declined on his behalf. She explained why: "He is in his 90th year and stopped doing interviews some time ago. He is becoming profoundly deaf . . . He thinks that he has been interviewed about 50 times, yet he has never been all that interested in recalling the past."[1]

Despite his reluctance, I handwrote and mailed an old school letter, asking Neil if I could at least meet him—perhaps in the home he shared with Itter in the city's Strathcona neighbourhood. The answer again was no. I was disappointed, but I understood. Neil expressed everything he wanted to say through his anomalous music, writing, and art, and in those many interviews, so it was pointless to invest some of the time he had left in helping yet another well-meaning inquisitor rummage through the past.

Itter gave me some suggestions for where to look for insights about Neil. I took her cue and made some discoveries. Then two people who were granted an audience with Neil kindly shared their interviews with me. Finally, I learned about a place with stacks of information about Neil. It's on the seventh floor of the Simon Fraser University W.A.C. Bennett Library that houses the Special Collections and Rare Books division. There I was spellbound by hundreds of artifacts from Neil's long life. It was as close as I was going to get to his creative spirit, so I drank it in, going back almost a century to retrace his steps.

• • •

Alan Douglas Neil was born March 26, 1924, in Vancouver General Hospital. One of six kids, he was a self-taught gymnast,[2] who studied classical piano with Glenn Nelson from 1933 to 1940. *Vancouver Sun* articles documented recitals by Nelson's "pianoforte pupils," listing the students including Neil, who performed at venues such as St. John's Church Hall at Nanton and Granville and the Peter Pan Ballroom at Broadway and Fir. Neil also completed Toronto Conservatory of Music exams and competed in festivals. In 1937, at an "Eisteddfod" [a competitive festival in Welsh culture] held at the Cambrian Hall at 17th and Main, Neil won first place in the "Piano solo, children under 12" category.[3] Also that year, in the British Columbia Music Festival, Neil earned second place in the under-14 piano category.[4] Adjudicator Arthur Benjamin commended Neil "for his touch and phrasing." Benjamin also gave high praise to the four finalists, including Neil, and their parents: "When your youngsters can play like that you haven't much to worry about."[5] What Benjamin didn't know was that Neil sometimes played hooky and went to theatres like the Orpheum and Beacon to catch vaudeville acts. And he grew up to be exactly the type of pianist you need to worry about.

The Second World War interrupted Neil's piano playing. Starting in 1941, as part of a project to build a military runway in Port Hardy on the northern coast of Vancouver Island, he worked as a surveyor for the Department of Transport. In June 1943, he enlisted in the Canadian Armed Forces. During wartime, newspapers reported on when individual soldiers arrived overseas. With a photo of Neil in uniform, a story in the *Province* reported that "Gnr. [gunner] Alan Douglas Neil, 19, son of Mr. and Mrs. W.T. Neil of 242 West Nineteenth, has arrived overseas with the R.C.A. [Royal Regiment of Canadian Artillery]."[6] He ended up being one of more than 156,000 Allied troops who landed on the north coast of France in the invasion and Battle of Normandy. More than 5,000 Canadians were killed in the Normandy campaign, but Neil survived. Almost three quarters of a century after D-Day, at Neil's memorial service, Gregg Simpson told people gathered at the Western Front how Neil stayed alive during the landing at Normandy. "He told me that, rather than get machine-gunned, he hid under this overturned lifeboat."[7] While that may have been an apocryphal story, Neil dying at twenty would have deprived Vancouver of one of its greatest cultural creators and characters. Neil received five medals for his military service, and his destiny played out.

In the Al Neil special collection at SFU, I was especially fascinated to read documents detailing his military record and assessing his future prospects. I can't quote from the documents because they're classified as "restricted in whole." What I can say is they paint a picture of an exemplary young man who seemed to be on a direct path for the straight life. Becoming passionate about jazz had a lot to do with why he strayed from that path.

While serving in Europe, Neil received issues of *Down Beat* from his mom. Articles in the magazine talked about the development of a new jazz form: bebop. After returning to civilian life, he studied again with Glenn Nelson and with Jean Coulthard, a pioneering composer. Along the way he took a few jazz lessons with pianist Wilf Wylie, but when it came to jazz piano, as with many other artistic disciplines, Neil mainly taught himself.

Neil worked downtown at Vancouver's main post office. At one point fellow musician Jack Reynolds suggested to Neil that if he stayed at the job, he could eventually be promoted from mail sorter to supervisor, and then manager. "He was aghast that I would even think that he would want to do something like that," said Reynolds. Neil told Reynolds that working at the post office was "mindless," and after leaving work, he didn't think about anything else except music.[8]

But at the post office, Neil met Harry Webb, a young Vancouver artist. Webb's wife Jessie was part of a group of young artists and writers who launched an arts magazine, *p m*, in 1951. Neil wrote "a short survey of new jazz" for the magazine's third and final issue, published in February 1952. In the forceful and intellectually rigorous piece, which touched on Dizzy

Gillespie, Charlie Parker, Lennie Tristano, Arnold Schoenberg, John Cage, and more, Neil engages right from the outset:

> Jazz lives for the now-moment, the unrepeatable instant of its insight. When it loses touch with the instant, it is lost, having denied its heritage. Herein lies a paradox. For the great jazz solo also has form, structure and meaning, has continuity and development, preoccupation with which, would seem to preclude the ecstatic insight of the moment. Not so. These elements of jazz are grasped intuitively, and unfold naturally, inevitably.[9]

Al Neil, circa 1949–1950. Photographer unknown.
Source: Simon Fraser University Library, Special Collections and Rare Books.

Neil clearly connected with Tristano's piano playing and composition. "The best of Tristano's music glows with an intense inner personalism," he wrote. ". . . and it expresses states of consciousness of a new level for jazz." Neil concluded the essay with ideas that presaged his future feelings on jazz:

> There are those who believe that Jazz is nothing but a rather more inspiring aphrodisiac, disseminating little more than banal and phallic musical images. But perhaps, even if this be to some measure true, jazz will eventually broaden sufficiently enough to enable it to express other, more subtle insights, in the realm of the sublime, the apocalyptic, and indeed there are moments in its tradition when this has come to pass.[10]

Her name goes unmentioned in Google and in the archival records I scanned, but Kitty Neil was an important person in Al Neil's life at this time. The married couple lived for a while near the Park Theatre cinema on Cambie Street, and on Sunday nights they hosted live music sessions in their apartment. I learned from Rod Wong, who attended a number of those sessions as a listener, that "Al was very different then. Brooks Brothers-clad, a very classy and upscale dresser," Wong said. As for Kitty, "She was always in the background as the supportive spouse," said Wong.[11] Al and Kitty had a shared passion for jazz, as confirmed by a long letter to the editor she wrote that was published in *Metronome* magazine, a competitor to *Down Beat*. Written entirely in lower case, the letter with the headline "Paean For Lennie," was an erudite and poetic appreciation of Tristano.[12] Despite their jazz affinity, the marriage eventually ended in divorce.

By the mid-1950s, word was getting around the city about Neil's emerging style and sound as a jazz pianist. Sandy Ross, a drummer and budding journalist at *The Ubyssey* student newspaper, wrote one of the first appreciations of Neil. Ross didn't hold back when he effusively proclaimed Neil as "one of the finest, most original jazz pianists in the world today. Somehow, Neil has managed to escape the fate of ninety-nine percent of all the jazz pianists playing today; he has not fallen into that semi-bop pianistic rut that has made nearly every modern jazz pianist West of Minton's, sound pretty much like every other." Ross somewhat rhetorically asked why people didn't know about Neil, whom he quoted as saying: "I just play for kicks."[13] An over-the-top assessment, but one that picked up on early signs of Neil's originality.

In 1955, Neil was part of a loose collection of jazz musicians who set up a jam space in rural Richmond called the Wailhouse that was an important precursor of things to come. On March 11, 1956, the Al Neil Septet debuted in a Vancouver New Jazz Society (VNJS) afternoon concert at the Georgia Auditorium. A *Province* article previewing the show noted that "Al still has to earn the family bacon by sorting mail at the Post Office. His dedicated group refuses to give up, and they hope that Sunday proves to be the start of a brilliant career."[14]

His career and the development of other aspiring local bebop players faced a serious hurdle: Vancouver didn't have a venue to catalyze the jazz scene. But around the time of the VNJS show, Neil and like-minded jazz musicians and artists committed to creating a real jazz club in the heart of Vancouver: the original Cellar. Neil, Harry Webb, architect John Grinnell, and guitarist/electrician Jim Kilburn were mainly responsible for readying the interior of the club at Watson and Broadway for the Cellar's opening in April 1956.

Musicians at the Cellar organized themselves into ensembles that regularly played in the club. Neil led one of those bands, which included Jim Johnson on tenor sax, John Dawe on trumpet, bassist Tony Clitheroe, drummer Bill Boyle, and other players. The group functioned like a collective, which was in keeping with the Cellar's cooperative spirit. Photos of Neil and musicians he played with show them wearing sharp suits and ties. Echoing Wong's memory, regular Cellar patron Gavin Walker said Neil was a "natty dresser."[15]

Neil's music evolved during the Cellar years, and the few recordings featuring his band that survived from that period document the metamorphosis. One of the recordings was made by the Al Neil Quintet in 1956 at a CBC studio for the *Jazz Workshop* radio program. "The jazz you'll hear today, well, it's very much present-day jazz," the show's host, pianist Doug Parker, said in his introduction. "Not experimental, but right up to the minute. It's not East Coast jazz, or West Coast, or even Midwest. It's jazz as it's being played everywhere. Al's purpose today, and I think the purpose of the group, is really just to swing." That was an accurate description of the dynamic session, and while Neil played melodically and within the songs' structures, there were subtle hints—notably the intros and solos in his original composition, "That One,"—of harmonic adventurousness.

Another session with Neil's quintet, possibly recorded for *Jazz Workshop* in 1957, included two tunes from the influential 1954 album *Clifford Brown & Max Roach*—"Jordu" and "Parisian Thoroughfare"—along with Horace Silver's "Room 608," Miles Davis's "Tune Up," and Duke Ellington's "Take the "A" Train." This session was just as vigorous as the first *Jazz Workshop* effort but sounded somewhat less original; it was a more direct homage to the source material. In a *Province* preview of a second concert that he was performing at the Georgia Auditorium on March 17, 1957, wryly titled "A different postman---he swings twice," Neil explained his motivations. "I try to keep a broad perspective on jazz as a whole, but right now I am keenly interested in the things we are hearing from the East Coast. In developing the book for our quintet, we have tried to keep everything in the swinging vein. Later on, we will try some of the far-out stuff, but not right now."[16]

Al Neil, Bob Frogge, Freddie Schreiber, Bill Boyle, and John Dawe, the original Cellar, circa 1958. Photographer unknown. Courtesy Walley Lightbody.

1957 was the same year Neil played with a jazz virtuoso at the Cellar, alto saxophonist Art Pepper. That gig went sideways, as Neil recounted to Marian Jago in her book *Live at the Cellar*, and in an interview in 2000 with Jane Gowan:

> I played with him myself for ten days. It was quite something. He was in one of his dope periods and so one way

or another, somebody had to be able to score for him or he just wouldn't show up. I think it had a profound effect on me personally because I really wasn't good enough to be playing with him. But I had every single one of his records at that time. Once we knew, maybe a month or so ahead of time, that he was actually coming, I'd got all his records and I picked out maybe a couple of dozen of the tunes. By the way, he played mostly standards. He was influenced by Bach and especially Charlie Parker, but he was old enough to have been influenced by, say, Lester Young too, even though he played alto. He liked standards and blues. He was traditional in that way, so it was a matter of getting the chord changes close enough that he'd accept them. We worked out a list and for the most part it was pretty good, because I more or less just backed him. I'd take maybe one chorus on each tune. But the trouble would be if he was really high, then he wouldn't pay any attention to the little slip with the tune list that we had, and he'd call out something which, well I knew the name of the tune, but I hadn't worked out the changes to them. I'd be groping around and maybe finally just stop.[17]

There's a lot to sort through in those words. Neil took the assignment of playing with Pepper seriously and prepared accordingly. But as he recognized, Neil wasn't at Pepper's level and didn't have a broad enough knowledge of repertoire at a time when there were no fake books. Walker remembered sitting close to the bandstand at one of the Pepper gigs and hearing the saxman ask Neil to refrain from accompanying him at times during the gig. Walker: "There were certain things that Al played that Art felt, 'Just leave that out.' Art simply said, 'Lay out on this tune. You can play your solo, but lay out behind me, I just want to play with the bass and drums.' Al took this very personally."[18]

Then Pepper went further. One night Chris Gage—not just Vancouver's best jazz pianist but among Canada's finest jazz players—was at the Cellar to hear Pepper. In the intermission before the last set, Pepper connected with Gage, and it was decided that the pianist would take over from his friend

Neil on the bandstand.[19] When I first learned about what transpired with Pepper, while I thought the experience must have stung and been at least somewhat humiliating, I didn't think the experience scarred Neil. I assumed he was resilient enough to shrug it off. Then I read what Neil wrote about the personal aftermath of the experience with Pepper in *Origins*: not long after the engagement, Neil had a nervous breakdown and turned to drugs.[20]

• • •

Kenneth Patchen was an important American poet who was underappreciated during his lifetime. He had a distinctive voice—both in his poetry and deep-timbred spoken delivery. Patchen was also an early officiant in the marriage of poetry and music. He collaborated with avant-garde composer John Cage on a radio play in 1942, and fifteen years later, released *Kenneth Patchen Reads His Poetry with the Chamber Jazz Sextet*. While the recording was an intriguing early example of jazz poetry, there was no direct interaction between the group and Patchen, as they were recorded separately.

Enter Al Neil. In his authorized biography of Patchen, *Kenneth Patchen: Rebel Poet in America*, Larry Smith wrote that John Grinnell was a Patchen fan and arranged for the poet to perform in Vancouver and Victoria with Neil, alto saxophonist Dale Hillary, bassist Lionel Chambers, and drummer Bill Boyle.[21] Neil's memory of how he connected with Patchen was different. Neil: "This is one gig that I myself put together. Somehow, I got in touch with Patchen, probably through his publisher. When I heard that he'd made a poetry-jazz record, and I heard it and I felt that the jazzmen were just playing what they'd ordinarily play, and I thought because I had an interest in this poetry, I might be able to come up with something a little closer to what he might want."[22]

So Patchen went to Vancouver, and on February 12, 1959, as recounted by Smith, he sent a note to his wife Miriam about a rehearsal the poet had with the band at the Cellar: "Worked out a lot of material, and things should pan out pretty well as far as readings-band combination is concerned. Neil is very versatile and quick, full of hero-worship of me; and [Hillary] the alto sax player (18 yrs. old) is almost as talented as Modesto [Modesto Briseno, who played on the *Kenneth Patchen Reads* album] . . ."[23]

In Victoria, they performed at Victoria College and the Scene, a club that Cellar co-founders Ken Hole and Walley Lightbody started. Future visual artist Eric Metcalfe, who was eighteen at the time, was at the Scene for the show with Patchen and Neil's quartet. Metcalfe loved what he heard at the performance, which he found "tremendously influential."[24] Then it was back across the Strait of Georgia to Vancouver for gigs at the Cellar and some other performances.

Patchen and the quartet were booked for a radio broadcast on February 17, 1959. Neil and the other musicians showed up at the CBC studio in the Hotel Vancouver's basement expecting to rehearse with Patchen for three hours. When Patchen arrived, he informed them that he had an appointment with a dental surgeon to fix a broken tooth—in an hour. "Well, Patchen had a major tooth surgery right on the spot as I waited," recalled Neil. "It was much more serious than any of us could have imagined. His jaw had to be chiselled away at, literally gouged out in an excruciatingly painful operation that took almost an hour." Patchen emerged from the dentist's chair with his mouth bleeding through cotton plugs and his face drained of colour. Yet after they got back to the studio, miraculously, Patchen was ready to do the session.[25]

Among the tunes/poems they did was "Four Blues Poems." It starts with Neil and the band playing the melody to "Laird Baird," a blues tune by Charlie Parker that the alto saxophonist recorded in 1952. As Patchen unhurriedly recites the four poems in low tones, Hillary solos in a straight-ahead bebop style while Neil and the rhythm section steadily swing. It was a fitting choice of music to accompany Patchen because Parker was a big fan of the poet. According to lore, Parker carried around Patchen's poems and recited them at some performances. Patchen and Neil's quartet also perform the slow "Four Song Poems" and jaunty "As I Opened the Window."

All of this builds up to "Glory, Glory," arranged by Neil, which features speeches from a play Patchen wrote: *Don't Look Now*. The piece begins and ends with the band briskly playing the melody of "Battle Hymn of the Republic." In between, as the band improvises over the chord changes to Parker's "Confirmation," Patchen delivers a rousing ten-minute spoken word tour de force. "In these times, when the only thing which circulates freely is a lie calculated to hurt all human beings, you're glad that the light is out, because today only in the dark, human beings still see one another for what they are: human beings, no more, no less. Glory, glory." Patchen recites/shouts those words, and others in the piece, with immense feeling, sometimes hectoring, sometimes lamenting, as the musicians' intensity rises and falls and rises yet again.

After the session, Patchen and the players had the energy to put on an unadvertised midnight show at the Cellar. An ad that ran in the *Vancouver Sun* three days later, promoting previously scheduled shows, said "HEAR … KENNETH PATCHEN READ HIS POETRY TO JAZZ AT THE CELLAR."[26] *Sun* reporter Mac Reynolds got in the poetic spirit when he reviewed the first night of the weekend Cellar shows: "He was reading his own stuff, about the lips of the moon and buttered Rolls Royces and landladies carrying sackfuls of smiling flies, to jazz that was cooler than the fishes that sleep in the grove."[27] Trumpeter John Dawe was at one of the Cellar shows, but he wasn't nearly so enamoured with Patchen. "I can remember that voice droning on and on and on. I was looking up at the ceiling and thinking, 'Let's go, man. This is not our scene.' That was the beatnik scene."[28]

For Neil, however, the experience with Patchen was meaningful because he connected with a like-minded creative soul. The feeling was mutual. On March 5, 1959, from his home in Palo Alto, Patchen wrote Neil a letter in big blue marker that said: "My pleasant memories of that [Victoria and Vancouver] jaunt fall into two categories 1) getting to know you (even under somewhat trying and confused circumstances), and 2) 'working' with that fine band you put together."[29] The same month, Patchen performed for two weeks with Charles Mingus and his band at the Living Theatre in New York City. Patchen was clearly at the epicentre of jazz-poetry.

But the Patchen-Al Neil Quartet collaboration had one more act. Just over five months later, a prominent New York City-based label, Folkways Records, told Patchen it was interested in distributing the CBC recording on vinyl. Patchen, stressing that it was a non-commercial label, told Neil that he suggested to Folkways owner Moses Asch that each musician receive $50 for the record. Patchen also asked if Neil could write liner notes,[30] which he did. Folkways released *Kenneth Patchen Reads with Jazz in Canada*, featuring the "Alan Neil Quartet," in October 1959.

The Billboard gave the album two stars, saying "it is no more valid than any of the other attempts" at fusing jazz and poetry. "However, the set does feature some good jazz by the Alan Neil Quartet, especially the work of alto sax man Dale Hillary, who is outstanding."[31] Ira Gitler gave it three stars in *Down Beat*. While Gitler wrote that "Patchen has a forced, somewhat melodramatic reading style," he also asserted that "Patchen's railing at the Atomic Age and the complacency and corruption in our society really generates some emotional power, and the group catches fire behind him."[32]

Despite the mixed reviews, *Kenneth Patchen Reads with Jazz in Canada* was one of the most successful jazz poetry recordings of its time and beyond. Patchen's poems, his singular voice, and the interplay between poet and musicians, elevated it from other efforts in the subgenre. For Neil, the experience reinforced his positive feelings about the poet's artistry and the music he and the band were crafting. In his creatively literary liner notes, Neil vividly described the recording of "Glory, Glory" and the resulting satisfaction he and his bandmates felt. It was a satisfaction he wouldn't always feel in his career as a bebop musician:

> We had all been caught up in the reading from the start - - we knew that something was happening, that this was "something else" - - but now he really went for it, he wailed! With our nerves, our hearts, we heard him coming on, ringing the changes, threading and pulling us in and out of the light – the King Cat making his scene! And on his face we could see that what we had to say back to him was making the same kind of "heart-sense." It was there.[33]

• • •

After the high of the Patchen shows and CBC session, Neil kept playing at the Cellar, in regular gigs and in a different context: experimental live theatre. Barry Cramer, a co-founder of the Cellar and occasionally emcee introducing musicians, came up with the idea of presenting one-act plays in the club on nights when the venue was normally closed. In 1959 and 1960, Cramer staged Samuel Beckett's *Endgame* and *Krapp's Last Tape*, Saul Bellow's *The Wrecker*, Tennessee Williams' *I Rise in Flame, Cried the Phoenix*, and other plays at the Cellar. Neil and Cramer were close friends, and the pianist supported these efforts to mount theatre, performing in the club on nights when plays were on, either before or after the theatrical shows. As he had shown with Patchen, Neil embraced art forms beyond jazz.

One of those other forms was film. In the summer of 1963, Acadian filmmaker Léonard Forest came to Vancouver to make a short documentary for the National Film Board of Canada featuring visual artists, poets, and musicians in the city. Painters Jack Shadbolt and Margaret Peterson, multidisciplinary artists Fred Douglas and Roy Kiyooka, and others appear in the twenty-seven-minute-and-forty-second film, written and directed by Forest and released in 1964. Bathed in sepia for the most part, *In Search of Innocence* is an oddly affecting film, and jazz has a lot to do with its strange allure. Neil, with Glenn McDonald on tenor sax and Don Thompson on bass, created the film's contemplative musical score.

There's a remarkable fifty-second scene filmed at the Cellar—the only known surviving footage of music performed in the club in front of an audience. It starts with a closeup of Neil's face while he plays a solo, looking and sounding entirely focused. Next the camera pulls back to show seated patrons in the foreground and the musicians on the bandstand in the background, giving a sense that the club had a serious vibe centred on listening. Then there are more closeups of patrons, some of them smoking. The smoke from their cigarettes lingers in the air like the band's music, which sounds modal and harmonically open—a fair distance from the bebop that dominated most nights in the club.

Neil developed an inimitable aesthetic, on and off the bandstand, which inspired strong responses from fellow musicians and patrons alike. Neil was a magnetic personality, and like a magnet, he could attract but also repel.

"I loved Al Neil," said Thompson. "He was one of my heroes." Thompson said Neil was reaching for a sound beyond what was typically heard at the Cellar. "I played with him a lot, and it was borderline free jazz. No, it *was* free jazz." Did other players appreciate it as Neil got freer? "No, they thought he was nuts. They thought he was crazy. He'd start off playing bebop like Bud Powell and then all of a sudden, he was playing this science fiction weird music. Some of the young guys really thought he was going nuts. But he wasn't. What he was playing was really interesting and at times bizarre, but he was definitely not crazy; he knew what he was doing."

Thompson said McDonald, who died in 1998, also appreciated Neil. "Glenn didn't know what to think. But he came to realize that Al was doing something. And Al really was doing something . . . he was working and creating something new with the music."[34]

Other views on Neil from fellow Cellar dwellers:

- "Lovely," said bassist Terry Hill. "Nuttier than a fruitcake, but just lovely."[35]
- "We used to think he was kind of a kooky guy but a good guy," said trombonist Jack Fulton. "I liked him, and his feeling for jazz came to the fore."[36]
- "He was one of the main guys that really got the place cooking," said John Dawe. "And he was mixed in with more than just the music because he was into the art scene and the drama scene." Neil did some "strange things" musically, and eventually went into "outer space," Dawe added.[37]
- When Neil found out Gavin Walker was interested in theatre, including experimentalists like Beckett, the pianist got excited. "Al immediately latched onto that," said Walker. "He would be surprised because he didn't get that kind of feedback from fellow musicians. They were like, 'What the fuck is that?'"[38]
- "He was the real thing," said saxophonist PJ Perry. "He was eccentric and not what you would call a great pianist, but he knew the idiom and knew what not to play, and he could solo quite ably with his right hand and sparsely with his left. He knew the tunes, knew the chord changes, and was brilliant in his own way. My favourite Al Neil story is that he got himself into a very intense solo one night and it was getting darker and darker and more heavy and more and more intense, and finally he got so intense that he leaped up from the piano bench and ran over to the wall and ran down the wall of the Cellar, playing the wall, the imaginary wall of the club."[39]

The Cellar closed in 1964, and six years after, Neil revealed how he felt about the underlying divide between himself and his cohorts at the club.

Neil told Bill Smith of *Coda* that he found himself playing with a "series of psychopathic horn players." He said "it got to be a drag searching something out within a chord formation, especially after Miles Davis put out that *Kind of Blue* album, and everybody got on the modal bag. You're hearing something and trying to play it and a horn player is going to lean over and say play the changes, Man. So you wait until four in the morning to try and do something like Monk."[40]

Then in 1979, David Rimmer released his forty-minute film, *Al Neil / A Portrait*, in which Neil traced the roots of his music, including ten years of playing bebop. Neil mentioned influences ranging from Bud Powell to French avant-garde writer Alfred Jarry and poet, essayist, dramatist, visual artist, and theatre director Antonin Artaud. The latter two didn't limit themselves to a single medium, and they prized experimentation. That approach resonated with Neil.

> I don't think at that time there were many jazz musicians that were dealing with that stuff. So I put it together that there was some other thing we could do. We could take the music up into other regions, other plateaus, or hopefully some space that wouldn't be possible as a bebop musician. And all those dudes that were playing with me, they got really upset about this, and they used to bang down atop of the piano on top of my hands almost and say, 'Play the changes, man.' I was trying to figure out something else.[41]

I'm guessing that when Neil talked about psychopathic horn players threatening the well-being of his hands, the words were embellished and delivered for dramatic effect. But what he said highlighted the gulf between the less adventurous Cellar beboppers and the cutting-edge that Neil craved. A long way from the days of being a full-on bebopper, Neil's inherent desire to search for a new sound made it untenable for him to stay within the structured forms where most of his peers resided. Freedom was the only option. This is where the story of Al Neil as a jazz pianist could have ended. But even as Neil pushed further and further out in the musical stratosphere, he kept a jazz sensibility.

• • •

The headline was unambiguous: "Pianist Guilty Of Drug Charge." Beneath it was a five-paragraph item in the *Vancouver Sun* on October 14, 1964, that began: "Jazz pianist Alan Neil was given a suspended sentence Tuesday when found guilty of possession of narcotics." According to the story, police officers followed Neil to a Main Street beer parlour, where they found him with a heroin capsule. He pleaded not guilty, and the judge ordered Neil to post a $1,000 bond and stay out of Vancouver's East End for two years.[42]

Changes, Neil's autobiographical novel first published in serial form by the *Georgia Straight* in 1970 and published as a book in 1975 and 1989, revolves around the graphic first-person narration of a character named Seamus Finn. The narrator represents Neil, and he gives an unflinching account of his rough life as a jazz pianist/hardcore heroin addict in Vancouver circa 1960, along with flashbacks to the horrors of war. There's a clear link between the narrator's wartime trauma and drug addiction. Just like Pepper, Charlie Parker, Fats Navarro, Miles Davis, Billie Holiday, John Coltrane, Chet Baker, Joe Pass, Gerry Mulligan, Anita O'Day, Bill Evans, and Sonny Rollins, and local heroes including Hillary and Perry, heroin caught hold of Neil. It wouldn't let go for nearly fifteen years.

By the time drummer Gregg Simpson met Neil in 1965, the pianist was a "chippie"—that is, someone who used heroin here and there before kicking the habit entirely.[43] After a musical hiatus, Neil focused on playing again. Simpson had seen Neil make music three times, including gigs at the Java Jazz on Locarno Beach and the Flat Five on West Broadway, along with an appearance on CBC-TV. At the Flat Five gig, Neil performed with Hillary, bassist Richard Anstey, and drummer Jim Chivers. They devoted themselves to George Gershwin's "Summertime" for almost an entire set. "He would take it into dimensions I'd never really heard," said Simpson about Neil's playing at the time. "It was just very stretchy. They really stretched stuff out, expanded the form. It was amazing."[44]

Then poet and visual artist Curt Lang brought Simpson to a cottage amid high rises on Chilco Street in Vancouver's West End to meet Neil and his second wife Marguerite Sanders. It wasn't long before Neil, Anstey, and Simpson were playing music together. Anstey and Simpson were nineteen; Neil was forty-two.

Simpson, who needed a space to pursue his twin passions of painting and music, rented a tiny, unheated storefront studio at 2951 West 4th Avenue in Vancouver's Kitsilano neighbourhood. He eventually named it the Sound Gallery, and late in the fall of 1965, Simpson, Neil, and Anstey started rehearsing there regularly.

On December 15, 1965, they performed at the studio for a small audience of invited friends. That was the same date astronauts in Gemini 6a and Gemini 7 achieved the first "space rendezvous"—maneuvering two spacecraft into the same orbit and at a very intimate proximity. "'We're Nose to Nose in Space,'" read the banner headline on the front page of that morning's *Vancouver Sun*.[45] The headline could have been written about what was recorded at the Sound Gallery that night. The trio freely improvised, with Neil ascending and descending to the outer harmonic limits of the piano, Anstey pulling away from gravity on bass, and Simpson raining down a meteor shower on his drum kit. Then suddenly Neil was the man who fell to Earth with the wispy melody of "Summertime," which contrasted perfectly with the swirling cacophony.

The lo-fi recording of the evening includes more than twenty-six minutes of bracing group interplay and individual expression in "Dreamers Exposed." The track appears on the Al Neil Trio's double album *Retrospective 1965-1968*, released thirty-seven years after the raucous session. The recording captures Neil and the trio at a transitional point. "You can hear he's playing bebop chords and we're still in a kind of swing mode for some of it, and then other parts are just tumultuous," said Simpson.[46]

By March 1966, the trio was playing a series of Saturday night concerts at the Sound Gallery. One poster facetiously announced, "AL NEIL AND HIS ROYAL CANADIANS PLAY AND SING YOUR FAVOURITES" and counterintuitively quoted Graham Humphries, owner of the Blue Horn jazz club that was in the same space the Flat Five had occupied: "THIS IS THE WORST GROUP I HAVE EVER HEARD." That month the trio also performed at the UBC Auditorium. The music was "nothing short of extraordinary," wrote Jim Banham in his *Province* review. "Most of these pieces reached a sort of frenzied climax a little past the half way mark during which Neil raced up and down the keyboard pounding out tone clusters with his fist and elbow and sometimes banging the keyboard cover up and down for emphasis."[47]

Above the review it said, "World of jazz."[48] Were Neil and his comrades still playing jazz? "He always had this saying. He said, 'I still like to think I'm playing jazz,'" recalled Simpson.[49] Although the trio's music was a long way from the Cellar's bebop, jazz was an important part of the group's aesthetic. There were fragments of melody and harmonic structure and endless improvisation, all of which kept it connected to jazz. No doubt there were also avant-garde jazz influences at play; Neil was fully familiar with Ornette Coleman and Paul Bley, having heard and met both free jazz icons at the Cellar. Neil was also aware of pivotal figures in American avant-garde jazz like Albert Ayler and Archie Shepp. As for one of the leading free/avant-garde jazz artists, pianist Cecil Taylor, people assumed he was a major influence on Neil. According to Simpson, that wasn't the case.[50] The biggest influences on Neil's playing were his own musical and life experiences, which shaped his one-of-a-kind sound more than anything.

Then there was the Trips Festival, which had next to nothing to do with jazz. Inspired by San Francisco's Trips Festival in January 1966, the Vancouver version took place July 29–31, 1966, at the PNE Garden Auditorium. The festival combined music—headlined by the Grateful Dead, Big Brother and the Holding Company (featuring Janis Joplin), and Quicksilver Messenger Service—film, slides, and a liquid light show involving more than fifty projectors and 25,000 square feet of screen. Al Neil & His Royal Canadians opened for Big Brother—who, like the other headliners, were not well-known beyond the San Francisco Bay area at the time—on July 30, and the Al Neil Jazz Trio (Royal Rascals) performed July 31. Both groups consisted of Neil, Anstey, and Simpson. There are no known sound recordings of Vancouver's Trips Festival. Yet even without documented evidence of the music Neil and his bandmates made at Trips, it's safe to say that it was far out from orthodoxy and, therefore, a perfect fit with the counterculture festival.

Meanwhile, the trio and a growing coterie of visual artists like Sam Perry, dancers such as Helen Goodwin, poets including Jamie Reid, and their audiences were outgrowing the Sound Gallery. After the Trips Festival, the trio moved downtown into the larger Motion Studio at 1266 Seymour. Together with collaborators, they staged multimedia sensory spectacles on Saturday nights that attracted large audiences. After one such performance, *Coda* Vancouver correspondent Sandy Lemon raved about Neil and the trio's

Journeys to the Bandstand

"amazing rapport," describing the musicians' individual sounds as "energy centres" coming together to "achieve an emotional pattern." As quoted by Lemon, Neil said: "I'm going beyond be-bop to my own music."[51]

Captain Consciousness presents....a Centennial Event
THE TRIP: AN ELECTRONIC PERFORMANCE
vancouver's first festival of sound & light
an ecstatic new space   total sense perception

Friday — the grateful dead — the acid test — weco multi-visual projection — the pH factor jug band — super-stroboscopic lighting   gerry walker tape music — the daily flash — the DANCE

Saturday — big brother & the holding company — gary lee nova's magic mirrors   liquid injection-projection — the daily flash — electronic music al neil & his royal canadians — jesse — the pH factor — the grateful dead & the unexpectable

Sunday — al neil jazz trio (royal rascals) movies: Charlie Chaplin: the vagabond — the gambler; Andy Warhol: Harlot; Harry Smith shorts! new film by sam perry shorts by gary lee nova michael mcClure does his thing   bill bissett the pH factor — big brother & the holding co. the grateful dead — the daily flash & DANCE

18 & over only

Is this your place in the rock revolution keep listening to C-Fun for more details

doors open at p.n.e. garden auditorium
8:30 p.m.
advance tickets $2.00 per nite $5.00 for series

The Blind Owl • **The Pot Shoppe** • **Positively Fourth Street**
2057 w. 4th   1420 w. pender   2137 w. fourth
736-6177

Record Gallery
936 Robson st.

black lite provided
wear your best
fluorescent clothes
& makeup

McLeods Books
350 w. pender

Tickets at the door
$2.50 per nite $6.00 for series

Trips Festival program.

• • •

At the end of 1966, Lemon reported in *Coda* that the Motion Studio had closed. "Al Neil is reported to be making fish nets," Lemon wrote. "Perhaps Al Neil will resume playing soon."[52] Thankfully, he did. The trio performed at UBC, the Vancouver School of Art, the Vancouver Art Gallery for Intermedia Nights, and at other venues until 1968, when Anstey left the group. *Retrospective 1965-1968* captures the Al Neil Trio's progression at these venues as the group went even further away from conventional forms and sounds, increasingly incorporating collage with tapes and other dissonant sounds.

In another *Coda* article, which was partially reprinted in Simon Fraser University's *The Peak* student newspaper before an October 1967 show at the school, Neil talked about how fulfilling it was to play this unrestrained atonal music. "I am so excited at the present time because, for the first time, after playing for 30 years, I am starting to play music where I am really expressing something that is valid and original, for me, rather than playing in someone else's style."[53]

Toronto writer and photographer Mark Miller—the dean of Canadian jazz criticism— characterized Neil's trio with Simpson and Anstey as "one of the first groups of its kind in Canada," which "slightly" predated Toronto New Music Ensemble and Montreal's Jazz Libre.[54] In Vancouver, the trio members were pioneers in the city's improvised music scene. Paul Plimley, Lisle Ellis, Paul Cram, Ralph Eppel, and Gregg Simpson formed the New Orchestra Workshop (NOW)—the next important improvised music group to emerge in Vancouver—in 1977. As Simpson saw it, "There's a thread that started with Al Neil and ran through the 1960s with his famous trio . . ."[55] That thread eventually wound its way to NOW. So Neil was at the creative forefront, as he had been years before at the Cellar.

After the original Al Neil Trio dissolved in 1968, Neil kept creating and exploring. He did so in a duo with the stalwart Simpson and in another version of his trio, with his then-wife Marguerite and Simpson, which got deeper into collage. In 1972, Neil briefly put aside collage and formed Al Neil Jazz Probe—with Anstey on soprano sax, Annie Siegel on alto sax and flute, and Simpson—and an expanded version called the Al Neil Jazz Probe Orchestra. "That was all playing," said Simpson. "There were no tapes, no readings."[56] Plus there was a plethora of other projects for Neil: solo concerts, collaborations with other musicians, multimedia performances, and art exhibitions of his collages, assemblages, and other works.

Montreal-born Michael de Courcy met Neil in 1967 at Intermedia, the multi-disciplinary artists' collective that established itself that year in the former Catelli pasta factory at 575 Beatty Street. For the next five years, de Courcy documented through his photography the visual artists, filmmakers, dancers, musicians, engineers, architects, and others who gathered, rehearsed, and performed in the building, at the Vancouver Art Gallery, and elsewhere.[57] So he had a front row seat to the cutting-edge Intermedia scene, which included Neil. "He was taking massive amounts of drugs in order to play the way he wanted to play," said de Courcy. "He saw drugs as kind of being the doorway to a certain kind of musical experience for him." Somebody would be responsible for "getting the right kinds of pharmaceuticals" for Neil. "Then he'd be out on the stage and he would just *go*. It would just be crazy. Crazy stuff."[58]

Of course, Neil was far from alone in getting high as a gateway to making creative breakthroughs. And like others who took a similar approach, at times he was too far gone to make music that was meaningful. Longtime *Georgia Straight* writer Alexander Varty said as much when he wrote that "on occasion, Al has been so looped that it was a struggle for him to stay on the piano bench, much less play to perfection."[59] At other times, though, even in a full-on altered state, he actually expressed something profound and impactful. Another thing that made him a rarity: the years of putting substances into his body didn't shorten his life. "He has outlived three of his physicians," said de Courcy. "All of whom predicted his early demise if he continued to live the way he was living."[60]

In the early seventies, Paul Plimley was finding his path as a young pianist. At that time, he studied classical piano with Kum-Sing Lee at the University of British Columbia, which didn't—on the surface—foreshadow Plimley's eventual calling as an avant-garde/free jazz torchbearer. Aside from being a professor of piano, Lee was a concert pianist who performed works by Brahms, Bartok, Bach, and other canonical classical composers. Plimley was also well aware of Neil, whose art didn't meet the rigid definition of any canon. "Al Neil did so much to really bring the music around in terms of the modern elements," said Plimley, who relished Neil's music and the man's completely uninhibited expression.⁶¹ Plimley summed up Neil this way:

> Al would have his football helmet with two alternately going on lightbulbs in his ears. And with his kind of football uniform on, chanting Taoist poetry, you know, sort of like throwing typewriters inside the piano, chanting and . . . what else? . . . Oh, I know, he had this big sort of rubber balloon that he would be sitting on, and then he would be bouncing up these stairs that had musical notes of the scale going up and going down. So he'd be doing tunes, so all this stuff, and he'd be playing this wild piano. So that's Al Neil. That was all going on. It sounds in a way almost completely contemporary today and it was thirty-four years ago. Isn't that wild?⁶²

I kept thinking about what Mark Miller wrote about Neil's significance. That it was "more symbolic than real." Miller acknowledged that Neil challenged standard approaches to jazz and music as a whole in Canada, and he was an inspiration to younger Vancouver improvisers. But in Miller's view, Neil didn't make "an altogether compelling case for his own generally distracted vision."⁶³ I concur with much of Miller's incisive sentiment on Neil. I also frame Neil's vision and importance in a somewhat different way. His aesthetic was truly multi-disciplinary and wholly unconcerned with receiving validation from the powers that be. The result was music that wasn't always enjoyable or even coherent, but I appreciated how it challenged my pre-conceptions and shook me out of my comfort zone, even decades after it was recorded.

Simpson, who played with Neil more than any other musician, summed up his musical collaborator and friend as a "free spirit" who was "extremely moral in a sense. A very strong sense of morality and political progressiveness." Also: "He didn't suffer fools gladly. It was a task sometimes to not make him think you were an idiot. He saw through people. He was a very perceptive person, and he knew where you were coming from pretty quick."⁶⁴

• • •

Though Neil's performances became less frequent, his legend grew. One thing he became known for was crossing the line that separates performers and audience members. Neil went to many concerts as the latter, including a solo show by Anthony Braxton at the Western Front on November 6, 1975. *Whispered Art History: Twenty Years At The Western Front* notes that while Braxton was improvising, Neil—without warning—started playing the piano. Braxton was surprised but continued his free improv.[65] Brian Nation, who put on the show as his first Vancouver Jazz Society presentation, doesn't remember Neil sitting in uninvited. But Nation has a clear memory of Neil doing that at a solo Steve Lacy concert about four months later, and several other times. Nation eventually banned Neil from attending VJS shows, which didn't stop the pianist from showing up with friends at the Vancouver East Cultural Centre on October 22, 1978 for a Sam Rivers concert. "They promised to sit with him and make sure he behaved, so I relented," said Nation. "Next thing I know Sam Rivers is playing a flute solo when Neil pops up about one foot in front of his face, dancing some kind of psychedelic jig." Nation swiftly "grabbed Neil without stopping (he wasn't a very heavy guy) and carried him to the exit and put him out, shutting the door behind him." Regardless of the ejection, Nation had much respect for Neil, and decades later made a point of visiting the elderly iconoclast at his Strathcona home. "I can't remember how the sitting-in episodes came up in our conversation [that day], but I remember him shaking his head and muttering, 'Stupid.'"[66]

A procession of writers paid homage to Neil in newspaper and magazine features that looked back at his milestones, sought his alternative perspectives, and invariably referred to the fact that he lived part-time with Carole Itter in the "Blue Cabin." A Norwegian craftsman built the cabin around 1927 in Coal Harbour. In 1932 it was towed across Burrard Inlet to a small cove next to North Vancouver's Cates Park, where it was placed on pilings. Neil moved in to the cabin in 1966, initially paying fifteen dollars a month in rent to McKenzie Barge & Derrick, the company that owned an adjacent shipyard. Then Neil stayed in the cabin rent-free in return for serving as a watchman for the shipyard. Itter joined him there in the 1970s. They made the interior comfortable and decorated the exterior with assemblage. Their beloved shoreline cabin—a true hideaway—enabled them to be reclusive and find silence.

2014 was bittersweet for Neil and Itter. Near the end of that year, they received an eviction notice from Port Metro Vancouver demanding that—at their own expense—they remove the cabin and any personal items from the land.[67] So not only did they have to leave their home of nearly half a century, but the cabin itself had to go or be demolished. It was a heartless edict for the two cherished, elderly artists to contend with, and a devastating loss to the couple who had long depended on the cabin as much more than shelter; it was sanctuary. That same year, the City of Vancouver honoured Neil with the Mayor's Arts Award for lifetime achievement. The prestigious tribute represented the establishment's 180-degree change of heart in its view of Neil. The man once seen as a beatnik, junkie, and musical reprobate, Neil was at long last formally recognized and celebrated for his original artistic vision and expression.

Surviving the invasion of Normandy, heroin addiction, and the miseries of advancing age, Neil outlasted even the most generous expectations for how long his pilot light would burn deep blue. Eventually, though, his flame flickered and Neil—who had weak lungs—passed away on November 16, 2017, in St. Paul's Hospital due to respiratory complications. He was ninety-three.

In 2015, three arts organizations came together to form the Blue Cabin Committee to ensure the historic cabin lives on. The committee arranged for the cabin to be moved to a temporary location and commissioned Jeremy and Sus Borsos to painstakingly restore it. After monumental fundraising and restoration efforts, the beautifully restored cabin was towed to a new home on a dock in False Creek, where it would serve as a floating artist residency.

I was there on August 25, 2019, when the organizations involved in the Blue Cabin project officially unveiled the cabin. I listened as various key players in the community initiative gave speeches and paid extra attention when Itter spoke. Then the organizers offered tours of the cabin, so I found myself inside the structure that Neil and Itter called home. As the people in my tour group walked around the cabin, I mainly focused on the spot where Neil's Farrand upright piano sat for years. The restoration preserved vestiges of the instrument: the boards underneath where the piano sat are a different colour from the rest of the floor, and there's also notch in the paint on the wall where the end of the piano rested. Looking at these ghost signs, there was only one way to interpret them—Neil's spirit lived on. Just like how the piano's presence remained in the cabin, Neil left a lasting mark on the entire city, through his music and art.

At one point everyone left the cabin except for Itter and myself. She noticed I was fixated on the area where the piano was and briefly talked to me about the instrument that was once there. I didn't identify myself as that writer who pestered her through email about interviewing Neil. That didn't matter anymore, and I didn't want to detract from the joy of the day, which I could see in her face. As for Neil, I never met the great man, but on this blue sky day, I came as close as I could to his enduring essence.

Carole Itter, in the restored Blue Cabin, False Creek, August 25, 2019. Photo by Chris Wong.

5 / FATHER AND SON: BARRY AND DYLAN CRAMER

THE CLUB IS full and if not for the liquor hidden in secret compartments under the tables from the no-fun morality squad, the audience of jazz devotees would be getting restless. But they know that things don't get going until late at the Cellar. Lateness is key to the attraction. If you didn't want to stay up late you would have cocooned at home, watching *Father Knows Best* on black and white TV before being safely tucked into bed. It's November 1958: the Canada of Prime Minister John Diefenbaker (JFK called him a "boring son of a bitch"[1]) and teen heartthrob singer Paul Anka (his first big hit, "Diana," was inspired by unrequited love for a girl he saw in church), that's overwhelmingly white and strait-laced. If you have a sense of adventure but not a lot of cash and want after-hours entertainment—to smoke, surreptitiously drink, laugh, and most of all, to hear great modern jazz—this is the place to be in Vancouver.

At last, the show is about to begin, and a man in his late twenties walks onto the bandstand. Barry Cramer isn't in the band. In fact, he isn't even a musician. Tonight, he's the emcee, an important role in the history of jazz clubs. Barry is also much more than the guy who introduces the band. He's one of the high-intensity, multi-talented characters who's making the original Cellar jazz club a once-in-a-lifetime hub of creativity and social connection.

The man does his thing: "For those of you who are interested in jazz, the name of Harold Land should ring a bell with you because Harold has appeared with all the greats of jazz in the United States. We are very privileged to welcome, the Harold Land Quartet."[2] The musicians launch into

"Cherokee," Ray Noble's jazz standard that separates the elite beboppers from the pretenders because the chord changes are difficult to improvise on—especially during the bridge—at the fast tempo it's played at. For just under eight minutes, Land relentlessly solos on chorus after chorus, a torrent of well-placed notes tumbling out of his tenor sax. Following Land's lead, each member of the rhythm section takes vigorous solo turns.

Barry gets back on the mic to introduce the band members—Land, Elmo Hope, Scott LaFaro, and Lenny McBrowne—before coolly intoning just four words: "Jazz at the Cellar."[3]

I've listened to a recording of that night's performance, including Barry's emceeing, dozens of times. Aside from the eternal pleasures of hearing Land and his band play raw and bracing bebop/hard bop, the sound of Barry's deep, distinctive voice has long transfixed me. Hearing it made me want to learn all I could about him: what brought this non-musician to the original Cellar, and where did he go after the club shut down? It became an obsession, and it took years to piece together the story—or more accurately, the extant parts that would reveal themselves—of this forgotten man.

About ten months before those boundless choruses of "Cherokee" rang out, Barry's son Dylan Cramer was born, on January 21, 1958. As a child, Dylan knew little about the Cellar, what his dad did there, or jazz itself. One cataclysmic event—the sudden and tragic death of his father—put Dylan on a long, often painful, and ultimately fulfilling passage that also fascinated me. Along the way, he found the keys to playing jazz on the alto saxophone, and to himself. It took decades to come to terms with Barry's decision to take his own life. Jazz, it would turn out, was the healing agent.

• • •

Morris Cramer, who was born in Russia, and Sofe Feinstein, who began life in England, married and raised a large family in Canada. Their son Barry Paul Cramer entered the world on March 9, 1929, in Winnipeg. The Cramers moved to Vancouver, where Morris followed his entrepreneurial instincts and established a retail clothing business.

In high school on Vancouver's West Side, Barry developed a passion for acting in live theatre. A photo in the *Province* newspaper showed Barry applying makeup to a fellow cast member for a three-act farce, "Convention

Go Hang," that the King George High School Players' Club staged in March 1948. Barry, one of the play's leads, looks right at the camera with an impish smile that conveys carefree youth.[4]

Just over three years later, at twenty-one, Barry married Beth (Betty) Faulkner, who wore "a pale beige silk suit with hat to match and accessories of caramel tones," according to the notice of the "pretty wedding" in the *Province*. After the reception, "the newlyweds left for a motoring honeymoon on Vancouver Island."[5] In the optimistic early 1950s, Barry and Betty seemed destined for a white-picket-fence existence.

Their first child, Gary, was born in 1952.[6] About two years later, Betty gave birth to their daughter Rhondi. As the household grew, Barry kept acting. One venue he performed in was the Avon Theatre, which was originally the Pantages, a classic vaudeville theatre on East Hastings. In 1953 and 1954, Barry was in the supporting cast for several of the Everyman Repertory Co's productions at the Avon: *Of Mice and Men* (with Lon Chaney Jr. and Bruno Gerussi), *Kiss and Tell*, *Burlesque*,[7] and *The Show Off*. In December 1954, he played the Tin Woodman in Theatre Under the Stars' production of *The Wizard of Oz* at the Georgia Auditorium. The *Vancouver Sun* ran a photo that showed the actors playing Dorothy, the Scarecrow, and the Cowardly Lion with big smiles, while Barry's Tin Woodman—ever in search of a heart— wore a downcast expression.[8]

Up to the mid-1950s, Barry's contributions to Vancouver's arts scene were dynamic and crowd-pleasing, primarily in mainstream settings. That abruptly changed in 1956, when he joined jazz musicians and others who cooperatively created the Cellar jazz club. This was an alternative milieu that provided a place to play and hang out for musicians who weren't the main instrumentalists featured in downtown venues. In the subterranean space accessed down a steep flight of stairs, Barry wasn't in Kansas anymore.

Not only was he part of the main organizing group that made the club happen, Barry was also one of the few non-musicians who made ongoing contributions to the club's development and success. He liked jazz but didn't especially care for bebop, one of the prevailing jazz sub-genres played in the club. Yet Barry was "almost always there," according to John Dawe, one of the Cellar's founding musicians.[9] The Cellar's appeal for Barry went beyond the music. Part of the attraction was being among the waggish characters—both musicians and patrons—that gathered at the club. Barry fit right in because he was an inimitable character himself. "He was a small man and bespectacled and kind of intellectual looking, but you knew you weren't talking to a nerd," said Gavin Walker, a frequent patron at the Cellar as a young jazz aficionado. "You were talking to someone who was really hip."[10]

Barry also found his niche as an emcee who introduced musicians. In that role, he showed that he was a "master of putdown humour," said Dawe.[11] Barry mainly aimed his barbs at local players like pianist Al Neil. Once when Neil's group was playing to a conspicuously sparse audience, Barry called the band the "Jazz Exterminators."[12] It was all in good fun, as Barry and the pianist were close friends. In fact, years later, Neil said Barry was one of his best friends.[13] For a period, Barry also represented Neil as a de facto agent, writing feisty letters to arts organizations that the pianist had a beef with.

When introducing prominent American musicians at the club, such as Harold Land, Barry struck a respectful tone. Almost fifty years after he introduced Land and the quartet, in 2007, Lone Hill Jazz released a bootleg recording of the show: *Jazz at the Cellar 1958*. While those behind the release dishonourably stole the music, the album provides rare documentation of the top-flight music played at the Cellar. It also placed Barry in the long tradition of distinctively voiced emcees making introductions on unforgettable live jazz recordings. Pee Wee Marquette, the wee MC at Birdland during its glory days in the fifties and sixties, had the best-known voice behind the jazz club mic. But there have been countless others around the world, including Barry.

He contributed a stellar idea that would expand the underground club's audience: on nights when the Cellar was normally closed, Barry would stage experimental one-act plays. To their credit, the musicians who ran the club supported the plan. Barry started off audaciously with *The Bald Soprano*, the first play published by Romanian-French playwright Eugène Ionesco. Barry sent a letter requesting permission to stage the play to Ionesco, whose reply, when translated, read: "Yes, you can use my play. Please send me the $10 right away."[14] Performed December 10–11, 1958, Barry directed the groundbreaking theatre of the absurd piece. Audiences got their money's worth; also on the bill were Al Neil playing jazz and Bud Wood reciting poetry.[15] Barry had suddenly put himself at the heart of an off-centre, multidisciplinary arts scene at the Cellar.

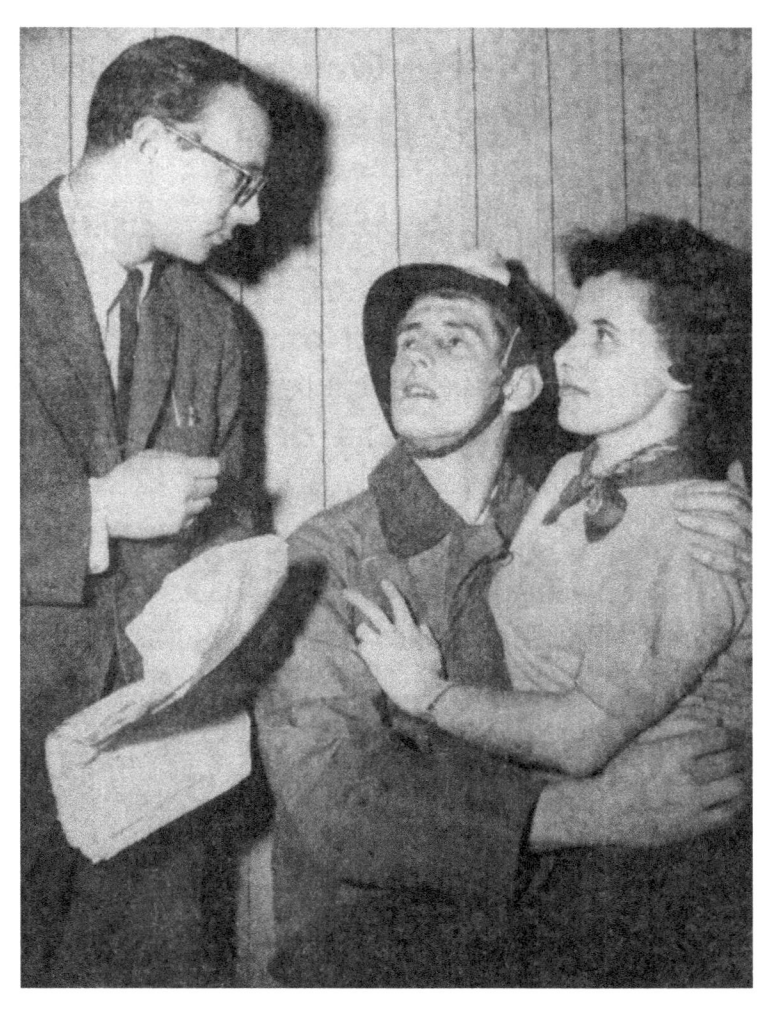

Barry Cramer, directing Glenn Beck and Joanne Walker in The Bald Soprano, the original Cellar, December 10-11, 1958. Photographer unknown. Source: Vancouver Sun (Postmedia Network Inc.).

He arranged for tickets to be sold in advance at Western Music, a musical instrument and record store where jazz lovers hung out, and at a place he knew well: 711 Shop, a men's clothing store at 783 Granville. The clothing business that his father Morris had established evolved into this store. Barry's brothers Jack and Harry ran the store and various Cramers, including Barry, worked there. Many musicians who played at the Cellar bought their suits, shirts, and accessories—advertised in newspapers as "natural clothes for men"[16]—at 711 Shop and looked sharp on and off the stage.

Another play Barry directed and acted in at the Cellar was Samuel Beckett's *Endgame*, the Irishman's follow-up to *Waiting for Godot*. It includes one character who's blind and unable to stand, another who's unable to sit, and two characters with no legs who are stuck in garbage cans throughout the play. The posters that Harry Webb hand drew for *Endgame* and other plays Cramer produced at the Cellar were also works of typographical art.

Barry's staging of Jean Giraudoux's *The Apollo of Bellac*, November 10–12, 1959, received positive reviews in the *Vancouver Sun* and the *Province*. The former called Barry "an astute young man with imagination" and praised the production "as one of the finest comedies in a long time."[17] In the latter, Wedman wrote: "With the minimum of sets and the barest of facilities, Barry Cramer's small cast—working in conjunction with nightly jazz presentations—do a smooth, satisfying run-through of this delightful, spry little satire."[18]

With *Krapp's Last Tape*, Barry went further than ever in presenting avant-garde theatre. Performed May 22–26, 1960, just nineteen months after Beckett's play premiered, the first twenty minutes or so features no dialogue and the lone character peeling, eating, and stroking, among other things, two bananas. Then the play alternates between the sixty-nine-year-old Krapp talking and the voice of his thirty-nine-year-old self, playing on a tape recorder. *The Vancouver Sun* said "it's questionable just how much theatrical impact it has" but declared the production "another boost for producer Barry Cramer, who persists in presenting experimental and offbeat plays."[19]

It seems *The Tender Edge*, performed August 7–11, 1960, on a double bill with the Al Neil Trio, was the last play Barry staged at the Cellar. I don't know why he stopped presenting live theatre at the club, but the body of work he produced in less than two years was way ahead of its time in Vancouver and had a significant influence on local theatre. "They got an amazing response," said Neil, about the plays, which he appreciated, along with the opportunity to perform for people who didn't normally go to the Cellar. "We found we got a whole new audience this way. We made valuable contacts at the CBC . . . who were quite surprised that Barry could put on a Beckett play that early, just a few years after it was written. The plays were favourably reviewed on CBC Radio. People attended these drama events and when they realized what was going on at the Cellar—we had abstract paintings on the black walls, and they heard a little jazz either before or after the play—they came back on Saturday nights for jazz, and then became regulars."[20]

June 1963. The Cellar was in its dying days because both musicians and patrons were moving on. And while two plays were staged at the club that year, Barry apparently wasn't involved. But the Cellar still had some music in it. Manager Dave Quarin booked underappreciated American saxophonist Monty Waters, drummer Jimmy Lovelace, and Don Thompson on bass to perform a weekend at the club. On June 9, 1963, Ray Sikora's terrific big band opened for Waters' group. Barry served as emcee that Sunday night, and his voice was captured on an unreleased recording made of both bands' entire sets.

Acknowledging its imminent demise, Barry riffed darkly about the Cellar's rise and fall for more than three minutes during his intro to Sikora's band. He said the club "did a lot of things first," such as bringing big name jazz artists to Vancouver. But the Cellar "can't seem to pay its way," Barry added. "I remember Harold Land landing in here and blowing beautiful jazz with Elmo Hope and Scott LaFaro, that brilliant young bass player who smashed himself up in New York. And I remember Charlie Mingus here, and I remember, you name it, Ornette Coleman. They were here and they were playing and, I don't know, nobody ever seemed to show up. But afterwards everybody said, 'Boy, isn't it a groove? Gee, imagine Ornette Coleman was here.' I guess if there's any kind of epitaph for the Cellar, the only thing I can think of is, 'Who cares?'"[21]

Barry often made people laugh; but after delivering that punchline, there was awkward silence. I don't think Barry believed everything he said that night. The Cellar meant a lot to him, especially during his run of plays, and he was likely proud of his and the club's successes. But as the resident satirist it was his job, so to speak, to lampoon and entertain. Barry succeeded in that with his theatrical direction and emceeing, and, in the process, told uncomfortable truths. In this case, he exaggerated a tad—people packed the Cellar to see Mingus and Coleman—but his commentary rang true, as it applied to the club's deathwatch. So, despite having nothing to do with music-making, he was an essential figure at the Cellar, which ceased to exist in February 1964. The question was, what next?

• • •

Barry's name continued to appear in newspaper stories about local theatre productions, but only in a trickle. Barry acted in a 1964 Gastown Players' production of *The Drunkard*,[22] and played the nebbish, poker playing Vinnie in a 1967 Arts Club Theatre production of *The Odd Couple*.[23] After about two decades of actively contributing to Vancouver's live theatre scene, he left that life to focus on earning a steady income to support his family. Barry's next role was as promotion manager at CHAN-TV's Channel 8, which began operating as Vancouver's first independent television station in 1960.[24]

At home, Barry and his youngest child Dylan developed a close connection. Their bond was the inverse of what Barry experienced as a child. "It was made very clear to him by his father that he was unwanted, so he clung to his mother and was very close to her, but it was difficult," said Dylan. "He grew up feeling really insecure, and I think that's why he doted on me so much. When I came along, he was ready to be a father. He and I had a connection that superseded his relationship with his wife. I would go everywhere with him; I did everything with him. I was his favourite. There was no mistaking it."[25]

Even though Barry spent countless nights in a jazz club, he didn't nudge Dylan toward instrumental jazz. Barry did, however, pass on a love for vocal jazz of the saloon singer variety. "When I was young, he used to invite his brothers over every Sunday to listen to Sinatra records, and I was the only one allowed in the room with them," said Dylan. "So my earliest training was Sinatra, and he also encouraged my brother. He [Barry] liked Bob Dylan and the Beatles, and he got my brother a guitar and harmonica."[26]

Spring 1967. Kitsilano, on 4th Avenue between Burrard and MacDonald, was nearing its peak as the hub for Vancouver's hippie counterculture. That's also when the city's first Be-In, a gathering of more than 1,000 hippies, happened in Stanley Park. And it's when Dan McLeod and others—including Barry—met to conceive an underground "free press" newspaper. On May 5, 1967, the *Georgia Straight* published its first issue.

Maclean's described Barry as an "advisor" who helped McLeod and an editorial collective produce that inaugural issue, whose coverage of police harassment rankled then-Vancouver Mayor Tom Campbell.[27] Canada's national news magazine went as far as crediting Barry with being the primary inspiration for launching the newspaper. *Maclean's* writer Robert Hunter wrote that "the paper got started as an amateur hippie venture because a non-hippie got angry at the police. Barry Cramer, 38, whose 15-year-old son likes to hang out in the 4th Avenue hippie district, grew disturbed by reports he was hearing about police harassment there. He took a closer look and was appalled." Barry told Hunter that "the cops were manhandling the kids, insulting the girls. When Dan McLeod suggested we do something about it, I jumped right in."[28]

Barry wrote film reviews for the *Straight* that, as described by *Vancouver Sun* columnist Jack Wasserman, contained "stinging criticism."[29] For a while his name was listed in the masthead next to "Strategy,"[30] and he also became the newspaper's business manager. Meanwhile, on March 31, 1968, the Vancouver hippies' underground government appointed Barry its "minister of media." His appointment was ratified during a meeting of about 500 hippies at the Retinal Circus, a music club on Davie at Burrard that was a vital part of the city's hippie community. Barry's job was to write press releases that would counteract mainstream media's portrayal of the hippies.[31]

As his involvement with the hippies grew, Barry evolved from supportive non-hippie to full-on participant. By the late sixties, the Cramer family was living in what Dylan described as a "commune," in various locations, including two houses at Sixth and Alder that had a geodesic dome in between. Dylan said numerous people lived in the commune, including his parents, siblings, Dan McLeod at one point, and others. The number fluctuated, depending on who Barry encountered on any given day. "He really loved the idea of picking up people," said Dylan. "We would be driving home and anybody who was hitchhiking, he would pick up and take home. He would allow them to stay at the house." As for what life was like in the commune, "It was non-stop sex, drugs, and rock and roll," said Dylan. "I was the only one who was not involved."[32]

So Barry went from being the experimental theatre wunderkind wearing a 711 Shop suit in a hip jazz club, to working for a mainstream TV station, to becoming socially conscious and transforming into a dyed-in-the-wool hippie. That transformation led to activism and a number of victories on social issues, but there were negative effects on the family. "He was unsatisfied in his straight job and wanted to make a difference in the world, and when he saw the movement in the sixties, he thought, 'I can do something. I can help people,'" said Dylan. "That is what he really wanted to do, so he ended up helping a lot of people at the expense of us because the family just disintegrated. And then he told all us kids you can go to school or you don't have to. You can do anything you want. It was sort of a communistic approach [to parenting and education], which doesn't work in reality."[33]

Throughout his life, Barry had been a visionary leader, someone who took decisive action to make things happen. With the Intermedia Society, he had one more leading role in him. In 1970, Barry went to work for Intermedia, a collective that brought together artists and others to produce influential, high-impact creative events and projects. The media noticed. The *Vancouver Sun* ran a long feature on Intermedia with a photo of Barry (captioned "new boss of Intermedia")[34] that matched exactly Dylan's description of what his dad looked like at the time: "A Russian revolutionary with a huge beard and crazy hair."[35] *Maclean's* also came calling again, interviewing the "black-bearded Barry Cramer" about Intermedia's mission. "Technology has made tremendous advances, and people have become dehumanized because of it," Barry presciently told the magazine. "We want people to understand that technology can be married to artistic impulses."[36]

Speaking of being dehumanized, in April 1971, an episode of *Mantrap* featuring Cramer aired on CTV.[37] Hosted and co-produced by Alan Hamel, the daytime panel show pitted three celebrity females against one celebrity male. When the male said anything that the females found offensive, they disparaged him. It was an interesting premise for a TV show. Dylan was in the studio audience for the episode with Barry, and he saw one panelist in particular mercilessly belittle his dad. For Dylan, witnessing this became a painful memory.

In a return to his original passion of acting, Barry also had one more supporting role. It was in *Madeleine Is*, one of the first Canadian, English-language, full-length, narrative films directed and co-written by a woman: Sylvia Spring. Set at the height of the counterculture in Vancouver, with many iconic shots of the city, the film is about the feminist awakening of a young woman. In a crucial scene, Barry plays a therapist who leads a group therapy session on "dreamwork," which he explains as "simply a question of learning, of uncovering yourself. Your authentic self." After that introduction, the therapist—with his glasses, slightly unkempt beard, and calm demeanour—sits in an armchair and listens as Madeline describes a meaningful recurring dream.[38]

Barry Cramer, 1970. Photo by Peter Hulbert, courtesy Vancouver Sun (Postmedia Network Inc.).[39]

"We needed someone who looks shrinkish and Jewish and intellectual, and he was perfect," Spring said of Barry, just before the movie opened at

Vancouver's Ridge Theatre on May 14, 1971.[40] The movie is an obscure and dated period piece, but all ninety minutes of it survive on YouTube for the few who know how to find it. As far as I know, it's the sole video footage of Barry that exists on the internet. The Cellar soundbites and the film cameo are the only real-life glimpses I got of Barry. They're haunting, especially in light of how he was about to exit the stage.

Barry and Betty were separated, and he was living away from the family. It was June 1, 1971: Barry and Betty's twentieth wedding anniversary. That's when Barry killed himself. According to Dylan, Dan McLeod was living with Barry in North Vancouver and found him that night. "Dan said that he broke every speed law in the book to try and get Dad to the hospital, but it was too late."[41]

Two days later, a brief and emotionless obituary for "Cramer – Barry Paul, of North Vancouver" ran in the *Vancouver Sun*. By the weekend Jack Wasserman included an item on Barry "Kramer" in his *Sun* column. Wasserman said Barry "died suddenly"[42]—a press euphemism for suicide. There was no mention of suicide because news media almost never reported on people taking their own lives for fear it would promote the act.

"A measure of the impact of his death on the people with whom he was most closely associated was the fact that his fellow staff members at the *Straight* couldn't bring themselves to write about his passing," wrote Wasserman. "They may have been right in their forbearance. What is there to say when confronted by the inference that there is no escape for that which we are – or may have been."[43]

More than 52 years after Barry took his own life, I found myself staring at the "Registration of Death" form that was filled out to document his passing. It came shockingly into view while doing an online genealogy search. Reading the cold facts about Barry's death typed on the form, signed by the coroner and Betty Cramer, was surreal and sad. I realized that those facts should be left undisturbed in the past.

Those who knew Barry from the Cellar days had their theories about what happened to the man they knew as a blithe soul. His suicide, some reasoned, was more than a response to marital troubles. "The consensus of opinion was he got on a bad LSD trip, like a lot of people," said Gavin Walker.[44] "He got mixed up with Al Neil," said John Dawe, referring to Neil's increased drug use and non-conformity post-Cellar. "He fell under the spell."[45] Those explanations weren't accurate. Dylan has his own theory: "I think what happened was he looked at himself in the mirror and he thought, 'Where am I going to go from here?'"[46] For forty-two years, Barry went to many fascinating places, but it was time. Time, in his mind, to come to a full stop and rest.

People who knew him from his diverse pursuits were shocked and saddened by Barry's death. "He was a great guy, a great talent," said trumpeter and Cellar regular Ed Roop. "Committing suicide at an early age—it was a tragic event."[47] No one was more devastated by Barry's death than Dylan. "His sense of humour, his kindness, everybody loved him," said Dylan. "And then when he died it was [Dylan made the sound of a huge explosion] like a big bang." He was just thirteen when his father passed. "I went through a huge change obviously because he was my ideal, he was my rock, and then when he died, a rug came out from under my feet because all of a sudden he was not there," said Dylan. "I just went into myself and walked out on my family, and I basically became homeless. I started sleeping in garages."[48]

Up to that point, Dylan aspired to become an athlete. Then something told him to pursue music. Dylan chose to do that through the alto saxophone, and he quickly developed an affinity with the instrument. Given a key to Eric Hamber Secondary School, which he continued to attend despite family upheaval and heartbreak, Dylan regularly practiced there late at night. He found this solitary exercise soothed him and helped him heal.

By 1971, Dylan's big brother Gary was making a name for himself as a singer, guitarist, and songwriter. That year he co-founded Brain Damage, also known as the Flying Hearts Family, which would become a legendary rock band in Vancouver and in BC's Kootenay region. About four years later, Brain Damage temporarily disbanded due to a love triangle, in which Gary formed one angle. Gary and the Brain Damage rhythm section started Ridgerunner with other musicians. Ridgerunner was a psychedelic cross between the Grateful Dead and Santana, primarily playing original music at festivals and in venues including Rohan's Rockpile in Kitsilano. In February 1976, Gary walked into his father's past. Ridgerunner got a gig at Ye Olde Cellar, which was in the exact same basement space that housed the original

Cellar jazz club.[49] It's an odd continuum, from Harold Land to Samuel Beckett to Ridgerunner, but Cramers left their mark in the hallowed space.

• • •

Around the time Gary was rocking the old Cellar, Barry's other son had his musical world rocked by a jazz veteran who would have been right at home at the original Cellar in its heyday. It happened when Dylan's best friend Joel Bakan gave him a 1975 record by Memphis-born alto saxophonist Sonny Criss. At seventeen, Dylan experienced that rare epiphany when one's life path is illuminated. Hearing *Crisscraft* was a complete revelation to Dylan. Criss' tone throughout the album is pure and gorgeous; his soloing is raw and captivating, shaped by years of playing bebop and hard bop with a mastery that Charlie Parker would have endorsed. In fact, Criss played with Parker, Sonny Clark, Howard McGhee, and other leading players over the course of his career as a respected but egregiously underappreciated West Coast jazz stalwart.

Five days after recording *Crisscraft*, Criss made another affecting album, the blues-soaked *Saturday Morning*, which also transfixed Dylan. Hypnotized, Dylan hatched an impractical plan to make his way to Criss' home in Los Angeles to take lessons at the feet of his new master.

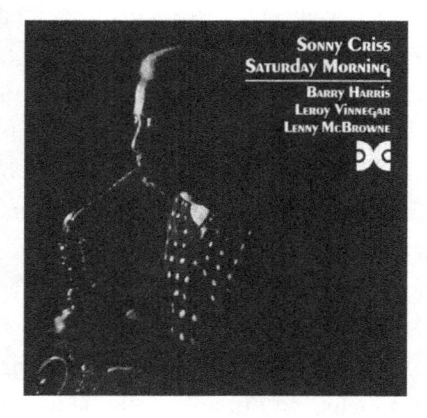

It took him more than a year, but Dylan made it to LA in 1977. You'd imagine he would have made detailed arrangements to begin what he saw as the next phase of his life. Wrong. At the very least you'd think Dylan would have introduced himself by letter or long-distance phone call before showing up on his idol's doorstep. Wrong again. Upon arrival, the nineteen-year-old simply looked up Criss in the phone book, cold called, and asked to study with the altoist. Criss gruffly said, "I don't teach!" and hung up. Variations on this scene repeated several times before Criss relented and told Dylan to come over.[50]

The first lesson sounds like something out of a Hong Kong kung fu flick in which a young initiate must face the stern head monk before gaining entry to the monastery. It began with a staring contest that became a cathartic therapy session. "He stared at me and looked at me really hard," said Dylan. "Sonny was the kind of guy that when he looked at you, you couldn't look away. So he looked at me forever, and then he said, 'What's wrong with you, boy?' He knew it. He knew something was wrong. He could read it because he was an artist. So I blurted out that my father had killed himself, and then I started crying, of course, and then he sort of just nodded his head."[51]

From that point on, Criss became a mentor and friend to Dylan. He was one of only two students Criss agreed to teach, said Dylan, and they met weekly for eight months. "I didn't realize this until later but, basically, he was my father all over again," said Dylan. "He had the same love, the same kind of person, the same energy, and then when he hugged you, it felt exactly the same as my father."[52]

A week before Criss was scheduled to go on tour in Japan, the unthinkable happened: on November 19, 1977, he shot and killed himself in his home. He was fifty. The *Los Angeles Times* published a story the next day by jazz critic Leonard Feather, who quoted saxophonist Benny Carter about Criss' death. "It's shocking that just when things were beginning to go well for Sonny after so many disappointments, his career had to be cut short so tragically," said Carter.[53] It was revealed later that Criss had stomach cancer. For Dylan, who didn't know Criss had been sick, the direct parallel with his dad was almost too much to bear. "It was like being shot twice in the heart," he said.[54]

Dylan stayed in LA and asked Dick Grove, who ran the well-known Dick Grove School of Music, for advice on what to do next with his alto sax studies. Grove suggested Dylan take a lesson with Phil Sobel, an in-demand woodwind teacher who played lead alto in the NBC Orchestra for years.

Right from the first lesson, Sobel taught like a drill sergeant. "It was exactly what I needed, even though I hated him for the first six months," said Dylan. "He said to me, 'You can't play anything. You don't know what you are doing.' And, of course, he was right."[55]

Dylan studied with Sobel for eight years of "gruelling torture." Aside from the tough love, Dylan absorbed an enormous amount of technical knowledge about playing alto sax that complemented what he had learned from Criss. "Sonny wasn't a teacher. Sonny was real. He was human. He taught you about love and commitment and trust, and he taught you that jazz is a brotherhood. Phil was a damn amazing teacher, a genius thinker, and he took the whole saxophone apart and figured it out."[56]

Sobel was also "a really possessive teacher," said Dylan. "You had to do everything his way, and you couldn't fuck around. I was so locked into him that it took me a long time to unlock myself. That was the beginning of finding me."[57] As part of the process of decoupling from Sobel, after a decade in LA, Dylan went to Toronto, and then returned to Vancouver. It wasn't time yet to make his own artistic statement. First, starting in the late eighties, he became a teacher to share the expertise he had accumulated. Plus, there was more soul searching. At one point he threw out Barry's memorabilia, including keepsakes he had saved from the Cellar. Why? "Well, why does anyone purge? I just had to get away from all of that stuff and find myself."[58]

In April 1997, Dylan was finally ready to express himself. Twenty years after going to LA to find Sonny Criss, he crafted an exquisite debut album. On ten songs that Criss had written and or recorded, Dylan struck an ideal balance between paying tribute to his sax hero in a heartfelt homage, and staying true to—in the words of Barry's final persona in *Madeleine Is*—his "authentic self." While the recording—*The First One*, which was re-released later as *Remembering Sonny Criss*—focused on another man's music, its emotional core was as autobiographical as it could be. There was no mistaking that Dylan's plaintive tone and blues-tinged solos on the sublime opening track, "Saturday Morning," were elegiacally inspired by Criss and Barry. Drawing from memories that were still raw after all those years made for an affecting and engaging sound, which could only have come from Dylan's horn.

Father and Son

Dylan was also inspired by the other musicians he gathered at Vancouver's Blue Wave Studios for the album. Landing Leroy Vinnegar was huge, as Vinnegar was a veteran American bassist who had played beautifully with many greats, including Criss. In fact, Vinnegar was in the rhythm section on Criss' excellent *Saturday Morning* album. Pianist Ron Johnston was in the pioneering Vancouver fusion group Pacific Salt and played standards for years with a melodic elegance before connecting with Dylan. "As soon as I started playing with him, I felt chemistry," said Dylan.[59] As for John Nolan, Dylan first played with him in LA, and the drummer contributed an ideal understated feel to the session.

Dylan Cramer (alto saxophone), with John Nolan (drums) and Ron Johnston (keyboard), Canada Place, June 21, 2013. Photo by Vincent Lim.

Dylan has gone on to release more albums, and while they haven't resonated as deeply with me as *The First One/Remembering Sonny Criss*, all have elements that made his first recording a success: an exceptional tone, the emotion in the altoist's interpretation of repertoire, and the strong interplay with the musicians. An interesting question arises: what would Barry think? "Everyone says that he would have been so proud of me," said Dylan. "I have no idea, but the thing about my father was, he said, 'Here's a dollar for allowance for being you,' and then he would give me a big hug. So I am being me."[60]

There would be more sorrow. Gary kept writing and playing music—with Gary Cramer and the Works, Brain Damage, and others—that was important in the development of the West Coast rock scene. While he never achieved commercial success, Gary was a magnetic performer who had star quality. Then he was in a horrific head-on collision on Galiano Island. "Gary was driving a Volkswagen van and some guy was charging down the hill at like 140 kilometres," said Dylan. "[The other driver] was going to kill himself and he was in the wrong lane, and my brother was going up the hill, and he just smashed right into him. You know there is no front [hood] to the Volkswagen van. He had to have his whole face [surgically re-] made with metal. I called him Terminator."[61]

Gary survived the accident, had facial reconstruction, and somehow resumed making music. It was liver cancer that would finally take his body and spirit. Gary passed away on March 28, 2006, at fifty-three.[62] Displayed on his Galiano grave was the portrait of him that appeared on the cover of his *Too Much Isn't More* album—his head tilted back, eyes hidden behind black shades looking skyward, and an exuberant, toothy grin.[63]

In 2008, Phil Sobel passed away. Dylan had kept in touch and stayed close with Sobel, who lived until ninety-one. Dylan's beloved teachers were gone, but he kept their life and musical lessons close.

• • •

It's December 2018, and I'm sitting with Dylan in a dimly lit room deep inside the Kerrisdale Community Centre, where he has taught alto sax and other instruments since 1993. He's just spent much of the last hour and a half talking about traumatic loss and grief. Yet after unloading all of that, he declares: "I'm in the best place I have ever been right now."[64] That unencumbered outlook was consistent with the vibe Dylan conveyed when I saw him perform at Frankie's Jazz Club a few months earlier. He looked and sounded relaxed and burden-free. In between tunes, Dylan joked with a black humour that was clearly inherited from his father.

In addition to sharing his jazz and alto sax knowledge through lessons, in 2019, Dylan also self-published a book he wrote: *Alto Saxophone Mastery*.

In it he shared insights learned from Criss and Sobel, including the latter's approach to technique, and elements of Dylan's personal story. The biggest breakthrough he achieved wasn't a musical one *per se*, but the final stage in his personal emancipation. "I finally have gotten to the place where I don't need anybody now," he said. "It's like a huge thing off my back. I don't need somebody to tell me they love me. I don't need somebody to tell me I am a great player. I don't need anything."[65]

As it did throughout our chat, the topic returned to his father. "I feel I am a lot like him. I feel like I carry his heart and his spirit and his [way of] thinking."[66]

In 1997, Dylan flew to Montreal to sign his first record deal. At the airport in Vancouver, while reaching the top of an escalator, Dylan clearly saw his dad among the crowd. "He looked exactly the same as he always did. He had an unmistakable look. I stopped, I froze, I stared at him, and he stared at me." Then Dylan's "rational brain" told him it was ridiculous to think Barry was there, so he started walking away. "I walked about four steps, and then my heart said, no. I turned around, and he was gone. He had just vanished."[67]

A doppelganger, a mirage, or something more? "I believe that was him," said Dylan. "I believe that he was there to say, 'I am with you.'"[68]

6 / MIND OF MINGUS: CHARLES MINGUS

IT'S A FABLED scene in Vancouver jazz history. Late one night in January 1961, Charles Mingus confronted football players at the original Cellar jazz club. The altercation was briefly reported on by media after it happened, and then shared as oral history for years. Decades later it was documented in a book. Those who witnessed the incident had divergent memories of what exactly happened. Regardless of the specific details, there's long been a fascination with the set-to. My question is, why?

The altercation has been compelling all this time in part because of who was involved: local athletes who played for the BC Lions football team, and Mingus, one of the most important and controversial figures in jazz. Plus, the setting was the city's quintessential jazz club at the time. Above all, it was a good yarn because it was a prime example of Mingus living up to his moniker, the Angry Man of Jazz. Or was it?

The story beguiled me for a long time, to the point where I needed to hear firsthand what went down. I may have been nearly a half century late to the party, but I was determined to talk to as many witnesses as I could find who were at the Cellar that night to learn what they saw and heard. Did Mingus really whack a BC Lion with a toilet plunger? Did the force of another blow from the bassist send a football player flying through tables? What triggered the dust-up, and how did it end? Then I had an epiphany: I was focusing on all the wrong things, and in the process, perpetuating the angry Black man trope. While the clash of the big men was a noteworthy anecdote in the story of Mingus' first visit to BC, more essential are the reasons why the jazz genius acted as he did, and the significance of the music he made during an extraordinary fortnight in Vancouver and Victoria.

• • •

By the 1950s, Mingus—who was born April 22, 1922, in Nogales, Arizona—was well-established as a prodigious jazz double bassist, bandleader, and composer. He had pioneered technique on his instrument; played with Louis Armstrong, Charlie Parker, Bud Powell, Duke Ellington, and other top-echelon musicians; adeptly segued from swing to bebop to contemporary jazz; led bands in various formats, including his Jazz Workshop with around eight to ten rotating members; composed acclaimed works; and recorded sublime albums, including *Pithecanthropus Erectus*, *The Clown*, *Blues & Roots*, and *Mingus Ah Um*.

Dannie Richmond was a New York City-born tenor saxophonist who played R&B before switching to drums. Alto saxophonist Lou Donaldson had recommended Richmond to Mingus, who hired him in 1956 and taught him how to play with a nimble adaptability. Richmond's drumming would become an essential element of Mingus' bands for more than twenty years.[1] In 1960, multi-instrumentalist Yusef Lateef gave Mingus the heads-up about two young talents who got their start in Detroit: alto saxophonist Charles McPherson and trumpeter Lonnie Hillyer.[2] Both would have long associations with Mingus.

On December 13, 1960, Mingus began an engagement at San Francisco's Jazz Workshop with McPherson, Hillyer, Richmond, and—starting the second night because of a delayed flight—pianist Duke Jordan. According to the *Oakland Tribune*, Jordan only lasted one night on the gig before Mingus sent him back to New York. "He's a good pianist," said Mingus. "But he just couldn't play my music and I couldn't train him on the job."[3] So the band continued the engagement as a piano-less quartet that drew large crowds and was held over. Meanwhile, Cellar Manager Dave Quarin had originally booked Mingus and his band to perform at the Vancouver club that same month.[4] With the San Francisco gig held over, Quarin rescheduled Mingus to the new year.

Journeys to the Bandstand

> **TONIGHT & SUNDAY ONLY**
> **IN THE**
> *Cellar*
> *"The Most Provocative Musician in Jazz"*
> **CHARLES MINGUS**
> **And His Quartet**
> TONIGHT
> 2 CONCERTS:
> 10 p.m. — 1 a.m.
> SUNDAY
> 1 CONCERT: 9 p.m.
> 222 E. Broadway   TR 4-9091

Vancouver Sun, January 14, 1961.

Opening night at the Cellar finally came on January 6, 1961, and the ad that appeared in the *Vancouver Sun* that day and on other dates during the run, referred to Mingus as "The Most Provocative Musician in Jazz."[5] It was smart marketing by Quarin, who was well aware of Mingus' reputation for being an intimidating presence, feared because of his temper, which could be directed at audience members, bandmates, journalists, and anyone else who might raise his ire. A preview in the *Province* noted that Mingus was known to "stop playing in the middle of a set and deliver a five-minute harangue on the foibles of an inattentive audience . . . But for a responsive and attentive audience, which The Cellar is famous for, Mingus will play deep, moving passages of original jazz with enormous power."[6] That description of the Cellar's audience wouldn't age well.

Tickets for the Mingus shows were $2.25.[7] One reason why the small, musician-run Cellar could afford Mingus was because the club and CBC-TV collaborated to make the economics work. They struck a fifty-fifty deal, with

Quarin paying about $750 to the musicians for performing at the Cellar, and the CBC providing the same amount to the band for participating in a television documentary.[8] That's James Carney's hazy recollection of the cost-sharing agreement. (The numbers don't correspond with detailed accounting records that Quarin kept, which show Mingus and his band were paid $2,086 for two weeks of Cellar performances,[9] but the difference is immaterial. While it seems like a low amount by today's standards, in 1961 dollars, it was sufficient for Mingus.)

Carney played trumpet and hung out with musicians who founded the Cellar in 1956. He didn't play gigs at the club. Instead, Carney worked at CBUT, CBC's TV station in Vancouver. He became a producer at twenty-five and started a dream project when Mingus came to town. Carney's bosses gave him the go-ahead to produce a series of mini-documentaries profiling jazz artists from Vancouver and the US. None of the programs have survived in the CBC archives, but Carney gave me a copy of the series' first show, *Mind of Mingus*. It aired on CBUT in the middle of Mingus' Cellar run on January 12, 1961, at ten-thirty p.m.[10] and as part of the national CBC network's *Quest* series on March 28, 1961.[11]

The half-hour black and white documentary is a fascinating and creatively crafted period portrait of Mingus. It consists of four tunes composed by Mingus and performed in their entirety by the quartet in a CBC studio, and an interview with a relaxed, affable, and thought-provoking Mingus in an empty Cellar. *Mind of Mingus* is an invaluable portrayal of the man and his music. It begins with a long establishing shot in the moodily lit studio, showing just Mingus in the background, unhurriedly improvising on the bass. At the same time, you hear a conversation between interviewer Bob Quintrell and Mingus, who says jazz "could be a mass music if it was handled right." As the camera slowly zooms in, and the quartet members emerge from the dark wings, Mingus continues: "I was searching for a new feeling. Not a feeling from myself but a new phrasing. You can phrase as much as you can take two notes and play them different all day long. Any two notes." To illustrate, he hums three sets of two notes in subtly different ways. "The same two notes can be done so many different ways." What's crucial: "Who does it, and how they do it."[12]

Then Mingus picks up the tempo and glides into a flawless walking bass line that begins the tune: "MDM (Monk, Duke and Me)." In October 1960, Mingus recorded a rollicking version of the song with a nonet that included McPherson, Hillyer, and Richmond. On this day in the CBC studio, the quartet members, wearing suits and ties, play the piece with a more understated but still buoyant approach. Each man takes meaningful solo turns, and a long section with just Mingus and Richmond shows the drummer's instinctive feel and their simpatico connection. The music conveys both cool poise and stirring vitality.

Charles Mingus, the original Cellar. Photo by Franz Lindner. Courtesy Barbara Lindner Coates, Tamina Lindner, and Dave Quarin.

Mingus talks about his quartet members with a level of detail that affirms he shaped the music with each player's specific strengths in mind. "My drummer, Dannie Richmond, I would not play without him. It would take a long time to replace him. Most people . . . don't understand what we have together. We have a beat that is like a railroad track or any straight line. But we don't play the straight line. We suggest this line. So you may hear a bass drum off of the line and you may think the tempo is staggering, but it's not, it's playing down to this centre."[13]

The quartet dials it down even more on "Vasserlean (aka Weird Nightmare)," which he first recorded in 1946 and re-recorded in the October 1960 session. A showcase for Hillyer, who plays exquisitely, the song evokes introspective melancholy that's the inverse of the dynamic and raucous pieces he's known for.

"You've used the words truth, honesty, and sincerity several times," Quintrell notes. "Are these the three things that you base all that you're doing in music?" Mingus, who's smoking a cigarette, gives an illuminating answer: "It depends on how truthful, honest, and sincere I am with myself. This is when it doesn't come off: If I get something kind of off the tracks that I believe in, then I can barely play. I can't play beauty for someone if I'm not feeling beautiful. But if they give me hate in return, I have much of that to give, and probably more, and I can also do that in music. But I don't enjoy it anymore. That's why I have an ulcer, that's why I have the milk." He smiles at the camera, raises a glass of milk while holding the cigarette in the same hand, says "Here's to the cows," and takes a refreshing sip.[14]

The next song sounds like a Charlie Parker tune—"Anthropology" comes to mind—but it's a rare bebop tune by Mingus called "Bugs," which he recorded in November 1960 and introduced during sets at the Cellar as "McPherson's in Person and He Ain't Rehearsin'." The alternative title is fitting because Parker was one of McPherson's biggest influences, and Mingus' altoist is up to the challenge of navigating the rhythmically tricky head and vigorously soloing at a rapid tempo. "Charles McPherson has kind of a warm heart . . . and a beautiful outlook on life, like Charlie Parker," says Mingus with an affection that belies his irascible tendencies.[15]

The made-for-TV set ends with the gospel-inspired Mingus favourite that was the infectious opening track on 1959's *Ah Um*: "Better Git It In

Your Soul." As the song builds in fervour, there's one more voice-over from Mingus, who gives Canada a shout-out. "Canada, I've always known it to be a little bit liberal and freer thinking than most of the United States because their environment won't let them think that I'm as good as they are. My experiences in any part of Canada, the people made me feel that they thought I was a man. And I've been places, many places, in America where I'm called not even a man, but less than that."[16]

As no footage or audio recordings are known to exist of the quartet's performances at the Cellar, *Mind of Mingus* is the closest I'll come to experiencing what the lucky patrons at the club heard. While it doesn't reflect peak Mingus innovation, the music has gravity and integrity. It gets close to you and stays there.

A review of the documentary called it an "interesting experiment." While it said "the words and music were eloquent and sincere," the reviewer was also confused at times. "The trouble with Charles Mingus talking is that, like his music, his thoughts leap ahead of his words, so ideas are inclined to tumble out end over end, making it hard for the listener to grasp exactly what he says."[17] I also lost Mingus' train of thought here and there, but the overall meaning was clear: creativity and authenticity were elemental to his being.

Mingus did at least one other interview while in Vancouver for the Cellar and CBC gigs. It was with Maurice Foisy of CHQM Radio, who said it was a "terrible" interview. "I just couldn't seem to get into his bag and he couldn't get into mine," recalled Foisy. "What I wanted to talk about was not anything he wanted to talk about."[18] So even with an always fascinating subject like Mingus, it wasn't a given that being granted an audience with him resulted in deep insights. He had to have a reason for believing it was worth revealing his soul for an inquisitor.

As for Carney, it was remarkable that he and the CBC team were able to quickly produce a cinematic work with an artistry that would normally take much longer to develop. Carney and Mingus also had an opportunity to grow closer than even work on the documentary would suggest. For part of Mingus' sojourn in Vancouver, he stayed at Carney's West End apartment. Carney retained a mental image of Mingus sitting on the apartment floor, with his back against a partition, drinking scotch with milk to soothe his ulcer. "He would sit there, and we would have these very, very earnest, intense conversations about jazz, life, and people," said Carney, who's still struck by what Mingus ultimately said in the documentary. "He's saying that all an artist can do is leave a little truth and a little beauty, and he was quite earnest and quite moving."[19]

Charles Mingus, the original Cellar, January 1961. Photographer unknown. Courtesy Dave Quarin.

• • •

Don Thompson arrived at the Cellar one night during Mingus' run, right when the music was about to start. "He glared over at me because I was standing in the doorway," said Thompson. "He said, 'Good evening, you're just in time to shut up.'" As for the music, it sounded "amazing" to Thompson.

"It was unbelievable," said the Cellar multi-instrumentalist about the whole experience. "I can remember that like it was yesterday."[20]

Thompson's friend Terry Clarke was fifteen when his revered drum teacher Jim Blackley—who spent time with Richmond while the quartet was in town—told Clarke he had to go to the Cellar to see Mingus and the band. Clarke, who put on a jacket and tie for what would be his first visit to the club, had no idea what to expect. "I remember after the first set being blown away and understanding, really understanding what the music was about," said Clarke. "Instinctively, it made perfect sense to me. It was completely bizarre but logical, it was beautiful, and it was huge."[21]

Clarke went back to the Cellar to see Mingus a second time, and it turned out to be the most infamous night in the history of the club. The story of what happened, first told in Jago's book, varies according to who's telling it, as memory is a malleable thing. Clarke's recollection: Mingus was playing a bass solo, without any accompaniment from Richmond, when the voices of football players sitting on a raised platform in the club could clearly be heard. Mingus noticed, and according to Clarke, he threatened them. "He said, 'If you motherfuckers don't stop talking, I'm going to come over there and beat the shit out of you.' And he keeps on playing, they keep on talking because, of course, they didn't hear him say that. They're not listening to anybody. Then he calmly put the bass down, and he walks right past me to the bathroom behind me. He runs out of the bathroom with a toilet plunger and goes over to that table, and all hell breaks loose. He starts whacking these guys. And the table flies, and people are scattering, and everything but tear gas was going on."[22]

Poet Jamie Reid recalled a somewhat different version, though it also featured football players on vocals and Mingus on toilet plunger. One of the footballers, Steve Cotter, went to the same high school as Reid—King Edward Secondary—and went on to play for the BC Lions and the Edmonton Eskimos in the Canadian Football League. Cotter was six-foot-three, 220 pounds, and "Mingus was a menacing looking dude," said Reid. "If you saw him on a street you wouldn't want to mess with him at all. So he said something to them, and they agreed they would be quiet. Mingus turned around, and then they made some scoffing noise. Then Mingus turned around and whacked Cotter on the head with the bathroom plunger. Cotter stood up and threw a punch at him. And Mingus just reached up and caught the punch like this and sort of twisted like this and Cotter went sailing. Literally sailing though about three tables, knocking them over. Cotter gets up and he's ready to go, and Mingus is ready to go—and in steps between them, Warren Tallman."[23]

Tallman was a very different kind of "lineman," a poetry-focused English professor at UBC. "He steps in between these two behemoths, and he says, 'Charlie! Charlie! Think about your career!' Mingus looks at him, and then veers off like a bull that has been distracted from his quarry. Somebody else grabs Cotter, and they rush him upstairs. And the encounter was over."[24]

I tracked down Cotter, who won a Grey Cup with the Lions in 1964. But Cotter's wife said he was too ill to talk to me. Cotter, who never publicly told his side of the story, passed away in 2022.[25]

Gavin Walker offered another variation on what he called "the night of the plunger." Walker went to the Cellar that night with a date. "I remember we sat right in front of the band. We were practically on the stage. It was a really exciting evening, a packed house, full capacity. Everything was going along really smoothly. The band was playing its ass off. Mingus and everybody seemed happy." Walker remembered that the quartet played one of Mingus' greatest songs, "Fables of Faubus," along with "Vasserlean (Weird Nightmare)." At one point Mingus announced that he and Hillyer were going to play a ballad together: "I Can't Get Started." "Mingus started alone with a long intro," recalled Walker. "Then Lonnie came in very quietly, starting to play the melody. Then there was this fucking noise. I guess no one noticed before because the band was playing so intensely, that these guys were making noise. But this was real quiet—no drums, just Mingus and Lonnie, and Lonnie playing muted trumpet, so really, really quiet. Then more noise. Mingus looked over, continued for a few bars more, then finally just stopped."[26]

According to Walker, Mingus told the noisemakers, "'You're louder than any jazz band at the highest volume, so if you don't mind, keep your voices down, we'd like to finish this.' He tried [playing] again, and then the noise continued. They just ignored him. So that was it. He put down his bass. Lonnie left the bandstand. Mingus headed over to the washroom. He came out with a plunger and put it on their table, with glasses strewn all over the place. I didn't hear any of the conversation. It happened fast. And these were all big football players. The football guys were confused, and Mingus was telling them it would be better if they just left. One of the guys pushed Mingus, and Mingus asserted himself. He didn't punch him, but he moved [as if to strike], and the guy knew he couldn't fuck with Mingus. They eventually agreed to leave. Mingus said, 'Get your money back at the door.' Then Mingus got back on the bandstand and said, 'Now we'll continue with what we started. Lonnie!'"[27]

Trombonist John Capon delivered yet another twist on the tale that got taller the more I asked about it. That night at the Cellar, Capon saw about five men he believed to be BC Lions players. Capon said the players were "very, very, very drunk" and making a lot of noise, which prompted Mingus to get mad and ask them to "shut up." When the noise continued, according to Capon, Mingus suddenly "whacked this guy in the face and knocked him right out. Bam! Just like that." Capon and his friends "thought we were all going to die. These big dudes could have wrecked the place, but they just quietly picked up the friend and left. We were just frozen solid, and the band just kept playing. They didn't even miss a beat. It was a moment, I'll tell you. It was a real moment."[28]

Finally, trumpeter Donnie Clark provided take five: "I didn't see any fight. But I'm pretty sure he took the peg out of his bass, and it was a threatening gesture." So, no plunger? "You know, I could be making this whole thing up in my head. So could five other people. There could be one of us who may be right, eh? And because it was such a kind of traumatic experience, something exciting happening at the Cellar, we've all developed a little story to satisfy our own curiosity." What's indisputable is that Clark used what little money he had as a UBC student to be at the Cellar every night of Mingus' run. His reward: hearing music that was modern and hard-hitting. "It had a lot of impact on me to make me want to be a little farther out with my playing. Now you must realize that me, as a young professional musician in Vancouver, I was playing with Lance Harrison's Dixieland band. That is probably the antithesis in a definition of jazz from what Charlie Mingus was doing."[29]

Bryan Stovell was a bass player hanging out at the Cellar, years before becoming a Nanaimo high school music teacher who greatly influenced

Diana Krall, Ingrid and Christine Jensen, and many other musicians. Like Clark, he heard Mingus night after night at the Cellar (except the infamous one), and it was transformative. "It was intense, just absolutely intense," said Stovell. "I mean, totally absorbing, and Mingus is yelling at the guys, urging them to play better, like nothing I'd ever seen before."[30]

Blaine Wikjord, another drummer who studied with Blackley, witnessed the kerfuffle between Mingus and the football players and thought the quartet was the "greatest band" the then-seventeen-year-old had ever experienced. He invited Richmond for dinner at the Wikjord family's home, and Mingus' drummer accepted the invite. "He was dressed up in a suit and really, really spiffy," said Wikjord. "I had my little niece staying with us at the time, and she had never seen a Black man before. She was in her high chair and was always trying to touch him . . . He was a real gentleman."[31] Yet another teenaged Blackley drumming pupil, Don Fraser Jr., was also at the dinner. After eating, the "personable and friendly" Richmond gave Wikjord and Fraser a drum lesson.[32] So even outside of the Cellar, Mingus and his band members' made an unforgettable musical impact.

But back to the fight. Jack Wasserman wrote about the fracas in his widely read *Vancouver Sun* column. "So far during his extended engagement at The Cellar, Mingus has had several discussions with customers who failed to pay attention," noted Wasserman. "The most memorable involved a giant football lineman who refused to shut up. After the show Mingus asked him to get his money back and leave. The footballer swung. Mingus, who weighs in at a comfortable 300 pounds, grabbed the arm aimed at his stomach and propelled the footballer across six tables. The footballer picked himself up, brushed himself off, and left. Afterwards Mingus apologized to the remainder of the packed house: 'I'm sorry, but I'm neurotic. My only defence is that I know it.'"[33]

I ended up dissecting the skirmish between Mingus and the football players at length, despite questioning whether the real and imagined events of that evening mattered. Yes, a complete about-face. I decided that thoroughly recounting what happened was needed for context. But I made up for the contradiction by getting the perspective of the only surviving member of the quartet who was on the Cellar bandstand that night: Charles McPherson.

More than fifty years after that turbulent night, I cold called McPherson, and he immediately recounted what was going through his mind during the confrontation. "I was thinking that there was going to be a horrible fight because there were three or four of them," said McPherson. "They were big, they were younger than him [Mingus]. I was thinking, I don't feel like going over there, fist fighting with people." But then it was an anti-climax. "It was very sad and quick . . . it didn't turn into anything, and it was over. Maybe a scuffle or something and it was broken up, and that was the end of it." McPherson remembered that the incident was covered in a local newspaper, but he mistakenly thought it involved a star quarterback. One detail McPherson got exactly right: the next night, patrons formed a long lineup to get in the Cellar to see for themselves what would transpire with Mingus.[34]

It was when I brought up Mingus' reputation as an angry man, and asked whether McPherson was ever the recipient of that anger, that my understanding of the event and the man at the centre of it transformed. "I guess anger can be one of the words that one could use to describe the person who has enough intelligence and awareness to know that there are some very screwed up things, and then to actually have something to say about it," said McPherson. "But you could just as easily use the term discontent. One could just as easily say dissatisfied or refused to accept."[35]

The next thing I knew, we were talking about the "cleansing of the temple" story, which is told in several verses of the Bible, including Matthew 21:12–13: "And Jesus went into the temple of God, and cast out all them that sold and bought in the temple, and overthrew the tables of the moneychangers, and the seats of them that sold doves, And said unto them, 'It is written, My house shall be called the house of prayer; but ye have made it a den of thieves.'"[36]

McPherson saw parallels with the biblical narrative. "I guess if you can say the most so-called beautiful man, Jesus . . . he can be angry, so I know somebody like Mingus, who grew up in a world where he couldn't drink water unless he went to a certain part of a restaurant, then I guess you could call that angry," said McPherson. "And he had issues with that. He spoke of it, he wrote music about it ["Fables of Faubus," a protest song about a racist Arkansas governor, for example], and he would have something to say about it. Basically, his attitude was, 'I'm not accepting the template that is supposed to be the template that everybody's following. I'm not doing it.' He actually had enough nerve to say no. So, he would be considered an angry man, I guess. But people like me would think of him as an honest man."[37]

While Mingus faced blatant racism at various times in his life, the incident at the Cellar didn't appear to result from overt discrimination. I would argue, however, it was a by-product of systemic racism that engenders attitudes of superiority and disrespect. That night at the Cellar, there was a lack of respect for the musicians and the music itself. Mingus demanded that respect, and when it wasn't forthcoming, he sprang into action. McPherson's analysis provided perspective that went far deeper than simply chalking up Mingus' behaviour to his anger.

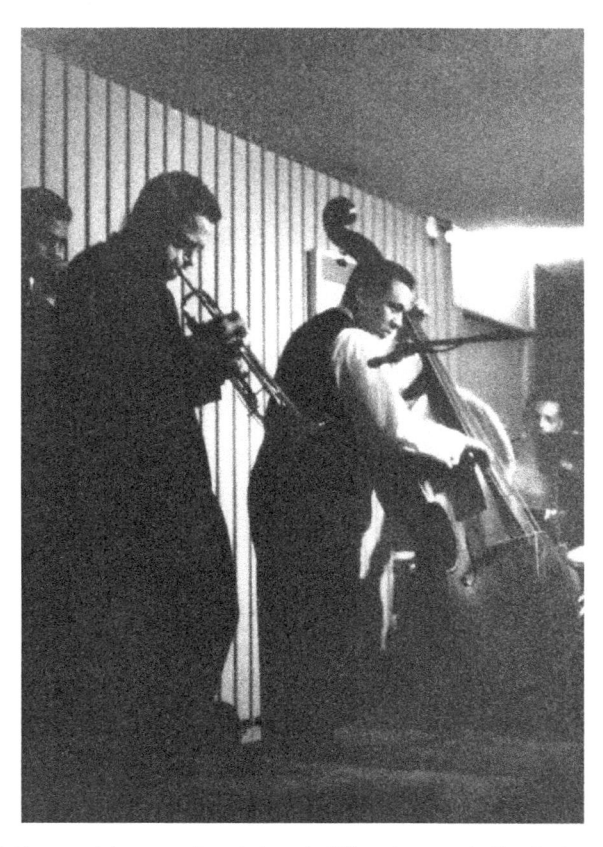

Charles McPherson (alto saxophone), Lonnie Hillyer (trumpet), Charles Mingus (bass), and Dannie Richmond (drums), the original Cellar, January 1961. Photographer unknown. Courtesy Dave Quarin.

Charles McPherson (alto saxophone), Charles Mingus (bass), and Dannie Richmond (drums), the original Cellar, January 1961. Photographer unknown. Courtesy Dave Quarin.

There were other memorable scenes from the Mingus visit. Near the beginning of a noon concert the quartet performed on January 13, 1961, at the University of British Columbia, Mingus noticed about a dozen people standing at the rear of the auditorium. Mingus suggested to Walker, one of the concert's main organizers, that he grab a hat and collect admission[38]—twenty-five cents for UBC Jazzsoc members, fifty cents for non-members[39]—from the latecomers. Walker demurred, so Mingus put down his bass and did it himself. "Now, up to a point, all this seemed quite hilarious, but he dragged it on to such an extent that one began to have an uneasy feeling about it, as if Mingus were determined that no one, not even an impoverished student, was going to hear Mingus for free," wrote *Coda* magazine's Vancouver correspondent John Clayton. "There was a certain tension."[40]

Independent of the Cellar's arrangements with Mingus, the Scene at 1306 Wharf Street in Victoria also booked the band. This was a jazz club started by Ken Hole and Walley Lightbody, two of the Cellar's founders who left the

Vancouver club over differences in artistic and commercial direction with other members. Edward Harvey and Garry Nixon bought the Scene from Lightbody for $100.[41] They "bet the farm" by calling Mingus' agent in New York, who had never heard of Victoria but still agreed to book his client to perform there at a fee that "seemed astronomical."[42]

Neither party had anything to worry about. The Mingus quartet performed to packed houses over four nights at the Scene, enabling the club to make a profit.[43] The group also played January 11, 1961, for a large audience at Victoria College (later the University of Victoria). A review in the *Victoria Daily Times* noted that the show went over its allotted time, and because a lecture was scheduled in the auditorium, Mingus, the band, and the "jazz-happy students" decamped to the cafeteria where the performance continued for another hour. "Centre of it all was Charlie Mingus, the rotund Negro from New York whose bass fiddle can play it hot, play it cool, and even come out with a Bronx cheer."[44] I was shocked to read the weightist and offensive description of Mingus in the review, which sixty years after the fact is overtly inappropriate. But at the time it was acceptable language.

Mingus' Victoria layover was successful, and for Harvey, Nixon, and the other young jazz aficionados who had the chance to spend time with him, the experience was so profound that it wasn't "quantifiable."[45]

Mingus returned to Vancouver to play at the Blue Horn in 1965 with the same band that he'd brought in 1961. McPherson believed that this version of the quartet was better than the earlier group. The names hadn't changed, but the virtuosity had. "Mingus would exact a certain level of performance out of people," said McPherson.[46] At the Blue Horn, the quartet was without Richmond for some of the nights because he was arrested for drug possession and deported. Mingus and the rest of the group played drummer-less after Richmond's drug bust.[47] The Blue Horn was the club where Don Thompson and Terry Clarke performed six months earlier with saxophonist John Handy, a Mingus sideman. They didn't just play with Handy in Vancouver—they toured with him, including performing at the Monterey Jazz Festival in a concert that was recorded and released to considerable praise. Hearing Mingus and his band perform live in 1961 was pivotal for Thompson and Clarke and that inspiration helped galvanize the young jazz players.

In the years after Mingus' first shows in Vancouver, he achieved many artistic heights. Among them: Mingus led an eleven-piece band for the recording of his epic six-part suite *The Black Saint and the Sinner Lady*, and his *Changes One* and *Changes Two* quintet albums were late-career gems. There were also painful lows. He went through periods of clinical depression, and got evicted from his Greenwich Village loft for non-payment of rent, a sad scene that was vividly documented in the film *Mingus: Charlie Mingus 1968*. Plus, Mingus infamously punched longtime sideman Jimmy Knepper in the mouth. The punch broke one of the trombonist's teeth and badly damaged Knepper's embouchure. Mingus was convicted of assault and received a suspended sentence. Yet years later, Knepper worked with Mingus again. All was not forgiven, but such was Mingus' contradictory allure.

There were two more Vancouver appearances: at Oil Can Harry's in 1976—critic Bob Smith said Mingus and his quartet gave a "stunning" performance[48]—and at North Vancouver's Old Roller Rink in 1977, after which a reviewer wrote Mingus "seemed subdued and perhaps even sulky."[49] That year Mingus received a devastating diagnosis—amyotrophic lateral sclerosis (ALS)—that progressively debilitated him. He kept creating as much as physically possible, including a collaboration with Joni Mitchell that led to the wondrous *Mingus* album, and staying true to his brilliant and complex self. Mingus was fifty-six when he died in Cuernavaca, Mexico, on January 5, 1979.

• • •

Rewind to early 1961. After the gigs in Vancouver and Victoria, Mingus and the band began a lengthy engagement at Copa City, a club in the Jamaica neighbourhood of Queens, New York. (The venue's name was immortalized in a tune Mingus wrote and performed live but never recorded in a studio, "Copa City Titty.") When the group started playing on the first night, a "FRUMPING, THUDDING SOUND" emanated from Richmond's bass drum. After opening the drum, Richmond took out "THIS FURRY THING THAT DANNY THOUGHT WAS SOME KIND OF ANIMAL." It was a fur coat that Mingus had purchased at G.L. Pop Fine Furs on Main Street in Vancouver. Mingus said he gave the coat to Dave Quarin's wife Ricci as "gratitude" for receiving extra gigs at the Cellar, and now it appeared that the Quarins surreptitiously returned the gift by sequestering it in the bass drum.[50]

All of this—and much more—is documented in a wide-ranging six-page letter sent in 1961 from Mingus to Ricci. It was handwritten in all caps on letterhead for Debut Records, the bassist's short-lived record label. The only problem: Mingus' description of the fur coat caper was part fact and a lot of fiction, said Dave Quarin. According to Quarin:

- Mingus did buy a fur coat in Vancouver, but it was for the bassist's third wife, Judy Starkey.
- When crossing the Canada-US border at Blaine, Washington, Ricci wore the coat so Mingus could avoid paying duty.
- Neither Dave nor Ricci put the furry jacket into the bass drum.

Mingus substantially embellished the tale in the letter for an unknown reason. So he used his artistic licence and imagination on and off the bandstand.

Also in the letter, Mingus described in detail a crazy dream that involved eating a lot of pie and ice cream in the Quarins' house, requested assistance in getting money that he claimed James Carney/the CBC owed him, and asked for information about jazz clubs where he could book himself. "WHERE IS THE YARDBIRD SUITE," Mingus asked about the Edmonton jazz club, without a question mark. "BETTER YET, WHERE IS EDMONTON ALBERTA. IS THAT CANADA OR U.S.A. CAN YOU GET BETTER ADDRESSES. IT'S VERY IMPORTANT SINCE I'M GOING TO BOOK MY OWN SELF TO COME OUT THERE. I NEED MORE SPECIFIC DETAILS, LIKE CLUB OWNERS OR MANAGERS."[51]

Dave Quarin kept the letter and the frayed-with-time air mail envelope that Mingus put it in. The former Cellar manager referred to the letter multiple times during our phone conversations over the years. When I met Quarin in July 2022, it was an indescribable feeling to actually hold the original missive and read what Mingus wrote in blue ink more than sixty years earlier. I pored over the relic as if I was doing a forensic analysis. While there were no stunning revelations, the letter was another illuminating window into the mind of Mingus. My key takeaways: Mingus was, at the time, an attentive businessman who stood up for himself and his band. And while he was known for his rage, he also had a playful sense of humour.

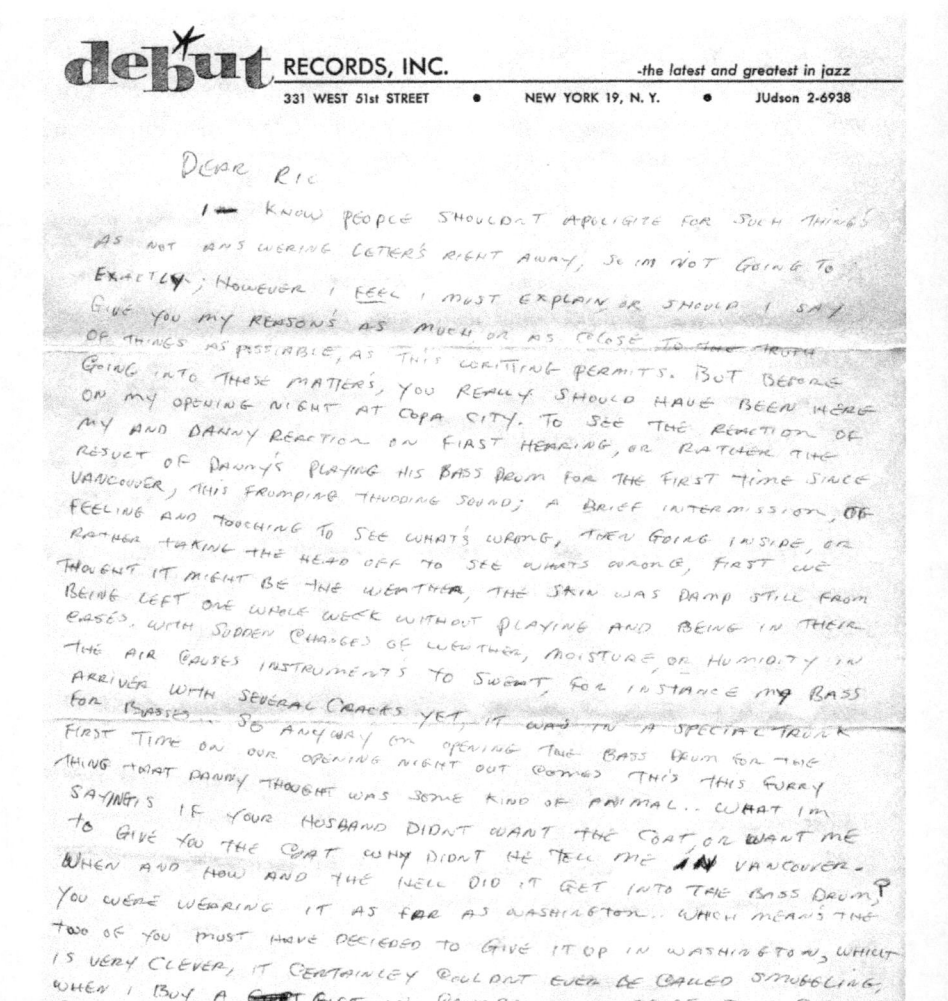

Page one of a six-page 1961 letter from Charles Mingus to Ricci Quarin. Courtesy Dave Quarin.

Rewind again, this time to 1976. That's when Rick Kilburn had a close encounter with Mingus. The setting was Bradley's, an intimate and beloved jazz club in Greenwich Village. Many great pianists performed there, and on this night, Jimmy Rowles was playing in his gorgeous style on an upright piano. Accompanying him on bass: Kilburn, a young, mild-mannered

Canadian who grew up listening to and meeting jazz musicians. He enjoyed an idyllic jazz childhood and adolescence in large part because his dad Jim was one of the founders of the Vancouver haunt where fireworks went off when Mingus was on the bandstand: the Cellar. Jim was there the night Mingus allegedly grabbed a toilet plunger, and the guitarist heard the master bassist utter, "Anybody talks when I'm playing, I'm gonna plunge them out!"[52]

At Bradley's, Rowles and Kilburn were playing a bossa nova, when the bassist closed his eyes and started a solo. "From the table right next to me there was this gruff voice saying, 'Don't freeze, motherfucker.'" Kilburn opened his eyes to see none other than Charles Mingus. What did Kilburn do next? "I froze. I followed his instructions to a T [except for the "Don't" part]. He stayed for the rest of the night and entertained the audience by giving me a lesson out loud all night long."[53]

During a set break, Kilburn asked Rowles to intervene. "I said, 'He's your friend. Tell him to shut up.' Rowles said, 'No, no, that's Mingus. I'm not going to tell him anything.' We made it through to the end of the night and by then I had built up my courage. I was going to go and just give Mingus hell. So I walked up to the table, he saw that I was mad, and he said, 'Hey, I'm sorry. I shouldn't have done that. I had no right to do it, but I'm high and, well, go get a piece of paper and a pencil and come back here, and I'm going to talk to you like an old man.'"[54]

Kilburn got the supplies, and Mingus wrote notations that were directly relevant to playing jazz on the bass. "It had to do with phrasing," said Kilburn. "They were devices to lock the time in, and it was invaluable. It took me about a year to get a grip on it." Mingus claimed that the only other person he showed this information to was Scott LaFaro, the great bassist who died young in a car crash.[55] Kilburn had met LaFaro at the Cellar when the bassist played there with Harold Land, so it meant a lot to receive this bespoke guidance from Mingus that apparently only one other musician had ever received.

The two bassists talked until Bradley's closed, and then went to Mingus' apartment nearby. Kilburn played Mingus' basses and explained his connection to the Cellar. Mingus remembered the Cellar and the "machinations" that went with his unforgettable visit. They ended up hanging out all night.

"He kept saying to me, 'I know you, man. I love you.' I guess he was trying to make up for shitting on me."[56]

After that night, when playing gigs, Kilburn would sometimes spot Mingus. "He'd be sort of sitting in a corner somewhere, like in the shadows, checking me out. I guess he was wondering if I was doing anything with the information he gave me. It turned out the next night [at Bradley's] I came back to play with Rowles, and I started trying to do the stuff that Mingus had said, and Jimmy said over his shoulder, 'Cut that shit out. Don't listen to him. Go back to the way you were playing.'"[57] Classic.

Mingus, when Kilburn encountered him, was both scoundrel and sweetheart. Heckling, dropping deep knowledge, and declaring his love.

• • •

In July 2013, I time travelled with James Carney, Gavin Walker, photographer/installation artist Michael de Courcy, and de Courcy's piano-playing son Johnny. Our vehicle: the subterranean space that had been the original Cellar and two other jazz clubs. The building in Vancouver's Mount Pleasant neighbourhood that housed the clubs was slated for demolition, to be replaced by a large condo and townhouse complex named "The Independent." The developer let us go in before local jazz heritage vanished.

After the Cellar door near Watson Street was unlocked, we walked cautiously down the steep, unstable stairs. Inside, there were piles of junk and scarcely any traces of what it was like in its prime as a smoke-filled, after-hours bebop club. But the layout was essentially the same and the bandstand was astoundingly still there, so while walking around and taking photos, I imagined. Especially about Mingus. There's the staircase that excited patrons descended with anticipation about hearing his music and experiencing his fury. That's where Mingus and his quartet played glorious modern jazz. There's the washroom where he charged headlong and grabbed the infamous toilet plunger. That's the spot where his candid interview took place for *Mind of Mingus*.

Carney and Walker didn't have to imagine because they were there those many years ago. Their smiles said it all. They were joyous about having the rare chance to revisit transcendent moments from their youth, Mingus prominent among them.

About eight months later, it was all gone. I watched, in a silent vigil, as a worker operated a hydraulic excavator to completely demolish the place where Mingus held court. Only rubble remained. By 2019, the gleaming complex was complete and ready for middle-class habitation. The only acknowledgement of the scrappy jazz club that was once there is a small public art piece that's displayed on the side of Watson Street: a reproduction of a newspaper ad that promised "jazz tonight" in the Cellar with LA saxophonist Bill Perkins, who played in the club in July 1960.

That was it. No plaque with historical context, and certainly no mention that Mingus was there. It didn't matter. Nothing could erase the beauty and soul of the unvarnished, forthright jazz that Mingus and so many others created right there on the holy bandstand.

Gavin Walker and James Carney, the former original Cellar, July 19, 2013. Photo by Chris Wong.

7 / FISHERMAN'S JAZZ: DAVE QUARIN

HALFWAY UP THE east coast of Vancouver Island, in a place that tourism brochures promote as the "Salmon Capital of the World," Dave Quarin lives in his sanctuary. Quarin's home in the small city of Campbell River doesn't have an ocean view, but it's just steps from a beach that overlooks Discovery Passage and Quadra Island. It's a beautiful vista and the perfect setting for two of Quarin's pastimes: fishing and self-reflection.

A half-day journey, by car and ferry, is all that separates Quarin from BC's mainland. But he's worlds away from his past life as one of Vancouver's finest and busiest jazz saxophonists. Quarin was a central figure at the original Cellar jazz club that had such a pioneering influence on the city's jazz scene. Yet when fellow musician and Cellar colleague John Dawe was researching the history of the club they created along with other local players, asking Quarin questions proved to be a dead end. "He doesn't seem to want to talk about it," said Dawe in 2013. "I don't know why. He's gone weird."[1] Marian Jago interviewed almost all of the primary characters that made the Cellar what it was for her definitive history of the club, *Live at the Cellar*, with one key exception. Despite repeated requests, Quarin was the sole holdout.[2]

Various people told me he's a recluse, and some said he's embittered. Then I talked to drummer George Ursan. "Dave Quarin's one of the sweetest guys I've ever known in my life," said Ursan, who played with Quarin at the Cellar and elsewhere. "He wasn't a recluse then. He was a guy that I just loved to talk to. Very social, very friendly, very giving. If you had a musical question for him, he was glad to answer it if he could."[3]

Those sentiments, along with fond reminiscences of Quarin from other musicians, made me wonder about reports of his disaffection and self-imposed exile. I had to see for myself the character of the man Ursan and others knew. In the process, I hoped to learn not only about Quarin's time at the Cellar, but about his entire long career in music. So I called Quarin and left messages, he called me back a few times, and we conversed briefly. I also wrote letters to him; he wrote back once. This cat-and-mouse game went on for months that turned into years, and all the while, I researched the hell out of his life. Despite my obsessive search for answers, many unanswered questions remained. I had to accept the fact that at best, I could capture an imperfect, somewhat blurry portrait of him. As I learned, there are no easy answers or absolutes with this man. Then, unexpectedly, Quarin became a willing participant in my quest. He helped me tell his story, which offers insights about passion, creativity, and integrity in jazz.

• • •

Giovanni (John) Quarin was born in northern Italy; Amabile (Mabel) Ceccon was born in Treviso, in the Veneto region. They immigrated to Canada and married in Princeton, BC in 1928. The Quarins had two sons: Dennis, born in 1929, and David, born August 26, 1934—the midpoint of the Great Depression—in Vancouver. Despite the tough economic times, Giovanni was gainfully employed as a foreman with forestry companies, including Bloedel, Stewart and Welch, which had logging camps in various BC locations. So the Quarins lived an itinerant life, moving between remote camps on Vancouver Island at places like Fanny Bay, Bowser, Union Bay, and Menzies Bay, just north of Campbell River. In the early 1940s, the Quarin brothers studied in a one-room Menzies Bay schoolhouse. For the younger Quarin, music came into his consciousness at this time through the magic of radio.

Before Commercial Drive became the heart of Vancouver's Italian district, Little Italy lay further west in the working-class neighbourhood that would become known as Strathcona. After he and his family moved back to Vancouver, Quarin's formative years were spent in this original Little Italy—absorbing the "wonderland" of vibrant life on Prior Street, Union Street, and other main drags in the area.[4] "They were the most important years in my life, actually," he said.[5]

Many of his Little Italy memories relate to music. He played in and listened to bands that performed at outdoor concerts in local parks. Strathcona is next to Chinatown, so the Chinese community also greatly influenced his worldview. "It was just so natural to live in the East End because everybody accepted everything that was there, and it was wonderful. Wonderful place. Where else could you go walk one block away and they have a whole family of gypsies living in the block? I always wanted to learn Chinese because I thought in the future, if I was going to continue playing, I'd want to play for the Chinese community."[6] Some of his earliest gigs were playing for Chinese dances.

There's a fuzzy photo from the 1940s of a pre-teen Quarin playing alto saxophone and standing right behind him, his brother Dennis playing clarinet. They wore matching jackets that their mother made. The photo conveys the exuberance of youth and joy of musical discovery. It took time, and his brother's influence, for that joy to come alive. "I didn't want to take music when I was a kid. I guess you could say my older brother whipped me into it." That was a Quarin quote from a 1968 *Vancouver Sun* feature on him by Bob Smith. Another quote: "I was about 11 years old when I started taking lessons on alto saxophone. Dennis, my brother, was playing pretty good tenor sax and clarinet but he quit to go into business and left me holding the bag."[7] Quarin was using a figure of speech when he said Dennis "whipped" him into playing music. Translation: his brother strongly encouraged Quarin to pursue music, and he followed that advice.

At an early age, Quarin also got interested in analog recording technology. He was particularly drawn to wire recording, popular in the late 1940s and early 1950s, in which audio recordings were made on thin wire. "Anytime Frank Sinatra had a movie on, I was carrying a forty-five-pound Webcor wire recorder and asking the manager of the theatre if I could go backstage. And I sat there for the whole movie holding a two-bit microphone that was [connected] to the wire recorder, and I would record the whole movie because Sinatra was [singing] in it."[8]

Jazz enthusiast Rod Wong first knew of Quarin in the mid-1940s. That's when a big jazz event happened in Vancouver. On October 9, 1946, American jazz impresario Norman Granz brought his Jazz at the Philharmonic tour to Vancouver's Strand Theatre, at Georgia and Seymour. The JATP bill for two shows at the Strand was astonishingly good: Roy Eldridge, Coleman

Hawkins, Illinois Jacquet, Helen Humes, Trummy Young, Buck Clayton, and other top jazz musicians performed. Wong saw twelve-year-old Quarin and his brother Dennis at the evening performance. The teenagers were part of the capacity audience of close to 2,000, which according to a review in the *Province*, included "rabid jazz fans" who "practically shouted the house down after each number."[9] A few years later, Wong got together with Quarin—an ardent record collector from an early age—to listen to music. "He was dismissive of musicians who were entertainers," said Wong about the conversation that day.[10] Even though he was still a callow high school student, Quarin conveyed an affinity with creative, intellectually rigorous music.

Quarin's childhood and adolescence weren't as idyllic as they sound. There was domestic strife. In October 1948, the *Vancouver Sun* reported that John (Giovanni) Quarin was arrested and sentenced to a month in jail for illegal possession of a gun.[11] According to the *Sun*, he was arrested "following a complaint of his estranged wife Mabel, 900 Jackson, that Quarin has threatened her with a gun."[12]

By the late 1940s, Quarin was playing in a rehearsal big band led by Bob Berglund that did arrangements of Stan Kenton tunes. Plus, Quarin performed in venues like the Debonair Ballroom and the Ukrainian Hall, both on East Pender Street. He was paid eleven cents to play at a dance—enough to pay for the streetcar ride home.

Quarin also performed with Ernie King, a dynamic trombonist and bandleader. King was a leading musician in Vancouver's Black community that was based in Strathcona, and the area's lively hub—Hogan's Alley—which Quarin explored. King recruited Quarin to play on a tour. As a teenaged high schooler, Quarin needed permission from his father to tour with King in his mostly Black band, which travelled in Cadillac limousines. Quarin relished the experience. King would go on to co-own—with his wife, Marcella "Choo Choo" Williams—the Harlem Nocturne Cabaret at 343 East Hastings. When it operated from 1957 to 1968, it was the city's only Black-owned nightclub.

After graduating from Vancouver Technical Secondary School, Quarin got deeper into music, learning from other local musicians. One of his first influences was Al Neil, who was developing a distinct jazz piano style in the early 1950s. "He was the very first person I studied any jazz with before I went to New York," said Quarin. "He was teaching me things that I should have known ten years earlier."[13] Quarin greatly respected Neil, who was a decade older and a World War II veteran. "That was always interesting, being around someone that had gone through what he had gone through."[14]

Dave Quarin (alto saxophone, second from left in sax section), Dennis Quarin (tenor saxophone, far right in sax section), McLean Park Dance & Talent Show, August 12, 1949. Photographer unknown. Courtesy Dave Quarin.

In 1952, Vancouver arts magazine *p m* published an essay Neil wrote—"a short survey of new jazz"—that included two long paragraphs expressing admiration for blind American pianist Lennie Tristano.[15] Another Vancouver musician who made an impression on Quarin, clarinetist Albert Del Bucchia, had studied with Tristano in New York. Quarin, who played with Del Bucchia, took note of Tristano's growing influence. After holding his own with bebop giants—including Charlie Parker and Dizzy Gillespie—Tristano developed an inimitable, technically striking style that incorporated counterpoint and contemporary classical elements. In 1949, Tristano led musicians, including his protégés Lee Konitz and Warne Marsh, on a session that introduced the first recorded free jazz tunes (nine years before Ornette Coleman's debut recording). Then in the early 1950s, Tristano controversially pioneered multitracking and overdubbing in jazz.

In 1951, Tristano established a jazz school in his Manhattan loft at 317 East 32nd Street. Quarin spent "quite a chunk of money"[16] to go on a three-day train journey to New York City in 1954 to study with Tristano for a month. Quarin's two main takeaways from his lessons with Tristano, an ultra-rigorous teacher who insisted on loyalty from his students: "Listen to the solos of trumpeter Roy Eldridge and saxophonist Lester Young, and learn the scales."[17] Quarin absorbed that advice, which would shape his approach to soloing.

It's long been rumoured that Quarin also had a lesson with none other than Parker. Several people repeated the story to me as fact. As it turned out, it's fictitious. Quarin said taking a lesson with Bird "didn't work out." But he heard him play in a manner of speaking. "I actually heard him behind closed doors, but I didn't see him."[18]

The mid-1950s were pivotal for Quarin. In 1955, with support from broadcaster Jack Kyle, he launched a series of jazz concerts at CJOR Radio's Playhouse in downtown Vancouver. "Called the Jazz Workshop, it has no officers or formal organization, but is being sparked by alto saxophonist Dave Quarin," wrote *Province* columnist Dan Ekman. "Dave's aim: to showcase every jazz musician on the local union's list." Ekman referred to the Jazz Workshop as a "new jazz group which feels the bustling Jazz Society has grown too big for comfort."[19] That likely caught the attention of those running the Vancouver New Jazz Society, the city's leading presenter of jazz concerts. Among the musicians who led bands in Jazz Workshop shows were guitarist Jim Kilburn, Del Bucchia, saxophonist Wally Snider, and Quarin himself. The series gave Quarin vital experience in being a jazz promoter. Also in 1955, Quarin was one of the musicians who started playing and hanging out in a jam space called the Wailhouse. That was a precursor to a momentous time for Quarin and the city's fledgling jazz scene.

• • •

Her name was Mildred, but she went by Ricci. Dave and Ricci fell in love, and they got married in 1956.[20] The Quarins' first child, Randy, was born that year. Ricci recalled a turning point in their marriage. "Dave came home and said, 'How do you feel about eating wieners for the next few years?' I said, 'Okay.' He said, 'Okay, I'm going to quit my [accounting] job and dedicate the rest of my life to music.'"[21] Exciting developments were unfolding in the scene, and Quarin wanted to participate fully.

Bassist and entrepreneur Ken Hole discovered a brand-new basement at 2514 Watson Street. Just off Broadway between Main and Kingsway, the subterranean space was the perfect setting for a jazz club. The same musicians who made a joyful noise at the Wailhouse, along with other players, artists, and jazz aficionados, created what would become the original Cellar jazz club. They registered the club as a non-profit society. Quarin, one of the club's charter members, was also part of the core crew responsible for the planning and physical preparations that enabled the Cellar to open in April 1956.

Dave Pike, Bill Schlossmacher, Carla Bley, Paul Bley, Don Francks, Ken Hole, and Dave Quarin, outside the door of the original Cellar, October 1957. Photographer unknown. Courtesy James Carney.

Quarin was also one of the musicians and supporters who cooperatively ran the club. Onstage, three groups led by Neil, Kilburn, and Bob Frogge emerged as de facto Cellar house bands.[22] Quarin occasionally led bands at the club but despite being in the club's inner circle, he didn't play there as much as the others "because he was not a bebop player," said John Dawe. "He kind of didn't fit in with that style," which predominated at the club. But Dawe and the others respected Quarin's playing. "Dave was a hell of a player," said Dawe.[23]

Kilburn gave me an unreleased recording led by Quarin that confirmed Dawe's assessment. It's a five-song session that Quarin's sextet played in 1957, with Kilburn and others, for CBC Radio's weekly *Jazz Workshop* show (which had nothing to do with Quarin's Jazz Workshop concert series). I've listened to those tunes countless times, and the repeat listens reveal a lot about Quarin's musicality. His original songs for the session showed he was an astute composer with a confident grasp of songcraft. The brisk melody for Quarin's hard bop gem "Little Quail," played in unison by the leader on tenor sax and Dawe on baritone horn, organically flowed with a satisfying impetus. Quarin's "Lampoon Blues" was entirely different: with just Quarin on alto and bassist Tony Clitheroe, it had a minimalist intro that segued seamlessly into the full band backing a solo by Dawe. Quarin wove creative stops and starts into the piece, a swinging blues with a twist of an ending. On those songs and the other tunes on the recording, Quarin's solos are harmonically engaging and carry a resolute momentum. The session offers a small sample size but expresses a lot about Quarin's already well-developed qualities and enormous potential.

Trumpeter Don Cherry performed at the Cellar multiple times, including a memorable engagement with Ornette Coleman, and would become a major voice on his instrument. Cherry and Quarin got along well and connected musically. Advertised as the "Don Cherry Dave Quarin Quintet,"[24] they performed together November 29 to December 1, 1957, at the Yardbird Suite in Edmonton,[25] with musicians including pianist Tommy Banks.

The gigs with Cherry were among the high points of a musically productive year for Quarin. It was also a difficult time. In September 1957, Quarin's mother Amabile died "suddenly"[26] at forty-seven. According to the Registration of Death form that was filled out, it was an accidental and traumatic demise.

Disagreement about the direction the Cellar should take led to discord among the members. By January 1958, tension had increased to the point where a decisive meeting was held. The majority of musicians, including Quarin, wanted to keep the Cellar primarily as a place where members could play, listen, and hang out. Ken Hole, who served as the first manager, along with law student Walley Lightbody, who originally registered the club as a society, and a few others wanted the Cellar to be more commercially viable. Said Quarin: "When we talk about Ken Hole or Walley Lightbody, they had ulterior reasons and motives for wanting to run that club, and it certainly didn't appeal to me and certainly not the rest of us. We decided we wanted to take our own journey. They were looking at a different kind of a situation. They were looking at the dollars and cents of it."[27]

Dave Quarin, the original Cellar, circa 1958. Photographer unknown. Courtesy James Carney.

As a result of the meeting, Hole resigned from managing the club, and he and Lightbody moved to Victoria, where they established the Scene jazz club. The Cellar membership voted Quarin in as the new manager with a small salary—about $100/month—that was all the club could afford. The Cellar was re-registered as the Cellar Musician and Artists Society, and the society issued a notice of appointment of directors on January 28, 1958. At the top of the list of six "First Directors"—"David Quarin, 3266 Grant Street, Vancouver, B.C., Clerical Musician."[28] That was a strange way to list his occupation, but it reflected Quarin's diverse accounting and music skillset that would serve the Cellar well during his tenure as manager.

Meanwhile, Quarin had performances lined up, including a high-profile one with his quintet: a concert May 26, 1958, at the Georgia Auditorium that was part of the Vancouver New Jazz Society (VNJS) 1958 Jazz Festival. The VNJS festival program included mini-bios of the featured performers. "Young, 24, personable Dave Quarin takes a serious attitude towards music," read his bio, which highlighted the fact he had twice gone on a "pilgrimage" to New York and furthered the falsehood that he had studied with Charlie Parker. "He left the east just a week before the great 'Bird' died. Quarin's dedication to music leads us to predict that Vancouver will soon take great pride in its native son."[29]

In late 1958, Quarin played another gig with Cherry at the Cellar. A scratchy black and white image captured Quarin that night with eyes closed, immersed in an alto solo, as Cherry and drummer Chuck Logan looked on. With hindsight, it's significant that Quarin played a number of times with Cherry, the future visionary. But in the moment, each time he gigged with Cherry was simply a chance for Quarin to play with a dynamic musician and further delineate his path in jazz.

Don Cherry (trumpet), Chuck Logan (drums), and Dave Quarin (alto saxophone), the original Cellar, November 1957. Photographer unknown. Courtesy Walley Lightbody.

In November 1958, Quarin in his manager role booked tenor saxophonist Harold Land to perform at the Cellar with a talented but doomed band: pianist Elmo Hope, bassist Scott LaFaro, and drummer Lenny McBrowne. (LaFaro, after playing brilliantly with Bill Evans and others, died in a 1961 car crash. Hope, a hardcore heroin addict, died of heart failure in 1967. McBrowne was forty-seven when he died in 1980.) Quarin went on to book prominent American jazz artists like Art Pepper and Carl Fontana. In 1960 alone, Quarin landed Pete Jolly, Howard Roberts, Bill Perkins, Joe Gordon, Barney Kessel, the Montgomery Brothers (Wes, Monk, and Buddy), Jean Hoffman, and other stellar American players to perform at the Cellar. This was in addition to lining up many gigs featuring Vancouver musicians.

Quarin negotiated fees with the artists, made their travel and accommodation arrangements, promoted the shows by placing ads in the *Vancouver Sun* and *Province*, and liaised with CBC-TV and Radio to book some supplementary gigs that would make visits to Vancouver more viable. He also served as chief babysitter/confidante for musicians who ranged from happy-go-lucky types to high-maintenance individuals with off-stage issues and a gift for finding trouble.

The accountant in Quarin meant it was a given that he would keep thorough records of Cellar gigs he booked. He recorded details on revenue and expenses on lined paper. An example: the Montgomery Brothers, who performed August 30 to September 4, 1960, were paid $800. The door take was $1,106. After accounting for concession revenue and expenses such as advertising and janitorial services, the profit was $149.95.[30] Another example: trumpeter Conte Candoli, when he performed January 27–29, 1961, was subsidized with $325 from the CBC. After adding that amount to the revenue and subtracting expenses, the gigs made $16.11 in profit.[31] Quarin documented all of the numbers meticulously.

The crown jewel among his Cellar bookings was brokering a lengthy engagement with the Charles Mingus Quartet, January 6–21, 1961. Quarin had to be at the top of his managerial game when convincing Mingus to play at this obscure little club on the west coast of Canada, and then ensuring that the jazz titan known for his volcanic temper was content during the extended stay. It worked in large part because of Quarin's friendly nature. "He was really good with people," said multi-instrumentalist Don Thompson about Quarin. "For instance, he became really good friends with Mingus. Now to become friends with Charles Mingus and get him to come to your club, that is a really big deal. That gives you an idea of how good he was, to get the trust of Mingus and people like that to come work at the club and then come back again. Those guys [musicians] really liked him, and there was a good reason for that: Dave was a really good guy."[32]

Thompson first showed up at the Cellar as a jazz-obsessed raw teenager, who travelled with a buddy from Powell River on BC's Sunshine Coast to Vancouver for a quick visit. Even though his skills were unformed, Thompson sat in on piano. Quarin was there and suggested they play "Just Friends." Thompson admitted he didn't know the standard. "So he [Quarin] says, 'I got the changes,' and he gives me this piece of paper with all these chords written on it, which I didn't know what they were," said Thompson. "They start to play and I just sat there and listened to it and figured it out. Then I sort of played too. But it was really exciting."[33]

Dave Quarin (alto saxophone), Don Cumming (drums), Chuck Knott (bass), and Harold Krause (piano), the original Cellar. Photographer unknown. Courtesy Dave Quarin.

Aside from being at a jazz club in a city that was like New York compared with his hometown, Thompson was thrilled to hear and play with Quarin, drummer Bill Boyle, and others. "Dave Quarin and all those guys could really play. They were really good players," said Thompson.[34] After moving to Vancouver in 1960 and playing with Quarin more, Thompson—who would become one of Canada's premier jazz instrumentalists on piano, bass, and vibes—realized the saxophonist was an "amazing" musician. "And just to play with him, I had never heard anything like it."[35] Thompson intuitively discerned that Quarin's aesthetic—shaped by influences like Tristano, Konitz, and Marsh—extended beyond bebop and hard bop. "Dave was a little out front of most of them," said Thompson about Quarin's playing compared with other Cellar musicians. "His mind was just different; he wasn't a bebopper. So when he played, it sounded really strange to me, but I really liked it."[36]

Dave Quarin. Photographer unknown. Courtesy Dave Quarin.

Saxophonist Gavin Walker, who was also a teenager when he started hanging out at the Cellar, said Quarin was important to the club on multiple levels. While Quarin was "very open to suggestions and listened to everybody," he also brought a "broader opinion" about what constituted worthwhile jazz, said Walker. "Because he was so respected as a musician, people listened to him."[37] Examples of Quarin's bookings of saxophonists that strayed from the bebop and hard bop that was mainly heard at the club: Lee Konitz (September 22–30, 1962), whose style ranged from bebop to cool jazz to avant-garde, and Monty Waters (June 7–9, 1963), who played at the Cellar with a free jazz spirit. Yet Quarin booked plenty of pure bebop and hard bop musicians too. As a programmer, Quarin was able to bridge varied approaches to jazz and always uphold the club's reputation for artistic integrity.

While a number of the club's founding musicians played only at the Cellar, Quarin had a busy performing schedule as a downtowner—one of the city's musicians who had the skills that qualified him to be hired for gigs at downtown supper clubs, on radio and TV, and in recording studios. "It's unbelievable the difference between what's happening now and then," Quarin said. "I mean I was working six nights a week and running the Cellar at the same time."[38]

Trumpeter Donnie Clark played alongside Quarin at the Cellar and at downtown gigs. "This is the thing: Johnny Dawe, Al Neil, Billy Boyle, Jim Johnson—all those guys never had the reading chops or the studio chops like Dave Quarin had," said Clark. "He was a fantastic alto player." Clark concurred with other musicians who praised Quarin's work as the Cellar's manager. He had a strong grasp of business and a "sense of understanding the plight of poor, struggling musicians," said Clark, referring to Quarin's generous unwritten policy of letting musicians in without paying. "He was a good diplomat and a really great guy."[39] Trombonist John Capon also lauded Quarin's managerial skills. "He was organized," said Capon. "Those other guys, I mean they played there but if it was up to John Dawe and Al Neil to organize anything, it wouldn't of happened."[40]

Quarin was also able to calmly handle stressful situations. He witnessed behind-the-scenes escapades with musicians performing at the Cellar and patrons, including some that involved drugs, gangsters, and cops. But even six decades after the fact, Quarin remained discreet and protective of individuals' reputations. "There are things that are incriminating. I just don't want to disclose any of this information," Quarin said. "There are a lot of things that happened that were questionable at the Cellar, and I'm not going to be part of that. They were great times, but most of the stories that happened are really quite personal."[41]

Since Quarin had a full schedule and a young family, when not working at the Cellar, he didn't always socialize with the local musicians who played there. He did, however, enjoy inviting musicians from out-of-town to visit, and in many cases, stay at the Quarin house on Grant Street in East Vancouver. "Just about everybody that came to the Cellar, if I could get them to come out to the house, I would," he said.[42] "The door was never locked," said Ricci, who helped at the club with tasks such as working the door and serving food. "I'd come home and find people in there helping themselves."[43]

The superb jazz, blues, and soul singer Ernestine Anderson, who Quarin booked twice to perform at the Cellar, was one of the artists who stayed at the house and became close with him and his family. "When she would get up in the morning she'd put a towel around her head," said Quarin. "She's big and she's Black, of course. And when she answered the door and somebody was confronted with Ernestine with a towel around her head, and she'd be, 'Yaza boss.' She'd talk just like that. It became a neighbourhood topic, believe me, that we had Ernestine staying at the house."[44]

Clyde Griffiths (bongos), Ernestine Anderson (vocals), and unidentified musician (bass), the original Cellar. Photo by Franz Lindner. Courtesy Barbara Lindner Coates, Tamina Lindner, and Dave Quarin.

Aside from playing in small ensembles, Quarin loved performing with big bands. "He could read anything and transpose anything," said Bobby Hales, who hired Quarin to play in the house band he led at Isy's Supper Club and in many incarnations of his large ensembles. "You'd give him a trombone part, and he'd play it [on alto] by sight . . . a very accomplished musician. I made him lead [alto] saxophone player in my big band." Awarding Quarin the first alto chair didn't sit well with some of the other saxophonists. "They would say, 'What are you doing putting him on the lead for? He's got this thin sound.' And I said, 'I like his style, his interpretation.' He was always individual."[45]

Clark, who played in the trumpet section of Hales' band at Isy's, understood why Quarin received the plum position. "There's a good example of a guy who came from the Cellar who was a real jazzer who really played. Bobby could tell that Dave was a good reader and a great improviser."[46]

Trombonist and big band leader Dave Robbins also relied on Quarin to be a sax section stalwart. Hearing rare recordings made in the early 1960s featuring bands led by Robbins enhanced my appreciation of Quarin's sound. One recording includes fourteen tracks of mostly large ensemble playing and a few small group tunes, including one Quarin wrote called "Popcorn." Accompanied by pianist Chris Gage—considered Vancouver's top jazz musician at the time—along with tremendous rhythm section players Paul Ruhland (bass) and Al Johnson (drums), Quarin shines. In three minutes and forty-one seconds—roughly the time that it takes to pop corn—Quarin adeptly navigates the up-tempo song's tricky melody, solos with complete authority, and robustly trades fours with Johnson before confidently restating the melody. Hearing the polished "Popcorn" makes me wonder what an entire record by Quarin would have sounded like. He had the prowess as both composer and player to succeed in crafting an album, and had something to say, so it's unfortunate Quarin never recorded as a leader.

Quarin was also in the sax section in trombonist Ray Sikora's big band that rehearsed at the Cellar on Sundays in the daytime and occasionally performed there. An unreleased recording of a June 8, 1963 performance at the Cellar captures the group in exhilarating form. The recording also picks up lively banter among the patrons. The exuberant vibe was, sadly, no longer reflective of the club's overall state. The Cellar was slowly dying, with musicians and patrons moving on to other venues such as the Flat Five, the Inquisition, and the Espresso Coffee House. In the September 1963 issue of *Coda* magazine, John Clayton reported that the Cellar appeared to be "going downhill" and that a change was needed. "For the sake of Dave Quarin and the others who have supported and guided what used to be the Mecca of the Vancouver scene it is hoped that a long needed transfusion of new blood will occur," Clayton wrote.[47]

The change came that month. Quarin was out as manager, and Bill Wright took over. It appeared to be an amicable handover. Bob Smith wrote in the *Vancouver Sun* that both original Cellar manager Ken Hole and Quarin "lent their help in an advisory capacity."[48] One of Wright's first moves was to book his wife Donna, a singer, to perform at the club. The Wright era at the Cellar didn't last long. The last listing in the *Vancouver Sun* for a performance by Donna at the club appeared on January 17, 1964.[49]

Then an ad appeared in the *Vancouver Sun* on February 1, 1964: "Mercury Recording Star ERNESTINE ANDERSON SINGS in the CELLAR FEB. 7-8."[50] A week after the shows, Bob Smith wrote that "good taste vocalizing prevailed" with Anderson, who sang at the club with the Chris Gage Trio "through the efforts of Dave Quarin." Smith didn't explain Quarin's re-emergence at the Cellar but took the opportunity to acknowledge his contributions as a presenter. "A resident saxophonist, Quarin has done a great deal in the past to keep quality and public acceptance akin in his bookings."[51]

The Anderson shows appear to have been a one-off for Quarin's involvement, and an epilogue for the Cellar. On April 3, 1964, Smith reported in the *Sun* that the Cellar had closed.[52] And in the April 1964 issue of *Coda*, Adrian Tanner wrote: "It may be a symptom of something, I don't know what, but the Cellar died quietly last month."[53] While the club had been in decline for months, one thing the closure affirmed was how crucial Quarin's adept management was to the Cellar. "I think it would have folded long before if Dave hadn't run the club," said Doreen Young, who sang at the Cellar and hung out at the club in the late fifties when she went by Doreen Williams.[54] For Quarin, the Cellar's end concluded a deeply meaningful time in his life; he accomplished a great deal on and off the bandstand.

In 1963, Ricci gave birth to their fourth child, Julie. All four Quarin children were born during the Cellar years. With the club waning, Quarin continued to work as a freelance musician and provide for his family, which meant playing at the main Vancouver supper clubs that were thriving and paying well—the Cave and Isy's—and taking various gigs that came his way. This was nothing new for Quarin; what changed for him was not having ready access to a real jazz club where he could play his own music and serve as an impresario.

In November 1964, the Louie brothers—Victor, Harry, and Alex—opened the Marco Polo at 90 East Pender in Chinatown. The Marco Polo shook up Vancouver's supper club scene, offering something different with its "Oriental Revue" and huge Chinese smorgasbord.[55] While trumpeter and valve trombonist Carse Sneddon was leading the Marco Polo's first orchestra, Quarin was the bandleader for groups playing in Chinatown venues. He played at the Kublai Khan at 442 Main—co-billed with Rae Dene who did a "sensational fire dance"[56] that involved juggling—and at the club that replaced it, the Shanghai Junk. Working in this part of town was a return to his childhood roots. By 1967, the coveted gig of bandleader at the Marco Polo was his.[57] Performing in supper clubs often didn't involve playing jazz, but it was steady work that enabled Quarin to make music for a living.

Vancouver Sun, January 28, 1966.

In May 1968, Bob Smith wrote a feature on Quarin for the *Vancouver Sun* that focused on his work at the Marco Polo and touched on his wider life in music. According to the article, then-thirty-three-year-old Quarin worked six nights a week at the Marco Polo. He brought with him every night an alto, tenor, and soprano sax, along with a flute and clarinet. Singers he backed at the supper club liked his playing enough to offer to take him on the road—offers he turned down. Smith observed that Quarin was "well prepared for his current challenging task, that of making a quintet, sometimes augmented, sound like a big band for visiting name performers who may or may not show up with the proper arrangements."[58]

Smith continued: "Fellow saxophonists give Quarin credit for being one of the best and fastest readers in town, the main criteria for a studio type musician. For me, Dave has an extremely personal sound – an almost oblique, original way of playing his solo statements which after all is the basis of jazz. In a word, the Quarin saxophone is instantly recognizable." He rounded out the piece with references to Ricci and their musically inclined children, painting a picture of domestic bliss, and concluding with a slice of Quarin's offbeat humour: "I once put an ad in the paper, 'Dave Quarin and his band, we play for divorces.' Nobody called."[59]

The stability that the Marco Polo gave Quarin was fleeting. After backing artists like Sam and Dave, the Platters, and the pre-disco Three Degrees, the gig eventually ended like they all do. By the early 1970s, because of challenging economics, Vancouver supper clubs were turning away from booking big acts, which meant fewer gigs for musicians. As he always did, Quarin adapted and survived. In January 1971, Isy Walters changed his Isy's Supper Club to Isy's Strip City. Quarin was there, playing alongside strippers, which prompted *Province* columnist Lorne Parton to ask: "What's a nice player like Dave Quarin doing in an arrangement like that?"[60]

Something else was at play with Quarin. "Well, you know Dave was an alcoholic, but nobody knew it," said Bobby Hales. "And I didn't know it either. I don't know how he managed to hide it."[61] John Dawe said almost exactly the same thing—he had no idea Quarin was a heavy drinker when the saxophonist was in the throes of his addiction. Hales noticed Quarin's demeanour change and found out it was due to alcohol. "He'd always show up, but he became more cantankerous and miserable, like what booze does to you," said Hales. "It changes your personality. You go one second past one o'clock and he'd say, 'I want overtime,' and I'd say, 'Come on, man, don't give me that horseshit. You know you can't time these shows out to the very second.' So he got really very, very miserable. I was told by the boss, 'Either he goes, or you all go.' So I had to let him go, but I always liked his playing. He was a great jazz player, very creative."[62]

Theories abound about why gigging musicians become alcoholics. According to the alcoholic musician trope, they play in clubs and, therefore, have ready access to booze. Or one of the following: they need to consume alcohol to be able to express themselves artistically; they drink to emulate their musical heroes; they feel rejected by commercial culture and need to dull their psychic pain. While there may be some truth to these notions, in many cases becoming an alcoholic has nothing to do with such pat explanations. Quarin grew up in a family with alcoholism. Quarin, then, had his reasons and eventually faced them, quit and got sober, relapsed, and finally quit again permanently.

Regardless of any hiccups in their relationship, Quarin and Hales maintained their connection. Hales kept hiring Quarin, and they shared enormous mutual respect. On September 14 and 15, 1975, Hales took a twenty-piece big band into Little Mountain Sound on West 7th Avenue to record *One of My Bags*, a collection of Hales' compositions and arrangements. Long out of print, the record's side two consists of a jazz suite, "Minor Event," that spotlights soloists in each of its four parts. On the prosaically named "Alto Sax Solo," Quarin plays as if it were his last-ever solo, with a fire that was still burning hot after more than two decades of jazz exploration. His solo intensifies, as do the horns and rhythm section behind him, to the point where the band suddenly drops out and an untethered Quarin blows with a bracing and cathartic mix of joy and melancholy.

There's one problem with my glowing assessment—Quarin wasn't at all happy with the record. He thought the band sounded "sterile" compared to its impact on a tour that happened before going in the studio. Plus, Quarin didn't feel good about his own playing on *One of My Bags*. Above all, he held himself to a high standard, and Quarin took it hard that—to his ears—the standard wasn't met. But he didn't complain, because Hales had been so supportive over the years. As well, in a radio interview he did after recording *One of My Bags*, Hales praised Quarin. "He's a very unique jazz player," Hales told radio host Gary Barclay about Quarin. "In my opinion, he's one of the most unique in Canada." Hales called Quarin "very unpredictable," and a musician "who just sticks his neck out and takes chances . . . He's one of the few people I know in Vancouver that I consider instantly creative and doesn't try to go the same route all the time."[63]

About five years after the recording with Hales, Hugh Fraser was forming a big band with a new sound that was startlingly different from conventional large jazz ensembles. Fraser's Vancouver Ensemble of Jazz Improvisation (VEJI), with its Duke Ellington meets Frank Zappa meets Alexander Scriabin sound, was set to play its debut concert on June 1, 1980, at the Western Front. But Fraser needed someone to play baritone sax. So he asked his mentor, trombonist Dave Robbins, for suggestions. Robbins recommended that he contact Quarin. He did, and Quarin agreed to play the gig.

"He played amazing!" said Fraser, adding that Quarin played with the band other times during its repertory period when VEJI explored classic works. "We did Mingus' *The Black Saint and the Sinner Lady* and he played alto, doing the Charlie Mariano parts, and he just ate it up," said Fraser. At the time, Fraser was finding his harmonic path, which was somewhere between McCoy Tyner and Ornette Coleman. "Dave would say, 'Oh yeah, that's that old in and out thing.' He had these really funny things he'd say but he was very encouraging, and he could play in and out."[64]

Though he was about a quarter century older than many of the VEJI members, Quarin fit right in because he was a "modernist," said Fraser. Quarin's improv was also still vital—a prerequisite for playing in VEJI. "He was the first guy I ever heard that played those really snaky lines," said Fraser. "He just made stuff sound great." When Fraser asked Quarin about his decades-long contributions to Vancouver's jazz scene, he was very "self-effacing," downplaying his impact.[65]

Campbell Ryga connected with Quarin when the two altoists played together in Hales' band, VEJI, and other contexts. One summer they both taught at a music camp in Kamloops, BC, where Ryga witnessed Quarin's unorthodox methods. At the first class, Quarin said, "Okay kids, as a musician you are going to have to learn to put up with a lot of crap in your life. So we are going to go out there and deal with that." He proceeded to hand out garbage bags before they went outside to pick up garbage while Quarin talked about his life as a saxophone player. "The concept, it sounds strange, but it was beautiful," said Ryga. "Not everybody thinks about doing things quite that way."[66]

Similarly, Quarin's sound wasn't "everybody's cup of tea," said Ryga. "I know some guys [musicians] that never enjoyed too much of what came out of his horn." Quarin wasn't a cookie cutter saxophonist. In fact, he was "one of the most innovative" musicians playing in the scene at the time, said Ryga. His unconventional, unpredictable nature could reveal itself on the bandstand. "He had an interesting and extremely funny way of looking at stuff," said Ryga, who heard an element of surprise in Quarin's playing. "He was extremely quick. He could be playing with people and when something unexpected happened, he could take that moment and turn it into something [musically original]."[67]

By now, a new generation of musicians like Ryga was coming up and receiving the calls for gigs that Quarin used to get. By playing together with them, he personified the if you can't beat 'em, join 'em philosophy. Quarin also wasn't done yet in the scene. In 1982, he led a quartet in concerts for young people that featured a program representing the history of jazz from 1940 onward. He described this endeavour to Bob Smith as "perhaps the most rewarding experience and opportunity in my short musical career." The next year, as part of the Whistler Jazz on the Mountain festival, Quarin played in a multi-generational "Big Band Extravaganza" that combined VEJI's brash insurgents with the Westcoast Jazz Orchestra's sage veterans.

A show Quarin presented at the Hot Jazz Club was a "highlight of his life." The 1985 concert featured his longtime friend, Ernestine Anderson, who sang beautifully in front of a big band with Ryga, Phil Dwyer, and others Quarin assembled, played with, and conducted. Anderson was still in the prime of her career as a leading jazz vocalist recording for Concord Jazz and touring internationally, so she didn't need to take the gig in the unadorned club. But Anderson was there because of her bond with Quarin, which says a lot about his rapport with jazz artists.

There was one more gig of note. The idea emerged from the creative mind of John Korsrud, leader of the Hard Rubber Orchestra. "I remember thinking it would be fun to get one of the older guys involved in some Hard Rubber shows," he said. So Korsrud recruited Quarin to play with the adventurous big band for *White Hot Core*, a collaboration with the experimental dance troupe Kokoro Dance that took place over four nights during the 1995 jazz festival in Vancouver.[68]

"We all really liked Dave because he was a good musician, he was a colourful guy, he was really funny, and he was quite quirky," said Korsrud. He cited one example of Quarin's eccentric humour: Ross Taggart, who was in Hard Rubber at the time, asked Quarin, "Hey Dave, what's your secret?" Quarin's response: "Keep your back to the wall and stay close to an exit."[69]

Dave Quarin, Coquitlam River, late 1980s. Photographer unknown. Courtesy Dave Quarin.

Quarin's first exit from Vancouver was by sea: he played music on cruise ships that took him to numerous ports of call in the late 1980s and nineties. There were still some gigs he did in the city, like one in 1996 at the Hotel Vancouver. Before that gig, a plumber he knew from Little Italy—Don Demetrio Santaga—urged Quarin to hear Santaga's grandson sing. So one day while Santaga worked on plumbing in the Grant Street house, Michael Bublé sang for Quarin, who was impressed. He hired the young singer for the hotel engagement—one of Bublé's first professional gigs.

In 2000, Quarin left Vancouver for good, starting a new life in Campbell River, not far from Menzies Bay where he spent his formative childhood years. The breakdown of his marriage to Ricci and dearth of gigs in the city were factors in convincing Quarin to move, said Gavin Walker. "There wasn't the kind of strong motivation for him to stay and suffer through having to play for the door. He did it for a little while, and I guess decided to seek more of a tranquil life."[70]

After leaving town, Quarin grew increasingly distant, according to some who knew him at the Cellar. The reasons why are simultaneously clear and murky.

• • •

In 2007, Spain-based Lone Hill Jazz released *Jazz at The Cellar 1958* by the Harold Land Quartet. It was recorded live at the Cellar in November 1958, when Land played there with Elmo Hope, Scott LaFaro, and Lenny McBrowne. The release was a stunning development for fans of Land and the other musicians, and those in the know about the Cellar, which was then a largely forgotten obscurity. Despite the mediocre sound quality—it lacks brightness plus LaFaro was severely undermiked and hard to discern in the mix—the album provides seventy-nine minutes and thirty-seven seconds of fervid bebop/hard bop. For jazz enthusiasts, the release was a gift.

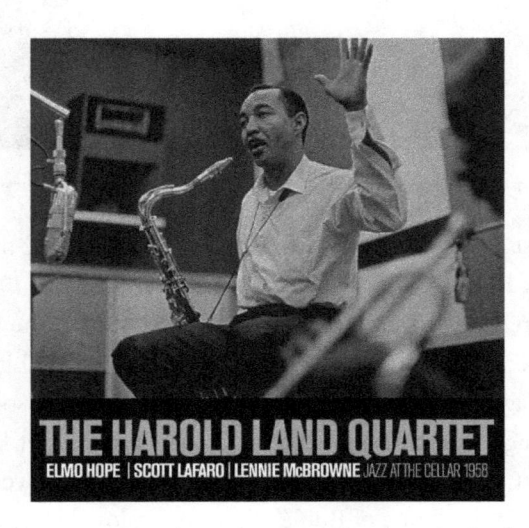

The problem: it was a bootleg. That was clear just by looking at the cover, which had a photo of Land that had already been used on the front of his *Jazz Impressions of Folk Music* album. Plus McBrowne's first name was spelled wrong. The story of how *Jazz at The Cellar 1958* was released is convoluted, and it starts with Quarin because he made the recording. The man who was fascinated with wire recording in his youth had systematically recorded shows at the Cellar. Quarin used a four-track reel-to-reel tape recorder to capture performances by visiting American artists and local musicians.[71] In *Live at the Cellar*, Marian Jago wrote that the recording equipment was hidden, and visiting artists were unaware they were being recorded.[72] As Jago outlined, bassist Tony Clitheroe said Lee Konitz became suspicious and went as far as searching the club—even the bathrooms—for recording devices.[73] But Quarin said visiting musicians were aware of his recordings, and he obtained their permission before rolling the tape. He cited Barney Kessel as an example. While Kessel didn't want any unauthorized recordings to come out, he also told Quarin, "'Just keep 'em [the recordings], don't worry about it.'"[74]

Quarin's intention was to keep the recordings for personal listening and not share them, but he dropped his guard with the Land recording. It happened during a period when Quarin rehearsed with drummer Audie Wong and two other musicians in Wong's parents' basement. At the rehearsals, Quarin told stories about the Cellar. One was about Mingus' drummer Dannie Richmond. Wong said Quarin told him and the others that he had found Richmond unconscious in the room where he was staying, and essentially saved the drummer's life. As for the Land recording, Quarin brought it to one of the basement rehearsals, and the musicians enjoyed listening to it. Strangely, Quarin just left the reel-to-reel tape there.

"At some point I guess we parted ways and it [the tape] was still in my possession," said Wong.[75] Then Wong told fellow drummers Gregg Simpson and Ian Hood about the recording and shared it with them. Simpson called Land in Los Angeles and told him about the recording. Land wanted to hear it, so Simpson sent it to him, and the tenor man was able to listen to his thirty-year-old self at the Cellar before he died in 2001. What followed was an opaque chain of events that led to the recording being privately exchanged by collectors for years before coming out on the Spanish labels. "I think somehow, maybe I lent a copy of it to somebody or traded [the tape]," said Simpson. "I shouldn't have. I don't know if that's where it came from, but it got released on Lone Hill. And that's an unauthorized edition."[76]

Word got to Quarin that the recording came out without permission, and worse, Land's estate wasn't benefitting from it. "I think it made him angry because he had lent that tape in good faith," said Walker.[77] While it was partially Quarin's inattentiveness that led to the Land recording being released into the wild, no doubt he felt burned by what happened with the recording. The bootleg also raised questions about all the other recordings he made at the Cellar—where were they, and would they ever be available for jazz fans to enjoy? The questions were in the minds of a number of people who knew about, or at least heard inklings of, Quarin's recordings that assumed mythic proportions.

Another musician who played informally with Quarin, guitarist Ray Piper, almost became guardian of the recordings. "We used to do duets, and I was just thrilled to play with him," said Piper. Quarin asked him to hold on to all of the recordings. Piper: "He said to me, 'Can I leave them at your house?' I thought, if I'm away and the house burns down, I'll be known as the guy who destroyed all the tapes. I said, 'No, I don't want the responsibility.'"[78]

Quarin initially told me he still had the recordings, and he had transferred reel-to-reel recordings to compact discs containing hundreds of hours of music. He also said that there were more recordings he planned to digitize if technical issues could be solved. When I heard Quarin describe this live jazz treasure trove my mind began to race. He was sitting on an extensive collection of historically important recordings that—aside from the Land recording—hardly a soul except himself had heard. So I asked Quarin if he would like people to hear these audio documents. "I don't know," he said. "I have mixed feelings on that for good reasons." His main argument for keeping them private: "They don't belong to me, really."[79] Meaning that, ultimately, they belong to the artists or their estates. Based on hearing Quarin's wariness about his recordings, I didn't think his fabled Cellar tapes would ever surface. I resigned myself to believing that they would eternally remain the sonic equivalent of Montezuma's lost treasure.

The Land tapes imbroglio was possibly one factor for Quarin to withdraw from people. Another was the unwanted interest in the Cellar that grew among academics and writers, many of whom came calling on Quarin. "I got rather annoyed with people asking questions about things, and I just kind of closed the door on it," he said.[80]

"I think it's just personal," said Walker about the ultimate reason Quarin removed himself from his old life and friends. "He had some tragedy in his family."[81] Quarin's son Randy died on June 27, 2007, at the age of fifty. An obituary that was published in the *Vancouver Sun* and *Province* said Randy "passed suddenly." Randy taught English to children in Thailand, and his co-workers "remember him as a fantastic teacher, a good man who loved to sing with the children." The obituary also listed surviving family members, including "his father Dave, who always had faith in Randy."[82]

I asked Quarin if trauma in his life had prevented him from going back to revisit periods of his life, such as the Cellar years. "Oh absolutely, that's part of it, Chris," he said. "These things have a way of coming around again, and then when they do, you have to take a stand on it and go through what you have to go through. It's too confusing at times, and too frustrating as well."[83]

After I first connected with Quarin in 2013, for the longest time my goal was to have a formal, face-to-face interview with him in his Campbell River home. I thought that was the only way to properly understand this complex man. On the phone and in letters, I gently but repeatedly requested the interview, but I came no closer to making it happen. Then in February 2014, after making my case yet again, he said: "Sure, let's do it,"[84] which shocked and excited me.

We agreed to reconnect and make plans after an upcoming trip I had to New York, the city where he learned so much fifty years earlier. So I called back in April 2014, but by then, Quarin had changed his tune. He said there was a family emergency that required him to go away, and that would be his sole focus for a while. Plus, he had other issues. "My situation is kind of dire, you might say," he said cryptically.[85] It was obvious that an interview wouldn't be imminent. Still, Quarin said I could send questions in a letter. Four years passed. In that time, I sent him questions and, in a role reversal, gave him Cellar recordings—not made by him—of Ray Sikora's big band (that he played in) and Monty Waters (who he booked). In a brief handwritten letter in all caps, he thanked me for the music, but didn't send answers to my queries.

October 2018. We talked on the phone for almost an hour and a half. The conversation hopped from topic to topic. For the first time, Quarin referred to his children. He said they knew nothing about his background and had never been particularly interested in finding out more. But Quarin did something about that. "My life became pretty interesting after I got letters from you because I ended up writing a whole bunch of things down for my kids."[86] Emboldened by the acknowledgement that I influenced him in a small way, I again proposed the in-person interview. Again, he demurred.

It finally dawned on me: this *was* the interview. I was convinced meeting him in Campbell River would never happen. I also realized that my Plan B, showing up unannounced at his doorstep, was a terrible idea. I tried one final time: "Even if I could just come and meet you and shake your hand, it would mean something to me," I said. "You don't have to do that," he replied.[87] We kept talking for a bit more, wished each other well, and said goodbye. I phoned a few more times and left messages, but he didn't return them. Something told me we would never speak again.

Despite the halting, intermittent nature of our connection, we developed a good rapport, and I learned a lot about him and Vancouver jazz and social history in the process. Why then was I left with nothing but worry? About his health, and if he ever reads this, whether he would see it as the homage I intended or a betrayal.

More than three years passed. I didn't even know if he was still alive. But something made me reach out to him again in May 2022. This time he picked up the phone. We talked for a long time about topics that had been broached before, and new themes. There were disheartening revelations. Quarin said that someone helped him with transferring the recordings he made at the Cellar to a computer and CDs. But that individual went to Cuba and his possessions—including those long sought-after recordings—were confiscated by Cuban authorities. Quarin said he didn't have any copies of the Cellar recordings other than two CDs with the iconic Art Pepper and one with the great underrecognized trumpeter Joe Gordon. It took some moments for that crushing news to sink in with me. The dream for me and other jazz lovers to hear his legendary recordings was effectively over. Yet he seemed at peace with it. Things in life come and go, he said.

At one point Quarin casually mentioned he was recording our call. A surprising admission, but it made perfect sense. The person who made wire recordings of Sinatra movies and systematically recorded jazz greats at the Cellar was a serial recorder. He didn't have nefarious reasons for recording our chat. Quarin simply wanted to have a document of our conversation that he could listen to as a way of jogging his memory for more insights about the past.

On this call, and a subsequent call, I mentioned that I would be on a road trip on Vancouver Island, and I popped the question yet again: could I see him in Campbell River? For the first time, he sounded receptive to the idea. After years of never giving up on reaching a deeper understanding of the man, we nurtured a mutual trust and respect. So we agreed to a date, but on the eve of the trip, Quarin said he wasn't well, so the visit wouldn't be possible. Then a few days later, while on the ferry, my phone buzzed. It was Quarin, who said he had a box of material ready for me to pick up. I wouldn't believe it until I actually laid eyes on him, but it felt like meeting Quarin was really going to happen.

On a sunny July day in Campbell River, I turned off a highway and drove the short distance to his home, which is across from an RV park. The surroundings looked pretty much the same as what I saw a number of times in Google Street View. Quarin emerged from the house and nine years after we first spoke, I shook hands with the man. We sat outside and picked up where our last conversation left off. The segue was seamless.

The topic of his sight-reading and transposition skills back in the day came up, and he shared a story about performing "Four Brothers," the song Jimmy Giuffre wrote in 1947 for Woody Herman's renowned saxophone section with three tenors and one baritone. For a big band radio recording, Quarin was playing alto sax, but he was handed music in the key of B flat for tenor sax. The task at hand was simultaneously sight-reading the music he was seeing for the first time and transposing the notes to the key of E flat that the alto sax is in. Some musicians who were present were skeptical about whether Quarin was capable of that, given the difficulty of sight-transposing and that the up-tempo tune featured the sax section on the note-intensive melody. With a hint of a proud smile, Quarin recounted how he absolutely nailed it.

After moving inside, Quarin presented me with a box and envelopes of material. I was stunned by what they contained: dozens of black and white photos of himself and other jazz musicians; newspaper clippings, programs, fliers, and other memorabilia from his career; a long letter from Charles

Mingus to Dave's wife Ricci, and letters to Dave from Lee Konitz, Barney Kessel, and Pete Jolly; the contract that Konitz signed to receive $600 and airplane tickets for performing at the Cellar (and at the CBC for a *Jazz Workshop* session); and Quarin's meticulous accounting records from numerous Cellar shows. There were few words exchanged about what I would do with these artifacts or when I would return them. He simply entrusted me with the one-of-a-kind documents of his life's work. I'm not sure why. Maybe his offering was a reward for my patience. Or he wanted the vestiges of his past to be with someone who appreciated their value.

Dave Quarin, Campbell River, July 12, 2022. Photo by Chris Wong.

Then I spotted them. Two burned CDs with live Cellar recordings of Art Pepper from 1959 and one with Joe Gordon from the same year. I

Fisherman's Jazz

asked to hear one of the Pepper CDs, and he put the disc in the carousel. First, I heard twenty-three-year-old Quarin briefly introduce Pepper. Next Pepper introduced the first tune of the evening's last set before local piano hero Chris Gage played a tasty four-bar intro, with subtle accompaniment from drummer Jimmy Wightman on brushes. Finally, the sound I had been waiting to hear, came out of the speakers: Pepper sweetly playing the melody to Cole Porter's "You'd Be So Nice to Come Home To," with bassist Stan "Cuddles" Johnson joining in. Sounding languid, Pepper stated the melody a second time before the band momentarily stopped to enable Pepper to play a solo break—brief unaccompanied improvising, with a sudden burst of well-chosen notes, that launched his solo. It wasn't at the epic level of Charlie Parker's famous solo break on "Night in Tunisia" from 1946. But Pepper's sound, despite his heap of troubles resulting from drug addiction and unsavoury living, was vigorous, impactful, and beautiful. While I had listened numerous times to Pepper play this same standard on *Art Pepper Meets the Rhythm Section*, recorded in 1957, this was a very different and exhilarating experience.

It meant a lot that the music was recorded live in the Cellar, and that no one except those who were there that night had heard it all these years, until now. And it was enormously meaningful that I was sitting across from eighty-eight-year-old Quarin, who made that high-quality recording sixty-five years earlier. Quarin and I had come such a long way in how we related to each other. I was privileged to be in the presence of history, of Vancouver's jazz scene, and one remarkable man.

• • •

Postscript: Almost six months after the Campbell River visit, there was one more revelatory moment. It had to do with a memorable work of art that anyone who went to the Cellar experienced. As soon as you stepped foot on the staircase that went down to the club, you saw a wall over part of the stairs that had an immense painting attached to it. Painter, muralist, and actor Frank Lewis, a tall man who likely needed to be careful about not bonking his head when going down the stairs, created and donated the painting to the Cellar. When John Dawe wrote about the club in the *Original Cellar Jazz Club* blog, he described the painting as a "fantastic floor-to-ceiling self-portrait."[88] Saxophonist PJ Perry said it was both "infernal" and "very beautiful."[89] Another sax man, Jack Reynolds, remembered that it was a "startling" painting that showed an individual in an "agonizing" state.[90]

Painting by Frank Lewis that hung over the stairs at the original Cellar. Photo by Chris Wong.

After the Cellar closed in 1964, the painting seemingly vanished. People I asked about it had no idea where it was, and no photos of it emerged. It turned out that Quarin was the self-appointed custodian of the painting. After our breakthroughs, he said I could see what Cellar dwellers saw when they descended the stairs. So I visited his son, Kevin Quarin, who showed me Lewis' creation that hadn't been viewed by more than a few people for almost six decades. Regardless of the blemishes it acquired over the years, the painting is as incredible as people described it. Just like when I heard the Art Pepper recording, seeing it—with its vivid colours and heroic (or tortured?) protagonist—was a profound experience that immediately connected me to the past. A time when walking down those stairs and under that painting was an affirmation of both jazz passion and a way of being. Gazing at it was also one more reflection of my bond with Dave Quarin, who was finally no longer a recluse in my weary eyes.

8 / THE ROAD FROM AVONLEA TO THE CELLAR: BOBBY HALES

AFTER DRIVING SLOWLY down a quiet crescent, I arrive at a nondescript bungalow, walk up the driveway and a short sidewalk, and gently knock on the door. The person I'm here to see emerges, and I'm immediately struck by two things: his big smile and small stature. I shake hands with Bobby Hales, who for years—as a trumpeter, big band leader, composer, and musicians' association president—owned this town.

I meet his wife Marj, who also affably greets me. They fell in love in Sylvan Lake—an idyllic resort town in central Alberta—and married in October 1957. Hales played there with the Paul Perry Orchestra at a classic venue called Varsity Hall, performing for up to 1,000 people on warm summer nights. Perry's orchestra included some of Vancouver's most dynamic jazz musicians, and playing in the dance band was essential to the foundation of Hales' long, exceptional career.

As we get settled in the den, I'm greatly aware that I'm sitting next to a leading figure in Vancouver's music history. It doesn't take long for him to start sharing a slice of that history. Within seconds of turning on my voice recorder, he conjures sights and sounds of a momentous experience at the original Cellar jazz club.

It was a Saturday night in 1957, and the Cellar was packed. Bassist Roy Hornasty landed the gig to play that night with Hales, pianist John Gittens, and drummer George Ursan, all of whom played together at Sylvan

Lake. This was Hales' first jazz gig in Vancouver, and his first time at the Cellar. "I had no idea what it was," said Hales about the club. "I just went the night of the gig."[1]

Bobby Hales, Burnaby, October 18, 2013. Photo by Chris Wong.

Numerous musicians—such as the sublime pianist Chris Gage—were at the Cellar that night after finishing their downtown gigs. They were there because word got around that a hot trumpet player from Los Angeles would be playing. The advance hype was a tad misleading. Robert Arthur Hales was born August 9, 1934, in the polar opposite of LA—the village of Avonlea, Saskatchewan, which was named after the fictional town in Lucy Maud Montgomery's novel *Anne of Green Gables*. At around age eight, he started playing his grandfather's cornet, taking lessons on the horn in Regina. About six years later, Hales and his family headed west to Chilliwack in BC's Fraser Valley. At sixteen, he led the White Spots, his own quintet that played dances in Hope at the Igloo Supper Club.

That same year Hales hitchhiked from Chilliwack to Vancouver—a distance of more than 100 kilometres—to hear Gage and his trio at the Arctic

Club on West Pender. Somehow the teenaged Hales talked his way into the private club. Once in, he heard about eight bars of a tune before the musicians—Gage, bassist Stan "Cuddles" Johnson, and drummer Jimmy Wightman—took a break. Hales bought drinks for the trio members so he could meet them. But all he got for his efforts was a quick thanks from Cuddles during the long break. Hales had to leave before the music resumed.[2] He hitchhiked back home, disappointed about hearing such a miniscule amount of jazz, but still excited about his big-city adventure.

One day he wandered into a shop in Chilliwack and spotted a trumpet made by F.E. Olds & Sons. Hales bought the instrument and bent the bell upward at a thirty-degree angle, inspired by how Dizzy Gillespie played a trumpet with the bell bent dramatically toward the sky. Hales would play the Olds trumpet for decades.

After graduating from high school, Hales toiled at the Bank of Nova Scotia before going on a holiday in California, where he serendipitously met a renowned virtuoso classical trumpeter: Rafael Méndez. After learning that Hales wanted to play jazz, Méndez suggested that he go to the Westlake College of Music in Hollywood. Long before jazz schools were ubiquitous, Westlake was one of the first American educational institutions to offer a music diploma that included jazz curriculum. Hales took an easy ear test, and Westlake accepted him. He studied there for two years with faculty who were working musicians in LA's thriving jazz scene. Hales absorbed their wisdom about playing and composing modern jazz. After graduating, he went to Sylvan Lake before ending up in Vancouver. So Hales was from LA in a very roundabout way, via Avonlea, Chilliwack, and Sylvan Lake.

Back at the Cellar, Hales "was scared shitless."[3] At the time of his Cellar and Vancouver debut, he and Marj were living in a basement suite, where he had a hard time practicing because noise wasn't allowed. Hales' workaround was ingenious: he practiced by playing his trumpet with a mute, inside a coat sleeve, while standing in a closet. Given that awkward regimen in a claustrophobic cone of silence, and lacking gigs, Hales worried his chops weren't in great shape.

Then there was the pressure of playing for the prominent musicians gathered in the Cellar. "I didn't know who was who, what was what," said Hales. "Roy Hornasty, he was so nervous he could hardly hold his bass."[4]

Their anxious pre-gig huddle went something like this:

Hales: "What's happening?"

Hornasty: "Everybody's here."

Hales: "What do you mean?"

Hornasty: "Every heavy in town's here."

Hales: "What do you mean by heavy?"

Hornasty: "All of the studio guys."[5]

Hales judged his performance that night harshly: "I mean, I wasn't playing that great. I didn't think I played worth a darn." On further reflection: "I guess I played well enough."[6] He and the band mainly did standards, and Hales also sang one tune, "Take Me Out to the Ball Game," which he phrased in a "lopsided" way. Most importantly, the audience that packed the Cellar knew whether the musicians were legitimate players or poseurs, and responded well. "The reception was good," said Hales. "They liked us."[7]

The gig was also Ursan's Cellar debut. Was he as nervous as Hales and Hornasty? "I guess I was, sure," said Regina-born Ursan, who became Hales' brother-in-law after marrying Marj's sister Bev. "But I always trumped my nervousness with bravado. If I went up there to play, I thought, 'I'm playing a loud instrument, I'm gonna play the fucker loud, and I don't care what they think.'" As for Hales' performance that night, "I thought he always played well," said Ursan. "He was a good player. He was somebody that I looked up to."[8]

I described Hales' Cellar debut to another trumpeter who frequented the club, John Dawe. "I know the gig," said Dawe, who was there that night. He remembered that Hales and the other musicians were new to town. "He sounded like a good trumpet player," said Dawe. "He didn't sound like a really *jazz* trumpet player. Bob could play good jazz, but he would prefer to make a living."[9] It's an interesting distinction that Dawe made, between playing jazz and playing in a style that made Hales employable.

Alto saxophonist Dave Quarin, who along with Dawe was one of the Cellar's founders, also noticed something different with Hales when it came to jazz. "He had spark, he was a great player, and he didn't practice jazz," said Quarin. "He didn't even know half of the musicians that we knew. He just wasn't someone that you could sit down with and talk about jazz particularly because he really didn't know much about jazz. I mean, I'm saying that with all the love I have for him. I worked with Bobby more than anyone else in Vancouver."[10]

Fascinating. Even though Hales had a passion for jazz from a young age, he didn't come across as being a hardcore jazzer. Yet he still played with appealing authenticity. Despite his misgivings about how he performed that unforgettable night, Hales made an impression. And the association with La La Land, as tenuous as it was, persisted. Not long after the Cellar gig, Hales' phone rang. It was Dave Robbins, the gregarious trombonist, bandleader, composer/arranger, and educator who had played in the orchestra led by Harry James, the hugely popular trumpeter and movie star Hales admired. Robbins heard that Hales was from LA. He offered Hales him a gig and asked whether the trumpeter had any original tunes he could bring. Hales had exactly one, written at Westlake. "So I brought it out, and he really liked it," recalled Hales. "And the people liked it too. It was a pretty good chart. I worked on it all year; it should have been good."[11]

Getting in with Robbins meant Hales landed gigs playing at the Cave on Hornby Street, Vancouver's top supper club. Robbins was leading the Cave's house band at the time. Robbins also hired Hales to perform on CBC shows and work in the city's recording studios. Then a chance encounter with the great saxophonist Fraser MacPherson at Isy's Supper Club on West Georgia Street led to another opportunity. MacPherson asked Hales if he wanted to be a bandleader, which got the trumpeter's attention. MacPherson revealed that he was taking his band over to the Cave, and Isy's was looking for new group. Hales did as MacPherson suggested and talked to Isy Walters, owner of the club, and promptly got the gig. Just one thing was missing—a band for Hales to play with. He recruited musicians including Cellar stalwarts PJ Perry on saxophone, Gittens, bassist Tony Clitheroe, and Ursan. Between the Cave and Isy's, Hales performed with a cavalcade of stars, from Sonny and Cher and Stevie Wonder to Tony Bennett and Buddy Rich.

The Road from Avonlea to the Cellar

Hales became exactly the type of musician that made him so nervous that first night at the Cellar: a heavy, otherwise known as a downtowner. But it wasn't an either-or situation for him. Hales was one of the minority of musicians busy working downtown—in supper clubs, at the CBC, and in studios—who also made it a priority to be at the Cellar to play, listen, and just be part of the club's scene. "I used to hang out there all the time," said Hales. "Any moment I had to myself, I had to go hang out at the Cellar. My wife can attest I was home late many nights because of the Cellar."[12]

Even in casual jam sessions at the Cellar, there was a freedom that energized Hales. "I could go downtown and play my commercial gigs, or do casuals, do a little commercial crap," he recalled. "Then I'd go down to the Cellar and play what I liked. Nobody told me what to play, and so we'd get up on the stage and just sort of wing it. Sometimes sessions turned out great, and sometimes it was sad. But mainly it was just a chance to play, to play what you wanted to play without having somebody call the tune for you."[13]

• • •

One of Hales' Cellar highlights was playing in Ray Sikora's big band that rehearsed on Sundays in the club. Sikora was an alumnus of Westlake, where he played in a jazz quartet with—of all people—Gordon Lightfoot on drums. Then Sikora became a trombone soloist with Stan Kenton and a superb big band composer and arranger. The musicians in Sikora's rehearsal band at the Cellar had the unique opportunity to play challenging charts without the pressure of having to perform them for audiences. Hales only remembers the band performing once, in Stanley Park, where Sikora's group played on the same bill as an ensemble led by Robbins. "We wiped their nose," said Hales. (Translation: Sikora's band handily outplayed Robbins' band.) "We were really hot because we rehearsed all the time."[14]

Actually, the band performed other times. Don Thompson, who played piano in the band, sent me an unreleased lo-fi recording of Sikora and company performing in front of a lively audience at the Cellar on a Sunday night in February 1963. One of the sax men in the big band, Glenn McDonald, recorded the band that night. Hales definitely played in the show because at one point in the recording, emcee Barry Cramer quirkily introduces all twelve members of Sikora's band, including the trumpeter.

Journeys to the Bandstand

I've listened to the recording of six tunes countless times because it's a rare artifact that conveys what it was like to be in the Cellar for an exciting gig. It also captures some of the most exhilarating big band music I've ever heard. Hales contributed to the powerful sound in a stellar trumpet section that included Arnie Chycoski, yet another Westlake-trained player with Sylvan Lake experience. It was a thrill for Hales to play alongside Chycoski, who nailed stratospheric high notes, in front of Ursan, whose forceful drumming was indeed loud as fuck, and next to stirring soloists like trombonist Ian McDougall and Thompson.

Bobby Hales. Photographer unknown.

The performance's raw vitality belied the Cellar's shaky viability at the time. After that blast of a show, the club had less than a year of life left. During this final period, musicians who had been at the heart of the Cellar moved on, and audiences dwindled. Hales thought the rise of rock 'n roll had something to do with the Cellar's demise. He also believed changes in the jazz world were at play. When Hales was sixteen, he snuck into a Louis Armstrong concert. "It was so packed, I had to sit on the stage, so I was right close to Louis and the whole group, his all-stars," said Hales. "I remember how much fun it was. People were having a really good time." He contrasted that experience with seeing Miles Davis at the Inquisition coffeehouse (726 Seymour Street) in early 1963. "Miles wasn't fun," said Hales. "He was all serious, all bitchy, and bad attitude. He didn't like the audience." Hales loved Davis' playing, "but for me, he changed the whole thing. Jazz sort of went inside itself."[15]

The Cellar's closure in 1964 created a void in Hales' life, but he found new ways to express his creativity and show leadership in the scene. In 1965, he formed the Bobby Hales Big Band. Three years later, Hales' fifteen-piece big band opened Jazz Alley on May 12, 1968. Jazz Alley was a short-lived club in the exact same space that housed the original Cellar. Hales also composed and performed an electronic jazz suite—an early attempt at fusion—with Thompson, Clitheroe, and Ursan at Jazz Alley. The suite was a by-product of an electronic music course he took at the University of British Columbia. "You twisted knobs and whatnot to make this music," said Hales about the course.[16]

A review in the *Province* of a 1970 concert he led at the Queen Elizabeth Theatre—with old friends Robbins, MacPherson, Quarin, Ursan, and others—praised Hales and the band for avoiding the "familiar floorshow formula," even with well-known tunes from the celebration of hippiedom, *Hair*. "Essentially the band proved that, with the aid of an imaginative arranger, namely Hales, even the most familiar of pop and show tunes can become aesthetically worthwhile," wrote Brian McLeod.[17]

There are some seventies artifacts on the Internet that feature Hales' big band. The CBC made 45 rpm recordings of the ensemble, with two short songs each, that were intended for radio broadcast. While Hales arranged the tunes with his usual professionalism and his musicians performed solidly, fifty years after they were recorded, the tracks—with elements like wah-wah electric guitar—sound dated.

John Dawe got it right when he said making a living was a priority for Hales, who succeeded at that by being versatile, adaptable, and resilient. He was music director of the Pacific National Exhibition—Vancouver's annual PNE fair—for a number of years. The gig meant Hales' big band played a lot at the fair, including a career highlight show backing Frank Sinatra at the Pacific Coliseum in 1976. But he also had to do other less appealing things like produce a beauty pageant. Hales did it because he was professional and pragmatic.

On YouTube, there's an approximately twenty-minute excerpt from the 1975 made-in-Vancouver film *Dogpound Shuffle*—co-starring David Soul before he went on to *Starsky & Hutch* fame—including a long party scene that Hales appears in. He essentially plays himself in the comedic film: a tuxedo-wearing trumpeter playing his horn with the bent bell and leading a quintet that did jazzy music Hales wrote. He was perfect for the part because after his years of experience, it all came naturally to him.

Bobby Hales Big Band. Photographer unknown. Courtesy Dave Quarin.

In 1976, CBC gave Hales what would be unheard of today: a one-hour TV special featuring his twenty-member big band in performance. Some videos of the show survive. All the band members—except for Hales—wore off-blue, too-tight turtlenecks. As for the music, at first, I thought it sounded a bit dated, like the CBC 45s. Then I listened closer and realized the turtlenecks clouded my judgement. Hales' arrangements, of standards like "I Love You" and "Watch What Happens" and his original tunes, were intricate and imaginative. The large ensemble—with stellar musicians like MacPherson, Stew Barnett, and Oliver Gannon—sounded tremendously cohesive, which was a by-product of performing together regularly. While Hales mainly conducted, he also soloed with finesse on some tunes. Above all, the musicians swung and played big band jazz with an effortless verve.

There were other gigs, like one in February 1978, when Hales and an eighteen-piece version of his big band played with American trombonist Bill Watrous at the Commodore Ballroom. The jazz show ran counter to prevailing sounds; it was the peak of the disco era. Yet according to the *Vancouver Sun*, "a large, enthusiastic" crowd attended to hear the virtuosic Watrous and the "spirited" band, which included Hales' longtime drumming sidekick Ursan.[18] Later, Watrous called to ask permission to record one of Hales' tunes. Hales considered that one of the "biggest compliments" of his life.[19]

In the early eighties on Friday nights, Hales and a slimmed-down band with ten musicians played swing—"String of Pearls," "In The Mood," etc.—for dancing couples in the Odyssey Room on the Hyatt Hotel's 34th floor. It wasn't exuberant jazz like what he did with Watrous, but Hales enjoyed the gigs, where he observed that people actually knew the proper steps for waltzes, mambos, and other dance styles. Something as simple as that gave him pleasure. He never seemed to suffer from existential angst about whether what he was doing was artistically legitimate. The sign beside the elevators in the hotel lobby read: "Bobby Hales Big Band Tea Dance Swings, 5 to 8 p.m., Friday. No cover. No tea . . . Thirst quenchers."[20] The sign's offbeat humour was pure Hales.

Hales might be best known for writing two non-jazz compositions: the iconic theme song for the CBC-TV series *The Beachcombers* that was heard on TV for eighteen years starting in 1972, and *The Beginning of the End*, a suite for the closing ceremonies of the 1988 Calgary Winter Olympics. Composition was a salve for Hales when diabetes curtailed his playing days. Because of the disease, he lost his teeth and couldn't play trumpet at a high level. "I had these Simpsons Sears teeth that didn't work very well." But the tooth and playing decay led to another type of gig. "I had to do something, so I thought, they need a president at the union."[21] Hales proudly served as President of the Vancouver Musicians' Association from 1996 to 2012.

As the conversation winds down at Hales' house, I get the clear impression that he enjoyed and appreciated all of his many musical pursuits. The dialogue returns one last time to the Cellar. "If I was a jazz junkie, that's where I got my shot," said Hales. "Hanging out there and listening to people play and playing with people, that kept me alive and thinking you're worth something. You know, you start playing these commercial gigs—you gotta read, you gotta play in tune, you gotta show up on time, you gotta wear certain clothes, and there's a ritual that goes along with that. You have to learn the routine. But there's nothing more satisfying than, after a gig, going down to the Cellar and hearing some live jazz players. You just came back to life again."[22]

After the interview, Hales walks me to the door, where I ask him to pose for a photo. He readily agrees, and flashes a toothy smile with choppers that are clearly an upgrade from the Simpsons Sears model. I've gazed at the few photos I took that day in 2013 a lot. Hales looked grandfatherly—because he was; he had three daughters and four grandchildren. But his expression also conveyed a vigorous presence that I could picture him radiating on those glorious Cellar nights. Bobby Hales died on October 15, 2016, just days before his fifty-ninth wedding anniversary, and almost six decades after his Vancouver and Cellar debut. He was eighty-two.

• • •

Two weeks after Hales passed away, trombonist Sharman King went on CBC Radio's long-running *Hot Air* jazz show to share remembrances of Hales, his former bandleader. "He had great organizational skills, he had a very fast mind, he could handle the pressures of business, and he had impeccable music training, so he would write charts very well, very quickly," said King, who played in that 1976 TV special. "It was such an honour to play with him," King added. "He was a very good trumpet player. Just a good all-round musician and more importantly, a great leader." King also noted that when Hales received "heat" from the bosses who hired the band, he never let it reach the bandmembers. Instead of transferring stress to the band, he kept the players laughing. "Bob Hales had a very acerbic sense of humour. He was very brutal and witty."[23]

Months went by, and I kept thinking about how fortunate I was to meet Hales and learn about the great man's career in his own words. I craved more insights, so I reached out to musicians who worked with Hales. Campbell Ryga, who subbed for saxophonists in Hales' big band, echoed King's point about the bandleader's sharp wit. "He didn't pull any punches ever," said Ryga about the quips Hales would suddenly impart. "These things would just come off the top of his head and right out of his mouth. It took the tension out of the room immediately."[24] Even Hales' obituary mentioned that he was "known to tell many corny and sometimes inappropriate jokes (which he often found himself giggling at)."[25] So the adorable grandfather I met was a master of scathing one-liners that kept his players—and himself—in stitches.

Often there was an affectionate intent behind Hales' comic manoeuvres. That was the case when he called Stew Barnett and asked him to show up for a big band gig at the Hot Jazz Club. The trumpeter made the gig, and after Hales counted off the tempo, on the downbeat Barnett—who never flubbed entrances—was the only one playing. As recounted by *Vancouver Sun* columnist Denny Boyd, "Hales mumbled, 'Jeez, what a way to start. Okay, let's try it again.'" The second time, Barnett again embarrassingly blew it, unintentionally starting the tune with a solo. The third time, Barnett held back a bit and the band finally played, but a different song: "Happy Birthday." That's when Barnett realized the "gig" and the false starts were all part of a clever surprise to celebrate his sixtieth birthday. Hales was "falling off the stage laughing."[26]

Dave Quarin said his former bandleader created many opportunities for musicians, and he was loyal and forgiving when band members made missteps. One opportunity for Quarin was being among twenty-one musicians who played on *One of My Bags*, the only jazz album Hales recorded with his big band. (Another album Hales put out a decade later, featuring singer Pat Hervey on three tracks, didn't have jazz; it had what Hales drolly called "SWOCK"—big band dance music combining swing and rock.) Recorded in September 1975 at Little Mountain Sound, *One of My Bags* consists entirely of tunes Hales composed and arranged. He released the album independently, which was atypical at the time, and had 1,000 copies pressed. Long out-of-print, you won't find *One of My Bags* in any streaming service, but someone digitized the record and posted it to YouTube. The historically important recording documents buoyant big band jazz. The album features various soloists, including Hales playing flugelhorn on the down-tempo "Talk Trap." His solo is lithe and soothing, like a perfectly steeped cup of tea with a dollop of honey.

Ryga, who said Hales was very supportive of VEJI—the large ensemble of jazz insurgents that Hugh Fraser started and Ryga played in—had one other insight. "Bobby always took care of business," said Ryga, echoing King again. "He was extremely professional and uncompromising, and he always stood up for the guys when something was going wrong. You never had anything to worry about in that regard because musicians were his life, music was his life, he was a leader, and he gave me so many great bits of advice over the years."[27]

Music was his life. So true, and even if it didn't come naturally to him, vibrant jazz was the lifeblood of this little man whose band had a great big sound.

9 / TOTAL HONESTY: PJ PERRY

ON AN IDYLLIC morning in 2014, I drove up a mountain to meet PJ Perry. What I learned that day about the saxophone icon brought my appreciation of his resilience and artistic legacy into sharp focus.

PJ had just arrived in Vancouver from his home in Edmonton to perform two much-anticipated concerts with an all-star Canadian quartet, including Renee Rosnes, Neil Swainson, and Terry Clarke. He agreed to do an interview on the morning of the first show (a performance that delivered on its promise), so I drove to meet him at his daughter's house in Coquitlam, a Vancouver suburb forty-five minutes to the east by car. The elevation steadily increased as I reached Burke Mountain. It's a master-planned community of cookie-cutter real estate developments. The large new homes I drove by had manicured landscaping and mass-produced elegance. The overall theme: well-to-do uniformity.

After arriving at a house in a cul-de-sac, meeting PJ at the door, and sitting down in the naturally lit dining room to revisit his jazz career that was approaching sixty years, I was struck by how these surroundings so starkly contrasted with his life in music. The environment outside of where we had convened was safe, conformist, and predictable, whereas his career had been the opposite: turbulent, unconventional, and singular.

His path wasn't at all pre-planned. PJ instinctively went with the flow, and it brought him to unexpected places—both dark and illuminating. As a very young and prodigiously talented saxophonist, PJ asserted himself with his urgent bebop sound. Self-doubt and other stressors led to addictions, which he wrestled with for decades. PJ gradually found the strength to become an addiction-free survivor, and he entered a renaissance that the saxophonist has sustained.

• • •

PJ's life in jazz was set in motion by his father. Paul Guloien, who went by Paul Perry, was an itinerant tenor saxophonist and big band leader who performed in western Canada starting in the 1930s. He and his wife Margaret Yeo welcomed their son Paul John Guloien into the world on December 2, 1941. Paul Jr. would become PJ, a whimsical name that suited him; later he would adopt the Perry surname that had been his grandmother's.

Varsity Hall, Sylvan Lake, 1940. Photo by J.H. Gano. Courtesy Red Deer and District Archives and Sylvan Lake & District Archives.

In 1947, Paul Sr. and two members of his band—his brother Jim and Geoff Hall—bought a storied hall in Sylvan Lake, Alberta. Varsity Hall was one of several dancehalls in Sylvan Lake, a thriving summer resort town equidistant between Calgary and Edmonton. The Perrys followed a yearly migration pattern: they lived in Vancouver during the winters and drove to Alberta in a station wagon with a hitched trailer in April and performed until Labour Day.

Unlike the thousands of tourists visiting Sylvan Lake, the Perry family was not enjoying a relaxing vacation; they were there to perform and entertain.

For close to twenty years, the Paul Perry Orchestra typically played seven nights a week at Varsity Hall in the summer. It was a pastoral place and time. Up to about 1,000 people of all ages would jam into the hall on a summer's night to dance and possibly find romance. They danced on a hardwood floor that was surrounded by a railing, which was perfect for leaning on when scouting out dance partners. PJ grew up in this setting where live music was ever-present night and day, and the musicians that played it were his role models.

Paul Perry Sr. (tenor saxophone) and musicians, Varsity Hall, Sylvan Lake, 1961. Photographer unknown. Courtesy Sylvan Lake & District Archives.

Inevitably, PJ learned to play multiple instruments, including piano, clarinet, and alto saxophone, the horn Paul Perry gave to his eleven-year-old son when he was in hospital recovering from polio. In 1955, Paul Sr. decided PJ was ready to join the dance band on baritone sax, a long, awkward, and heavy instrument for a slight teenager. At fourteen, PJ replaced Millard

Ringdahl, a gruff old saxophonist who had been in Stan Kenton's orchestra. "When my dad was introducing me to the baritone chair, I remember Millard coming and sitting on the bench in the dancehall and listening to the first rehearsal that I was playing," said PJ. "He sat with his cane and beard, and he sat in the shadows alongside the wall of the hall. After the intermission of the rehearsal, I had to walk past him to get off the stage. So, as I was walking past him, he said, 'Son.' And I said, 'Yes, Mr Ringdahl.' He said, 'If you're going to play the baritone saxophone, blow it!' And I said, 'Yes sir.'"[1]

Paul Sr. recruited some of Vancouver's finest jazz musicians to play in the orchestra: drummers Jerry Fuller and George Ursan, bassist Bob Miller, trumpeters Bobby Hales and Arnie Chycoski, pianists Ron Johnston, Ralph Grierson, and John Gittins, and multi-instrumentalist Don Thompson were among them. At night, they played danceable swing and some rock tunes for the masses that came to the hall. During the day, they used the empty Varsity Hall to play the jazz they were passionate about. PJ wandered into the hall one day and heard a glorious sound. It was his first experience hearing full-on jazz. PJ called it a turning point in his life and knew he had to learn how to play this compelling music. "I could sense the freedom, the commitment, and the virtuosity that was required in order to perform such magical feats on their instruments," he said.[2]

Miller, Fuller, and others encouraged PJ to join them in the daytime jams, and he did—with much struggle. PJ learned melodies to jazz standards by rote and, as advised by the musicians, listened to records by Charlie Parker, Sonny Rollins, Clifford Brown, and other greats. Parker's bebop mastery made the biggest impact, and PJ would eventually study Bird's solos like a monk devoting himself to Buddhist philosophy. "I dove in. The love of trying to play the music carried me through all the frustration of not really being able to do it. I found it an extremely frustrating and a very difficult process to work my way through the chord changes, and I just kept trying and put up with the disappointments."[3]

What PJ considered setbacks were revelations to other musicians, who marvelled at his rapid musical development. "He was unbelievable," said Hales. "It got so you had to solo before he did because if not, he'd use all your licks. He'd memorize every lick you had, and sound exactly like you did. The guy had very good ears and could play any goddamn thing."[4]

Back in Vancouver, PJ continued his music education in high school bands, first at Gladstone in East Vancouver and then at Como Lake in Coquitlam. But he learned the most from gigging in rough cabarets like the Smilin' Buddha and the New Delhi, well past school-night bedtimes. "I wouldn't get home until three in the morning and then I'd try to go to school, and I was sleeping through class. That pretty much put the kibosh on my education, so I dropped out of school." PJ's adoption of a nocturnal lifestyle at an early age wouldn't have thrilled most parents, but his folks weren't typical. "My dad had started me playing when I was young, probably with the intention that I become a musician. He was very supportive."[5]

PJ played tenor sax in R&B groups and in one of Vancouver's early rock bands in the late 50s, the Stripes, which at one point included a then-unknown Ian Tyson on guitar. PJ experienced rock and roll mania with the Stripes—"the screaming teenagers thing" as he put it—and had an opportunity to tour with the band in the US. "I had to make a decision about whether I wanted to do that with my life or whether I wanted to stay. I had been getting the occasional gig at the Cave Supper Club, backing up these lovely big-name acts that were coming through, like Lena Horne, Ella Fitzgerald, Peggy Lee. I was playing baritone with the Chris Gage Big Band that was hired to play [as the house band] at that time. I decided that that was where my heart really lay, to play with that calibre of musicians."[6]

So he quit the Stripes and focused on playing Vancouver supper clubs alongside top musicians like Gage, Fraser MacPherson, and Stew Barnett. While there were elements of jazz played in these clubs, the music wasn't always truly jazz. The focus wasn't on playing melodies and taking turns improvising solos; the players' task was to accompany the featured act in a way that ensured all eyes and ears stayed on the visiting stars. To listen to and play full-on jazz, PJ turned to the celebrated basement club that opened in 1956: the original Cellar.

His first memory of the Cellar was seeing the "infernal red, yellowish, and orange large oil painting of kind of grotesque figures" by Frank Lewis that immediately confronted patrons walking down the stairs into the club. "It was very beautiful," said PJ.[7] "It said it all: it was modern, abstract, very colourful, and quite large." Beyond the painting, he remembered "a basement club with no windows . . . and it was perfect. It was dark. It was kind of romantic. It was a place where you felt you were in a special little community of non-commerciality. It was a place where one could devote their time and energies toward their art form."[8]

That's precisely what he did at the Cellar. He heard visiting greats like Charles Mingus and the Montgomery Brothers, and sat in whenever he could. It was bliss because most nights the emphasis was on bebop, and he was a devotee of the style. Before long, young PJ had made an impression on patrons and especially fellow players. "PJ blew me out of the place," said tenor saxophonist Jim Johnson. "He was a saxophone player, and he played what I played: the alto and tenor. And he was a really good musician, and so was his father. When PJ came to the Cellar, he became very popular and probably the best player in town."[9]

So while several musicians like Johnson and trumpeter John Dawe had established themselves at the Cellar, when PJ—who was still in his teens—appeared like a blazing meteor, the scene shifted. "He showed up there with a whole lot of technical skill but not a great amount of anything else," said Dawe. "But man, he learned so fast it was scary. He was in a real hurry to catch up."[10] So fast, in fact, that PJ was soon booked to lead bands at the Cellar. His main ensemble there was the PJ Perry Quintet, with Dawe, Al Neil on piano, bassist Tony Clitheroe, and Fuller. Playing together for two-and-a-half years, the band developed an intuitive rapport.

"It was everything." That's how PJ, in his consistently modest way, described what the Cellar and its regular players meant to his rise as a jazz artist. "Without the musicians that were hanging around in the Cellar, without that core dedicated group of jazz musicians playing and practicing, there would have been no way that I could ever have learned how to play."[11]

The December 1961 issue of *Coda* included a review of a performance PJ's quintet had given the previous month before a packed UBC Auditorium. "If you like the maximum number of notes it is possible to play in any given bar at any given tempo, you will like Paul Perry," wrote John Clayton. "Personally, I felt vaguely uncomfortable. He tries so hard and gives his all to such an extent that I feel rather embarrassed that none of it reaches me. This is probably my fault, not his, but I must confess to a feeling of relief when on the scheduled round of solos he let up and was replaced by the cool and comparatively remote trumpet of John Daw [sic]. There is also a tendency, hardly surprising, to produce honks and sundry reed notes."[12]

The harsh review failed to mention that the sax player and band leader was only nineteen at the time of the concert. PJ, however, never gave himself a break based on his age, so if he read the critique, the self-critical perfectionist likely took it hard. Still, negative responses like that didn't slow his forward momentum.

The Cellar wasn't all about togetherness on the bandstand; it also featured some intense competition. PJ built a friendly rivalry with the superb alto saxophonist Dale Hillary, another Cellar stalwart who was just one year older. "They were like two gunfighters in the West," said Dawe. "Great respect for each other but also watching each other."[13] Thompson observed their musical battles. "Dale and PJ had some kind of bizarre competitiveness between them that was comical," said Thompson. "Lots of times if one was playing, the other one would show up and there would be a cutting contest on stage. On the bandstand, they would get really competitive trying to outplay each other. Off the bandstand, they were really good friends, and PJ was crushed when Dale died [in 1992]."[14]

The two saxophonists had more in common than prodigious technique and a shared competitive streak—they were both hardcore drug addicts. "I found one of the attractions of altering my perception and state with drugs and alcohol was it helped me cope with the difficulties of my inadequacies and what I was trying to do," said PJ. "I also found that I was frightened. I was dealing with stage fright and nerves. If somebody had been able to explain to me and made me believe it was just a natural process, that everybody gets scared, that it is something that passes, and that it's ok to feel like that, then perhaps I would have dealt with it in a saner way."[15] PJ turned to drugs and alcohol at a young age, and they exacted a savage toll on his life.

In 1959, PJ moved to Toronto, where he played with Rob McConnell, Ron Collier, Sonny Greenwich, and others. By 1962, PJ was performing with Maury Kaye in Montreal. Then it was on to Europe in 1963. In Berlin, his life crash-landed horrendously. PJ was arrested for suspicion of smoking marijuana. Under a draconian law that is now hard to imagine, PJ was held without bail in solitary confinement in the town of Bad Kreuznach for eight months before being deported back to Canada.[16] Surviving the traumatizing imprisonment was tough; his addiction struggles continued, which meant there were more grim times.

In an incongruous effort to escape his troubles, he joined the Canadian Coast Guard in 1967 and served a six-month stint as a seaman. Eventually PJ returned to music, which sustained him. In 1968, he joined Tommy Banks' band in Edmonton. In the early 1970s, PJ was part of the pioneering Vancouver jazz rock fusion group Pacific Salt. Back in Edmonton, PJ recorded his first album as a leader in 1977: *Sessions*. On the recording, PJ plays with a fierce intensity in the bebop spirit, such as on "Autumn in New York." He stays true to the standard's intent as a ballad, but at the right moments delivers quick and incisive improvised lines on alto, just as his hero Charlie Parker did. Near the end of the tune, the robust band—George McFetridge, Torben Oxbol, and Claude Ranger—lays out while PJ goes it alone, furthering his impassioned expression with a keen edge.

Sessions earned PJ recognition. The *Edmonton Journal* devoted an entire page to profiles of two top jazz players in the city: Tommy Banks and his friend and collaborator PJ Perry. While *Journal* pop music critic Graham Hicks described Banks as a "cool, collected customer,"[17] he saw PJ as a "self-driven musician, whose ability comes through the trials of continual inner struggle."[18] PJ confirmed as much in the 1979 article, which was a window into his state of mind. "I should be as happy as I can be right now," he told Hicks. "I'm working regularly. I'm married, with a beautiful daughter. I'm doing what I want to do. Millions of musicians would cut off their arms to be in my situation. But I still feel a tremendous amount of frustration." He elaborated: "Jazz is obsessive. You're dealing with a major vital force, a total honesty that is frightening in its purity. It's not like memorizing an arrangement and leaving some room for solos. You put yourself on the line every time you go out to play. To always be hot is tremendously demanding psychologically. It's so uncertain. It ceases to be fun. But a higher reward comes with it."[19]

In the eighties, PJ put in more years as an outstanding but underutilized player in Toronto before returning to Edmonton. In the Alberta capital, he had a revelation: if PJ couldn't love himself, he couldn't love his family and his life as a musician that still had untapped potential. PJ finally walked away from alcohol and drugs.[20] When I met him, he described his duel with the latter as "thirty-five years of heroin addiction that I'm proud to say is long gone."[21] PJ was nervous before playing his first gig drug-free and sober, at Sid's on Jasper Avenue. While his wife Rhonda was there to support him, PJ didn't know if he could play well substance-free. "I found I could play ten times better," he told Nick Lees of the *Edmonton Journal*. "It was an amazing feeling of accomplishment."[22]

More than a dozen years went by after *Sessions* before PJ returned to recording as a leader. In late 1990, PJ made two albums with elite musicians: *Worth Waiting For*, with Kenny Barron, Chuck Deardorf, and Victor Lewis, and *My Ideal*, with Mulgrew Miller, Neil Swainson, and Lewis. While PJ swings hard on the recordings, there's a tangible sense of calm, especially on *My Ideal*. On that album's title track, he takes his time exploring the meaning of the slow song, and the result is emotional and exquisite. The album's cover photo, which shows a smiling PJ standing on a rock by the sea with an umbrella held in one hand and his baby daughter Kira held close with the other, said it all. Here was a man at peace.

My Ideal came out in 1992, the year when PJ's father passed away. Paul Perry, who led bands that brought bliss to many, died from cancer and a bad fall. Just a few months after, PJ won a 1993 Juno Award for *My Ideal*, in the Best Jazz Album category. Almost forty years after joining his dad's band to play bari sax, PJ received one of the highest accolades in Canadian jazz.

• • •

Cory Weeds first heard PJ perform live at Hollywood North in downtown Vancouver. "From note one I was in awe of his unapologetic in-your-face sound and relentless hard-swinging groove," wrote Weeds in liner notes about PJ. "He is a true bebopper in every sense of the word, and there is nothing quite like sitting in front of him in a jazz club getting pummelled by that beautiful sound."[23]

Journeys to the Bandstand

PJ Perry and Cory Weeds, the Cellar. Photo by Jesse Cahill.

By the time Weeds opened his Cellar in 2000, PJ was still only fifty-eight, with a lot of music still to express. Weeds booked PJ to perform at the Cellar multiple times throughout the club's history. Live recordings of two engagements PJ played at the club were released on Weeds' Cellar Live label. The first one, recorded October 15, 2007, was an alto summit with Campbell Ryga, backed by Ross Taggart, Neil Swainson, and Terry Clarke. The performance documented on *Joined at the Hip* wasn't a gunslingers' duel *à la* PJ and Dale Hillary. Instead, it was a joyous meeting of like musical minds that affirmed the two altoists' mutual respect and mastery of lyrical, hard swinging, bebop. Fourteen years after he recorded with PJ, Ryga remembered the experience clearly. "The sound that he is able to create out of the horn, it's unbelievable," said Ryga of his longtime collaborator and friend. "I have stood beside many guys, and there is nobody that can play like PJ. The guy is eighty years old, and he still plays so strong. It's just uncanny."[24]

Ubiquitous, the second live recording, made May 20–21, 2011, captured PJ in a frontline alongside Montreal trumpeter Kevin Dean, and backed by pianist Mark Eisenman, Swainson, and drummer André White. Their playing is more hard bop than bebop on the all-original set of mostly medium to slow tempo tunes. If the *Coda* writer who criticized PJ in 1961 could have heard this, I expect he would have revised his opinion of PJ's playing. PJ had aged very well. He wasn't breaking new ground, but PJ still sounded fiery and passionate, and now his notes came with space and nuance.

PJ is one of a select number of musicians—along with Charles McPherson, Buddy Montgomery, Don Thompson, Terry Clarke, and a few others—whose longevity meant they played in both the original Cellar and Weeds' Cellar, and whose talents withstood the thirty-six-year interval between the clubs. PJ believes both iconic clubs played an invaluable role in enabling musicians and audiences to experience an intrinsic axiom: "that there's no end to the magic it [jazz] can conjure."[25]

PJ Perry, André White, and Kevin Dean, the Cellar, May 20, 2011. Photo by Vincent Lim.

Just as it takes special musicians to make jazz that connects and reverberates through generations, PJ believes that a special kind of jazz listener, such as those who attended the Cellars, is what keeps the music from becoming overly niche. "The world is full of people that don't know anything about jazz, and a lot of times [those who dismiss the music] don't get the opportunity to hear good jazz, so they're at a bit of a disadvantage in terms of not being exposed to this incredible art form," said PJ. "But there's always been a group of people that hear the journey. They can hear the emotion. They feel the music and can understand the freedom yet the discipline, the virtuosity, the tonal quality, the communication. There's always been a very select audience for jazz, and I believe that's the way it is today. There are people that care: the people that run the clubs and the musicians that persevere through all the crap of not being able to earn a living but somehow are able to keep the fire burning. It's the reason I know it's never going to go away."[26]

There's a YouTube video with highlights from *Come Fly Away*, a musical directed by dance legend Twyla Tharp featuring Frank Sinatra songs, which ran on New York City's Broadway in 2010 and toured to other cities. The video shows the mighty big band—including PJ who was a featured soloist—that played behind the show's dancers. It includes a snippet of PJ playing a solo during Count Basie's "Jumpin' at the Woodside." The scene lasts only twenty-six seconds, but it's enough to confirm that PJ—who was close to seventy at the time—kept playing with an enthralling sound and an appreciation for where life had taken him. Interviewed about the Broadway experience by Roger Levesque of the *Edmonton Journal*, PJ said: "There were a couple nights at the beginning of the run when I was overwhelmed with emotion for finding myself in such as wonderful situation."[27]

In the summer of 2018, PJ talked about finally getting over the cycle of self-doubt. "I feel now that I can be human," he said to Mike Devlin of the *Times Colonist*. "I'm allowed to make mistakes, and take chances, and have fun at this stage of my life. It has been a very important transformation for me."[28] A few months later in December 2018, just after turning seventy-seven, PJ played alto in a duo recording session with pianist Bill Mays. The album, recorded in a house on the West Side of Vancouver and released on Weeds' label, has perfect bookends. PJ approaches the opening tune, Bud Powell's "Parisian Thoroughfare," with a suitably robust energy. On the closing title track, Michel Legrand's "This Quiet Room," PJ's sound is contemplative. It's still intense, like his playing on virtually every piece he's ever recorded, but with a deep sense of autobiographical reflection that's poignant and resonant.

"I think I have music in me," he said when we met in that perfect Coquitlam neighbourhood. As that major understatement showed, PJ was proud yet humble when taking stock of his prodigious career that day. "I believe that I feel the music and that I try to play honestly." Honesty, he said, was "one of the characteristics of jazz music that I treasure and admire, and that had convinced me that it was what I wanted to devote my life to. You

PJ Perry, Coquitlam, April 18, 2014. Photo by Chris Wong.

can't fool anybody on the stage: you're either being honest and sharing your feelings and soul with the audience, or you're not. I believe I was able to do that. I worked hard at it. I devoted my life to learning the tunes, I listened to jazz music continually, and I played all the time. So there must have been the occasional good night."[29]

Seven years later in October 2021, I was at the Vogue Theatre for the pandemic-delayed celebration of life for Hugh Fraser, who passed away more than a year before. At times over the years, PJ played with Fraser's VEJI big band, plus the two musicians did small ensemble gigs together here and there. Fraser also once wrote a concerto that featured PJ. The two Canadian jazz greats shared a massive mutual respect. PJ was at the Vogue to pay his respects and play in honour of Fraser. When PJ came on stage and brought the alto to his mouth, the notes that streamed out of his horn sounded potent and beautiful. I'm sure everyone who was there felt the power of PJ's musical eulogy for his friend. PJ's performance also affirmed for me the saxophonist's innate and enduring gift for playing jazz that deeply and unequivocally moves people.

PJ turned eighty near the end of that year, and he continued to perform and record in Edmonton and elsewhere in 2022. As articulate as ever in yet another newspaper interview early that year, he told Levesque that he "never felt stronger and more capable and more in command of my instrument than I do now. It's taken me all my life to experience the freedom to spontaneously create music and play what I hear in my head."[30]

I read that quote a number of times to absorb what he was essentially saying. That after sixty-six years as a working musician, he was finally able to break through and completely free himself to authentically express himself. For those of us taking a long time to find creative satisfaction, that's an incredibly inspiring statement, and one that I'll keep close to me.

10 / JAZZ DREAMER: CAROL FOX

THE ADAGE THAT explains why people become musicians—*You don't choose music, music chooses you*—seems absurd and illogical. But there's truth to it, as evidenced by the inexorable path of many jazz musicians. Here's a variation on that maxim: *You don't choose to become a jazz club owner, jazz club ownership chooses you*. Again, it's ludicrous, but there must be something to it because why would someone of sound mind want to own a jazz club, given the economic challenges, tiresome hassle of complying with city bylaws, and headaches of dealing with temperamental musicians and demanding patrons?

Despite the stacked odds against success, something pushes a rare breed to create and run jazz joints. Carol Fox was among those jazz dreamers. Fox ran a jazz club that's long forgotten, but she and her club earned a place in Vancouver's music history.

When the original Cellar closed in 1964, it marked the death of a great jazz club. That major loss didn't, however, change the fact that the space that housed the Cellar had perfect bones for a jazz joint. Although the basement at 2514 Watson Street housed the Steering Wheel car club in the mid-60s,[1] [2] [3] its history as a jazz venue meant it retained the muscle memory for live music inside its walls. It was too young to die. Someone was bound to recognize the potential for vital jazz to be played and heard there.

Outside those walls, the city's economics and demographics worked in a new club's favour as well. Though more and more young people were fans of the hippie counterculture movement and its psychedelic rock soundtrack, jazz still had a considerable audience that was employed and had disposable income in pocket. And at the time, some other clubs that featured jazz players had shut down.

One of the people to recognize the possibilities for the old Cellar was Carol Fox. She wasn't a musician, and Fox never went to the Cellar. In fact, she hadn't even really experienced city life. Fox was from Trail, a small blue-collar city in southern BC's West Kootenay region that was home to a lead and zinc smelter so polluting that the locals and its ice hockey team were known as the Smoke Eaters. She studied anthropology at Notre Dame University of Nelson for about three years before making her way to Vancouver. Working as a lifeguard for a summer got her into jazz. A fellow lifeguard had a jazz collection, including an oddity that caught her attention: *Modern Jazz Performances from Bizet's Carmen* by guitarist Barney Kessel. "Since I had taken classical piano, I knew a little bit of the score," Fox told Bob Smith of the *Vancouver Sun*. "It made it easier for me to dig."[4]

Fox heard about the Cellar's legacy and that the car club was no longer parked in the subterranean space on Watson Street, which to this day feels like an alley because it's behind buildings. She saw her opening and arranged with the building's owners to rent the basement. To raise money for renovations, Fox worked double shifts in sixteen-hour days as a cook and waitress in the part of Vancouver's Kitsilano neighbourhood known as the Greek Village. In about four months she saved almost $1,600, enough to spruce up the former Cellar.

Some musicians who played at the original Cellar, like trumpeter John Dawe, helped Fox set up the club. While doing so, they found artifacts from the past, including "a carton of Cellar matchbooks and a door sign-in book with lots of names of musicians and folks that were required to sign in," said Dawe.[5] These vestiges symbolically represented the continuity between the jazz devotees who energized the Cellar and Fox, who idealistically pursued her dream of opening a jazz club.

She christened the new club Jazz Alley, which opened Sunday, May 12, 1968—Mother's Day—with Bobby Hales and his big band playing to two near-capacity houses. Tenor saxophonist Ross Barrett said it made sense that Fox booked Hales for opening night. "She would have got Hales to open the club just because he was more or less God in the jazz scene. And that made a statement that this was a [serious] jazz club opening."[6] As for the name, Fox's club began life more than a decade before Seattle's Jazz Alley started its long run that still continues, and also before a short-lived Jazz Alley opened at the back of the Istanbul Restaurant in Vancouver.

The first house band consisted of multi-instrumentalist Don Thompson, bassist Dave Fields, and drummer Rocky Weems. *Vancouver Sun* jazz critic Bob Smith popped in "late one night, early one morning"[7]—Jazz Alley opened at midnight on Fridays and Saturdays and nine p.m. on Sundays—to hear the trio play Horace Silver's "Nica's Dream," Charlie Parker's "Scrapple from the Apple," and other tunes. Tenor saxophonist Nick McGowan, trombonist Dave McMurdo, and drummer Don Fraser Jr. also sat in. Smith's verdict? "Take my word for it, the Jazz Alley and its cats are worth your support."[8]

On another night, Smith heard an eight-piece ensemble with musicians who regularly played at the original Cellar years before: Dave Quarin, Tony Clitheroe, George Ursan, Hales, and Thompson. Experiencing their calibre of musicianship in the club prompted Smith to write: "Carol is keeping the faith. So should you, if you call yourself a jazz fan."[9] Smith's counterpart at the *Province*, Brian McLeod, wrote that "more and more people are being turned on to the club and the modern music scene in general."[10] *Coda* magazine also declared that Jazz Alley "has become a thriving club with nightly jam sessions with musicians in all jazz-related areas . . ."[11]

Optimism always seems to accompany the birth and early days of a jazz club, and it was in ample supply with Jazz Alley. Intimate Vancouver jazz venues were in short supply at the time: The Cellar was long gone; the Black Spot was history; the Flat Five and its successor the Blue Horn were memories; and a fire destroyed Nield Longton's Espresso Coffee House on December 15, 1968. "There was a vacuum that she wanted to fill," said Barrett. "Guys like [alto saxophonist] Dick Smith and I would have made it clear to her that there was no place that you could play." For more than two years, she succeeded. "It became like a hangout," said Barrett. "It was definitely the central jazz club in Vancouver at that time."[12]

Barrett described Fox as having short black hair, wearing turtlenecks, and being part beatnik, part Audrey Hepburn. "She was quite reserved and quite shy," he said. "But she was no bullshit, that's for sure. She had her own opinion."[13] In a photo that appeared in the *Vancouver Sun* on March 21, 1969,

Fox's hair is hidden under a headscarf, her left hand rests under her chin, and her closed lips and big eyes convey a faint smile. The photo accompanied a piece by Bob Smith on the death of Longton's Espresso, and the progress of Fox's club, which by that point she was simply calling "the Alley."

"It's been tough, living and paying bills almost from day to day, doing the cooking, cleaning, checking the door, waiting tables," Fox said in the article. "But I've learned a lot about myself with all these responsibilities. I figure it's been good for me."[14]

Carol Fox, 1969. Photographer unknown. Source: Vancouver Sun (Postmedia Network Inc.).

• • •

In 1969, after enduring struggles and achieving some success in programming dynamic local jazz musicians, Fox reached her first anniversary of running a jazz club. Not long after, in the summer of '69, Fox was driving her Volkswagen Beetle in Keremeos in BC's Similkameen Valley when she picked up two hitchhikers. It was sixteen-year-old Coat Cooke and his best friend, who were hitchhiking in BC before thumbing their way back to Winnipeg, where they lived. Fox drove them to Vancouver and on the way there, they discovered something in common. The boys found out Fox ran a jazz club; Fox found out Cooke was a jazz buff who was listening to Charlie Parker, Thelonious Monk, Ornette Coleman, and others.

Fox turned onto Watson Street and parked the car in a small lot behind the nondescript building that housed her jazz club. She told the teenagers that they could listen to the band booked for that night and sleep on the bandstand after the music stopped, so they followed Fox down the club's steep stairs with their duffel bags. They heard late night sets of jazz before sleeping on the bandstand at about five a.m. They repeated that routine for about two weeks. "I had never heard live jazz at that point, so it was very exciting," said Nikita Carter, who was Coat Cooke before changing names and coming out as a trans woman almost fifty years after that highly influential fortnight.[15] After turning seventeen, Carter started playing saxophone. Later, Carter became an important player in Vancouver's improvised music scene and co-led the New Orchestra Workshop (NOW) Society. Fox's kind generosity, and her feisty jazz club, made a significant impact on the saxophonist.

The Alley wasn't just a great place for straight ahead jazz musicians to do their thing. Fox also offered the bandstand to musicians playing other forms of music. One such band was Mock Duck, a psychedelic rock/blues/jazz band led by guitarist and vocalist Joe Mock that included Barrett. Another prime example was Greta Poontang, led by Bob Turner on electric bass and including Barrett, Dick Smith, guitarist Henry Young, pianists Gerry Caunter and Bob Murphy, and drummer Paul Grant. Turner described the band's music as "experimental" jazz or "fusion."[16] Barrett recalled that Turner wrote "really dark, heavy pieces," somewhat similar to what Miles Davis was doing at the time on albums like *Bitches Brew*. Greta Poontang was provocative in both its name and music. Letting the group play as essentially a house band said a lot about Fox and her club. "It was the only place you could really play alternative music," said Barrett. "She definitely developed such a love of music and the whole notion of providing a venue for it to happen."[17]

Gavin Walker went to Fox's club as a patron, and he remembered her "sincerity about the music and what she wanted to do," which was simply to give creative musicians opportunities to perform. "She was really dedicated. She wanted to keep it like a real jazz club."[18] Sincerity and dedication are essential but, as countless club owners before and since have learned, they don't pay the bills. In September 1970, Bob Smith reported that the Alley was no more. "After two or three years of hard work, innocent mistakes and, most often, lack of co-operation from you and me, the jazz public, she called it quits," wrote Smith.[19]

What silenced the Alley? The usual factors that doom jazz clubs. "Carol had a hell of time keeping it open, and sometimes you wouldn't get paid," said Young, who started touring with Nina Simone in 1968. While he experienced the high life on the road with Simone, there were nights at the Alley, like the one where she was reduced to bartering. "I think she gave Bob [Turner] a tea kettle, and I just said, 'That's fine.'" He and the musicians playing that night had steady gigs elsewhere, so they could afford to forgo payment at the Alley, at least for one night. They did so because they understood Fox's challenges and personal sacrifices and appreciated her musical openness. "We could play what we wanted to play [at the Alley]," said Young.[20] Of course, not all of the musicians who played at the Alley could afford to be so generous.

Another reason for the Alley's demise was the "downtown heavies" didn't support her," said Turner.[21] He was referring to veteran musicians with steady gigs at the downtown supper clubs and with CBC. Bobby Hales was among the exceptions of downtowners who supported Fox. Hales loved bebop and other jazz forms that didn't always get played downtown, and prized the freedom the Alley gave him to listen to and play what he wanted.

Regardless of why Jazz Alley/the Alley ceased to exist, it became part of what Jeani Read grimly referred in the *Province* to as the "corpse-strewn recent history" of Vancouver jazz clubs that shut down.[22] But despite the enormous challenges of running a small jazz club, the music refused to die in the Watson Street basement. Not long after the Alley shut down, Ron and Shirley Small took over the space and opened the Old Cellar. Local musicians—including a number that had played there in previous incarnations—and big names like Herbie Hancock and Ornette Coleman would perform in this third life of a jazz club.

Fox's iteration didn't last long enough to develop a distinct vibe like jazz venues with more longevity that came later—such as the Classical Joint—said Dick Smith, who was in and out of a relationship with Fox. But the club and Fox still had a singular character.

Fox and Shirley Small were among of handful of women who owned or co-owned Vancouver jazz clubs over the years. Others included Marcella "Choo Choo" Williams, who co-owned the Harlem Nocturne with her husband Ernie King, and the two women who owned and operated the Cotton Club from 1997 to 2000. For decades the city's community of jazz musicians was male-dominated, and the same was true of jazz club owners. As an outlier, Fox likely encountered a degree of entrenched sexism. She wasn't intimidated about being in the minority. "Carol was a tough woman and did what she wanted," said Smith.[23]

Fox gave Barrett a brand-new Selmer Mark VI tenor sax, which he still plays today. In return, Barrett created a painting that documented their relationship. It shows Fox, looking insouciant, and Barrett, gazing lovingly at Fox and playing the Selmer sax. For years the painting hung in Taf's Cafe on Granville Street in downtown Vancouver, where the patrons had no clue about who inspired the artwork. "I adored Carol," said Barrett. "Loved her. When that fell away, it was very sad."[24] After their romantic relationship ended, her presence remained with Barrett. "I loved her dearly, deeply, and I always acknowledge her whenever I play because I'm playing her horn."[25]

Barrett said that after leaving the jazz scene, Fox had a daughter. Smith said Fox went back to school but couldn't finish her studies because of a severe illness that she eventually succumbed to. I couldn't find an obituary or any mention of Fox's passing in Vancouver newspapers. But to those who knew her as a hard-working, ahead-of-her-time jazz club owner—and an inspirational muse—she made a lasting impression.

Painting of Carol Fox by Ross Barrett, courtesy Ross Barrett.

11 / THE VOICE: RON SMALL

IT WAS A rare occasion. Three legends of Vancouver's arts community—Ron Small, Denis Simpson, and Bob Murphy—were together on stage at the Vancouver East Cultural Centre to celebrate Black History Month in music and conversation. Small's contribution was personal and mesmerizing. When he reached deep into his life experience and soul that afternoon to sing the elemental words to "Ain't Nobody's Business," which Bessie Smith, Jimmy Witherspoon, and others immortalized as a blues standard, it was an enthralling statement. As Murphy eloquently set the perfect blues mood on the grand piano, Small sang with a full-throated conviction that enveloped the theatre. Eyes closed, the vocalist held on to the "no" in "nobody" for what felt like an eternity until the point was made—the protagonist in the song defiantly does as he pleases.

Small knew of what he sang; he was both in character and singing autobiographically when he delivered this powerful performance. After decades of being on stages like this one and living a hard life offstage, the then-seventy-year-old sounded strong and authentic. Small embodied Black history in his storied tenor voice and presence. Not enough people knew it, but he contributed immeasurably to that history. As for the personal history that was the subtext to his artistry, perfectionism and struggle shaped Small. He insisted on the highest standards and had zero tolerance for mediocrity. The blunt way in which he communicated these rigid standards was hurtful at times, but his uncompromising approach brought out the best in this proud, elegant man and those he collaborated with and mentored.

When I wrote about Small in 1999, his jazz singing caught my ear, but I couldn't have predicted that he would become much more than a one-off story subject. Years later I went far deeper into examining his oeuvre, and the more I learned about Small, the more I became captivated with his music and character.

It was initially challenging to put together the fragments of Small's life. Information about his career in the performing arts and private life was available but scattered. Then after much effort, I gradually tracked down details of his experiences as young R&B/doo-wop singer, club co-owner with his wife Shirley, jazz singer, gospel singer with the Sojourners, vocal mentor, and friend to a chosen few. But there were still gaps in my knowledge of Small, such as about his final years, after Small moved to Toronto and cut most of his Vancouver ties. He died at St. Michael's Hospital in Toronto on November 3, 2018. It's a glaring injustice that if you Google his name, not a single search result about Small's passing appears. He was a remarkable man who deserved much better. It became clear to me that I had to answer, as thoroughly as possible, a fundamental question: who was Ron Small?

• • •

Ron Small was born December 7, 1937, in Chicago. The middle child in a family of six boys and three girls, Small grew up in poverty on the city's South Side. He was close to his mother Hester, who died when Small was in his early teens, but not especially close to his father Plemon. Small discovered music at a young age. "Once he learned to sing, he was singing all his life," said Small's daughter Collette Hackl. "Even as a child, at the church and on the street, he just sang away." Small also lived in a milieu where jazz, blues, soul, R&B, gospel, and doo-wop thrived. "He was into a whole lot of different music because of his introduction, not just from the church but from the street, to all of the music that was out there," said Hackl.[1]

At seventeen, Small enlisted in the US Air Force and was stationed at McChord Air Force Base in Tacoma, Washington. He joined an R&B/doo-wop vocal group at McChord that became known at various times as the Fabulous Pearls, the Four Pearls, and simply the Pearls. The quartet members were among the winners of Tops in Blue, a prominent air force talent contest, which got them an invite to perform on *The Ed Sullivan Show*.

The program notes for the show that aired August 31, 1958, indicate that while other contest winners did comedy routines, swallowed razor blades, and yodelled, the Pearls sang "My Love." The notes also list the Pearls' members, including "A3-C [Airman Third Class] Ronald Small."[2]

In February 1959, the quartet drove to Los Angeles and auditioned for record producer Dootsie Williams, who signed the group to his Dootone label. As the Fabulous Pearls, they recorded five tracks for Dootone in LA. When the label released "Jungle Bunny" and "My Heart's Desire," Williams predicted that "both sides of this record will explode."[3] That didn't happen, and Dootone didn't put out the other tracks. So the group went home to Seattle and cut two tracks for Dolton Records: "Look at Me" and "It's Almost Tomorrow." That was the end of the quartet's recording career. Two of the unreleased Dootone tunes—"I Laughed So Hard" and "Baby Top Drop"— didn't surface until the 1990s on doo-wop compilations that UK-based Ace Records released. More than half a century after making the recordings, all of these songs live on in digital music streaming services and still sound vibrant. They're intriguing vestiges from an era when R&B and doo-wop vocal groups were in their prime. It's unclear whether Small sang lead on any of the tracks, but he was certainly at the core of their robust harmonies.

Ron sang with the Fabulous Pearls at Isy's Supper Club in Vancouver in 1959.[4] Two years later, as the Four Pearls, the group performed at Isy's again[5] before disbanding. Being in the quartet was a formative experience for Small, influencing his emerging musicality and bringing him to Canada. Becki L. Ross interviewed Small for her book *Burlesque West: Showgirls, Sex, and Sin in Postwar Vancouver*, and she wrote that he stayed in Vancouver due to a simple reason: falling in love.[6]

Her name was Shirley. Born in 1936 in the village of Herne in southeast England, she moved to Canada in 1952. As a couple and business partners, Ron and Shirley Small would become key to bringing top jazz, blues, and folk artists to intimate venues in the city. Before that happened, Small—known at the time as Ronnie—was a singer and emcee at nightclubs such as the Smilin' Buddha Cabaret at 109 East Hastings Street and the New Delhi Cabaret at 544 Main Street in Chinatown.

The Smilin' Buddha ran ads in the *Vancouver Sun*, and many mentioned Small. One ad from 1966 gave Daiquiri St. John, "The Biggest Name in

Burlesque," top billing. At the bottom of the ad: "Ronnie Small Singing Sensation."[7] Other artists Small performed with included LaWanda Page, who was known as the "Bronze Goddess of Fire" because her act included fire tricks such as lighting cigarettes with her fingertips, and Kay Nelson,[8] sometimes billed as "Hawaiian Lovely."[9]

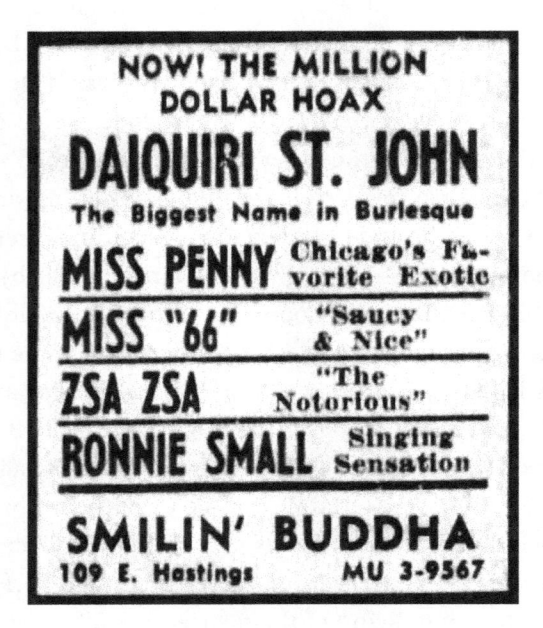

NOW! THE MILLION DOLLAR HOAX

DAIQUIRI ST. JOHN
The Biggest Name in Burlesque

MISS PENNY Chicago's Favorite Exotic

MISS "66" "Saucy & Nice"

ZSA ZSA "The Notorious"

RONNIE SMALL Singing Sensation

SMILIN' BUDDHA
109 E. Hastings   MU 3-9567

Vancouver Sun, October 5, 1966.

Ross' book is a landmark study of the history of erotic entertainment, including burlesque, go-go dancing, and striptease, in Vancouver.[10] Ross quoted Small a number of times in the book, which reflected how his experiences at east end clubs like the Buddha gave him insight into the fascinating social dynamics of a milieu that included burlesque artists/strippers with diverse ethnicity and sexuality, musicians who played jazz and other genres, comedians, club owners and patrons, prostitutes and pimps, drug dealers, and police officers. Those experiences compelled Small to find a way to make his mark in the city's entertainment scene.

The Riverqueen began in June 1968 as a folk coffeehouse at 1043 Davie in Vancouver's West End. It was a small space that started big, with a grand opening featuring Gordon Lightfoot, who by then was a star in Canada and becoming one in the US. Then bluesmen Sonny Terry and Brownie McGhee did an engagement. Later that year, Ron and Shirley Small, along with pianist/organist Mike Taylor, became co-owners and operators of the Riverqueen. They continued the folk and blues programming, while adding jazz and—in a decision that they would come to lament—live theatre.

Small and Taylor performed regularly at the Riverqueen, doing nocturnal sets between midnight and six a.m. as a duo and with other musicians. *Vancouver Sun* jazz critic Bob Smith wrote that Small had a "deep, scooping chocolate milkshake of a voice."[11] Interesting choice of words. *Province* music writer Brian McLeod was less enamoured with Small's voice. "Small is a vocalist with some interesting improvisation inclinations, one who makes up in enthusiasm for what he lacks in resonant expression," wrote McLeod. He also took issue with Small's drumming, which he did at times. "I really don't think Ronnie Small can hack it on drums."[12]

Then Taylor bowed out of co-ownership and the Smalls were the only ones running the Riverqueen, which was also known as Ronnie's Riverqueen or just the Queen. Shirley played a central role, collaborating with Ron on booking performers for the club, working the door, cooking, and serving as a de facto bouncer, among other duties. She was a "hard-nosed Brit and a big woman," said saxophonist Gavin Walker. He recalled one night at the Riverqueen when an inebriated patron tried to get Taylor to play a certain tune. When Taylor didn't oblige, the drunkard crossed the threshold and lunged at drummer Al Wiertz on the bandstand. "Shirley came bounding out of the kitchen," said Walker. "She basically just picked this guy up and threw him out."[13]

Shirley had a boy and two girls from a previous marriage, and she and Small also had a child together, Ronald Jr. According to Walker, Small "doted" on the children,[14] who spent a lot of time at the Riverqueen helping out, eating, and listening to music. In many ways it was an idyllic time for the Small family. But the interracial couple and their kids also faced ugliness. One day on the lawn in front of their Templeton Drive apartment, someone placed what looked like a cross and set it on fire. "There was no doubt about it," said Hackl about the frightening racist message the burning cross sent.[15]

The incident didn't affect their resolve to present important Black artists. On that front, 1969 was a very good year. They brought back Sonny Terry and Brownie McGhee in January, presented Odetta—the folk, blues, jazz, and spirituals singer and a leading light in the civil rights movement—in June and December, and booked the incendiary John Lee Hooker for October. Admission to see Hooker: $2.50. In his glowing review of the show, Bob Smith said he was "regenerated" by the blues singer and electric guitarist, and he added kudos to the proprietors: "Shirley and Ronnie Small are to be complimented on the good feeling aboard the Riverqueen."[16]

Then, about a month after the triumph of Hooker's shows, came a stunning blow. Following a performance of Michael McClure's play *The Beard*, on November 5, 1969 at the Riverqueen, the Smalls and three others were arrested and charged with unlawfully presenting an obscene performance. A capacity crowd, including three plainclothes members of the Vancouver Police Department's morality squad, attended the performance by the Gallimaufry Theatre company. Charged were leading lady Angela Slater, leading man Wayne Robson, Ron, Shirley (described in newspaper accounts as "cashier and ticket-seller"[17]), and Henry Yeager (technical director and lighting operator). "Police trim Beard's run" read the headline for a story in the *Province* about the show's final performances being cancelled due to the charges.[18]

The play revolves around an imagined meeting between movie star Jean Harlow and outlaw Billy the Kid. It was controversial because of numerous expletives in the dialogue and a final scene where oral sex was simulated. After being charged, the Smalls somehow found themselves embroiled in a major examination of obscenity, morals, and censorship—in the courtroom and in the community—for more than three years.

But the legal fracas didn't stop them from presenting vital music. Just five nights after the last performance of *The Beard*, the amazing multi-instrumentalist Rahsaan Roland Kirk—known for often playing several saxophones and other wind instruments simultaneously—began a run at the Riverqueen. Bob Smith was there, and he wrote that Kirk played "fiery, uncompromising music."[19] Also at one of Kirk's performances was seventeen-year-old Ken Pickering. Seeing Kirk was a watershed moment for Pickering. So the Smalls' programming had an indelible influence on the path of a young man who would go on to become artistic director of Vancouver's Coastal Jazz & Blues Society and the city's jazz festival.

In March 1970, the Cannonball Adderley Quintet performed three nights at the Riverqueen. Pianist Bob Murphy led the Riverqueen's house band at the time, and the first Rhodes electric piano Murphy played was the one that Adderley's pianist Joe Zawinul performed on at the club. The shows Adderley, Zawinul, Nat Adderley, Roy McCurdy, and Walter Booker played there, and their interactions off the bandstand with locals, had a significant impact on Murphy, Walker, and others who were present. This was the kind of inspirational influence that a jazz club was meant to have.

There was also disappointment behind the scenes. Plans to present Miles Davis, Charles Lloyd, and Freddie Hubbard fell through. Plus, there was the unavoidable stress and exhaustion of running a club. "I know they worked themselves to death," said Hackl about her parents.[20] Financially, the Riverqueen was a house of cards. "They were weeks behind in paying us," said Murphy. "They would give us a little bit of money. They were scrambling the whole time. I think they just ended up so far behind on so many bills that they just sort of bailed on the club. And then a while later, much to my surprise, they were trying again at the [Old] Cellar."[21]

• • •

In its September/October 1970 issue, *Coda* magazine noted that "the Riverqueen people, Ronnie and Shirley Small, have gained access to what used to be Jazz Alley but renamed the club, The Old Cellar."[22] The basement club also once housed the original Cellar jazz club in the late fifties and early sixties. So it was a big development for Vancouver's jazz scene that the Smalls were reviving the space where Ornette Coleman, Charles Mingus, Art Pepper, and many other American and local jazz musicians played.

Murphy set aside any resentment about being stiffed at the Riverqueen and was in the Old Cellar's first house band, along with his then-wife Joani Taylor on vocals and others. Incredibly, the first big name the Smalls landed for the Old Cellar was none other than Coleman, who performed in early September 1970 at the club with titans of contemporary jazz: Dewey Redman, Charlie Haden, and Ed Blackwell. The second major artist they booked was Herbie Hancock. He played a Rhodes at the Old Cellar, September 28 to October 3, 1970, with an astounding sextet: Eddie Henderson, Julian Priester, Bennie Maupin, Buster Williams, and Billy Hart.

Journeys to the Bandstand

As Hancock recounted in his autobiography, *Possibilities*, before arriving in Vancouver, the musicians had not yet played as a unit. On the afternoon of the first show, Hancock, Williams, and Hart rehearsed in the empty club, while the other three went over the music in the hotel. During that night's first set, the players slowly got into the music and became familiar with each other.[23] Bob Smith caught that seventy-minute set, and he wrote that the three tunes they played "alternately soared, swept or rumbled by" despite some sound issues.[24] As the night went on, and they played Hancock compositions including "Speak Like a Child," the musicians' comfort with each other grew, and the music got freer. It felt like they had played together for a long time. Hancock thought it was one of the most transcendent nights in his career, and after two hours of music, the jazz men looked at each other in amazement about what just transpired.[25]

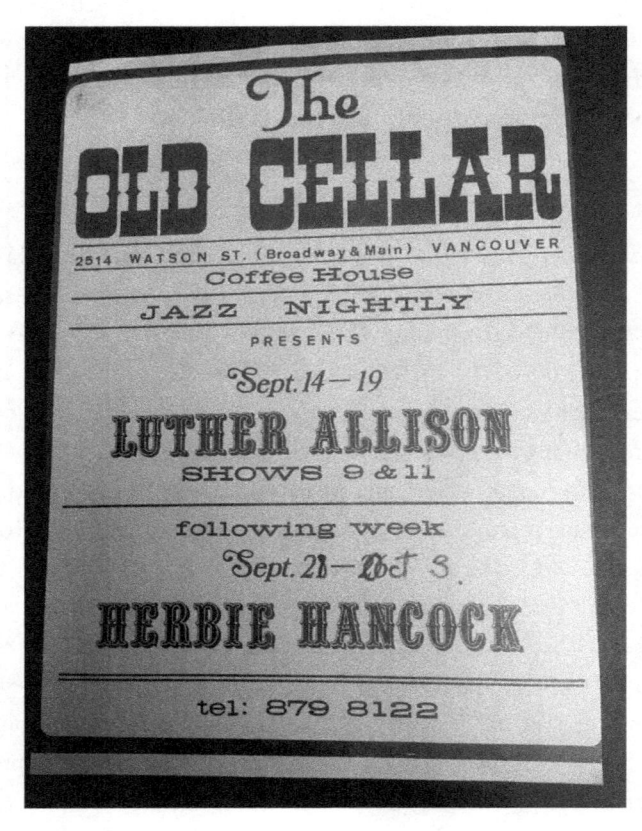

Courtesy Kevin Mooney.

Over the next two years, Hancock and these same musicians would become known as the Mwandishi band and go on to record three influential albums that beautifully and cerebrally melded adventurous avant-garde jazz and funky jazz-rock fusion. It's a little-known fact that the band started in Vancouver at the Smalls' Old Cellar. And Murphy got to open for Hancock and the band, just as he did for Coleman. Thanks to those plum gigs, and the opportunities to hear and meet other artists at the Riverqueen and Old Cellar, Murphy credited his close friend Ron for being instrumental to his growth as a jazz artist. "Ron was kind of responsible for a big part of my jazz education," said Murphy.[26]

Just over two weeks after Hancock's run, American blues-based singer-songwriter and guitarist Tim Williams crossed the border from Blaine, Washington, into Surrey, BC. Williams, who was twenty-two at the time, drove from Los Angeles to Canada to permanently leave the US in protest to the Vietnam War. After arriving in Vancouver, Williams found out that Ramblin' Jack Elliott, a great folk interpreter influenced by Woody Guthrie, would play at the Old Cellar in a few days. One thing led to another, and Williams was suddenly opening for Elliott at the Old Cellar. Then the Smalls booked Williams to perform his own gig the following week.

Williams got to know the Smalls well. What made Ron tick? "He was a highly intelligent man who had a wicked sense of humour," said Williams. "He was a little bit cynical, but there was a sort of joy to him that was like a twelve-year-old boy. He could have a very bawdy sense of humour sometimes, which he took great delight in. I think he enjoyed shocking people with it. And there was always a dignity to him." Above all, Williams saw Ron as a sincere man. "I never saw him do anything mean to people, but I always saw him telling the truth about their talent or their actions." And Shirley? "She was kind of like a den mother. She was extremely kind to me. She always had a million plans, and only some of them worked out."[27]

One plan the Smalls pulled off was bringing the tremendous blues singer and guitarist Johnny Shines—an associate of Robert Johnson—to the Old Cellar in November 1970. Bob Smith was struck by Shines' bottleneck slide guitar technique. "The effect is striking, a kind of dying gliss at phrase's end, like the sight of a lit match travelling through space on a dark night, eventually going out," wrote Smith with a metaphorical flourish.[28] Another plan they carried out: getting the brilliant but ill-fated Tim Buckley to perform at the Old Cellar January 11–16, 1971. Just two months before the gigs, Buckley released *Starsailor*, which had an uncompromising sound incorporating avant-garde jazz and free experimentation that was far from his folk-rock roots. As always, Bob Smith was there, taking in the music with an open mind. "It is reminiscent of how it must feel to hop alternatively right foot then left foot atop warm coals – very interesting, but challenging," he wrote.[29] Buckley died of a drug overdose four year later.

Interestingly, Small rarely booked himself at the Old Cellar, which was also known as the Olde Cellar or Ye Olde Cellar. When he did perform, Small dazzled. "One of the highlights of working in those two clubs [the Riverqueen and the Old Cellar]," said Murphy, "was that every once in a while, Ron would come up and say, 'Hey, can I sing?' And he always killed. He killed back then; he still kills."[30]

From jazz, blues, and folk to the avant-garde, the Smalls' programming at the Old Cellar was diverse, visionary, and a reflection of the times. "That kind of orientation was a smart one because at that time, with the social turbulence and the political changes that were going on, there was a lot of interesting music that was tied together," said John Orysik, Ken Pickering's high school buddy and fellow jazz fanatic who wrote about the Coleman and Shines gigs in *Coda* magazine. "That [music that went together] included jazz, blues, and folk, and a lot of the people that were into [one of] those genres liked the other genres and supported them too. That's why a lot of people would go to an Ornette Coleman concert and then go to a Johnny Shines concert and then go to a Tim Buckley concert. There was a real openness at that time."[31]

While that Catholic spirit defined the Smalls' musical life, a close-minded Puritanism wreaked havoc on them away from the club. On May 28, 1971, Provincial Court Judge Larry Eckardt ruled that the production of *The Beard* staged at the Riverqueen was obscene. Eckardt convicted the Smalls of allowing an obscene performance in their coffeehouse.[32] It was no small irony that a *Vancouver Sun* story on the ruling appeared right next to an ad for the Factory Show Lounge. The Factory, which was across the street from the Riverqueen, offered "Continuous & Dynamic TOPLESS" entertainment . . . The classiest topless show lounge in North America," according to the ad.[33] Just under a month later, Eckardt fined Ron and Shirley $350 each for their convictions.

With support from a defence fund that the arts community donated to, the BC Civil Liberties Association launched an appeal. On January 12, 1972, County Court Judge Graham Ladner set aside the fines but allowed the convictions to stand. *The Beard* wasn't the only problem for the Smalls. The economics of running the Old Cellar were as bleak as the Riverqueen's had been. "I can tell you with absolute certainty they weren't getting rich," said Williams. "I think it was a struggle month to month for them."[34]

The March/April 1972 issue of *Coda* confirmed the inevitable—the Old Cellar was dead. "It would indeed be an understatement to say that this town is starving for the elusive music we have come to know as jazz," wrote Orysik in the magazine. "In view of the fact that there are very few (almost nil) clubs that operate on a jazz policy, it is even more disheartening to report that the Old Cellar has now joined the ranks of the defunct. Economic frustrations (what else?) among other considerations are cited as reasons for closure."[35]

The Smalls were in the news one more time after a ruling on a second appeal related to *The Beard*. On April 12, 1973, the BC Court of Appeal overturned the obscenity convictions in the case. The saga of *The Beard* finally ended for the Smalls.

At one point their relationship was also done. The anxiety of running music venues and the worry from the court cases were hard on them. Plus, there was a fundamental reality that prevented them from continuing as a couple: Small was gay. Hackl said her father wasn't ashamed of who he was, and some people knew his orientation. But he was discreet about his sexuality, and after going through the shock of the burning cross and the ordeal of an obscenity trial, Small read the room. "To him, being a Black man was a strike," said Hackl about Small's view on intolerance in society at the time. "Being gay was a second strike."[36]

• • •

After the Old Cellar's demise, Small decided to move to Toronto. With opportunities diminishing in Vancouver, it made sense for him to relocate to a larger city. But even though he and Shirley were no longer together, it was tough to leave the family. "I remember him coming to me and saying even though he was leaving and going to Toronto he did not want to lose touch with me," said Hackl, who was fourteen when her dad left. Small told her that "he loved me very much and that he was just a phone call away." Despite his absence from her life for long periods, and Small being "damaged" by hardship and struggle, Hackl considered him a good father.[37]

Small pursued and landed acting and singing parts in theatre, TV, and movies. One film he acted in was a 1978 dramatization/documentary, *Fields of Endless Day*, which focused on the history of Black immigration and slavery in Canada. Small showed off his acting chops in a scene where he played a fiery preacher. The whole fifty-eight-minute movie is available on YouTube, and it's an example of a Ron Small artifact that's hidden in plain sight. He also had a leading role in a 1992 theatre production of August Wilson's *Fences*, staged in Ottawa and Calgary. His longest gig was touring in the cast of *Show Boat* for six years in the nineties. Small, who did not know how to read music, affirmed his talent, well-honed instincts, and resilience throughout these years.

In September 1999, I called Small, who had returned to Vancouver the previous year. I wanted to talk to him about a four-night stand—a rarity in the city—that he was about to do at the Cotton Club. But I got his answering machine message, which included a snippet of Small singing "Scandalize My Name," a traditional song that Paul Robeson recorded. "Small sings the tune with a gospel-like fervour," I wrote in the *Vancouver Courier*—my only ever review of an answering machine message. "In fact, his soulful passion left me speechless when it was time to actually leave a message."[38]

I eventually interviewed Small. We talked about what he had been up to with acting, glanced back at the Riverqueen, and looked ahead to the Cotton Club shows where he would perform with Bob Murphy, Ross Taggart, and others. Small had two long sets of material planned for each night, with a focus on songs by Duke Ellington. I didn't ask a single question about the Fabulous Pearls, the Smilin' Buddha, *The Beard*, the racism he encountered, or the Old Cellar because I had zero awareness about these scenes from his life. I wish I could have a do-over on that encounter; I would have probed these and other topics. Instead, I have to be content with knowing that I at least got a glimpse of his persona.

Small gave me an unreleased CD that he recorded at the Cotton Club earlier in 1999. Backed by Murphy and bassist Miles Foxx Hill, Small sounded relaxed and comfortable singing fourteen jazz standards. He sang the first two minutes of "Lush Life" a cappella, which brought into focus how—instead of sounding weary—Small's voice had aged well with a sage quality. Forty-five years after leaving his hometown, he sang "Chicago" with meaningful vigour. On "Come Rain or Come Shine," Small reached emotional heights as he crescendoed at key moments.

In the 2000s, Small performed several times at Cory Weeds' Cellar with Murphy and other musicians, often selling out the club. "He would sing his ass off [at the Cellar]," said Murphy, who was always Small's go-to pianist. "He sang so beautifully."[39] A video posted on YouTube captured Small performing at the Cellar on February 25, 2007. Wearing a tuxedo and white bow tie, he sang "Them There Eyes" with impeccable phrasing and humour. Just over a year later, plans were hatched for live recordings to be made March 7–9, 2008 at the club with Small, Murphy, Tom Keenlyside, and other players. The performances went exceptionally well, but the hard drive containing the recordings—planned for release on Weeds' Cellar Live label—failed, and all of the music was irretrievably and heartbreakingly lost. It was a devastating turn of events for Small, who never ended up releasing an album as a leader.

Marcus Mosley, Bob Murphy, Jim Byrnes, Ron Small, and Will Sanders, the Cellar, circa 2007. Photographer unknown.

Ron Small, the Cellar, March 7, 2008. Photo by Steve Mynett.

Julie Brown's close friendship with Small began when Brown asked actor and original member of a cappella group the Nylons, Denis Simpson, if he could recommend a vocal coach for her to study with. Simpson said he knew the perfect person—Ron Small—but added a caveat: "This is not an easy guy. He has a chip on his shoulder the size of Manhattan." Brown wasn't deterred and went to Jazz Vespers at St. Andrew's Wesley Church to hear Small perform with Murphy. Brown's reaction to Small's singing: "The minute he opened his mouth, I went, 'Oh my God, why has he been such a secret? This guy is phenomenal. He should be in New York.'"[40]

Small became her mentor, and he came as advertised—unequivocally forthright about Brown's singing and how she could improve. Brown knew some other singers who tried lessons with Small and ditched him. "They never went back because they couldn't handle what they called his negativity. But his negativity was his honesty, and you had to get below your ego to understand the man is trying to help," said Brown. "He's not going to say nice cute little things. He already knows what you do well. Now he is trying to get you to break through."[41]

His strictures weren't just about singing. "I remember I did a gig and Ron came, and I think I was wearing jeans and a blouse," said Monique Van Dam, a singer who was Murphy's partner and Small's friend. "He was like, 'What's this about?' He was pissed at me. He was like, 'Why aren't you dressed up?' That was really a big deal to him. Ron was a fantastic dresser."[42]

Small's elegance, however, didn't reflect material wealth. When Brown met Small, he was living in an apartment on Victoria Drive in East Vancouver. The apartment was above a dentist's office, and Small struck a deal where he paid low rent in exchange for cleaning the office. Being poor was an unavoidable reality for Small, especially given his unyielding approach that sometimes hurt not just feelings but also his livelihood.

Brown was a member of Good Noise Vancouver Gospel Choir, co-founded by Texas-born Marcus Mosley and Gail Suderman in 2004. Mosley was "blown away" the first time he heard Small perform. "The man had one of the most exquisite tenor jazz voices I could think of, and his phrasing and his understanding of how to deliver a song were stellar," said Mosley about his immediate impressions. Case in point: Small's rendition of "Angel Eyes" that night. "It was like a master class listening to him deliver that classic song."

Mosley and Suderman invited Small to join the choir, which he was initially reluctant to do. Small saw himself as a jazz singer, and he wasn't a religious man. Small also wasn't physically well at the time. But the choir directors, Brown, and others encouraged Small to join, so he did, becoming a key soloist with the choir. Someone posted on Soundcloud a rehearsal recording from 2005 of Small singing lead on "Since I Met Jesus." For more than two minutes, Small sang with just piano accompaniment from Suderman, and his pure voice powerfully soared. After the choir joined in, Small elevated the intensity even more. He masterfully demonstrated his command of *passaggio*—seamlessly transitioning his voice, in the moment, to a higher register—and gloriously sustained pivotal notes. "It would just make the hair stand up on the back of your neck when he was vocalizing," said Mosley.[43] Choir members embraced Small, whose health improved as he became a much-loved elder statesman with Good Noise.

Then singer and guitarist Jim Byrnes decided to record an album that emphasized gospel music. Byrnes wanted to record with a true gospel vocal group, and he thought of getting the renowned Soul Stirrers. After that plan didn't come to fruition, he turned to Mosley, who recruited Small and another choir member Will Sanders to join him in singing with Byrnes. The resulting 2006 album produced by guitarist Steve Dawson, *House of Refuge*, resonated strongly with vigorous contributions from the singers and won a Juno Award. That led to them forming the Sojourners, which was the name Byrnes had called the vocalists.

The Sojourners' debut album, *Hold On*, came out in 2007. Also produced by Dawson, the recording features the trio's glorious vocal harmonies in the tradition of heavenly gospel groups like the Blind Boys of Alabama, the Soul Stirrers, the Swan Silvertones, and the Dixie Hummingbirds. In June 2007, when the group performed with Byrnes in an opening set for the Blind Boys, and almost exactly a year later when the Sojourners opened for the Dixie Hummingbirds, it was an honour for Mosley, Sanders, and Small to be billed together with progenitors of traditional Black gospel.

When the Sojourners worked on their music, Small would use his highly attuned musical ear to find "fine points" that would "shape the Sojourners' sound," said Sanders.[44] Mosley concurred. "Pop [Mosley's nickname for Small] was the architect of the Sojourners' sound," he said. "He was the one that listed all of the different components and elements and brought it together."[45] In other words, Small was essentially the Sojourners' arranger. "We would all put in ideas," said Mosley, "but Ron was the final authority on how to do the harmonies, who would sing what range in what we would call the stack [the bottom, middle, and top of their vocal harmonies]." One day at rehearsal Small paused, got emotional, and thanked Mosley and Sanders for collaborating with him. Mosley: "I guess he never felt recognized [in the past] for his ear, his sense of musicality, and [Small's talent for knowing] how to bring voices together."[46]

Offstage and away from rehearsal rooms, these were halcyon days for Small and fellow American expatriate, Vancouver-based, Black singers like Mosley, Sanders, Lovie Eli, and Sibel Thrasher. They would get together to play cards and dominoes, eat delicious soul food, and tell stories from their long careers in show business. At these gatherings, Small "could be very, very charming and be very delightful to be around when he was in a really great mood," recalled Mosley. Small could also be triggered and flash his temper.

"You had to kind of watch what you said around him sometimes because it would set him off and then he would not mince words."[47]

Tommy Babin (bass) and the Sojourners: Marcus Mosley, Ron Small, and Will Sanders, February 2008. Photographer unknown. Courtesy Kathy Campbell.

Small had that rare personality type of someone who was completely unselfconscious about expressing his honest feelings and wishes, whether they were harmonious like the Sojourners' voices or discordant. On a European tour with Byrnes and the Sojourners, they were in a car halfway to their destination when Small suddenly announced that he forgot his beloved red shoes in the hotel they were staying at. He stubbornly insisted that they had to double back and retrieve the shoes. Small was serious; the others wanted to keep going. It was only resolved that they would take the highway and not Small's way when their manager Kathy Campbell promised to arrange for the hotel to send the shoes to the next tour stop.

Mosley said Small "was very well known for going off on the rhythm section" if the musicians didn't keep what he considered a steady tempo. "He would get outright belligerent if the tempo varied." Near the end of an outdoor performance in the Netherlands attended by about 5,000 people, Small had a mic drop moment. After something upset him, he emphatically dropped his mic, left the stage, and went to the hotel where the Sojourners were staying, recounted Mosley. Another scene Mosley witnessed: in Belgium during a sound check, Small "screamed at the sound man, 'Get the shit right!'"[48] As Hackl explained, "My dad was blunt and only spoke the truth, or he said nothing at all."[49]

• • •

In January 2010, the Sojourners' self-titled second album came out. The sophomore recording goes even further than their first release in capturing the intensity of raw gospel. At the album's midpoint, Small sings lead on a classic gospel hymn, which Elvis Presley recorded: "Lead Me, Guide Me." With minimal backing from Dawson on electric tremolo guitar, Small opens with a stirring solo:

> I am tired and I need thy strength and power
> To help me over my weakest hour
> Let me through the darkness thou face to see
> Lead me, O Lord lead me

The words he sang with such feeling mirrored real life. "He would say little things here and there from his past, but he wouldn't talk a lot about the details," said Mosley. "But I got the sense he had been very, very wounded, and music and singing were his release from that."

Two months after the album release, the Sojourners were among the artists who performed in a pair of extraordinary concerts that were part of the Cultural Olympiad accompanying the 2010 Winter Olympics. The shows held March 12–13, 2010, at the Capilano Performing Arts Theatre, paid tribute to the Mississippi Sheiks: a sublime string and vocal group from the 1930s that had elements of Delta blues, jazz, and country in their influential music.

The Sojourners also contributed to a tremendous 2009 tribute album to the Mississippi Sheiks—*Things About Comin' My Way*—that Dawson and his wife Alice dreamed up and coordinated. For the album produced by Dawson in various studios, the trio expressively harmonized the lyrics to "He Calls That Religion," about a preacher with dubious morality. In the

2010 concerts, the Sojourners were equally resonant on "Sweet Maggie." I doubt anyone cared that Small got a few words wrong during an excellent solo on the tune. His behaviour before the first show, however, was disquieting. Small wanted a large number of comps for friends; Kathy Campbell informed Small that wouldn't be possible with the sold-out concert, which angered him. When it was time for the group to do a soundcheck, Small was nowhere to be found. Mosley said Small arrived about two hours late, "scowling at Kathy as he walked past her and to the stage, and he did it all for show. He did it all to make a point."[50]

Steve Dawson (National Tricone guitar) and the Sojourners: Will Sanders, Ron Small, and Marcus Mosley, release party for Things About Comin' My Way, 2009. Photo by Kathy Campbell.

Although no one realized it at the time, a concert in March 2010 in Ghent, Belgium, was Small's last full performance as a Sojourner. In June 2010, when the Sojourners celebrated the release of their second album with a concert at St. James Hall, Small wasn't on stage. Khari Wendell McClelland subbed for Small. Sanders revealed why in an interview before the show. "He [Small] went through a major, major surgery, and he got through it," said Sanders. "He's doing much better now. He's on the mend. He has a real strong constitution, so we're not worried about him coming back."[51]

Small had a life-threatening condition—"his bowels burst," said Hackl[52]—that required surgery and kept him in hospital for about two months. After being discharged, Small's recovery continued, and he wanted to eventually return to the Sojourners. But McClelland became Small's permanent replacement. Small's time with the Sojourners was over. "I think in one way it just destroyed him," said Hackl about her father's exit from the group, which she characterized as a dismissal.[53]

Mosley categorically denied that Small was kicked out of the group. Mosley said Small's departure from the Sojourners went down like this: Small's recuperation took some time, and while recovering, his voice was raspy, which prevented him from singing. Mosley and Sanders came up with the idea of having Small continue to coach the Sojourners and receive an income for that, while bringing McClelland in so they could keep functioning as a working group. Mosley and Sanders also saw the possibility that after Small was strong enough to sing again, McClelland could stay with the Sojourners as a "fourth voice, which would free us up to have a lead singer and tight three-part harmony behind." According to Mosley, Small wasn't at all receptive to these ideas. "He thought we were trying to nudge him out of the group, and we were doing just the opposite," said Mosley. "We were trying to make certain that he was being taken care of."[54]

September 19, 2010. Small sang one final time with the Sojourners—including McClelland—on one song during a Vancouver gospel cruise on the Queen of Diamonds. Regardless of the circumstances behind Small's exit from the Sojourners, this much is clear: being a Sojourner was enormously important to him. Despite that, Small suddenly moved to Toronto without telling many people in Vancouver—including Mosley and Sanders—effectively ending his tenure in the group.

In 2012, I started searching for Small. His phone number and address were listed in the 2011 Vancouver Musicians' Association Directory, but the number was out of service. I didn't know at the time that Small had moved to Toronto, but eventually I got a number for him there. The number worked, but no one picked up. I kept trying it without any luck. I also didn't know that in March 2011, Hackl had brought her ailing dad to Wahnapitae just outside Sudbury—where she lived on a hobby farm with her mom, Small's ex Shirley. In ill-health, he would live in Wahnapitae and Toronto during his final years.

The second Sojourners' album, which Small sang on, was nominated for a 2011 Juno Award in the best blues album category. Mosley, Sanders, and McClelland performed in Toronto at Hugh's Room as part of the festivities. Small was invited to the gig, but he didn't show up. Then they met Small outside of the award ceremony and briefly talked. "He showed up and then disappeared, and I never saw him again," said Mosley.[55]

More than seven years later, in October 2018, Sanders told me it had been years since he had talked to Small. Sanders had heard that Small was in a Toronto hospice.[56] Just over one week later, I saw this Facebook post from Dawson: "Sorry to hear about the passing of the mighty Ron Small. I got to know Ron pretty well working on albums for the Sojourners, James Byrnes and at countless gigs and festivals over the years. I learned a lot from him in our times together. He was very set in his ways, but those ways were rooted in deep gospel and jazz music, and he always wanted the music to be right. I respected him for that. We had lots of laughs and talked about cool music often. He'll be missed."[57]

When Mosley heard the news, he was "sad that the amazing gift [of Small's voice and spirit] was gone from the earth," but he was also relieved to hear people who loved Small were with him when he died, at the age of eighty. Mosley wistfully remembered how the Sojourners used to talk about how they would vocalize side-by-side eternally. That they were "going to be coming with our walkers up on stage to sing our songs. We envisioned singing together forever."[58]

Many people, including those who sang with Small in the Good Noise Vancouver Gospel Choir, posted tributes to him on Facebook. One of them was Clifton Murray, a member of The Tenors vocal group, who wrote a moving farewell that recognized Small's "magical voice" and his role in Murray's gospel education. "My friend and a music mentor Ron Small has passed on to the great choir in the sky. Although I knew him for a short while, he strongly influenced my approach to music and the meaning I put into it . . . This world treats you mean Ron Small, but you turned it into crushed velvet and gold. Rest In Peace. May god bless and keep you always."[59]

When Murray wrote "the world treats you mean Ron Small," he was referencing the traditional spiritual "Sweet Little Jesus Boy," which Small soloed on every Christmas with the Good Noise Choir. There's a key moment on a recording of the choir rehearsing the song at a slow tempo. The choir and drummer stop, and Small—accompanied just by the pianist—sings the age-old lyrics with an astonishing and unforgettable spirit:

The world treats You mean, Lord
Treats me mean too
But that's how things are down here with me
We didn't know it was You

Hackl followed her father's only wish and took his ashes home to Chicago, placing them by his mother's final resting place. As for Hackl's mother, who was so important in Small's life and career—"My mom is the only woman that he loved," she said[60]—Shirley died in November 2020.

After hearing about Small's passing, and then learning about his deep artistry and complex character from Collette Hackl, Julie Brown, Marcus Mosley, and others, I reflected on why I spent years resolutely digging for information and obsessively searching for insights about the man who had become a spectre in my life. While his artistic accomplishments inspired me to share his untold story, I also found the indications of his prickly nature unsettling. For a long time, I couldn't reconcile the two sides to Small. Then I had an epiphany: I was fascinated with Small precisely because he was both a great, gifted artist who strove for perfection, and also an imperfect being who at times "let his demons get the best of him," as Mosley put it.[61] Those aspects weren't mutually exclusive. They were the overlapping circles of his life's Venn diagram, which I was determined to decode.

About six months after Small passed away, about forty people gathered in a Vancouver community centre to celebrate his life. Mosley, Sanders, Brown, Murray, a former neighbour who witnessed the cross burning, Small's prize student Haisla Collins, and others were there to pay tribute to their fellow artist, mentor, and friend in words and song.

The man they lovingly described sounded very consistent with the person I got to know after years of tracing his life story. Small's immense impact as a performer and teacher, how he didn't suffer fools, how he could exasperate, his heavenly voice—the speakers covered all of this in their tender homages. They had a clear consensus about Small's essence because although he was a private person, his beliefs, opinions, and his very way of being were transparent. Ron Small was truly an honest man, and when he sang, it was a heartfelt expression of his extraordinary life, the likes of which we'll never see again.

12 / DEEP CONNECTION: BOB MURPHY

IN THE UNITARIAN Church of Vancouver's sanctuary, brightly illuminated with natural light, people filled every pew. They kept arriving until both the sanctuary and vestibule were full. Those who were there quietly gathered and made space for each other to celebrate the extraordinary life of a partner, brother, father, grandfather, friend, musical colleague, and mentor: Bob Murphy.

Emotions were raw. Murphy passed away only a week before, on October 22, 2015, far too young at seventy. Unlike the death of his close friend and collaborator Ross Taggart, who died in 2013 just weeks after his terminal diagnosis was made public, Murphy left this realm unexpectedly. There was a shock of sudden loss when the sad news spread through the jazz community. Coming to terms with his departure would take time, and this day was an important part of the healing process.

"He was a very loved man, very loved by his family and by his friends," said Murphy's sister Margo more than five years after the celebration of life.[1] She was listed as a speaker in the program for Murphy's wake, but Margo was too emotional to say anything on that day of both sorrow and fond remembrance.

Few in the church had ever known a Vancouver jazz scene without Murphy. He contributed so much to the scene as a pianist, organist, composer, and teacher for about half a century. Several of the Vancouver musicians he was closest to—Tom Keenlyside, Hugh Fraser, and Campbell Ryga—spoke that day about Murphy's musicality, compassion, dark humour, zest for life, and much more. Plus, they and others performed beautifully in his honour. "What a massive legacy this man left in a lot of different ways," said Keenlyside.[2]

About forty-six years earlier, Murphy performed in the same spiritual space. On April 13, 1969, the then twenty-three-year-old Murphy played a concert in the Unitarian church with guitarist Terry Frewer, bassist Jon Washburn, and drummer Al Wiertz. "Frewer, Murphy: Big names-to-be," read the headline in the *Province* the day after the show. A full-length review reported on the "latest chapter in young jazz" and focused on Murphy and Frewer, "two talented and serious young jazz-modern music players." On Murphy: "He is fast, proficient, progressive in a funky way, and soulful," wrote Brian McLeod. "Instead of copping all the old tunes, riffs and general leftovers from the legacy of jazz piano, Murphy has incorporated a Jimmy Smith R-and-B organ thing into the piano and added his own technical mastery in the high right hand. Every time I catch one of his gigs he gets faster."[3]

I thought a lot about the connection between the heartfelt sentiments of love and admiration at the gathering for Murphy and this forgotten review that documented the extraordinary promise of young musicians. Murphy fully realized that promise, becoming one of Canada's finest jazz pianists. Along the way, he nurtured an astonishing number of relationships, both musical and personal. That's what it was all about for him—making the deep connection that led to transcendent music.

• • •

Dalton Murphy and Margaret Walker married in 1941 in Vanderhoof, near the geographic centre of BC. Four years later, on May 28, 1945, their son Robert was born in Vancouver. As per family tradition, Rob, as he was called in the family, was given the middle name "Neil" that his father, grandfather, and uncle shared.

Dalton's vocation was accounting, but his passion was music. He was a multi-instrumentalist and singer who had a minor role in one of Vancouver music history's most endearing success stories. Elizabeth Clarke was a nurse at Crippled Children's Hospital in Vancouver who was inspired to write a song after seeing a sparrow perch on the windowsill near a patient's bed.

213

Initially, she sang "(There's A) Bluebird On Your Windowsill" only to patients. Then Clarke was invited to sing it on CKNW radio.

Seeing the positive response to the song, Clarke paid for Vancouver's Aragon Records to record and release her composition in 1948.[4] Aragon, run by radio and recording pioneer Al Reusch, found someone to sing and play guitar for a seventy-eight RPM single, with "Bluebird On Your Windowsill" on side A and Paul Robeson's "Ma Curly Headed Baby" on side B. It was Don Murphy,[5] a pseudonym for Dalton Murphy. His version of "Bluebird On Your Windowsill" also came out on Savoy Records in the US. The song would be a hit several times over, covered by Doris Day, Tex Williams, Wilf Carter, Stompin' Tom Connors, and others. In 1950, Aragon released two more songs featuring Don Murphy: "Jasper Lullaby" and "(When It's Summer) In Green Gables."[6]

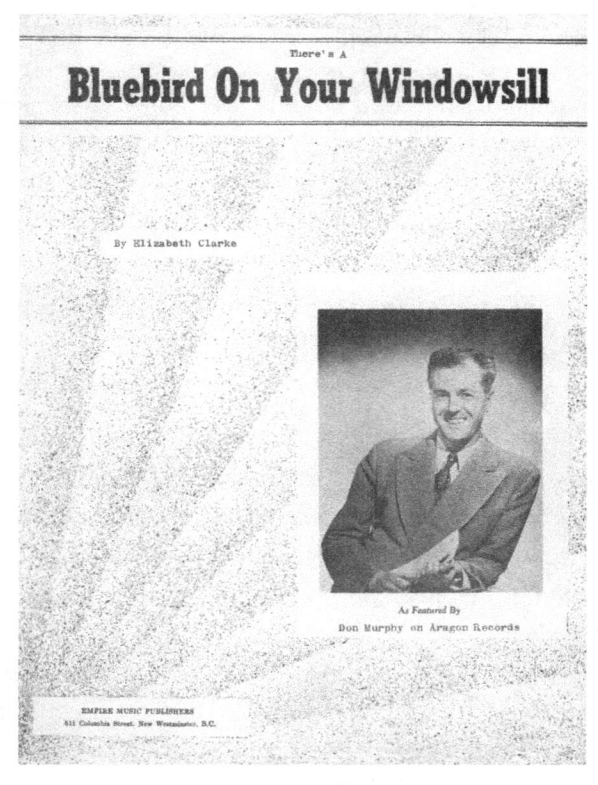

Sheet music for "(There's A) Bluebird On Your Windowsill", courtesy York University Libraries, Clara Thomas Archives & Special Collections.[7]

Dalton aspired to become a full-time professional musician, but his music career didn't advance much beyond the Aragon recordings, so he chose the more practical path of number crunching. Music, however, was still ever-present in the Murphy household: Dalton sang and played instruments, and Margaret sang along at gatherings in their home on Maple Street in Vancouver's Kerrisdale neighbourhood. They also had a summer place in Sechelt on BC's Sunshine Coast, where the animal-loving Murphy befriended snakes, lizards, and winged creatures. "He cared for birds that had been hurt," said Margo. "He'd take them into the basement and help them heal. He was very caring."[8]

By age five, Murphy was taking his first piano lessons from his father. As he progressed, Murphy studied classical piano with Vera Radcliffe and other teachers throughout the 1950s and into the 1960s. At one point, he initiated the conversation that many kids have with their parents about dropping piano lessons. Dalton said that was fine; his mother, however, shut down the idea. As recounted by Margo, who overheard the conversation, Margaret told her son: "'You're not a quitter. Murphys aren't quitters. You're not going to stop.'"[9]

It was a pivotal moment. Continuing with classical lessons helped shape Murphy's playing and kept him engaged in the lifelong discipline of mastering his instrument. At the same time, he learned the rudiments of jazz from his father, along with boogie woogie and other styles. That led to another turning point in 1959: his first professional gig, at the Smilin' Buddha Cabaret on East Hastings Street. Murphy was fourteen.

Years before it became a notorious punk rock haven, the Smilin' Buddha opened six nights a week from about nine p.m. to four a.m., featuring an orchestra that played dance music and main performers. The afternoon of the gig, Murphy went to a rehearsal with the band and "some guy" who appeared to be the star of the show. "That night we started off with a dance set, and then the band leader counted in the music we had rehearsed that afternoon," wrote Murphy on his website. "The guy we had rehearsed with was nowhere in sight. Instead, a very exotically dressed woman came out from behind some curtains and started to dance. She proceeded to take her clothes off until she was down to bra, g-string, and high heels ..... and then she took off her wig and her bra ..... surprise! .... no tits! .... and, of all things, it was the guy from the rehearsal. I thought it was a comedy act. My career in the music business was launched."[10]

As an unlicensed "bottle club," where patrons surreptitiously brought in booze to get around draconian liquor laws, it was legal for Murphy to work at the Buddha. He also had his parents' blessing to perform there and at other clubs. They supported his growing desire to play music for a living. When Murphy was in junior high school, his parents built a music room in the house. "He practiced all the time. He always had people over, and they were playing music," said Margo.[11]

In senior high at Magee Secondary, he played trumpet in a school band until the ineffectual music teacher kicked him out of music class. "I was part of a group that was fairly disenchanted with what was going on," said Murphy. "One day I finally expressed it in a way that upset him."[12] His mom arranged for Murphy to change schools for grade twelve, transferring him to Prince of Wales Secondary, which had a better music program and where she was a teacher. PW was also where Murphy met Bob Turner, a budding bass player who would become a close pal and key musical co-conspirator.

Turner said he bonded with Murphy because they shared a love for jazz and both were "bored with the status quo." They fantasized about moving to Toronto to attend Oscar Peterson's Advanced School of Contemporary Music together. "Oscar Peterson at that point was the role model for us, to be replaced shortly afterwards by Bill Evans," said Turner. They didn't fulfill the dream. Instead, Murphy became a music student at the University of British Columbia, where classical music was taught. "He signed up for first year, hated it, came over to my place every day, hung out, and we played," said Turner. "And then the chicken came home to roost when he got his non-grades at the end of the year."[13]

Classes and practices were all well and good, but what the Bobs really aspired to was the rush of playing gigs. "When I started playing gigs as a young teenager, it was easy to find work," said Murphy. "And as I got a little older, by the time I was in my late teens and out of high school, I was working all the time. It was like there were gigs on every street corner." At the corner of Main and Keefer in Chinatown, Murphy played at the New Delhi Cabaret, where one night the whole band dropped acid before playing "Sophisticated Lady" for a stripper's routine. Murphy could see his hands moving on the organ but otherwise lost all sensory perception. Aside from that hallucinatory experience, he played rock, R&B, country, jazz, and other genres at weddings, dances, bowling banquets (yes, that was a thing), bar mitzvahs, and other functions. "I loved it," he said of that time.[14]

When not playing, Murphy relished listening to live jazz at the original Cellar, the Black Spot, Java Jazz, Flat Five, and other Vancouver venues. "When I first started going to these places, I was a teenager, and it was a big thrill for me," he said. "It all seemed exotic to walk into a place like that, see a bunch of musicians playing, and drink coffee and smoke cigarettes."[15]

Cue Joani Taylor. She's another jazz artist who started performing at a young age. Her first professional gig was at the El Mocambo ballroom in Burnaby when she was fifteen. A chance encounter that her father had at the Espresso Coffee House, a downtown jazz venue, profoundly impacted Taylor's life. "He was there in the afternoon one day, and these two guys were sitting next to him talking about that they needed a singer," said Taylor. "My dad turned around and said, 'My daughter's a singer.'" The two guys were Murphy and Turner. "And I remember my dad saying, 'Well, this guy [Murphy] is coming to get you, and you're going to go to a rehearsal,'" recalled Taylor. "I said, 'So now you're picking my boyfriends? He's probably driving his mother's car, and he wears glasses.' He came to the door with horn-rimmed glasses, and he drove his mother's Volvo."[16]

Murphy and Turner were in the J.B. Trio, a group with drummer John Le Marquand. Taylor joined the band, which gigged at the Pillar and Post, the Vancouver Lawn Tennis Club, and other spots. Even with the addition of Taylor, the band name held true: "J" stood for John and Joani, and "B," the two Bobs. Off the bandstand, Murphy and Taylor fell intensely in love and got married in February 1968. Murphy was twenty-two, and Taylor was twenty-one. Young and talented, the prime of their careers lay far ahead; personal breakthroughs in developing a jazz sound were gestating.

Vancouver supper clubs were important sources of gigs for jazz musicians. For those with the sight-reading skills to back name artists after minimal or no rehearsal, the clubs were a steady source of income. Murphy landed a plum gig as the pianist and organist in the Isy's Supper Club house band, led then by trumpeter Bobby Herriott. Typically, they played four sets a night: two dance sets, and two show sets with the featured performers. Between

Isy's and shows Murphy played at the Cave, he shared the stage with stars like Chuck Berry and Dusty Springfield. Some shows were more demanding than others. One night at Isy's, the pianist in vibraphonist Lionel Hampton's quintet was delayed in transit, so Murphy filled in on short notice.[17] Every night was a blast in large part because the musicians on the bandstand were larger-than-life characters with wicked humour. "They were a pretty crazy bunch," said Murphy. "It was a party every night, drinking and yahooing."[18]

For all the good times, Murphy's memory of Vancouver clubs in the sixties and seventies was unvarnished and clear-eyed. "In those days, all the clubs were always filled with smoke. And whether they served alcohol or not, there was always alcohol in there. If they didn't serve alcohol, people brought it [in under the table]. Drinking was a different thing in those days. Drinking and driving was a different thing in those days. Back then if they emptied the ashtrays and swept the floor, the place was tidy. If we walked into a club from that era nowadays, we'd probably turn around and run out. The Cave and Isy's were just dumps, but they were tarted up to not look like dumps."[19] Regardless of how he felt about the clubs, playing in them paid the bills. Murphy was making more money than his mother, who then worked for the Vancouver School Board.

Bob Murphy, circa 1968. Photographer unknown.
Source: Vancouver Sun (Postmedia Network Inc.).

The *Vancouver Sun* published a three-page spread that recognized twenty-two people (and Skana the whale) who stood out in 1968. Murphy and Taylor were the only artists featured in the "Pop Music" category. Next to a headshot of twenty-three-year-old Murphy with a healthy head of hair and those horn-rimmed glasses, the write-up said he made the list "because he knows today's pop music ingredients instinctively [proven by his position at Isy's] and is rapidly becoming oriented in the stronger antecedent, jazz."[20]

While Murphy reached this level of recognition largely through his own independent study and practice, he also absorbed wisdom from outstanding teachers. In his late teens, he studied jazz piano with Lloyd Abrams, a local teaching legend. Later, he took lessons with the masterful multi-instrumentalist and original Cellar regular Don Thompson. Perhaps if Murphy had emerged a decade or two later, he would have studied in a college or university jazz program. But he never took that route. Murphy developed an individual style on his own the hard way: practicing alone, playing in smaller jazz-focused clubs, listening to and learning from other musicians, experimenting, and reflecting on his purpose in music and life.

Among the jazz clubs Murphy played in during this period were the Riverqueen on Davie Street and Jazz Alley, which was in the basement space that once housed the original Cellar. At Jazz Alley, Murphy was part of the politically incorrectly named band Greta Poontang. With various personnel, including Turner and guitarist Henry Young, the group played experimental fusion.[21] After the Alley closed and the Old Cellar opened in the same subterranean space in 1970, Taylor, Murphy, Wayne Kozak, and Tommy Doran played as the new venue's house band. "We were playing pretty free stuff," said Murphy. "Quite out there."[22] Not long after, Murphy had the rare honour of opening for Ornette Coleman (with a supergroup including Dewey Redman, Charlie Haden, and Ed Blackwell), and then Herbie Hancock (with his Mwandishi band) at the Old Cellar.

It was galvanizing for Murphy to open for these jazz geniuses and hear their monumental music in an intimate club. But getting these dream gigs didn't magically elevate Murphy's career or enable him to let up his near constant playing. The nightly grind of being a working musician, and one with ambitions to craft original music, continued. Plus, he still had the challenge of wrestling—with help—his ridiculously heavy Hammond B3 organ down and back up the stairs at the Old Cellar, on the treacherous fire escape outside the multi-floor Oil Can Harry's at 752 Thurlow, and in and out of other venues.

At one point Murphy and Taylor lived in a three-storey shared house with other jazz musicians and their partners in Vancouver's Kitsilano neighbourhood. Drummer Al Wiertz and his partner were on the ground floor, Murphy and Taylor were on the middle storey, and pianist Ron Johnston and his partner were at the top. I imagine it was a fun house with epic jam sessions and domestic dramas. Unfortunately, the good times as a couple didn't last for Murphy and Taylor. Their marriage ended, but they got through the emotional pain and remained friends and musical collaborators. Maintaining their connection would pay artistic dividends years later.

• • •

In 1975, the Vancouver Jazz Society led by Brian Nation started presenting creative contemporary jazz concerts, performed by acclaimed musicians from the US, South Africa, and Vancouver. The sixth VJS concert, on May 20, 1976, featured Murphy playing seventy-five minutes of fully improvised solo piano at the Western Front. Listening to the entire performance recorded that night and kept unreleased in archives, it's striking how long parts of it were completely dissimilar from the melodic and contemplative style that Murphy became known for. Cannonball runs of notes at breakneck speed and thunderous chords in burst mode crescendo into maelstroms that have much more in common with the anarchic dissonance of Vancouver pianist Al Neil than with the impressionism of one of Murphy's primary influences, Bill Evans. But there are ruminative moments in the concert where elements that became his hallmarks as an improviser shine through—Murphy's sustained flow and his impeccable intuition for when to accentuate the space between the notes.

"People either loved Bob or hated him back in those days," said Taylor. "He'd get inside the piano and bang on the strings, and sometimes he'd put his feet up on the keyboard."[23] As he entered his thirties, Murphy embraced freedom while also developing his essential, melodic sound.

Murphy's next VJS show came about in the most grassroots way possible: a long-distance cold call. Nation knew from reading *The New Yorker* that Lee

Konitz had a regular Monday night gig at the Village Vanguard. So, in a bold move, Nation called the Vanguard roughly in sync with a set break and, after several tries, got Konitz on the phone. Nation proposed presenting Konitz in Vancouver, and the alto saxophonist not only said yes in a subsequent call, he also committed to bringing along tenor saxophonist Warne Marsh. This was a huge coup for Nation and the Vancouver jazz community because Konitz and Marsh, who both studied and recorded with "cool jazz" visionary Lennie Tristano, were important artists who hadn't performed together in years. Nation chose Murphy, Torben Oxbol, and Blaine Wikjord to serve as the local rhythm section for the shows, March 9–12, 1977, but when Wikjord pulled out George Ursan got the gigs.[24]

The four-night stand was also significant because it launched a new venue: the Vancouver Jazz Society Auditorium, at 2611 West 4th. For the new hall, Nation managed to acquire the Yamaha grand piano that jazz virtuosos—Ahmad Jamal, McCoy Tyner, and Cecil Taylor, among many others—played at Oil Can Harry's before the club closed and went into receivership. So that was the sanctified instrument Murphy played for the shows that cost five-dollars to get in. Nation said Murphy and Oxbol made positive impressions on the sax icons. "Konitz and Marsh loved them, loved both their playing, but didn't like the drummer," said Nation.[25] Marke Andrews' *Vancouver Sun* review confirmed Nation's appraisal: "Murphy sparkled at the piano, soloing and comping with graceful ease. Oxbol maintained his usually high standard on bass, adventurous, creative and tasteful."[26]

There was more to the story. Saxophonist and jazz fan Gavin Walker was there for two of the shows, including opening night when he witnessed the following:

> Bob played his usual inventive solos and approached each tune with energy. He backed Konitz well and Lee, of course, delivered and seemed to like Murphy's comping and responded to it. Marsh soon delivered his wishes after a few of the opening night tunes that Murphy lay out during his solos. It actually was a nice contrast and as Marsh's solos were more abstract and delivered with his austere tone, it worked musically.[27]

So Marsh didn't feel Murphy's comping meshed well with the saxophonist's improv. Murphy could have taken that as a slight, but I think he was savvy enough to understand that visiting artists and local rhythm section players sometimes don't click. There's a grainy black and white photo of Murphy, Konitz, and Marsh sitting at a messy table, filled with backstage bric-a-brac. The very seventies image conveys what must have been an exciting experience for Murphy, who would have drawn on his musicality and self-belief to substantively contribute and feel good about his contributions. The shows were also historic—Konitz and Marsh would only perform together one more time, in Edmonton, the night after the last Vancouver show.

Murphy went from performing mostly standards with two sax masters to something completely different for one more VJS happening. Murphy and Wiertz approached Nation about playing in the jazz society's hall when concerts weren't booked. Nation said yes, and they put in motion something bigger than a piano-drums duo, which was a rarely heard format they performed in at Oil Can Harry's and elsewhere. For several weeks in June 1977, they played alongside improvising modern dancers, including Murphy's second wife Carol. "I think there were maybe half a dozen or ten dancers that showed up every night," said Nation about the performances, which were open to the public. "It was amazing." As for the music, it was "right out there. It was totally improvised, free-form duos and sometimes trios. [Alto saxophonist] Dick Smith would sit in with them." During a break one night, Smith admitted to Nation: "God, I hate this shit."[28] Nation in fact loved it, as did Murphy, Wiertz, and the dancers.

The bond between the pianist and drummer exemplified the depth of musical alliances and friendships that Murphy made. Playing live, recording, hanging out, and living together meant Murphy and Wiertz were like brothers. Wiertz was a tremendous drummer, whose volcanic energy erupted on the bandstand. He also had a reputation for playing loud that turned some people off, like Andreas Nothiger, the proprietor of the Classical Joint in Gastown where Murphy and Wiertz often played together. Murphy wasn't exactly an innocent bystander. He liked it when Wiertz played loud and "would basically egg on Al," said Nothiger. It got to the point where Nothiger banned Wiertz from drumming at the coffeehouse.[29]

Undeterred, they played at the Spinning Wheel, which was across the street from the Joint. That's where bassist Rene Worst witnessed a rare physical fight between the jazz brothers. "Al was being particularly Al" one night with his volume, remembered Worst, and this time Murphy didn't appreciate the high decibels. "Bob got so mad at Al that he jumped over the drums at Al, and they ended up slugging each other on the stage," said Worst, who added that this was totally out of character for the gentle Murphy.[30] But they made up and remained pals and musical comrades until Wiertz's death in 1997.

Nothiger considered Murphy to be one of the most dynamic players to perform at the Classical Joint. Playing on an old Heintzman upright that lived at the Joint, or on his own Rhodes electric piano that he sometimes brought there, Murphy was free-flowing and intense. "He was just improvising all the time, very, very fast," said Nothiger. "He was very exciting."[31] That's how Murphy sounded on *Improvisational Communications*, a double album he recorded in 1979 with Oxbol and Wiertz. On seventeen tracks, Murphy is both melodic and free as he caresses and coaxes the piano, going deep inside the instrument. The album was never widely distributed.

In 1980, the *Province* included Murphy in a feature called "Six players without fame." "I'd like to be successful, but I'm kind of afraid of it, too," he said in the piece.[32] It was an intriguing statement that may have meant he feared success could detract or distract from his artistic impulse. Just over two years later, there were two nights of farewell concerts for Murphy at the Classical Joint before he made a major change—moving to Toronto. Was he chasing the sweet smell of success? If he was, it was a different brand. Murphy thought there would be more opportunities in TO. He played in Toronto's jazz venues, but Murphy mainly worked with guitarist Pat Coleman on composing and recording music for film and television, along with serving as musical director and accompanist for TV shows. He and his wife Carol were also raising two young children.

I was curious about what Murphy was like as a father, given how ultra-focused he was on music. "He wasn't over the top cuddly," said Carol, but "he was always there when they needed him."[33] Her observation brought to mind something drummer Buff Allen said about Murphy—that while he seemed cynical, flippant, and dark, he was a tender and caring person with a "big marshmallow centre."[34]

Murphy was content to stay in Toronto but Carol hated that city, so they moved back to Vancouver in 1986. After returning, they drifted apart and eventually split. Despite their differences, Carol treasured her time with Murphy. "My life was wonderful with him," she said. "I feel enriched because of being with him."[35]

The Classical Joint welcomed him home by providing gigs, and Murphy found other stages as he always had. Above all, it was comforting to have him back, resuming old partnerships and creating new ones. Then in 1988, Murphy began what would turn out to be a lengthy run at Carnegie's, a restaurant on West Broadway. It was a rarity: a six-nights-a-week gig. Murphy served as both the featured performer and booking agent, who lined up musicians to play with him in duos and trios (and sometimes quartets) and to perform when he wasn't there. Saxophonist Campbell Ryga played many nights with Murphy at Carnegie's, and even in a restaurant gig where few patrons were actively listening, it was a meaningful experience. "We got a chance to just stretch out on kind of a little island there," said Ryga. "It was really fun because he would constantly play and experiment with time, and all the bar lines in anything we were playing would just disappear."[36]

Aside from playing plenty of standards, "Bob was also a prolific writer, so we would take these opportunities on a steady gig like that to go through some of his new compositions, and it was always great, it was always musical," said Ryga.[37] Tom Keenlyside had similar experiences when playing with Murphy at Carnegie's. "Nobody could care less about the music," said Keenlyside about the Carnegie's crowd. "So we just played whatever we wanted. And Bob would whip out his [original] tunes." They were "ridiculously epic" pieces, "big long forms with sweeping melodies, incredible harmony."[38]

Keenlyside's friendship with Murphy dated back to 1969. That's when Murphy showed his "magnanimous spirit" by encouraging the teenaged Keenlyside when they jammed together at the Riverqueen.[39] Ryga and Murphy also went way back. "Our whole relationship and musical interaction just grew over the years," said Ryga. Their rapport heightened to the point where the line between making subtext-heavy conversation and playing metaphor-rich music blurred. "I could say something to him, and he would kind of look at me for a while a little bit sideways because he wouldn't quite know how to take it. He would be laughing for the next five minutes when he finally figured out what I really meant, and actually it was that very approach that we took to music in a lot of ways. Just trying to figure out these messages that were there hidden in the music."[40] Off the bandstand, Ryga—like many other musicians who looked up to Murphy—turned to him for advice, which he happily dispensed.

In 1994, Carnegie's halved the gig to three nights a week, which was indicative of a continuing reduction in the number of places and nights where Vancouver musicians could play jazz. When reporters invariably did stories on the dearth of jazz venues, they often called Murphy, who obliged with quotes like: "Live performance as a profession has virtually gone out the window."[41] Murphy saw what was happening as a sign: to be viable as a musician, he had to get serious about recording and releasing music that he and his collaborators had been shaping for years.

First up was *I Have a Dream*, an exquisite duo recording with Murphy on piano and singer Christine Duncan. Next: *B3*, a terrific vehicle for Murphy's robust Hammond B3 organ playing, alongside Bill Runge on saxophone and Buff Allen on drums. Then on *Come Rain or Come Shine*, Murphy delves further into his stirring organ style with a quartet he co-led with Pat Coleman, including John Gross on sax and Allen. Again, on Hammond B3, Murphy soars throughout the Ross Taggart Quartet's *Thankfully*, recorded live at Cory Weeds' Cellar in 2001. Murphy's improv on Taggart's song "Shorter Days" is especially sublime. It's a two-minute model on how to build an exhilarating, chills-giving solo that conveys the character and soul of the vintage organ, and especially of the organist playing it.

Two duo recordings in 2001 strike resonant chords with their empathetic musicality and raw emotion: *Mysteries and Tall Tales* with Taggart and *The Art of the Jazz Ballad* with Taylor. Without the safety net of playing in an ensemble, all the subtle nuances, unique turns of phrase, and untethered interplay in rubato passages on these captivating albums magnify. The latter release was the first of three Taylor-Murphy collaborations, also including *The Wall Street Sessions* and the singer's *In My Own Voice*. "We were meant to play together," said Taylor. "That's our connection. Our connection was always very spiritual, a deep musical connection. Never lost that, no matter what."[42]

Taylor on Murphy's way: "His music touched so, so deeply. Whenever he would play, he would always play his way. He'd never do what you expected.

But if you stood rigid and expected him to change or play something your way, if you're trying to be strong as a singer or as a lead player, he would just go the opposite way. But the minute you gave in to what he was doing, you'd go to a place you couldn't go with anybody else."[43]

Murphy became a go-to pianist for local singers. Whenever Ron Small had a gig singing jazz, he always lined up Murphy to play with him. Small, who was fastidious with musicians, felt well-supported and understood by the pianist. Murphy and bassist Rene Worst played on Jennifer Scott's engaging *Something to Live By*. "It was called the Jennifer Scott Trio but man, I tell you that was a huge collaboration," said Scott. What was it like for Scott to collaborate with Murphy? "Bob had a famous saying: 'Every time you play, you want to start from zero.' He didn't believe in preordaining anything when you were going to create and improvise."[44]

Bob Murphy, the Cellar, March 7, 2008. Photo by Steve Mynett.

There was a period in the mid-2000s when I lost touch with what Murphy was doing. I didn't make the effort to go to his gigs and admittedly took him for granted. Maybe it was thanks to people like me that Murphy told his partner, singer Monique Van Dam, he sometimes felt "obsolete."[45] He was far from it. In 2007, he released *Downtown East Side Picnic*, with his quartet: Keenlyside (flute and tenor sax), Doug Stephenson (bass), and Allen (drums). Although the album didn't receive anywhere near the attention it fully deserved, this is his masterwork; the very personal expression for which Murphy's decades-long life in music had prepared him.

The first thing that struck me was the word "picnic" in the name of the album and title track. It seemed like an oxymoron, given the poverty, mental illness, drug addiction, and other heartbreaking sources of pain and suffering in the Downtown Eastside neighbourhood Murphy was referring to. But after repeatedly listening to the recording's eight tunes, all composed by Murphy (including a number he had workshopped at Carnegie's), the title's meaning became clear. It's a declaration of support for the neighbourhood he lived near and worked in over the years. That awareness is shared by the entire quartet; the music alternates between dark introspection and sunny hopefulness, reflecting the community's intractable realities as well as the unobvious beauty that's there if you know where to look.

The opening track, "Free on the Inside," resonates in an autobiographical way. In his younger days, Murphy experienced the challenges of the human condition that engender regret: dalliances with drugs, breakups, selfish self-absorption, and financial struggles. Through music, his relationship with Van Dam, support from family, friendships, meditation, and tai chi, he achieved an inner stillness and absolution for past missteps. Murphy—a seeker who read the philosophy of George Gurdjieff and Jiddu Krishnamurti as well as the spiritual teachings of Paramahansa Yogananda to find answers about life's purpose—also connected with a celestial being. "I don't think he ever used the word God, but he really felt when he played the piano that he was in touch with the source, the higher power," said his sister Margo.[46]

That's one interpretation of "Free on the Inside." Another: although he was a long way from the free jazz he explored in the seventies, Murphy felt entirely liberated in his musical expression. You can hear it during his "Free on the Inside" solo, when he extends his improvised phrases just the right amount, a longtime Murphy trait that creates a momentum that Jennifer Scott described as "breathless."[47] Also faintly audible: Murphy accompanying his own solo with a low-pitched moan, similar to that of one of his piano heroes, Keith Jarrett, but quieter. During the solo, Murphy—perhaps more than anywhere else on the recording that was made in the basement studio at Keenlyside's Kerrisdale house—is fully immersed and lost (in a good way) in the music.

• • •

In December 2013, I arrived at the studio on Wall Street where Murphy and Van Dam lived. It's the place where Murphy practiced for hours on end. It was also the scene of a weekly ritual that lasted for more than a decade: a Thursday jam with the musicians who played on *Downtown East Side Picnic*, and others. It was one of Murphy's favourite things—the simple act of playing jazz for pure pleasure with dear friends. The studio was also where he taught, and that day he was finishing a lesson. The student was Linda Lee Thomas, principal pianist with the Vancouver Symphony Orchestra and the city's finest tango piano player. Aside from Murphy and Thomas being friends, later I realized another connection between them: her husband Jon Washburn played with Murphy at the Unitarian Church decades before. Murphy's presence really was tightly woven into the fabric of Vancouver arts and culture.

Sitting near his beloved grand piano, the powerful instrument Murphy called his "racehorse," we talked about his life in jazz and the thing that "rescued" him: teaching. His focus on teaching began in the late 1990s, when opportunities for gigs were at a low point. Murphy discovered he was passionate about sharing his knowledge. "One of the things I love about teaching is I feel like I'm doing something very subversive," said Murphy. "Some of the people who really influenced me, who I got to see when they came through here, were Cannonball [Adderley] and Bill Evans. Both were jazz evangelists. They were preaching that this music should be able to change the consciousness of the planet. I guess I still think that's possible."[48]

Bob Murphy, Wall Street studio, December 3, 2013. Photo by Chris Wong.

Then he talked about present-day young players and the multi-generational dots were connected. "Listen. One of the things that's knocked me out and always knocked me out, is that every few years you turn around and there's a new crop of young players coming up. It's like you can't kill this music. It's like morning glory. You can't stamp it out. You can defund it, and you can try and kill all the education and all that sort of stuff. It doesn't matter. Kids keep coming out and want to play."[49]

Murphy was so right about the steady stream of young musicians who want to play jazz. About six years after Murphy died, when Vancouver's jazz scene was reviving itself following the loss of gigs caused by the COVID-19 pandemic, it felt like a generational inflection point. Many younger jazz musicians were establishing themselves in the scene with a high skill level, passionate energy, and abundant creativity. As a player and teacher, Murphy helped ensure the scene—despite being vulnerable at times—had a strong foundation that would endure for future generations.

In 1980, he shared another insight about his voyage of discovery into jazz and himself. "I've spent most of my time finding out what function music serves. I believe there is something in music that serves people, and I want to be able to put that out in as straightforward and workable way as I can."⁵⁰ Murphy seeing himself as a servant to jazz says all you need to know about the philosophy and motivation that informed his music.

• • •

Bob Murphy, Tangent Café, July 24, 2014. Photo by Vincent Lim.

One of the best gigs of Jennifer Scott's career took place June 6, 2015, at the Silk Purse Arts Centre, with Murphy and Keenlyside. It didn't look promising beforehand as Scott was sick, but the show went on without a set list and each trio member calling tunes. As it turned out, all three performed wonderfully. Murphy was "fully expressive" that night, recalled Scott. "He would be playing, and he would just start growling. He was so physical over the keyboard." At the end of the show, they knew something special had happened. "We were emotional, the three of us, and we looked out into the audience and people were just like, 'Holy fuck, what just happened?' It was really like that. Very emotional and expressive. So grateful to have had that last gig with him and to have it be a quintessential Bob gig where you don't have any plan. You just go in, and you start from zero."[51]

On September 26, 2015, Murphy posted a standard gig promo on Facebook: "I'm playing at Pat's Pub (403 East Hastings) today from 3 to 7 with Bill Runge, Hugh Fraser, Miles Foxx Hill, and Buff Allen. We're going to have a great time. Please join us if you can. There's no cover."[52] It ended up being his final full-length gig. Someone posted a video on YouTube of a song Murphy's quintet played that day. It's remarkable to be able to click a few times and be back at the show, experiencing a Bob Murphy solo. On his fire-engine red keyboard that emulated the sound of the Hammond B3 he quit lugging around years before, Murphy soaked that solo in blues licks with finesse. And yes, he was growling.

He played on the same bandstand one more time, on October 5, 2015, when Murphy accompanied Van Dam for one song at the Pat's Pub vocal jam. Close to that date, the couple realized their long-held dream of recording together. The result was *Beautiful*, a duo album with gorgeous interpretations of standards. The experience of recording together affirmed to Van Dam what an exceptional listener Murphy was, despite being half deaf from years of playing. She wrote in the liner notes that the music they made would "always take flight."[53]

Murphy disliked hospitals and preferred alternative medicine, but about ten days after his last trip to the bandstand, he landed in hospital. Murphy had a series of strokes before he passed away at Vancouver General Hospital.

Tributes flooded into Facebook about Murphy. "I always looked up to Bob Murphy," wrote Renee Rosnes, the jazz pianist from North Vancouver who discovered her sound in blessed spaces like the Classical Joint and made it in New York. "Before I left Vancouver years ago, I heard him perform often, and would marvel at his lyrical flow and connection to the instrument. His music was inspired and soulful—just like he was. It's difficult to grasp he's no longer here."[54]

On Joani Taylor's *In My Own Voice*, she sang "You Are My Sunshine" with warm backing from Murphy and bassist Miles Foxx Hill. At Murphy's celebration of life, for the last song, Taylor and Hill performed "You Are My

Sunshine" for the man who meant so much to them and everyone there. While his absence was profoundly palpable, it felt like Murphy was somehow there in his customary place at the piano, sounding great and supporting the others to be at their best by deeply connecting.

13 / LET YOUR VOICE BE HEARD: HUGH FRASER

A WILD SCENE is unfolding before my eyes and ears in Edmonton's Citadel Theatre. It involves a group of young and rebellious musicians, led by an energetic and visionary twenty-two-year-old: Hugh Fraser. As I'm witnessing their unforgettable performance, I have no idea that Fraser—the bandleader, pianist, trombonist, and composer—will go on to become one of Canada's greatest jazz musicians and ambassadors. All my seventeen-year-old self knows is that he and the band members are the coolest jazz musicians I've ever seen.

It's May 1981, and there's a buzz in the packed theatre hosting the Canadian Stage Band Festival's national finals. Though most of the competing ensembles are high school stage bands from across the country, the festival has an "open class" category consisting of bands with older but still youthful musicians. One of these groups is the thirteen-member ensemble that's on stage—Vancouver Ensemble of Jazz Improvisation, or as it says on the t-shirts most of the players are wearing: VEJI.

"Sax Freeabin" begins quietly with just electric bass, cymbals, and sustained tones from the three-tenor sax section. Suddenly Fraser, who is conducting the intro with his left hand, accelerates the tempo and the three tenors launch into a swirling succession of harmonically disarming notes that prompt applause from the audience. After the whole group comes to a dead stop, the saxophonists deftly play an altissimo line that, as written by Fraser, seems impossibly high before segueing into the song's catchy melody. Then come the solos. With an agile right hand, Fraser delivers a strong improvisation on a Rhodes electric piano. Patric Caird, conspicuous in his black leather jacket that exudes rock and roll attitude, follows with a tenor solo that ascends to the stratosphere and elicits more cheers. Campbell Ryga and Perry White contribute their own rousing sax solos before all three of them combine in a raucous group improv that once again has the crowd cheering. When Fraser's tune ends, all of us in the predominately teenaged band geek audience—including a sixteen-year-old Diana Krall— immediately spring to our feet in an exuberant standing ovation. In that moment they are rock stars because what they just played demolished the quaint notions of what we had been taught a large jazz ensemble should sound like.

Forty years after, I asked Ryga about the significance of the band's astonishing performance. "These kids were hearing their instruments being played in ways they didn't even realize were possible," he said.[1] The festival's adjudicators were similarly impressed—VEJI outperformed ensembles from Canada's top post-secondary jazz programs and won the open class division. It was the first major triumph for the band and its wunderkind leader. For Fraser, there would be many more in the decades to come.

Over the years, I marvelled as Fraser, VEJI, and his quintet harnessed their creativity and dynamism to make impactful jazz. At the same time, Fraser was a remarkably inspiring jazz educator. Nurturing meaningful, lifelong relationships was key to his success in playing and teaching. There were gaps where I fell behind in my awareness of what he was doing. Whenever I caught up with him, though, it was clear Fraser never stopped contributing with his music. He also went through immense personal challenges: battling debilitating cancer and other conditions while processing memories of trauma. Despite the physical and emotional pain, it didn't stop him from composing, playing, and leading—his life passions—before taking his last choruses. Above all, he held on to his irrepressible positivity and hopeful romanticism that were at his core.

• • •

The story begins with Kenneth Fraser, who was born in England and immigrated to Canada. Following stops in Montreal and Banff, he settled in Vancouver. Kenneth owned a printing shop and landed a percussionist job with the Vancouver Symphony Orchestra. He played jazz at W.K. Chop Suey on East Pender in Chinatown, which offered dining and dancing. Trained as a tenor choirboy, Fraser also sang as part of CBC Radio's first coast-to-coast broadcast in 1936. Three years later, Kenneth married Mary Fraser (*née* Deeley) in West Vancouver. Their wedding announcement said the Frasers would live in West Vancouver,[2] but the Second World War changed those plans. He was in the army and assigned to the Fort Rodd Hill artillery fortress in Colwood near Victoria on the southern tip of Vancouver Island. Kenneth ended his music career, and they lived in the Victoria area for the rest of their lives.

The youngest of three sons, Hugh Alexander Fraser was born October 26, 1958. Scenes from his childhood: At about age six, Fraser started a private club with its own hiding place. As the club leader, he charged friends a nickel to join. Around the same time, he started taking drum lessons from his dad. When Fraser was ten, his aunt made an audio recording, which she sent to relatives in England. On it, Fraser said in a chipper voice: "Hi, this is Hugh, and I'm playing my drum better and better."[3] A few years later, he joined the cadets and became a marching band drummer. Before long, Fraser was promoted to sergeant, which meant leading band members who were considerably older. Whether it was innate or a learned quality, Fraser was destined to be a leader.

At twelve, Fraser took classical piano lessons, which provided him with a musical foundation but didn't motivate him to play professionally. Far more influential was attending a jazz-rock fusion concert at Victoria's Royal Theatre in the early seventies. The band was Pacific Salt, and trombonist Ian McDougall, co-founder of the group and a first-call player in Vancouver's music scene, was married to Fraser's cousin. Talking to McDougall and especially hearing him perform with Pacific Salt inspired Fraser. Seeing his cousin-in-law play the trombone with a wah-wah pedal upped the badass quotient. "I got a trombone, and I started figuring stuff out right away," said Fraser, who learned by fanatically listening to and playing along with the latest jazz records that he got from his audiophile uncle.[4]

After Kenneth died in 1972, when Hugh was thirteen, Mary Fraser enrolled her youngest son in St. Michaels University School. "There was no jazz there," said Fraser about the private school's music program.[5] There was, however, a scholarly teacher who studied at the Royal Academy of Music in London. With that teacher's help, Fraser started learning how to analyze symphony scores. While still in high school, he progressed on the trombone by taking private lessons and playing in ensembles at the University of Victoria (UVic). But jazz was in his blood now, so Fraser looked for a place to play it. "This great guy taught at Esquimalt High School," said Fraser.[6] Jerry Bryant, an African-American pianist from Kansas City, started one of the first stage bands in Victoria. Playing in the Esquimalt High stage band led by Bryant was a formative experience. At seventeen, Fraser also started a sixteen-piece big band: the Left Bank Express. The teenager transcribed some of the band's charts himself. Fraser's musical talents and ambitions were starting to emerge.

This was the "big mesh of stuff" that led Fraser to focus on music as his career path and apply to UVic.[7] Amazingly, even though Fraser had informally studied at the university for two years, he didn't get in because his high school marks weren't good enough. Then Tom Eadie, Fraser's trombone teacher, told him about a great trombonist and teacher leading a stage band at Vancouver Community College (VCC). Dave Robbins was born in Greensburg, Indiana, and played for six years in trumpeter Harry James' big band/orchestra. After moving to Vancouver in 1951, Robbins became principal trombonist with the Vancouver Symphony Orchestra and one of the city's premier jazz musicians, big band leaders, composers/arrangers, and educators. Studying with Robbins at VCC, together with other young jazz devotees, would change Fraser's life and start delineating his musical flight path.

In 1977, eighteen-year-old Fraser left home, sailed on the ferry that connects Vancouver Island with BC's mainland, and made his way to the city on the horizon: Vancouver. At VCC's Langara campus he met musicians who would figure in future endeavours, including Patric Caird and Don Powrie. The first mention of Fraser's playing in a newspaper appeared in a December 1977 *Vancouver Sun* review of a VCC Jazz Ensemble performance at the Hot Jazz Club. "Of the four trombones, Hugh Fraser had the biggest sound."[8]

Before Bill Clark showed up at VCC as a student in early 1978, friends told the trumpeter, "You've got to meet this guy, Hugh Fraser. What a character, and what a musician." The hype was real. "It was just one of those things where, as soon as we met, we hit it off and a life-long friendship began on multiple levels," said Clark.[9]

Let Your Voice Be Heard

Hugh Fraser, Vancouver Community College, circa late 1970s. Photo by Graham Ord.

Clark knew his new friend was a rare and special talent when Fraser brought in an original piece for the VCC band to play: "Trombone Freeabin." Fraser's imaginative tune was an exhilarating thrill ride to play and listen to, with complex harmonies, intricate rhythms, and compositional flourishes that unleashed the force and fervour of a big band in full flight. Clark was astounded that someone so young could write a chart that advanced. Clark: "It was like, 'What the heck? This guy wrote this already?'"[10] The song would eventually be part of a suite that included "Sax Freeabin" and "Trumpet Freeabin," all inspired in part by the Russian pianist and composer Alexander Scriabin, who was a pioneer in atonal classical music. Fraser included a solo in "Trombone Freeabin" that was meant to be played completely free, and later it would be earmarked for Clark.

Vital to Fraser's development during his time at VCC was Robbins. In his gentle and positive way, Robbins encouraged Fraser's burgeoning creativity. "He supported me, and he made space," said Fraser. Robbins was open-minded about his students playing avant-garde jazz, even though it wasn't something he had done in his career. Robbins let players including Fraser, Clark, and Perry White play small ensemble sets at VCC big band concerts. "He'd say, 'What are you going to do?'" said Fraser about his always smiling mentor. "I'd say, 'We are going to play free for fifty minutes.' He'd say, 'Go ahead.'"[11]

That experience contributed to the creation of the Jazzoids, a mighty band with Clark, White, Fraser, and others. Heavily influenced by the Art Ensemble of Chicago, the Jazzoids played free and fierce, with rock grooves driven by Fraser on drums in the group's first version. "Hugh was a ferocious drummer," said Clark. "A lot of people don't know that."[12] Similar to how the Art Ensemble performed in lab coats, the Jazzoids wore surgical scrubs procured by White, who worked in a hospital laundry room. The band performed at rent parties in City Space, a former warehouse, where Clark lived alongside new wave and punk musicians.

There's a line connecting Robbins and the Jazzoids' unconstrained expression because while Robbins was more than thirty years older than many of his VCC students, there was no generation gap. Fraser, Clark, and the other emerging musicians at the college deeply respected Robbins, who gave them a crucial bit of advice: "I remember Dave said to us, 'You've got to make your own scene,'" said Clark.[13] No one Clark knew took that advice more to heart than Fraser.

While still at VCC, Fraser was becoming a go-to musician in the city. He played drums in Studio 58's production of *Jacques Brel is Alive and Well and Living in Paris* and wrote and played jingles for the Army & Navy department store, which paid lucratively. Fraser could have kept working gigs like these, but he was creatively restless and yearning for something much more profound. He quit school and made plans to step away from the scene to attend the Creative Music Studio (CMS) in Woodstock, New York. Before he went in 1979, Fraser pledged to Clark they would form a band after he returned from Woodstock.

CMS was another pivotal experience. Learning from, playing with, and listening to artists like Jack DeJohnette, Carla Bley, Julius Hemphill, Lee Konitz, and Ronald Shannon Jackson was mind-expanding. Fraser soaked up insights from these icons at the forefront of avant-garde and contemporary jazz, and he embraced the CMS concept of world jazz that focused on global musical traditions and improvisation. Both would be essential to his near and distant futures.

• • •

It was Christmastime 1979, and Fraser, back from Woodstock, was at City Space making plans with Clark. At CMS, Fraser conceived the blueprint for the ensemble he wanted to create: a little big band including sax, trombone, trumpet, and rhythm sections of three members each. While it could expand or contract as needed, the group Fraser had in mind was smaller than a traditional big band. "The idea was to form a band where everyone was an improviser, yet there were enough horns to create powerful ensemble passages," said Fraser.[14] They talked excitedly about that and another important life decision that would help the band enormously: moving in together in a shared house. That same night they saw a house in East Vancouver, on Mons Drive, and signed a rental agreement.

Fraser, Clark, and a few other musicians moved into Mons House in January 1980 and started rehearsing in the basement with players they mainly knew from VCC. Those rehearsals marked the birth of VEJI. Fraser provided material for the band to play. He arranged the title track from McCoy Tyner's orchestral *Fly with the Wind* album, which had a huge sound and energy that appealed to Fraser. Plus, he transcribed some charts played by nonets with a wonderfully raucous sound, including: Tyner's "Mode for John" and "Utopia" from his *Tender Moments* album, and "Seven for Lee" (in 7/4) by the English saxophonist Elton Dean and his Ninesense ensemble from *Happy Daze*. Fraser also contributed a handful of his own early tunes, like "Trombone Freeabin" and "Vortney Sprazits." "When we first started playing, he was already ready with a pretty strong book of material, so we really felt like a band quite quickly," said Clark.[15]

Another musician who took part in the Mons rehearsals was Campbell Ryga. "Hey, groovy guy!" were the first words Fraser, wearing a leopard skin vest, spoke to Ryga when they met at VCC.[16] They became fast friends, and it was a given that Ryga would be part of VEJI and join in the basement sessions that went well into the a.m. hours.

Journeys to the Bandstand

Rehearsing continued for five months until VEJI's first concert in front of about one hundred people at the Western Front on June 1, 1980. The band unleashed most of the aforementioned tunes plus Bill Runge's "Helen," an entirely improvised (guided by cues) sonic re-enactment of the massive Mount St. Helens eruption that happened exactly two weeks before. VEJI's whole set was volcanic. An unreleased recording of that first show documented VEJI at this embryonic stage—rough, free, loud, and thrilling. Fraser played the piano hard and fast. The recording, which I've listened to, confirms the audience almost matched the group's intensity. "It was a really responsive audience—they were blown away," said Fraser. "The band was raw. The sheer energy of all the players who finally had a chance to get the music out was just overwhelming."[17]

Vancouver Ensemble of Jazz Improvisation (VEJI). Top row (left to right): Dave Quarin, Don Powrie, Henry Christian, Patric Caird, and Campbell Ryga. Third row: Ron Thompson, Hugh Fraser, Rod Borrie, and Rudy Petschauer. Second row: Brad Muirhead and Bill Clark. First row: Don Barker, Mike Lent, and Joe Bjornson. City Space, 1980. Photo by Graham Ord.

While VEJI's debut was successful, it took time to get gigs and attract media attention. So the band kept rehearsing parallel to Fraser paying his dues as a gigging musician. In 1981, Fraser, Clark, and White joined the Night Train

Revue as the band's forceful Tritones horn section. Playing R&B and soul up to six nights a week in clubs was a blast. "We played with the right amount of rock attitude," said Fraser. "We were just hell bent on blowing our brains out."[18] Low-resolution videos of the band that survive online confirm their exuberance. There was a downside to the good times while they rode the Night Train—playing at a high volume and intensity night after night may have contributed to health conditions that emerged later in life. "Hugh's firm belief was that [playing Night Train Revue gigs] damaged all three of us," said Clark.[19] Fraser got Bell's palsy, a form of paralysis of the face; Clark blew a nerve in his lip and got dystonia, a movement disorder that causes muscles to contract uncontrollably; and White ended up with severe tinnitus (ringing in the ears). But at that time, they were young and resilient, so they carried on with the musician's life.

As word spread about VEJI, more gigs came, and the ensemble stayed true to developing a sound that upended big band norms. "When we started out, we had an insatiable appetite to learn about playing free and avant-garde, playing really loud and fast, and just doing a lot of things that were against the textbook ways of getting into the music," said Fraser.[20] Sometimes before playing the faster tunes, Ryga reminded Fraser about sticking to a sane tempo. "I said, 'Okay, there is the playable speed and then there is eleven, and if we are going to do this, please don't get really excited while you are counting it in and make it twelve, right?' He said, 'Oh, yeah, yeah, yeah,' and sure enough he would be excited, and he would be counting it in, and it might as well have been shot out of a cannon."[21]

VEJI also paid attention to performative aspects of the band's vibe. After Fraser, Clark, and others in the group saw Sun Ra and his Arkestra in Seattle, where the musicians with far out headgear ventured into the audience as they played otherworldly free improv, VEJI did the same. Meanwhile, Clark would jump off the trumpet section riser and dance in a popping and locking street style that he learned from avidly watching *Soul Train*. Fraser loved to see Clark dance with the band because he thought it broke down barriers and brought audiences closer to the music.

Offstage, Fraser looked after business, like making sure the band got paid. At a festival, the promoter stiffed Fraser. The musicians didn't find out until much later that Fraser selflessly sold his Rhodes to do the right thing and pay the band himself. He was also the social convenor. "Wherever Hugh was going, that was the hang for the night," said Clark. "'Where are you going? Okay, I'm going too.'" Fraser created a social scene wherever he went. "If he was sitting at a table, it was kind of the table everybody wanted to be sitting at," Clark added. "That's where the party was."[22]

In 1981, VEJI recorded its self-titled debut record at Bullfrog Studios. While it captured Fraser's compositional prowess and the band's vigour, it was uncharacteristically slick and failed to convey the raw spirit of VEJI's live shows. This was largely because the band tried to squeeze the recording into two days of free studio time, and Fraser didn't have full involvement in shaping the final tracks. He learned from that experience the importance of having full autonomy in the recording process.

• • •

Not long after VEJI's watershed performance in Edmonton at the stage band festival, Fraser was playing at the after-hours Basin Street club in Vancouver's Downtown Eastside, and he was frustrated. "I had just finished a really fast tune," said Fraser. "I had thrown my trombone because I was pissed off my tongue wasn't working." At that exact moment, a "short gentleman with glasses and a moustache" introduced himself to Fraser.[23] It was Michael Century, coordinator of the Jazz Workshop at the Banff Centre for the Arts, who was in the amped-up Edmonton audience for VEJI's tour de force show. As Century explained at Basin Street, and in a meeting with the whole band crammed into Fraser's apartment, he was offering an all-expenses-paid three-month residency at the Banff Centre to Fraser and up to nine other musicians in VEJI. "From our perspective, this was just kind of unheard of," said Clark. "This is what you offer classical musicians. Only classical musicians get to talk to international art schools. Not a bunch of us rounders. At that time, we were quite literally, to a man, all college dropouts."[24]

Then Century asked who the band would like to have as clinicians in Banff. Clark recalled that when he suggested a veteran Vancouver jazz musician, "Mike said, 'I don't mean to diminish your respect of this person at all or how great he no doubt is, but I mean, *who* do you want your clinicians to be? Like anybody.'" Clark cheekily suggested Miles Davis. Century said it could be pretty much anybody short of Davis.[25] And then Fraser and the band understood what he was getting at. The clinicians Century eventually confirmed for the 1982 residency, who each spent about a week with VEJI in Banff, formed a dream roster: Joe Henderson, Frank Foster, Slide Hampton, and Don Thompson. The residency went exceedingly well.

I met Fraser for the first time in November 1983. It was late afternoon in his East Vancouver suite, and jazz was playing loudly through the stereo that was next to a shelf laden with hundreds of records and tapes. Fraser was eating bacon and pancakes. "This is kind of a late breakfast," he explained. "It's the jazz life."[26] The then-twenty-five-year-old, who hadn't done a lot of interviews up to that point, spoke articulately about VEJI and the Vancouver jazz scene, which he was actively contributing to as a member of numerous groups. While he only made enough from gigs to pay rent, eat, and not much more, Fraser said with a smile: "I'd say I'm making a good living because I'm enjoying life."[27]

The Banff Centre brought VEJI back for another three-month residency in 1984, with a different set of top-notch clinicians: Dave Holland, Dave Liebman, and Julian Priester. Both Banff residencies were life-changing for Fraser and the others, giving them the rare opportunity to learn from and perform with jazz masters, play together as a band on a daily basis, play in a non-musical sense (at social events including toga parties), and tap into their creativity in an idyllic place far away from distractions and quotidian stresses like hustling for the next gig. As a result, they strengthened their bond and resolve.

At the second residency, Fraser met American classical harpist Jan Walters, who was doing her own residency at exactly the same time as VEJI. Fraser's energy and curiosity about the harp made an impression on Walters. "He just seemed so curious, musically, and just full of life, fun to be around," said Walters.[28] After the residency, they kept in touch and started a long-distance relationship. Fraser and Walters both dreamed of living in New York. Fraser received a Canada Council grant to study there, which enabled the couple to live the dream.

They lived in a big old storefront in Brooklyn's Park Slope neighbourhood. Fraser made the most of his grant, studying trombone with Slide Hampton and contributing to big bands led by Maynard Ferguson and Clifford Jordan. Fraser had the wherewithal to organize the New York Ensemble of Jazz Improvisation, which performed a show in June 1985 at a fabled jazz club in Chelsea co-founded by pianist Barry Harris: Jazz Cultural Theatre.[29] New York musicians, along with Perry White and Phil Dwyer, played the gig. The New York sojourn showed that a much bigger stage didn't at all faze Fraser. Regardless of the locale or the occasion, he dove right in and made things happen.

Back in Vancouver in 1986, Fraser still considered VEJI his main priority. That year the band put out its second album, *Classic VEJI*, and this time the recording conveyed the group's true sound. Then Fraser got a gig for the band at CBC, which promptly cut the original budget for the show in half. He adapted by re-arranging VEJI tunes for a quintet. The smaller group, which Fraser put together with VEJI members, had a big sound. It included two saxophonists—Ryga and Dwyer (who also played piano in the group)—Fraser on trombone when he wasn't playing piano, bassist Chris Nelson, and drummer Buff Allen. Fraser quickly saw the potential for the band, which shared VEJI's passion but in a more agile format. The Hugh Fraser Quintet came into being.

By the next year, Walters was serving as Fraser's manager, and they entered the quintet in the high-profile Alcan Jazz Competition that was part of the Festival International de Jazz de Montréal. The group won the Pacific region semi-finals at the Sheraton Landmark Jazzbar in Vancouver and flew to the festival for the finals. The quintet proceeded to win the 1987 Concours de Jazz Alcan, earning generous prizes, starting with a plum performance right after the award was announced. The quintet opened for Dave Brubeck before a full house with close to 3,000 people in Salle Wilfrid-Pelletier at Place des Arts. When the band members came on stage to receive the award, just before their opening set, Fraser's neat and clean look with a jacket and tie seemed a long way from the jazz rebel in a VEJI t-shirt. But the renegade spirit was still there, and Fraser would keep expressing it in new and captivating ways.

Another reward for winning in Montreal was a recording contract, and the first release in the deal established an expansive approach the group would explore and extend in subsequent recordings. *Looking Up*, released in 1988, included both vigorous hard bop and beguiling reflective pieces, all composed by Fraser. Both styles engaged me as I absorbed the melodic expressions on vinyl. In the liner notes to the record, which won the 1989 Juno Award for best jazz album, Don Thompson recalled first hearing a tape of VEJI, and then meeting Fraser and the band in Banff. That's where he "began to understand where all this music was coming from." As Thompson wrote: "Hugh Fraser is much more than a gifted musician who plays piano and trombone and writes tunes. He is a person who is so passionately obsessed with music, it's as though he's in love with it."[30]

As for VEJI, the difficult-to-obtain elements that enable great large ensemble jazz—soaring compositions and arrangements, top level personnel, and the ideal environment to perform in—came together December 16 to 19, 1989, in Banff. That's when and where Fraser and eighteen other musicians recorded *VEJI NOW!*, encompassing *Mass in C Minor for Jazz Orchestra*, *The Freeabin Suite*, and other works. Fraser's original vision for VEJI—fusing mighty ensemble playing of imaginatively written music with vigorous solo and group improvisation—came alive more intensely than ever.

Vancouver Ensemble of Jazz Improvisation (VEJI). Back row (left to right): Blaine Dunaway, Robin Shier, Walter White, John Korsrud, Ross Taggart, and Rob McKenzie. Middle row: Don Powrie, Brad Muirhead, Rod Borrie, Dennis Esson, Perry White, Patric Caird, PJ Perry, and Blaine Wikjord. Front row: Bill Clark, Hugh Fraser, Campbell Ryga, and Chris Nelson. Luscar Recording Studio, Banff Centre for the Arts, December 1989. Photo by Neil Taylor.

• • •

August 1988, in another of Fraser's apartments, I spotted a curious drawing perched on his piano. At first glance it looked like a pentagram surrounded by an outer frame of Spirograph-like loops. It had two outer rings, each with different sets of letters representing musical notes. The loops connecting some of the letters seemed to indicate relationships. The inset pentagram was covered with lines that converged in the middle like bicycle spokes. The spokes and the five points of the star radiated out to cryptic numbers and letters. To a lay person, John Coltrane's "circle of tones" drawing is indecipherable; to Fraser, it was a fascinating window into the mind of one of his jazz heroes. "It's just a piece of paper with a drawing on it, but it represents a link with Coltrane's devotion and searching through music," said Fraser.[31] It also represented Fraser's own thirst for acquiring and sharing jazz knowledge.

So much had happened on those fronts since we last met almost five years prior. The most significant development: his move with Walters to London, England, in September 1987. In London, Fraser studied with the masterful Toronto-born trumpeter and composer Kenny Wheeler. The extroverted Fraser and shy Wheeler could have been a mismatched pair. But mutual respect bloomed between the two as they played and discussed each other's tunes on the piano and worked together in Wheeler's big band. With guidance from Wheeler, Fraser expanded his harmonic vocabulary.

Fraser multi-tasked, as always. He wrote the first version of his five-movement "Mass in C Minor," which a choir performed in London. The quintet went on a number of European tours. Fraser and Walters (who played harp on *VEJI NOW!*) brainstormed and collaborated to actualize the tours and other projects. "It was almost kind of like this combination where he would say, 'Let's do this.' And I'd be like, 'I can make that happen,'" said Walters. In pre-internet and cell phone times, making it happen involved preparing grant applications on typewriters, mailing venues records and cassettes, making "a million" landline phone calls, and squeezing every penny out of "shoestring" budgets.[32] They specifically waged a campaign to get the quintet a gig at Ronnie Scott's, the world-famous jazz club in London. Their main tactic: frequently dropping off music by the quintet at the Soho club for Scott to listen to.

When he finally did, Scott surprised Fraser and Walters with an amazing opportunity—opening for the iconic Cuban jazz band Irakere for two weeks in the summer of 1988. The plan was for Fraser's group to play the first and third sets, and for Irakere to perform the second and fourth sets. While Irakere was the main attraction, wowing audiences who packed the club, the quintet was also a big hit with the sophisticated London patrons. Scott would go on to re-book the two bands to share engagements multiple times. One night the droll club owner showed his appreciation for the quintet's ability to retain and entertain audiences by handing Fraser a "thick wad of twenty-pound notes with a rubber band around it"—a bonus of several thousand pounds, which Fraser split with the guys in the band.[33]

On another night, none other than Dizzy Gillespie showed up at the club. Because fans were swarming Gillespie, he stayed in Scott's office, where the quintet left their instrument cases. When they went to retrieve them, Fraser and the boys met Gillespie and exchanged small talk. Gillespie and Blaine Wikjord, the veteran Vancouver drummer with the nickname "Wacker," who was in the quintet at the time, got along especially well. Seeing that, Ryga said: "Hey Wacker, why don't you show Dizzy what happens when you drink too much scotch?" On cue, Wikjord, who had his back to the trumpet legend, displayed one of his uncanny talents: transforming into a silverback gorilla. "He turns around slowly and looks at Dizzy with his face all curled up, and the smile on Dizzy's face was unbelievable," said Ryga.[34]

Over the course of the quintet's parallel runs with the Cuban supergroup at Ronnie Scott's, Fraser developed a strong rapport with Irakere's leader, pianist Chucho Valdes. They had much in common—striking technique and a high-spirited life force were at the top of the list. Valdes informally taught Afro-Cuban music to Fraser, who took to it intuitively and joyfully. Fraser returned the favour after becoming head of the Banff Centre's summer jazz workshop in 1991, by recruiting Valdes to teach in the workshop. A highlight for Fraser was performing with Irakere and revered Cuban percussionist Changuito as part of the 1994 Afrocubanismo festival in Banff. Valdes followed up by bringing Fraser's quintet to the Havana International Jazz Festival several times and one time programming VEJI. Scott's fateful decision to program acclaimed Cubans with relatively unknown Canadians paid countless musical dividends for many years.

Fraser's love affair with Cuban sounds spoke to his curiosity about a range of music. "He was excited about so many different things, so many different aspects," said Ryga. "Often when we hung out, we would listen to a lot of different music, and he would get an inspiration from it, and then track it to its source. If those people who were involved in it were still alive, he would go spend time and get to know those guys and study with them, try to figure how they felt about music and where they were going next, and then take that energy and put it back into his own work."[35]

Fraser and the quintet performed at other renowned jazz clubs, including Yoshi's in San Francisco during a 1990 west coast US tour. Plus, the quintet performed at the Blue Note in New York City's Greenwich Village. Fraser and Walters set up the gig as a showcase for the group, inviting A&R reps from American major labels to attend. The quintet—including the excellent drummer Keith Copeland—was in strong form after a European tour. There were high hopes that the showcase could lead to a record deal and more opportunities stateside. It didn't play out that way, which was disappointing, but Fraser found other ways to keep himself and his ensembles active and fulfilled.

From the late 1980s and all through the 1990s, Fraser was full on with an internationalist approach to music. Articles published about him during that period read like travelogues. Fraser amassed a jumbo jet's worth of frequent flyer points while shuttling between Victoria, Vancouver, Banff, London, New York, Toronto, Havana, and other cities in Europe and Latin America for touring, leading international jazz orchestra festivals, teaching, and recording.

London continued to be an important base for Fraser because he taught at the Royal Academy of Music (RAM) for more than a decade. His teaching appointment at the prestigious school came about in an unconventional way. Walters sent—unsolicited—the *Classic VEJI* record to Graham Collier, head of RAM's jazz program. Collier, a bassist, composer, and educator at the leading edge of British jazz, who embraced both melodic and dissonant sounds, liked what he heard on the VEJI album. Fraser and Collier did lunch and "they ended up hitting it off," said Walters.[36] Collier arranged for Fraser to teach a workshop, which eventually led to substantial work, especially in teaching composition. Fraser's knowledge and passion resonated with Collier, and vice versa, so the jazz men were close colleagues and friends.

Hugh Fraser Quintet: Ross Taggart (piano), Hugh Fraser (trombone), Ken Lister (bass), Dave Robbins (drums), and Campbell Ryga (alto saxophone), Antigua Guatemala, 2003. Image on the cover of Concerto. Photo by Lorae Farrell.

Fraser and his groups also resonated with at least one cabinet minister. During Lloyd Axworthy's tenure as Canada's Minister of Foreign Affairs, Fraser and the quintet were flown to Panama City, Bogotá, São Paulo, and other cities to perform one-nighters hosted by Canadian embassies. "Lloyd Axworthy was a huge fan of the Hugh Fraser Quintet, and he thought that we could be the ambassadors of Canadian jazz," said Ryga,[37] who, aside from Fraser, was the constant in the group that seamlessly transitioned when Ross Taggart, Ken Lister, and Dave Robbins (not Fraser's VCC guru, but the drummer with the same name) joined. Fraser mentored all of them by simply giving them opportunities to express themselves. "I wanted to create a fun, safe space where they could do what they do," he said.[38] It wasn't all merriment and good times over the quintet's lifespan; at times, as the leader, Fraser needed to address challenges as they emerged. I don't know how effective he was at that, but I'm guessing he erred on the side of forgiveness when there were missteps. His humanist philosophy: "Any human doing the best they can is the best human on the planet at that moment."[39]

Some of the missteps were his own. In the early nineties, Fraser and Walters had a second stint in New York that was demonstrably different from the first time they were there. "He had his demons," said Walters, referring to what she described as a serious drug addiction during that time. It involved "casual encounters with certain drugs" that became "a much bigger part of his life."[40] After being together for eight intense years, Fraser and Walters broke up in New York, ending a momentous chapter in both of their lives.

When I talked to him on the phone in January 1999, a few months after turning forty, Fraser estimated he had flown somewhere at least once a week in the previous year. Yet he sounded energized, not jetlagged. Since 1993, Fraser had led the Banff Jazz Orchestra Workshop, for which he recruited Muhal Richard Abrams, Maria Schneider, Wheeler, Valdes, and others as guest faculty. Fraser also staged jazz orchestra workshops and festivals in Vancouver and other cities in Canada and Ireland. My sense was that he enjoyed this nomadic life because it was ultimately all about the music. But there were reasons to dial back the travel. Fraser became a father in 1994. While he and his partner Agnes eventually separated, Fraser wanted to spend more time with his son Jimi James. Fraser also wanted to be close to his mom, who lived with dementia in a care home until she died in 2004. So, after more than two decades chasing the jazz dream around the world, he committed to a quieter life back where it all started, Victoria.

Fraser found himself back in his childhood home, and he thought it would be an ideal living situation. Unlike the waterfront view he had of Esquimalt Harbour, however, life wasn't idyllic. Fraser felt uneasy because repressed emotions were starting to surface. For a long time, he didn't understand what was happening, but Fraser knew it was causing him pain. His response was to self-medicate by drinking to excess and using cocaine. The infectiously gregarious man who was on top of the jazz world at Ronnie Scott's, and who wrote the ballad "Fairy Tales" in 1992 to express "the hope that everything in one's life will work out in the end, like a fairy tale,"[41] had gone through challenges before. Fraser had always bounced back from setbacks with his usual spirit, but now he was troubled. It would take years to disentangle why.

• • •

While Fraser's life had slowed down, there were still significant concerts to play. In June 2001, the Hugh Fraser Quintet opened for Legends of the Bandstand—Hank Jones, Curtis Fuller, Gary Bartz, Ray Drummond, and Louis Hayes—at the Vogue Theatre as part of Vancouver's jazz festival. Fraser was chuffed to open for jazz musicians who had truly achieved legendary status.

In December 2001, a friend visited Fraser in Victoria and she brought along Lorae Farrell, a trumpeter who first met Fraser backstage at the Legends of the Bandstand concert. "By the end of the weekend he said, 'You know what? We're going to spend the rest of our lives together,'" recalled Farrell. Every day the next week, Fraser sent roses to Farrell. On Valentine's Day 2002, Farrell moved to Victoria to live with Fraser.[42] The following year, Ian McDougall retired from teaching music at UVic and Fraser became the university's jazz professor. Things seemed to be looking up.

At the same time that Farrell came into his life, a megaproject that Fraser conceptualized and worked hard to make a reality was coming to fruition. He gathered an expanded version of VEJI, string players, and singers to record in Vancouver's Armoury Studios for three days in December 2001. They had an ambitious agenda: recording both Fraser's *Mass in C Minor*, which he had written years before in London and previously recorded in Banff, and a new five-movement work he had composed with a solitary focus in Victoria: *Concerto for Jazz Orchestra*. Hiring thirty-two instrumentalists and singers, a producer, engineers, and others, and releasing the recording on his Boathouse Records label cost about $60,000.

It was well worth it. *Big Works* is a sublime achievement that affirmed Fraser's virtuosity as a composer and bandleader. The suites also convey the breadth of his vision. The Concerto's "Duke's Circle" is a tender traditional ballad with a gorgeous trombone solo by McDougall. "Credo" from the Mass builds up to a cacophonous frenzy that climaxes with Bill Clark's entirely free solo. During the sessions, Clark consciously appreciated the significance of what was being recorded. "As I'm playing this, as I'm hearing it, and as

I'm listening to the other players do their parts, I just feel like I'm part of an orchestra that's playing a major piece of jazz writing," said Clark.[43]

Big Works led Fraser to write other long-form pieces and find the resources to present them. The Ottawa Jazz Festival commissioned Fraser to compose a suite celebrating both the festival's and VEJI's twenty-fifth anniversaries. VEJI premiered the eight-movement *Canadian Dedication* on June 24, 2005, in Ottawa's Confederation Park. The hour-long suite was Fraser's longest work, and his composing for it was just as stunningly inventive as *Big Works*. Although it wasn't recorded in a studio, VEJI performed *Canadian Dedication* on a cross-Canada tour. "That tour, it was phenomenal," said Clark. "I felt like everywhere we played, we were lifting the roof. From the beginning of the tour, we were playing that way."[44]

A CBC recording of the tour's second-to-last show, October 28, 2005, at the Vancouver East Cultural Centre (the Cultch), captures a particularly vibrant performance. "It sounds like someone flying over Canada and hearing a party in all these cities," said Farrell.[45] Once again, Fraser excelled at balancing compelling writing for a large ensemble with providing ample spaces that let soloists shine. Singer Christine Duncan didn't hold back in her exquisite solo that traverses the last two movements, "Founding Mothers" and "Her Majesty the Blues." She never held back when performing with VEJI, as Fraser "would ramp it up and he would just basically egg you on" to try to elicit the most passionate performance, Duncan said. "Things could get pretty crazy and intense," she added. "You could find yourself really going for it."[46] On Clark's music for one of the tunes, Fraser indicated a solo for him and added an odd notation that he knew the trumpeter would understand: "And they freaked out at 3415 Mons"—the address they shared a quarter century before when VEJI was blowing hard in the basement.[47]

Over the next decade, Fraser didn't work at the frenetic pace of his younger days. He kept a lower profile but still contributed at his high standard on noteworthy projects. In 2005, Kenny Wheeler mounted a UK tour with an all-star twenty-one-member big band to celebrate his seventy-fifth birthday, and he chose Fraser to conduct. The band featured Lee Konitz, and many of the elite musicians who fifteen years earlier had performed on Wheeler's *Music for Large & Small Ensembles* album on ECM Records, including Dave Holland, Norma Winstone, Evan Parker, and Julian Argüelles.

Fraser also played on that superb recording. He considered it an honour to conduct the band, and it was a joy for Fraser and Farrell to ride on a tour bus with Konitz and the cream of contemporary English jazz for two weeks.

Then Fraser received a commission to compose a triple concerto to be performed by the CBC Radio Orchestra, with him on trombone, Wheeler, and Ryga as soloists. Fraser and Farrell worked as a team to prepare the music for the orchestra. Fraser wrote the music by hand and gave it in segments to Farrell, who put it in music notation software. "That was scary because Hugh was very much a procrastinator," said Farrell. "If he had a deadline he would wait pretty much to the end, and then write through the night. So, I had to stay up through the night copying at the same pace he was writing because we had to be there the next day for the first rehearsal."[48] Premiered March 26, 2006, at the Chan Centre for the Performing Arts in Vancouver, "Primary Colours" is a beautiful cinematic meditation on "Blue," "Yellow," and "Red." It went further than any of his major works in crafting compositions that encompassed classical music and jazz. Fraser's orchestration gave the soloists space to soar, and they came through with compelling improvisations.

Hugh Fraser, the Cellar, December 20, 2006. Photo by Steve Mynett.

Fraser had multiple musical personas he could shapeshift between. He was as at home collaborating with the introverted and gracefully understated Wheeler as he was with vibrant and technically awe-inspiring Latin jazz musicians. A once-in-a-lifetime concert on January 12, 2010, in Havana exemplified the latter. Fraser first met Orlando "Maraca" Valle in 1988 at Ronnie Scott's when the virtuosic Cuban flutist and percussionist was in Irakere. They maintained a connection as Fraser progressed in his career, and Maraca became a top Cuban artist. After Maraca decided to put on a concert at the resplendent Gran Teatro de La Habana, he assembled an exceptional eleven-member band—the Latin Jazz All Stars—including drummer Horacio "El Negro" Hernández, percussionist Giovanni Hidalgo, saxophonist David Sánchez, pianist Harold López-Nussa, Fraser on trombone, and other players with chops galore. Fraser and violinist Sayaka Katsuki were the only non-Latinos in the group. "He was really thrilled to be asked to do that," said Farrell. His delight in being there translated into ardent playing, as the concert's subsequently released DVD and live album *Reencuentros* confirm. During "Afro," with an eyes-closed focus, he delivers a quintessential Hugh Fraser trombone solo that bursts with ebullience and is strikingly in sync with López-Nussa's montuno rhythm.

Including Fraser in the all-star group made sense. "He was like a superstar there," said Farrell, who witnessed the sold-out Havana show with Maraca and company and went with Fraser on tours with the quintet and VEJI to the island nation. "A lot of the students would always come backstage and flocked around Hugh."[49]

After the exhilaration of the Latin Jazz All Stars' extravaganza in Havana, Fraser and Farrell returned to Victoria and resumed their quiet lives by the sea. He was back to dreaming up new projects, applying for grants, composing, and grabbing chances to play. But the discomfort Fraser started feeling after moving back to the home where he grew up increased and manifested itself in emotional and physical pain. At the same time, his purchase of the house saddled him with debt. Being a jazz professor at UVic also didn't turn out as Fraser had hoped, so he left the job. Heavy drinking, which he had successfully cut back, re-emerged at times. Fraser asked himself, "What the hell is happening to my karmic life? There is something wrong here."[50]

In need of a change, Fraser and Farrell repeated the move he made thirty-five years earlier: going across the water to Vancouver. A prime advantage of making the move was the pick-me-up of reuniting with musicians Fraser had led for years in VEJI and the quintet. Though he had linked up with some fine players in Victoria, Fraser and his Vancouver comrades were a brotherhood. One person Fraser was especially looking forward to spending time and playing with was Ross Taggart. It didn't turn out that way. Taggart had renal cancer and went into Vancouver General Hospital (VGH) in October 2012. Fraser and Farrell visited Taggart at VGH and shared some laughs, respinning old tales of times on the road. He passed away in January 2013. "That was really hard on Hugh," said Farrell.[51] "I think about Ross a lot," Fraser told me more than six years after his friend's death.[52] When visiting Taggart in the hospital, Fraser had no idea that he would face his own overwhelming health battle.

• • •

"One, two, one, two, uh, uh!" That's how Fraser counted in one of the last songs performed at the Cellar on February 26, 2014, the beloved venue's final night. The piece: one of Fraser's signature tunes, "Thank You Very Much."

The song differs from most of his more than 200 compositions in several ways. Fraser didn't sit at the piano to write it. During a teaching stint in Toronto, he camped out in noisy Paupers Pub in the city's Annex neighbourhood, and with just a Bic pen and paper composed two of his most enduring songs: "The Key of Love" and "Thank You Very Much." I can imagine Fraser sitting there, humming the melodies he was creating and envisioning how they would sound. On the surface, "Thank You Very Much" is a straight ahead, swinging twelve-bar blues in B flat that was more straight forward than his complex works. "That was realizing and respecting the power of the blues and simplicity," said Fraser about the tune's inspiration.[53] Because it was Fraser's, there were intriguing components. Inspired by Joe Henderson's "Isotope," the song's first ten bars are straight blues, and then in the last two there's an angular turnaround with chords and notes you don't expect in a blues. So, in just two bars Fraser managed to create harmonic interest and pay tribute to a mentor from his Banff days.

Journeys to the Bandstand

Hugh Fraser (piano), Jennifer Scott (vocals), Cory Weeds (tenor saxophone), Adam Thomas (bass), Chris Davis (trumpet), and Julian MacDonough (drums) performing "Thank You Very Much," the Cellar, February 26, 2014. Photo by Steve Mynett.

Vancouver Ensemble of Jazz Improvisation (VEJI). Back row (left to right): Bill Runge, Kent Wallace, Dennis Esson, Jim Hopson, Miles Foxx Hill, Daniel Miles Kane, Brad Muirhead, Bill Clark, and Campbell Ryga. Middle row: Jack Duncan and Dave Robbins. Front row: Lorae Farrell and Hugh Fraser. The Warehouse Studio, April 12, 2015. Photo by Vincent Lim.

"Thank You Very Much" was also one of the few songs for which Fraser wrote lyrics:

Thank you very much for all you've said
Thank you very much for all you've done
But no thanks
No thanks
I can manage very well on my own so don't phone
Just please go home

The tune is about someone who undeservedly took credit for "discovering" and "making" the careers of certain jazz musicians. Fraser was fascinated with the idea that "you can make music that's really fun and happy and it's about a negative thing."[54] He also loved to extend the shelf life of his strongest compositions by re-recording them in new ways; "Thank You Very Much" was a prime example. Versions of the song ended up on four albums, including recordings by the quintet, VEJI, the quintet + Slide Hampton, and Fraser's Bonehenge project that featured five trombonists. In performance, the tune was often the last song because it was a great closer. If there was a singer on the gig, like Christine Duncan, Fraser was sheepish about the words. "Hugh felt really self-conscious about it because he felt bad that he's saying to the crowd, 'I don't need you, go home,'" said Farrell.[55]

When Jennifer Scott heartily sang it that last night at the Cellar, with Fraser on piano, Weeds on tenor, and other players, I doubt any of the patrons analyzed the meaning. They likely thought "Thank You Very Much" was an ideal expression of gratitude to Weeds and the Cellar for providing a special place to play for countless Vancouver jazz groups, including Fraser's quintet and VEJI. Regardless of the rollicking song's devilish intent, hearing it always brings to mind Fraser himself—his upbeat disposition, sense of humour, and gift for musical storytelling.

•

When the diagnosis came in June 2016, it was devastating. Fraser had colorectal cancer, the second leading cause of cancer death in Canada. From that point on, Fraser and Farrell had to focus on a daily struggle to maintain his physical and mental health. Treating the cancer required surgery, chemotherapy, and radiation, but doctors discovered that Fraser had serious heart disease, which his father also had. Heart surgery was the first priority.

His condition and the treatment regimen ruled out playing gigs or working on any recording projects. For the first time in Fraser's life, he was in significant financial need. In August 2016 at Pat's Pub, a benefit was held for Fraser, in which he was able to play with VEJI. Then at the end of the year, planning was underway for a larger fundraiser with VEJI and the quintet. This time, though, Fraser wouldn't be able to play; he was just too ill. Ryga was the primary organizer for the benefit concert on January 14, 2017, and Fraser agreed to let his longtime pal and bandmate look after all the details. That didn't last. Fraser got involved in selecting musicians and shaping the setlists. "He wanted to do all of this stuff, so I had to let him because he was a controller and he was an organizer and it was his music and who was I to stand in his way?" said Ryga. "I just wanted to help him and I guess as things went on, the best way to help him was to let him help himself."[56]

From my seat in the packed theatre at Capilano University, I had a clear view of Fraser sitting in the wings just off stage left during the show. I assumed it was very hard on him to sit out while *his* bands played *his* music—the first time that had happened in their parallel histories. It was in fact tough, but he also enjoyed the experience. The concert proved that his music "had a life of its own if he wasn't there," said Farrell.[57]

Fraser's cancer surgery happened in February 2017, and describing it as a major invasive operation is a huge understatement. Surgeons removed part of his colon, bladder, prostate, and seminal vesicles, and he had a blood transfusion, colostomy, and urostomy. Seven months later, surgeons reversed the colostomy in another procedure, but the urostomy was permanent. These were the hard realities Fraser and Farrell faced. Then it happened. Triggered by the surgeries and anesthesia, he experienced vivid flashbacks. Repressed memories of being physically and sexually abused by an older boy painfully surfaced. "I've never been a victim, and I never will be," said Fraser. "I just take what I've got, and I do the best I can with it. But my God, I can't believe the stuff I have lived through."[58]

There are complex layers to Fraser's abuse and recovered memory story. I'm not qualified to peel back those layers and analyze them. But it's clear that while Fraser harboured acute trauma, and suffered from many serious health conditions, he remained exuberant and positive onstage and in the company of friends. It both astonished me and made perfect sense that he maintained that duality. Fraser held on to his inherently happy nature; his ebullience was authentic. At the same time, the suppression of dark memories was a "defense mechanism that protected him from the horrors of what really happened," said Farrell.[59]

Fraser needed help to work through issues that emerged after the abuse realizations. Some original VEJI members provided critical support. Rod Borrie, a psychologist and trombonist in Long Island, New York, was one of them. Another was Patric Caird, the dude wearing the leather jacket who played the wild tenor solo in Edmonton at the Canadian Stage Band Festival. Caird, who had moved to Los Angeles and became a successful composer for film and TV, paid for a health care professional to provide counselling to Fraser. "She has just saved my life," said Fraser. "So the irony now is this lady is being paid for by a guy in the Hollywood Hills and the other guy who helps me is in New York, so I am getting free psychological medical care from the USA," he added with a laugh.[60]

Then there was Farrell, his partner, caregiver, manager, and member of the VEJI trumpet section. She was selflessly there for Fraser twenty-four-seven, while working full-time as a paralegal. "She has been my keel through this whole thing," Fraser said.[61] He wrote notes to Farrell, mini love letters left around their apartment for her to discover. On December 19, 2018, he wrote: "I Love You more than anything in the universe!!! I'm turning a corner – 2019 will be our year!!! (of many!). All my love, life + music, Hugh."[62]

Fraser was declared cancer-free at one point, which bolstered his optimism. Farrell, however, intuitively suspected something was still wrong. "But, of course, Hugh would be so positive and energetic," she said. "He'd go into the cancer agency to meet with the oncologists and Hugh would be like, 'You're doing a great job, you're wonderful, thanks so much, I appreciate what you're doing. I'll highly recommend you to anyone.' As if they needed business. And I'd be in the background behind Hugh, waving at the doctor, going 'It's not good.'"[63]

In spring 2019, they drove to West Vancouver and found St. Francis-in-the-Wood, the idyllic little Anglican church in the forest where his parents had exchanged vows almost eighty years before. "We walked around the grounds, we walked inside, and then he said, 'Let's get married here in the fall,'" recalled Farrell. She phoned the church to ask about availability, but it never happened because Fraser's condition worsened. "I wish it had," said Farrell wistfully.[64]

Not many weeks later, in May 2019, Farrell posted an update on Fraser's health on Facebook. In the post, she confirmed that his cancer had metastasized to spots in both lungs and lymph nodes in his abdomen. This was part of a long and disconcerting list of Fraser's health concerns and procedures Farrell detailed. I looked at that list a long time. It was hard to reconcile what she wrote with my earliest memories of Fraser—the young and fearless jazz insurgent with his whole creative life ahead of him. But Farrell struck a reassuring tone for the many worried members of his tribe. "He is so positive and confident that he is going to beat this," she wrote.[65]

Fraser was sanguine enough to commit to a prominent concert: VEJI performing on June 23, 2019, at Pyatt Hall as part of Vancouver's jazz festival. Saying yes to the show meant there would be no half measures. Fraser intended to fulfill all his duties as band leader—choosing the musicians and repertoire, leading rehearsals, conducting the band when needed, playing piano and trombone, and talking to the audience—regardless of his shaky health. "He was in the kind of pain that made it almost impossible for him to play, but he always considered himself to be pretty invincible," said Ryga. "Somehow, he was going to pull it out of the bag, even if it was going to hurt the next day or the next week, which it always would. But he would never back down from the opportunity to play."[66]

Fraser and VEJI delivered. The band sounded as explosive as ever and Fraser, performing his first gig in three years, played with total ardor. Also, a momentous thing happened: Fraser's son Jimi James played piano on a few tunes. Fraser was incredibly proud of James, who had emerged on the Vancouver scene as a fine pianist well versed in jazz history. He lives in Jazz House—a scruffy shared house well known, especially among younger musicians, for its late-night jam sessions. Here was the Clan Fraser updating Mons House history in a new guise.

Something else happened that singular night: rather than save precious energy for playing, Fraser, who was a master of long and funny between-song banter, talked even more than usual. At Pyatt Hall, he riffed on Scriabin's "mystic chord" and the Fibonacci sequence, praised the musicians and friends on stage and some who had passed, acknowledged the bliss of being there—"It is so wonderful to be in a room with so much love and music,"—and looked ahead to the future: "We will do a lot of stuff next year . . . I am going to be here for a long time."[67] No doubt he believed these hopeful proclamations, but something compelled him to leave nothing unsaid. As it turned out, this was the last show Fraser performed with VEJI.

. . .

Hugh Fraser, the Classical Joint, circa 1980. Photo by Graham Ord.

In the early to mid-1980s, if you wanted to hear the hippest, most happening jazz played by Vancouver musicians, you went to the Classical Joint on Sunday nights. That's what I did on many Sundays to hear musicians like Ted Quinlan, Patric Caird, Shannon Gunn, Bob Murphy, and Fraser. The

Joint's proprietor, Andreas Nothiger, loved to book Fraser at the coffeehouse in Vancouver's Gastown district because of his playing and personality. "One word: exciting," said Nothiger about what Fraser was like at the Joint. "Very, very exciting. Very, very involved. He couldn't sit still, moving all the time."[68]

Images of sitting on a bench at the candlelit Classical Joint, listening to an enthused Fraser, were in my head on September 17, 2019. That day I walked across old Gastown cobblestones to Fraser and Farrell's condo building, kitty-corner from where the Joint had stood. Fraser greeted me warmly at their high-ceilinged loft. He had a black eye and other smallish injuries from a recent fall outside the building, but that and his other more serious ailments weren't slowing him down. Twenty years had passed since my last interview with him, and Fraser had a lot to say. Similar to his onstage banter at Pyatt Hall, Fraser speed-talked through his life story. Not in a linear way, but with sudden U-turns and detours. I could barely keep pace. To emphasize points, at times he excitedly started sentences with "Dig this." Other times, Fraser proudly showed me artifacts—a framed photo of him with McCoy Tyner, his first drum, and a sterling silver card certifying that his dad Kenneth Fraser was a life member of Vancouver Local 145 of the American Federation of Musicians, among other treasures.

The recurring themes that afternoon were clear. "I've had a really tough time," Fraser said. "It's amazing I am alive. I think I am alive because of the power of music." Looking back at his life, Fraser felt "lucky" about receiving opportunities. "But I will say that I did take advantage of the opportunities," he said. "I am amazed sometimes that people have opportunities, and they don't go for them. You have to put yourself physically in that space." Fraser meant that artists need to believe and invest in themselves, to be ready to answer when opportunity knocks, something he did for himself and many others. He also had no regrets about his musical choices. "I feel very proud of myself for continually putting music first. Art music."[69]

Three days later, on a sunny fall day, I picked up Fraser and drove us to an East Van house that was crucial to his survival. It's where saxophonist and VEJI member Daniel Miles Kane lives and hosts frequent jam sessions. Along with Kane, veteran players were there: Tony Wilson, Allan Johnston, Wayne Stewart, and Nels Guloien (PJ Perry's brother). It was obvious in Fraser's demeanour how happy he was to be there with the guys, having beers, yakking, listening to records, and above all, playing. They crammed into a tiny room off the living room and blithely jammed on standards: "I Love You," "Mahjong," "Gemini," and more. Fraser was sweating and didn't feel like he had his trombone chops that day, but it didn't matter. I was witnessing what has always happened when jazz musicians are off the bandstand and have time on their hands—they get together and play more jazz, just for fun. As Fraser put it, "This is the most exclusive jazz club ever."[70]

Participating in the jam was much more than a simple pleasure for Fraser. "That was his regular and only place to really play in the last two or three years," said Bill Clark.[71] The gatherings inspired him to keep composing; he brought in new tunes for the musicians to try out. Plus, it gave him the musical and social stimulus that was as necessary to him as air. "I've just got to play because I live to play and be with people," said Fraser.[72] Clark recalled the times he showed up for the jam and a seated Fraser yelled out "B'Dort!", the nonsensical nickname Fraser and Ryga attached to Clark. Fraser would then jump up and, with a big smile plastered on his face, hug Clark. "Keep in mind, he's deadly ill when he does this," said Clark. "He's well into the cancer, he's well into losing his teeth, and he's well into not being able to control his bowels. And that's his reaction to seeing me walk into the room. It's just like we're twenty-one-years-old again."[73]

Around the time of those two indelible days that I hung out with Fraser, he was preparing for a set of dates that stood out on his calendar. Cory Weeds had booked Fraser and his quintet to perform October 25–27, 2019 at Frankie's Jazz Club. The plan was to record the gigs, which would focus on new material from *Gastown Chronicles*, a collection of about thirty songs Fraser had composed since getting sick. Fraser would just be on piano; he didn't have the lung power to play trombone. Campbell Ryga on alto and soprano saxes, bassist Ken Lister, and drummer Dave Robbins would also be there as they had for years whenever Fraser convened the band.

The only question was, who would fill Ross Taggart's tenor spot? Fraser decided to ask Weeds to take on the role. Weeds, whose sound reminded Fraser of a young Taggart, was honoured and floored. When he was an emerging saxophonist, Weeds worshipped the quintet and aspired to play at the group's level. He also saw Taggart, previous member Phil Dwyer, and Ryga as sax heroes. Fraser knew all of this and unburdened Weeds from the weight of expectations and his usual frontman duties. "I want to be in charge of the band on stage," Fraser said. "I don't want him to talk. I want him to think about playing and just enjoy himself and loosen him up that way."[74] Fraser was still very much a mentor.

I went on the last night, and Frankie's was filled to capacity. Many familiar faces from the jazz community were present. Sitting at the bar with Farrell was Patric Caird, who was there to support his lifelong friend. Fraser played beautifully, and the musicians meshed well. In the first set on the up-tempo "Kenny," dedicated to Kenny Wheeler, Fraser was all over the piano during his fiery solo. Then Fraser gifted us a classic from his oeuvre: "Dusk," a ballad from the *Concerto for Jazz Orchestra* suite. Ryga and Weeds played their parts with fitting gravity. Between sets, Fraser lay down in a hotel room next door, which Weeds had arranged at Fraser and Farrell's request. That's how draining it was to perform. But not a soul in the audience noticed. In the second set, Fraser really went for it on the last tune: "Our Man Ross in Havana," an homage to Taggart. Fraser found the energy to play a montuno pattern and improvise with supreme abandon. Chucho Valdes would have dug it. Clark said Fraser always set the standard by embodying the philosophy that "I'm going to play today like there's no tomorrow."[75] On this, the final song ever performed by the Hugh Fraser Quintet, he did exactly that.

I saw Fraser one more time, six days before Christmas 2019. I was walking near the shadow of the Classical Joint, by now shuttered nearly thirty years, when I spotted Fraser and Farrell. Fraser walked slowly and gingerly, holding on to Farrell's arm as they crossed the street and went a short distance down the sidewalk before ducking into their favourite watering hole, the Blarney Stone. I thought about going in to say hi but decided against interrupting their time together. I regret that decision.

No one knew then that COVID-19 would soon have a devastating impact. After it was declared a pandemic, the live jazz scene shut down for months. For Fraser, that meant losing the jam sessions that buoyed him. At the same time, he was getting sicker. But he had a coda in him. It came about because the Hard Rubber New Music Society organized An Earful of Vancouver, a series of videos made during the pandemic featuring creative musicians in Vancouver's jazz scene.

Hugh Fraser (piano) and Campbell Ryga (soprano saxophone), Frankie's Jazz Club, October 25, 2019. Photo by Vincent Lim.

Hugh Fraser, Frankie's Jazz Club, October 25, 2019. Photo by Vincent Lim.

In April 2020, Farrell shot a video of Fraser in their place performing a song for the series. Of course, Fraser had to introduce the tune with his usual joie de vivre. Fraser says he is going to play his reworking of "Stella by Starlight." He explains that his interest in Béla Bartók led him to phi, also known as the golden ratio, a mathematical form expressed in many of nature's most beautiful shapes, and which became associated with the Italian mathematician Leonardo Fibonacci. Talking about phi and Fibonacci was so Hugh Fraser. Intellectually curious about realms beyond jazz, he was always looking for ways to translate theory into enchanting music. "So you're going to hear everything about two-thirds away from where the chords regularly are, if that interests you," he tells the video audience. "Just listen to it, and it sounds really cool, it's really fun. This is 'Bella by Bar Light,' by Hugh Fraser, coming to you live from downtown Gastown." It is, indeed, cool and fun. On his grand piano, Fraser transforms the jazz standard with a re-harmonization that has lived on in my consciousness ever since. Fraser, the impeccable showman, then shares some final words: "'Bella by Bar Light.' Thank you. Peace, love, and music. Be safe to everyone. Love you."[76]

• • •

In early June 2020, Farrell brought Fraser to St. Paul's Hospital, where he was diagnosed with an intestinal blockage. Fraser was also once again riddled with cancer. Farrell could see that her life partner, who was in enormous pain, didn't have long. So she focused on ensuring James could say goodbye to his dad. With COVID-19 restrictions, however, Farrell was the only visitor allowed. A sympathetic employee let James in a back door and brought him up to Fraser's room. "I was holding Hugh's hand, he was still alive, and then James walked in," recounted Farrell. "I gave James a hug, I looked back down, and he was gone."[77] Fraser, who hung on until James arrived, passed away on June 17, 2020, at approximately four a.m. The time of death was significant. Fraser enjoyed composing at that time. He also listened extensively to John Coltrane's *Suite*, whose third movement is titled, "Prayer and Meditation: 4 A.M."

For Farrell, it was a heartbreaking conclusion to their time together, which included "a lot of great memories and a lot of great music that we made together. It's just amazing when I look back. I'm pretty darn fortunate to be part of all that."[78]

Later that morning, Ryga was riding his motorcycle to the hospital, where he was also going to be snuck in to see Fraser. En route, Ryga received the call he was dreading. It came from Dr. David Esler, a trumpeter and caregiver/friend of Fraser, confirming that the end had come. Ryga had played more gigs with Fraser than any other musician, but they had shared more than music; they were like brothers, who spoke almost daily and had sweet monikers for each other—Fraser was "Blue," Ryga was "Red." Ryga had prepared for this moment, but coming to terms with the loss would take months. During that time, Ryga thought about the wisdom he had gained from Fraser, including this: "'You don't fall in love with somebody and have a backup plan if it doesn't work out. You have to get into this [musical life] unreservedly and wholeheartedly and without hesitation and embrace it. And if you fall, you fall. You just get back up and continue doing it.' That was his philosophy."[79]

More than thirty years after Jan Walters and Hugh Fraser parted, Walters summed up her thoughts about Fraser's musical significance: "Hugh distinguished himself amongst his musical colleagues in every way. He was well respected, admired, and loved by the jazz greats he met throughout his career and was definitely in that league of musicians, composers, and bandleaders who are far more well-known than he was."[80] Walters emphasized that Fraser was "inclusive of other players, other ideas."[81] She also believed that "it's a real shame Hugh didn't get to realize his full potential."[82]

Farrell achieved a goal she and Fraser had: releasing both *Canadian Dedication*, the 2005 live recording of VEJI's incendiary performance at the Cultch, and *Gastown Chronicles*, a live recording of the Hugh Fraser Quintet's meaningful last performances at Frankie's in 2019. There wasn't much fanfare about the albums coming out, just as there hadn't been enough acclaim in the past when Fraser put out recordings. But that didn't mean they went into a void. Jazz artists from a younger generation, like Dean Thiessen—pianist, composer, and leader of the Stranger Friends Orchestra—have heard and been influenced by the ingenuity in Fraser's music. Thiessen recounted to Will Chernoff of *Rhythm Changes* what it was like to hear Fraser's music for the first time: "'Oh, *that's* what a big band can sound like!'"[83] Thiessen's response, years later, to *Canadian Dedication* after Farrell released it: "It has Hugh's wit and comedy and it sounds like a composer who trusts his band with everything."[84] Even after Fraser was gone, he was inspiring emerging artists.

The COVID-19 pandemic eased sufficiently to enable Farrell to hold a celebration of life for Fraser. When it finally happened on October 17, 2021, at the Vogue Theatre, befitting Fraser's propensity to go big, Farrell went all out to ensure it was an event to remember. She curated a program that mainly consisted of emotional performances of Fraser's music, by VEJI, the Hugh Fraser Quintet, the James Fraser Trio, Farrell and James in a duo, and James performing solo. Fraser's legacy of compositions he wrote and community he built—more than 300 people were in the audience—was front and centre. As James' remarkable playing that day showed, his father's musical passion was left in very good hands.

There were also heartfelt words, including a speech by Clark that captured Fraser's spirit. Among many things, Clark learned from Fraser the symbolic importance of believing in yourself not just as a musician, but as an artist. After listening to the words and music that resonated that day, I tried but struggled to distill Fraser's essence.

Then something else Clark had described to me earlier came to mind. Clark and other musicians that were part of the VEJI/quintet circle taught with Fraser at many music camps. Even if Fraser wasn't the director at these camps, "there was no question who the lead teacher was, ever," said Clark. It was always Fraser. He incorporated in his teaching the influence of Abraham Adzenyah, a master drummer from Ghana whom Fraser had met at the Banff Centre in the 1980s. Every morning, and at the end of every camp's final concert, Fraser led students in an ancient Ghanaian folk song that Adzenyah taught him: "Let Your Voice Be Heard." It was quite the sight and sound—teenagers singing, dancing, clapping, and playing this Ghanaian song. "It was one of the most magical things I ever experienced as an educator," said Clark.[85]

The 2019 VEJI show at Pyatt Hall didn't close with "Thank You Very Much." Fraser knew the moment called for "Let Your Voice Be Heard." He explained to the audience what the song was all about. "The thing is, all of us wake up one morning and we say, well you know I can just look at my instrument or my life or what I'm doing and go, this is not very good. Or you can look at it and say that I might as well just let my voice be heard and do the most I can with the hand I have been given. And make it really positive."[86]

Jack Duncan on congas and Dave Robbins on drums got the groove started. Then the rest of the ensemble came in with a jubilant sound. Then the band stopped, and it became an a cappella sing-along. Until the end of the song, the musicians and audience jointly let their voices be heard. The voice I could hear clearest was that of Hugh Alexander Fraser.

14 / THANKFULLY: ROSS TAGGART

And if I ever lost you
How much would I cry?
How deep is the ocean
How high is the sky?

- *"How Deep is the Ocean?" by Irving Berlin*

When Ross Taggart walked onto the bandstand at Cory Weeds' Cellar on a warm July night in 2002, he was well aware of the sense of occasion. Taggart was about to play piano with a visiting alto sax great: Charles McPherson. Taggart's jazz history knowledge was vast. He knew all about McPherson's long tenure with Charles Mingus and the altoist's track record as a bandleader and keeper of the bebop flame. At that time, when the club was less than two years old, McPherson was one of the most prominent jazz musicians to perform there. Plus, Weeds and Brad Turner were recording the two nights of performances. Taggart knew he and the other members of the local rhythm section Weeds lined up for McPherson's Cellar engagement had to deliver.

It happened during a long version of the classic ballad Irving Berlin wrote seventy years before, "How Deep is the Ocean?" Taggart achieved transcendence. Over the course of an entrancing four minute and twenty-two second improvisation, Taggart reached deep within to craft a gorgeously lyrical solo. His hands were in sync, playing crisp lines with the right and resonant, well-timed voicings with the left. Throughout, Taggart incorporated a range of elements, from blues licks to dense block chords, and cascading runs that spanned multiple octaves. Just when it seemed like the improv would end, he kept giving more, continuing to shape melodic and harmonic contours until the last note.

Elegant and swinging, Taggart's solo consisted of sublime moments in time. Those moments weren't just ephemeral. The recording that documented McPherson's shows with Taggart, Jodi Proznick, and Blaine Wikjord resulted in a live album that Weeds released on his Cellar Live label. In my streaming platform of choice, I've been able to repeatedly transport myself to the club and this specific performance. While Taggart played countless majestic solos on piano and tenor saxophone with myriad ensembles in his career, this one grabbed hold of me as an emblematic expression of his artistry. It hasn't let go.

Taggart started developing his sound as a lanky teenager in Victoria, and he quickly progressed to the point where—across the Strait of Georgia in Vancouver—he became one of the city's and Canada's pre-eminent jazz musicians. As a multi-instrumentalist, Taggart played beautifully in local jazz joints and venues around the world. Taggart was also one of the Vancouver jazz scene's most-loved characters, with the gift of making people smile and laugh.

His death from cancer at a young age in early 2013 was devastating to all who knew him. When someone so extraordinary dies prematurely, the natural impulse is to try to hang on to a piece of the person. For me, the "How Deep is the Ocean?" solo is that piece, and it's a window to a luminous body of work made over a remarkable jazz life.

• • •

William Taggart was born in Glasgow, Scotland, and grew up in Winnipeg, where he met Helen Shaw.[1] They married in Vancouver in 1954.[2] The Taggarts raised three children, including the youngest: Ross Thomas Taggart, born November 24, 1967, in Victoria on Vancouver Island.

Taggart started piano lessons at a young age and did typical boy things, like join Cub Scouts. In Cubs, he met Reece Metcalfe Rehm, who was born four days after Taggart. They became best friends. In 1981, Metcalfe Rehm's father Eric Metcalfe gave his son a record that had come out the year before: *The Trumpet Summit Meets the Oscar Peterson Big 4*. Aside from Peterson, the album features a three-trumpet frontline of Dizzy Gillespie, Clark Terry, and Freddie Hubbard.

"I put it on and the expression on Ross's face was like it was a eureka moment," said Metcalfe Rehm. "His face went white, and his eyes went like deer in the headlights. It was like, 'Oh my God.'"[3] For fourteen-year-old Taggart, hearing the high-octane recording was a revelation that kick-started his love for jazz. "I remember immediately falling in love with the exciting, swinging, and foreign sounds of these legendary musicians then unknown to me," Taggart wrote in liner notes years later.[4]

He jotted down the names of the jazz stars who made this music that astounded him and showed the list to his father, a music lover who worked at the University of Victoria's library. The next day, William borrowed a stack of Peterson records from the UVic library and presented them to his son, who again embraced what he heard. Taggart enjoyed going to Victoria's Sweet Thunder Records to buy jazz treasures. Taggart and Metcalfe Rehm also frequented the jazz section in the Victoria location of A&B Sound. They bought albums by Miles Davis, Dexter Gordon, and many other jazz greats. When listening to the music, the pals stood in front of a mirror and pretended—air-band style—to play and improvise.

It wasn't just make-believe. Metcalfe Rehm played trumpet and Taggart played piano, clarinet, and an instrument he picked up around the same time as his jazz epiphany: tenor saxophone. Taggart took jazz lessons with various teachers to begin the lifelong process of learning the music's intricacies. His band teacher at Claremont Secondary School also encouraged him to improvise and introduced Taggart to the music of top Canadian jazz artists, like PJ Perry, Fraser MacPherson, and Oliver Gannon. Taggart was clearly the best musician at Claremont, said Metcalfe Rehm. "There were some other very talented people, but Ross was exceptional."[5]

At sixteen, Taggart started sitting in with bands at Pagliacci's, a popular Victoria restaurant. Metcalfe Rehm remembered seeing a tall, skinny Taggart calmly wait for his opportunity to play at the busy restaurant. "It would be time to play and suddenly, you could hear a pin drop," said Metcalfe Rehm about the surprising quality of Taggart's sax playing and the effect it had. "It was just amazing. Even the band members were like, 'Who's that kid?'"[6]

The childhood friends, who had long been inseparable, grew apart. "I was running with kind of the cool kids, and he was pretty nerdy," said Metcalfe Rehm about Taggart, who didn't have a girlfriend at the time or go out much.[7] While Metcalfe Rehm was out partying, Taggart was at home practicing and listening to jazz. On Sunday nights, he tuned in to Co-op Radio's broadcasts of shows at the Classical Joint in Vancouver's Gastown that featured fiery players like Hugh Fraser, Renee Rosnes, Bob Murphy, Perry White, and Phil Dwyer. "This exposure fueled the fire that was burning inside me to play like them and, one day, with them," said Taggart. "I realized that I was learning a language."[8]

It's important to note that after graduating from high school he didn't follow the path that most young jazz musicians take these days—completing a multi-year university or college jazz program. Instead, Taggart took the old school route: self-study, apprenticing with mentors, and learning on the bandstand.

Inevitably, Taggart made his way in 1985 to Vancouver, where there were substantially more musical opportunities than Victoria offered. His first gig in Vancouver was playing in a militia band based near Jericho Beach. While in the city, he connected with jazz singer June Katz, who happened to be dating the man who shared the record that changed Taggart's life: artist Eric Metcalfe. The following year, around the time Taggart permanently moved to Vancouver, the Alma Street Café opened just a few kilometres away from where he was stationed with the militia band. Katz was a partner at the restaurant and programmed live jazz there. Katz arranged for a "very shy" and "deferential" Taggart to sit in with Campbell Ryga, Gannon, and other superb local musicians at Alma Street,[9] which became a beloved straight-ahead jazz venue that lasted a decade. The experience Taggart gained and connections he made from the age-old tradition of sitting in led to landing gigs as a leader and establishing himself as a rising talent on tenor sax and piano.

Taggart then focused on learning from mentors. For several months in 1987, he studied with multi-instrumentalist Don Thompson and pianist Bernie Senensky in Toronto. "I want to learn how to play better, learn as much as I can," Taggart said about that time of discovery.[10]

Reece Metcalfe-Rehm, Ross Taggart, and Eric Metcalfe, Western Front, circa 1987. Photo by Hank Bull.

In July 1988, Taggart played piano with the Bill Clark Sextet in the finals of the national Alcan Jazz Competition at the Festival International de Jazz de Montréal. Watching almost an hour of video capturing the group's performance in Montreal provides insights about where Taggart was in his development. His solos confirm the twenty-year-old already had an extensive jazz vocabulary. They also show that he improvised with a raw intensity. In many moments, Taggart pummelled the keys with a barrage of notes and chords that both impressed and indicated room for growth. His idea generation and execution weren't always in sync and there wasn't much breathing room. Taggart would eventually excel at both.

By the beginning of 1990, the Hugh Fraser Quintet was well-established as one of Canada's most exhilarating small jazz ensembles, having recorded two albums and toured extensively. Then wunderkind saxophonist and pianist Phil Dwyer left the group. Enter Taggart. He was an ideal choice to step in because, like Dwyer, Taggart was a compelling saxophonist and pianist, with the latter coming in handy on tunes where Fraser swapped piano for trombone.

Initially, though, Taggart searched for his identity in the band because replacing Dwyer created self-expectations for playing at the departing musician's high level. "But I did pull him aside and I said, 'You don't have to be anybody but you, and that is the way you need to play in this group,'" said quintet member Campbell Ryga.[11] Fraser was equally direct in his advice:

"Ross, he just wanted to play like Phil," said Fraser. "And I said, 'Don't play like Phil. Play like you do what *you* do!'"[12]

Taggart, who was also a member of Fraser's Vancouver Ensemble of Jazz Improvisation (VEJI), proceeded to express his personality on and offstage. In performance, especially with the quintet, Taggart played with a robust passion he had been harnessing since listening to the *Trumpet Summit* record as a kid. When travelling on national and international tours, recording, and hanging out with his bandmates, Taggart's active sense of humour revealed itself. Taggart and Ryga, in particular, developed a comic rapport. Ryga remembers being in recording sessions with Taggart "where I would look at him in just a certain way and he would say to me, 'Oh don't, and then he would start laughing, and we would have to stop the session until he composed himself. We were always testing the boundaries and limits."[13]

By the early nineties, Taggart and Metcalfe Rehm had reconnected and become roommates in a second-floor apartment at Main and East 20th in Vancouver. "When we were roommates, he was out almost every [day and] night playing or recording or teaching or doing something," said Metcalfe Rehm. "He was busy, and he was a hard worker," he added about the in-demand Taggart who was playing with Fraser's groups, the Bill Clark Sextet, Hard Rubber Orchestra, and other bands. Just as he did in the Hugh Fraser Quintet, Taggart doubled on piano and tenor with the Bill Runge-led Creatures of Habit, which won the finals of the Alcan Jazz Competition in 1990. When Taggart wasn't making music locally or touring, the pals recaptured a mutual love for listening to jazz. Metcalfe Rehm: "He'd get an album and say, 'You got to listen to this. You hear that? This is what he's doing.' And I'd be like, 'How do you know that?' He could dissect every note and know what was happening."[14]

• • •

In the summer of 1991, then-seventeen-year-old Sharon Minemoto met Taggart, who was twenty-three. In his beat-up Honda, he drove to the house where Minemoto lived with her parents, and Taggart gave jazz piano lessons with a kinder, gentler teaching style. "He was really supportive and found a lot of positive things to say about students' playing," said Minemoto. "He would say, 'You could try this,' and he would say it in a real gentle way. I was kind of impatient to get better, so I was sort of hoping that he would be harder on me, but that was just not who he was."[15] Minemoto was mesmerized by the virtuosic music that flowed out of Taggart and struck by how kind and polite he was. But there was only time for a few lessons: she was headed to Iowa for music school, and he was going to the ultimate place to learn more about the intricacies and soul of jazz.

The Canada Council for the Arts gave him a grant to study from 1991 to 1993 in New York City with three great tenor men: George Coleman, Clifford Jordan, and J.R. Monterose. In New York, Taggart also regularly gained insights from piano virtuosos—like Tommy Flanagan, Hank Jones, Cedar Walton, and Barry Harris—not in formal lessons but by simply listening to them in jazz clubs.

After a year, Ryga also got a Canada Council grant to study with Coleman and joined Taggart. Eventually, the two would share an apartment in a Puerto Rican neighbourhood on the Upper West Side. On Ryga's very first day in the city, Taggart and trumpeter Joe Magnarelli took the new arrival to a bar. Ryga ordered a beer and the bartender responded, "We don't serve Mexicans here." Ryga, who had features that would later cause New Yorkers to think he was Puerto Rican, froze. "I looked at my first bartender in New York, and I looked at Ross, and then he couldn't hold back the laughter. He had set me up. So that was my first experience in New York, and every day after that there was always some element of that. We had a great time in New York."[16]

Three years after their New York sojourn, Taggart was the best man at Ryga's wedding in Summerland, BC, and he showed up wearing a rubber chicken mask. He even wore the mask while giving a speech. It's the kind of person Taggart was, at least on the outside—unselfconscious about being the resident merry prankster.

Journeys to the Bandstand

Ross Taggart (tenor saxophone) and Rene Worst (bass) with Creatures of Habit, Théâtre Port-Royal, Place des Arts, Montreal, July 6, 1990. Photo by Mark Miller.

Ross Taggart and Campbell Ryga, Vancouver Island. Photo by Neil Taylor.

Taggart's greatest humorous moments may have been on stage, when he performed with Hard Rubber Orchestra on September 24, 1994, at St. Andrew's Wesley Church. That night Hard Rubber presented *The Elvis Cantata*, a satirical, kitschy, and hilarious examination of Elvis Presley. John Korsrud, the big band's leader, wanted the ensemble and guest artists to interpret Elvis-related songs in every imaginable style. He tapped Taggart to do a "lounge jazz" version of an Elvis tune. Taggart didn't reveal before the show what he would do. "It was 100 percent a surprise," said Korsrud of Taggart's solo performance, which involved singing and playing piano on "Hound Dog Blues," a bluesy variant of "Hound Dog." I've watched and re-watched a low-res video of Taggart's number, and I can see why Korsrud said it was the "highlight of the show." Aside from playing killer blues piano, Taggart got fully into the spirit of the evening's offbeat humour with his singing. While not exactly a polished vocalist, he incorporated both subtle comic timing and deliciously over-the-top falsetto, which made the audience laugh heartily. Only someone with ample self-assurance and an instinct for absurdist hilarity could have pulled it off, and Taggart—who Korsrud described as "the funniest person I've ever known"—was perfectly cast.[17]

Then there were his renowned imitations of local musicians. Ryga recounted a story about Taggart calling Oliver Gannon and successfully pretending he was Fraser MacPherson. It's an astonishing yarn given that Gannon had played with MacPherson for years and knew, better than most, the distinctive sound of the saxophonist's ultra-low voice. Monique Van Dam talked about the first time Taggart played with guitarist Pat Coleman. Bob Murphy, Van Dam's partner, let Coleman know in advance that Taggart was a funny man. During the gig, Coleman enjoyed Taggart's playing but didn't think he was especially witty. "Then at the very end of the night, after the gig, Ross did an impression of Bob, and Pat just lost it," said Van Dam, describing how Taggart nailed Murphy's mannerisms. "It was exactly Bob, and Pat roared."[18]

Taggart wasn't just out for laughs, though. His proficiency in impersonating people reflected a genuine interest in and affection for fellow musicians. "I always found him very courtly and very loving to other musicians," said Katie Malloch,[19] who hosted the national Sunday night *Jazz Beat* show on CBC Radio that recorded a number of groups that Taggart played in. Simple gestures, like sending Christmas cards and taking photos of musicians and later presenting them with prints, were acts of kindness and gratitude.

Older musicians appreciated Taggart because, among other traits, he strongly respected tradition. One such elder was Vancouver pianist Linton Garner, the older brother of pianist Erroll Garner. One night Linton played with Taggart on tenor and bassist Russ Botten at the Cellar. A recording of that's evening music—released on Cellar Live as *Quiet Nights*—showed that while there was a more than fifty-two-year age difference between Linton and Taggart, they shared a warm, contemporaneous sound.

Another veteran player who cherished Taggart: Ronnie Scott, the British tenor saxophonist and owner of the renowned jazz club in London's Soho district that bears his name. Scott loved presenting the Hugh Fraser Quintet, and he was a kindred spirit with Taggart. "He had all these pictures [of musicians] up all over his club and Ross could identify every single one, plus Ross's tenor playing was right up Ronnie's alley," said Ryga.[20] "Every year the week after we played with my quintet, he and Ross would hang out and play chess until four a.m. every night," added Fraser. According to Fraser, Taggart was one of the last people to see Scott before the Brit jazz legend died on December 23, 1996, from an accidental barbiturate overdose.[21]

That same year, Minemoto and Taggart started dating. Their mutual friend, singer Shannon Gunn, didn't like how some of Taggart's previous girlfriends had treated him and suggested he ask Minemoto out because she was "normal."[22] Their relationship and professional lives as working musicians blossomed. The year 2000 was pivotal for the couple. That's when Cory Weeds opened the Cellar, which would be a crucial venue for both of their careers. Weeds, like a number of musicians, saw Taggart as a hero. So Taggart was the first person Weeds told about buying the club. Some were skeptical when Weeds, then-twenty-six, announced the purchase and his plans to run a real jazz club. Not Taggart. "He was extremely encouraging to me," said Weeds about Taggart's reaction. "Everything that I said, he took seriously. That had a great impact on me."[23]

It's also the year Taggart and Minemoto got married in Victoria. They tried to indirectly support the Cellar by hiring Weeds' business partner, Don Guthro, to cater their Vancouver wedding reception at the WISE Hall. "We thought if he's Cory's partner, he needs money to keep this club running, so if we pay him for the catering for our wedding, that's going to hopefully come back to us as far as keeping the club open for one more month or two more months or whatever it might be," she said. "So we hired him, and he totally screwed the whole thing up. He forgot to bring cutlery and plates. It was a total gong show. My parents were running around Commercial Drive trying to find Chinet for our guests. We were so mad."[24] And madly in love.

About two years before the paper-plate wedding, I was driving to Vancouver's Cotton Club to attend a gig. It was the CD release celebration of Taggart's debut album, *Ross Taggart & Co*, and in an amazing coincidence the opening track—"After You"—came on the car radio. It's the most winsome tune on the recording. In Taggart's tenor playing on the song, he embraces the clear influence of Dexter Gordon's big tone and deliberate phrasing, while still making the sound his own. In three of four originals by Taggart, there's also an understated melancholy in his compositions that intrigues and engages.

His next album as a leader was a duo collaboration with Bob Murphy, *Mysteries and Tall Tales*. The recording had a long gestation. Soon after Taggart moved to Vancouver as a nineteen-year-old, he started playing tenor with Murphy, the accomplished pianist who was twenty-two years older. "I was pretty scared," said Taggart about making music for the first time with the far more experienced Murphy.[25] They clicked, as musicians—working sporadically on a recording for about a decade—and dear friends. The chums would hold court among musicians who often gathered at Wong Kee restaurant on East Broadway after gigs. "You would be howling your butt off a long time because the two of them were so funny," said vocalist Jennifer Scott about the Wong Kee sessions.[26] Taggart and Murphy were like "big goofy kids," concurred Metcalfe Rehm.[27]

As it turned out, *Mysteries and Tall Tales*—with photos by Metcalfe Rehm on the CD sleeve—was nothing like Taggart and Murphy's side-splitting repartee. "All of a sudden, we hit this zone," said Taggart about the intense two-day session in January 2001, where they recorded all-original tunes emphasizing improvisation.[28] It's the most introspective and farthest away from swinging tradition that Taggart would ever sound on a recording. The whole package—the title, photography, and music—had a cinematic feel, which was consistent with Taggart's love for movies. This was a musical direction he could have explored more if his destiny had unfolded differently.

• • •

A month after making the duo album, Taggart played at the Cellar with a new quartet he led: Taggart on tenor sax, Murphy on Hammond B3 organ, guitarist Mike Rud, and drummer Bernie Arai. "It was their first night as a band, and I knew that Ross had hit on something very special," said Weeds,[29] who booked Taggart and the band for a return engagement June 1–2, 2001. Drummer Morgan Childs, who was listening at the Cellar all three nights, was thirteen when he first met Taggart through family friends: Kate Roach and her husband Don "D.T." Thompson, the wonderful tenor saxophonist (not the Don Thompson who once taught Taggart). Childs had heard Taggart, whom he idolized for years, confidently perform many times, so it was interesting that his hero seemed nervous just before the two-night stand began. "I had never really seen him that on edge about playing music before," said Childs.[30]

The nerves may have been because the shows were being recorded, and Taggart wanted to be at his best for this prime opportunity to document the music. Weeds would put out the recording as *Thankfully*, the very first release on his Cellar Live label. It still holds up as one of the best recordings on the label. "Taggart and his bandmates radiate an extraordinary spirit of melodic joy," I wrote about *Thankfully* in the *Vancouver Courier*. "Taggart plays with the warmth, finesse, and unerring sense of swing that make him such a valuable contributor to our jazz scene."[31] Those words still hold true. Twenty years after first hearing it, the music continues to captivate, especially the album's apex: "Shorter Days." It's a beguiling tune by Taggart that I've listened to hundreds of times. Taggart, Murphy, and Rud solo with an ecstatic intensity, and the whole group achieves a next-level kinship on the song.

Murphy, who passed away in 2015, said playing in the group was consistent with all the projects he did with his friend and colleague. "Ross's approach at that time was what I always experienced with him. Not much was ever said. It was a very open and supportive playing situation. He played the shit out of the saxophone and said yes to what everyone else was doing."[32]

"It was like getting into a hot tub," said Rud. "It was just so easy to play with these guys."[33] Arai referred to himself as the "least experienced and least capable" member of the quartet. "I think he [Taggart] was giving me a chance that nobody would, to give me the opportunity to play with these people. He saw something that he thought was worth nurturing."[34]

Minemoto, who wrote the exquisite waltz that's the title track, can still visualize the band's chemistry at the Cellar. "I can picture them all being up there on stage, and just hearing the organ and the interplay between the four of them was pretty magical. They were searching for something together and it didn't feel like, 'Oh, they are just playing a swinging tune here.' There was so much interaction between them."[35]

Journeys to the Bandstand

Ross Taggart, the Cellar, July 27, 2007. Photo by Steve Mynett.

Aside from frequently playing at the Cellar with Vancouver bands, Taggart was a first-call choice for Weeds to book as a sideman for visiting jazz greats who played at the club. "Even if I thought Ross wasn't necessarily the best choice [stylistically], Ross always was the best choice because he had this way of relating with the older guys," said Weeds. "He was such a student of the music. These old guys would come in, and they'd be a little uptight. 'Who's this young, white, punk kid?'" he said, referring to what the legends may have thought about Weeds. "Ross would be able to just make everything cool. And before you knew it, they would be laughing and having a good time."[36]

Weeds hired Taggart to play with Charles McPherson in 2002 and 2004, Benny Golson in 2003, and Frank Wess in 2005. "They always loved Ross," said drummer Dave Robbins, who played on the Golson and second McPherson gigs. "Ross would know so much about the person's career. He could name probably all of the records, if not most of the records the person had been on. Certainly, all the records as a leader. He had a great idea of the tunes that the person liked to play and the keys that they liked to play them in. I think that always put the guests at ease. Ross would say, 'Oh, you know, I was just listening to such-and-such a record, and I really loved your playing, and do you want to do this tune from that?'"[37]

The performances with McPherson were the only ones of these high-profile shows that Weeds released as a live recording, straightforwardly titled *Live at the Cellar*. Taggart sounds completely at home on the extended bebop treatments of four standards—including the version of "How Deep is the Ocean?" that has so entranced me—and two McPherson originals. Taggart comps empathically during the leader's long solos, and his piano solos convey the right amount of heft. "I can remember it being comfortable with him [Taggart] and liking to listen to his solos," recalled McPherson.[38]

"He did enjoy it because he had such a love and respect of jazz history and the people who created the history," affirmed Minemoto about Taggart's experiences with visiting artists at the Cellar, like McPherson. "But sometimes he would say, 'It's so stressful because you just don't know what's going to happen.'"[39]

In 2004, Weeds booked Taggart, André Lachance, and Robbins to play with bebop saxophonist Frank Morgan. His life and career were legendary:

Morgan had been anointed the heir apparent to Charlie Parker; he struggled with heroin addiction and was in and out of prisons, including notorious San Quentin; and Morgan made a successful comeback. Taggart knew this history, of course, but that awareness didn't prepare him for what happened during Morgan's three-night engagement. "Frank tried to give Ross piano lessons in the break," said Robbins. "That was pretty weird. He yelled at me too. He just turned around at the end of one tune and started yelling, 'I played with fuckin' Charlie Parker! This isn't a fuckin' big band!'"[40] That was Morgan's irascible way of telling Robbins to turn down the volume on drums.

Lachance said Morgan turned to Taggart and repeatedly yelled "Stroll!"[41] Taggart didn't know that "stroll" is an old school jazz term that means the pianist should lay out. When Taggart kept playing, Morgan got pissed off. Taggart was in a funk after the first night—he wanted to stroll right off the gig. Minemoto: "He came home and he said, 'I think he really hates my playing. I think somebody else should be on this gig because I can't do whatever he wants me to do.'"[42] Weeds saw all of this going down. "He [Morgan] was unimpressed with Dave Robbins, and he was unimpressed with Ross, which very rarely happened. Ross threatened to walk off, which is also very rare. That's how upset he was. And I had to call him and say, 'You can't walk off. I'll do whatever it takes, but I need you to just get through the next couple of nights.'" Taggart did exactly that, and the gigs played out without incident. In fact, Weeds thought the music was outstanding. "It was some of the most beautiful music that had ever been made at the club."[43]

Regardless of the tension with Morgan, Taggart—with his enormous knowledge of tunes, ability to play them in any key, and affable manner— was at the top of Weeds' musician call list for the first half of the Cellar's thirteen-year run. "I think he always excelled in those situations where he was the piano player playing with some heavy guy from New York," said Bill Coon. "I remember many times listening to him play with people from New York, and he was always such a strong and supportive piano player in all of those situations."[44] New York saxophonist Ian Hendrickson-Smith confirmed Coon's observation. Hendrickson-Smith said he played "fantastic gigs" with Taggart at the Cellar. "Ross and I just had a real hookup [musical connection]. It was really telepathic. Whatever he played, I enjoyed, and I think vice-versa."[45]

Then came the incomparable George Coleman. Weeds booked Coleman and his tenor protégé Eric Alexander to play two nights at the Cellar in September 2006, with Taggart on piano, bassist Jodi Proznick, and drummer Jesse Cahill. The night before the Cellar shows, with Chuck Deardorf playing bass, they performed at Seattle's Triple Door. Coleman and company were playing "Cherokee" at a breakneck tempo when something unexpected happened. During the solos, Coleman and Alexander kept improvising in different keys, going up a semitone with each chorus. At one point, Deardorf and Cahill stopped playing; Cahill said they came to a halt because Alexander indicated stop-time. But Taggart feverishly kept going, somehow keeping up with the marathon solos in the proper keys. "I remember he came off the stage, and he said, 'I can't believe that just happened,'" said Minemoto. "And then he said, 'I think I suck.' And I said, 'No you didn't suck because that was the weirdest thing I have ever seen in my life. Nobody played with you. You did an amazing job.'"[46]

What happened in Seattle harked back to a time when it wasn't uncommon for premier jazz musicians to improvise in different keys during a tune as a way of weeding out mediocre musicians in jam sessions or just for kicks. An unreleased recording of Art Pepper playing with a local rhythm section at the original Cellar in July 1959, documents a situation where the saxophonist did it. The musicians improvised on a medium tempo twelve-bar blues, with a twist "to make it a little more interesting," as Pepper put it.[47] The twist: Pepper began by soloing in the key of F for three choruses before switching to B flat and eventually eight more keys that aligned with a key concept in music theory known as the "circle of fifths." When Pepper switched keys, pianist Chris Gage and bassist Stan "Cuddles" Johnson did the same. Arguably, what Taggart pulled off with Coleman and Alexander was more challenging because the chords for "Cherokee" are more complex than a blues progression, and they played the standard at warp speed with the choruses whizzing by in a blur. So Taggart patently did not suck.

• • •

Playing in big bands was key to Taggart's development and musical life. After he arrived in Vancouver in 1986, Taggart auditioned on sax and piano for a Capilano College big band led by Fred Stride, becoming the large ensemble's pianist. Starting in the mid-nineties after returning from New York, Taggart sat in the piano chair for the Fred Stride Jazz Orchestra. In 2006, Stride and twenty-two musicians in the orchestra went into Factory Studios to record an album for Cellar Live: *Forward Motion*. Stride wrote complex original charts for the two-day session, including fully notated rhythm section parts. Taggart deftly played what was written and improvised individual touches that complemented the music. On "Oddly Enough," Taggart plays a dynamic piano solo that has an inspired spontaneous moment: he suddenly inserts a quote from "Hooray for Hollywood" that's off-key yet somehow meshes perfectly. "For me this solo sums up a lot of Ross Taggart the musician and the person," wrote Stride in a remembrance of Taggart. "We can hear his sense of musical tradition, his impeccable time and rhythmic sense, his vivid and creative imagination, and, for those of us that spent any time around Ross, his great sense of humour."[48]

In 2008, Taggart realized a dream when he recorded a piano trio album. On originals and standards, Taggart, with Ken Lister on bass and Craig Scott on drums, distills his years of experience—including those nights in NYC listening to jazz masters and the evenings at the Cellar playing with them—to deliver a master class in crafting beautiful jazz piano from the tradition. On both softly engaging and hard swinging performances, Taggart conveys a comforting romanticism with his sure touch.

Weeds put out *Presenting the Ross Taggart Trio* as Cellar Live's fiftieth release in 2009, eight years after *Thankfully* launched the label. The jazz club and record label owner and fellow saxophonist was delighted that these recordings were milestone releases for the label because Taggart "has easily been the most supportive of me and my endeavours," said Weeds in the liner notes.[49] Brad Turner, another good friend, recorded the album in his studio, and Eric Metcalfe created the album's abstract cover art. It would be Taggart's final recording as a leader.

"Special thanks to Sharon – I love you," wrote Taggart in the liner notes.[50] It was a bittersweet declaration; in September 2008, he and Minemoto separated. Although Taggart and Minemoto didn't see much of each other for a few years after splitting up, they remained on good terms. But Metcalfe Rehm said Taggart "was devastated" and "heartbroken" about the end of the marriage.[51]

Thankfully

*Ross Taggart, Vancouver Community College Auditorium, June 16, 2008.
Photo by Judy Chee.*

Many in Vancouver's jazz scene knew and enjoyed Taggart's whimsy. That he revelled in doing imitations, telling jokes, leaving long and amusing answering machine messages, and playing practical jokes. Like the classic prank in which he convinced musician friends they were needed as an emergency sub for a gig, when no such gig existed. Few, however, were in the know about any troubling issues Taggart dealt with below the surface. "Ross had a lot of demons that he was fighting," said Weeds. "But unless you were really close to him, those demons never really came out." Taggart "struggled way more than people ever realized," he added.[52]

"I don't know what his demons were," said Hugh Fraser. He did know that Taggart had exceptionally high artistic standards and was hard on himself. "I would get upset with him because he would get so down on himself, and I'd say, 'Lighten up,'" said Fraser. "But you can't just say that and have it happen, so I challenged him and wrote stuff."[53] Meaning Fraser wrote demanding tunes with Taggart in mind, including one simply called "Ross Taggart." It featured him on piano, and when Fraser's quintet with Slide Hampton performed it for a live recording at Rossini's Gastown that was released as *A Night in Vancouver*, Taggart came up with an inspired, meaty solo filled with imaginative ideas.

Fraser had one more observation, based on spending countless days with Taggart on the road, in Vancouver, and in Victoria, their hometown. "He wanted to be this ideal person, to Sharon and to his family, yet he liked to go crazy, and I don't think those two people ever met. I think that is what the problem was."[54] By "go crazy," Fraser meant that Taggart wanted to allow himself to let loose—to not be the virtuous young man he was in high school.

"I wish that he hadn't had so many things brewing in him, but I helped as best I could just [by] being his friend," said Ryga. "We talked pretty much daily. It never got to the point where I was worried about him, but I could see sometimes he suffered." Occasionally Taggart would take criticism or even offhand remarks as personal slights, and then let them fester. As Ryga recalled, "I would spend a lot of time saying, 'It [the negative remark] doesn't matter.'" Ryga also witnessed Taggart's harsh self-critiques. "He never felt that he was proficient enough, which to me was kind of crazy. I mean none of us ever do. He was just a really true musician and garnered the respect of everybody."[55]

So there were incongruities between Taggart's outer self and inner life, but as Metcalfe Rehm pointed out, Taggart was authentic. "What we saw was real. He wasn't fake. He was a real person."[56] Whatever demons he had within didn't undermine his endearing nature. Jennifer Scott summed up Taggart's persona best: "Like a great many intensely creative and intensely gifted musicians, you can't have the light without the dark, and Ross did have both those sides to him. And it is important to have those sides because, I think when you have a genius-level musician like that, you need to go to both of those places [to create], and he was capable of that."[57]

With someone as widely adored as Taggart, there's a temptation to focus on and preserve just the warm memories of his being. That would be inaccurate hagiography. That said, Taggart was an extremely private person, and it's important to honour that. Minemoto saw Taggart's personal battles up close and for years has been steadfast in respecting his privacy. The first time we talked about a source of his demons, that part of the conversation was off-the-record. The second time, years later, Minemoto felt more comfortable about divulging some details, only because they could serve as a cautionary tale for others.

Taggart was in a car accident at Main and 16th in Vancouver. The accident put him in substantial pain for the rest of his life. Trying to ease that pain was an ongoing, sad struggle. A doctor liberally prescribed OxyContin for Taggart. OxyContin, a brand name for oxycodone, is an enormously addictive opioid pain medication. And while the drug is effective in providing short-term relief from pain, it also causes a litany of side effects. OxyContin changed Taggart. The man who was much-loved for being an ebullient spirit became constantly fatigued and drowsy.

• • •

In 2011, Taggart's world was upended when he was diagnosed with renal cancer and underwent surgery, which initially seemed successful. Taggart played on the familiar bandstand at the Cellar in April 2012. But a month later he was diagnosed with the same cancer a second time. Taggart and Minemoto, after all they had been through together, mutually agreed that she would become one of his primary caregivers.

Despite his condition and bleak prognosis, Taggart still accepted gigs. In fact, he was booked weeks in advance for two engagements on November 10, 2012. In the morning he had a recording session in Vancouver with drummer Albert "Tootie" Heath, pianist Jeb Patton, and Jodi Proznick; in the evening he was scheduled to play in Victoria at a Duke Ellington Sacred Music concert with the Fred Stride Jazz Orchestra.

Ross Taggart, the Cellar, September 19, 2012. Photo by Steve Mynett.

In October 2012, Kate Roach accompanied Taggart on one last trip to New York, to attend a celebration for George Coleman. Taggart had dinner with Coleman at one of the city's top steak joints, Keens Steakhouse. The mutual respect at the table was palpable. "Ross Taggart was a good friend of mine," said Coleman. "He was a fine, excellent student," Coleman said about mentoring Taggart.[58] But during the trip, Taggart became very ill and never made it to the celebration. He flew home and was admitted into Vancouver General Hospital.

Family and friends visited Taggart at VGH, including Brad Turner. There was a piano in the palliative care unit, and Turner played it for Taggart. Born in the same year, both multi-instrumentalists had accomplished an immense amount in jazz. "We'd known each other since we were seventeen or eighteen and came up together," said Turner.[59] All that time, Turner looked up to Taggart as a hero. When Bob Murphy and Monique Van Dam visited at the hospital, Murphy and Taggart—the long-time collaborators and buddies—spent some time alone together and just like old times, they giggled. After the visit, Van Dam asked Murphy what they were talking and laughing about. "He [Murphy] said, 'I asked Ross, what does he think is on the other side? What does he think it's all about?'"[60] I don't know if Taggart had the energy to think of an answer to Murphy's deep question. But I can imagine it was a quintessential moment for the two men, reflecting their years of friendship and shared interest in the quest for fulfilment.

Musicians and jazz fans showed their support for Taggart by attending a sold-out benefit concert at Capilano University in November 2012. Taggart had served on the Cap faculty for years, teaching many musicians. Among his students, at Cap and outside of the school, were Bruno Hubert, Amanda Tosoff, Jillian Lebeck, and Jon Bentley. On stage for the benefit were six ensembles—ranging from duo to big band—that Taggart had played with, representing the vitality of the scene, and reminding everyone how he was at the very heart of it.

Although Taggart couldn't play the concert with Stride's big band or the session with Heath that he had been looking forward to, Weeds came up with an idea: bringing Heath to the hospital for a visit. Weeds asked Minemoto if this would be a good plan and she was unsure, given Taggart's weak state. But Minemoto asked Taggart. "She said Ross lit up like a Christmas tree, sat right up in his bed, and was the most coherent he had been in days," said Weeds. Minemoto asked Weeds to bring Heath. "We went down there and you would have never known Ross was sick. Tootie was so gracious. I felt like that was kind of my gift to Ross. That was the last time I saw him."[61]

Weeds was on tour when Taggart was in his final days. Knowing that his close friend was near death, Weeds kept his cell phone under his pillow at night. In Portland, it vibrated when a message came from Ryga: on January 9, 2013, Taggart passed away at the age of forty-five.

In Vancouver's jazz history, there have been musicians essential to the scene who died far too young. Among them: Chris Gage, Hugh Fraser, Chris Nelson, Natasha D'Agostino, and Ross Taggart. After Taggart passed—as was the case with all of these artists—the loss was devastating, the grief profound, and the tributes to him heartfelt.

"The guy was like an encyclopedia on jazz," said Ryga. "I've only met a couple other guys like him. He was a real historian of the music, the art form, and the tradition, and that's what he wanted to live. He wanted to be a part of that and contribute to it, and as far as I am concerned, he really, really was. He really was a beautiful player."[62]

"I actually never played with Ross when he phoned it in," said Coon. In other words, Taggart never just went through the motions or sounded perfunctory. "He was always playing really strong."[63]

Eric Metcalfe described Taggart as "a very, very capable player, and a very gifted player." As for where Taggart was in the continuum between being an interpreter and an innovator, Metcalfe said "he could have taken it much further, I think, if he had lived."[64] That's an intriguing viewpoint. In many ways, Taggart was a traditionalist, who had far more Dexter Gordon than Dewey Redman or Michael Brecker in him. I agree he could have gone further in exploring adventurous sounds if fate had taken a different course. I also strongly believe that when Taggart approached a standard like "How Deep Is the Ocean" that had been played thousands of times, and still came up with a fresh perspective, that was a form of invention.

Cory Weeds: "Ross was such a central figure. He was the main person in a lot of people's bands. There was a huge void when he passed away, not only because of his playing, but just his personality. He was always this gregarious, happy, encouraging guy. When a personal presence like that leaves the scene, it leaves a huge hole."[65]

Weeds went further in illuminating Taggart's impact, particularly as a bandmate. "There's a lot that goes into playing jazz music. We're all very insecure and always questioning ourselves, but when you got on the bandstand with Ross, it didn't matter how I played. Whether it was good or bad, I always felt comfortable. I always felt like everything was going to be okay. Ross was a consummate professional and always made everybody around him play and sound better."[66]

Minemoto looked after spreading Taggart's ashes in multiple meaningful locations: behind his family's house in the Cordova Bay area of Victoria; in Vancouver's Queen Elizabeth Park where he liked to go; and several places in New York. That's where musicians including Minemoto, Michael Blake (who, before moving to New York, regularly played with Taggart in Vancouver),

Ian Hendrickson-Smith (and his wife Jenny Larisey, who managed Weeds' Cellar), Rudy Petschauer, Evan Arntzen, and Joe Carello gathered to pay their respects to Taggart.

In the months and years that followed, there would be live and recorded tributes and dedications to Taggart. Minemoto expressed her tender remembrances of Taggart on her absorbing, all-original *Safe Travels* album that she dedicated to him. The song titles—like "Rice Cooker," "The Secret," and "Possible Theme Song for the Aunt Jemima Show"—and the tunes' evocative moods can be interpreted as allusions to life with Taggart, including his outer kindness and humour, and his interior realm. Then there's *A Bowl of Sixty Taxidermists* by Waxwing (Tony Wilson, Peggy Lee, and Jon Bentley). Bentley, who regularly visited Taggart in hospital, named the title track and the album after something Taggart said while in his palliative care bed. As the story goes, a friend visited and asked if she could get him anything. Taggart replied that he would really like a "bowl of sixty taxidermists."[67] His quirky humour was intact until the end.

Weeds had one more gift for Taggart: an ambitious project that involved commissioning Jill Townsend, Coon, and Bill Runge to arrange ten of Taggart's songs for Townsend's big band (yet another ensemble Taggart had played in), recording the band's performance of the arrangements at Capilano University's theatre, and playing the tunes for an audience. Weeds initiated a Kickstarter campaign that exceeded the fundraising goal for the project. *Legacy, The Music of Ross Taggart*, which came out on Cellar Live in 2015, is a moving homage to Taggart the composer, musician, mentor, and sweet friend to many.

Taggart got the last word all to himself. The album concludes with "Apple Cider Vinegar – For Jill," a two minute and forty-eight-second document of Taggart slowly playing heavenly solo piano. His enchanting melody, delicately shaped chords, and meaningful spacing between the notes resonate and soothe. Like the man and his music always did.

15 / HERE NOW: BRAD TURNER

ON AN OVERCAST Saturday morning at summer's end, Brad Turner is behind the wheel of his red 1965 Ford Mustang, and he looks relaxed. Turner has owned the car for thirty-six years, since he was sixteen, and barely legal to drive. By now the Mustang is an extension of himself, and a repository for memories, good and bad. We're cruising near his home in the Vancouver suburb of Port Coquitlam, and while he's smoothly shifting the four speed, Turner is recalling epic experiences with the pristine car. I'm in the passenger seat, intently listening over the loud engine noise to make out these formative tales. The more I hear, the deeper I realize that the car is a fitting metaphor for Turner, Vancouver's most accomplished and compelling jazz musician.

Turner drove the Mustang from Vancouver to Denton, Texas, and back. Twice. Denton is home to the University of North Texas, where he did his master's and was a stud on trumpet in its renowned big bands. Another time he was driving from Portland to Bellingham with his roommate, when the classic car's accelerator cable snapped. That meant the gas pedal was out of commission, so, on the side of a busy highway with traffic whizzing by, Turner and his buddy devised an ingenious workaround. It involved grabbing an extension cord from the trunk, splitting it in half, connecting one end to the carburetor, and threading the other end through the firewall and under the dashboard. "I pulled it by hand to do the gas and my roommate shifted from the passenger seat, and we drove home to Bellingham that way," said Turner, laughing at the memory.[1]

I can picture it: Turner calmly assessing the dire situation and coming up with a solution on the fly. The man is an analytical thinker and a resourceful improviser. After Turner describes his car as being "pretty analog," I suggest that maintaining the Mustang in working order is like keeping another analog classic he knows well—the Rhodes electric piano—in playing shape. "It's analogous," he agrees, with a Spockian rationality, and no pun intended. "To an extent, you can jerry-rig a solution [with the Mustang], same with a Rhodes," he said. "Even the worst sort of falling-apart-Rhodes, you can resurrect it."[2]

Brad Turner, Port Coquitlam, August 31, 2019. Photo by Chris Wong.

Let's squeeze some more mileage out of the car and keyboard analogies. Like a vintage vehicle or instrument, Turner has a singular character. It's in his trumpet and piano playing, drumming, composing, and contributions as a bandleader and educator. Turner shaped that character by dedicating years to study and practice, applying a laser focus to composition, embracing demanding performance opportunities, and being musically curious. But far removed from his striking solos and audiences' hearty applause, he secretly had a severe problem that nerdy ingenuity couldn't fix. Turner was drinking himself to death. His description of a "worst sort of falling-apart" instrument directly applied to him. This could easily have been a soul-crushing obituary. With support from people who knew and cared, and by focusing his sharp mind on epiphanies that brought him face-to-face with the root of his addiction, Turner transformed the premature obit into a redemption story.

• • •

His musical bloodline runs deep. Turner's great grandfather wasn't a musician, but he was the type of man who knew a vast number of songs, which he sang and whistled wherever he went. Fred Turner, Brad's grandfather, played trumpet in bands on Saturday nights during the Great Depression and became a music education legend in BC. As Assistant Music Supervisor in Burnaby, and then Music Supervisor in Vancouver, Fred recruited band directors to start school bands, a new concept at the time. His pioneering efforts enabled scores of kids to play in bands.[3] Starting in 1941, he also led the New Westminster Junior Band, which evolved to the New Westminster and District Concert Band. Competing in festivals and touring the world, the band became an institution, with some alumni that went on to play jazz professionally: trumpeter Arnie Chycoski and trombonist Ray Sikora were among them.[4]

In 1964, Fred passed the director's baton for the New Westminster and District Concert Band to his son Kerry Turner, who was just twenty-two at the time. Kerry first joined the band in 1949, as an alto saxophonist. Just like it was with his dad, music education was Kerry's life. He taught music at various schools and became Director of Fine Arts in Abbotsford, the main city in BC's Fraser Valley. So two generations of Turners set high musical standards and were respected in the community.

Kerry's wife Gail gave birth to Brad, their first child, on January 29, 1967. In the year of Canada's centennial and the nation's signature celebration, Expo 67, the mood was optimistic and confident. There was certainly a lot to be optimistic about with Brad. He was a bright and inquisitive child.

His affinity with music emerged early. At seven Turner started lessons on his first instrument, piano, at the Langley Community Music School. He was an atypical kid who didn't mind practicing. Influenced by his uncle Vince Ricci, who had toured with Del Shannon, played with local bands as a drummer, and had a great record collection (Miles Davis, Chick Corea,

Weather Report, etc.), Turner also had a thing for drumming. As a preschooler, his kit consisted of overturned ice cream buckets. But when he had to select an instrument to play in the school band, Turner chose trumpet, which his grandfather Fred and his uncle Tom played. Fred gave his grandson a vintage cornet, which the younger Turner began playing at ten in the fifth grade. Not long after, Turner followed the lead of his dad and grandpa by joining the New Westminster and District Concert Band. He played with the band for more than a decade.

"I was a quiet, shy kid," said Turner, who was also small compared to his peers. "I had friends, and I played soccer and lacrosse. I was a good athlete. In a way, that was a blessing and a curse because I found myself in these circles where none of the other kids were really sensitive and would cry at the drop of a hat [like Turner would]. I was quite a sensitive soul when I was a little boy. My teenage years, oh man, if it weren't for music and sports, but particularly music because it gave me that expressive outlet, I think I maybe might've lost my way."[5]

Being small, shy, and sensitive was a recipe for getting bullied, and Turner was on the receiving end for some of that. He was also highly attuned to struggles schoolmates were going through in their lives, and their angst vicariously became his angst. None of that slowed his musical progress. He was a top student musician at Langley Community Music School and at R.E. Mountain Secondary School in Langley. A photo—published in 1977 in the *Langley Advance*—showed scholarship winners including a ten-year-old Turner and "Irene Rosnes," who would later be known as Renee Rosnes, acclaimed jazz pianist.[6]

Solos and awards came Turner's way because of the musicianship he showed on his instruments and his high academic standing. After graduating from high school in 1985, Turner went to Western Washington University in Bellingham to do a double major on classical trumpet and jazz studies. On top of the heavy course work at WWU, Turner aspired to practice three hours every day on trumpet and as long again on piano. He finished the double degree and considered taking a break, but instead did his master's at the University of North Texas. UNT has long been known for its technically formidable big bands, and by his second year, Turner was playing trumpet in the university's flagship One O'Clock Lab Band, directing the Three

O'Clock Lab Band, and writing charts that the school's ensembles performed and recorded.

"The level of the reading, the difficulty of the music that we played in there, I could tell right away that probably not again in my career was I going to see music that challenging," said Turner about the One O'Clock Band.[7] In 1991, Turner and the rest of the One O'Clockers played in Vancouver. That was the first time that bassist André Lachance heard Turner perform. "They were all amazing young players," said Lachance, whose first memory of Turner—who played multiple solos—is indelible. "It was just this young guy in the back playing the trumpet with huge hair that just played his ass off."[8]

The following year, Turner turned twenty-five and completed his UNT studies. He could have made a go of it in New York City but decided to come home. A major reason for returning was to provide support to his girlfriend, who had just emerged from a coma after being in a bad car accident. His job and gigging prospects in Vancouver's jazz scene were, however, uncertain. After years of studying in the States, he was virtually unknown in his hometown. Then Capilano College (now Capilano University and referred to as Cap) in North Vancouver hired Turner to teach trumpet.

As a performer, his first break happened when singer Jennifer Scott hired him to accompany her at Santos restaurant on Commercial Drive. "I had played piano all through school but trumpet was my main thing, so I hadn't really done the due diligence that jazz piano players need to do," said Turner "So I was quite exposed on that gig, let's just put it that way. But she was super gracious."[9] It led to more piano gigs, including other opportunities to accompany vocalists. Then he started subbing in as a trumpeter with big bands, including the one led by Fred Stride. "As soon as that happened, and people heard me play the trumpet, then it was like everybody knew who I was."[10]

Years of rigorous practicing and performing, and endless hours of listening to the likes of Miles Davis, Wayne Shorter, Herbie Hancock, Freddie Hubbard, Chick Corea, Woody Shaw, Wynton Marsalis, and fellow Canadians such as Ingrid Jensen and Seamus Blake, had prepared Turner for a pivotal moment: It was time to do his own thing. In 1993, he started the Brad Turner Quartet, with Turner on trumpet and flugelhorn, pianist Bruno Hubert, bassist Chris Nelson, and drummer Dylan van der Schyff. They recorded four songs by Turner that he put out on a cassette that year, and then a full CD—*Long Story Short*—in 1994. Listening to the tunes about a quarter century after they were recorded, I can make out the influences and seeds of an aesthetic that the quartet would spend years honing. From that beginning, there was a distinct group sound. While Turner's fluid trumpet playing was at the core, every player made vital contributions. None of them could have predicted the quartet's longevity.

It was significant that Nelson was in the band. He was one of Vancouver's most respected jazz musicians, and his presence spoke highly of the new kid in town leading the group. But Nelson soon left the quartet for the Vancouver Opera Orchestra, and Lachance entered the group. With that change, the band's lineup was set for years to come.

While Turner wrote extensively for the quartet, he also needed other outlets for his compositions and musical energy. In 1996, he and Chris Tarry co-founded Metalwood. They assembled the band with members living in different cities—Turner on keyboards and trumpet (Vancouver), saxophonist Mike Murley (Toronto), electric bassist Tarry (Vancouver, and then New York), and drummer Ian Froman (New York)—and made it work. The Brad Turner Trio—with Turner on piano, bassist Darren Radtke, and drummer Bernie Arai—began life the following year.

Metalwood boldly asserted itself from the beginning with a sound that fit in the tradition of electric-era Miles Davis, Weather Report, the Brecker Brothers, and other jazz-rock fusion groups, while avoiding the excesses of that genre. The first Metalwood song I heard was "5 Minute Margin," the lead track on the band's self-titled debut album that was recorded after minimal rehearsal and only two gigs at Vancouver's Chameleon Urban Lounge. It begins with a hypnotically repeating bass pattern and robust drumming. Then, just seconds in, Turner starts a keyboard solo. The first thing that struck me was the captivating sound of the electric keyboard, which Turner set to a shimmering tone. Throughout the four-and-a-half-minute solo, he steadily elevates the harmonic interest and intensity. Over the years, I've kept going back to hear what Turner played at the beginning of the song because it's a compelling example of how to shape an electrifying solo.

That 1997 album and the following year's *Metalwood 2* both won Juno Awards for best contemporary jazz album. It was a busy and gratifying time for Turner. In December 1997, I interviewed Turner for the first time, and he described an enviable performance schedule. Wednesday nights he had a regular gig at the Mojo Room, alternating from week to week between his quartet and trio, which gave him and these ensembles the opportunity to develop. He played fun soul/R&B two nights a week with Soulstream at Bar None. Turner also found time to play with Namedropper, a drum 'n' bass/hip hop/ambient band. "I'm really lucky," he told me. "Not everyone gets a chance to enjoy what I'm enjoying now with these gigs." I ended my piece by declaring Turner was leading a "wonderful life" as a musician and educator.[11]

Despite my Capra-tinted view, there was much that I and even his close companions didn't know about Turner's life. One thing was his deepening relationship with alcohol. Liquor wasn't part of Turner's life when growing up; he had his first drink at twenty-one. Soon after, though, Turner found out he had a dangerous superpower. "I realized right away that it didn't seem to have the same inebriating effect on me that it had on my friends."[12] As he increasingly played in clubs and other licensed venues, Turner was exposed to the age-old occupational hazard for gigging musicians: ready access to alcohol. For many, drinking doesn't become a problem. For Turner, it gradually became a life-or-death struggle.

But the music seemed to be no problem at all. On January 14 and 15, 2000, Turner and his quartet, plus tenor saxophonist Seamus Blake, were booked to perform at the Cellar Jazz Café on the West Side of Vancouver. Lacking a noise policy to discourage loud chatter, it wasn't a venue for attentive listening. But it was a chance for the quartet and Blake to perform Turner's original music and to record the gigs. They were crisp recordings that Maximum Jazz released on *Live at the Cellar*. It turned out to be an important and influential album. Cory Weeds, who was in the audience for one of the nights at the Cellar Jazz Café, was "flabbergasted by what they were playing and how they were playing it." And then he heard the live recording. Weeds: "To this day, the music stands up as some of the best recorded in this city."[13] I agree. Turner, Blake, Hubert (on Fender Rhodes), Lachance, and van der Schyff struck an engaging melodic/harmonic tone and maintained a bracing rhythmic pulse that confidently declared Vancouver jazz at the end of the twentieth century was in good hands.

Just over eight months after those momentous shows, the same group performed at the grand opening of the Cellar, a promising jazz club in the same basement space where the Cellar Jazz Café had existed. Now owned by Weeds, the club would—especially in its early years—become an important venue for Turner and his various projects. His quartet and trio both played regularly at the Cellar, developing further in the listener-friendly club, where Weeds gently enforced a no-talking policy for audiences during sets. Turner also played there with Ugetsu (co-led by Bernie Arai and Jon Bentley) and bands led by Sharon Minemoto, Ross Taggart, Mike Allen, Kevin Elaschuk, and others. "Life was just amazing because it seemed to revolve around us making music all the time in every aspect of our existence," said Turner about Vancouver's jazz scene in the early 2000s. "I just remember it being a really vibrant, productive time on the scene. The Cellar existed as a focal point and sort of an end result. We could work on our stuff, get it together, and then present it to people."[14]

Brad Turner, the Cellar, November 23, 2006. Photo by Steve Mynett.

Then it was Metalwood's turn to make some noise. In January 2001, there was an exciting announcement: Universal Music Canada signed the band, committed to releasing two new Metalwood albums, and re-releasing the quartet's first three albums that originally came out on Vancouver-based indie label Maximum Music. It was a big deal for an adventurous Canadian jazz group to sign with a major label, so this was a feel-good story for Turner and his bandmates. The other big news: three high-profile American guests—guitarist John Scofield, percussionist Mino Cinelu, and turntablist DJ Logic—would play on a number of tracks on the band's Universal debut, *The Recline*. The night before the two-day recording sessions began, I witnessed Metalwood, Cinelu, and Logic deliver loud and memorable sets at a sold-out Cellar. There were rumours that Sco—a bona fide jazz star—would show, but that didn't happen.

Four months later, I heard *The Recline*. There was a lot to like about the album; as the group always had, Metalwood played electric jazz with depth and integrity. But the greater emphasis on groove, and the contributions from the special guests, didn't resonate with me. Plus, the more polished, mature sound made me pine for the raw and impetuous early Metalwood. It was a rare instance when something Turner was part of didn't fully engage.

With help from the group's touring, Scofield's star power, and a marketing push from Universal, *The Recline* sold well. "Other than [albums by] Diana Krall, that was the highest selling [Canadian] jazz record in Canadian history," said Turner. But how much did the band pull in? "I never got a dime. And that's how it works. People are like, 'What? Really?' No, that's how it works."[15] So Turner and his Metalwood bandmates didn't get rich and famous because of the success they achieved. In fact, aside from the band's gigs being more consistently well-attended, their careers were not much different than before.

. . .

He carried on with life in the Vancouver scene and kept doing Brad Turner things. Like playing with his quartet and Joe Lovano, the New York-based consummate master of the tenor saxophone and other woodwinds. The concert was set for September 19, 2001, at what was then known as Capilano College Performing Arts Theatre. Then came the terrorist attacks on 9/11 that changed the world. As initial dates on Lovano's west coast tour were cancelled one by one, there were serious doubts that the sold-out Cap concert would go ahead. But just one day before the show, Lovano's manager confirmed that in a true act of faith, the saxophonist would make the effort to travel from his traumatized city for the North Vancouver performance. Thankfully, he did, and Lovano, Turner, and the others played wonderfully, providing succor at a time when it was very much needed. Lovano played at his high standard, with an added emotional impact given the circumstances. Turner and the quartet were "on fire, especially Brad," said Cap Director of Programming Fiona Black. "His virtuoso trumpet chops were in full flight." Lovano was impressed with Turner, Hubert, Lachance, and van der Schyff, "but he thought they dressed like 'dock workers,'" added Black. "Joe was dressed impeccably."[16]

Another Brad Turner thing: alongside Lachance, he played drums in a trio led by Hubert, his singular quartet member. Those who knew Turner but didn't know he played drums did a double take when they saw him behind the kit for the trio's gigs. For their Cellar shows, the decision was made to record the sets. As it turned out, the performances were top-notch, with animated playing by Hubert, Lachance's usual solid bass foundation, and spirited drumming from Turner. In addition to playing, Turner co-engineered, mixed, and mastered the live album. He had tinkered with the recording process but never recorded a whole record until then. *Get Out of Town* ended up selling well for Weeds' Cellar Live label.

Around this time, Turner went on leave from his teaching position at Cap College. While he would continue to teach privately, Turner wanted to focus on his own music. Then he found out that his wife Tia was pregnant with twins. Evan and Theo Turner were born October 14, 2002. Turner would describe the joy of that event through music and photography on the quartet's strong 2007 album, *Small Wonder*. The cover featured a beguiling photo Turner took of the tiny boys holding yellow flowers and inquisitively examining bugs in the driveway. But the arrival of the twins brought something else to Turner; it felt as if life had thrown him a serious "curve ball," as he described it.[17]

In the decade after Turner returned to Vancouver, he racked up a remarkable number of accomplishments, including becoming a first-call musician and, as described by Weeds, "The Man, the musician we all strived to be."[18] There were, however, signs of trouble, even if only Turner could see them. He second-guessed himself for choosing Vancouver over New York and measured himself against Canadian jazz musicians who went to the Big Apple and succeeded there—artists such as Rosnes, Jensen, and Blake. He also wasn't having the time of his life as the father of twin sons. "Right at that time, I really started to think I ended up with a life that I felt like I didn't deserve," said Turner about doubts that crept in. "The great irony is that what was happening all around me at the time, particularly my two baby boys, that should have been the greatest and most inspiring time of my life. But I couldn't see it."[19]

So the curve ball was a gradual realization about his beautiful infants. Turner: "They don't care about that interesting motif you wrote into that last tune that's so clever. They don't care about the Junos. They don't care about the fact that you had a gig and got home at three-thirty in the morning." What they cherished was "the extra level that's more about being a good human."

Turner's leave from Capilano College, which started before the twins arrived and extended a number of years, was intended to enable him to focus on playing and composing music. If awards and commissions were any indication, despite growing inner strife, Turner was succeeding in his vocation. In 2005, Turner won musician of the year in Canada's National Jazz Awards. In 2006, he received the Victor Martyn Lynch-Staunton Award—a $15,000 prize—from the Canada Council for the Arts. Just after receiving the prestigious award, Vancouver's Hard Rubber Orchestra performed an entire evening of Turner's music, including a thirty-minute commission, *Bitter Suite*.

The suite's title wasn't just a play on words; in his late thirties, Turner was increasingly feeling embittered about his lot in life. He lacked fulfillment in his career and struggled with the daily realities of domestic life with two young boys and a mortgage. Ego, self-doubt, guilt for not being a good enough partner and dad, drinking, and blaming others for his situation were accelerants for a "bonfire of self-pity" that engulfed Turner.[20] At the core of his crisis he saw making art as his birthright, which the applause and acclaim only reinforced; but, in truth, Turner no longer knew why he was an artist.

Still, the music played on. While the quartet and trio were his main vehicles for jazz expression, it was tough to find places for those groups to play. He kept the bands going with gigs here and there, including some at the Cellar with prominent American musicians. His trio played at the Cellar with saxophonist Ernie Watts in February 2009, a show in which his chops were put to the test. "I've never played a faster tempo than I played that night with Ernie Watts," said Turner. The blazing tempo was on "Hot House," Tadd Dameron's bebop classic. "I knew it was going to be brisk because we rehearsed it, and [before playing the tune during the gig], he turned around and looked over at me with his eyes opened really wide, and he goes, 'Get ready, man.'" Did Turner get through it unscathed? "Oh yeah. I killed it."[21]

Brad Turner, the Cellar, February 19, 2007. Photo by Steve Mynett.

Journeys to the Bandstand

Brad Turner, Derry Byrne, and Campbell Ryga, the Cellar. Photo by Jesse Cahill.

• • •

Considering he's primarily a self-taught composer and arranger, the quantity and quality of Turner's output as a composer for his own bands and other ensembles have been impressive. Vancouver's Turning Point Ensemble, a sixteen-member contemporary classical chamber orchestra, commissioned him to compose a major piece. "One of the mandates I have put on myself as a composer is to basically say yes to whatever anyone asks me to do and figure it out later," said Turner. "Because of that, I have put myself in a few interesting situations where I have looked at them as opportunities."[22] One of those situations was composing for Turning Point Ensemble, and a turning point it proved to be.

TPE premiered the twenty-four-minute, seven-movement *Scenes from Childhood*, March 30, 2012, at the Langley Community Music School's Rose Gellert Hall, followed by a performance of the suite two days later at SFU's Fei and Milton Wong Experimental Theatre. Turner delivered an exceptional work. *Scenes from Childhood* affirms Turner's intuitive ability to compose an extended classical piece filled with engaging melodic, harmonic, and rhythmic ideas, transporting sonic textures, and whimsical humour. His own assessment of the piece is unequivocal: "It's the best thing I've ever written in my life. The thing I'm most proud of."[23]

That the suite got written at all was a major accomplishment given what was happening in Turner's life at the time. While his mom and dad's wisdom inspired each movement in the suite, during the time Turner composed it, Gail Turner was in the advanced stages of early onset Alzheimer's. "When things get rough sometimes the feelings get just too much to handle. So writing that music was a nice, positive outlet for me," said Turner. "But there were a lot of negative paths that I took at that time."[24] Starting in about 2011, Turner's drinking grew more serious. Then in May 2012, Turner's good friend Ross Taggart was diagnosed—for the second time—with renal cancer. "I remember playing piano for him in the palliative care unit, and I was drunk as a lord in there," said Turner. "I couldn't handle Ross dying."[25] Taggart passed away in January 2013.

In November 2013, Turner went into a sixty-day, live-in rehab program in Langley—the Vancouver suburb where he grew up. The timing of the rehab stay meant he had to temporarily stop teaching and directing the A Band at Capilano University. "It was never announced that's what it was," said Turner. "It was just, 'Brad's sick.'"[26] It was both a vague and accurate explanation. "I treated it [rehab] like a college course, like I was going to get an A+ in rehab," Turner recalled. "I did all the things that were asked of me." One requirement was to keep a journal, which he excelled in because he could write well. Turner also skillfully drew, so he sketched scenes from the treatment centre. All of this impressed his counsellors, which was the plan. "I manipulated the counsellors to think I was doing fine," said Turner. "And in the back of my mind, I knew that as soon as I had the chance, I was going right back to it [drinking]."[27] After spending Christmas 2013 in rehab, he got out in January 2014. Within twelve days, Turner was back on the bottle.

Turner's alcoholism grew progressively worse. While some people knew, many didn't because Turner was a classic high-functioning alcoholic—someone who, on the surface, is a productive and successful member of society but secretly has a serious alcohol problem. He was masterful at hiding it. At this point, though, not even Turner could completely cover up his addiction. In October 2014, Turner received yet another major honour:

the Mayor's Arts Award for Music. There's a photo taken at the award ceremony with Turner, pianist Matt Choboter (the emerging artist in music selected by Turner), and then-Vancouver Mayor Gregor Robertson. Turner's eyes were glassy, his hair and complexion were "fucked up," he was bloated and overweight, and his clothes were rumpled. "That picture speaks a thousand words," said Turner, whose dad, aunt, and uncle were at the ceremony to support him. "They all knew I was in the throes of this."[28]

Turner played a November 2014 concert with premier electric guitarist Bill Frisell. "I remember just feeling strong enough to play," said Turner, who recalled that "certain aspects" of that show went well.[29] My memory is that though there were many exquisite moments, I also distinctly remember thinking that Turner lacked his usual dynamism on trumpet. By this time, I had heard talk that Turner was a drinker, but I had no idea he had a severe addiction or that he was reaching a breaking point. In hindsight, going on stage with Frisell at a time of debilitating crisis was a risky move that could have blown up in Turner's face. It was also an amazingly brave gesture in service of the music.

Around that time, Turner was isolating himself and taking fewer gigs, but he said yes to playing familiar repertoire with pianist Sharon Minemoto and her quintet at Seventeen89. Before the gig, he had numerous drinks, and by the time the first set started he was in rough shape. "These are tunes that I could play in my sleep. I'm getting lost, and I'm sort of losing interest." It hadn't been obvious on many gigs, but it was this night. Turner was "hammered" and couldn't play anywhere near the standard that his fellow musicians and audiences expected of him. After the gig, Minemoto took him to task. "She sent me an email that night. She said, 'It's obvious that you're not doing well. People were asking me [about Turner]. Your dinner came and your face was almost in your plate. Are you on medication that I don't know about, or are you just drinking too much? What's going on with you?' Everything she said was right on the money and it was to the point." His reply to Minemoto—a longtime friend and former student—was also direct, but in a caustic way. He clicked send on a nasty, defensive response that got personal. His words were rooted in the fear of admitting he had a problem and in a larger fear. "The biggest thing when you're addicted to something is the fear of not having it," said Turner. His mindset at the time: "'I can't live without it [alcohol]. I can't function. I can't do anything without it.'"[30]

Turner has long meant the world to André Lachance because of their friendship and the sheer volume of bandstands they've shared. "Brad's probably the musician I have played the most gigs with," said Lachance. "It's a four-figure number of gigs we have played together. You can't put a value on that." As Turner descended further into his quagmire, Lachance and others were aware of their friend's precarious condition, and they grew increasingly concerned. "There was a circle of friends, and we would call each other up. 'Hey, do you know what he is up to tonight? Have you seen him?' We were very worried."[31]

Bruno Hubert also knew about Turner's state but took a hands-off approach. "Actually, I never worried about him," said Hubert. "Because, to me, he's the guy who was so in control, who had such control of his ability, and was so talented. It never had crossed my mind that this is going to be terrible. To me, it was just like, he has to go through this wall, but he will go through this wall."[32]

Hubert was initially only half right: it was going to be terrible, and Turner smacked right into that wall in November and December 2014. "I was drinking around the clock," said Turner. "I'd sleep for an hour, and then drink. I couldn't walk. So I basically would crawl to get myself to the couch." Plus, he wasn't eating. "My digestive system was all messed up. I couldn't keep food down, and all I could do was drink. At that time, I was drinking a twenty-sixer, one and a half of those a day of vodka. That was an average day. I would just drink it like water." The toll on his body was pronounced: harsh vomiting and dry heaves, coughing up blood, heart palpitations, and yellowing eyes, among other physical manifestations that should have landed him in hospital. "I never went to the hospital because I was too ashamed," he said. "This isn't like appendicitis where it's blameless. This was on me, so I didn't want anyone to see it." On top of all that there was depression from the shame of addiction and the loss of family. "Tia, for good reasons, said you've got to go, and I couldn't see my kids." The decline in his playing was the least of Turner's concerns. "There was no ladder out of that pit that was apparent to me at the time," said Turner. "I was on a conveyor belt to checking out. And then, things changed."[33]

On December 19, 2014, at about five a.m., Turner ended up in the driveway of the place where he was living. Turner doesn't know what led him out there, but that's where he had a life-changing epiphany. At one level, Turner recognized that if he kept on his self-destructive path, he wouldn't live to see the New Year. At another level, he realized a confluence of truths: It's not all about him, there's something bigger in the universe, and—the surprising gamechanger—music, which brought him adoration, doesn't define him. "I realized that, no, music is not me," said Turner. "I go deeper than that. This [music] is something that I do. For a lifetime it defined me, and when life was putting demands on me that called for more than just being a really good jazz musician, that's not going to cut it. You need to be more. You have to be more of a dad. You have to be more of a husband. You have to be a better son. You have to be a better employee. You just need to be a better person."[34]

In that moment of truths, Turner immediately quit drinking. In one sense, he climbed out of the pit and achieved sobriety that morning by himself. Turner sees it another way. He let go of a hardwired propensity to try—on his own—to control everything, and he began to simply let life happen.

It wasn't a made-for-Netflix lightning bolt. "It's not like God opened the clouds," said Turner. Instead, he used an analogy relevant to Vancouver's jazz scene to explain what happened. What transpired with Turner that cold December morning was as if his friend and bandmate Bruno Hubert, who's known for not having lenses in his glasses, suddenly popped lenses in his frames. "And in fact, they're trifocals," said Turner, describing the clarity of vision he attained. "I can see things up close, I can see mid-range, and I can see far away."[35]

A long list of family, friends, and colleagues helped him get to that point. "As long as I'm on this planet, they're going to feel the love from me," said Turner. "Tia is at the top of the list. Sharon is right up there. And there are a number of people." Turner deeply apologized to Minemoto. "Sharon gave me what I needed, which was a reprimand," said Turner. "She knew that people were walking on eggshells around me and not wanting to say anything. It was obvious that there was a problem. And I had hidden it like crazy, but then when it starts to come out, it's at the point where it's a monster. So God bless Sharon. I'll always be grateful."[36]

His apology was just one repair to damage that had been done. Turner started following the concept of "living amends"[37]—committing to a new, healthy approach to life for himself, and to healing relationships that were strained during the dark, tumultuous times.

Just nine days after Turner's watershed moment, he played with the Jill Townsend Big Band in an important recording session at Capilano University. Turner was one of seventeen musicians who recorded tunes composed by Ross Taggart and arranged for big band by Townsend and guitarist Bill Coon. The session was for an album paying tribute to Taggart that Weeds was putting out on Cellar Live. On the solemn ballad "Light at the End of the Tunnel," Turner had a substantial written and improvised flugelhorn solo. "If you listen you can hear my tone shaking," said Turner about the solo. "I had just recently stopped [drinking], and I had the shakes, and I could barely keep the horn on my face. So that's documented evidence of my condition."[38] I could hear some tremors in Turner's tone after he told me about what happened that day, but I doubt the average listener picked up on his withdrawal symptoms. Turner—always striving for high standards, even in his weakened state—was, however, painfully aware of how much his form was off. I could also detect Turner's fragility in the black and white band photo on the CD sleeve for *Legacy, The Music of Ross Taggart*. Crouching in the front row, with eyes hidden under the dark shadow of his hat's brim, Turner was neither smiling nor gloomy. If his eyes were the red Mustang's stick shift, they indicated Turner was in neutral, a liminal space that represented real progress after his time in hell.

After taking some time off from teaching at Cap, Turner returned to campus with a rejuvenated outlook. "I did observe him being calmer and a more settled person," said Fiona Black. His return was meaningful for both Turner and his students. "You can see that it means the world to the students to nail a solo in performance with Brad, and it also means the world to Brad to see his students raise the bar," Black added. "I believe it's a really important part of Brad's life to mentor the Cap students. It grounds him and allows him to give back in such a meaningful way."[39]

While difficult times continued—his mother passed away in March 2015—in Turner's first year of sobriety, he rededicated himself to the craft of playing music. Turner also returned to what he had always excelled at:

Journeys to the Bandstand

writing dynamic, autobiographical music and recording it with his long-time bandmates and friends. On November 6 and 7, 2015, an extraordinary event took place at Frankie's Jazz Club: Turner celebrated the simultaneous release of new albums by his quartet and trio by performing with both groups both nights. Given his condition on the same dates a year before, this was an immense feat.

Both albums hit hard from the first note. The quartet's *Over My Head* begins with the title track, where Turner plays a fast-moving, serpentine melody on muted trumpet before soloing with utter conviction. He based the changes for "Over My Head" on the chords for Irving Berlin's "How Deep is the Ocean?" That wasn't by chance. The album's cover shows a startling black and white photo of Turner, in full suit and tie and black-framed glasses, clutching a trumpet while standing very much alone in the ocean. Water is up to his elbows, covering the bell of his trumpet. The photo clearly conveys the drowning man metaphor, reflecting Turner's near-death descent. The image's ultimate message, however, is buoyant: Turner isn't in grave danger of drowning anymore. He's keeping his head well above water and looking intently toward the shore and the life ahead of him.

Album cover photo by El Dunfield.

Over My Head was nominated for a Juno, which meant a lot to Turner. His trio's *Here Now* also opens with the title track, for which Turner plays on piano a rhythmically tricky, harmonically satisfying, and hopeful melody line. "Here now" is something Turner said during roll call at Alcoholics Anonymous meetings. "Meaning, I'm here, and no, I haven't had a drink since the last time I saw you."[40] As for the album cover, it's a close-up of Turner holding a Polaroid showing a street sign for "O Avenue," which represented his fresh start in life.

Releasing both albums at once was "shooting up a signal flare just to remind people, if they were curious, 'What's up with that guy? Last time I saw him, he didn't look well, and he didn't sound that great,'" said Turner.[41] The twin releases were, among other things, a way to tell the music community: I'm all right. Plus, it was a pledge that he was going to rededicate himself to reaching his potential as a musician and do so without crippling insecurity. "I'm not a very self-assuring person," reflected Turner. "A lot of what I do, the achievements that I've been able to realize, in large part stem from that motivation. Meaning, I'm not sure of myself, so I've got to have some stuff that's solid that I can stand on or hide behind. But now, I don't have to hide."[42]

• • •

Cellist Peggy Lee is one of Vancouver's most compelling instrumentalists and composers, in large part because she's uncategorizable. She incorporates and segues with finesse between melodicism, free improvised music, contemporary classical, and other creative forms. Turner has played trumpet with the Peggy Lee Band since it began, contributing to the group's 1999 self-titled debut recording and the ensemble's subsequent releases. It made sense, then, that when Coastal Jazz & Blues Society commissioned Lee to compose the *Echo Painting* suite, Turner would be part of it.

Lee and nine other musicians premiered the suite on June 25, 2016, at Ironworks, as part of the Vancouver International Jazz Festival. The suite's second movement, "Out on a Limb," is a gorgeous piece with mesmerizing, increasingly intense interlocking rhythms counterbalanced by stately horns. A video taken of the entire concert zoomed in close on Turner for much of a three-minute-and-thirty-five-second solo he played on "Out on a Limb." The video captured his eyes-closed concentration and how he alternately furrowed his brow and, especially on higher notes, raised his eyebrows. These facial expressions had nothing to do with their stereotypical meanings and everything to do with how Turner viscerally responds to playing profound music, which Lee composed with his specific voice on the trumpet in mind. The video also documented the powerful arc of his solo, encompassing both short bursts and long lines, all personifying the movement's title. Nearly ten months later, the same musicians recorded *Echo Painting* for an album that was released on Songlines Recordings, and Turner shapeshifted the solo into a trippier expression than the one he had delivered at the concert. Both versions are gripping.

2018 was a productive and important year for Turner. On two days in May, Turner on trumpet and flugelhorn, tenor saxophonist John Gross, Chris Gestrin on Hammond B3 and Moog bass synthesizer, and drummer Joe Poole recorded nine songs by Turner. The songs, released as *Pacific* on Cellar Live, were unlike anything his quartet or trio had recorded or performed live. The personnel, instrumentation, songcraft, and mood were all bold departures for Turner. While there were parallels with organist Larry Young's important *Unity* album, *Pacific* was hard to categorize and unassumingly original. "I'm super proud of that record," said Turner. "All the things that I've been working on came to fruition, and it's a totally different experience with John Gross [who has played and recorded with Shelly Manne, the Toshiko Akiyoshi-Lew Tabackin Big Band, Howard Roberts, and many others] on there."[43]

Then came a pivotal project that had its beginnings in the hyperactive brain of Cory Weeds. Almost twenty years after Turner's quartet and Seamus Blake had recorded a live album at the Cellar Jazz Café, Weeds had a vision of the same musicians recording together again, this time for Weeds' Cellar Music label. He approached Turner with the idea. "I think Brad feels a lot of pressure sometimes," said Weeds. "Everyone thinks of him as a God-like figure that can do no wrong, but coming up with nine tunes, I think it made him . . . nervous is not the right word—he was a little bit apprehensive about it. And of course, in Brad Turner fashion, not only did he do it, he exceeded every expectation, perhaps even his own expectations."[44] Turner started writing songs for the album a year in advance and came up with about twenty-five tunes that were "auditioned" until nine made the cut. He's long been a prolific and focused composer. "If I'm in writing mode, it's always with me, and it's constantly going through my head," said Turner. "It's hard to explain, but I can't not think about it."[45]

The quartet and Blake performed the tunes at Frankie's with a euphoric intensity, and they recorded them at The Warehouse Studio, pop star Bryan Adams' state-of-the-art recording studio. Weeds' label released the album in May 2019 as *Jump Up*, the most cohesive and absorbing collection of tunes that Turner has conceptualized and shaped in his career as a recording artist.

The title track exemplifies the album's quality. "Jump Up" starts with Hubert and Lachance punctuating a distinct rhythmic figure while van der Schyff keeps a solid pulse on a cymbal. Then overtop, Turner and Blake play the melody that has an engaging harmonic tension in unison. Soon the tempo changes to a swift swing feel before it goes into a transition that segues back to the original rhythm. As the song proceeds with hearty solos by Turner and Blake, the players repeatedly switch between the two rhythmic patterns. It's a tricky tune that could implode if not executed precisely. The elements come together fluidly and strikingly because Turner composed it with each musicians' strengths in mind, and they play it with a rapport developed from years of making music together. Plus, I appreciate how "Jump Up" evokes post-bop touchstones, including Miles Davis' second great quintet that played from 1964 to 1968, while also coming across as contemporary and resonating with a sound that's unique to this band.

The title relates to the interval Hubert and Lachance repeat in the rhythmic figure. "Leaping intervals tend to be uplifting and create a positive kind of vibe," said Turner. "So I thought, well, that sounds cool, and it sounds like it's jumping up. So I just called it that. The only other deeper meaning is that it's just meant to be a positive, enthusiastic, upbeat kind of tune. A happy tune."[46] If art was imitating life, and it inevitably does with Turner, "Jump Up"—the song and album—represented a declaration of hard-won contentment and an affirmation of making art for the right reasons. I also got the clear sense that Turner didn't necessarily see *Jump Up* as his capstone; there's so much more music in him to explore and express. He showed that four years later by again putting out two releases in quick succession: a radiant session with Turner's trio (*North Star*) and a recording with a new, exceptional quintet that lived up to the album title (*The Magnificent*).

Journeys to the Bandstand

Brad Turner Quartet with Seamus Blake: Bruno Hubert (piano), Seamus Blake (tenor saxophone), Brad Turner (trumpet), André Lachance (bass), and Dylan van der Schyff (drums), Frankie's Jazz Club, December 28, 2018. Photo by Vincent Lim.

Things were also looking up in other ways. Over the years Turner had mentored many young musicians, teaching them at Capilano University, playing on their gigs and recordings, and providing advice. With his inner burden lifted, Turner had more energy and focus to bring to his important role as a teacher and mentor. During the years before and after he quit drinking, I saw the Capilano A Band—the university's top student big band that he led and conducted—perform a number of times. I noticed a change in his presence at those shows—he went from looking stoic to conveying in his body language the joy of working with fledgling players.

At Tangent Café, there was a table next to the bandstand where musicians playing at the restaurant sat, drank, ate, and yakked before the music began and between sets. One night I sat nearby, with my back to the band's table, and eavesdropped on a conversation between Turner and three younger players who all benefited from his mentorship at CapU. The talk was wide-ranging—touching on music, movies, and more—and Turner clearly led the discussion by animatedly sharing anecdotes. I couldn't see their expressions, but I sensed the smiles and heard the laughter from the other three. Dad jokes didn't inspire the mirth. Instead, Turner simply expressed his measured ebullience, which was infectious.

As for Turner's relationship with his twin sons who had grown up to become young men, when we talked, I could hear in his voice and see in his demeanour the positive change that had come about. There was quiet pride, about everyday stuff like getting their first cars, and their growing interest in activating the Turner music gene.

• • •

In March 2019, Turner played the Vancouver Improvised Music Meeting at 8East, an artist-run space in Chinatown. These gigs—including Americans Eyvind Kang and Sara Schoenbeck and locals such as van der Schyff—called for free improvisation without the safety net of the jazz forms that Turner had mainly played within. "There was a time where I thought all of that was pretty much bullshit," said Turner about improvised music. "I looked down my nose at it." His attitude shifted years before when van der Schyff invited Turner to participate in Coastal Jazz & Blues Society's Time Flies mini-festival. "They put us together in bands or duos or even solo, and you went out and just played. I realized on that occasion how difficult it really was to do that well."[47]

November 2019 was an important time for Turner. Turning Point Ensemble would play "Scenes from Childhood" three times over the course of one weekend—the first performances of the suite since TPE premiered it in 2012. In the seven intervening years, Turner's life had transformed, so I had to experience one of the concerts to get a sense of what the remount meant to him. I chose the November 23, 2019, show at Langley Community Music School because that's where Turner's musical journey began in 1974. Also, a string quartet piece he was commissioned by the school to write— "Music for an Occasion"—would premiere that night. Outside the school's Rose Gellert Hall, as rain drove down hard, I saw Turner's Mustang in the parking lot. Inside the hall, there was a buzz about the evening's concert, the last in the school's fiftieth anniversary season. Townsend and Coon were there to support their friend. I overheard the elderly lady sitting next to me speak to her friend about Turner—a local boy who succeeded—with pride. They likely had no idea about the torment he had been through.

Turner introduced "Scenes from Childhood" with a sweet story about one of the suite's whimsically titled movements: "You'll Change Your Mind (About Girls)." Turner said it was inspired by a talk his mom gave him about girls, and then what happened after. "You can hear in that piece when my mind was changed." It was in ninth grade, after a canoe trip where he hung out with his classmate Debbie, who gave Turner a small kiss before he biked home. "The rest of that piece is me, you can imagine in Steven Spielberg style, riding home. I think I took the long way home that day."[48] While the first half of the piece was majestic and serious, the last half exuded the fast-pedalling optimistic momentum Turner had described. It was one of the highlights of the performance. Another was the exquisite rendition of the affecting movement "It's Ok to Cry," inspired by another piece of advice from his mom, for which Turner steadily brushed a snare drum at the back of the stage.

"My compositional approach is not one based in technique or any sort of systematic approach," explained Turner that night. "I need to have imagination; I need to have something going on in my head that motivates me to write." Later, when introducing his stirring string quartet composition, Turner shared more insights about his writing style. "A lot of it [composing "Music for an Occasion"] was me improvising at the piano for hours and hours and hours and recording it, and then going through it and finding things that I felt that were interesting to me."[49] It was all there that rainy night in Langley: an endearing return to innocence, beauty in music inspired by real life, insights into the creative process, and Turner's sense of serenity and humour that were telling about his sanguine state of mind.

Eight days later, Turner was one of the busiest musicians performing at the Shadbolt Jazz Walk, Weeds' inaugural jazz festival at the Shadbolt Centre in Burnaby. Turner was booked to play with four different groups in the one-day festival. At one point during a quintet set—his quartet plus tenor saxophonist Jon Bentley playing music from *Jump Up*—the band wasn't rhythmically in sync. So Turner showed leadership and called an audible. He put his hand on his head as a cue to the musicians to repeat the melody an extra time. "In that case I felt we were a little unsettled possibly, or I thought it would do us good to play the theme one more time and just restate things and get the groove," he said.[50] Half an hour after the quintet set, Turner played piano with Weeds' quintet featuring drummer Roy McCurdy, and the group was on point with their renditions from Cannonball Adderley's repertoire.

Turner's next obligation at the festival wasn't a performance. Weeks in advance, he agreed to participate in a festival workshop with me previewing this book. At the workshop, I planned to read an excerpt from this chapter and conduct a live interview with Turner in front of festivalgoers. A number of days before the session, I asked him if he wanted to read the excerpt in advance, or if there were any topics that I should steer clear of in the interview. Turner didn't take me up on my offer to read my words, and he said he would "be completely comfortable with discussing anything at all."[51] With that in mind, I planned to read at the workshop the opening paragraphs, which referred to Turner "drinking himself to death."

While the interview went well, just before it was time to read the excerpt, I panicked and called my own audible. I disingenuously told the audience that I couldn't share the excerpt due to time constraints. Turner suggested that he could go get ready for his next performance and I could read the excerpt without him being there, but I demurred. At that exact moment, after years of studying Turner, I transformed from objective chronicler to someone who wanted to protect him and his story. It was a well-meaning but unnecessary manoeuvre because Turner wasn't ashamed of his addiction narrative and didn't need protection. After everything he had been through, his resilience and self-belief were unshakable.

A couple of months after the Shadbolt Jazz Walk, Turner played trumpet at 8East with the Peggy Lee Band. The show was significant for a trio of reasons: the band performed beautiful new tunes from a suite by Lee; it was the last performance Turner played with his longtime bandmate van der Schyff before the drummer moved to Australia; and it was three days before the fifth anniversary of Turner's sobriety breakthrough. By the time I arrived, the only seats available were in the front row, a few feet away from Turner. It was the perfect spot from which to absorb his contributions during ensemble sections and solos. Turner's playing was strong and clear. He looked and sounded at ease, grounded, content. Brad Turner was in a good place.

16 / LIFE OF BRUNO: BRUNO HUBERT

ON A WARM August night, Bruno Hubert is in classic form. Bruno sits behind the upright piano that's next to a brick wall at the Libra Room, the restaurant on Vancouver's Commercial Drive where he's been ensconced for years. He's hunched over with his head bowed near the keys. Perched on the piano is a wide piece of tattered paper with curious markings. It's not sheet music, but it's all about music. Written in different shades of felt marker are around forty song titles, along with the names of two jazz artists and one classical composer. Some of the songs and artists have blue highlight on top, and some have solid or broken lines above, below, or beside them. He doesn't look at the paper. Bruno's concentration remains on the keyboard, where his fingers create beguiling sounds that are uniquely his.

Over the course of about twenty minutes, Bruno cycles through a dozen or so songs, playing their melodies beautifully and improvising gorgeous inflections. Among the tunes he explores: Keith Jarrett's "The Windup," Charlie's Chaplin's "Smile," the Bee Gees' "How Deep Is Your Love," Billy Strayhorn's "Lush Life," and Bach's "Prelude and Fugue No. 6 in D Minor." In lesser hands, this song cycle would be a shmaltzy mess. Not with Bruno. There's a carefully conceived aesthetic at play where he simultaneously interprets and creates anew. And please don't call it a medley. It's an organic flow. The renditions segue seamlessly into each other. The curious paper now makes sense. It's both a road map and a treasure map that's a reassuring guide for Bruno. When he completes his solo odyssey, there's a smattering of applause, mainly from me and one other man—the only ones listening.

The ten or so other people in the restaurant are drinking, talking, and totally oblivious to the art that just transpired. He acknowledges the clapping by putting his hands together, prayer-like, in a sweet gesture that's pure Bruno. Then he starts again on another solo flight.

Bruno Hubert's musical road map. Photo by Chris Wong.

Just over twenty-four hours later, Bruno is on another bandstand with his trio—including bassist James Meger and drummer Joe Poole—at Vancouver's main jazz joint: Frankie's Jazz Club. Bruno doesn't typically play gigs two nights in a row. In a perfect world, he would present his craft multiple times a week; in this imperfect world, Bruno performs for audiences here and there when opportunities arise. So for Bruno fans, it's a lucky week. Tonight he's wearing a black shirt, red pants, and a colourful novelty tie.

> **Brunoisms #1**: Instead of following tie etiquette and having the narrow end of the tie almost the same length as the wide end, Bruno often asymmetrically keeps the tip of the narrow end not far below the Windsor knot.

He starts the set with "Fly Me to The Moon," reshaping the familiar melody in dense chord clusters and mining far below the surface for harmonic insights in his solo. Next up: "Love for Sale," with a robust "Night in Tunisia" intro. As the set proceeds, he plays "Take Five," "Birdland," "My Favourite Things," "Goodbye Pork Pie Hat," and other standards either in their entirety or as quotations within tunes. Just like in the solo setting at the Libra Room, Bruno's interpretations uphold integrity and a cliché-free hipness. Those who know his approach would very likely identify his playing in a blindfold test—his musicality is that singular. Plus, if you just say "Bruno" to anyone in Vancouver's jazz scene, chances are the person will instantly conjure a mental image of the man, whose character can't be properly distilled with prosaic words like "eccentric" or "unconventional." Understanding Bruno's persona requires peering into his creation story.

• • •

It all began for Bruno in a town in southwest Quebec at the confluence of the Désert and Gatineau rivers: Maniwaki. In 1925, Joseph-Olivier Hubert founded the J.O. Hubert general store in Maniwaki. J.O. Hubert evolved to become a modern department store and an institution in the town. Hubert and his wife Thérèse had twelve children, including his son Armand, who became one of the store's owners. Armand and his wife Bernadette also raised a large family. Their youngest of eight children, Bruno, was born April 22, 1964.[1]

In Maniwaki—population approximately 4,000—Bruno grew up in a milieu of strong French, Irish, and Algonquin cultures. He played hockey with kids from Kitigan Zibi Anishinabeg, an Algonquin First Nation reserve where future Vancouver Canucks fan-favourite Gino Odjick was born and lived, not far from the Hubert home. Bruno was a decent and somewhat tough hockey player, who made the local all-star team. "I'm a defenceman, so the puck can go through me, but not the man," he said. "The man is going to go flying up in the air."[2]

Home movies that Bruno's aunt Lucille made with a Super 8 camera in the sixties and seventies convey an idyllic childhood for Bruno and his siblings in Maniwaki. When young Bruno appears in the frame, he looks like a happy boy with a mischievous glint in his eyes.

One day, when Bruno was about twelve, he was sick and stayed home from school. Because his parents were working and couldn't look after him, he went to his oldest brother Pierre's apartment. Pierre had a powerful stereo system, including two gigantic speakers and a massive record collection. Bruno sat in a La-Z-Boy chair when Pierre cranked up the speakers as Keith Jarrett's *The Köln Concert* played on the turntable. After ECM Records released the live recording of Jarrett's bravura solo piano improvisations as a double vinyl album in 1975, it went on to become the best-selling solo album in jazz history. At the time, Bruno knew nothing about Jarrett, jazz, or piano (other than tinkling on the family upright at home), but he reacted viscerally. "This to me . . . it was a revelation," said Bruno, who clearly remembered his response to the music: "My God, piano can actually sound like this?"[3]

Though he wasn't at all ready to act on the inspiration that Jarrett's dazzling improv gave him, Bruno was already devoted to music. His passion was being among the ranks of La Fanfare de Maniwaki, the town's marching band. He initially played trumpet and trombone in the band, which had about seventy-five members, before earning a coveted spot on the drumline. Young Bruno played snare and bass drum in the band for about five years, and he was proud of his contributions to La Fanfare. But his path was far from set.

Bruno Hubert (bass drum) with La Fanfare de Maniwaki. Photographer unknown. Courtesy Bruno Hubert.

The Incredible Escapades of Bruno #1: Aside from going to school, playing hockey, and drumming in the marching band, Bruno took part in the family tradition of hunting and fishing. He was in the forest with friends on a hunting expedition, armed with his father's double-barrel shotgun, when the unthinkable happened as darkness approached: the sixteen-year-old tripped and accidentally shot himself in his stomach. One friend ran to the nearest phone to call an ambulance while the others carried Bruno out of the woods. He was taken to the only hospital in Maniwaki, where surgery was performed on him. "I am lucky to be alive," said Bruno about surviving that horrific day.[4] Although the surgery and post-op treatment were successful, there were limits to what the Maniwaki medical team could do. Bruno and his family were advised that there was essentially an expiry date on his treatment, and he would need to be re-checked and possibly operated on again later in life.

Bruno resumed his carefree life that increasingly focused on music. Within a year of the hunting accident, he became the drummer in Ad-lib, a rock band playing gigs in local venues. By the time he graduated from high school, Bruno envisioned pursuing a career as a professional drummer. But he wanted to study music first, so Bruno enrolled at Cégep de Sainte-Foy, a college in Québec City. Thus began his protracted trek through post-secondary music schools.

Like all drummers at the cégep, Bruno had to take piano. He soon realized that piano resonated with him more than drums, so Bruno decided to switch instruments. As an inexperienced pianist, he wasn't at the requisite level to enter the classical piano program. But Michel Franck, a pianist on the music faculty at Cégep de Sainte-Foy, agreed to teach Bruno privately and help him meet the standard. Another teacher at the cégep significant in Bruno's musical development was Réjean Marois, a trombonist, guitarist, singer, and composer/arranger. There's a group photo taken of the Cégep de Sainte-Foy stage band, directed by Marois, at the 1985 Canadian Stage Band Festival in Québec City. Bruno is in the front row, with afro-like hair and wire-rimmed glasses, looking blissful with his life ahead of him. The following year, Marois took an ensemble—including Bruno—to Vancouver to compete at the same festival, which was held as part of Expo 86. The trip foreshadowed career and life directions for both Marois and Hubert.

Bruno ended up spending about seven years at the cégep—far longer than most students—while he unsuccessfully auditioned for university music programs in Québec City and Montreal. Then Bruno met bassist André Lachance in 1988. They performed together for the first time when Bruno was brought in to play in the rhythm section of the vocal jazz choir at Lachance's Québec City high school. Lachance said Bruno was so busy as a musician that he needed two keyboard rigs to play gigs at different venues on the same day. "He was involved in many different things: a lot of jobbing stuff, a lot of casuals," said Lachance. "It wasn't all jazz. Over the years he has gradually dropped that whole jobbing thing and just worked on his own voice and his own sound, and he has been crafting that ever since."[5]

By 1988, Marois had moved across the country to teach at Capilano College in North Vancouver, and he encouraged Bruno to apply there. He did and was accepted. Bruno thought Lachance should go too. All he had to do was convince both Lachance and the bassist's mother that it would be wise to travel more than 5,000 kilometres to attend an English-speaking music school. "He came to dinner at my house and gave this whole speech on why we should go to Vancouver," recalled Lachance.[6] It worked. At the end of the summer of 1990, Bruno, Lachance, and three other friends moved to Vancouver. Bruno and Lachance becoming Cap music students, and then working musicians in their adopted west coast city, would greatly impact Vancouver's jazz scene.

At Capilano College, Bruno studied with pianist Miles Black for five years, and that was an illuminating experience. Black plays beautiful jazz piano and possesses an encyclopedic knowledge of standards. So he was an ideal mentor for Bruno. "He was definitely the one that opened all the doors for me," said Bruno[7] about how Black helped him unlock jazz harmony, interpreting standards, and much more. Bruno also studied with Ross Taggart—another musician with far-reaching knowledge of repertoire and jazz piano—and re-connected with Marois, who led the college's NiteCap jazz vocal ensemble that Bruno played with. Another influence: veteran pianist, tenor saxophonist, and Cap teacher Al Wold. "Al would say, 'From one to ten, your playing is at eight, eight point five. Your reading is at two. You have some work to do there.'"[8] This was part of a recurring theme in Bruno's schooling. He was a quick learner on piano; Bruno's playing far surpassed what his experience level suggested. Contributing to an ensemble's sound, accentuating fellow players, and improvising are at the heart of jazz performance, and he excelled in these areas. But he struggled with sight reading and was befuddled by theory, composing, and arranging.

• • •

After years of being away, Brad Turner returned to Metro Vancouver in 1992 with impressive credentials. He left in 1985 to complete undergraduate and graduate music degrees, including a master's from an institution with a lot of cachet in the jazz world: the University of North Texas. In addition to playing at a high level on three instruments, Turner showed a knack for arranging and composing. In other words, apart from both having big curly hair and a hunger for jazz, Turner and Bruno were polar opposites. Despite all of his schooling, Bruno hadn't earned a single degree, and composing was his kryptonite. Yet after Turner started teaching at Capilano College and encountered Bruno, he heard something in the pianist. When Turner formed a quartet in 1993, he chose Bruno for the piano chair. It was an astute choice. Right from the band's first recording, a four-song cassette, there was an unmistakeable chemistry between Turner, Bruno, Chris Nelson, and Dylan van der Schyff. That rapport deepened on the quartet's full-length album debut, *Long Story Short*. Bruno contributed enormously to the group's engagingly thought-provoking sound. Then Nelson left the band, and Lachance replaced him. They didn't know it at the time, but the Brad Turner Quartet was poised to go on a long and fulfilling run.

At thirty, Bruno was making progress in his jazz vocation. He also had ambitions that went beyond the local scene. Bruno heard about the Great American Jazz Piano Competition that was part of the Jacksonville Jazz Festival. This was a prominent event—Marcus Roberts (who would go on to play with Wynton Marsalis before becoming a solo artist) won the first edition, and Harry Connick Jr. came in second. Bruno was among many pianists who auditioned for the fourteenth edition of the competition, and he was selected to be one of five finalists to perform in Jacksonville in November 1996. Each finalist had to play three tunes: one solo piece and two trio songs with upper-echelon players—drummer Danny Gottlieb (who was in the Pat Metheny Group) and bassist Jay Leonhart (who had played with Duke Ellington and many other well-known artists)—after a twenty-minute rehearsal.

There's a low-quality YouTube video, taken from WJCT public TV, of Bruno's eighteen-minute performance in the competition. A skinny and short-haired Bruno, in suit and tie, walked onto the Florida Theatre stage and absolutely nailed all three jazz standards, giving a stirring performance. Winning could have changed the course of his career, but that didn't happen. He came in third, which was still an outstanding accomplishment. While the strong showing didn't elevate Bruno's status, it gave him affirmation of his personal conviction that he was on the right track. That fueled him moving forward.

The same year as the piano competition, Bruno applied for a grant from the Canada Council for the Arts to study at the University of North Texas. Inspired by Turner, who spoke highly of his experience at UNT, Bruno wanted even more education. His application was successful, and he went to Denton, Texas, in 1997 to work toward a degree. It's hard to imagine Bruno, with all of his irregular traits, in conservative Texas. But he studied there with UNT piano guru Dan Haerle and other faculty for two years. Bruno fell short of getting a degree, once again, because he couldn't pass the required arranging and composing classes. Those classes "destroyed me," he said.[9] Plus, after his Canada Council funds ran out, staying in the expensive program was out of the question.

With Bruno, for every door that closes, another (generally) opens. Bruno received a surprising call. It was from one of his idols, Gino Vannelli, whose soft-pop/rock hits like "I Just Wanna Stop" made him a star in the 1970s. The Montreal-born singer/songwriter achieved fame in Quebec and internationally. So it was a big deal when he contacted Bruno about going on a world tour as a keyboardist in Vannelli's band. Vannelli initially offered the gig to Miles Black, who turned it down because a baby was on the way. Black referred Vannelli to Bruno, and before long he was on a plane to Portland to join Vannelli in his studio to work on songs. The Quebecers got along well and connected musically, but Bruno faced a familiar predicament. "He really wanted me to do the tour," said Bruno. "I worked as hard as I could to learn his music. He made me write [down] everything I was playing, which was my nemesis. That's why I failed school. So here's Gino going, 'We need to write all this down, and when you play, you have to play what you wrote down.' And that's where I fell apart because I had trouble [repeating pieces note for note]."[10]

So Bruno didn't go on the tour, which would have helped his CV and bank account. It especially stung because two other idols—bassist Alain Caron and drummer Paul Brochu from the chops-heavy Quebec fusion band UZEB—were in the rhythm section.[11] But just having the opportunity, which led to some studio work with Vannelli, was meaningful to Bruno. "Gino was sort of this huge door that opened for me," he said. "I was playing the piano a certain way, and Gino loved my playing, but I was not quite ready for it."[12] It was another case of being tantalizingly close to something big, but not quite making it, which prompts his admirers to root all the harder for him.

Bruno's father Armand was incredibly supportive of his son's pursuit of music. Armand died in 1999, and his obituary included a list of the Hubert children that referred to "Bruno et son piano."[13] Armand had helped Bruno financially for years. But after his father's death, Bruno was struggling with a large student loan debt. During that time, he visited Québec City and met with the dean of music at Université Laval. "At the end of our meeting he opened his chequebook and wrote me a cheque for a very significant amount of money," recalled Bruno. "He just gave it to me. And he said, 'Go back to Vancouver. I hope you're going to graduate someday.'" Bruno was floored by the generosity and faith shown by the dean and told him straight up that he wouldn't be able to repay him. "He said, 'Don't worry about this.' This was a present to me to say, 'Go and become a piano player.'"[14]

• • •

In the late nineties, when Bruno wasn't in Texas, he gigged around Vancouver as much as he could. With the Brad Turner Quartet, his own trio, and other groups, he played at the Mojo Room, the Glass Slipper, the Purple Onion, and other long-gone venues. Cory Weeds' launch of his Cellar jazz club in 2000 gave Vancouver players a desperately needed boost by providing a welcoming place where they could play and hang. Bruno was on the bandstand with Turner's quartet and Seamus Blake in September 2000 for the club's grand opening.

> **The Incredible Escapades of Bruno #2**: The following didn't happen to Bruno *per se,* but a tangential connection to fires that gutted jazz venues only adds to his legend.

The Glass Slipper, in East Vancouver's Mount Pleasant neighbourhood, was an important venue for creative music. Housed in a former church, it was a cherished, uncurated hub for jazz—from straight ahead to avant-garde, roots music, and more. On December 19, 1996, Eastwind—led by Henry Boudin and including Bruno—performed what would be the musician-run venue's last show. The next morning, at 11:37 a.m., fifteen emergency units responded to a large fire at the Slipper. They couldn't save the turn-of-the century building, or the musical instruments and other equipment valued at about $20,000 inside it.[15] Losing the Glass Slipper devastated Vancouver musicians, including Bruno.

The Blue Note Jazz Bistro, at 2340 West 4th in Kitsilano, was an upstairs restaurant that featured jazz in the late nineties. While it wasn't beloved by a number of musicians because it paid less-than-generously (not unlike the Libra Room), the Blue Note was a dependable source of gigs for some. Bruno played at the restaurant's previous location and performed regularly at the Blue Note on 4th after it opened in 1996. On July 3, 1999, Bruno played there with his trio. Just a few hours after his last set, at around three a.m., about twenty-four firefighters responded to a two-alarm blaze at the Blue Note that started in the rear stairwell and caused extensive damage to the interior.[16] Bruno had borrowed Turner's rare fifty-four key Rhodes electric piano, used it at the Blue Note on that fateful night, and left it there. "I went through the police tape a few days later to go in and get it, and it was sitting there," said Turner. "It was like angels had guarded it. Everything around it was charred, but it wasn't burned."[17] Was Bruno a fiery bad luck charm or a bringer of good fortune because the precious Rhodes was spared? Only the jazz gods know.

As part of Turner's quartet, Bruno played with the great saxophonist Joe Lovano in a September 2001 concert at Capilano College Performing Arts Theatre. "He played his ass off," remembered Turner about Bruno's performance and Lovano's reaction. "That was an instance of, 'Who the fuck is this guy? Where did this guy come from?' Because he's that unique."[18]

Weeds gave Bruno and his trio a regular Sunday night gig at the Cellar. Weeds even sprung for an ad, featuring Bruno, appearing in 99 B-Line express buses that stopped near the club. "There was this picture of me at the Fender Rhodes, and it was all in blue," said Bruno. "It was very well designed. A lot of times I would go to my gig on Sunday on the bus and find where the picture was, and I would just sit right under it. Eventually some people would be sitting and watching and go, 'That guy looks awfully like the guy in the picture there.' And then some people asked me, 'Is that you?'"[19] Quintessential Bruno.

Weeds, who has a propensity for coming up with ideas and acting quickly on them, suggested recording the Bruno Hubert Trio live at the Cellar for possible release. It happened January 13–14, 2002, with Bruno, Lachance on bass, and Turner on drums. The recording was much more than good enough for Weeds to release on his new Cellar Live label. Bruno's playing those nights magically displayed his interpretive artistry—the fruition of years of work to absorb the elements of jazz piano and develop his self-expression. *Get Out of Town* leaves an impression from the first notes on the opening track "Cost of Living" by Don Grolnick. Bruno transforms the tune that Grolnick, Michael Brecker, and others played as a ballad. He starts alone with a vigorous left-hand pattern before Lachance and Turner join in at a brisk pulse. Bruno suffuses the melody and his improvising with kinetic soul. On that tune, and others like "Simone," the title track, and "The Man I Love," Bruno and the trio enter an enchanting and affecting realm. No wonder *Get Out of Town* was unexpectedly a strong selling album. (Quirky fact: it sold exceptionally well in Japan.)

"I think what we all try and do in this world of music is have a unique voice," said Weeds. "So if that's the criteria, he certainly reached the top of his game because you know Bruno the second you hear him, whether it is his touch or whether it is the lines he plays. Just listen to that first record. There's nobody that really plays the piano like that. There are so many influences coming into play."[20] In his liner notes to *Get Out of Town*, Ross Taggart cited some of those influences: Duke Ellington, Thelonious Monk, Errol Garner, Bill Evans, Herbie Hancock, Cedar Walton, Kenny Drew, and Keith Jarrett. "He is, however, his own man musically and in turn has influenced countless players that have heard him," wrote Taggart,[21] a fellow gifted pianist.

> **Brunoisms #2:** Since he was young, Bruno has worn glasses. "If I don't have glasses on, I feel totally naked." For years, however, Bruno has worn just the frames with no lenses in them. The lack of lenses is primarily due to not having enough money to buy them, he explained, alarmingly. The result is blurry vision; he can't recognize people across the street and can have trouble reading music. But, as with many other aspects of life, Bruno experiences this unlike most of us would. He believes that merely wearing frames helps each eye focus. "Just having a circle around your eye helps," according to Bruno. A number of people have offered to buy lenses for him. Mike Allen did exactly that while on tour with Bruno because he was standing up behind the piano and leaning over so he could read Allen's original music. (Those lenses are long gone.) I've come to the conclusion that he prefers to be lens-less. "I started to appreciate the fact that [without working glasses] you can't see that far. You're just concerned about what you have around you, and everything else is kind of blurry. So then it doesn't disturb you. If I'm performing, if I look around, I don't see anything, I don't see anybody. So it helps me focus on only what's in front of me."[22] Which is the sublime music within him.

Bruno Hubert, Frankie's Jazz Club, May 6, 2022. Photo by Vincent Lim.

Brunoisms #3: "Even though he can't really see, he has to have music on his piano stand," said Turner. "And not only that, he has to have the music, but he folds the title over so that he can't see it, which he couldn't see anyway because he can't see. All these strange, idiosyncratic tendencies just developed over the years. And the beautiful thing is, maybe in a different scene, somebody who's a unique personality like Bruno might possibly get marginalized a little bit because of his eccentricities. But not here. Bruno is a fixture."[23]

Brunoisms #4: When not playing pianos, Bruno is tuning them, and often the two things overlap. Given the chance, Bruno will tune a piano before playing it in a gig. I've watched him do so in painstaking fashion, with every key, right up until curtain time. Sometimes to his detriment.

"He would push his luck," said Weeds about Bruno's tuning before Cellar gigs. "He would be tuning into the dinner hour, and I repeatedly told him not to. Finally, I just lost my cool in the back of the club in the hallway, and he started crying. He was so upset and so apologetic, and I've never felt so bad in my life. He never did it again, so that's what it took him to stop. But I felt so awful, and at that point I realized what a sensitive guy he is."[24]

Regardless of the times Weeds lost patience with Bruno, they've always had mutual respect. That's why Weeds invited Bruno to record a second album. *Live @ The Cellar*, released on Cellar Live in 2008. While the album didn't shine as luminously as *Get Out of Town*, it's another resplendent document of Bruno's inimitable approach. The CD's cover photo shows a tricycle with one of the rear wheels askew. "I see it as two solidly planted wheels (Brad Turner and André Lachance) and one slightly off-kilter wheel that looks like it could collapse at any moment (Bruno)," Weeds wrote in his perceptive liner notes. "There is no chance that Bruno and the trio will actually collapse, but it's the crookedness, the wobbling and the unpredictability of that wheel that represents the musical direction of this trio and the personality of its leader."[25] Weeds explained further: "He's a very unique talent, extremely unique talent, but he is also extremely idiosyncratic and a quirky human being. That quirkiness has probably kept him back a little bit, but it also is what makes him a super beautiful guy."[26]

The Incredible Escapades of Bruno #3: The odds of a Vancouver jazz pianist being the star of a feature film are infinitesimal. But it happened to Bruno. The long process that led to a movie all about Bruno began when filmmaker Michael Simard went to Bukowski's on Commercial Drive. Seeing and hearing Bruno play made an impression on Simard. After getting to know the man behind the music, and witnessing his artistically rich but monetarily poor life, Simard saw the potential in making a comedy. Filming began in 2003, but it took years to complete and received a limited theatrical release. Finally, in June and July 2012,

Bruno's Blues briefly played in a few Vancouver, Toronto, and Montreal cinemas.

As a music mockumentary, *Bruno's Blues* is no *This Is Spinal Tap*. It has a student film feel to it, with amateurish acting and unpolished cinematography. But the fictional feature, which Simard produced, wrote, and directed, captures Bruno's real-life essence: part gifted jazz musician, part lovable train wreck. He first appears in a shower scene, though not of the *Psycho* variety; Bruno simply emerges from the shower in a cruddy bathroom with a towel around his waist and brushes his teeth. Then, in between many scenes of Bruno and mostly young musicians playing satisfying jazz, the story unfolds: he ignores messages from bill collectors; he decides to launch a magazine called *Underground Jazz* with neither a plan for the content nor money to publish it; he runs up beer tabs on gigs that exceed the pay for him and his bandmates; Bruno witnesses the demolition of his house due to his financial neglect; he ends up homeless and dirt-encrusted, comforted only by the bottle; and, finally, Bruno climbs out of the abyss, achieving musical success.

"It's sort of a fairy tale, but there are lots of real elements in there," said the bona fide Bruno. "Bruno loses everything, he's on the street, and he has no more money. It was kind of true. It kind of did happen in some ways, not to the point where I'm in the alleys. But there was definitely a time when it was like, 'Okay, what do I do now?'"[27]

As well as conveying Bruno's ineffable aura, the film documents Vancouver's burgeoning jazz scene in the 2000s. Bruno was the casting director, recruiting musician friends to act and play music in the movie. Brad Turner has a prominent role as a slimy record label head. Réjean Marois shows up in an off-the-wall cameo as a street food vendor/

Life of Bruno

folk guitarist selling repulsive hotdogs. Cory Weeds plays himself as the jazz club owner owed money by Bruno in a scene filmed at the Cellar. And saxophonist Daniel Miles Kane plays a quack doctor who gives Bruno an antidote for his long list of ailments, which the doc sums up as "Totally Fucked Up." While these ridiculous scenes are amusing in an infantile way, the movie's lasting value is its music. The scenes of Bruno and others playing at Bukowski's (with the same Rhodes that escaped incineration at the Blue Note) and in jam sessions capture Bruno's peerless sound. Musically, *Bruno's Blues* peaks in a recording studio scene near the end of the film, where Bruno performs with singer Denzal Sinclaire and other musicians. They imbue new meaning to "Cost of Living," which evolves from the funky tour de force it was on Bruno's first album to a melancholic meditation in the movie's dénouement. The latter version of the tune raises a delicate question: what's the real-life human cost to being Bruno?

The Incredible Escapades of Bruno #4: If you spend any amount of time with Bruno, it quickly becomes clear that he's a gentle man who wouldn't hurt a soul. That's why I shuddered when I heard about a doozy of a bar fight he got in the middle of. It happened in Whitehorse, the capital of northern Canada's Yukon, in October 2005. Bruno had landed a great, multi-day gig for his trio at the time, including bassist Sean Cronin and drummer Sam Cartwright. It involved performing and recording an album at the sizeable Yukon Arts Centre theatre in Whitehorse.

On the third night, Bruno wanted to shoot pool. The band was directed to a bar that had one pool table, being used by some people, and our man subtly made it known that he wanted to play next. Conversation among the people at the pool table got louder and suddenly they attacked the three musicians, using bar stools as weapons. After the brawl was over, the trio had black eyes, swollen jaws, and other significant injuries. "We looked like we had a fight, and we lost," said Bruno. All three ended up in a Whitehorse hospital, and despite looking and feeling horrendous, they still played a performance scheduled for the next day. It turned out the assailants were major drug dealers. Bruno decided on behalf of the band not to press charges because he realized "we won't get anything out of this other than trouble."[28] To add insult to their injuries, Bruno wasn't happy with the recording, and it never came out.

Bruno has had other escapades, like the time he had a high-speed bike accident at the bottom of a steep hill, and then-University of North Texas student/future star Norah Jones was among his rescuers. Bruno's valuable hands were fine, but his face was "demolished" and his glasses broken.[29] I won't get into any more details because by now you get the point—serious trouble finds Bruno, yet he survives and his bewitching music plays on.

• • •

Bruno started having stomach issues about thirty years after his surgery for the hunting accident. It got so bad that he couldn't eat at times because it was too painful. Bruno needed another operation, but he didn't have the wherewithal to navigate the healthcare system to get it done. Guardian angels stepped up. Among them was a jazz fan who's married to a physician. The good doctor organized the surgery for Bruno. On the eve of his operation, a benefit was held at Frankie's, with proceeds that would help Bruno subsist while he convalesced and went without gigs. The club was packed with jazz fans and musicians who wanted to hear a double bill of Turner's quartet and Bruno's trio and support the man who a preview of the benefit referred to as "one of the most-loved misfits of the Vancouver jazz scene."[30]

Almost precisely two years later, in December 2018, Bruno played three nights at Frankie's with the Brad Turner Quartet and Seamus Blake. The gigs were an opportune tune-up for a recording they made at The Warehouse

Studio the day after the Frankie's run. *Jump Up*, the album that resulted from that session, was a triumph for Turner and all of the musicians involved. Turner wrote tunes with each musician in mind, and Bruno executes written parts and comping—on acoustic piano and Rhodes—with verve. As for his solos, Bruno shapes them in his style, which emphasizes harmonic quality over volume of notes. On the album's one live track from Frankie's, "Catastrophizer," he ventures out of his melodic comfort zone into another dimension. "I can tell you *Jump Up* has some of the finest piano playing he has ever done," said Weeds,[31] without equivocation.

Lachance, who played alongside Bruno on *Jump Up* and other recordings and gigs dating back twenty years, doesn't try to place his friend and bandmate according to conventional standards. "He is so unique," said Lachance. "You can't judge that guy according to the parameters of how you would compare other people because he's a brilliant artist. An amazing, unique voice on the instrument, more as an interpreter." Lachance also understands better than most that while his "weird brother" is undeniably quirky, it doesn't define Bruno. "Underneath all that charm and personality there is still this core. There is still this heavy musician and to me, there is still the guy I met in 1988."[32]

I asked Turner for a definitive statement on Bruno. "I don't know anyone like Bruno as a piano player, as a friend, as a human, as a character. He's one of a kind, truly, which is really saying something, particularly in terms of his piano playing because there are a lot of piano players out there. There are a lot of great piano players out there. But there aren't a whole lot of originals, in my humble opinion, that play jazz and have found a way to play modern music straight ahead—in fact in Bruno's case quite traditional jazz—in a unique, personal way with his own language, his own rhythmic feel and approach, his own articulation on the piano. It's just unique."[33]

Everyone I talked to about Bruno used the word "unique" to describe the man and his music. Most also referred to Bruno's distinct "voice" on the piano. Both descriptions speak to how *sui generis* he is, and they raise the question, what was it about the life of Bruno that led to his individual sound? "I think it happened because of being so late in the game in playing piano," said Bruno. "I think I had to make it work for me, so I had to find a way to play."[34]

Bruno Hubert, the Cellar, April 30, 2008. Photo by Steve Mynett.

• • •

At the Libra Room, Bruno is pacing. He's exuding the nervous energy that rears itself usually before gigs. Bruno showed up late for our interview, and now he's on the phone, organizing musicians to play in the restaurant. Eventually we enter a patio oasis out back that he calls his "office," and he relaxes a bit. We talk about his musical and non-musical lives—where he's been and where he's going. Bruno is drinking a rum and Coke, or "breakfast" in his lexicon. "I call it breakfast because it's the first drink of the day. All vitamins are in there."[35]

In Bruno's history with the Libra Room, which began in the early 2000s, he went from playing every Friday to performing twice a week—solo and in small groups—to sometimes casting his spell even more frequently. Along the way, he became the booker lining up musicians to play and the sound man who diligently adjusted levels as they played. Seeing all the assistance Bruno was providing his restaurant for free, the Libra's owner proposed a barter: in return for playing and his ancillary services, Bruno would receive free rent, food, and beer. He took the deal. Then in 2016, the Libra suffered a catastrophe. No, another fire didn't follow Bruno, but a sewer backup closed the joint for a year and a half. Again, though it could easily have deteriorated into a case of life imitating art à la *Bruno's Blues*, Bruno adapted. "For a few years, I had to borrow money left and right. That was tough. Then [piano] tuning just slowly got better. I'm at this point now where the Libra Room is changing. I don't really predict what's happening, but I've been here for fifteen years, and there might be some changes."[36]

I wonder if the cumulative challenges—his health, falling short of earning a degree, almost but not quite making professional breakthroughs, persistent money worries—have ever led Bruno to consider giving up on his passion. Bruno doesn't answer directly. Instead, he recalls a prediction a piano teacher in Quebec made about him approximately thirty years ago: "He said, 'By the time you get to your late forties, you're going to start seeing the clouds separate. The piano's going to start making more sense. Everything in music, it's like a pyramid upside down. The next level is that much harder to get, but it's exponential. If you make it to the next level, then it's that much more knowledge. And it keeps going like this.'"[37]

In other words, Bruno is optimistic about continuing to musically evolve and has no thoughts of giving up. "That thirty years of piano is now starting to make more sense. I see better things coming. What's been happening the last twenty years has been amazing. I still think there's more that's going to come . . . I kind of think my late fifties and sixties will actually be more intense, even more beneficial for me than all those [previous] years. I think my sixties will be the time where I will start getting out there with more confidence."[38] Bruno's tone of calm conviction makes me believe that his prognostications will come true.

Jump up four and a half months, to January 4, 2020. Bruno's premonition about change has come true. It's the last night of the Libra Room before it closes. There's a holiday season window painting on glass panes at the front showing smiling Bruno behind a piano and "Season's Greetings" in whimsical writing. Bruno is inside playing with young musicians, as he always did at the Libra. The people packed in the restaurant during its final hours don't seem to recognize or care that it's the end of one man's musical era that unfolded right where they sit. For me, knowing that this is his windup makes the night bittersweet. Still, I savour hearing Bruno one last time in his haunt.

Life of Bruno

The countless songs he coalesced here, and the singularity he brought to his interpretations, will warmly remain in memory.

The Libra Room, January 5, 2020. Photo by Chris Wong.

It took six weeks for Bruno to reset. That's when "Bruno Schubert," as he's known on Facebook, posted a dark photo of the former Libra Room piano. A different version of the piece of paper that's never out of sight but never in focus was on the piano as it should be. Many of the familiar songs were on it, but Bruno colour coded it differently. Musical hieroglyphics, Bruno style. Just like an earlier piano that was wheeled down Commercial Drive from Bukowski's to the Libra Room years before, the Libra upright was moved to Sopra Sotto, a block away from its former home. Bruno got a brand-new gig playing solo piano in the Italian restaurant. Then, not long after, the COVID-19 pandemic exploded and closed the restaurant to dine-in guests. The gig was up barely after it began, but this time Bruno was not alone. Every live music venue shut down during the pandemic's first stage. For weeks. While it was happening, I wondered yet again how he would survive. I feared the worst.

December 20, 2020. It took nine months, but the Sopra Sotto gig is back on. Bruno's on the same piano bench where I last saw him almost a year ago, and he's facing another wall, both literal and metaphorical. While piano tuning work has lessened but continued, he's only had a handful of gigs since limited live music resumed. Bruno also hasn't managed to get a cent of COVID relief funds, even though he surely qualifies. Local arts management expert Diane Kadota is going to help him get government support, he tells me. In the meantime, Bruno is two months behind in rent. If he's stressed about any of this, it doesn't show during glorious solo sets that afternoon or comforting trio sets that night at Frankie's during his annual Christmas show.

The last song at Frankie's is "Silent Night," and like the timeless words say, "all is calm, and all is bright" in Bruno's world. So far he has survived the pandemic and vaccines are on the way, so there's hope. Resilient and phoenix-like, Bruno has an uncanny and innate ability to park life's messy realities and concentrate on what he naturally does best: dig deep into the music, make melodic discoveries, and impart both heartfelt meaning and a touch of grace.

Epilogue: Fifteen years passed after Bruno's second trio recording came out. In August 2023, drummer/Bruno's biggest fan Keith MacLachlan and Tim Reinert launched an Indiegogo campaign to raise funds for the pianist to record an album with James Meger and Joe Poole. Guardian angels stepped up again. Bruno's prediction that the best is yet to come had a fighting chance to come true.

17 / HOW MY HEART SINGS: KATE HAMMETT-VAUGHAN

SINGER. THAT'S WHAT the small sign with cast iron letters says on the gate outside Kate Hammett-Vaughan's music studio. Never mind that it's from a vintage sewing machine. For Hammett-Vaughan, it's a lifelong statement of purpose that guides her thoughts and actions and delineates every waking hour and each blissful dream.

"At the end of the day, I'm a singer," Hammett-Vaughan declares inside the studio at the bottom of her East Vancouver heritage house. "Somebody asks, 'What do I do?' I say, 'I'm a singer.' And then if they ask, 'What music do you sing?' I say, 'Well most people know me as a jazz singer, but I like certain kinds of pop music, and I like certain kinds of classical music, and I like art songs, and I like this and that, and I'm really happy to sing anything, as long as I am singing.'"[1] The woman with an email signature that quotes Ella Fitzgerald—"The only thing better than singing is more singing"—couldn't be any clearer about her raison d'être.

I remember what it was like to meet Hammett-Vaughan for the first time, in another home with old bones. It was early 1983 when I interviewed her in a duplex at the corner of 12th Avenue and Burrard where she lived. Hammett-Vaughan was friendly, confident, and intriguing during the interview, one of the first she had done.

My angle was, what's it like to be a female artist in jazz? That approach made sense as a profile of her would appear in *The Ubyssey* student newspaper's International Women's Day issue. "I feel like I've been fortunate," she said that day, forty years ago. "I'm living and working in a fairly enlightened environment. I haven't had to deal with a lot of the garbage that people in the past had to . . . Most of the men I deal with are open toward thinking of me as a musician, a working partner."[2]

Hammett-Vaughan went on to talk about one of the groups she was part of at the time: Badazjazz. I had seen the ensemble perform a few months earlier at the Commodore Ballroom, and the vocalists in it were strikingly dynamic. The group offered something Vancouver had never seen before and never saw again after it disbanded: eight high-spirited female singers in the frontline. Forming Badazjazz in 1981 solidified a bond between the singers, which included some of the city's premier vocalists like Hammett-Vaughan, Colleen Savage, Lovie Eli, and June Katz. As Hammett-Vaughan explained, "[Before forming Badazjazz] we weren't aware there were other women dealing with the same problems and the same walls to get over."[3]

But facing less outright sexism than her foremothers and having the mutual support of her bandmates in Badazjazz didn't change a fundamental fact: "I'm really poor," Hammett-Vaughan said. "She is not exaggerating," I wrote in the story headlined "Jazz artist makes it in man's world." My callow concluding prose: "Walking up the steps of her home, one gets the feeling it is the humble abode of a punk rocker, not one of the city's finest jazz vocalists."[4]

Looking back, "humble abode" incredibly making it into print wasn't the only surprising aspect of the article. The photo that accompanied the article was also curious. The photographer captured Hammett-Vaughan in black and white, with short hair and a barely perceptible shadow of a smile as she sat in front of her well-worn Winterroth piano. In the decades to come, her shock of red hair, exuberant toothy beam, and fearless approach to singing would become familiar and comforting touchpoints in Vancouver's jazz and improvised music scenes.

• • •

Kathy Vaughan was born May 1, 1957, in Halifax and grew up on the west side of the Nova Scotia peninsula in the small town of Windsor. She and her older brother and three younger sisters were "free-range kids" living in a tranquil setting.[5] Their parents were passionate about music and art, and Vaughan grew up listening to her mother Muriel's soundtracks to musicals, her father Garth's folk music, both parents' Nat King Cole records, and her brother Alex's rock albums by the Beatles and others.

*Muriel and Kathy Vaughan, circa 1959.
Photographer unknown. Courtesy Kate-Hammett-Vaughan.*

When Vaughan was about fifteen, she received a meaningful gift from her mother: *Ella Fitzgerald Sings the Rodgers and Hart Song Book*. Recorded and released in 1956, the double album was a vocal jazz classic, with Fitzgerald's infectious interpretations of many durable standards from the Great American Songbook. The year after giving the gift, Muriel died of cancer. To honour the memory of her mother, whose pre-marriage surname was Hammett, Kathy—who would become known as Kate—changed her surname to Hammett-Vaughan.

There's a small poster from 1975 with a photo of a stoic, eighteen-year-old Hammett-Vaughan, who had long straight hair—think Joni Mitchell or Emmylou Harris back in the day. The poster said Hammett-Vaughan was an Acadia University student and a candidate in the competition to become "Princess Windsor," which was part of the Annapolis Valley Apple Blossom Festival. The poster described her interests as ". . . music, music, and more music."

Hammett-Vaughan sometimes sang backup in Alex's rock band, and she was the lead singer in a disco group, Uptown Saturday Night. But her first real group was JADA, which she formed with Acadia University pals. JADA played some gigs at Halifax's Odin's Eye, an upstairs hippie cafe. Hammett-Vaughan also performed a bit with Bucky Adams, a veteran jazz tenor saxophonist, who was well-known and respected in Halifax. These were small but influential experiences in Hammett-Vaughan's growth as a singer.

Then she and her boyfriend Stephen Anthony made the pivotal decision to leave Nova Scotia and hitchhike across Canada until they arrived somewhere they liked. "We gave away all of our stuff. Our families drove us up to the highway with our packsacks, watched us stick our thumbs out, and waved at us as we got into the first car," said Hammett-Vaughan.[6] They went from coast to coast, arriving in Vancouver on September 4, 1979. That's where they decided to stay, and, at twenty-two, Hammett-Vaughan's path was set.

At that point, however, she hadn't even considered becoming a professional jazz singer. While she used her small amount of spare money to build a vinyl and cassette collection, Hammett-Vaughan was essentially a blank slate when it came to jazz vocals. "I knew nothing," she said. "I liked to sing, and I knew some songs. But I didn't really know anything about what a jazz standard was."[7]

She learned on bandstands. Like the one at the Classical Joint, the Gastown coffeehouse that figured prominently in Vancouver jazz history. One night at the Joint, Hammett-Vaughan took part in a jam with musicians including guitarist Michael Guild. "I started singing some tune that

I had learned off a Betty Carter record. I didn't have sheet music for it and, of course, Betty's phrasing is so wild and her note choices are so nutty, but I just got this tune in me, and I started singing. I could feel the band behind me going, 'Oh oh, should we save her?' I could feel all this uncertainty and Michael, bless him, turned around and said to the band—I heard him say this—'It's ok, she knows. She is not lost.'" Hammett-Vaughan got through the song. "I am very grateful to Michael for that. He taught me a lot."[8]

Hammett-Vaughan worked as a "ticket girl" at another important venue, the Sheraton Landmark Jazz Bar on Robson, and she started getting gigs there. She sang at the club with Gettin' Off Easy, which included two of her co-singers in Badazjazz: Colleen Savage and Bonnie Ferguson. Plus, Hammett-Vaughan did her own gigs, including one that two young jazz nerds with big plans—Ken Pickering and John Orysik—caught. "They came up to me one night at a gig, and they said, 'We really like you, and we are thinking of starting a jazz festival. We'd like you to be the opening act.'"[9]

Gettin' Off Easy: Bonnie Ferguson, Kate Hammett-Vaughan, and Colleen Savage, circa 1980s. Photographer unknown. Courtesy Kate Hammett-Vaughan.

Hammett-Vaughan opened the Pacific Jazz & Blues Festival—a precursor to the city's international jazz festival—on August 19, 1985, with a show at the Town Pump, another venue where she worked. With a quintet that included tenor saxophonist Michael Blake, who would go on to establish himself in New York's jazz scene, Hammett-Vaughan sang what was characterized by Marke Andrews in the next day's *Vancouver Sun* review as a "smooth-as-silk set of jazz standards." Describing Hammett-Vaughan as "a tall, lithe woman with a sunburst of red hair," the review said she had a "sensuous voice that slides easily into ballads."[10]

The references to her looks and sensuality of her voice weren't uncommon; others picked up on those refrains, like whoever wrote a gushing paean to Hammett-Vaughan in *TV Week*. Exhibit A: "This woman is a homewrecker, and a lot of college boys are gonna leave the farm for those downtown lights once they get an earful of this lady's earthy singing style." Exhibit B: "There's a terrible kind of compromised innocence in seeing an attractive woman in black leaning against a piano singing them 'getting sentimental over you's.' Hammett-Vaughan knows that and is as much an actress as anything else—something a lot of this town's other aspiring singers ought to consider."[11]

Reading those words more than thirty years after they were printed, I was taken aback by how the writer sexualized and stereotyped Hammett-Vaughan. In the mid-eighties, that was an acceptable media portrayal of a woman. Hammett-Vaughan could have stuck to singing standards and gone along with being typecast as a sultry torch singer. Instead, and much to her credit, she followed less lucrative but more creative impulses.

• • •

When Hammett-Vaughan applied to attend the 1986 Banff Centre for the Arts international jazz workshop, she submitted a tape of herself singing standards. After receiving a scholarship and spending four weeks at the workshop, she was no longer just a standards singer. Her experience studying at the Banff Centre with faculty like singer Jay Clayton, bassist Dave Holland (who ran the workshop at the time), pianist Muhal Richard Abrams, and saxophonist Dave Liebman transformed her perspective about improvisation and musical risk-taking.

One Banff moment in particular—when she encountered George Lewis, the acclaimed avant-garde trombonist, electronic musician, composer, and scholar—was a leaping off point. "So I found myself in this room with George, who I knew nothing about, and there was a big circle of us in chairs.

I happened to be sitting next to or very close to George and people were improvising. George looked at me and said, 'Sing something.' And I said, 'Who me?' And he said, 'Yeah you.' And I said, 'What?' And he said, 'Just sing something.' So I just improvised some garbled thing. And then the class was almost over, and I was totally freaked out, so I went straight to the bar. I'm over at the bar and having a glass of wine and George comes up to me and says, 'Can I sit down?' and I said yes, and so he sat down, and he says, 'What makes you so tough?' I said, 'I don't know. I guess I was just born that way.'"[12]

Maybe being born with a tough gene explains how Hammett-Vaughan was emboldened to leave home and hitchhike across Canada, get on bandstands to sing jazz without any training, and—starting in Banff—improvise outside of the standards comfort zone. Regardless of the reason, after returning to Vancouver, she had a new resolve to create opportunities for herself and like-minded performers who wanted to takes risks in their music. By December 1987, she was co-curating with her musical and romantic partner—guitarist Ron Samworth—a series of Wednesday night gigs at the Grunt Gallery on East 6th Avenue. "Jazz at the Gallery" featured local musicians and emphasized improvisation. Hammett-Vaughan would go around the city putting up posters for the Grunt shows, which didn't always result in large turnouts. "Often we had more people in the band than we had in the audience."[13] But the series gave a vital boost to the improvised jazz scene.

1988 was a momentous year for Hammett-Vaughan. She and Samworth—a tall, striking couple with an affinity for creating inventive sounds—formed Turnaround. That year she also began her association with the New Orchestra Workshop (NOW). And she co-created Garbo's Hat, an improvisatory jazz trio with saxophonist and flutist Graham Ord and bassist Paul Blaney. With all of these groups, on recordings and in performance, she embraced dissonance and a no-holds-barred rethink of what it meant to be a jazz singer.

Garbo's Hat was where all of Hammett-Vaughan's musical passions came together. The trio's 1993 album, *Face the Music*, begins and ends with standards: "Let's Face the Music and Dance" and "Angel Eyes." Yet both have a non-standard aesthetic; she phrases with a unique fluidity, reharmonizes where it feels right to do so, and expands the tunes' melodic and harmonic possibilities. On the original songs in-between, some co-written by Hammett-Vaughan who rarely composed, she goes further with vocal experimentation and free improv. Halfway through the album, "New Directions" epitomizes the group's appeal. After the three musicians establish the song's melodic structure, Hammett-Vaughan goes for it with operatic trills and absurdist playfulness in her call-and-response interchange with Ord's elevating soprano sax and Blaney's grounding bass.

Kate Hammett-Vaughan, 1988. Photographer unknown. Courtesy Kate Hammett-Vaughan.

As Hammett-Vaughan went deeper into improvised music, her love for singing standards didn't actually diminish. But some booking jazz rooms failed to see it that way. "There was a thing when I started to play free music that suddenly people didn't want to hire me for [straight ahead] jazz gigs anymore because clearly [in their eyes] I was no longer a standards singer because I was singing free jazz," she said. "And I thought, 'Well that doesn't make any sense to me because I am just me, and these are things that I do.' It's like saying, 'I'm not going to buy your paintings because you started painting oil now, and I only liked your watercolours.'"[14]

"Lots of people would be, 'Oh, is she going to be singing weird stuff?' Some would say, 'I see you are playing at such and such a place. I hope you are singing standards,' and I'd be, 'Well, it's going to a be a mix.'"[15]

Vocalist Jennifer Scott has long admired her friend Hammett-Vaughan's resolute daring. "That is something you have to recognize about Kate: she is pretty freakin' fearless," said Scott. "That has always served her incredibly well as a musician and singer and really along her trajectory as a performer. She has never been afraid to take chances."[16]

If there was another Vancouver jazz singer who was the polar opposite to Hammett-Vaughan, it was Kenny Colman. The man whose story was well-known—discovered by Sarah Vaughan, performed on prominent TV shows and at big resorts and clubs, and endorsed by no less than Frank Sinatra—came close to making it big. In December 1990, Denny Boyd wrote a column in the *Vancouver Sun* that told his story and included bitter quotes from Colman about how he had to leave Vancouver because there was no work for him in his hometown.

Hammett-Vaughan wrote a letter about the column that the *Sun* published. While she acknowledged in the letter that Vancouver audiences and club managers can be reluctant to support their own, and sometimes artists need to go elsewhere to pursue their craft, Hammett-Vaughan presented a counter-argument to Colman's sob story. "If we artists wish to survive, we must present a united front. We must prove that our art is worthy of support, and we must market ourselves in ways that are appealing to audiences and the media . . . I worry that Kenny's self-indulgent attitude, and the support Mr. Boyd gives it, is damaging to other non-commercial artists working in

Canada. Surely you could dedicate space to something more constructive to the arts than Mr. Colman's endless griping."[17]

It was brave of her to publicly diss the older, more established Colman, whose bad books you didn't want to get into. Hammett-Vaughan said Colman was "a little pissed" about the letter but got over it. The two singers actually had more in common than it appeared. They both respected tradition, felt frustrated about being overlooked for gigs, and understood the hustle that was needed to survive.

Starting in the mid-nineties, Hammett-Vaughan led a Sunday jam at the Latin Quarter on Commercial Drive. Samworth, bassist André Lachance, and drummer Tom Foster were among the musicians who initially performed with there. Then pianist Chris Gestrin joined, along with saxophonist Jim Pinchin. Gradually a quintet with Hammett-Vaughan, Pinchin, Gestrin, Lachance, and Foster took shape. The players knew each other well—Gestrin and Lachance were both members of Soulstream and other groups; Pinchin and Foster were from Edmonton and had played together extensively. With Hammett-Vaughan, they built a singular rapport.

The quintet recorded in April 1999 at the Western Front, and the album that resulted was a stunner. Entirely consisting of standards, *How My Heart Sings* has the melodicism and in-the-pocket swing that Hammett-Vaughan had moved away from on recordings with Garbo's Hat and NOW. She still makes room for adventure; Hammett-Vaughan and the band revamp Duke Ellington and Peggy Lee's "I'm Gonna Go Fishin'" as a free romp. But after two decades of paying her dues and exploring inside and outside of straight-ahead forms, on *How My Heart Sings*, Hammett-Vaughan affirms her place in the melodic vocal jazz tradition.

I wondered if the album also represented a personal passage. I construed Hammett-Vaughan's unhurried and melancholic interpretations of tunes like "The Meaning of the Blues" and "You've Changed" as metaphors for the end of her twelve-year relationship with Samworth, since the breakup roughly coincided with the recording. Hammett downplayed that connection. "It was probably more subliminal than real," she said. "I just liked those songs that happened to coincide with that time in my life." The point is, Hammett-Vaughan sang words like "You've forgotten the words, I love you," with affecting meaning that made me think it was non-fiction.

The quintet recorded two more albums: *Devil May Care* and *Eclipse*, recorded live at the Cellar. They combined affecting vocals and hard-hitting playing from the band. Throughout the three releases, there was abundant space for the musicians to express themselves. "I liked that band because we did a bit of everything," said Hammett-Vaughan, who sang the melodies and scatted with a honed certainty on the recordings. "I felt we could be crazy improvisors, but we could also be a straight-up standards band. Those guys were so flexible and wonderful." She added: "I think they liked the fact that I was not telling them what to play. We would just count it in and go."[18]

"She let us play a lot," said Lachance. "And the material that she chose, especially in the beginnings of the group, it was pretty open. There was a lot of room for us to find the band's sound." The repertoire included less-performed tunes from the standards canon and luminous folk-pop songs by Joni Mitchell and Nick Drake. Lachance: "She's not just singing 'All the Things You Are.' She's digging deep in the book and knows a lot of music and would dig in these really deep-catalogue Duke Ellington tunes and that kind of stuff to pull out."[19]

Few Vancouver singers during the quintet's prime were putting in that amount of effort to research material, added Lachance. And virtually none of the other vocalist-led jazz groups conveyed a free sensibility while melodiously staying within the contemporary jazz idiom like Hammett-Vaughan's band achieved. "We played pretty free, especially in the earlier years," he said. "That was a different way to present a group with a singer than what was around at the time, certainly in Vancouver."[20]

When Cory Weeds opened the Cellar in 2000, local musicians rejoiced. After so many lean years, the city at last had a full-time jazz club. At first, however, Weeds didn't give a lot of gigs to singers. "It's not that I didn't want to give singers gigs, it's that I wanted first priority to go to instrumentalists," said Weeds. That said, Hammett-Vaughan was an exception. "I think Kate started getting booked at the Cellar pretty much from day one simply because I had, and continue to have, a ton of respect for her," said Weeds. "She always did a great job, she is a great musician, and her band was killing, so it was a no-brainer to involve Kate."[21]

While Weeds acknowledged he wasn't "aligned musically" with Hammett-Vaughan, "Kate was a very well-respected person on this music scene, and she was very supportive of me, so it was never hard to give her a gig."[22] Plus, he liked the fact that the quintet was a working band rather than a group of individual players who just came together for certain concerts. Hammett-Vaughan knew she was one of the few singers that Weeds booked back then. "I felt very lucky because he would give me gigs," she said. "I think he knew that people knew me, and I could bring people into the club."[23] She was also grateful that after pitching Weeds on presenting her two main mentors—Sheila Jordan and Jay Clayton—at the club, he said yes.

In the 2000s, other projects that stood out included contributing two songs to *Poor Boy: Songs of Nick Drake*, a tribute to Drake put out by Songlines Recordings. Hammett-Vaughan's quintet had done "Poor Boy" for *Devil May Care*; she re-recorded it with Gestrin, Samworth, and Simon Fisk for the tribute album. That title track, and their rendition of "Clothes of Sand," were two of the album's absolute highlights.

She took another left turn with *Conspiracy: Art Songs for Improvisers*. Hammett-Vaughan's fascination with art songs, which incorporate contemporary classical, improvised music, jazz, poetry, and other elements, dates back to the late nineties. After she unsuccessfully applied for funding to support an art song recording project, Vancouver composers such as Mark Armanini, Rodney Sharman, and François Houle volunteered to write art songs for her. Hammett-Vaughan first performed the tunes at the Western Front in 2000 and the Vancouver East Cultural Centre in 2001. About five years later, she recorded the pieces with three members of her quintet plus saxophonist Mike Braverman and violinist Cam Wilson. Listening to the music they recorded for *Conspiracy* was arduous at first. To my ears, the trio of quintet albums she released pre-art songs were her most successfully realized recordings. *Conspiracy* challenges listeners on tracks like "Aon" and "Oh Yeah (go Johnny!)," which have moments of sheer lunacy. It requires open-minded listening to appreciate, for example, "Shattered Mind," with music by Houle and words from Jane Bowles' deathbed letters to her husband Paul Bowles. Through her halting recitation of the jumbled phrases, Hammett-Vaughan compellingly captures Jane's fractured, post-stroke state. After listening to these tracks many times, I gained an appreciation for her art song side.

In typical Hammett-Vaughan fashion, she took another banked turn for her next recordings: standards albums, including two trio sessions and one with guitarist Bill Coon. Her most recent release of the three, a playful and soothing collab with Coon and Adam Thomas—*Sanzaru*—came out in 2012. I wonder if Hammett-Vaughan has any more recordings in her. It's an open question.

• • •

On July 1, 2015, at nine-thirty p.m., Hammett-Vaughan closed that year's edition of Vancouver's jazz festival. Thirty years earlier, also at nine-thirty p.m., she opened the first incarnation of the festival. The symmetry was perfect. In the intervening years, Hammett-Vaughan performed many times at the festival, and she elegantly served as emcee at numerous shows during the annual event. On this night at Performance Works on Granville Island, Hammett-Vaughan radiated joy while fronting her quintet.

They began at the very beginning with "I Could Write a Book," one of the Rodgers and Hart tunes on the Ella Fitzgerald record that Hammett-Vaughan's mom Muriel gave to her years earlier. Then came Ornette Coleman's "Lonely Woman," which the singer and instrumentalists stretched out on. Next: Antonio Carlos Jobim's "Desafinado." When introducing the bossa nova standard, Hammett-Vaughan translated the title as "slightly out of tune." While listening to her, I thought about what has always drawn me to Hammett-Vaughan's singing over the years. In the spirit of one of her biggest inspirations, Betty Carter, Hammett-Vaughan isn't the type of singer that automatically lands flawlessly on a note. From time to time, she's intentionally and subtly off-key before gliding into the correct note, which adds a satisfying nuance to the music. Was she as adept at pulling that off in 2015 as she was in 1999 when recording *How My Heart Sings*? No, but remaining frozen in a particular moment in time is not the point of long-lived artistry. Her voice has naturally evolved, reflecting where she is in life, with her many qualities and occasional imperfections. Not pitch-perfect but honest and authentic.

About a year and a half after that festival concert, in Hammett-Vaughan's studio, she showed me a stack of meticulously assembled binders with articles, photos, fliers, posters, and other artifacts from her career. "I look at it and say, 'I did all that?'" she said. In a way, the collection of memories, including documentation of the broad range of her performances, says as much about her as it does about the resourcefulness that Vancouver's jazz scene has long demanded. "I have been here for a long time, and I have seen it continue to happen that people just take it upon themselves to create a scene," Hammett-Vaughan observed. "People want to talk about factions in scenes. There is always that to a degree, but I think Vancouver has been remarkably interactive and sharing and humane and kind in a really big way."[24]

Hammett-Vaughan often applies her own twist to a well-worn expression to explain what the city has given her: "It's that old joke where someone gives you just enough rope to hang yourself. Vancouver has just been doling out the rope. Vancouver has been fantastic for me that way. It has been so open-minded and open-hearted. It's been interesting to watch the city grow for better or for worse over all these years and to feel that I made a family here. All these amazing musicians and students that I have met and teachers that I have worked with."[25]

She briefly studied music at Acadia University in Nova Scotia and Humber College in Ontario and never earned a music degree, but Hammett-Vaughan became a dedicated teacher at Capilano University and Vancouver Community College. She also kept studying, with Jay Clayton, Sheila Jordan, and others. Clayton and Jordan have had long and distinguished careers as creative jazz singers and educators. I wondered whether Hammett-Vaughan envisioned singing and teaching well into the future. She reiterated that "I love to sing," and then casually said: "I've been having memory problems. Did I tell you that?" She hadn't. "My short-term memory is very bad, so I am taking [prescription] drugs for it. They don't know what it is. I can tell you all this stuff about my childhood, but what did I do yesterday? Hmm. I had breakfast because I know I had to have breakfast. What day was it? It was—so don't tell me—it would have been Tuesday."[26]

While Hammett-Vaughan was right about the day, I asked if her health care providers raised the possibility of Alzheimer's. She said tests hadn't confirmed the disease, but she joked that for the longest time she's had "CRS—Can't Remember Shit."[27] Yet she has always been able to remember lyrics. Jennifer Scott confirmed Hammett-Vaughan's gift for keeping lyrics close to her. "I remember being on a gig and somebody requested a tune that

I had forgotten to learn," said Scott. "I knew the tune, but I didn't know all the lyrics, and she had an absolutely ridiculous capacity and photographic memory for lyrics." This was before people had cell phones and internet access, so Scott called Hammett-Vaughan on a pay phone and sent an SOS for the lyrics to "Weaver of Dreams." Hammett-Vaughan started singing into the phone: "You're a weaver of dreams, you and your strange fascination . . ." and she proceeded to sing the whole tune for Scott. Her perfect recall of the song was not a one-off. Over the years, said Scott, her friend would "just rattle them [lyrics] off. No problem."[28]

As our chat on the fragility of memory continued in her studio, I must have looked increasingly worried. Perhaps sensing that, she again summoned levity to the subject. "I won't know anybody or know where I am, but I will still be able to sing a whole bunch of standards," she said, smiling. "I say to Guy [her supportive husband], 'I'll just be singing at you,' and he said, 'And that will be different how?'"[29]

We both laughed, and afterward she asked, "Well, what am I going to do? Go lie down in traffic?" I played along with the gallows humour, suggesting Hammett-Vaughan could lie in the road if she gets lost on the way to the Pilates studio she frequents. The inside joke: the Pilates place is across the street from her house. "That's funny. One day on the way to Pilates I'll just go, 'No, this is it. I'll just lie down in the road and someone will run over me.' No, I don't think that's going to happen. I'm having a lovely life. Yeah, having a beautiful life. It's a little weird, but my life has always been a little weird. So I'm okay."[30]

• • •

December 22, 2019, downtown in the First Baptist Church Vancouver. We Three Queens—featuring vocalists Karin Plato, Scott, and Hammett-Vaughan—perform a Christmas Jazz Vespers concert in the church. Though she doesn't carry the performance, Hammett-Vaughan looks and sounds joyous. Observing them on and offstage, it's clear the Queens' singing sisterhood is strong.

We Three Queens—Kate Hammett-Vaughan, Karin Plato, Jennifer Scott and band—the Cellar, December 19, 2010. Photo by Vincent Lim.

February 8, 2020, Hood 29. Hammett-Vaughan sings with a trio in this Main Street music joint. Plato is there to support her friend and colleague. I'm there once again to not take Hammett-Vaughan's deep alto voice and gift for storytelling-through-standards for granted. Despite some sound problems and noise from chatty diners, which Hammett-Vaughan diplomatically shushes, the gig goes well. Hearing her sing the Beatles' "For No One" and Irving Berlin's "Be Careful, It's My Heart" particularly resonates.

It turned out to be her last performance before COVID-19 abruptly shut down live music around the world. On her sixty-fourth birthday, Hammett-Vaughan planned to sing "When I'm 64" and other songs by John, Paul, George, and Ringo at an all-Beatles gig she lined up at Pat's Pub, but it was cancelled due to COVID restrictions. During the pandemic, I kept in touch by email, pestering her with questions that she gladly answered. Then I caught up with her on a FaceTime call with wonky connectivity. Before we were abruptly cut off, Hammett-Vaughan mentioned her continuing memory challenges and confirmed she had received a diagnosis: early onset Alzheimer's. Despite the confirmation of her condition, sitting at the piano in her studio, Hammett-Vaughan looked and sounded upbeat and optimistic. She acknowledged moments of fear, but the person I had known for thirty-eight of those sixty-four years was completely at peace.

Kate Hammett-Vaughan, 120 Diner, Toronto, July 19, 2018. Photo by Mark Miller.

October 28, 2021, Frankie's Jazz Club. After months of the pandemic blues, it's her first gig in a long time. Despite the prolonged absence from local bandstands, Hammett-Vaughan looks at ease and enthused about finally performing. She has a music stand in front of her with charts for the two sets. When it's time to do "Alice in Wonderland," she realizes there's no chart with lyrics for the tune. After a moment of hesitation, Hammett-Vaughan goes ahead and delivers the song without a hitch, just like she does with "Lament" and "Moon and Sand"—two of the evening's highlights. At one point, Hammett-Vaughan expresses what her body language has been saying all night: "I'm so in my happy place right now."[31]

As Vancouver's jazz community returned to and surpassed pre-pandemic activity, I could see in the growing gig listings that Hammett-Vaughan wouldn't have a big role in the scene's reawakening. There's a time that comes in most musicians' lives when they're not often called for gigs like they used to be. Maybe that time came prematurely for Hammett-Vaughan. But it doesn't change what she's accomplished as an intrepid artist, insightful teacher, and dedicated leader in the scene. Hammett-Vaughan helped lay the groundwork for today's healthy jazz community. It bothers me that young, emerging artists likely have low awareness of those accomplishments. I don't think it bothers her. She found her calling long ago, and regardless if she's on a bandstand in front of an audience or in her home studio alone, singing still gives her invaluable bliss.

Sifting through our many conversations, two recurring themes emerged: the spontaneous nature of her life in music, and gratitude. Apart from the decision to leave Nova Scotia, Hammett-Vaughan has rarely told herself, "I need to make this thing happen. And I don't think I ever set out for it to be the great learning experience that it has been. It's been organic, also known as flying by the seat of your pants. Reaching out, grabbing opportunities when they came my way. I have been incredibly lucky. Really blessed."[32]

18 / HARDEST WORKING MAN IN JAZZ BUSINESS: CORY WEEDS

PART 1: HOW TO SUCCEED AS A JAZZ CLUB OWNER

Over three nights at the start of a new decade, it all came together for Cory Weeds. His Cellar jazz club was jam-packed and pulsating with excitement. The patrons came to hear Weeds play tenor sax, lead a mighty quartet with jazz star Joey DeFrancesco on Hammond B3 organ, and make a live recording. The music enthralled each evening's audience and pumped up the musicians. While there were scores of similar weekends at the Cellar, this one—and the album that resulted—epitomized Weeds' innate ability to make the seemingly impossible an exciting reality.

In the early years of owning the Cellar, Weeds thought artists like DeFrancesco—who had played with icons like Miles Davis and John McLaughlin and built a tremendously successful career as a leader—were unattainable for the small, scuffling club. That changed when Joey D accepted Weeds' invitation to play at the Cellar in 2007. Near the end of a second engagement in January 2009, DeFrancesco asked Weeds to sit in with the band, which went well. Then DeFrancesco casually said to Weeds, "Hey man, you know we should make a record." Weeds' reply: "Why would you make a record with me?"[1] It was an emblematic response from Weeds, who had achieved a lot as a player but had also perfected the art of self-deprecation. DeFrancesco replied that he enjoyed Weeds' playing and sincerely wanted to collaborate.

Weeds still wasn't convinced. He emailed DeFrancesco to ensure the organist meant what he said. "What you need to know about me is that I am a doer, so when you say something to me, I do it," Weeds wrote. "If you were just blowing smoke, it's cool, no hard feelings. But if you are serious, let me know, and I will make it happen."[2] One more time, DeFrancesco definitively confirmed he was completely serious about his suggestion. "All musicians are that way to an extent," said DeFrancesco, years later, about Weeds' self-doubt. "We have a certain level that we're always striving for, and in our minds, we're never going to approach that." But his answer to Weeds about why he suggested recording together was clear: "Because you play your ass off, and I want to make a record with you, so let's do it!"[3]

Their plans came to fruition January 8–10, 2010, when they played with DeFrancesco's drummer Byron Landham and local trumpet stalwart Chris Davis at the Cellar. Despite Weeds' initial disbelief about performing and recording with DeFrancesco, he checked his anxieties at the Cellar door. "It felt like I was playing with another musician who happens to be a virtuosic player," said Weeds. "I wasn't nervous, I wasn't scared, I wasn't tentative, I wasn't lacking confidence, I wasn't questioning anything."[4]

Chris Gestrin, who himself played organ many nights at the Cellar, sat in the miniscule, dishevelled office next to the club's bar on two of the nights to engineer the live recording that would come out six months later on Weeds' Cellar Live label as *The Many Deeds of Cory Weeds*. The cover photo shows Weeds, eyes closed, playing tenor at the Cellar, with his then-nine-month-old son Noah strapped to him in a BabyBjörn carrier. In the blurry background: Weeds' wife Alana stands with arms crossed, looking somewhat displeased, in front of a painting of Duke Ellington. The album title and photo convey a message: Weeds juggles numerous priorities at once, which creates stress for him and those close to him. But he also accomplishes most of what he sets out to do. While the art direction was meant in good humour, there was truth to it.

As for the music, the album's infectious second track—"Goin' Down" by local hero Brad Turner—encapsulates the album's bite. DeFrancesco and Davis spiritedly improvise on the tune, and Weeds shapes a blues-immersed solo with confident dexterity. While there would be much more musical growth for the saxophonist in the years to come, on that song and others played during the three nights, Weeds left no doubt about whether he could perform at a high level with DeFrancesco and the other musicians on stage. He belonged.

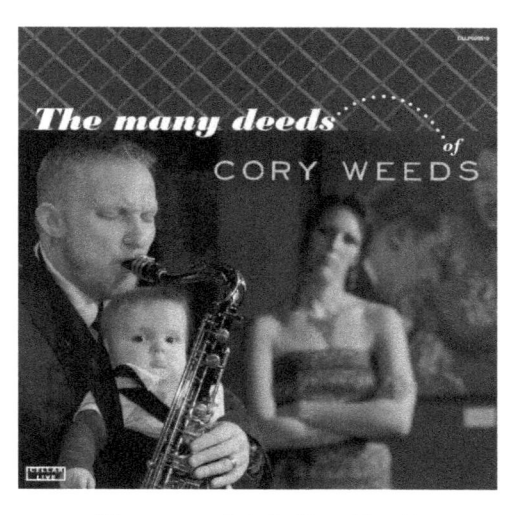

Album cover photo by Steve Mynett.

That dream weekend was a microcosm of a remarkable run for the Cellar as a treasured jazz club in Vancouver and for Weeds as one of the most important figures in the history of the city's jazz scene. Before, during, and after the Cellar's thirteen-and-a-half-year lifetime, Weeds has evolved from being a cocky kid who winged it to becoming an expressive saxophonist, passionate club owner and impresario, astute record label owner, and producer with musically satisfying instincts. There have been massive challenges along the way, including economic ones and anxiety that has been severe at times. Weeds has met those challenges and realized ambitious jazz dreams, through his talent, sheer will, and daring, with help from his supporters. Plus he has more big ideas to actualize.

Someone like Weeds, who has made a significant difference in the lives of Vancouver jazz musicians and jazz artists further afield, doesn't come along often. So I exhaustively retraced his steps, followed him in real-time, listened to him make music in a variety of contexts, and talked to some who know him best to document and understand Weeds' significance to the community. I also tried to look beyond his very public persona to see who's really there.

• • •

Weeds' work ethic began the old-fashioned way: he was born to it. Bill and Betty Weeds, a salt-of-the-earth couple, got married in 1971. Bill worked in commercial printing; Betty had jobs including executive secretary at IBM. Their first child, Cory, was born December 5, 1973.

At a young age, Weeds was extroverted and resourceful. He had an arrangement with a friend's father: Weeds sold the dad's sports cards, paid the man the amount he wanted, and kept the rest. "Cory made a ton of money," said Bill about the scheme. When Weeds had a newspaper route, there was a contest to win a ghetto blaster for selling a certain number of subscriptions. "You'll never win that," Bill remarked to his son. "But sure enough, at the end of the evening he was packing this great big ghetto blaster on his shoulder." When the family held garage sales, Weeds was put in charge. "He had a hustle about him," said Bill. "When I think back, it was quite unique. I'm not saying he had confidence in school, or he was the most popular guy. He wasn't. But he always had that ability to find something and to be able to hustle it in a good way."[5]

Bill was raised in a family that loved listening to music, and he created a similar environment when Cory and his sister Cindy were growing up. Bill also played guitar. For Bill's high school graduation, his parents gave him a cheap but playable acoustic guitar from Woodward's department store, which he noodled on for years. Hearing the Vancouver jazz trio of Fraser MacPherson, Oliver Gannon, and Wyatt Ruther on the radio was a revelation. "I just stopped the car, and I said, 'That's it.'"[6] While he endeavoured to unlock the mysteries of jazz, his teenaged son went the opposite way, gravitating to the likes of Iron Maiden, Judas Priest, and Mötley Crüe. But Bill played jazz records in the house, including *Wes Montgomery Plays the Blues*. One day the metalhead heard a hip tune on the album, Montgomery's "Sun Down" that the guitarist played with a big band, and something clicked. Just like that Weeds was hooked on jazz.

Weeds started playing alto sax in grade nine and took lessons with Wayne Diggins. Weeds heard his dad struggling to play Clifford Brown's "Joy Spring." "He went to Wayne Diggins," recalled Bill, "and said, 'I want to learn 'Joy Spring.' Show me the buttons to push.'" Around that time Cory played his first gig with his dad and Doug Jackson in a mall. For grade twelve, with his proficiency rising, Cory switched schools to attend Vancouver Technical Secondary in order to join a band program led by two strong music teachers. One of the teachers introduced Weeds to recordings by Charlie Parker, Paul Desmond, and other alto greats. "At that point, from a listening standpoint, Cory was miles ahead of everybody in the class," said Bill.[7]

Bill was "thrilled to death" after realizing his son wanted to be a professional musician.[8] He lived vicariously through his son's pursuit of music, something Bill would have done himself if not for the realities of being a working man. Weeds took some private lessons with saxophonists including Tom Keenlyside and Campbell Ryga and enrolled in the music program at Capilano College in North Vancouver, where he studied for three years. Musically, Cory held his own, but he didn't stand out or portend future success.

Then Weeds did one year in the jazz program at the University of North Texas, a prestigious music school known for its award-winning big bands. He learned a lot at UNT, but the program's emphasis on modernity over tradition didn't appeal to him.

While at UNT, Weeds got a dose of public humiliation. The incident involved the great baritone saxophonist Gerry Mulligan, who was an artist-in-residence at the school in 1995. Weeds was playing second alto in the UNT Jazz Repertory Ensemble on a day when Mulligan directed the band while many other student musicians, including the hotshots in the university's top One O'Clock Lab Band, watched and listened. The time came to play an arrangement of "Rocker," a tune Mulligan wrote and Miles Davis recorded with the bari player and others for the seminal *Birth of the Cool* album. Weeds' part had a solo, and he had a quick decision to make: play Lee Konitz's solo from *Birth of the Cool* as written out on the chart or improvise. Weeds decided on the latter. Bad choice. "I sounded like a complete idiot," said Weeds. "I was nervous, my eyes were watering, and Gerry Freaking Mulligan was standing right in front of me. He stops the band and looks at me and says, 'Son, what's your name?' 'Cory,' I reply. He says, 'Well Cory, if you're not going to play what Lee played, I suggest you learn the changes."' Mulligan proceeded to count the song in—after the solo section.[9] He clearly didn't award mulligans. Musicians in the band were laughing, as were others in the audience. Mulligan's reproach—gruff like his bari playing—was embarrassing for Weeds. But he didn't let it defeat or haunt him and simply moved on, which reflected his resilience.

After UNT, Weeds returned to Cap briefly before leaving school for good to tour internationally and record with the unfortunately named People Playing Music. I heard Weeds play live and met him for the first time in 1998, at Café Deux Soleils on Commercial Drive. Weeds performed there with Crash, a band he co-led that had just released its debut album. I was primed to dislike the group because I snobbishly assumed they weren't jazz enough. But Crash's fusion of funk and soulful jazz won me over, and I said as much in an article.

The next time I saw him we met to discuss a project Weeds was planning with a partner. The concept was to launch a music magazine, called *Groove City*, which would cover jazz comprehensively. While Weeds was enthusiastic about the publication, I had my doubts about whether he could launch and sustain it. With no track record, Weeds probably encountered other doubters like me. As it turned out, he took another path.

In April 1999, he presented New York trumpeter Brian Lynch at the Cat's Meow, a restaurant on Vancouver's Granville Island. This was Weeds' first promotion of a prominent jazz artist as well as the first time he matched an out-of-towner with locals, in this case Brad Turner, André Lachance, and Dylan van der Schyff. It went well on all fronts. He followed that up in October 1999 by booking an infamous show in a basement space on the West Side of Vancouver that would become supremely important to Weeds and Vancouver jazz life.

• • •

At the western edge of Vancouver's Kitsilano neighbourhood, the north side of the 3600 block of West Broadway and some nearby blocks have a history of housing dynamic venues that presented live jazz and other music.

The Alma Academy opened in 1929 at 3695 West Broadway as a ballroom that featured dance bands, and in the fifties, jazz musicians who played in the dancehall would go on to launch the original Cellar jazz club that operated about seven kilometres to the east. In 1963, the Flatted Fifth opened at 3623 West Broadway. It soon became the Flat Five and later the Blue Horn. This was an important jazz space where Eleanor Collins, Don Thompson, Terry Clarke, John Handy, Charles Mingus, Philly Joe Jones, Freddie Redd, and many others performed. Also in 1963, Tommy Chong (who would later gain fame as half of the stoner comedy duo Cheech & Chong) co-established with Tommie Melton the Blues Palace in the former Alma Theatre at 3719 West Broadway. Melton and Chong performed at the nightclub with their R&B band Little Daddie and the Bachelors, which later became Motown recording artists Bobby Taylor and the Vancouvers. The headliners at the venue's biggest show: Ike & Tina Turner. City Council shut down the Blues Palace in October 1963 because of residents' concerns about "noise and rowdyism" near the venue.[10] That same year, the Attic at 3607 West Broadway emerged as a folk music venue. The Attic cultivated the folk coffeehouse tradition that the Question Mark, at 3484 West Broadway, maintained from 1959 to 1961.

Intersection of Broadway and Alma, Vancouver, 1951. The second floor of the corner building housed the Alma Academy ballroom. Photo by Jack Lindsay. Source: City of Vancouver Archives.[11]

Skip ahead to 1980. That's when Joanna's Gallery Café at 3667 West Broadway started presenting jazz musicians on the freer side, including Bob Turner and Raymon Torchinsky (who would become important in Weeds' life). Six years later, the Alma Street Café at 2505 Alma Street began featuring live jazz. Over the next decade, it became a crucial spot for straight-ahead jazz played by premier musicians.

In 1978, Nick Liapis bought a brand new, multi-level building at 3617 West Broadway that was once the location of a bowling alley. He leased the main floor to retail stores and shifted his White Tower Pizza and Spaghetti House from across the street into the basement at 3611 West Broadway. Eventually White Tower moved upstairs, and the downstairs space was either rented by various tenants or unoccupied. His son Stephanos (Steve) and other family members persuaded the family patriarch to let them run an establishment in the basement. Stephanos dreamt of opening a jazz club, and his Cellar Jazz Café opened August 7, 1997.

The Cellar Jazz Café offered a mix of jazz, hip hop, and stand-up comedy. Regardless of the genre, the vibe was consistently boisterous. "It was really loud," said Brad Turner, who played in the venue. "It was more like a little nightclub that had less to do with the live music and more to do with the social aspect. But it was pretty vibrant."[12] Pianist Chris Gestrin, who played at the club a lot, described the audience din there as "constant white noise."[13] Guitarist Bill Coon, who also played there, agreed "it was a very noisy club. There was no noise policy at all. He [Stephanos] didn't really care about that. He wanted to bring [musical] groups in, but he just wanted people to have fun, talk, and drink, which is fine, but you never really felt like you connected with the audience."[14]

October 27, 1999, was the fateful night Weeds—calling himself C.W. Productions—co-presented with Prussin Music a show at the Cellar Jazz Café featuring hard-swinging New York tenor saxophonist Eric Alexander. Weeds, who had arranged with Stephanos Liapis to present Alexander in the club, booked Vancouver musicians—Ross Taggart on Rhodes electric piano, Lachance on bass, and drummer Dave Robbins—to play with Alexander. Weeds knew that Diana Krall was performing in Vancouver that night with her trio at the time: guitarist Peter Bernstein, bassist Paul Gill, and drummer

Joe Farnsworth, all contemporaries of Alexander in the New York jazz scene. Plans were hatched for Bernstein to sit in with Alexander and the band.

Joe Farnsworth, the Cellar. Photo by Jesse Cahill.

The first set at the Cellar Jazz Café unfolded without incident. Then Bernstein, Gill, and Farnsworth arrived, and it was decided that all of them would play the second set with Alexander and Taggart. Weeds asked

Alexander to ask Lachance and Robbins if this would be okay. That communication didn't happen. After it became apparent that Lachance and Robbins would have to sit out, without the bandleader formally asking if that would be cool, the locals weren't thrilled. The New Yorkers and Taggart played an extra-long set. "It was burning," said Weeds, whose inexperience prevented him from recognizing that as noses were getting out of joint, he needed to finesse the situation. Then Lachance and Robbins got back on the bandstand for a third set. "Farnsworth is now [seated] at the front, drunk as ever, saying all kinds of shit to Dave," said Weeds.[15]

By the end of the set, tensions were high. "Before the last ring of the cymbal is out, Dave's got it basically off the stand," recounted Weeds. "He's got all his cymbals off, and he's out the door. I don't even think Eric knew. Eric just started playing "Cherokee" super-fast. Dave isn't even there. Farnsworth, now completely inebriated, gets up and kind of stumbles and trips over the drums to try to get back there and play. Dave sees that and runs back to the stage. It sounds like somebody pulled the plug on a record player. And they're nose-to-nose, screaming at each other. I'm freaking out. I don't know what to do." No punches were thrown, and the anger dissipated. "Things calmed down, and that was it," said Weeds.[16]

Robbins' memory of the incident is slightly different: "He [Alexander] was giving us lots of attitude, that he was this heavy guy. And fair enough, whatever. But then he wasn't being helpful to try to bridge the gaps [between what Alexander wanted and what the local players provided]. Ross was doing what Ross does, and suggesting tunes, and Eric was really, really not being helpful at all. That kinda got things off to a bad start." Then Alexander told Robbins that he didn't like the drummer's playing. At all. When Alexander wanted to keep playing after the apparent end of the gig, Robbins wasn't receptive. "He started playing a tune, the time was done, and I was having a horrible time. I just said, 'I'm finished.' I put my cymbals away and left the stage." Re-enter Farnsworth, who "got up on stage without asking me and set up my cymbals. I didn't like that too much, and I told him to get off the drums. And he didn't like that too much. But he did get off the drums."[17]

Drummer Morgan Childs witnessed the whole evening, including the "breach of drummer etiquette." Aside from the tense moments, "people were eating it up, going absolutely crazy," said Childs about the audience reaction to the music.[18] As for Weeds, the newbie jazz promoter saw firsthand the tensions that can result when local musicians and visiting players don't mesh. On the other hand, Weeds experienced the exhilaration of promoting a slamming jazz gig in a small, intimate club packed with satisfied listeners. A 100-watt bulb went off in Weeds' head. That night he gave his card to Liapis and said, "If you ever want to sell this place, please call me first." Liapis' response: "Oh no, not in a million years."[19]

• • •

The late 1990s to the first half of 2000 was a barren period for live jazz venues in Vancouver. Alma Street Café, where Weeds heard local players who became heroes to him, closed in 1996. The Glass Slipper, which programmed a range of creative music including jazz, went up in flames at the end of 1996. The Blue Note had a similar fate in 1999. The Cotton Club closed in 2000 after a run of about three years that had mixed results. There were other jazz joints in the city, including the Hot Jazz Club and restaurants such as O'Doul's Restaurant & Bar and Rossini's, but the scene badly needed a fulltime venue that was dedicated to presenting live vital jazz. Weeds framed the issue this way: "I was thinking about people that I wanted to hear play that I hadn't heard in a long time. Why can I not hear Olly [Oliver Gannon]? Why can I never hear Campbell [Ryga]? Where's Ross [Taggart]? Why can't I go hear Hugh [Fraser]? Like, what's the problem?"[20]

It was a classified ad that caught Weeds' eye. In the April 6–13, 2000 issue of the *Georgia Straight*, under the "Businesses for Sale" section, the ad read: "Popular West Side Jazz Bar for Sale! High income with very steady clientele. Priced to sell immediately."[21]

A Vancouver jazz bar with "high income?" This wasn't exactly truth in advertising, but Weeds knew right away what the ad meant: Liapis' million years were up, and the Cellar was for the taking. Weeds called Liapis' realtor, Alex Tsakumis, the same day the ad appeared and told him he wanted to buy the club; Tsakumis said Weeds needed to fax a letter of intent. "I hadn't talked to my dad. I hadn't talked to anybody. I just faxed the letter of intent," said Weeds.[22] A few days after sending the fax, Weeds went on a ten-day Vipassanā meditation retreat in Ethel, Washington, that required "noble silence"—minimal communication with the teacher was allowed and any form of communication with fellow students was strictly prohibited. In a scene straight out of a sitcom, just after taking the first step toward a life-changing commitment, the motor-mouthed Weeds had to somehow stay in almost total silence and isolation.

After surviving being incommunicado at the retreat, Weeds had to match his bravado with the $70,000 that Liapis was asking for. What's more, he had to quickly figure out how to run both a jazz club and restaurant. Weeds met and befriended Don Guthro, a chef and restaurant owner, at an East Vancouver jazz venue that Weeds had played at and Guthro had worked at: the Mojo Room. Weeds partnered with Guthro, who would look after the food program at the Cellar. Neither man had the funds to contribute to the purchase. A bank loan wasn't in the realm of the possible. Weeds had only one option: ask his dad to lend the money.

It was a tough ask because a print shop Bill ran with two partners had failed, forcing him to declare business bankruptcy in 1993. Seven years later he was still feeling raw from the trauma of losing a business. Putting his hard-earned savings into a jazz club wasn't a high-risk gamble he wanted to take. "My dad just said 'No, I'm not giving you any money.'" Weeds' mom Betty intervened. "Long story short, my mom got in there. She said, 'This is our son, this is what he wants to do. We need to support him.'"[23] Bill loaned his son $50,000 and co-signed with Cory a $30,000 loan from the bank that the elder Weeds committed to cover if needed.

While the deal was in the works, Coon went with Weeds to the Cellar Jazz Café to hear some music. They had previously met when Weeds subbed for Jack Stafford in the sax section of the WOW Jazz Orchestra that played Tuesdays at the Hot Jazz Club. Coon, who played in the big band filled with veteran Vancouver jazz musicians like Paul Ruhland and Jack Fulton, remembered that Weeds showed up to play at the Hot Jazz with a "bad mohawk" (not technically a mohawk, said Weeds, but spiky enough for people to compare him to Bart Simpson). Coon thought Weeds' playing sounded "okay." At the Cellar Jazz Café, Weeds told Coon he was going to buy the club. "I was skeptical because that's the only playing I heard by him, and he just seemed so young," said Coon. "I thought, how could such a young guy make a club work?"[24]

Liapis believed that Weeds had the wherewithal to succeed with the club. "He knew everyone in Vancouver's jazz scene, he played in three or four or more different projects, and he's a personable guy, so I knew that from the point of view of getting the right music in there and artist relations, he had the skills to do that," said Liapis.[25]

For the club's opening night, scheduled for July 13, 2000, Weeds booked a group created for the occasion: Midnight Special, with Gestrin, James Danderfer, Dave Sikula, and Bernie Arai. On the afternoon of the maiden gig, there was a knock at the Cellar door. It was a liquor inspector, who told Weeds that he couldn't open because of transgressions on the last night of the Cellar Jazz Café. "They [the previous owners] got their liquor licence taken away because they had this big blowout party," said Weeds, who had to turn away people who showed up for the new Cellar's launch. He and his friends also availed themselves of the liquor purchased for the opening. "We sat there and got absolutely, beyond all recognition, drunk. I was so depressed."[26] Midnight Special never played a single gig.

The next day, Weeds—still smelling of alcohol—went to the Liquor Control and Licensing Branch to start dealing with the liquor licence problem. Then there were issues raised by a health department inspector that Liapis had to address, as per the sale agreement. Weeds wondered whether these issues would kill the deal, and he started thinking about finding another space. Weeds was driving near Broadway and Main when he saw a "For Rent" sign for a basement in the building next to alley-like Watson Street. It was the space that housed the original Cellar jazz club and other jazz clubs. Weeds left a message for the owner. "The owner called me, and we went and looked at it," said Weeds. "At that time, it was so dilapidated. But you walked down the staircase and it was the old Cellar."[27]

Weeds decided against renting the hallowed space, where the ghosts of Mingus, Art Pepper, and Ornette lingered, and committed to completing the purchase of the West Broadway club from Liapis. The licensing issues meant that Weeds had to delay the opening by more than three weeks. He used that delay as leverage to reduce the purchase price.

Weeds' Cellar opened for real on August 8, 2000, with the Mike Allen Trio. Allen was "completely exhausted" that night because he, among others, helped Weeds get the club ready. Allen couldn't have predicted that he was helping to launch a long run for the Cellar, given the meagre resources available to get it up and running. The tenor saxophonist, however, was impressed with Weeds' "gumption" in opening the club despite all the obstacles.[28] Call it gumption, cojones, or audacity. But at twenty-six, Weeds pulled off the purchase and launch of his own jazz club. There would be many more hurdles for Weeds to get over and so much fine jazz to be played and experienced at the club. This was just the beginning.

• • •

The original capacity of the club, which was now simply called the Cellar or Cellar Jazz Club (and later, Cellar Restaurant and Jazz Club), was sixty-seven. Opening night, with a five-dollar cover, drew a large crowd that filled the club. The next night: about four souls showed up. Then roughly eleven patrons the following night. So right away, Weeds was strapped into the stressful emotional rollercoaster of being a jazz club owner. At the same time, he had to learn the fundamentals of his job. After all, the sum total of his jazz programming experience consisted of promoting Crash gigs and putting on two shows with New York players.

Weeds began by booking musicians he was familiar with and admired. He gave Allen a regular Tuesday night gig. Ross Taggart, Campbell Ryga, Chris Tarry, Bruce Nielsen, and Chris Gestrin were among the strong Vancouver jazz players who performed on other nights in the Cellar's initial weeks. Sometimes Weeds booked himself, but in moderation. When Gestrin—who played on weekly Cellar organ nights with fun names like "Organ by Donation" and "Green Eggs and Hammond—performed at the club six nights after it opened, he earned a miniscule twenty-two dollars. Weeds had a long way to go before audiences grew to the point where he could pay musicians decently.

These early days built up to the Cellar's grand opening, September 28–29, 2000, featuring the Brad Turner Quartet with Seamus Blake. The two nights also celebrated the release by the Maximum Jazz label of a superb live CD the group recorded in the same space eight months earlier when it was the Cellar Jazz Café. Weeds was there one of the nights the album was made, and the music wowed him. He saw the musicians as young and brash, which appealed to him. Weeds wished he had put out the recording. Mike Allen's

Change Is, also released in 2000, similarly made a big impression on him. Weeds inevitably started fantasizing about running his own label.

Bill Weeds (guitar), Cory Weeds (alto saxophone), Jodi Proznick (bass), and Blaine Wikjord (drums), the Cellar, fall 2000. Photographer unknown. Courtesy Cory Weeds.

Weeds embraced introducing musicians at the beginning (and often again at the end) of sets. As part of that, he did something novel for Vancouver's live music scene: articulate a noise policy. "When Cory got up and said, 'Please keep your talk to a minimum in respect of the music that's being played and those around you,' that was a key moment for many of us," said Coon. "We were like, 'Okay, this guy is serious about the music.' I can't remember anyone else getting up on stage and saying that."[29] While some patrons had to learn how to adapt to the policy, it worked—the curb on chatter created a rare listening environment for musicians and audiences to enjoy. Often the only things you could hear other than the music were clinking glasses at the bar and other ambient sounds that reassuringly told you this was a real jazz club. Still, Weeds initially worried a bit about whether the noise policy deterred people from coming to the club at a time when he desperately needed their business.

Mike Allen's Tuesday night gig, which continued for close to a year, was indicative of the club's fortunes in its first months. Musically, it was amazing for Allen and his bandmates to have a weekly opportunity to develop a sound. Financially for the club and the musicians, it was hit and miss. "It kind of struggled to get people in," said Allen, who sensed that some in the jazz community were thinking "we will see how this goes" about whether the Cellar would have any staying power.[30] That was understandable, given how so many Vancouver venues—even with the best intentions—had come and gone into the jazz club graveyard.

It wasn't encouraging that one of Weeds' first bookings of an American artist at the Cellar, Brian Lynch in November 2000, was a bust. After the poorly attended first night, seeing that there was zero chance the low turnout would offset the Cellar's costs of putting Lynch up in a hotel, feeding him, and paying the musicians, the trumpeter jokingly remarked to Weeds: "That's a nice shirt. You just lost it this evening."[31] Despite badly miscalculating, Weeds appreciated the humour. But the slow nights discouraged and scared him.

While there were evenings like those that bombed, progress was also being made. Weekends, when Weeds began booking stronger groups that could draw, were getting busy. Weekdays also started to improve. As a player, Weeds is a dyed-in-the-wool hard bop man, whose first priority is making the music swing. But as a club owner, he offered gigs to bands that didn't fit neatly into the standard definition of jazz. One such group was Emergency Broadcast System (EBS), which performed in the club May 3, 2001. EBS included Turner and Gestrin playing racks of digital and analog keyboards— "Me and Chris had every keyboard we owned [at the Cellar]," said Turner[32]— Lachance on electric bass, and drummer Randall Stoll. The electronic music they created that night sounded like the soundtrack to a cyberpunk film.

Turner, who helped Weeds with setting up and fine-tuning the club's sound system, remembered another Cellar night with Seamus Blake when they played electric funk. "Seamus had three laptops, an iPad, and his EWI [electric wind instrument], and I had two keyboards and my Rhodes," said Turner. "We did some crazy stuff. Cory was really open, especially on certain nights of the week. Then on the weekends, typically, he would try to present something that was a little more unified."[33] In a similar vein to EBS,

Elevator Head performed a few years later. "It was Scott Sanft, Dave Sikula, Jon Bentley, and myself, and we were all playing different combinations of electronics and other instruments," said Bernie Arai. Elevator Head earned a dubious achievement with one of the band's gigs at the club. "I think maybe it was the only time there was a zero person turn-out at the Cellar," said Arai.[34]

By late spring 2001, the Cellar had some momentum. May 15–16, 2001, Weeds presented saxophonist Gary Bartz, the most prominent jazz artist to perform at the club up to that point. After the shows, Weeds and Morgan Childs drove Bartz to the Seattle airport. On the way back, Weeds bemoaned having to be the Cellar's bartender to save money. "Morgs, I really love running a jazz club, but I fuckin' hate bartending," Weeds said to Childs. That was Childs' cue to become the bartender for a spell. "At that time, the Cellar had one of those typical early 2000s cocktail menus of like one hundred different drinks made with all these liqueurs and shit, which was just disastrous," said Childs. "When we would get busy you would have to make ten of these ridiculous drinks. So I was scrambling and mostly trying to pay attention to the music."[35] Childs was behind the bar when the Ross Taggart Quartet gave stirring performances in June 2001. A recording of the shows would become key to Weeds' dream to have his own jazz record label.

After more than ten months of breaking in the club, Weeds was feeling optimistic about its prospects, and the Cellar was ready to be part of Vancouver's jazz festival for the first time. All went well until June 29, 2001, the first of two nights a quartet led by Kurt Rosenwinkel and Mark Turner was scheduled to play as part of the festival. Just before the second set and in front of a full house of patrons, three uniformed police officers, two city officials, and a fire marshal suddenly showed up. They weren't there to dig the jazz. It was a raid that came about because of a complaint from another restaurant. The officious interlopers conducted a spot inspection and found deficiencies, including an inadequate sprinkler system. If Weeds didn't make the necessary improvements, getting shut down was a possibility. "I was more upset than I had ever been in my life," said Weeds,[36] who was in tears after the incursion. But he quickly figured out how to gain support: go to the media. Sympathetic articles about the Cellar's plight appeared and, in the end, the club only had to spend about $6,000 on the upgrades—a lot of money for the cash-strapped club but not an apocalyptic amount.

Journeys to the Bandstand

Kurt Rosenwinkel and Mark Turner, June 2001, the Cellar. Photo by Cory Weeds.

While dealing with the fallout from the raid, someone slipped an envelope under the club's door. It contained a cheque for $1,000 from one Joan Mariacher. For decades, Mariacher had regularly gone around town with her friend Mary Jean "Bunny" Moreton to hear live jazz. After Weeds' Cellar opened, Mariacher showed up—sometimes with Bunny, and sometimes alone, sitting at the bar. Weeds had exchanged casual conversation with Mariacher over the bar counter, but they barely knew each other. Weeds didn't even know her name. So it was a pleasant surprise to receive the cash infusion, which Mariacher contributed to help cover costs resulting from the raid. She was the first investment angel who came into Weeds' life. Her gift was also the first act in a longtime friendship that would become essential to the Cellar's ability to survive and thrive.

Just over a week after the raid, the Cellar reached a milestone: the club's first anniversary. Weeds planned to celebrate with shows in September 2001 featuring vibraphonist and pianist Buddy Montgomery. Then the 9/11 terrorist attacks happened, and Weeds had to postpone the engagement until near the end of the following month. Montgomery was one of a small number of musicians who performed in both the original Cellar jazz club and Weeds' Cellar. Presenting Montgomery introduced audiences to a terrific but underappreciated veteran player—something Weeds would make a priority over the decade to come.

Another milestone was the release on Maximum Jazz of the first full album of music captured at the club: *Maximum Jazz Presents Live at the Cellar*. The album included eight tracks that Kory Burk, Turner, Gestrin, and Weeds had recorded at the club, mostly in 2001. Even though he didn't have a record label yet, early on Weeds made it a priority to document Cellar shows. The tunes chosen for the collection reflected the club's focus at the time. The emphasis was on instrumental bands; none of the tracks included singers. The aesthetic was straight-ahead jazz, with some groups playing more harmonically complex tunes. Initially, the club was male dominated; no women performed on the album's tunes. Weeds didn't play on any of the tracks, which reflected how he prioritized building the Cellar over promoting his own career as a saxophonist.

Weeds got a huge thrill out of putting together the Maximum compilation. There was no avoiding it—he had to create a record label. "I wanted to start a label, but I had no money, and when I say no money, I really had no money," said Weeds. "I was being paid nearly zero dollars from the club." He met with a loan officer at a bank on a Friday to ask for $10,000 to start the label. "It was a very, very short meeting. The answer was very quickly no. They were very polite, but I had nothing, no back-up, no assets." The following Monday he coincidentally received a promotional offer in the mail from the same bank that said, "You have been pre-approved for a $10,000 line of credit."[37] Weeds quickly went back to the bank and in an instant he had $10K to establish a record label.

Weeds lined up Burk to record the Ross Taggart Quartet's two nights of Cellar shows in early June 2001. After securing the line of credit, putting out the recording became a reality that meant a lot to Weeds. This was his chance to honour a musician and friend he revered. The release of *Thankfully* by the Ross Taggart Quartet in February 2002 marked the birth of the record label Weeds dubbed Cellar Live.

Around the same time that the label was coming together—with distribution from Maximum Jazz—Weeds connected with Raymon Torchinsky, a jazz fan and saxophonist. Torchinsky wanted to support Weeds and the Cellar by making an investment. To the tune of $25,000. There was, however, one significant condition: Weeds needed to recruit three other people willing to invest the same amount. Weeds was excited but thought his chances of finding a trio of investors for a jazz club were remote. Yet one by one, in just a few weeks, they fell into place. Bill Weeds changed half of the $50,000 loan he had given his son to buy the club to an investment. Mariacher, after hearing the investment plan, said "I'm in."[38] Despite not having a long history with Weeds, she didn't hesitate. "There weren't many bums in the seats," said Mariacher. "I had been to the Cellar when the band out-numbered the audience. It's a tough racket. I had some money, and I just wanted to help."[39] Bob Syme, who Weeds worked with at the Prussin Music store and school next door to the Cellar, also signed on. Incredibly, the little jazz club that could found itself flush with $100,000. Part of that money was used to pay off a bank loan, buy out Don Guthro (who was no longer involved), and pay back Bill Weeds for the rest of his original loan. The balance was money in the bank that could be used as operating capital. "We were rocking, so to speak," said Weeds. "We had some money, and everything was cool."[40]

• • •

The headline: "Club owner accepts fear factor." The lede by Marke Andrews: "In living a life of danger, Cory Weeds ranks right up there with James Bond and Austin Powers. No, he's not a spy. The 28-year-old Vancouver native runs a local jazz club, The Cellar ... an occupation with a high attrition rate." That was part of a short Q&A with Weeds published in the *Vancouver Sun* in February 2002. In the piece, Weeds admitted he didn't know what he was doing the first four to five months of running the club, and it was only after figuring things out that it got "really scary." Eighteen months into his life as owner, he enjoyed the successes of packed shows, but Weeds was weighed down by the high stress inherent in the job. "The Cellar's doing well, but I'm not making a living right now," he said. "I'm living at my parents' house." Final question: "In a perfect world, how do you see the future?" Weeds' response: "I'd like to see the Cellar flourish. I'd like to see it turn a profit. I'm quite happy to run this place for a long time if it's turning a profit. I'll keep doing this until I'm bored."[41]

Boredom wasn't an option because he had too much to do. Weeds put in long days dealing with countless duties, including many that were tedious. It wasn't glamorous to get the beer cooler fixed, schedule kitchen and serving staff, and fill out paperwork to enable Americans to play at the club, but these were all essential tasks. Managing the restaurant proved especially challenging then and throughout the Cellar's life, with the food being a frequent target of naysayers. The fun part was being in the position to give friends and heroes gigs, see them flourish in the club, and record their music for release on the new label. In 2002, that's exactly what happened with the Bruno Hubert Trio, Oliver Gannon Quartet, and Sharon Minemoto Quintet. They all delivered stellar two-night stands, and Weeds released recordings of the performances on Cellar Live.

There was one more Cellar Live release in 2002, and it was a significant one. *Live at the Cellar* featured alto saxophonist Charles McPherson, the former Charles Mingus sideman and longtime bandleader/recording artist. It was Weeds' first release of an album led by a prominent US jazz musician, and the first that paired a visiting artist with a local rhythm section. That set the template for future recordings. It also captured scorching bebop-rooted playing by McPherson and the Vancouver musicians.

One of the local musicians Weeds recruited to play with McPherson was bassist Jodi Proznick. At the time, she hadn't played with someone as high-profile as McPherson. "One of the greatest things about Cory is that he has so much faith that it [the gig he's lined up] is going to be great," said Proznick. "He just says, 'Okay, you are going to do this, play with Charles McPherson. Yes, he was Mingus' saxophone player, but you sound great, and it's going to be great, and now we are going to record it too.' And there is no chance for me to go, 'Ah, excuse me, wait a second, can we talk about it?' He's just, 'We are going to do this!'"[42]

When Joanne Clifton made a reservation for one of the nights McPherson performed, she thought it was odd that Weeds emailed her back to confirm the reservation. Clifton assumed the club owner would delegate a task like this. "So I emailed him," recalled Clifton, "and said 'Why are you doing that? I would have thought you were too busy.'" Weeds responded with a somewhat flippant response: "'Well, do you want to do it?'"[43] To Weeds' surprise, she did. As a volunteer no less. They met and Weeds welcomed another angel into the Cellar.

Clifton started by helping to seat people on Friday and Saturday nights, which lessened the load on servers Jennifer Hart and Sarah Bondo and other staff. That's all Clifton did for a while until she took on reservations, which she ended up looking after for twelve years. "If you took minimum wage and multiplied it by the number of hours she worked, it would have been in the thousands and thousands of dollars that we would have had to pay out," said Weeds. "Any time in a small business you can get a person that comes and actually puts in hours you don't need to pay, that's huge. So yes, it was a massive help."[44]

Joanne Clifton, June 2, 2014. Photo by Chris Wong.

Help came in other forms, including contributions from Weeds' close friend Steve Mynett, who took photos used as artwork on Cellar Live releases. Mynett once asked Weeds who his favourite alto sax players were. Weeds said Maceo Parker and Kenny Garrett. "Kenny Garrett was my man, he was it for me," said Weeds about the American saxophonist who broke through as a significant artist in the early nineties. He was stoked after booking Garrett and his band to perform at the Cellar May 12 and 13, 2003. His high hopes were deflated. Garrett played well, but he and Weeds didn't hit it off. "I wanted to become friends with Kenny Garrett, but that's not always the way it works," said Weeds. "There were the musicians who would come into the Cellar and understand the vibe of what the club was, that it was run by a saxophone player. It was run by somebody who cared very deeply about the music. It was essentially a musician-run club . . . Kenny Garrett was probably the only one that didn't get that and never warmed up to that kind of vibe."[45]

Contrast that with the connection Weeds and New York organist and pianist Mike LeDonne made when they first met. "Usually, club owners are a little standoffish," said LeDonne. "They know you are going to hit on them for a gig, so they are just waiting in fear of that moment. But he wasn't like that at all. He is a musician. That's the difference." Weeds and LeDonne went on to build a strong friendship and working relationship that, while not always conflict-free—"We had some definite shout downs, I am ashamed to say, but it happens," said LeDonne—it has endured to this day.[46]

George Colligan also had a good impression of the club and its owner when the pianist played at the Cellar for the first time in August 2003. Performing with saxophonist Noah Becker, Colligan was struck by how "the vibe of the place was great, and the sound was great." Weeds' role as a musician/jazz club owner resonated with Colligan. "I just like the idea of a musician running a club because they understand, they just have a more sympathetic approach." In the years to come, Colligan would return multiple times to perform at the Cellar, always finding Weeds to be "straight up" and "respectful" with him and other musicians,[47] which isn't always the case with jazz club owners. "He really looks out for the musicians that he brings in and he's very fair, taking care of business," added drummer Jeff Hamilton. "There's no shady dealing. He doesn't leave you stuck at the border."[48]

George Colligan, Portland State University, August 4, 2014. Photo by Chris Wong.

Then there were the mutual admiration societies that Weeds forged with two major artists who made their Cellar debuts in 2003. Hammond B3 organist Dr. Lonnie Smith played with Weeds' band Crash for the Cellar's third anniversary. After an awkward start in a rehearsal due to Weeds' apprehension about performing with such a high-profile artist, Smith offered some kind words of support, and they made a lasting connection. Succeeding on the bandstand with Smith was a breakthrough for Weeds. "That's when I realized I'm not just a club owner, I'm a musician," said Weeds.[49] Smith would end up playing at the Cellar and touring with Weeds and other Vancouver musicians multiple times over the years. "Whether I play here or not, we're going to always be close," Smith said about his connection with Weeds.[50]

The second legendary musician he forged a bond with that year was David "Fathead" Newman. The saxophonist/flutist played at the Cellar November 28–29, 2003; it would be the first of five wondrous Cellar engagements before he passed away in 2009. Weeds and Newman became close. "I think he was kind of like a big brother to Cory," said Karen Newman about her late husband's connection with Weeds. "He [Newman] was a private kind of man, but if he liked you enough, he really opened up to you, and Cory got that out of him, which is beautiful."[51]

One morning the Newmans went with Weeds to his parents' house for breakfast. Bill Weeds made pancakes, sausages, and bacon, which prompted Karen to announce that David didn't eat red meat. "David puts two pancakes on his plate, and I look over, and he is sneaking bacon and sausages from the tray and putting them in between the pancakes, putting his syrup and butter on the pancakes, and not saying a word," said Cory. "He looks over at me and gives me this glare and puts his lips into the shush position. He is just sitting there with this big smile on his face eating bacon and sausage, all while Karen is going off about why David doesn't eat red meat."[52] Weeds and Newman had an affinity that went beyond spoken words.

Though Weeds developed lifelong attachments with many artists who performed at the Cellar, I'm especially fascinated by the deep friendships he built with older, Black musicians including Smith and Newman, and later with George Coleman and Harold Mabern. Weeds and these musical greats were unlikely chums. The age difference was more than thirty years. The social milieus they grew up and worked in to establish themselves were completely different. Career-wise, Weeds and these men were in very different places. It wouldn't have been surprising if the elders had kept some distance with Weeds. But they were genuinely drawn to each other. Weeds saw Smith, Newman, Coleman, Mabern, and other jazz greats who played at the Cellar as underappreciated heroes. Legendary keepers of jazz tradition. So he was thrilled to have them perform in his club and to tour with some of them. They appreciated the Cellar's warm vibe, the appreciative audiences, and Weeds' musician-friendly approach. Plus, they saw in him an old soul who could really play.

Frank Morgan, the bebop alto saxophonist, brought his legendary presence to the Cellar April 23–25, 2004. There were some issues between Morgan and the local players Weeds had booked for the gigs. But Weeds thought Morgan and the band "played beautifully." Off the bandstand, Morgan indulged in BC bud. After the shows, Weeds drove Morgan to Seattle and asked if the saxophonist got rid of the weed. "No, no, I've got it right here," said Morgan, who then rolled a joint and smoked it. "Now my car smells like weed, and we're probably like fifteen minutes from the border," said Weeds. "I have an eighty-two-year-old high Black man in my car. I said, 'You've got to get rid of the rest of the stuff.' So he holds the plastic bag out the window and it all blows back into the car. Now I'm at a rest stop right before the border with my door open, brushing the seats off. This is it. I'm going to jail. At this point there's no way around it. I'm done."[53]

At the border, as Weeds explained how he knew the man in the passenger seat, "Frank Morgan interrupts me, leans over with his bloodshot eyes and just looks up at the border guard and says [imitating Morgan's high-pitched voice], 'Isn't it beautiful to be alive?' And I was like, 'That's it, I'm done.' And the border guard just looked at him and said, 'Okay great, have a good day' and pushed us through."[54]

A few months before the nerve-wracking Frank Morgan experience, Weeds brought trumpeter Tom Harrell to the Cellar. Weeds was "very, very nervous" about the two-night stand,[55] booked for January 30–31, 2004. Instead of bringing his quintet at the time, Harrell planned to perform with just two of his band members, bassist Ugonna Okegwo and drummer Quincy Davis. Weeds agreed to pay the musicians a significant fee, which reflected Harrell's stature as a well-respected jazz artist who composes and plays exquisitely. One other thing: Harrell has schizophrenia, for which he takes medication to limit symptoms such as hearing voices. Weeds didn't know what to expect from the engagement.

On the first night after Weeds introduced Harrell, he picked up his trumpet and looked ready to play. But for what felt like the longest time, "nothing was happening," and "you could definitely feel the tension rise in the room," recalled Weeds. Many local musicians were in the club, and like Weeds, they were wondering what would happen next. Harrell calmly put the trumpet down and just stood on the bandstand, looking down. "Then he grabbed the flugelhorn and brought it up to the microphone and just went crazy," said Weeds. "He just ripped, and it was amazing, so there was this collective sigh of relief. It sounded beautiful." As the performance progressed, Harrell mainly played flugelhorn, and then after pausing, "played some of the most beautiful piano ever."[56]

That night with Harrell encapsulated the duality of Weeds' life as a jazz club owner: his trepidations never went away, but there was always the chance of hearing profound music that temporarily eased his mind. I was there too, enraptured by Harrell's playing, as I was on other nights with the purposeful sounds of Mulgrew Miller, Benny Green and Russell Malone, Danilo Pérez, and other visiting and local artists. The Cellar was in a groove. The club had proven its staying power, with Weeds as the visionary public face, the behind-the-scenes investment team, reliable and friendly staff, and supporters like Joanne Clifton volunteering their assistance. Musically, the club had contributed so much to the local jazz scene. Weeds' mom Betty lovingly assembled large scrapbooks, with posters, brochures, newspaper articles, and other mementos that documented these early Cellar years. Holding and looking at Betty's scrapbooks years later, it's clear that the club—and her son—were growing up and already evolving during this momentous time.

But as always, margins were tight, and the Cellar's finances were at the mercy of fickle audiences. There were some lean times. Even though it wasn't his money on the line, Weeds felt responsible—guilty even—for the initial $100,000 infusion and additional cash calls that were made to the investors. Weeds internalized the stress and anxiety of being the steward of their investment in a venture that was dicey by nature. He simply couldn't deal with that anymore.

Weeds set up a summit meeting in 2004 with his benefactors to talk about something he never envisioned but was serious about going ahead with: exiting from the club's ownership, which likely would have killed the Cellar. Then Michael Grunewaldt conferred with Weeds just hours before the meeting. Grunewaldt had become a Cellar investor in 2003, replacing Bob Syme. Since then, Weeds and Grunewaldt had clashed over their different approaches. Grunewaldt wanted proper accounting and planning; Weeds ran things looser and more ad hoc. Ironically, Grunewaldt talked Weeds out of quitting. He asked Weeds if he was truly ready to give up the benefits of running the Cellar, which included a salary and the opportunity to play with excellent jazz musicians.[57] Torchinsky, who was a key mentor for Weeds, also helped convince him to reconsider his exit strategy. Weeds realized he didn't want to walk away. "I owe it to them to run this club as long as I can," he said to himself.[58] Weeds knew, however, that the investors could take this opportunity to back out. If they declared, "'We're not giving you any more money,' we would have been done."[59]

That didn't happen. The investors had his back. Instead of the Cellar's heart and soul walking away and the club prematurely ending its run in Vancouver's jazz scene, everything was in place to enable many tremendous players—including Weeds himself—to ardently express more extraordinary jazz, and with even greater conviction.

18 / HARDEST WORKING MAN IN JAZZ BUSINESS: CORY WEEDS

PART 2: FIN DE L'AFFAIRE, LIVING THE JAZZ DREAM

Cory Weeds and the Cellar survived the tough early years of operating as a small but tenacious jazz venue. It was time to celebrate the Cellar's fourth anniversary, and Weeds went big. He found out that New York jazzmen Eric Alexander, Peter Bernstein, Mike LeDonne, and Joe Farnsworth were heading west for some gigs. Weeds grabbed the chance to book them at the Cellar, September 17–18, 2004, for the anniversary celebrations.

It was also another anniversary: close to five years earlier, Weeds presented Alexander at the club that preceded the Cellar in the same basement space. That's the night when Bernstein and Farnsworth sat in, and fireworks ensued after a disagreement on whether it was closing time. Back then Weeds was a complete jazz promotion neophyte. So much had changed. Despite the obstacles, he had established himself as a capable jazz club owner with staying power and promising label head. There was much more to come, including his breakthrough as a capable musician collaborating with top players. First, though, Weeds needed to keep nurturing the Cellar.

In a jazz club, the bandstand is the focal point. At the Cellar, the bandstand had to move. With a renewed commitment from the club's investors and Weeds after he nearly quit, there was a shared resolve to better position the Cellar for success. That involved doing a substantial renovation: moving the bandstand from the kitchen side to near the front door; making the kitchen smaller; increasing the capacity to around ninety, installing new sound equipment, and more. The work was completed quickly, at considerable expense, with great hopes that the changes would pay off.

Aside from Weeds and the room itself, the Cellar staff also had a lot to do with shaping the club's vibe. Jenny Larisey walked into the Cellar one Friday night in the fall of 2005, right at opening time, and handed her resume to Weeds. He was working behind the bar and didn't have time to talk to her. But Weeds called her the next day and asked if she liked jazz. Larisey wisely said yes, and he hired her on the spot. While Larisey was in fact a jazz fan, at the time she didn't know the difference between an alto and tenor sax. Larisey's first night on the job was a busy one; she handled the high volume well. She also fit right in with the staff and customers. Soon Larisey was working full-time in the club. Over time she went from being a bartender and server to managing the club.

Early in Larisey's Cellar tenure, New York saxophonist Ian Hendrickson-Smith performed at the club. She and Hendrickson-Smith, one of Weeds' closest friends, clicked after meeting at the Cellar and began a long-distance relationship. It meant that Hendrickson-Smith performed relatively frequently at the Cellar, which was good for the club and audiences because he's a dynamic and soulful saxophonist. Musicians and patrons also had a lot of affection for Larisey. She radiated a calm and friendly presence that people connected with.

During one of Joey DeFrancesco's gigs at the Cellar, the club was sold out, and the band needed somewhere to eat dinner between sets. The cramped office behind the bar, where many musicians ate and hung out, was too small. "I remember setting up a table in the parking lot," said Larisey, referring to the covered lot behind the club. "I made it nice. I put a candle on the table, put out some napkins, you know, made it as decent as possible."[60] Simple yet meaningful gestures like this were endearing and built lasting bonds with visiting musicians. "She fostered at the club exactly what I wanted to be fostered, which was an inclusionary place, a meeting place, and a community place," said Weeds.[61]

Larisey became friends with regulars like Rose Hook, a jazz lover in her eighties. Hook always sat at the end of the bar closest to the cash register, and she sported wraparound sunglasses during the sets. The two women, with an almost fifty-year difference in their ages, became pen pals after Larisey moved to the east coast. Another regular, Vincent Lim, who took thousands of photographs in the club, always had two beers—one of the customer tendencies she got to know so well. "He wouldn't even have to ask for his beer," she recalled. "It would just show up on the bar for him." Yet another regular Larisey got to know was Doreen Young. Unbeknownst to most people who met Young at the Cellar, when she was known as Doreen Williams, she sang at Vancouver's original Cellar jazz club.

As Weeds' touring increased, along with his desire to be at home more with his young family when he was in town, Larisey—yet another angel in Weeds' life—filled the void at the Cellar. "Jenny was instrumental in enabling me to be away from the club, without question, and for me to have full trust in what was happening in my absence," said Weeds. She also knew how to handle her boss, whose mood and stress level openly fluctuated with busy and slow times for the club. "She was a sweetheart, so she coped just by being who she was, by not coming on the rollercoaster with me," said Weeds.[62]

Jenny Larisey, the Cellar. Photo by Jesse Cahill.

• • •

Sometimes the issues that sent Weeds around the bend were self-inflicted. In 2005, he impetuously released *You'll See, The Anniversary Quartet Live at the Cellar*, a live recording of Eric Alexander and his NYC compatriots made during the club's fourth anniversary celebration. The only problem: Weeds didn't ask for permission from the label that two of the band members had exclusive recording contracts with: HighNote Records. Joe Fields, HighNote's co-founder, slapped a cease-and-desist order on the Cellar Live release and Weeds had to pull it from circulation. Seven years later, history repeated itself, only the names had changed. That's when he re-released *Cellar Groove* with David "Fathead" Newman listed as leader above the Tilden Webb Trio, and not the other way around like it was when it first came out in 2005. Weeds received permission from HighNote for the 2005 release, but he didn't have authorization before the 2013 version. Newman passed away in 2009, but he was under contract to HighNote at the time of the recording, so once again Fields issued a cease and desist, and the 1,500 pulled CDs became collector's items.

"Why do I seem to make shit hard on myself? Why?" Weeds wailed. Because his inner voice almost always tells him to forge ahead. "In ninety-nine percent of the time, that forging ahead has been the right thing to do," he said. "But that one percent of the time, it's a real pain in the ass." I sarcastically suggested an alternative—he could just be a musician, teach, and have a quiet life. "God! That would destroy my will to live."[63]

In early 2005, the Cellar launched a regular night that went far outside the straight-ahead sweet spot that Weeds cultivated at the club. It came about after Raymon Torchinsky discovered tenor and alto saxophonist Nikita Carter (then known as Coat Cooke) playing at 1067, an underground creative jazz venue in downtown Vancouver that one entered through an alley door. Torchinsky explained his role as a financial backer of the Cellar to Carter and proposed that the saxophonist play there every Monday, a night the club was closed at the time. Torchinsky assured Weeds and the other investors that he would cover costs, and Carter ended up playing avant-garde jazz with bassist Clyde Reed and drummer Kenton Loewen on Mondays at the Cellar.

Carter and her bandmates built a rapport that they wanted to document in a live recording. Surprisingly, it was Weeds who served as recording engineer. Weeds hadn't been to any of the previous Monday night gigs with the trio, which wasn't unexpected because it would have been unlikely for "a leopard to change his spots," as Carter aptly put it.[64] Someone needed to record the trio, and Weeds did so professionally. Still, the image of Weeds sitting in his tiny office and listening through headphones to completely improvised free jazz that was polar opposite to his swinging and melodic bag, was one of the unlikeliest in the Cellar's history. Just as surprising, the recording—*Up Down Down Up*—came out on Cellar Live. With Torchinsky footing the bill on top of his commitment as a Cellar investor, however, it all made sense. It's also a fine recording, which captured the trio's adventurous sound.

By 2006, Carter switched gears by having her group play once a month and booking improvised music artists the other weeks. The Monday night series continued until 2008. Over the course of the series, whenever Carter crossed paths with Weeds, the Cellar owner was supportive. "He was saying, 'That's great that you are doing it. You are managing to keep this going for a long time on a night that was traditionally in Vancouver such a dead night.'"[65] Carter was grateful to Torchinsky and Weeds for the chance to perform and provide a showcase for Vancouver's burgeoning improvised music scene.

In a completely different vein from improvised music, Weeds landed a gig playing baritone sax in a big band backing Paul Anka on a 2006 tour. Then before the seven-city tour started, Hendrickson-Smith made an enticing offer. It was for Weeds to sub on bari and play alongside Hendrickson-Smith in the Dap-Kings, the dynamic band backing the remarkably powerful soul singer Sharon Jones, for a multi-week tour. It was tempting, and there was a potential for Weeds to become a permanent Dap-King, but he said no to his pal Hendrickson-Smith. Weeds was dating his future wife Alana at the time, so he didn't feel it was the right time to go on a lengthy tour. Plus, another friend—producer, record label veteran, and saxophonist Scott Morin—lined up Weeds for the Anka gig. Weeds didn't want to bail on Morin. The gut decision, which reflected Weeds' loyalty, paid dividends years later when Morin took on writing grant applications for Weeds that led to significant funding for his record label. It's interesting to speculate how Weeds' life could have changed if he had gone on the road with Jones, then a rising star. Another exit from the Cellar averted.

In November 2006, Weeds led a trip to New York that was both a sweet dream and a nightmare. He landed funding to showcase two Vancouver groups—the Chad Makela Quartet and Ugetsu–in NYC. They played at Fat Cat, a West Village jazz club, and were well-received. So the trip was musically exciting and successful. But Weeds had booked inexpensive accommodations in Queens that turned out to be a "ragtag house," which looked nothing like the pictures of a beautiful brownstone he saw before booking. The Vancouver musicians were "looking at me like, 'What are we going to do,' and I had nothing," said Weeds. "I was speechless. I was scared. I didn't know what to do." Then he relocated the whole crew to a hotel that also ended up being an "absolute dump." Weeds said the accommodations missteps constituted "friendship-ending stuff," but the musicians kept cool and didn't mutiny. The trip epitomized two sides to where Weeds was at. He was devising bigger initiatives and creating opportunities for musicians. Weeds was also still learning how, with scarce resources, to execute these projects. Sometimes—like in New York—shit happened, which elevated stress for Weeds and others.

By 2007, the year Cory married Alana—a perfect union in part because her calm balances his angst—the Cellar had some financial stability. The 2005 renovation that resulted in more seats was paying off. Those seats were more frequently getting filled for gigs with visiting artists and Vancouver players. At this point Weeds had more connections and confidence to bring in US players, who generally drew well. Landing tenor titans George Coleman and Eric Alexander to play together, for example, was a coup. The club was building up its base of regular clientele, who could be counted on to support higher-priced shows. That year, Music on Main led by David Pay also started presenting a series of Tuesday night classical and contemporary music shows at the Cellar, which often filled the club and bolstered the venue's role as a community hub. While Weeds still believed the Cellar was always just "two or three bad weeks away from being in trouble,"[66] with support from the investors he could relax a bit about the club's survival and focus on something that was right in front of him but not fully explored: playing and recording music as a bandleader.

As a club and label owner, Weeds had ample opportunity to book himself for gigs and make recordings. During the first half of the Cellar's existence, he held back. While Weeds performed in the club regularly, he didn't dominate the limelight. Gradually, Weeds played more with locals and name visitors, and his self-assurance grew. Weeds came up with an ambitious plan: playing

Cory Weeds (alto saxophone) and Scott Hamilton (tenor saxophone), the Cellar, September 7, 2007. Photo by Steve Mynett.

alto and tenor, January 11–13, 2008, at the Cellar with three New Yorkers he knew well—guitarist Peter Bernstein, organist Mike LeDonne, and drummer Joe Farnsworth—and recording the last two nights. Weeds' position at the Cellar gave him the chance to play with heavy hitters for his first album as a leader, but he still had to execute. *Big Weeds*, released on Cellar Live in July 2008, is a solid debut recording (although years later, Weeds wasn't enamoured with it). The musicians play the eight straight-ahead tunes, including six originals by Weeds, with exuberance and reverence for jazz tradition. When playing the melodies and soloing, Weeds sounds entirely unambiguous about his mission: making music with a swing-first mentality.

Almost exactly a year after making his first album, Weeds followed up in 2009 with a second recording, this time in a very different setting. He recorded a session in a New York City studio with superb NYC musicians, including trumpeter Jim Rotondi and one of Vancouver's finest: Ross Taggart on piano. The music captured that day, released on Cellar Live as *Everything's Coming Up Weeds*, advanced what *Big Weeds* had established as Weeds' core components—unerring swing, melodicism, and deep respect for hard bop and related genres—and upped the sophistication.

Journeys to the Bandstand

I've thought a lot about these intrinsic elements of Weeds' sound that have been evident since his first recordings. I asked others and myself: Is it fair to say that Weeds, because of his resolute devotion to straight-ahead jazz, is a conservative musician? "Those kinds of arguments go nowhere," said baritone saxophonist Gary Smulyan, another American jazz musician who bonded with Weeds through the Cellar. "To call someone conservative or adventurous, what does that mean really?" Smulyan believes that if a musician plays genuinely from the heart with skill and craft, that's what counts, as opposed to either-or labels. And to his and my ears, Weeds "plays beautifully."[67] For DeFrancesco, knowing how to swing and staying connected to tradition were key. "And that's what I love about Cory," he said. "You know, he's a bebopper, and that is so important. That's the basis of everything you do. Before Coltrane played *Om* and *A Love Supreme*, he was playing bebop . . . Even Miles [Davis], when he was in the seventies playing all that wild stuff, the basis and the phrasing and everything he did, the feeling, the elements of the blues, all of that stays into play because these guys had the tradition. That's why Cory, I really dig him, musically."[68]

Gary Smulyan, the Cellar, January 18, 2014.
Photo by Chris Wong.

Hardest Working Man in Jazz Business

Joey DeFrancesco (organ), Byron Landham (drums), and Paul Bollenback (guitar), the Cellar. Photo by Jesse Cahill.

Aside from Weeds' emergence as a bandleader, things were clicking for him in other ways: In April 2009, Cellar Live released the label's fiftieth album: *Presenting the Ross Taggart Trio*. Not only was it a milestone release, but it was also especially meaningful for Weeds because it showcased Taggart, who continued to be an important player at the Cellar, friend, and confidant. Putting out fifty albums in seven years was momentous for Vancouver's jazz scene because while a handful of those releases were by artists from other parts of Canada or the States, the vast majority featured local ensembles. In past eras, recordings of the city's jazz musicians came out sporadically, with limited distribution. For the first time in Vancouver jazz history, someone was thoroughly documenting the sound of the scene. And doing so with increasingly sharp design, emulating how classic labels like Blue Note created a look.

• • •

In 2010, the year the Cellar celebrated its tenth anniversary, the club made a small but significant change to its name. It became Cory Weeds' Cellar Jazz Club, with the name placed on a sign outside the club and on a banner at the back of the bandstand. It was a smart, strategic move that made plain what had long been the reality: the Cellar's brand was synonymous with Weeds. "The club flows out of the personality of the club owner," said Spike Wilner, owner of Smalls and Mezzrow jazz clubs in NYC and Weeds' friend. "If the club owner has no personality, the club will have no personality."[69] Weeds never had that problem—he always projects a big personality, and the Cellar embodied that.

Part of being so front and centre at the club was the frequency that Weeds booked himself to play in the club's second half. "I think he maybe overexposed himself in the playing department there, I would say," said Tom Keenlyside. "For a while it was Cory Weeds and everybody else. I think people wanted a little more variety. And it's not that he isn't a great player because he is."[70] Weeds booked Weeds because—aside from it being his prerogative as the club's owner—he drew well, which was always important at a jazz club with tight profit margins. That said, other musicians could pack the club too. So there was more to it. After holding back in the early Cellar years, Weeds gradually built his confidence as a player and he was simply enthusiastic about getting on the bandstand.

James Danderfer, the Cellar. Photo by Jesse Cahill.

Weeds has maintained long-term friendships with many musicians. Sometimes mixing fellowship and business can be tricky. Clarinetist and saxophonist James Danderfer and Weeds, who are very close friends, once had a tiff over money. Danderfer's exuberant Hummingbird Brigade, inspired by New Orleans brass bands, packed the club one weekend. But the larger-than-average group was playing for the door and those were nights when the Cellar was accepting two-for-one cover coupons that quite a few patrons used. Danderfer, who put in many hours writing charts, wanted to pay the musicians decently. So he was going to lose money unless Weeds increased the band's take. Weeds seemed reluctant to do that at first. Eventually the two men talked, both conceded some fault in the matter, and the compensation was increased.

This was a minor quarrel, but it showed how occasional conflict goes with the territory of being a jazz club/label owner and impresario. It also exemplified competing forces Weeds has had to balance. As a musician who understands what it's like to be in an economically vulnerable profession, Weeds has empathy for his fellow players. As a businessman, he has to keep musicians' fees and other costs under control. When negotiating with Weeds, if there's an impasse, he doesn't forcefully try to break it, said Ian Hendrickson-Smith. "If he wants to do business with somebody, he will offer them the terms of whatever that transaction is, and if they are not okay with it, he's okay with them not being okay with it. He's a hustler, but in a very gentle way."[71]

Then there's Weeds' inherent nature to publicly speak his mind when he sees something wrong. Like when three of Weeds' favourite New Yorkers—Mike LeDonne, John Webber, and Joe Farnsworth—played at the Cellar from November 30 to December 2, 2012. On the last night of the weekend run, the lack of attendance by students set Weeds off. That night he wrote "AN OPEN LETTER TO MUSIC STUDENTS IN VANCOUVER." In the letter, Weeds said student attendance on discounted Sundays "has been appalling and quite honestly embarrassing." He got to the crux of the matter: "I'm trying hard to make the music accessible for you, I'm trying to make it affordable for you, I'm trying to encourage you to come and be able to soak up everything that there is to soak up. I'm starting to think that it's really not about how expensive it is. It's about that fact that there is . . . a general lack of caring by students and I'm not sure why."[72] After clicking publish, it didn't take long for the replies from students to flood in. Some said the Cellar had become too expensive and was too far to get to on transit. Weeds replied that there was never a cover for students attending second sets, and not being able to get to the club on transit was just another excuse. It went back and forth in the blog comments and on Facebook, with intensity.

Just under four months later, Weeds was leading forty-three jazz lovers on his annual New York with Weeds tour, and everything was cool until near the end of the eight-day trip. Weeds had arranged for people on the tour to go to the the fabled Village Vanguard to hear Kurt Rosenwinkel. Weeds and some tour members exchanged words with certain Vanguard staff at various times that night. The Vancouverites thought the service was poor and rude. Naturally, Weeds blogged about it—multiple times. Weeds didn't mince words about the venue or the music. "Kurt Rosenwinkel and friends are very, very popular and are all fantastic musicians but I'm not a fan of the music and last night did nothing to change that. Again, I stress that I have great respect for them but it just doesn't float my boat. Having said all that, the vibe in what is supposedly the most famous jazz room in the world ruined any chance at all of anyone enjoying themselves."[73]

He expressed a view about an acclaimed artist that went against the prevailing opinion and criticized a venue that's sacred in the jazz world. Not surprisingly, the blog posts sparked a heated exchange of comments, including volleys between Weeds and Rosenwinkel's manager. As a result of the kerfuffle, Weeds said the Vanguard "banned" him. The episode illustrated Weeds' penchant for voicing his opinions honestly, without letting trepidations about how they would land dissuade him. He could have avoided a lot of jazz world tension by staying silent, but that simply wasn't in his nature.

• • •

In 2013, on the surface, the Cellar was stronger than ever. One of Weeds' ultimate coups was booking the Christian McBride Trio to play in the club February 21–24, 2013. McBride could have filled much larger Vancouver venues, but he chose to play in the small club. Weeds was also thrilled that McBride asked him to sit in. Weeds said yes and played solidly. Six weeks later,

Hardest Working Man in Jazz Business

Weeds pulled off another dream booking with a jazz star. George Coleman played at the Cellar with a local trio to honour the memory of his former student and Weeds' close friend, Ross Taggart, who died in January 2013.

Christian McBride, the Cellar, February 22, 2013. Photo by Steve Mynett.

Taggart died on the first day of a tour that was another seemingly unachievable endeavour that Weeds pulled off: nineteen engagements for a quintet he led, featuring himself on tenor sax, New York trombonist Steve Davis, and a strong Vancouver rhythm section. It concluded with a gig at Smoke, the Upper West Side Manhattan jazz club that Weeds had an affinity for because of the programming and vibe that influenced what he nurtured at the Cellar. The live recording that Weeds released of the Smoke show, *Let's Go!*, conveys the swinging fluidity of the Weeds-Davis frontline on melodies and the two friends' hard bop literacy on solos. Davis saw Weeds' growth as a musician and his self-effacement. "He is not walking around with his chest out about what a great saxophone player he is, and he is a wonderful player," said Davis in 2013. "I mean, he really takes a back seat to nobody. He is just an excellent musician, and he is getting better to my ears just in the last two, three years."[74]

Harold Mabern, the Cellar, September 27, 2013. Photo by Steve Mynett.

As the year went on, the Cellar was up and down financially. Weeds' gloomy assessment: May was slow, jazz festival gigs in the club were well-attended, August was "horrible," and September "got off to a plodding start."[75] Still, he had Harold Mabern to look forward to. Weeds booked an

Hardest Working Man in Jazz Business

ambitious tour and recording session in which he would play with Mabern, the premier pianist. The tour included four nights at the Cellar, September 26–29, 2013, planned as the club's thirteenth anniversary celebration.

It was a rewarding fortnight, capped off with a recording session in Victoria that produced *As of Now*, Weeds' most vital and engaging album to date. But two mini-floods in the Cellar during the Mabern run put Weeds back into mega-stress mode. For some time, there had been a problem at the club with water coming in when it rained a certain amount. Patrons at the Mabern shows had to walk around a soaking wet section of carpet to get to the washrooms. For Weeds, it was another stressor that gnawed at him.

・・・

October 25, 2013. On the Cellar bandstand, alto saxophonist Mike DiRubbo and pianist Larry Willis projected a hearty sound. I was especially drawn to Willis' vigorous style. The pianist exemplified the kind of unsung jazz musician—someone who played with many jazz greats and, though lesser known, was one himself—that Weeds loved to present at the club. But the Cellar owner wasn't among the patrons enjoying the music. He was in the office, where he often sat over the years during sets, half listening to the music and half obsessing over the latest threats to the club's survival. In the office, Weeds picked up one of the club's monthly printed calendars and verbally annotated individual dates with his memory of what the attendance had been: "Bad, bad, good, okay, bad, bad . . ." and on he went. By that point, Joan Mariacher was the only investor left, and she generously kept helping. But Weeds didn't feel he could keep asking her for more to prop up the club. His blunt assessment: "We are bleeding. We are more than bleeding."[76]

In many ways, nothing had changed. Weeds was stressed from the moment he purchased the Cellar, and the anxiety never really went away. But on this night, something was different. I could see in his face and body language, and hear in his tone, that the fun was gone.

Mid-November 2013. After surviving all the giant challenges and achieving myriad triumphs, Weeds confirmed in emails, social media posts, and phone calls that he was closing the Cellar. Weeds told me on the phone, but I could picture an enormous weight being lifted from him. He felt liberated and was already looking ahead to what would come next. Weeds thanked international and local musicians who played at the Cellar. "There was always a lot of hoopla made about the international stars that came to the Cellar, but without a strong local jazz community you cannot have a 'real' jazz club," Weeds said to Vancouver musicians. "It is YOU who have made The Cellar what it is."[77] Weeds was also sad about the finality of his decision. "This is the end of something very special and very unique and something that will never be repeated."[78]

Cory Weeds, the Cellar, February 17, 2014. Photo by Chris Wong.

After Weeds announced the closure publicly, supportive messages flooded in from hundreds of musicians and patrons. In the five stages of grief, people were in different places. "First of all, I was in denial," said Smulyan. He responded to Weeds' announcement by asking his friend, "'Come on, you aren't really going to close?' And then it was kind of grief. I think there is a grieving period that you go through, especially if you look at what he has presented through the years and his track record, and to know that's going to come to a stop is kind of a sadness."[79]

Tenor saxophonist Steve Kaldestad, who played at the Cellar many times, was also in denial at first. Here's why: His introduction to the Cellar seven years earlier was unique. Jodi Proznick asked Weeds if he would pay for flights from London, England, and back for Kaldestad so that he could be a sideman with her band for a Cellar weekend to celebrate the release of her first CD. Weeds, who had never heard Kaldestad play before, said yes to the longshot request. Why would he make such a blind investment? He trusted Proznick, who said Weeds would love Kaldestad's playing, which turned out to be the case. Plus, Weeds will "go to the ends of the earth for music."[80] The two sax men became instant friends, Kaldestad moved to Vancouver, and he became a Cellar regular.

So the club was crucial to Kaldestad's life. But then he accepted the loss and savoured memories of listening to and playing with great musicians at the Cellar, especially older ones. "I really like learning from older musicians that have been playing the music that I love because to me, they have some of the secrets," Kaldestad said. He could have easily cited some of the prominent American jazz artists that played at the club to illustrate his point, but instead, highlighted local guitarist Oliver Gannon. "When I hear Oli Gannon, I'm like, 'Oh yeah, the way you play that chord, no one does that anymore. What is that?' It's kind of like I want less of the music to be buried. I want those mysteries to stay alive."[81] For Kaldestad and many others, the Cellar bandstand was an altar for those spellbinding jazz mysteries.

For Bill Coon, hearing the Cellar was closing prompted an even heavier metaphor. "It was interesting for me to go through that process of mourning the loss of the Cellar," said Coon. "It was like someone had died."[82] That someone was a jazz club where the music had high standards and integrity. The Cellar was also a welcoming, warm place where—like the corny *Cheers* song said—"everybody knows your name." In that vein, the news had existential meaning for Morgan Childs. "That room is part of music history now and holds memories so essential to my being. I can hardly imagine it not being there."[83]

I was struck by how Dr. Lonnie Smith used the word "hurt" to describe how he felt about the end of the Cellar, which he treasured for its rare intimacy. "I really do miss it," said Smith. "I think about this place all the time." But he put it in perspective by quoting another song, "The Gambler": "You have to know when to fold 'em." Another reason for Smith's strong feelings was his heartfelt gratitude for Weeds. "It wasn't about the money to him," said Smith. "It was something he enjoyed doing. And that's real—you can't beat that. Real soul, real heart in the belief in what he does. That type of person will go on and on. I'm never worried about him. He's going to be fine."[84]

Luckily for the musicians and patrons, it wasn't a sudden death. Weeds announced the Cellar's end more than three months before time was up. That enabled a long goodbye, which Weeds made the most of by presenting some of his favourite musicians: Steve Davis, pianist Jon Mayer, Louis Hayes' Cannonball Adderley Legacy Band, and others performed dynamically on the Cellar bandstand in November and December 2013.

Hayes saw the impending loss of the Cellar as part of a lamentable trend. "When I was a younger person playing this art form, you had more venues to play in, in a lot of the cities in America, where now you don't have that anymore," said Hayes. He appreciated Weeds for engendering the Cellar's "warm environment and atmosphere" and presenting what he called the "special creative art form" of jazz to audiences.[85]

Mayer talked about Weeds in valiant terms. "I see him as a hero, a jazz hero," said Mayer, another of the below-the-radar musicians Weeds featured at the Cellar. Mayer described Weeds as heroic because he's "carrying the torch" for jazz. Mayer went on to say that Weeds is "a very unusual guy, but he has great forward movement." I'd heard many descriptions of Weeds—hard-working, determined, brash, opinionated—but not unusual. "Unusual in believing in this particular music, combined with his perseverance and industriousness," explained Mayer, who put the Cellar's passing in perspective and was optimistic about Weeds. "I learned there's always a beginning, a middle, and an end to people, places, and things. Clubs are born, and clubs die. People are born, and people die. It's sad when it happens, but I have faith in Cory. I think that he's going to reinvent something."[86]

Ian McDougall described Weeds in yet another way: "He's got bulldog qualities," said the veteran trombonist. "I think he's done a magnificent job of trying to keep the old flame burning, and I have the highest respect for him."[87]

On New Year's Eve, organist Mike LeDonne played with Weeds and other local players. The music was swinging, but Weeds was in a dark mood, and it showed on and off the bandstand. Before the first set, Weeds told me he'd had it with running the club, especially the aspect of dealing with high maintenance people. Between the second set and an abbreviated third set, Weeds facetiously suggested a title for this chapter: "Angry and Bitter."[88] Clearly Weeds was done.

Bill Coon, Joan Mariacher, Jodi Proznick, and Miles Black, the Cellar, February 5, 2014. Photo by Vincent Lim.

Or so it seemed. After the New Year's downer, Weeds fulfilled the role of jazz club owner, musician, and emcee, and did so impeccably from my vantage point. He understood that patrons and musicians wanted to experience the club's magic before the end, and Weeds did his best to give the people what they wanted. The club was packed every night as Cellar favourites—like Peter Bernstein, Smulyan, and Joey DeFrancesco with Weeds—and local stalwarts played their final choruses in the club. The last major shows, February 23 and 24, 2014, featured a powerhouse trio: pianist Monty Alexander, bassist John Clayton, and drummer Jeff Hamilton. Musically, it was exciting to experience three masters interacting with each other. Emotionally, it was bittersweet because the end was so near. That didn't stop Mariacher from joyously relishing every note. At various points Mariacher, seated with friends at the front, closed her eyes as if she was committing to memory the splendour of each swinging moment.

Journeys to the Bandstand

• • •

It finally arrived: closing night at the Cellar, February 26, 2014. It was the most challenging night in Joanne Clifton's years of handling reservations because everyone wanted to be there. But she used her intimate knowledge of the club to cram in more than ninety people, who would witness a momentous event. Half an hour before the festivities began, I looked around and saw so many familiar faces. Many of the regular patrons I was used to seeing at the Cellar were there, along with numerous key contributors to the jazz community.

"It is really hard to imagine that these walls are no longer going to vibrate with wonderful jazz," said Margaret Gallagher, then host of CBC Radio One's longstanding *Hot Air* jazz show, in her remarks that opened the evening.[89] She thanked and introduced Weeds, who walked up to his comfortable place behind the microphone and delivered a speech for the ages. Weeds eloquently recounted key events in the history of the Cellar and his own evolution. "I was young, I was brash, maybe a little bit cocky, maybe a little bit arrogant," he said about his former self who bought the club in 2000. "Many things have happened. Not the least of which is that I grew up." Weeds recognized key people who helped the Cellar survive and flourish. He also acknowledged himself in his characteristic way of simultaneously being unselfconscious and self-deprecating. "Another funny thing happened, and I feel a little weird saying this, but I actually became a real musician."[90] He was in fact a "real" musician when the club opened, but he went from being a jazz club and label owner who happened to play, to being a musician first, who learned from experience to create his own voice.

Weeds arrived at the sad juncture where he recited the Cellar noise policy one last time: "So without further ado, welcome to the Cellar. Thank you for coming down. If you have a cell phone, please turn it off. Put it to the vibrate mode. If it does go off, please answer it outside. And Joan, this one's for you: If you feel the need to talk, don't."[91]

What followed was the only thing that could: magnificent jazz, performed with an exuberant spirit by a rotating cast of musicians who had been key Cellar contributors. It was fitting that one of the last tunes was "Fin de l'Affaire" by Hank Mobley, one of Weeds' biggest influences. Aside from the relevance of the title, it's a ballad—Weeds' specialty—and he played it with feeling alongside friends including the veteran guitarist he revered and often featured at the Cellar: Oliver Gannon. As the final notes wafted from the storied bandstand, everything was as it should be.

Jesse Cahill was walking around the Cellar with his camera and flash taking portraits of people. Two months after that memorable night, I asked Cahill to sum up Weeds' method for growing the Cellar. "Whether it was intentional or not, he really came at it like an improviser, because that is what he is," said Cahill. "He made it up as he was going along, and he took a lot of chances, and just like when we play, sometimes the more chances you take and the more risk you take, the better the result." Cahill added: "We got to see all these great bands and, in some cases, play with some great bands. And then, as local musicians, we got a venue to play our own music. So admiration and appreciation for the guy."[92]

On the bandstand that final night, Mike Allen lauded the Cellar and Weeds as incubators of bands finding their way. "The Cellar has been a test tube for a lot of different groups that I've been part of, and a lot of great music has been incubated here on this stage. It's really aided and led to the development of a lot of local groups, so we all owe appreciation to Cory for providing a space for music and bands to create their music and to try out their music to figure out what they're really going for artistically."[93]

Hearing the analysis from his colleagues/friends of how Weeds approached curating the Cellar brought to mind something he said to me just before announcing the Cellar's end. "It's about [getting] people in the seats," Weeds said. "You [a band he books] can get up there with a friggin' ukulele and a hula hoop, I don't care. You bring eighty people down, all your friends, I don't need to justify anything. Where it gets tricky is you get up there with a ukulele and a hula hoop and you bring twenty people. Then I have a lot of explaining to do."[94] I knew right away that Weeds was being hyperbolic to make a point about the slippery art of programming a jazz club. A few years later, Allen offered more insight into what made the club a lasting success: "The Cellar never seemed to suffer from that problem that some jazz clubs have, which is they can't decide if they want to have great music or music that sells. I think Cory always found the sweet spot between having great music and music that does well."[95]

Journeys to the Bandstand

The morning after the last night, Weeds, Larisey, and some volunteers began the crummy but necessary task of cleaning up the detritus of thirteen-and-a-half years of jazz clubbing and disassembling the Cellar. Weeds was standing on a stool, taking down the sound system, when he fell and badly broke his elbow. In a weird way, the injury was symbolic of his split from the Cellar: a painful but clean break. "It [closing the Cellar] was one of the few things that I have done where I just knew without a shadow of a doubt that it was the right decision and everything would be okay," said Weeds.[96]

A one-armed Weeds in pain wasn't going to get the job done, so Larisey looked after most of the teardown. By March 3, 2014, the once jumping joint was a lifeless, hollow shell. Weeds could have taken a moment that day to gaze one more time at the reservoir of memories. He was having none of that. Weeds, wearing a Cellar hoodie and his arm in a sling, walked to the front double doors and locked them at the top and bottom. Then he walked past the bar and, without looking back, shut off the lights before going out the back door and turning the key. "So it's adios," I said. "Yeah, that's it," said Weeds. "Bye-bye."[97] We both laughed at the irony that an emotionless, two-syllable valediction was the final farewell to a place that meant so much to him and the community.

Cory Weeds, the Cellar, March 3, 2014. Photo by Chris Wong.

Hardest Working Man in Jazz Business

• • •

After winding down the Cellar, Weeds immediately dove into post-club ownership life. Even before the Cellar closed, Weeds had created the non-profit Cellar Jazz Society as a vehicle for presenting performances and music education. He swiftly lined up two series, one at a restaurant (Seventeen89), and another at a venue that Weeds recognized as a promising place for jazz: Pyatt Hall. At no point was he out of the game. Then just two weeks after closing the Cellar, his New York with Weeds jazz tour began. I decided to go on the tour to learn more about what made Weeds tick.

The insights started revealing themselves the night before the tour started. That's when a few tour participants went with Weeds to Smoke jazz club. As soon as we walked in the packed room, Weeds was in absolute heaven. David Hazeltine was leading a quartet with Eric Alexander, David Williams, and Joe Farnsworth—buddies of Weeds who performed at the Cellar a number of times. Handshakes and hugs all around. Holding court in the corner was none other than George Coleman, who received a steady stream of admiring musicians, including Weeds. Sitting by himself in the middle of Smoke was the renowned alto saxophonist Lou Donaldson, who had also played at the Cellar. Weeds went over to say hello to Sweet Poppa Lou, as he's known. When Weeds came back, he had a sheepish grin on his face. As Weeds explained it, Donaldson remembered the Cellar and Weeds, and in fact had heard some of Weeds' albums. Donaldson's kicker, repeated by Weeds in a high-pitched voice that simulated the jazz legend's timbre: "Those records you're putting out in Vancouver, that's some sad shit."[98]

Weeds reacted to Donaldson's putdown by laughing. Weeds knew Donaldson wasn't necessarily kidding. But Weeds was also aware that the then-eighty-seven-year-old Donaldson doesn't hold back from bluntly critiquing jazz musicians. "I thought it was a rite of passage to get ripped by Lou Donaldson," said Weeds. "As insulting as it was, it made me feel good."[99] Weeds' blasé response showed me that he didn't take himself overly seriously, and he was savvy when navigating the sometimes harsh give-and-take with crusty jazz artists from much different eras. Perhaps steering a sky-high Frank Morgan past a US Customs and border protection officer equips one with a lifetime of unflappable composure.

Lou Donaldson, the Cellar, January 10, 2007. Photo by Steve Mynett.

The next day, Weeds started herding more than forty people around New York to experience jazz in mostly unique settings. Simultaneously, he was completely in his element and "in a very emotional space," observed Katie Malloch. The former host of CBC Radio's *Jazz Beat* and *Tonic* national jazz shows was on the tour for the third time as co-leader with Weeds, so she knew him well. He was still in pain from the broken elbow. Closing the Cellar had happened so close to the trip that there hadn't been time to process what it all meant. "It was like a huge breakup with someone you love," said Malloch about Weeds' decision to shut down. "And then he had to deal with taking care of all these guests [on the tour] and making sure they had a good trip. It was an awful lot on his plate."[100]

Malloch was accustomed to seeing Weeds juggle priorities during the Cellar years. "It's almost like if he stopped too long to think about all the stuff he was trying to do, he would have said to himself, 'This is nuts. I shouldn't be doing this,'" said Malloch. "But he never stopped. He never took that breath and that breathing time. He just said, 'I wanna do this, and I wanna do this, and this has to get done, and so-and-so's gotta be recorded 'cause they're great.' It's like he just poured it on. Certainly, the Vancouver jazz scene would not be what it is today if he were not there."[101]

One of the New York trip's highlights was making a pilgrimage to the American Legion in Harlem, where Weeds had brought many previous tour groups to hear soul jazz by organist Seleno Clarke and others. "He [Weeds] has a certain vibe, a certain spirit that most club owners do not have," said Clarke, who performed twice at the Cellar. "He doesn't hide from nothing. He gives you his word, and that's it. He's a very sensitive person like me." With a serious look on his face, Clarke pledged to help Weeds raise funds to revive the Cellar. "If I get some money, I'm going to send him a million dollars. New York is one of the richest cities in the country—I'm going to ask around and see what I can do."[102] I don't doubt Clarke sincerely meant it, but a Harlem-to-Vancouver cash infusion didn't happen before Clarke passed away in 2017.

Another New York highlight for the tour participants was witnessing back-to-back recording sessions that Weeds organized for two Cellar Live releases. He booked the Unity Center in midtown Manhattan to record the albums with plenty of time for both. But the first session for a Steve Kaldestad recording with Renee Rosnes, Peter Washington, and Lewis Nash was delayed because of unanticipated jack hammering next door. As the musicians waited and the delay continued, Weeds looked stressed. Not just the type of stress he suffered from while owning the Cellar, but a DEFCON 1-level anxiety. He knew another set of first-rate players—John Webber, Harold Mabern, Nat Reeves, Joe Farnsworth, and special guest George Coleman were due to arrive soon for the second session. During the wait, Nash reminisced about the Cellar. "It would rank among the best and most rewarding playing experiences of any of the clubs [he played] in the world," said Nash, who didn't see the end of the Cellar and other great jazz clubs as absolute. "Certain things that happened in those places are part of our lore and experiences, so the clubs never really die in the memories of the people: the musicians and the patrons who went there."[103]

After the trip, Weeds carried on with multiple presenting, recording, and performing projects. While the weight of ownership responsibility had lifted, the stress didn't dissipate. "I am still running around like an idiot," he said. "I am still totally stressed out."[104] As Weeds explained a few years later in a video for AnxietyBC, he has suffered from anxiety and depression for much of his adult life. "It has, at times, completely debilitated me and been a very, very serious thing in my life," he said. "I was one of the lucky ones in that for some reason I was able to talk about it from a very early stage, and so I got the help that I needed to best cope with the symptoms of anxiety and depression."[105]

He was clear about one thing: Weeds didn't pine for the Cellar. "I definitely don't miss it," he insisted.[106] I did. I went out of my way to do drive-bys of the shuttered club to evoke memories. One night I went to the Royal Canadian Legion 142 at the other end of the block where the Cellar once was, just so I could hear music that swings on the street that had some form of live jazz dating back to the fifties. Gannon was playing in the WOW Jazz Orchestra at the Legion that night, so mission accomplished.

Then in September 2014, I discovered the former Cellar had become the "Cannabis Cellar." It had gone—cue cheesy joke snare drum hits and cymbal crash—from Weeds to weed. I made the mistake of texting Weeds about seeing what the Cellar had become. His curt reply: "You and 9,000 other people . . . Everyone seems to think I care."[107] Half an hour later he posted on Facebook: "I can appreciate the desire to tell me about it [Cannabis Cellar], but I have really moved on from that part of my life. Please stop telling me about it."[108] Raw nerve touched, message received. Weeds had no time for nostalgia; he had too much to do in the jazz biz.

The weed joint didn't last. I went back a few years later to find a Brazilian jiu-jitsu school had moved in. I was shocked by how the space was completely transformed, leaving no trace of its earlier incarnation as a jazz paradise.

• • •

In November 2013, when Weeds announced the Cellar closure, he knew that he would feel a "massive itch" to keep presenting music. Ideally, it would be in a jazz club setting but without the "million-pound weight" of financial and other responsibilities on his shoulders.[109] He scouted locations, held meetings, and looked for potential. Weeds found it at 755 Beatty in what was then a sports bar owned by Raffaele Aiello. There was some music venue history in the area—in the early 1970s, the Egress blues-folk-jazz club was across the street, and the after-hours Nucleus where Lenny Breau once played was two blocks away.

It took a lot of discussion and negotiation, but a dream situation for Weeds emerged at the one-hundred-seat Frankie's Italian Kitchen & Bar. An agreement was struck whereby Aiello would run and be financially responsible for the restaurant; Coastal Jazz & Blues Society would pay for musicians to perform there and put its marketing resources behind it; and Weeds, who would become a Coastal employee, would program the music. He would also help program Coastal's annual jazz festival, deliver jazz education, and be free to pursue his own projects. The only question I and others like Malloch had was, would working for Coastal—working for anyone, really—be a good fit for the independent-minded, strong-willed Weeds? "He's always a little bit on the edge, kind of out there by himself," said Malloch. "It's very demanding, but it's his personality, who he is. He's not going to be a kind of organization-type guy."[110] Cory Weeds, company man, wasn't in the cards. But the arrangement went ahead and the elements fell into place. Frankie's launched live jazz October 8–10, 2015, with Weeds' quintet, featuring pianist David Hazeltine.

Weeds' instincts for booking a jazz club kicked in immediately. Carrying on from where he left off at the Cellar, for the restaurant that would become known as Frankie's Jazz Club, he started programming a mix of strong musicians from the Vancouver area, other parts of Canada, and the US who could swing, shape expressive solos, and draw an audience. Among the Americans who have been featured at Frankie's are top players Weeds had previously presented at the Cellar, like Mabern, Roy McCurdy, George Colligan, Peter Bernstein, and Eric Alexander. At one point, I realized Frankie's had become the new Cellar. While it didn't have the intimacy and vibe that I missed so much from the Cellar, Frankie's was an improvement in other ways—much better location, bigger room with a longer bar, and more consistent food. It soon earned the distinction of being a real jazz club. Somehow Weeds had done it again, creating the city's go-to jazz spot.

Parallel to nurturing Frankie's, Weeds kept elevating his career as a musician. A high point was assembling the eleven-member Cory Weeds Little Big Band with musicians from Vancouver, Edmonton, and New York to record and perform live, and commissioning Bill Coon and Jill Townsend to deftly arrange charts for the band. Weeds didn't let the daunting economics of the project stop him from pursuing it. While taking in one of the gigs at Frankie's, I was struck by the band's deep talent, including accomplished bandleaders and soloists. A younger Weeds would have been apprehensive about making himself the featured performer in such proficient company; forty-three-year-old Weeds relished the opportunity and confidently delivered a robust tenor sound. Between songs, that night and many others, he was polished and relaxed while talking to the patrons and making jokes—often at his own expense.

Weeds also reorganized and expanded his record label by releasing live recordings through Cellar Live, studio sessions through Cellar Music, and archival recordings through Reel to Real, all under the Cellar Music Group umbrella. Archival recordings are enormously challenging to produce and release. Weeds partnered with the right man for this niche: Zev Feldman, co-President of Resonance Records—one of the leading labels releasing archival jazz—and consulting producer for archival and historical recordings with Blue Note Records. For Weeds, collaborating with another Type A personality in Feldman could have been a recipe for combustion. But complementing each other's knowledge and passion, they launched Reel to Real with a bang in January 2019 by putting out excellent previously unreleased live recordings by the Cannonball Adderley Quintet and Etta Jones. The rescued recordings came complete with gorgeous art and informative booklets covering the history of the performers, the original live performances, and the venues where they happened.

Right at the time when it seemed that Weeds' life was in perfect harmony, just before midnight on May 31, 2019, he sent his Cellar Sound email newsletter out to more than 2,000 subscribers. It said he would leave Coastal Jazz & Blues Society in two months and continue to program music for Frankie's by working directly with the club. "I had a great run at Coastal Jazz & Blues working with some really wonderful people, making some good friends and learning a lot," he wrote. "They afforded me a great opportunity after I closed the Cellar and I will be forever grateful." Weeds added that he would be a "proud member of the programming team at Coastal Jazz" until the end of his contract.[111] On the surface, it was no big deal, just an administrative change that wouldn't affect the scene at Frankie's. But Weeds' public statements belied what was happening behind the scenes. There was major discord between Weeds and some Coastal Board members, which played out in meetings that got very heated.

Weeds pivoted without missing a beat. He focused on planning and promoting his new creation: the Shadbolt Jazz Walk, a one-day jazz festival at the Shadbolt Centre for the Arts in Burnaby, December 1, 2019. It wasn't a festival like the one Coastal Jazz presents annually, which features artists ranging from straight-ahead to avant-garde who record for different labels. Weeds programmed eleven performances with American and local musicians who emphasized his favourite things—straight ahead, swinging, and melodic jazz—and almost all were Cellar Live and Cellar Music recording artists.

Even though the City of Burnaby funded the event, given the scale of the festival and high expectations, Weeds' reputation was on the line. It seemed inevitable, then, that anxiety would rear itself in the days leading up to the festival, and it did. But a good turnout and strong performances that satiated the attendees meant the Jazz Walk ended up being one of the high points in his career as an impresario.

There was a palpable sense at the inaugural Shadbolt Jazz Walk that Weeds had come up with a winning template for a jazz festival, so he was already looking to do it again in a year's time. What no one could know was that in just two months BC would have its first diagnosed case of an infectious disease called COVID-19. On March 20, 2020, in response to growing COVID cases, the BC government ordered all restaurants in the province to cease dine-in services. Two days earlier, Frankie's had proactively suspended performances and all operations for a two-week period. The closure stretched into the summer, and the city's other jazz venues similarly closed. It quickly became clear that the pandemic, in addition to changing the lives of every citizen, would have a devastating impact on musicians. Now Weeds, who had long been able to get more gigs than most because of his sax appeal and extensive connections, was in precisely the same position as every other player: shut down.

With more free time than ever, Weeds started a Facebook Live series called "Tales of a Club Owner." Weeds sat in front of his massive jazz record collection and shared stories from the Cellar, life on the road, and other aspects of his career. I watched almost every session, and they reaffirmed how the notions of being guarded and mysterious are so contrary to his nature. "I wear my heart on my sleeve," he once said. "I can't pretend. If I'm not doing well, everybody knows about it. And that's not because I want everybody to know about it. It's just because I can't be someone that I'm not. This is how I'm feeling, so this is just how I am. Deal with it."[112]

In late June 2020, Frankie's announced that it was reopening with limited seating, and Weeds would perform on the first two nights. At the same time, Weeds revealed on Facebook that the club wasn't rehiring him as programmer "and there is no indication" he will be brought back.[113] The announcement explained why Weeds was a bit subdued on reopening night at Frankie's, where he switched things up by playing baritone sax. I was surprised when Weeds told me between sets that he had applied for a job as a letter carrier. After all of Weeds' accomplishments in jazz over two eventful decades, was this really his final chorus?

I should have known better. He pivoted again. Weeds put on pay-per-view "Cellarstream" concerts from Vancouver and New York. They included shows from the Shadbolt, replacing the second edition of Weeds' Jazz Walk that couldn't happen, and a free, six-hour virtual festival. Weeds obtained funding that ensured the musicians were paid, so even in a pandemic he was serving as a provider and giving musicians opportunities. In September 2020, Weeds showed again that he's a jazz phoenix by announcing that he was "excited to be back booking music at Frankie's Jazz Club!"[114]

Then came sad news. In October 2020, Joan Mariacher passed away at eighty-nine, after a two-year struggle that began when she had a stroke at Frankie's while sitting at the corner table that was always reserved for her. Mariacher's discreet philanthropy—whether it was subsidizing live shows, funding recording sessions and album releases, or hosting jazz parties in her home with Harold Mabern, Jimmy Heath, and many others—supported many in Vancouver's jazz scene, especially Weeds. "She allowed me to live out EVERY single one of my jazz dreams," wrote Weeds on Facebook. "We did it all. Anything and everything, we did it! Nothing ever stopped her."[115]

Hardest Working Man in Jazz Business

Joan Mariacher and Cory Weeds, Cuba, February 2008. Photographer unknown.

There were other losses to grieve. Great artists (and one future star) Weeds had presented at the Cellar and at other venues, played and toured with, and spent many hours soaking up their wisdom and character, passed away. 2019: Harold Mabern and Natasha D'Agostino; 2020: Jimmy Heath and Bucky Pizzarelli; 2021: Dr. Lonnie Smith; 2022: Joey DeFrancesco. Weeds mourned each person's passing and affectionately looked back at his meaningful time with them.

• • •

As the pandemic persisted into 2021 and continued to create economic challenges for the jazz scene, Weeds seemed unfazed and kept executing a dizzying array of large projects. With Feldman, his Reel to Real partner, Weeds put out previously unreleased, historically important, and musically nourishing live recordings featuring Harold Land and drummer Roy Brooks. Weeds and former Cellar investor Raymon Torchinsky had not been on speaking terms for years after a bad falling out, but they reconciled and Torchinsky helped fund the archival releases. Plus, with help from various funding sources, Weeds continued to release a steady stream of albums through Cellar Live and Cellar Music. Weeds still had an uncanny knack for getting people to invest in his dreams. Artists leading the sessions also increasingly entrusted Weeds to produce their recordings, which reflected their belief in his instincts.

Weeds realized two elaborate projects as a leader with strings. One was his take on the 1950 *Charlie Parker with Strings* recordings, which he performed live with the Kamloops Symphony. Among the tunes in the Parker concert: "Rocker," the song with the solo he botched years earlier in Texas. This time, Weeds improvised with aplomb. The other project was recording his eighteenth recording as a leader, *What Is There To Say?*, with a rhythm section and thirteen strings players. Despite the logistical complexity of making the recording happen with so many musicians, particularly during a pandemic, Weeds sounds completely at ease in the lush orchestrations of mostly ballads—his sonic sweet spot. Later in the year, he played superbly on a Cellar Music recording with a quartet led by Hammond B3 organist Brian Charette at legendary Van Gelder studio in New Jersey, where Weeds has produced a number of albums.

In mid-November 2021, Weeds made a big announcement: Jazz @ The Bolt, his second jazz festival at the Shadbolt Centre, would take place February 11–13, 2022. He booked a significant number of New Yorkers to perform at the festival, along with many locals and musicians from elsewhere in Canada. Then the Omicron variant of the virus that causes COVID-19 hit hard, causing COVID cases to skyrocket and prompting government restrictions. I thought, this is it—Weeds will finally need to concede defeat on something and cancel or postpone the in-person and streamed festival. Instead, he held his nerve, cases abated, and the show went on. It turned out to be a satisfying, decently attended event that was a tonic for jazz fans who had been deprived of live listening experiences.

The festival only happened because he's a virtuoso of getting shit done and making things happen. Weeds systematically announces and provides updates on all of his projects, current and future, on social media and in emails with his well-honed PR mastery. He doesn't take on all of the tasks himself—over the years Weeds learned how to delegate. Plus, he constantly makes alliances, like the one he forged later in 2022 with jazz promoter Tim Reinert (aka Infidels Jazz), which led to an ongoing series of late-night shows at Frankie's.

During the third Jazz @ The Bolt, February 4–5, 2023, more insights about Weeds came into focus. It was the most successful edition of the festival, with clearly the best attendance, and not just because COVID-19 was no longer a significant factor in influencing whether jazz fans showed up. Weeds demonstrated his ability to adapt. Inviting Reinert to program part of the festival, with an emphasis on younger and edgier local artists, was a smart move that expanded the audience and its demographics. Pretending to dislike each other—in social media and when introducing artists on stage—is also a savvy tactic by Weeds and Reinert to generate buzz about their collaborations and inject humour into the proceedings. While I've heard some people complain that the fake feud is a stale shtick, I appreciate the mock insults because what they ironically signify is a deep mutual respect. Weeds' willingness to play along and bear the brunt of his counterpart's especially enthusiastic gibes is further evidence that he's no narcissist.

Weeds also only played once during the festival, in an easy-going performance with the Nightcrawlers, which was another astute decision that freed him up to focus on the many logistical details and lowered his stress. But Weeds still multi-tasked. With support from Scott Morin, Weeds obtained funding to make five recordings for his label with American and Canadian Jazz @ The Bolt artists right after the festival. More than ever, I understood the Cory Weeds ecosystem that interconnects live performance, touring, and recording with support from funding, media relations, and social media marketing.

David Caballero (bass), Bill Weeds (guitar), and Cory Weeds (tenor saxophone), Frankie's Jazz Club, January 22, 2023. Photo by Vincent Lim.

On day one of the festival, some other key elements of that ecosystem were front and centre during a trio performance that begin in the late morning. The bandleader was immensely talented multi-instrumentalist John Lee, who played piano with New Yorkers Joe Farnsworth and John Webber. The circumstances: Lee had never played with Farnsworth and

Webber before; their set was as spontaneous as it could be, with next to no rehearsal; and Lee thought about cancelling from the festival because his mother passed away unexpectedly five days before. But the twenty-nine-year-old in deep sorrow decided to play. The result: stunningly beautiful and impeccably swinging piano trio jazz. It worked so well because of the musicians' proficiency and heart. Weeds' contributions, aside from making the festival happen: mentoring Lee for a number of years; hiring him whenever Weeds could, which gave Lee vital experience; and having the foresight and trust to bring the seasoned New Yorkers and blossoming Lee together.

By the festival's second day, Weeds looked elated and—incredibly for him—almost serene. The event surpassed expectations, and so many friends and family—including his parents Bill and Betty, wife Alana, and children Noah and Kayley—were there, which made it extra meaningful. That afternoon, Weeds received great news: an album by the Generation Gap Jazz Orchestra, which Cellar Music released, won a Grammy for Best Large Jazz Ensemble Album. While Weeds didn't produce the recording, the high-level validation meant a great deal. As for myself, experiencing wondrous festival performances by Farnsworth and Mark Turner—who were part of Weeds' very early adventures as a jazz impresario (the tension between drummers and the city officials' raid)—reminded me how far he had come and how much he had accomplished.

Five months after the festival, Weeds received fifty votes and placed second in the "Rising Star Producer" category of *DownBeat* magazine's annual Critics Poll. Weeds received more votes than many noteworthy producers/musicians. Twenty-two years after Weeds used a precarious line of credit to start a record label, top international jazz critics held his production on Cellar Music Group releases in high regard.

In November 2023, an unlikely gig happened. For his "After Dark" series of late-night Frankie's shows, Reinert booked KneeJerk—Brian Horswill, Karlis Silins, and Kenton Loewen—to perform with Weeds. At the trio's core, KneeJerk plays immersing free jazz that's by turns feral and minimalist. When Reinert told me about this mad scientist programming, I was shocked and had no idea what it would sound like to pair the band with swing-is-the-thing, melodic Weeds. I could only imagine that it would be like adding fiery hot sauce to a beautiful plate of pasta. Would it be palatable?

In a set that lasted just over an hour, Weeds obliterated my conception of how open-minded and capable he could be while playing outside of his comfort zone. On alto sax, Weeds counterintuitively clicked with KneeJerk. During tunes with both structure and ample room for free-form soloing, Weeds got into the spirit of the band's vibe, mostly avoided familiar licks, and freely improvised. His satisfying improv didn't come across as forced. Above all, it looked and sounded like he was having fun. After the gig, Weeds wasn't going to suddenly trade his Hank Mobley records for Ornette Coleman vinyl. But he proved to himself and witnesses that he's multidimensional.

Over a decade, I conducted more than thirty interviews with Weeds and read or listened to many other things he said while putting himself out there. I combed through the mountain of material to see if I had missed anything central to his character. I never found a hidden layer he kept under wraps. He's the most WYSIWYG person I know. The closest I came to glimpsing something unforeseen happened one day after we visited Mariacher in the long-term care home where she spent the final months of her life. While just chatting casually, Weeds cryptically suggested that he doesn't see friends very often. That didn't correspond with my impression of the man who has very close to the maximum number of 5,000 Facebook friends. Weeds never said anything like that again, and it may have been a throwaway comment, but it hinted that being Cory Weeds is more solitary than one would assume.

This much I know: jazz is the lifeblood that sustains Weeds, giving him purpose and joy. Playing and presenting passionate jazz that swings is *it* for him. He certainly has ego and enjoys being acknowledged, but those things don't motivate Weeds or make him whole. What ultimately inspires Weeds? In his speech on the final night of the Cellar in 2014, he said: "There are not too many people that love this music more than I do." It was one of those big, sentimental statements that Weeds is wont to make. While his declaration was impossible to verify, it rang true given his towering efforts to elevate jazz over the years. So it's simply old school love—for family and friends, and for jazz as an art form that moves people and makes them happy. That's what drives Cory Weeds to be the hardest working man in jazz business.

19 / THE DOCTOR AND THE AMBASSADOR: DR. LONNIE SMITH AND SELENO CLARKE

AFTER THE LAST note of the show reverberates, Dr. Lonnie Smith gently moves his skilled hands away from the keys, the lucky recipients of his singular verve over the last ninety minutes or so. A mischievous smile subtly appears on his face. As he had done thousands of times before in a career spanning half a century, Smith just performed a miracle. He electrified the audience from his familiar operating theatre—twin keyboards with numerous keys and more than twenty bass pedals, all of which Smith somehow manoeuvred to make exultant music.

On this Vancouver night in December 2015, his instrument wasn't the Hammond B3 organ that he'd been associated with throughout his career; it was a close cousin, the Hammond A100. The milieu was atypical too—Smith played with the seventeen-member Jill Townsend Big Band, which matched his immense, swirling sound. Aside from these departures, all was as it should be this winter evening. The good doctor was in fine form, serving up heaping dollops of soulful jazz.

After the show, I approach Smith and ask if I can interview him the next day. He says yes on one condition: I take him to a place where he can get a decent plate of eggs. Smith declares that the eggs at the hotel where he's staying are substandard. The next morning, I pick him up at the hotel and

Journeys to the Bandstand

take him to Helen's Grill, an old-world diner on Vancouver's Main Street. A greasy spoon for the master of greasy jazz.

Dr. Lonnie Smith, Helen's Grill, December 5, 2015. Photo by Chris Wong.

Smith and I cross the old checkerboard floor and slide into a booth, where a mini-jukebox exudes nostalgia. The seventy-three-year-old grew up in an era when jukeboxes were ubiquitous, but he ignores the coin-operated antiquity. Other diners select "I Got You Babe," "These Boots Are Made For Walkin'," and "Let It Be," and Smith focuses on the task at hand: enjoying the scrambled eggs with American cheese he ordered. After several tastes, he flashes that understated smile. The eggs meet his standard. Between bites, Smith talks about his special connection to this city that began twelve years earlier and the destiny that carried him to a lifetime of playing arguably the most powerful instrument in jazz.

• • •

Smith's Vancouver debut started with a cancellation. When Ravi Coltrane's manager nixed gigs for the saxophonist that included two nights at Cory Weeds' Cellar Jazz Club and a festival performance in nearby Surrey, Weeds needed to find a replacement on short notice. Enter Dr. Lonnie Smith. Weeds knew about the B3 great's stature in jazz and was keen on booking him, but Smith needed a band to play with him. Booking agent Jeff Turner suggested that Crash, which Weeds co-led, back Smith. "I was excited but scared," said Weeds, who worried he might be seen as an opportunist for booking his own group to play with such a big artist. "Who am I to be booking myself with Dr. Lonnie Smith? But at the same time, I wasn't going to pass up the opportunity."[1]

So booking Smith, who had never heard of Weeds and the Cellar, was confirmed. Weeds suggested to Smith that they play funky, James Brown-inspired tunes from an album the organist recorded in Detroit with guitarist George Benson, baritone saxophonist Ronnie Cuber, and others in 1970: *Live at Club Mozambique*. Smith agreed to that but asked that Weeds transcribe the songs. Chris Gestrin, who often played B3 at the Cellar, had already transcribed some of them. Weeds and his Crash co-leader Jerry Cook "ferociously" transcribed the others.[2]

After Smith arrived, they went into a rehearsal, where Weeds presented the transcribed music. The following exchange ensued:

Smith: "What is this?"

Weeds: "This is the music."

Smith: "I don't need the music. I can't read music."

Weeds: "Why would you make me transcribe all the tunes for you?"

Smith: "That wasn't for me, that was for you. I want to make sure you know the music."[3]

Once that was cleared up, they began rehearsing. Weeds was on edge, as he had never played with a musician as prominent as Smith. "I was so nervous and uptight, I was going to blow a gasket," said Weeds. "Lonnie stops the rehearsal, and he says, 'Weeds, you and me, we've got to go talk.' I go, 'Shit, he hates the band, he hates the club.' So we go into the back, and he's like, 'Look man, this is music, this is not brain surgery. We're not saving lives, we're playing music. I'm not going to have any fun if you're like that, and you're not going to have any fun, so just relax. Just chill out. You sound great, the band sounds great, we're going to have a good time. Just play the music, and don't worry about it.'"[4]

With the weight lifted from Weeds, Smith and Crash "tore the house down" on the first night at the Cellar.[5] At the end of the evening Smith noticed CDs piled up in the club's cramped office. Weeds explained that he ran a label, and Smith suggested recording the next night's show. On September 6, 2003, Gestrin recorded Smith with Crash: Weeds on alto sax, tenor saxophonist Jerry Cook, guitarist Dave Sikula, bassist Mark Humeniuk, and drummer Bernie Arai.

The following year Weeds released *The Doctor Is In*, featuring Crash with Smith, on his Cellar Live label. Listening to the album years later, it more than holds up. There's a great loose feel, unrelenting funky energy, and bright sound to the tracks, all written by Smith except one by Weeds and Cook. Despite having just met and barely rehearsing, Smith and Crash lock into fierce grooves. Individually, the playing is strong, with Weeds, and the other band members contributing raw and vigorous solos. Smith thoroughly exudes his B3 mastery.

Smith begins "Play It Back" alone, teasing what's to come by stroking the organ's keys with a light touch. Then suddenly, he stops and implores the audience: "I want some help there." That's their cue to start clapping, and they oblige, keeping it going until Smith and band kick into gear. Later in the tune, while characterfully singing along off-mic, Smith solos all over the organ's keys, keeping the grease quotient high. Then there's his ardent playing and singing on "Your Mama's Got a Complex," with putdown lyrics consisting entirely of the title and "She thinks she's hot, but hot she's not," which along with his between-song banter, keep the audience smiling.

It was a coup for Weeds to release such a solid recording on his then fledgling label and for him and the band to play so well alongside Smith. "I think that record put the club on the map, it put the label on the map, and it put me on the map," said Weeds.[6]

To cover Smith's fee and recoup the investment in the recording, Weeds struck a deal with Smith to tour with Crash. They played shows across the

Pacific Northwest and got to them in a rented motorhome. On the long drives, Smith wore doctor's scrubs because he found them comfortable, and he often shared his idiosyncratic humour. "Lonnie's crazy," said Weeds. "He's totally nuts but in a normal and fun way."[7] One day Cook lived up to the band's name and crashed the motorhome into a restaurant overhang, which freaked everyone out, especially Smith, who was sitting in the front seat. Luckily, there were no injuries except to Cook's pride. That expedition led to more Cellar shows and two other tours, including one with Crash and another where Weeds switched some of the musicians, enlisting Ross Taggart on tenor sax and guitarist Bill Coon. "I've never met a performer who could raise the stage like Lonnie Smith," said Coon. "I mean literally, you felt like he could raise the stage. The stage was levitating at times."[8]

• • •

Dr. Lonnie Smith was born July 3, 1942, in Lackawanna, New York, near Buffalo. His virtuosity in conveying the warmth and resonance of the instrument he's devoted his life to mastering started taking shape when Smith was about twenty. That's when he hung out for hours at a time in a music store on Buffalo's Fillmore Avenue owned by Art Kubera. "One day he says, 'Son, may I ask you a question?'" recalled Smith. "I said, 'Yes sir.' He says, 'Why do you come in here and sit every day until closing time?' I looked at him in his eyes and said, 'Sir, if I had an instrument, I could work. If I could work, I could make a living.'" One day not long after, Kubera showed Smith a back room. "There was a brand-new organ. And he said, 'If you can get this out of here, it's yours.'"[9] On a snowy day, Smith heaved it onto a pickup truck. He sat in the bed of the truck, holding on to his pristine Hammond B3.

He taught himself how to play the B3 by ear, listening to records by organists Wild Bill Davis, Bill Doggett, and Jimmy Smith, among others. When the doctor was still an intern he played in Buffalo's main jazz club, the Pine Grill, and connected with rising star George Benson. Smith played on two of Benson's early albums, and the guitarist did the same on the organist's first record as a leader, *Finger-Lickin' Good Soul Organ*. With Smith's emerging style and stellar contributions from Benson, Blue Mitchell, and King Curtis, it was a strong debut. By 1968, Smith had a record deal with

Journeys to the Bandstand

Blue Note Records. He would make five albums for the high-prestige label that solidly established the organist in the soul jazz genre.

Dr. Lonnie Smith, the Cellar, December 27, 2005. Photo by Steve Mynett.

Dr. Lonnie Smith, the Cellar, December 27, 2005. Photo by Steve Mynett.

Smith eventually played in a style with a slow, laid-back groove, which Blue Note co-head, producer, and photographer Francis Wolff wanted him to stick to. But Smith, who considered himself a "rebel," had other ideas. He left Blue Note and went on to record for other labels and to tour, which often involved moving his humongous instrument weighing close to 200 kilos. I asked if he had to lift B3s on his own. "Did I lift? I remember it was time to leave [a gig], and a guy would say, 'I have to go, uh, get somethin' out of my car,' or 'I have to go to the bathroom.' And I'm standing there. I had to learn how to move that thing by myself. You know, I'd drag it and pull and tug."[10]

But the nightly risk to herniated discs was worth the feeling that playing the B3 gave Smith throughout the years, even during the downtimes when his music didn't fit with trends and he faded into obscurity. "It's like electricity," he said about playing the B3. "It's like a fire that burns throughout my body when I play. And I can feel that. It's part of me."[11]

Smith's discography shows that he took a hiatus from recording as a leader for most of the 1980s. But he kept performing and in 1985, Smith recorded an album in Paris, France—*Lenox and Seventh*, with guitarist Melvin Sparks and drummer Alvin Queen—that showed the fire was still burning. By the end of the decade, hip hop artists were acknowledging Smith's relevance and influence by sampling him. A Tribe Called Quest twice sampled his interpretation of the Blood, Sweat & Tears hit "Spinning Wheel," from Smith's 1970 *Drives* album. Recording two mighty albums in 1993 and 1994 with guitarist John Abercrombie and drummer Marvin "Smitty" Smith, paying tribute to John Coltrane and Jimi Hendrix, signalled that Smith had a lot more music to contribute.

Fast forward to 2015. A month before the Vancouver show with Jill Townsend's big band, Blue Note announced that Smith would release his first album for the label in forty-five years. That superb recording, *Evolution*, came out in early 2016 with high-profile contributions from Joe Lovano and Robert Glasper. The year after that Smith was one of the recipients of a 2017 National Endowment for the Arts Jazz Masters Fellowship, the highest honour bestowed on jazz musicians in the US. Four years later, Blue Note released *Breathe*, including two tracks on which Smith collaborated with—of all people—Iggy Pop. Not a bad late-career run for the rebel who can't read music, is a self-proclaimed doctor, and is known for mysteriously wearing a Sikh-style turban.

So what's the story behind the turban, which first appeared on the cover of his 1976 *Keep On Lovin'* album? "That's personal, and I will never tell you," said Smith about the headwrap. "I've been wearing a turban since I was about fifteen years old."[12] Smith told *JazzTimes* that he didn't know why he started wearing a turban, and after wearing one for so long, it became an essential part of his being that people expected.[13] Taking it off would be like the Lone Ranger, Batman, and Zorro removing their masks. Greg Bryant, a broadcaster and musician who presented Smith, believes the organist wore turbans "as a symbol of universal spirituality, love, and respect."[14] Regardless of the reason, Smith enjoyed maintaining the enigma. But where did the Dr. honorific, which he started using in the 1970s, come from? It's "honourary from the musicians," he told me. "I always doctor up their music."[15]

Smith's musical elixir was pivotal to the healthy growth of both Weeds the club owner and the musician. They also forged an unlikely but deep friendship. "That will remain in my heart forever as one of the most beneficial and one of the most heartfelt associations in my life," said Weeds. "I learned so much from him on the bandstand every night. He's just a real beautiful soul."

Near the end of my time with Smith at Helen's Grill, he started reminiscing about the Cellar, which closed more than a year earlier. "I miss it," Smith said. "It hurts. I think about the place all the time." Smith believed it wasn't just serendipity that brought Weeds and the Cellar into his orbit. In his view, it was preordained that he would connect with Weeds in Vancouver and make music together. "There's a reason for everything, and that was the reason," said Smith. "Isn't that beautiful? That's something beautiful."[16]

In June 2021, during a live stream celebrating the twentieth anniversary of the Cellar Live/Cellar Music label, there was a startling moment: Weeds announced that Smith was very sick and likely wouldn't survive his illness. Smith, who had pulmonary fibrosis, passed away in Fort Lauderdale on September 28, 2021, at seventy-nine. With his personality that inspired joy, the hands of a surgeon, and electric soul-jazz genius, the likes of Dr. Lonnie Smith will never be seen again.

Three months later, I saw on Facebook that guitarist Peter Bernstein posted a lengthy and wholehearted tribute to Smith. Bernstein knew Smith well, and he deeply respected him. "He was there for some firsts for me: my first record date with Lou Donaldson in 1990 and the first time I went overseas to play," wrote Bernstein. "I remember on that trip one gig had an organ for him to play in a big outdoor space that was literally a toy, I think it said 'Fisher-Price' on it, maybe four octaves. He saw it and laughed and then made it sound incredible and spread joy to the entire place." At a festival, Bernstein had lunch with Smith and a gospel choir director. "He [the choir director] was a pretty strait-laced fellow and asked Lonnie where he had received his doctorate from. To which Lonnie replied deadpan, 'New York.' The choir director then said, 'NYU?' Lonnie shook his head and said 'No, just New York . . .' There was a long silence after that. He was hilarious and loved to put people on."

Many idioms are overused, but one that Bernstein used directly applied to Smith, and it summed up his essence. "He was truly larger than life," said Bernstein. "He embodied the deepest things about expressing oneself through music. He had total commitment. He didn't just make amazing sounds, he was pure drama, complete immersion. It was all LOVE."

• • •

It's Sunday in Central Harlem, so that means the American Legion on West 132nd Street—also known as Post 398—is jam packed and loud. Inside the brownstone basement on this early evening in March 2014, more than forty enthusiastic jazz lovers that are part of Cory Weeds' New York with Weeds tour have congregated. Leading Harlem Groove on the bandstand, as he has for years, is Seleno Clarke on the Hammond B3—what he refers to as "The Beast"—playing juicy organ riffs. Tenor saxophonist Peter Valera is roaming the Legion while playing, even blowing his horn from the floor, much to the delight of the crowd that's enjoying delectable southern food and digging the soulful music. Then sax men from the Vancouver contingent—Weeds and Steve Kaldestad—get in on a jam. Meanwhile, about every ten minutes or so, a local regular at the back yells out, "Yeah, baby!"

It's a raucous scene that's giving everyone here indelible memories. Clarke, the man in a suit and tie known as Harlem's Jazz Ambassador, calmly holds it all together with his classy playing and bandstand dialogue. I quickly realize I need to talk to him to learn more about his life and the musical institution he has nurtured at Post 398. So on a break, we drift to an empty back patio—an oasis from the party in the Legion—for a brief chat.

Seleno Clarke, American Legion Post 398, Harlem, New York, March 16, 2014. Photo by Chris Wong.

Born September 30, 1930, in Poolesville, Maryland, near Washington, D.C., Clarke was the son of a preacher man and grandson of a pianist who taught him how to play. Clarke began his music career as a twenty-four-year-old army veteran who arrived in New York City in 1954, when jazz joints were jumping. He started as a saxophonist, who studied with George Coleman, and performed at the Apollo Theater and various clubs in Harlem. Clarke played in Count Basie's top-flight band. Then he was drawn to the organ and the instrument became his passion. Growing up, Clarke had known the organ solely as a church instrument until he heard Jimmy Smith's jazz wizardry on the B3. After buying his own B3, and realizing that it didn't fit in his Bronx apartment, Clarke asked the commander at Post 398 if he could store it there. The commander agreed on the condition that Clarke play at the Legion.

"We had it [jazz performed in clubs] on every corner in Harlem years ago," he said. "When I bought that organ, I put it in here fifteen years ago to rekindle or redevelop what Harlem used to be about."[17]

Like Dr. Lonnie Smith, Clarke connected with George Benson and the musicians forged a bond. Unlike Smith, Clarke didn't record much or get signed by a big label. Instead, he released obscure 45 rpm 7" singles. Like "Soulful Drop," which came out in 1970 with "Memphis Boogaloo" on the B side. Then released the same year was "Exploitation of Soul," paired with "Stimulation." The songs were short blasts of hard funk and soul, with Clarke's vibrant organ swelling at the core.

It's interesting to ponder why Smith became an international jazz star, while Clarke's reach mainly consisted of a local following at classic Harlem venues like the American Legion, Showmans, and Minton's Playhouse. Saying there's a fine line between making it big and staying in relative obscurity is dramatic, but it's a pat and inadequate explanation for the organists' divergent trajectories. Smith, who also paid his dues in Harlem at the Palm Cafe and Minton's, had an innate ability to convey the organ's warmth and power along with his inimitable style. Clarke also had an intuitive feel for transmitting the organ's resonance, but breakthrough opportunities simply never emerged for him. Despite not making it big, he found fulfillment playing the loop of joints in his beloved Harlem, elsewhere in New York, and on the occasional tour. Above all, Clarke was instrumental in the revival of organ jazz in Harlem. "I feel good," Clarke said about where he was in life. "I'm more laid-back now. When I was younger, I took things a little differently."[18]

When Weeds experienced a Sunday at the Legion with Clarke and Harlem Groove, he knew it would be perfect for his annual New York tour. So Weeds made repeat visits to the Legion with his tour groups and booked Clarke to perform in Vancouver at the Cellar on two occasions.

During Clarke's first engaging appearance at the Cellar, an amusing turn of events became part of the club's lore. Before one of the shows in 2009, Clarke planned to make his own way to the club. Rather than take a cab, Clarke chatted with a limo driver who offered to take him there. But instead of delivering him to Vancouver's West Side, the driver took him to a vanilla downtown establishment that was the exact opposite of a jazz club. Confusion arose because it shared the same name as Weeds' place. After sorting out Clarke's true destination, the driver set out for the right Cellar. In the meantime, Weeds and the rest of the band were worried about the missing Clarke. Weeds, standing on the sidewalk outside the club with the other musicians, would never forget the welcome sight of an enormous stretch limousine pulling up to the curb and a nonchalant Clarke emerging to casually greet them.

Seleno Clarke, the Cellar, January 4, 2013. Photo by Steve Mynett.

Three years after the amazing experience at the Legion, I went back to Harlem to get another soul infusion. While the vibe wasn't as boisterous as the first time, it was satisfying to once again soak up the atmosphere, hear Clarke do his thing on the B3, and chat with the man who was all class. On my way out, from his perch behind the organ, Clarke emphatically asked me to tell Weeds to make sure he returned to Post 398. I promised to do so.

The Doctor and the Ambassador

Seleno Clarke (organ), Cory Weeds (tenor saxophone), Ian Hendrickson-Smith (tenor saxophone), Julian MacDonough (drums), and Dave Sikula (guitar), the Cellar, January 4, 2013. Photo by Vincent Lim.

Just a short month-and-a-half later, on December 28, 2017, Clarke passed away at eighty-seven. More than 500 people signed a petition to rename the portion of the street where the Legion sits as "Seleno Clarke Way." The petition describes his legacy:

> Traditionally a local veterans organization on a small street in Harlem, the American Legion Post 398 transformed into a popular and crowded spot for local and international guests to hear top-quality music, free of charge. He [Clarke] hosted "jam sessions" where musicians of all ages, from children to the elderly, had the opportunity to perform with his band. He mentored many who became professional musicians. Many of his prominent friends visited him and participated in the jam sessions, including George Benson, Lou Donaldson, Eddie Henderson, Jimmy McGriff, Joey DeFrancesco, Dr. Lonnie Smith, Michael Torsone, and Russell Malone, to name a few.[19]

That's a fine legacy, and one that I'm grateful to have experienced firsthand. Being at the Legion with Seleno Clarke holding court was an authentic and glorious experience. It's hard to fully convey what it was like, but perhaps the man at the back eloquently summed it up best: "Yeah, baby!"

20 / BIG G: GEORGE COLEMAN

THE MYSTERY AND magic of jazz are about to unfold. Three of Vancouver's most capable jazz musicians—pianist Miles Black, bassist Jodi Proznick, and drummer Jesse Cahill—are on the bandstand at the jam-packed Cellar. They're primed to play at an especially high-level tonight in the club. Seated in front of them is a giant of the music: tenor saxophonist George Coleman.

For many jazz aficionados, he's best known for performing as a sideman on albums made more than fifty years earlier. As a member of the Miles Davis Quintet in 1963 and 1964, Coleman played on four vital live recordings with the trumpet God: *Miles Davis in Europe*, *Live at the 1963 Monterey Jazz Festival*, *My Funny Valentine*, and *'Four' & More*. He was also a key contributor to Davis' splendid *Seven Steps to Heaven* and Herbie Hancock's modal masterwork, *Maiden Voyage*. Those who go deeper into the music know that Coleman has recorded with many other greats and had a lengthy, consistent, and underrated career as a leader. Over the course of that career, he's forged one of the most distinctive and recognizable sounds on the tenor sax. Certain artists come to mind when thinking about tenor saxophonists born in the 1920s and 1930s who developed a singular sound: Dexter Gordon, John Coltrane, Stan Getz, Johnny Griffin, Hank Mobley, Sonny Rollins, Wayne Shorter, Joe Henderson, and Charles Lloyd, among others. George Coleman indisputably belongs on that list.

After Cellar owner Cory Weeds gives a rousing introduction, the audience applauds warmly and sits silently in rapt anticipation. Coleman blows air through his horn without playing and rapidly presses the keys—his pre-game ritual. Then Coleman decisively calls "Green Dolphin, E-flat, vamp." To the non-musician, these instructions would be incomprehensible. To these players, who are fluent in oral jazz shorthand, they immediately know what to do. Their mission: start the set by playing the 1947 jazz standard "On Green Dolphin Street," in the key of E-flat major (one of two keys it's typically played in), with a piano intro. Without hesitation, Black sets off for eight bars. Then Proznick and Cahill seamlessly join in for another eight bars before Coleman enters. As the rhythm section alternates between a Latin feel and swing, which is how the song is supposed to be done, Coleman plays the tune's timeless melody. Then he improvises a fascinating, one-of-a-kind solo before the other musicians each take solid solo turns. It doesn't feel long, but they explore "Green Dolphin Street" for sixteen absorbing minutes.

For the rest of the set, Coleman doesn't say a word before each tune; he gives no hint about the upcoming song, its key, or tempo. Coleman just starts playing and the musicians figure it all out in a few quick bars. A couple times at the beginning of a tune, Proznick subtly glances at Black, looking for confirmation of where they're heading. The pianist has an exhaustive knowledge of standards and flashes a hand signal to indicate the key. At one point during Coleman's three-night stand, it was Black who needed help from Proznick, who also has an extensive internal database of repertoire. "He only stumped me on one tune," said Black. "That was a fairly easy samba and Jodi knew it, so we got it together."[1]

It all sounds harmonious and rhythmically in sync, even though there hasn't been any prior discussion or rehearsal except for a loose jam, and there's not a scrap of music in front of them. This is the essence of jazz. Only learning hundreds (or for some, thousands) of tunes in different keys, practicing in groups or in solitude, and years of experience performing for audiences can prepare an instrumentalist to confidently play like this. At this echelon, musicians aren't encumbered by having to think about the mechanics of what they're doing. Instead, attuned to each other's every musical gesture, they're playing with a deep intuition that's sublime to witness.

Three months after playing with Black, Proznick, and Cahill at the Cellar, Coleman said this old school approach wasn't meant as a test for the players. "I've just always felt that if you can play, you don't really need a lot of rehearsing," he said. "If you know the songs, and if you're experienced, that's all you need to know. Just play."[2] Coleman has followed that credo throughout his prodigious performing career that's spanned about seven decades.

Miles Black (piano), Jodi Proznick (bass), George Coleman (tenor saxophone), and Jesse Cahill (drums), the Cellar, April 5, 2013. Photo by Vincent Lim.

• • •

George Edward Coleman was born March 8, 1935, in Memphis, Tennessee. He played in bands at Manassas High School around the same time that future jazz men Hank Crawford, Harold Mabern, Frank Strozier, Booker Little, and Charles Lloyd did the same. Early in his career Coleman played alto sax with Ray Charles, and then tenor with B.B. King, but his body of work isn't associated with the idioms of his hometown or points south, such as the Mississippi Delta. That said, there's something very southern and soulful about his sound. And compared with saxophonists who emphasize torrential phrases overflowing with notes, his expression is more nuanced, sounding abstract at times and never hurried.

He paid his dues in Chicago before moving to New York in 1958, when Max Roach came calling with an invitation for Coleman to join the drummer's quintet. It's interesting to listen to six albums Coleman recorded with Roach and Little that year and the next. The tenorist's sound was still developing, but his distinguishing features—his warm tone, fluid phrasing, and harmonic edge—were palpable.

In early 1963, Miles Davis had some vacancies to fill in his band. He had engagements booked but no second or third horn player, and pianist Wynton Kelly and bassist Paul Chambers had left Davis' group. Only drummer Jimmy Cobb remained from the trumpeter's previous ensemble. So Davis hired Coleman, fellow Memphians Strozier on alto and Mabern on piano, and bassist Ron Carter. April 1–3, 1963, this version of the Miles Davis Sextet that was never recorded played in Vancouver at the Inquisition on Seymour. Davis drove himself to Vancouver in his Maserati.

Gavin Walker was at the Inquisition for two of the three nights and recalled that "the band sounded fabulous." Walker sat at one of the shows in the intimate coffeehouse with pianist Al Neil, who played regularly at Vancouver's original Cellar jazz club. (While in Vancouver for the gig with Davis, Coleman and Mabern went to the Cellar, where they heard the fine tenor saxophonist Glenn McDonald, and Mabern played some tunes.) "One thing that really sticks in my mind was Al Neil's prophesy that Miles would keep George and Ron Carter but dump Mabern and Strozier," said Walker.[3] That's exactly what happened, and Coleman would go on to make the magnificent recordings with Davis.

In the early 1970s, Coleman started focusing on leading groups and by 1977, he was recording for the first time as a leader. Waiting close to twenty-five years after he began working as a professional jazz musician to put out his own albums may seem like a very long time, but Coleman wasn't uptight about it. During that quarter-century no one offered him the right terms to do a recording, and—despite having recorded and performed live with the top names in jazz—he didn't feel his playing was at the requisite standard.

His first release—an album of relentlessly exuberant duets with blind Spanish pianist Tete Montoliu that came out as both *Meditation* and *Dynamic Duo*—still holds up tremendously well. On Coleman's second record, released as *Revival* and *Big George*, he leads an octet including Mabern, Strozier, and others. Long out-of-print, it's criminally hard to find the rare album. But if you dig deep enough, you can find snippets of it on the internet. Someone went to the trouble of putting the entire first track, "Green Dolphin Street," on YouTube and pairing it with cute photos of dolphins. Once I came to terms with that goofy juxtaposition, it sunk in that the music hits gloriously hard, in large part because Coleman and the three other saxophonists play ferociously as a unit and as soloists.

Organist Shirley Scott wrote the tune "Big George" for Coleman, and a short version of the title —"Big G"—became his nickname. It's the perfect moniker. While there are tenor saxophonists with a bigger sound or physical stature, there aren't many with a larger presence. When Coleman is merely sitting in a jazz venue (as I experienced at Smoke Jazz Club in New York in 2014), and especially when he's playing, you feel his immense aura.

In 1979, Coleman performed in Victoria on Vancouver Island. That's where then-thirteen-year-old Miles Black lived, and the show was the very first jazz concert Black went to. "At the end of the night I was covered in his spittle, I was sitting so close to his sax," said Black. "So I always say I was baptized in jazz by George Coleman."[4]

In the early 1990s, two Vancouver saxophonists—Ross Taggart and Campbell Ryga—studied with Coleman in New York. The lessons gave both an enormous amount of knowledge that influenced their aesthetic. A key takeaway for Ryga: the imperative to challenge himself, whether that meant learning tunes in twelve keys or exploring harmonic possibilities in improvisation. With the latter, that involved learning a certain rigour when soloing. That, as Ryga explained it, the soloist can "make it angular, and be able to cause tension in the listener's ear, so long as you can resolve it, resolve the idea. I think that is a big part of what I learned from George."[5]

Leap ahead to March 2006. Weeds was taking a lesson in New York with tenor saxophonist Eric Alexander, who Coleman mentored. Weeds handed Alexander a piece of paper with a figure on it. Then Weeds said: "You and Big G at the Cellar for this amount of money. Here are the dates. Do it."[6] The gambit worked. Coleman and Alexander agreed to play at the Cellar for the club's sixth anniversary shows, September 22–23, 2006. Weeds matched the powerful two tenors with Coleman's former student Taggart on piano, Proznick, and Cahill.

Over the years Weeds chose Cahill more than any other Vancouver drummer to play with top artists at the Cellar, and for good reason. Cahill always seemed at ease playing with prominent musicians at Coleman's level. But Cahill was "terrified" the week of the Cellar gigs with Coleman and

Alexander, which also included a night at the Triple Door in Seattle, where the two saxophonists intensely improvised on "Cherokee" in twelve keys. Aside from not revealing many of the tunes they were playing, Coleman didn't count in most of the songs to establish the tempo, a crucial bit of intelligence for any drummer. Off the bandstand, Coleman didn't share whether he liked the locals' playing. Cahill realized, however, that Coleman's taciturn ways weren't meant to be dismissive. There was similar silence when Cahill played at the Cellar with other older musicians like Charles McPherson, Eddie Henderson, and initially with David "Fathead" Newman. "I learned later if they don't say anything to you, then everything is cool," said Cahill.[7]

Proznick vividly remembers how the gigs with Coleman began. "The first set of the first night he turned his back to the audience and just stared at me," said Proznick. "The whole set. And I kept looking up and seeing that he was staring at me, with not really an expression. Just staring. So I closed my eyes." Coleman called "Ceora," a not particularly well-known bossa nova by Lee Morgan. "I was so thrilled when he called 'Ceora,' and I said I know it. I could tell in his face he was like, she knows 'Ceora.'"[8]

Proznick clearly made an impression on Coleman—he described her as a "phenomenal" bass player—as did the other local players. "Vancouver, you're in pretty good shape," said Coleman. "The guys, they can play, and the girls too."[9]

Weeds, who developed a warm friendship with Coleman, observed the bandstand dynamics and gained insight into the tenor titan's motivations. "George isn't demanding perfection," said Weeds. "It's not about whether you know the tune right away and can play it perfectly. It's about can you adjust, do you have ears, and do you know what's going on? I don't think George would have done it if he wasn't confident that the guys—and gal in Jodi's case—could handle it. That's George's vibe. He's a very intense guy, and he's got a very intense aura and persona about him. Once you get past that gruff exterior, that protective exterior, he's a real sweetheart."[10]

Weeds conceived Coleman's second Cellar engagement—April 5–7, 2013—as a tribute to Taggart, who passed away in January 2013. Even though Coleman had essentially retired from touring by that point, he travelled to Vancouver and played the shows. Coleman wanted to honour Taggart, who he saw as a fine student, strong player, and friend.

George Coleman, the Cellar. Photo by Jesse Cahill.

George Coleman, the Cellar. Photo by Jesse Cahill.

Journeys to the Bandstand

• • •

On the Cellar bandstand, Coleman takes things a step further from starting tunes without revealing them. He segues mid-tune into another song, again without advance notice. The band still doesn't miss a beat and stays right with him. In these moments, they're showing their knowledge, listening skills, and proficiency. At the same time, they're learning from a master, receiving unspoken mentorship in the jazz tradition the way it used to be passed on. Witnessing this alchemy brings to mind something Harold Mabern said when talking with him about the elemental pleasures of playing jazz, and why they can't be experienced by everyone. "We jazz musicians love what we're doing because it's a special kind of music," said Mabern. "Where does it come from? You tell me. Does it come from Buddha, Allah, Jesus, or—who's the evolution man? Charles Darwin? But the point is it's special. Jazz musicians are special people and very smart people too. This music is not for dumb people [to play]."[11]

Tenor saxophonist Steve Kaldestad was in the audience when Coleman performed at the Cellar in 2013. Kaldestad watched and listened carefully as Coleman soloed on each tune. "He would play a chorus and it wasn't all genius, but it was kind of probing and feeling his way around, and then another chorus and another, and you realized that he was really getting inside his trip," said Kaldestad. "He's really getting inside his head and going somewhere." Kaldestad was observing and absorbing Coleman's improvisational process, shaped by decades of musical and life experience, unfold. "George Coleman doesn't worry about, 'Oh, I better only take two choruses.' One of the solos might have been ten minutes long, and by the end of it, you are like, 'Man, that was the deepest thing ever.'"[12]

After the show, some Cellar patrons crowd around Coleman at the bar, asking him to sign records. Someone asks what it was like to play with Miles Davis and Herbie Hancock. Coleman signs the records but doesn't say much. Three months later, when I cold-call Coleman and he agrees to do an impromptu interview, Coleman speaks more about those heady days. "It was a good experience, and I took it for what it was worth, and, you know, I survived it."[13]

Survived? "I had a problem with them for a while. With Herbie and Ron [Carter] and Tony Williams. There were certain little things happening in the band that they didn't like. They wanted me to play a certain way, and I didn't want to play that way. I wanted to play along the lines of what Miles had wanted me to play. They wanted to go into the so-called free, avant-garde thing, and I didn't want to do that. But one night I did it just to prove to them that I could do it. After that I didn't play that way anymore. But I did it one night and everybody was surprised, including them, because they didn't know I could do that."[14]

Davis talked about that exact situation with Coleman in the trumpeter's autobiography. According to what Davis and Quincy Troupe wrote, Williams was primarily the one who was negative about Coleman because the saxophonist played almost perfectly instead of being willing to make mistakes. While Davis thought Coleman was a stellar musician, Williams preferred players like another Coleman—Ornette—and Archie Shepp who were at the frontlines of the avant-garde at that time in the sixties. Coleman played according to the chords. But there was that one time he went free with them, in San Francisco, and Davis said that messed with Williams' head.[15] I can picture Coleman calmly going about his business, and then suddenly and forcefully playing completely outside to unequivocally prove a point. Quiet pride, letting his horn do the talking, and resolutely delivering with an individual expression have long been among his hallmarks.

In December 2020, Weeds realized a major project. He and Zev Feldman—his partner in Reel to Real, an imprint of Weeds' Cellar Music Group label—released *The George Coleman Quintet in Baltimore*. It's an archival recording of a performance, presented by Baltimore's Left Bank Jazz Society, that Coleman gave on May 23, 1971, at the Famous Ballroom. Weeds and Feldman went all out, assembling extensive liner notes that honour Coleman.

It's worthy of the deluxe treatment. The historically important recording captures Coleman leading a band six years before his first albums as a leader came out, and he sounds raw and formidable. Weeds: "Coleman is playing with reckless abandon, not concerned with perfection or even precision."[16] That's especially true on the album's version of "Joy Spring," one of the great tunes from *Clifford Brown & Max Roach*, the 1954 hard bop masterpiece. Coleman and the ace band on the Baltimore recording play the melody at a blazing tempo. Then during his solo, after Coleman shifts from playing with the whole band to a drum and sax duo with Harold White, Big G improvises with an unbridled urgency.

Contrast that with the first time I heard Coleman, when—as a teenager—I listened to the title track of Hancock's *Maiden Voyage*. His solo on the tune isn't especially long, but he improvises so melodically and exquisitely, with focused control, that the perfection Davis spoke of when referring to Coleman is within reach.

From his time at the top of the jazz world with Miles, to that wild night in Baltimore, to being down in the Cellar with local heroes, Coleman has played with integrity, harmonic vitality, and a clearly conceived sense of self. Sharing all of that has been a precious gift, for audiences and fellow musicians, that will profoundly endure.

21 / THE RHYTHM SECTION: TILDEN WEBB, JODI PROZNICK, AND JESSE CAHILL

ON A WINTER'S night in December 2004, David "Fathead" Newman and the Vancouver musicians playing with him at Cory Weeds' Cellar Jazz Club begin "Cellar Groove," and the connection is immediate. Right from the first bars of the tune, with a fitting title given the locale and what they're doing, pianist Tilden Webb, bassist Jodi Proznick, and drummer Jesse Cahill are in sync with each other and with the renowned saxophonist they're sharing the bandstand with. Their vibrant union of melody, harmony, and rhythm starts strong and grows over the course of the evening into something exceptional.

Just over seven years later, in February 2012, a similar thing happens. The featured performer is different—ace guitarist Peter Bernstein—but the rhythm section and the venue are exactly the same. As they play Bernstein's "Bones," a tribute to his dog, Webb, Proznick, and Cahill are preternaturally aware of each other and the sublime artist Weeds hired them to complement. They play as a cohesive unit and with the personal expression that's intrinsic to momentous jazz.

It's no wonder that "Cellar Groove" and "Bones" are the opening tracks on live recordings Weeds released of those wondrous performances. The songs epitomize Newman's and Bernstein's artistry, and how Webb, Proznick, and Cahill jointly deliver the elements of a great jazz rhythm section. There were scores of stellar rhythm sections that performed at the Cellar during its long run. Among Vancouver players, this one went the deepest in developing a rapport with premier artists and articulating a distinct, compelling sound. Weeds called the trio "one of the tightest units to ever grace the stage at the Cellar. They make the perfect team because they're so in tune with what one another is doing."[1]

There are clear reasons why this rhythm section is so striking, starting with shared history. They all studied at McGill University in Montreal. After graduating, they eventually went west and joined the Vancouver jazz scene, where they have performed alongside each other regularly. The Cellar was an essential venue for them, as a rhythm section and as members of other ensembles. They are also family: Webb and Proznick are married, and Cahill's partner is Proznick's sister. Aside from all of these commonalities, their individual histories and experiences have shaped the trio's compelling sound.

• • •

Webb was born in Regina, where he had an inspirational band teacher at Sheldon Williams Collegiate, who influenced his decision to pursue music. That's also where he became friends with tenor saxophonist Steve Kaldestad, who would follow a comparable career trajectory. Starting in the 1980s, McGill established a degree-granting jazz program that attracted talented young musicians from across the country. In 1988, Webb enrolled at McGill. Kaldestad, Christine Jensen, Joel Miller, and Kelly Jefferson were among the other jazz talents studying there. For Webb, the school and the Montreal scene formed the perfect environment in which the pianist could learn and gain experience.

While working toward his bachelor's and master's degrees at McGill, Webb gigged with contemporaries and old-guard players in the city's jazz rooms, such as the Upstairs Jazz Bar & Grill and Biddle's Jazz and Ribs. At the inversely named Upstairs, located in a basement, Webb played with visiting artists like saxophonist Mark Turner. "With the Mark Turner thing there was no rehearsal at all," said Webb. "It was just, 'Ok, what songs are we going to play tonight?' It was very much an impromptu kind of thing."[2] Gigs like that would serve Webb well. Playing in singer Ranee Lee's band for about six years was key to his development, as it involved touring internationally and recording with heavy hitters including Ray Brown, Ed Thigpen, David

Murray, Jeff Hamilton, and John Clayton. Webb half-jokingly called these "scary experiences,"[3] which he succeeded in at a young age. Regardless of any spine-chilling junctures, Webb developed a noteworthy style, with melodically eloquent lines in his improv.

Tilden Webb, the Cellar, February 8, 2013. Photo by Steve Mynett.

After beginning on piano and making a miserable attempt at learning oboe, at thirteen, Proznick started playing an instrument she hadn't seen many girls or women play: electric bass. Proznick's father was her band teacher at Semiahmoo Secondary School in the Vancouver suburb of Surrey. David Proznick was a legendary music educator known by his students as "Proz," who also taught his other children Tim and Kelly Proznick (now Cahill's wife) and many others like Jillian Lebeck and Amanda Tosoff, who became professional musicians. During the Lionel Hampton Jazz Festival in Moscow, Idaho, thirteen-year-old Jodi sat near the stage in complete delight as master double bassist Ray Brown played a solo that was one of the most joyful things she had ever heard. By sixteen, she was playing upright bass, and her path was set.

Like Webb, Proznick embraced the opportunity for intensive learning at McGill and playing gigs in Montreal. While she switched from majoring in jazz performance to music education in her second year, with thoughts of becoming a high school music teacher like her dad, Proznick wanted to keep playing. She met Webb when he coached an ensemble that she was in. "He was a very young master's student, so we are not that far apart in age," said Proznick. "He was really impressive. Articulate, and a very good teacher."[4]

Right after graduating from McGill, Proznick got a gig playing several nights a week at Kaizen Sushi Bar on Sainte-Catherine with two storied Montreal jazz musicians: guitarist Greg Clayton and tenor saxophonist Paul "Boogie" Gaudet. There were never any charts, and initially she didn't know all the tunes they played. Over time she learned core jazz repertoire. "Playing with Greg and Boogie gave me this real-time experience that I then brought here [to Vancouver]," she said. "Basically, the seeds were planted, and the Cellar was the garden where this information got to grow and get a chance to be nurtured."[5]

Webb and Proznick moved to the West Coast in 2000. They were among McGill alumni, including Mike Allen, Dave Robbins, Denzal Sinclaire, Mike Rud, Steve Bokudo Holy, Kaldestad, Cahill, and others—along with Concordia grads such as Bill Coon and Jill Townsend—who migrated to Vancouver in the nineties and the following decade. All would make immense contributions to the city's jazz scene. The timing was perfect for Webb and Proznick: the Cellar opened the year they arrived.

Not long after they settled here, I met Proznick in the unlikeliest of circumstances. I was on the board of my daughter's bilingual preschool, and I was tasked with interviewing applicants for a music teacher position. In walked Proznick for an interview. Given her McGill degree and outgoing, enthusiastic manner, she easily got the gig and "Miss Jodi" was a hit with the children. When I think back to that time, it's a reminder of how hard Proznick worked to build a self-sustaining musical life while establishing herself in Vancouver's jazz scene.

Then there's Cahill. Born in Victoria, he grew up immersed in music. His father David Cahill was a master guitar technician, luthier, and musician who ran Old Town Strings for forty-seven years. At home, R&B, blues, rock, and bluegrass albums spun on the record player. Cahill got a snare drum at twelve and borrowed a drum set the next year. Jazz drew him in, and Cahill learned how to play it the old school way: listening to countless records borrowed from the library and emulating what he heard.

Attending month-long Banff Centre for the Arts' jazz workshops in the summers of 1993 and 1994 was important and ear-opening for Cahill. Core and guest faculty at the workshops included Hugh Fraser, Kenny Wheeler, Jim Hall, Don Thompson, and others. "I remember it was very, very intense and you played all day, every day," said Cahill. He was mostly "terrified" and "trying not to suck." It was also Cahill's first experience of "when people don't like what you're doing [playing], and having them really tell you they don't like what you're doing."[6] Cahill was a green and unformed drummer at the time, but he was already building his confidence armour, so the frank critiques didn't throw him off.

Jesse Cahill, the Cellar, August 20, 2010. Photo by Steve Mynett.

Cahill, who started at McGill at the same time as Proznick in 1993, said students in the university's jazz program at the time had a shared passion for playing "in a very specific kind of way."[7] Cahill explained what he meant by referring to Miles Davis' two great quintets that were active from the mid-1950s to the late sixties, with the likes of John Coltrane, Bill Evans, Paul Chambers, Herbie Hancock, Wayne Shorter, Tony Williams, and other top musicians. In other words, Cahill and his McGill compatriots dug the hard bop and post-bop that those seminal ensembles played so transcendently.

Putting into practice what he listened to and learned was another matter. Cahill figured out that if he went to his instructors' gigs and waited until the last set, often as late as one or two a.m., opportunities would arise to sit in. He was never shy about seizing those opportunities.

After graduating, Cahill worked on cruise ships and moved back to Victoria, where he got busy as a freelance drummer. But he wanted more. Cahill cold-called Weeds, whom he hadn't met, and landed his first gig at the Cellar. While leading a band with Brad Turner, Mike Rud, and Proznick at the club, Cahill took note of what he observed. It was a bona fide jazz club, where people truly listened. The Cellar wasn't the only reason why Cahill moved to Vancouver, but it was an important factor. For the first few years, though, things were slow, and he mainly played R&B. "I was lucky if I had two or three [jazz] gigs in a month."[8]

• • •

Transitioning from music student to professional jazz musician is a gradual process without fixed demarcation lines. That said, there are shit-is-getting-real moments that can arise suddenly. For Proznick, it was when Weeds asked her to play at the Cellar with longtime Charles Mingus sideman Charles McPherson, Ross Taggart, and Blaine Wikjord in July 2002. She called the gig "scary"[9] because it was her first time playing with an historically important musician like McPherson, and on top of that, Weeds recorded it for release on his Cellar Live label.

Despite the pressure, the shows went tremendously well. "He [McPherson] was really, really kind to me but also really direct about what I could do to move forward," said Proznick. "He was very encouraging, but he was also, 'You need more vocabulary in your playing.'" Looking back at the performance that Weeds released as *Live at the Cellar*, and some other recordings at the time, Proznick gave a candid self-assessment. "The first few records on the label [that Proznick played on] I have a hard time listening to, to be honest. Because you know, I would have been twenty-three, twenty-four at the time, so really still growing."[10] Clearly Proznick played well enough, as she was chosen to perform with the alto saxophonist again in 2004. I also asked McPherson about Proznick, and he praised her. "Jodi was very good," McPherson said emphatically.[11]

Jodi Proznick, the Cellar, December 13, 2005. Photo by Steve Mynett.

"I wouldn't have done so well on the Charles McPherson gig," said Webb. "There were certain gigs that he [Weeds] wouldn't call me for, and I think for very good reason. I would have probably melted down in that situation. I would have been in the fetal position in tears in the middle of the stage by the second set."[12] Webb knew himself well enough to recognize that a piano assignment that called for mainly playing up-tempo standards with a bebop vibe was better suited to Taggart.

Weeds excelled in figuring out which local musicians were the best fit to play with visiting artists at the Cellar. When he booked tenor saxophonist and flutist David "Fathead" Newman to perform November 28–29, 2003, Weeds' intuition told him to line up Webb, Proznick, and Cahill for the gigs. It was an astute decision that would pay major dividends.

Newman—known for his dynamic playing with Ray Charles, accomplished career as a leader, and endearing nickname—came prepared with thoughts about songs he wanted to play and sheet music for those tunes. "Fathead showed up with a mountain of charts," said Webb. "In the grand scheme of things, he was pretty well-organized compared to a lot of the guys [other visiting artists at the Cellar]."[13] But before the first downbeat, Newman was unsure about the locals' musical level. As it turned out, the shows went very well and by the end of the weekend, Newman was impressed with their playing. "They're exceptionally talented young musicians, and they've worked very well with my musical plan," Newman said.[14]

Weeds thought the music they performed together was sensational, so he booked Newman for a return engagement—with the same rhythm section—December 11 and 12, 2004. Weeds arranged for keyboardist/recording engineer Chris Gestrin to record both nights for a Cellar Live release. As Newman was under contract with HighNote Records, the workaround that emerged was to release the recording as the Tilden Webb Trio, with "Special Guest David Fathead Newman."

All went well except for hiccups with two songs Webb wrote: "Lady J" and "Round About." Webb wanted to do a few original tunes. He had sent Newman the music in advance but at a rehearsal, an issue emerged: "David didn't read music," said Weeds, so Newman struggled to play Webb's unfamiliar melodies. "Tilden was trying to do damage control," added Weeds. "'Let's just do a standard, let's just do something that you know,'" Webb said to Newman, as Weeds recalled. "And David was, 'No, no, I really want to do your tunes.' He just would have none of it. He had to do those tunes because David's vibe was that he learned on the bandstand. That's the way he had done it his whole life, so needless to say, the tunes didn't go very well at the actual gig," explained Weeds. "Of course, the solos were amazing, but the melodies he had trouble with just because he didn't have enough time to learn them. But at that point, we needed them to be on the record because it was Tilden's record. So we literally stayed after the gig had ended and played through those tunes about seven or eight times until we could get it [close] enough to the point where we [Gestrin] could piece together the melodies."[15]

The soft-spoken Webb and the other trio members stuck with the process, while staying ever mindful to show respect to Newman. As it turned out, the final versions of Webb's songs were more than fine, and there were no perceptible glitches. *Cellar Groove*, released in 2005, is the aural equivalent of deeply satisfying comfort food. It's a musically nourishing album because of each player's vigorous contributions and the tangible, cross-generational rapport between Newman and the rhythm section.

The album ends with "A Night in Tunisia," and after the fiery version of Dizzy Gillespie's classic, Newman introduces the band in his soft voice: "Mr. Jesse Cahill, ladies and gentlemen, Jesse Cahill on drums . . . The young lady on the bass, the awesome Miss Jodi Proznick . . . And the leader of this trio, ladies and gentlemen, Mr. Tilden Webb . . ."[16] Even in these concise introductions, you can hear in Newman's tone his genuine admiration for the three. Newman, Webb, Proznick, and Cahill "really, really connected"—on and off-stage—said Newman's wife Karen, who travelled with her husband to Vancouver. "They [the trio] became a real intense part of our lives."[17]

Newman performed a third time with what was now essentially his Vancouver band at the Cellar November 4 and 5, 2005, to celebrate the release of *Cellar Groove*. He also briefly toured with the trio, including two nights at Seattle's Triple Door and a night at Portland's Blue Monk. The rhythm section members were proud and honoured that Newman, a celebrated American musician, chose to perform in the US with them (Canadians who required paperwork to legally play in the States). Webb saw Newman's gesture as an invaluable gift to him and his bandmates.[18]

Playing consecutive nights with Newman, the trio got to see the saxophonist/flutist elevate his playing. "He kind of put it in an extra gear, maybe after we played a third night consecutively," said Webb. "I remember a couple of times, after having played a few nights with him, going, 'Wow, I hadn't heard that before; that's something new, he's turning it up a notch tonight.'"[19]

Cahill concurred. "One of the things I noticed with David is every night would be better. The first night would be good, but by the last night he would be getting to this other level, and you would sort of start to see and hear this whole other depth of musicality that I think people of my generation have really missed out on."[20] Cahill went deeper with his analysis, noting how the opportunities to play for consecutive nights to live audiences have decreased since the years of Newman's heyday:

> When Fathead would have been twenty years old, to the time he was say forty, for a twenty-year period it was probably highly unusual that he went two or three days without playing. I don't mean just practicing. I mean being on the

bandstand in front of a big audience playing at the highest level with Ray Charles, with a really great band. Playing in the same place for a week, two weeks in a row, three weeks, or a month at a time at the same club, playing three sets a night every night, then rehearsing during the day or recording. The amount of performing that people of his generation did versus what guys like me have available to us is a whole other thing. And I felt when I would play with somebody like him [Newman] or George [Coleman] or any of these people [other greats Cahill played with at the Cellar and elsewhere], when it would start to hit, you could see it, and then you are like, 'Oh, it's almost there, I can almost touch it.' I would be like, 'Pull me up to your level.'[21]

Fascinating insights that Cahill discerned because he's a lifelong student of non-academic jazz history, plus the drummer was right there on the bandstand with Newman, fully engaged with a performer who conjured soulful greatness.

Newman wanted to tour more with the Vancouver players and record with them in the US. Those plans didn't come to fruition, however, because he passed away January 20, 2009, of pancreatic cancer at seventy-five. "He was a gentleman—kind hearted and so supportive on the bandstand. I miss him dearly," said Proznick.[22] "It doesn't always happen this way, but there was a genuine human-to-human connection. I really felt that with him."[23]

Ottawa Citizen jazz critic Peter Hum contacted Webb not long after learning that Newman had passed, and the pianist shared warm remembrances. "What strikes me looking back today was how kind, supportive, and generous a person he was," Webb told Hum. "He was so encouraging to Jodi, Jesse, and myself, always treating us with the utmost respect. He gave us lots of room to stretch out on the bandstand and often encouraged me to take another chorus. His vibe on stage was so great. It was an absolute privilege to play with him." Also: they called him "David."[24]

The Rhythm Section

David "Fathead" Newman, the Cellar, March 28, 2007. Photo by Steve Mynett.

• • •

Over the years, there were many other indelible moments the rhythm section delivered at the Cellar. In 2004, Weeds booked New Yorkers Eddie Henderson and Ian Hendrickson-Smith to perform with the trio. The day of the first gig, the Cellar's piano collapsed after a leg buckled, so Webb had to switch to a Rhodes, which was no problem because he's capable on the electric piano. Although few patrons showed up, the music was fantastic.

About two years later, Proznick recorded her debut album, *Foundations*, with Kaldestad, Webb, and Cahill. Released on Cellar Live, *Foundations* is an absorbing first statement from Proznick as a leader. On originals by Proznick and interpretations of tunes by Joni Mitchell, Duke Ellington, and others, her bass playing sounds assured and warmly evocative. Proznick's solos on the album illustrate that she's a stirring improviser. The quartet played the repertoire during memorable shows at the Cellar and on a Canadian tour.

Kaldestad doesn't have family ties to Webb, Proznick, and Cahill like they have with each other, but the saxophonist developed a close familial bond with the rhythm section. In 2000, Kaldestad moved to London,

England, where he became a busy freelance musician. Despite the distance, Proznick wanted Kaldestad to play on *Foundations* and in performances. While remaining committed to London, he returned to Canada to play with Proznick and the band. Kaldestad soon realized how satisfying it was to make music with them.

"I had been in Britain playing with all sorts of great musicians, but as soon as I played with Jesse, Tilden, and Jodi, I just felt like, 'I feel so comfortable playing with these people,'" said Kaldestad. "I didn't need to ask myself, 'What is my style, how should I play, how should I approach the music?' . . . I was in such a supportive environment that I could just be myself."[25] His connection with the rhythm section, re-connecting at the Cellar with another Jodi he knew from years before who came to hear him play (they would eventually marry), and the vitality of the club and its owner Weeds all compelled Kaldestad to move to Vancouver in 2008.

Over the years, Kaldestad—along with other musicians and Cellar patrons—saw how Webb, Proznick, and Cahill were indispensable to the club. It seemed at times the trio was the Cellar house band. Weeds trusted the musicians implicitly. As Webb was regularly booked for gigs in contexts outside of jazz and the Cellar, variations of the trio heard at the club could include Proznick and/or Cahill with other players. The bassist and drummer, along with Ross Taggart, backed up tenor titans George Coleman and Eric Alexander in 2006. Proznick, Cahill, and Miles Black also accompanied Coleman in 2013. Both engagements were challenging, think-on-your-feet situations. The locals met the standard required.

Proznick and Cahill played at the club with Alexander and the magnificent pianist Harold Mabern in 2011. "I enjoyed playing with both of them, especially the young lady on the bass because I've always been pro females playing music because they don't get a lot of respect the way they should," said Mabern.[26]

For Proznick, receiving respect from male musicians hasn't been an issue, with rare exceptions. One of those happened during a two-night gig at the Cellar with some visiting musicians. On the first night, one of the musicians behaved inappropriately. Proznick felt so uncomfortable that she debated whether to come back the next night. The bassist returned, and there were no further issues.[27]

Proznick was one of the few female instrumentalists who played frequently at the Cellar, especially in the club's early years. When she performed with McPherson for the first time, being in such a clear and visible minority made her somewhat insecure:

> I felt very self-conscious that I was a woman, and having a picture of Mingus on my bedroom wall in university and knowing what he looked like and that I didn't look like him, I was imagining Charles McPherson walking in the room, seeing me, and thinking, 'What the hell, Cory? Really? This was the best you could do?' I often would feel that when they would meet me because I looked like a kindergarten teacher. For the most part, everyone was really polite and the minute we started to play, they were super encouraging and really celebratory; they were thrilled that I could play because, at the end of the day, they just wanted to play good music.[28]

As we sat in a café talking about this, Webb gallantly downplayed his partner's "I looked like a kindergarten teacher" line: "They [visiting musicians] were probably looking at me in the same way. 'How's this guy going to screw up my night?' kind of thing before they heard me play."[29] Webb also concisely noted something essential about Proznick: "People always respond to what she does." She emits both energy and musicality that inspires that response.

From Kaldestad's perspective, he witnessed Webb's steady growth—from high school to McGill to the Vancouver scene—as an exemplary jazz pianist and diligent professional. Like Webb's perfect posture he always has when sitting behind a piano or electric keyboard, primary elements of his playing—empathic comping and flowing improvisation—are continually in alignment with what's being performed and who's with him on the bandstand. "And the other thing that's really interesting about Tilden is that it is never, ever, ever about him," said Proznick. "It's always about the music."[30]

The one time I saw Webb shine a light on himself was subtle. Jazz promoter Tim Reinert posted a Facebook appreciation of David Murray's glorious tenor sax playing, and Webb replied with a screenshot showing credits for Ranee Lee's beautiful *Seasons Of Love* album. Webb played piano on the recording and arranged the tunes, including four tracks featuring Murray.

Reinert was amazed and asked how he didn't know about this. Webb responded: "Haha. I'm the jazz Forrest Gump."[31] True to form, Webb was modest and downplayed his accomplishments.

As for Proznick, she kept adding to her résumé, playing with McPherson, Ed Thigpen, Oliver Gannon, Coleman, Newman, Mabern, Bucky Pizzarelli, Russell Malone, Sheila Jordan, PJ Perry, and others. That top-level experience helped Proznick get "thick-skinned" and bolstered her confidence, observed Kaldestad. "So then you stop being fazed by anybody, which I think she has arrived at. Jodi can play with anybody."[32]

Tilden Webb (piano), Jodi Proznick (bass), Russell Malone (guitar), and Jesse Cahill (drums), the Cellar, February 9, 2013. Photo by Vincent Lim.

Meanwhile, perhaps more than any other musician who performed at the Cellar, Cahill constantly initiated ideas for projects that led to gigs and recordings. "He was calling me like every week, 'Oh man, we should do this,'" said Weeds,[33] who appreciated—for the most part—receiving the drummer's pitches. It helped that their musical tastes are simpatico and Cahill always delivers behind the drum kit, swinging like crazy, which is why Weeds keeps hiring him. During my first few times hearing Cahill, I wondered if he was too loud. Then after getting to know his sound, I realized I confounded his active drumming style with excessive volume. Cahill, when keeping time or soloing, is never tentative; he strikes the drums and cymbals with intention, which invigorates any band he plays with. "He's just a really awesome, very, very knowledgeable, and committed musician," said Proznick about her bandmate and brother-in-law,[34] who does in fact play at the right volume.

An example of Cahill's enterprise is the Nightcrawlers, his soulful quintet that dishes out greasy jazz. Co-led with Weeds, the group played numerous shows at the club and released albums on Cellar Live, and continues to perform and record. Then there was the brilliantly named Creed Taylor Appreciation Society (C.T.A.S.), which Cahill and Weeds put together to play at the Cellar as an homage to Taylor's CTI Records label.

Weeds booked Hammond B3 organist Pat Bianchi and drummer Ralph Peterson Jr. to perform two nights with guitarist Bill Coon at the Cellar in April 2011. Cahill was looking forward to hearing the band on the second night. An excellent photographer, Cahill was getting his camera equipment ready so he could photograph the band when Weeds called. "Weeds is like, 'Hey man, can you come and do this gig? Ralph's kind of getting deported.' And I'm like, 'What?!' So I went down there, and we played."[35] Weeds recorded that night's performance and released what Cahill calls an "accidental recording" on Cellar Live in 2012 as *Crazy*. Cahill's fearlessness and ability to quickly pivot saved the gig and recording, and the organ trio burned hot.

Jesse Cahill, April 27, 2014. Photo by Chris Wong.

In the Cellar's final years, Webb, Proznick, and Cahill played less at the club as a unit, but the trio still had some more standout gigs there. Weeds chose them to play with Peter Bernstein, February 24 and 25, 2012, and it was arguably the rhythm section's quintessential performance at the Cellar. As documented on a crisp recording of the shows that Weeds released in 2013, the musicians create an exquisite sound. While Bernstein plays the melodies beautifully and improvises with the unwavering focus that makes him a master jazz guitar player, the other three do their thing: Webb comps with a supportive touch and improvises fluid lines; regardless if she's playing a walking bass line or soloing, Proznick radiates musical bliss; and Cahill both keeps time precisely and shows his self-assured personality through fills and solos.

Veteran jazz critic Bill Milkowski gave the album a four-star review in *DownBeat* magazine. "They did great," said Bernstein about the trio. He knows that playing with local rhythm sections doesn't always work. "You never know what to expect. But I heard them on CD, and I had heard Jodi play live before and Jesse too, so I knew that they were cool."[36]

There were parallels between playing with Coleman and Bernstein. Both New Yorkers generally took an old school approach of starting songs without either giving a heads-up of what they were going to play or having much discussion. It wasn't as stressful as it sounds. In fact, playing this way created an edgy vibe that positively impacted the music. "With guys like Peter and George it's very much just keeping the energy on the edge a little bit," said Proznick. "It's almost like the cat chasing the mouse, kind of chasing each other to realize the music."[37]

• • •

After the Cellar was no more, I wondered if the loss of gigs would hit them—especially Proznick and Cahill—harder than other Vancouver jazz musicians. They didn't seem to miss a beat, continuing to substantively contribute to the scene. Weeds' launch of live jazz at Frankie's in 2015 helped fill the void and gave them a dependable outlet for their talents. Plus, they are versatile and in-demand musicians: Webb has played tons of reggae and other genres; Cahill has delineated a rockabilly beat with Cousin Harley; and Proznick's upcoming gigs lists are always very long because she's called on for numerous projects that can be pure jazz or cross-genre, such as

Vetta Chamber Music (tango/klezmer/jazz) and SGaanaGwa (traditional Haida music/jazz/blues/folk/rock).

In November 2017 at Frankie's, Proznick, the same musicians who had played on *Foundations* eleven years earlier, and singer Laila Biali gave a heartfelt performance to celebrate the release of an album they recorded together that year. *Sun Songs*, Proznick's second recording as a leader, shows how much her perspective evolved over its long gestation. While *Foundations* is upbeat, like her personality, *Sun Songs* is an intensely personal meditation on birth and death. Proznick composed almost all the music—combining resonant jazz and intelligent pop—and some of the lyrics. All told, the songs represent an affecting expression of her artistic vision and emotional self-awareness.

Sun Songs also conveys the rhythm section's synergy that's stayed intact and grown. "I think you hear on the recordings [they've made together] that there is a connection and an understanding of each other's personalities," said Proznick about the progression of the trio's sound over the years. For *Sun Songs*, Proznick wrote some tunes with Cahill's musical persona—his vigorous character on the drumkit and the grooves he excels at—in mind. As for Webb, Proznick said he's been the "secret sauce" for recordings she's put out as a leader.[38] Her pride in their partnership comes clearly across.

Playing together with family also brings its own pressures and setbacks. "Like any relationship, it's not all just rainbows and butterflies," said Proznick in 2018. "Sometimes it's challenging. We have gone through loss, deaths in our families, and challenges with my mom [who was diagnosed with early onset dementia not long after Proznick and Webb's son Tristan was born]. It's hard to just put that all aside and get on the bandstand together. The relationship has been generally really great, but it isn't always easy. Tilden and I playing, it is not always easy, but it's a long game. We will be playing together for many, many, many years to come, I am sure."[39]

Jodi Proznick and Tilden Webb, April 15, 2014. Photo by Chris Wong.

Three months after Proznick spoke those words, her mom Patricia died. Cahill's dad David passed away the year before, and in 2020, Webb's father Stan—who sang in choirs and played trombone—also died. It was a rough few years, where they all experienced loss. Then the COVID-19 pandemic transformed musical life as they knew it. When live music was shut down, they adjusted as much as they could, performing on live streams that Weeds organized.

As the pandemic continued, Proznick adapted further. The bassist, Toronto pianist Amanda Tosoff, and arts administrator Francesca Fung launched Music Arts Collective, an online music school. Conversations between Proznick and Tosoff that engendered the collective solidified their sisterhood. "It's hard to meet true, true friends," said Tosoff. "Not only is she [Proznick] that, she's like family, but she is also just an amazing musician who I admire and learn so, so much from. We have endless brainstorms about things we want to do, and it's pretty awesome to have her in my life, so thank you COVID."[40]

As part of the collective's work and in musical projects she took on, Proznick advocated for women in music more assertively than ever. Just

The Rhythm Section

before the pandemic began in 2019, I saw her perform with the all-female Sister Jazz Orchestra in the big band's debut concert, which felt like an important moment in elevating the profile of women in jazz.

Observing from afar, I could see Proznick was in a harmonious place, energized to share her knowledge and continue to creatively evolve as a performer. A post she shared on Facebook in September 2020 confirmed her self-actualization:

> Sometimes when I am playing, I feel an immense sense of peace. It's taken years to get there. I had to unpack and work through my deep feelings of fear and inadequacy. Thankfully, playing music has now become a space where I can dwell in all of the good things about being human—flow, joy, tranquility, imagination, spirit, sensuality, connection. So much of my passion for music education comes from a desire to mentor others so that they can taste this state of being—and to understand that they are already walking, talking, works of art.[41]

• • •

It came out of nowhere, an artifact from the not-too-distant past. During the pandemic, Weeds had time to reflect on the Cellar years, and he remembered a live recording of baritone saxophonist Gary Smulyan and trumpeter Joe Magnarelli with the rhythm section. Weeds had intended to release the recording after it was made at the club in 2011, but it got lost in the jazz life. After a decade passed, he put it out in November 2021. There's nothing groundbreaking about the music. It's a blowing session including five hard bop tunes with cool titles like "Eracism" and "Conundrum." But I was surprised by how strongly I responded to the music. It was thrilling to discover a document of Webb, Proznick, and Cahill hitting hard in their robust support of a kick-ass frontline and one another. Hearing the applause after solos and at the end of songs transported me back to the magical time when the trio was the beloved, go-to unit at the Cellar.

Three months later, I witnessed all three members of the rhythm section in action. The setting was Weeds' three-day Jazz @ The Bolt festival in Burnaby.

I kept seeing Cahill on stage that weekend because he was booked to perform with so many bands, which affirmed his continuing value to Weeds and the scene. As always, Cahill's vital pulse propelled the ensembles he played with.

Proznick and Webb were also busy at the festival. Proznick enjoyed a pivotal moment: the first public performance of an all-female septet that came together in large part because of her vision and co-leadership with Tosoff: the Ostara Project. Named after the Germanic goddess of spring and dawn, the Ostara Project includes outstanding musicians from various Canadian cities. While listening to the band play original compositions with absolute joy in their stirring set, it was clear that like Artemis—the Ostara Project's all-female equivalent in the US—the Canadian group makes a strong statement about the collective power of women who have chosen to express themselves together.

Co-developing Ostara Project is consistent with Proznick's evolution on gender disparity in jazz. In the early Cellar days, she didn't think a lot about why there weren't many women playing alongside her; her priority then was simply playing at the standard that was expected. These days, while that disparity is slowly changing, Proznick critically questions why there aren't more women playing jazz. She's also doing something about it, through her work as an educator and music with Ostara Project, which will inspire young women and men. The day after the ensemble's striking live debut, Ostara Project went into a studio to record a heartening album that Cellar Music released in November 2022. The group's emergence felt significant and inspired optimism about the possibilities of jazz to change and progress.

When I saw that Peter Bernstein would perform at Weeds' festival in various configurations, including a quartet with Webb, Proznick, and Cahill, I got excited. It had been almost exactly a decade since they last played together, at the Cellar when they made their live recording that has absorbed me so profoundly. In the intervening years, Bernstein kept delivering his evocative jazz guitar sound, and each of the rhythm section players continued to develop their instrumental voice.

The Ostara Project: Amanda Tosoff (piano), Jocelyn Gould (guitar), Joanna Majoko (vocals), Jodi Proznick (bass), Rachel Therrien (trumpet), Sanah Kadoura (drums), and Allison Au (alto saxophone), Shadbolt Centre for the Arts, February 13, 2022. Photo by Vincent Lim.

Just before their festival set began, I had a hopeful premonition that they would start with "Bones." Sure enough, the reunited musicians immediately slid into the paean to the guitarist's best canine friend. Just like how they did it back in the day, Bernstein played the tune's first two notes alone before the rest of the band joined in. Despite not meeting on a bandstand for years, they were comfortably in the pocket. Their connection was immediate, meaningful, timeless.

22 / KEEPING IT REAL: ROY MCCURDY

IT'S 1963, AND Roy McCurdy is working the night shift at the sprawling Eastman Kodak factory in Rochester, New York. His work as a film tester involves spot checking giant rolls of film for defects. It's more graveyard than even the shift's hours imply: to avoid exposing the film, he works in near total darkness. The job is thoroughly tedious and soul-crushing.

On breaks, McCurdy listens as his co-workers—many of whom have worked there for years—talk about making enough money to go on holiday somewhere special like Europe or Asia. McCurdy thinks to himself, 'That's what I was doing, traveling all over the world playing music and getting paid for it. And here I am, back here doing this.'[1]

Self-aware moments like this told McCurdy that life had to have much more in store for him. Before working this dead-end job, he had established himself as a world-class jazz drummer, capable of holding his own with some of the artform's masters. Yet McCurdy put down his sticks and brushes, choosing instead to toil in a dark place. He would soon find out what fate would decree for him.

• • •

Roy McCurdy was born in Rochester on November 28, 1936. When he was eight years old, McCurdy started playing drums. By his teenage years, McCurdy knew being a drummer was what he wanted to do with his life. While still in high school, he started studying with William Street at the

Eastman School of Music. By sixteen, McCurdy was working professionally, playing in bands such as a blues group with a whimsical name: Count Rabbit and his Bunnies. He was also called to play in rhythm sections with visiting artists. One such artist was exceptional trumpeter Roy Eldridge. Another was the legendary alto saxophonist and singer Eddie "Cleanhead" Vinson. Because McCurdy was still a minor, his father had to accompany him to clubs where the drummer played.

After a stint in an Air Force band, McCurdy connected with fellow Rochester natives and Eastman students Chuck and Gap Mangione. They played together at the Pythodd, one of Rochester's main jazz clubs. When they heard that Cannonball Adderley would play at Toronto's Town Tavern, the friends drove three hours to make the show. They ended up meeting Adderley on the trip and must have made the most of the opportunity because soon after, the star saxophonist recorded the Mangione Brothers Sextet—including twenty-three-year-old McCurdy—for the "A Cannonball Adderley Presentation" imprint of Riverside Records. Adderley produced the 1960 New York City sessions that resulted in *The Jazz Brothers*. The music was straight-ahead hard bop, which in no way foreshadowed the smooth jazz that Chuck blew through his flugelhorn seventeen years later on the mega-hit "Feels So Good."

Roy McCurdy, second from the right.

In New York City, McCurdy played with the Mangione group for two weeks at the historic Five Spot. It was there that trumpeter/flugelhornist Art Farmer heard the band. Back in Rochester, a few weeks later, McCurdy received a telegram from Farmer. In it he asked McCurdy to go to New York and join the Jazztet, a sextet co-led by Farmer and tenor saxophonist Benny Golson. McCurdy went, and when he saw a long line of musicians outside the original Birdland on Broadway at 52nd St., he realized Farmer's invitation was actually to participate in an audition.

The jazz planets were aligned for McCurdy that day. He auditioned, got the gig, rehearsed with the band for a few days, and then made his Jazztet and Birdland debut. "It was incredible," he said about playing in the hallowed club for the first time. "It was a club you had heard about all your life, and here you are playing there."[2] That night, premier jazz drummers Max Roach and Philly Joe Jones were in the audience. That was the equivalent of a young dancer performing at the Metropolitan Opera House with Mikhail Baryshnikov and Rudolf Nureyev sitting in the front row. It was also a double-bill with John Coltrane and his quartet that included another extraordinary drummer, Elvin Jones. No pressure.

McCurdy stayed with the Jazztet for about a year, recording *Here and Now* and *Another Git Together* with the group in 1962. McCurdy also played on an album led by Farmer, *Perception*, alongside pianist Harold Mabern. Plus, around that time, McCurdy started performing with vocalist Betty Carter.

Then tenor sax colossus Sonny Rollins asked McCurdy to join his group, including Canadian pianist Paul Bley and bassist Henry Grimes, and they performed in July 1963 at the Newport Jazz Festival. That's where a tenor titan who Rollins idolized, Coleman Hawkins, played a few tunes with the band. About a week later, the same musicians (plus bassist Bob Cranshaw) went into an NYC studio to record *Sonny Meets Hawk!* The two-day session, encompassing both tradition and the avant-garde, begat a landmark recording. "There was no preparation," said McCurdy about the session. "It was basically going in and doing those tunes."[3] On one of the songs, "All The Things You Are," Bley played a solo that Pat Metheny, Lee Konitz, and others have lauded as one of the most transformational and profound improvisations in the history of jazz. McCurdy is never mentioned when the solo is discussed, but he was right there, laying down a sturdy rhythmic foundation.

In 1964, McCurdy played on Rollins' next album—*Now's the Time*—alongside Thad Jones on cornet, pianist Herbie Hancock, and bassists Ron Carter and Cranshaw. The first time McCurdy played outside the US was with Rollins and Betty Carter in Japan. McCurdy went on to tour extensively with Rollins internationally. McCurdy was clearly ascending rapidly.

Despite the many high-level situations McCurdy had already excelled in, he walked away from all of it. McCurdy returned to Rochester and drifted away into the Eastman Kodak factory job to "save a marriage." He explained: "Although I was out there playing with Sonny and those people at that time, she [his wife at the time] kind of wanted me to just stay home and not play. We had a kid, so I decided to go back to Rochester and try it."[4]

It wasn't working. Accustomed to the excitement and creativity of the bandstand and recording studio, McCurdy's factory work bored him. It didn't help that while listening to jazz radio at work, McCurdy would occasionally hear tracks that included himself on drums. Meanwhile, New York was calling. Numerous musicians asked him to return to NYC and play. Horace Silver was one of them. Incredibly, McCurdy turned the pianist down.

Then this happened: Louis Hayes left Cannonball Adderley's Quintet to join Oscar Peterson, creating a plum job opening behind the drum kit. Adderley, who remembered McCurdy from the Mangione Brothers band, called the drummer at his house in Rochester when some friends were over. This wasn't another Jazztet situation, where McCurdy was just getting a chance to audition. Adderley, who wanted a hard-swinging drummer to bring fire to his band, got right to the point—could McCurdy join the group, almost immediately?

McCurdy kept Adderley on the line, put his hand over the phone, and told his friends what was happening. McCurdy's buddies gave clear advice: "Listen, you gotta take this one," they said.[5] "If you don't take this one, we're going to kick your butt."[6] McCurdy said yes to the offer. A few weeks later, McCurdy was playing in Atlantic City with Adderley, his brother Nat on trumpet, keyboardist Joe Zawinul, bassist Herbie Lewis (replaced later by Victor Gaskin, and then Walter Booker), and tenor saxophonist Charles Lloyd (who was briefly in the band). So in 1964, not far removed from living a soulless existence, McCurdy joined one of the top bands in the jazz universe.

As for his marriage, it eventually crumbled. McCurdy later married a woman who was completely supportive of his life as a touring jazz musician.

• • •

As a teenager discovering jazz in the late seventies, my first introduction to Cannonball Adderley's fervent alto sax sound came from three seminal albums recorded in 1958 and 1959. They include: Miles Davis' *Milestones* and *Kind of Blue*, which Adderley contributed to as a sideman, and the saxman's *Somethin' Else*, for which Davis returned the favour and played as a sideman. While Adderley was magnificent on those essential recordings, they didn't prepare me for the euphoria of hearing *Mercy, Mercy, Mercy! Live at "The Club."* "Once again ladies and gentlemen, let's swing with Cannonball Adderley and the quintet."[7] That was the emcee's authoritative introduction at the beginning of the album that captured a crackling live performance by the quintet, including McCurdy. After buying the 1967 album on vinyl, I heard that introduction and the music that followed, hundreds of times.

The liner notes on the back of the record sleeve, which I also read repeatedly, said the album was recorded at The Club—formerly Club De Lisa—in Chicago's South Side. "The Club seats 800," wrote E. Rodney Jones in the notes. "Cannonball drew in better than 1200 customers a night, and we were seating the overflow out in the lounge. Everybody went away gassed. That Quintet of his is five giants, all climbing up the beanstalk at once."[8] For years I had no idea that parts of that were pure fiction. It was actually recorded at historic Studio A inside the Capitol Records Tower, in the Hollywood area of Los Angeles. "They set the studio up like a club and invited people in," said McCurdy. "We played two or three sets, and they recorded the whole thing that night."[9]

The artifice doesn't invalidate how the band's robust and soulful vibe on the album mesmerized me as a young jazz fan. That feeling was evident right from the up-tempo first track, "Fun," which McCurdy drove with his assertive and fiery drumming. McCurdy described his playing at the time as more "bombastic." "Back then I was probably dropping a lot of stuff [rhythmically], doing a lot, and being pretty active. You could probably hear it on the album."[10] I could, and I soaked it up.

The funky title track, written by Zawinul and featuring his infectious groove on Wurlitzer electric piano, became a hit and the album won a Grammy. Adderley was already immensely popular because of his bravura playing and eloquent/funny between-song banter. "Mercy, Mercy, Mercy" elevated Adderley to a level of stardom that was rare for a jazz artist, and McCurdy was a low-profile but important player in this success. "He was a huge star in the jazz world and outside the jazz world," said McCurdy. "I mean the bands that he had, which I played in and Louis [Hayes] and all those other guys played in, were incredible bands. We drew people in lines down the street. [Those lines appeared twice in Vancouver at Cannonball gigs McCurdy played: in 1970 at Ronnie's Riverqueen, and in 1974 at Oil Can Harry's.] He was an incredible player. His sound, it was beautiful."[11]

The beautiful sound fell silent on July 13, 1975. McCurdy was with Adderley in Gary, Indiana, that day when Cannonball had a stroke that partially paralyzed him and left him unable to speak. "If we called an ambulance it was going to take a while, so we put him in a car and started blowing the horn to alert people that we were coming," recounted McCurdy. "Just a block or so from the hospital we got hit by another car—T-boned in the middle of the street. So I had to get Cannon out. I had him actually, physically in my arms, and we put him in another car."[12]

They made it to the hospital, where Adderley received care until he passed away August 8, 1975, at forty-six. In more than a decade of music and friendship with Adderley, McCurdy learned how to be a "real musician." Translation: "I mean, how to conduct yourself. It wasn't all about the music. It was about the music, but it was also about the person. Cannon said, 'You don't have to be the best musician in the world to be a part of a band.' But if your personality is such that you can get along with everybody in the band, that's very important."[13]

About thirty-six years later, Roy McCurdy entered Cory Weeds' life, thanks to pianist Jon Mayer (not to be confused with John Mayer, the unexciting pop artist). Weeds booked Mayer to perform at Weeds' Cellar Jazz Club December 2–3, 2011. Mayer is an interesting figure. He recorded with Jackie McLean and John Coltrane in 1957 and 1958 respectively, and he performed with prominent artists in the sixties and seventies before entering a thirteen-year Rip Van Winkle period of musical inactivity. After he resurfaced in the Los Angeles jazz scene, Mayer eventually connected with McCurdy, who moved to LA following Adderley's death. As they were regular playing partners, Mayer brought McCurdy to the Cellar. "I have to admit that I was not really aware of Roy's happenings, and I wasn't aware of his playing," said Weeds. "He wasn't on my radar at all."[14]

Brad Turner (piano), Cory Weeds (alto saxophone), Michael Glynn (bass), Thomas Marriott (trumpet), and Roy McCurdy (drums), Frankie's Jazz Club, January 18, 2019. Photo by Vincent Lim.

That changed quickly. "First of all, he is a beautiful, beautiful guy," said Weeds. "Just a super nice man, and he swung his ass off. He sounded phenomenal. There is something about these old drummers. I don't know if it's playing the drums that keeps them young and physically fit, but they have so much power."[15]

Old jazz drummers who play with a young, vital sound is a thing. Roy Haynes, who got his start playing with the likes of Lester Young and Charlie Parker in the 1940s and years later led the aptly named *Fountain of Youth* band, has kept playing in his late nineties. Jimmy Cobb continued to play almost up until he passed away at ninety-one. Louis Hayes, the man McCurdy replaced in Adderley's band, is still active in his eighties. McCurdy doesn't have the name recognition of Haynes, Cobb, and Hayes, but he's at their level in terms of rhythmic impact and staying power.

After his time with Adderley, McCurdy worked with everyone from jazz-rock pioneers Blood, Sweat & Tears to jazz vocal great Sarah Vaughan to another singer, the elegant and sassy Nancy Wilson, who he accompanied for more than thirty years. All along he kept fine-tuning his craft, which meant McCurdy was in superb playing shape when he arrived at the Cellar. Vancouver bassist André Lachance, recruited by Weeds to play with Mayer and McCurdy in a trio at the club, saw McCurdy shift into his game face when songs were counted in. "That amount of focus was there from beat one," said Lachance. "There was no, 'Oh, it takes a couple of bars to get into it.' He was seventy-five. He looked like he was fifty-five. He was playing his ass off. Game on, right? You don't often get to experience that kind of thing."[16]

Weeds told McCurdy he had a proposition and even before the Cellar owner explained it, McCurdy said, "I'm in."[17] The idea: Would McCurdy be interested in returning to the Cellar to do a tribute to Cannonball, alongside local musicians including Weeds on alto sax? The answer was still yes. So Weeds booked McCurdy for June 1-2, 2012, and assembled a band with trumpeter Chris Davis, Brad Turner on piano, and Lachance.

The plan was to play *Mercy, Mercy, Mercy! Live at "The Club"* almost in its entirety as well as other tunes from Adderley's songbook. When Weeds drove McCurdy to a rehearsal, the drummer made a specific request: that they don't play "Sticks," a tune on *Live at "The Club"* with a gospel-like intensity that moved the LA audience to clap along throughout. Weeds: "I was like, 'Okay, cool, can I ask why?' And he said, 'Because that beat is really physically demanding, and I don't think I can do it.'" Secretly, Weeds was crushed because he loved the very up-tempo, bluesy-funky song and was hoping to do it. Then at the rehearsal, after successfully running through a number of tunes, McCurdy suggested they try "Sticks," but that they play it slightly slower than how it's usually performed. Weeds: "So we took it a little bit down, and Roy nailed it," which prompted McCurdy to say: "Okay man, we can do it full tempo on the gig."[18] Which they did, and he was precisely on the beat again.

The back-and-forth on "Sticks" was telling. It showed that McCurdy wasn't insecure or self-conscious about questioning whether he could play at the level required for a tune that his younger self handled effortlessly. Even though it turned out to be a non-issue, McCurdy's demeanour affirmed his character: honest, humble, and grounded.

Roy McCurdy, Frankie's Jazz Club, November 30, 2019. Photo by Vincent Lim.

The shows paying tribute to Adderley were jubilant experiences for all involved. "I enjoyed the club and the people," said McCurdy. "The club was packed, and the people were coming to listen. So I had a good time there."[19] McCurdy told Weeds that he receives numerous requests to do Cannonball tributes but usually turns them down. The drummer explained why he made an exception: "'I got a great vibe from you, and I kind of thought you would do it right,'" McCurdy told Weeds. "'And I just wanted to let you know you did it right. You guys sound great, and I will do this anytime.' This is Roy McCurdy, who played with Cannonball, saying this to me, and I just about started crying. The validation I felt when he said that, it was so phenomenal."[20]

• • •

Six and a half years passed before McCurdy and Weeds collaborated again. Much had changed in that interval: the Cellar closed, Frankie's Jazz Club—booked by Weeds—opened, and Weeds launched with partner Zev Feldman Reel to Real Recordings to put out archival jazz recordings. One of the label's first releases in 2018 was Cannonball Adderley's *Swingin' in Seattle, Live at the Penthouse 1966–1967*. The euphoric album includes tunes from two sets of live recordings that were made slightly before and after the one-night stand that resulted in *Mercy, Mercy, Mercy! Live at "The Club."* This was Adderley and his quintet at their apex as a unit, and McCurdy was the propulsive force at the core of the music.

Roy McCurdy, Frankie's Jazz Club, January 18, 2019. Photo by Vincent Lim.

To celebrate the release of *Swingin' in Seattle*, Weeds organized shows with McCurdy—the only surviving member of Adderley's last quintet—including January 18–19, 2019, at Frankie's. At one of the gigs, I sat near the band and mainly watched eighty-two-year-old McCurdy. What I observed: He's a physical specimen, who stays lean and toned due to a regular gym routine that McCurdy even maintains on the road. The man is also so calm and relaxed behind the drum kit, seemingly barely moving his upper body because of his well-honed economy of motion, yet McCurdy plays with intensity.

"That's the way I learned to play," said McCurdy. "I was taught to play relaxed. That's how my teachers taught me and guys that I met later [played]." Then he imparted two keys to his style, which he shares with young drummers when teaching at the University of Southern California's Thornton School of Music: "When I play it's all from the wrist. And I learned how to breathe. You know drummers need to breathe, too, and be calm."[21]

When McCurdy talked about the drumming insights he has acquired and self-developed throughout his career, I finally fully appreciated that the soft-spoken, gentle man sitting across the table from me embodied more than sixty-five years of learning, growing, and passionately playing heartfelt jazz. From the sixteen-year-old playing with Roy Eldridge, to the present day respected elder still contributing and making an impact, his longevity and consistency are remarkable.

Ten months later at Weeds' Shadbolt Jazz Walk festival, I heard him play with the same band I caught at Frankie's, and McCurdy did it again—he performed vigorously with barely a bead of sweat showing.

When I learned the Rochester Music Hall of Fame's 2020 inductees included McCurdy, I quietly gave thanks that all those years ago, McCurdy chose to leave that gloomy factory floor for the vibrant musical life he was destined to lead.

23 / SENSE AND SENSIBILITY: AMANDA TOSOFF

HOW DO YOU build a productive, creative, and fulfilling career as a jazz musician, composer, bandleader, and educator? In Canada? In the middle of a pandemic? These are complex questions that eluded pat, one-size-fits-all answers. The tremendous pianist Amanda Tosoff reflected on these questions and put in the work to identify her direction. While she comes across as having a deliberate nature, Tosoff didn't overthink her options for delineating a sustainable path in jazz. When completely new possibilities emerged, she's trusted in herself and embraced them.

The onset of the COVID-19 pandemic rocked Tosoff's professional life. Like all freelance musicians, the shutdown of venues meant that suddenly all of her gigs vanished. This included the cancellation of a tour with singer Emilie-Claire Barlow. Tosoff also had to postpone the release of her years-in-the-making sixth album, *Earth Voices*. Plus, she had to learn the technology to quickly shift from teaching in-person to online.

While those were significant challenges, Tosoff made artistic breakthroughs and meaningful pivots that will shape her blossoming career for years to come. How she got to these junctures connects back to her formative beginnings in jazz, when Tosoff started the long process of developing her knowledge, technique, and expression.

. . .

Born December 9, 1983, Tosoff grew up in White Rock, BC, in a musical family. Her mom Wendy plays classical piano and sings; Tosoff's dad Lloyd is a longtime country singer/songwriter; and her uncle Ted is an experienced performer, songwriter, and producer steeped in the blues.

In Metro Vancouver there are some high schools with a tradition of strong music programs that have produced musicians who are making an impact in jazz and other genres worldwide. One is Handsworth Secondary—Bob Rebagliati was the music teacher there who helped inspire a number of students to perform and compose jazz at a high level: Renee Rosnes, Laila Biali, Brandi Disterheft, Darcy James Argue, and others. Tosoff went to Semiahmoo Secondary—known as Semi—where band teacher David Proznick set high standards for decades. Proznick's daughter Jodi, Jillian Lebeck, Tristan Paxton, and JP Carter are other Semi graduates who have gone on to forge strong careers as musicians. Tosoff also studied privately with Lloyd Abrams, who taught scores of pianists in the Vancouver area, including Bob Murphy and Brad Turner. Abrams' methodical approach of breaking down the fundamentals of jazz theory and improvisation, documented in his book *The Art of Jazz Improvisation: For All Instruments*, greatly influenced Tosoff.

After her positive experience at Semi and studying with Abrams, it was inevitable Tosoff would go to music school. In 2001, when she began studies at Capilano College, becoming a jazz musician wasn't her goal. From a young age, she wanted to be a band teacher, even taking attendance in her pretend play as a child. When Tosoff arrived at college, the band teacher ambition was still her focus. Then at Cap she started studying jazz piano with Ross Taggart and other instructors. "He had a real impact on me," said Tosoff about Taggart. "He was super encouraging and definitely a huge influence and inspiration."[1] Taggart saw her as a dream student. "Not only would she complete the assignments I gave her for the week, but she would always bring in other songs, ideas, original compositions, and transcriptions she was working on," he said.[2]

Equally important to Taggart's mentorship: meeting and playing music with fellow students, including drummer Morgan Childs, clarinetist and saxophonist Evan Arntzen, bassist Sean Cronin, trumpeter Bria Skonberg, pianist Cat Toren, bassist Josh Cole, drummer Dan Gaucher, and others.

Childs described the key players in this generation of Cap student musicians in an interesting way: "I was lucky to come to Cap College at a time when there was a very strong peer group of people who were really interested in playing jazz."[3] Interesting because it seems self-evident that students in a jazz program would want to play jazz. It ain't necessarily so. "I still have students that say that they don't like swing," said drummer Dave Robbins, a longtime Cap faculty member.[4]

Certain years of Cap students have had more individuals with primary musical interests outside of jazz. Not this bunch. While the specific sub-genres that resonated with each player varied—from Dixieland to hard bop, post-bop, and improvised music—Tosoff's cadre at Cap shared a solid work ethic, seriousness about jazz in its various forms, and initiative to make things happen.

Robbins and other instructors encouraged Tosoff and her pals to hear as much live jazz as possible. "That's what makes the difference between it being an exercise in study and being a real, living, breathing thing—is to see the music the way it's supposed to be done," said Robbins. "I think that made a dramatic difference in their development."[5] André Lachance, who studied at Cap in an earlier generation, regularly saw Tosoff and friends at jazz haunts around town. "I would see them at the Mojo Room [a venue with jazz nights that were popular with students], and they were so enthusiastic," said Lachance. They were "obviously so focused and motivated."[6]

They quickly went from listening at jazz venues to performing at those joints. Over the years, they played at places like the Libra Room, Rime, and the WISE Hall in the city's Commercial Drive area. The central place for listening to top-flight jazz and playing plum gigs, however, was across town at Cory Weeds' Cellar. Childs hung out at the club all the time, and Weeds hired him to bartend. Tosoff also frequented the Cellar to listen to Taggart, Brad Turner, and other top musicians in the scene. Their first chance to play in the Cellar came in 2002, when Childs—a dynamic presence on the drum kit—led a quartet with Alvin Cornista, Tosoff, and Cronin. "I was really, really nervous," said Tosoff about the gig. "All my heroes played there."[7]

The young musicians gradually organized themselves into bands. Tosoff formed a quartet with Arntzen, Cronin, and Childs, who was also her boyfriend at the time. Tosoff discovered she had it in her to lead a band. Childs, in turn, created a quintet with exactly the same personnel plus trumpeter Chris Davis. Both groups regularly played at the Cellar. They prepared well for the gigs, meeting an unspoken expectation of the more established musicians and teachers that Childs and the others looked up to. "They never said this explicitly to us, but it was understood that if we were going to go out there and try to get the same gigs they had, we better present something worth presenting," said Childs. "We better take care and do it properly. And I feel like we really did."[8]

The Tosoff and Childs' ensembles drew well at the Cellar. "I think that was a very defining time for the scene," said Weeds, who himself went to Cap College in the early nineties. Weeds saw how the young musicians maintained a high quality in their performances and also advanced the promotion game. Weeds specifically recalled a conversation with Childs about getting a gig at the Cellar. "He [Childs] is like, 'Is there a guarantee?' And I said, 'No, there's no guarantee, it's a door gig.' He's like, 'Oh, you can't give us a hundred bucks each?' And I'm like, 'No, I can't give you a hundred bucks each.' They [Childs and the band] charged $10 [at the door]. They brought [attracted] ninety people to the club. I wrote them a cheque for $900." The wily jazz club owner had underestimated their ability to pack the Cellar. "That to me is when the shit started to change a lot," said Weeds. "Now we've got these young people using all of these things like Facebook and Twitter and mailing lists. A 'We promote ourselves' attitude. That was when that started to happen, and they were responsible for that."[9]

The next step for each group was developing a sound to the point where music could be recorded. In April 2006, Tosoff and her quartet recorded over two days at the Cellar without an audience. Weeds released Tosoff's debut recording on an imprint of his Cellar Live label that he set up to feature emerging artists: Cellar Live Futures. *Still Life* captures the group playing with confidence and drive on the tunes, including six by Tosoff that convey appealing moods, by turns cerebral and invigorating. Weeds was especially struck by Tosoff's compositions. "They sound penned by someone far older and more mature than a twenty-two-year-old pianist right out of college," he wrote in the liner notes.[10]

Amanda Tosoff, the Cellar, April 18, 2006. Photo by Steve Mynett.

That same year, the October Trio—Arntzen, Cole, and Gaucher—recorded *Day In*, also released on Cellar Live Futures. Co-produced by the group and Brad Turner, the album projects a searching sound, both melodic and free with committed improvisation and creative use of space in the pianoless trio format.

Advance to 2008, when Tosoff's group plus Turner on trumpet and flugelhorn recorded at Factory Studios. *Wait and See* shows the musicians' progress over the two years since Tosoff's first release, individually and as a cohesive unit. Ross Taggart could hear it in the album's ten songs, nine composed by Tosoff and one by Cronin. "Amanda was always inquisitive and loaded with questions for improving herself," said Taggart in the liner notes. "She understood right away that you can't begin to learn this difficult art form simply from reading about it in books. One must immerse oneself into the idiom whole-heartedly, listen to the music all the time and fall in love with it." Taggart believed Tosoff had "come into her own as a player and composer."[11]

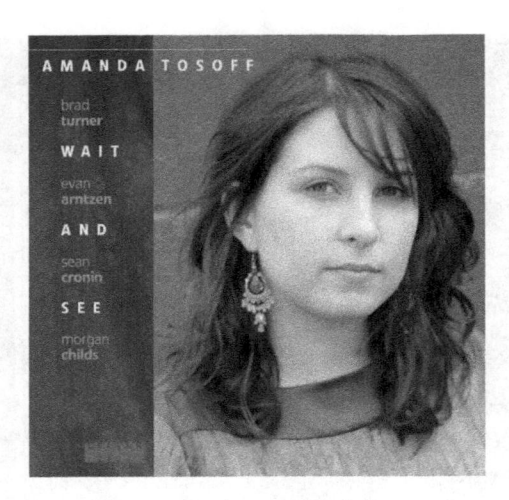

Album cover photo by Angela Fama.

Earlier in 2008, Childs and his quintet performed shows at the Cellar that were recorded for a release on Cellar Live. Including two tunes by Richie Powell from the classic 1956 album *Clifford Brown and Max Roach at Basin Street*, three originals by Childs, and one by Tosoff, *Time* is authentically and passionately delivered hard bop. Also in 2008, Cat Toren released her debut album, as did Bria Skonberg in 2009.

Here, then, was a confluence of budding ingenuity from this self-assured generation of young musicians. "Looking back at Vancouver, it is a really special scene, with a lot of great bands," said Tosoff, who fondly recalled the rapport between her quartet members back in the day. "I felt like at times we could read each other's minds. And that's the wonderful thing with playing all the time with people who you jell with."[12]

"I honestly don't think I'd be doing what I'm doing if it weren't for the group of musicians that I played with and Cory and the Cellar," said Tosoff. The chance to perform her own compositions at the club was key. "That was really instrumental in helping me get more experience doing that because it's quite terrifying playing your own music at first."[13]

Weeds was more than content to keep booking young and hungry players like Tosoff, Childs, Arntzen, and Cronin. "The problem is, they all friggin' left," said Weeds. "And that left a huge void for me when they left."[14] Eager to make a go of it in a new environment, Tosoff and Childs moved to Toronto in 2009. It was a risky move, trading the comfort zone of Vancouver for a bigger city with more musicians. As it turned out, it was a decision they wouldn't regret.

Morgan Childs, the Cellar. Photo by Jesse Cahill.

• • •

Tosoff made a concerted effort to establish herself in TO. "It always takes time to build," she said. "It was probably a year of really hard work trying to book gigs, and meet people, and play sessions with people before I was actually working a lot."[15] While she was introducing herself to the jazz scene, Tosoff kept composing. It wasn't long before she was ready to record her third album, *Looking North*, with nine of her compositions. By recording again with musicians in her Vancouver quartet—Arntzen, Cronin, and Childs—and expanding the group to a septet with more horn players, Tosoff both maintained continuity with her artistic through-line and advanced the elements of her developing compositional approach and sound. Those elements include harmonically beguiling textures, judicious use of space, and fluently crafted written and improvised playing that engaged my attention, especially on the bravura final track of *Looking North*: "Got It."

Journeys to the Bandstand

It's interesting to compare the cover art of Tosoff's first three albums, side-by-side. She was photographed for the covers of all three, and like the music's advancement, the portraits show an artist who's increasingly comfortable with herself and sage beyond her years.

Amanda Tosoff, 2011. Photo by Angela Fama.

Tosoff periodically returned to Vancouver for gigs, like one at the Cellar in July 2012, which was recorded and released as simply *Live at the Cellar*. Playing with bassist Jodi Proznick and drummer Jesse Cahill, Tosoff sounded so assured playing supple melodies and soloing with conviction. "The cool thing about it was just showing up and playing through these tunes with them, and there was [an] automatic band vibe because they had played together so much," said Tosoff. "I was feeding off of that, and it was just so easy to play with them because of their connection."[16]

Following the live trio recording, Tosoff started something completely different: a master's at the University of Toronto focused on music theory and musicology. "It was a lot of paper writing and reading and analyzing some classical music, which was great," she said. "I learned a lot and grew a lot from that."[17]

After a quartet of releases, Tosoff's route seemed set. Rigorous contemporary jazz, composed and played with intelligence and vitality, was her thing. Then came a big departure with *Words* in 2015. For the first time, Tosoff composed music to go with poetry and lyrics. It started with a "random composition exercise" that involved writing a melody to a short poem, "Owl Pellet" by Canadian poet and novelist Tim Bowling.[18] Tosoff liked the results, which catalyzed the words and music project. She chose other poems and lyrics—by Canadian poets, William Wordsworth, her dad, uncle, and sister— and improvised melodies and chords on them that led to songs.

I had followed Tosoff's career since the early Cellar days, but after her live album at the club, I lost track of where she was artistically. Hearing *Words* months after it came out was an enchanting revelation. While I had to find my bearings at first—*Words* swings but not in the traditional sense—listening to how she juxtaposes jazz, pop, folk, classical, and art song and expands her tonal palette by including violin and cello resonated with me. There's a lovely, coming-into-bloom quality to the music.

Tosoff wanted to go deeper with this approach, so she dreamed big, conceptualizing a recording—*Earth Voices*, released in January 2021—that would encompass eight songs performed by seven singers and ten players. Again, Tosoff paired poetry, this time by Rumi, Edgar Allan Poe, Pablo Neruda, and others, with blissful music. What she and the many contributors delivered is breathtaking.

"*Words*, I was terrified to share that because it was so different," said Tosoff. "It was a little bit more of me. The poems I chose spoke to me and felt more personal, and so that was really terrifying."[19] The experience of making *Words*, receiving positive feedback, and gaining confidence in putting out music with this aesthetic reached another level that's closer to full bloom with *Earth Voices*.

The compositional centrepiece of *Earth Voices* is the least jazz-sounding song on the album: "To a Stranger," with words by Walt Whitman from the poem of the same name. Tosoff through-composed the tune's music for string quartet and Felicity Williams' vocals. It was her first completely notated tune without improvisation. "I can't really call it a string quartet because when I think of string quartets I think of Bartok and Debussy, the real string quartet pieces," she said. "But it is a string quartet with voice, and it was really fun to labour over every single note and not leave anything up to improvising, which I love of course."[20]

I'll go further: "To a Stranger" encapsulates in six minutes the breadth and depth of Tosoff's artistry. If the song were a movie or novel, "To a Stranger" would be *Sense and Sensibility*. Like Elinor, the main character in Jane Austen's classic, who's intellectual and rational, the song's compositional detail is rigorous and pitch perfect. Like the other lead character, Elinor's sister Marianne, who's a romantic free spirit, the evocative melody and moving words about human connection convey intense feeling. Tosoff's ability to express all of this in just one song speaks to her progression as a reflective artist and person.

• • •

After going through the stress of seeing the pandemic wipe clean her performance calendar, Tosoff refocused her energy. She set herself a goal to launch an educational YouTube channel and began by creating a how-to video on reharmonization in jazz. Commissioned by JazzYYC, it's an excellent primer on a key tactic in jazz, especially for pianists. It succeeds in presenting complex concepts in a comprehensible and friendly way. Jodi Proznick loved the video, which led to conversations between the two musicians about music education, something they're both passionate about. The discussions resulted in Tosoff, Proznick, and Francesca Fung establishing Music Arts Collective, an online music school.

It's apt that Tosoff connected with Proznick so closely. After all, the bassist's father David was a major inspiration to Tosoff back at Semiahmoo Secondary. Plus, Tosoff has long looked up to Jodi. "There are so many great female musicians coming out [now], but really there were a handful of [female] musicians that I knew about in high school, and Jodi was definitely one of them," she said. I wondered if Tosoff was inspired by Proznick's achievements as a musician in general or as a woman in jazz. "As a musician, period," Tosoff said. But then she acknowledged the significance of gender. "I think what I am trying to say, for me being a woman seeing another amazing musician who happens to be a woman was very inspiring."[21]

In her high school, Tosoff was one of only about five girls who played in jazz ensembles. "I was the only one that ever played in the combos and wanted to actually improvise." As she progressed in music, Tosoff minimized the focus on her gender. Her inclination then was "kind of wanting to be one of the guys and not acknowledging I am a woman, if that makes any sense." Things have changed, with herself and the jazz world. Artemis, a supergroup of top female jazz artists (including Canadians Renee Rosnes and Ingrid Jensen) named after a Greek goddess, released its first album in 2020. Tosoff thinks Artemis' success and what the group represents are significant. "It's like saying, 'Hey, here we are, we kick butt, and we are women, and we are proud of it,'" she said. "I think that is the difference I am seeing now. I feel like in the past there was a little bit of women shying away from even acknowledging their gender, and I feel like that is changing now."[22]

Why is it that people like me always ask female jazz musicians about what it's like to be . . . female jazz musicians? Admittedly, one reason is laziness—asking the standard questions from a binary perspective to get good quotes. But one valid reason for this line of questioning is because their minority status remains conspicuous. There's still much work to do on better supporting and recognizing women in jazz. When the day comes that such questions no longer feel relevant, we'll know that true progress has been made.

I asked how Tosoff stays so positive. "I am not always positive," she said. "Right now, I seem positive, but you know there is always that fear in the back of your mind. But I think having projects has brought me a lot of—I want to say joy, but it's not like joy—but I guess satisfaction in having projects and seeing them through."[23]

I assumed, based on her trajectory and personality, that Tosoff makes detailed, long-term plans. It was surprising to learn that it's challenging for her to think about the future. "Thirty years from now, where do I see myself? Well, thirty years from now is quite a while. Even ten years from now, where do I see myself? I have a hard time with that. I don't really know, and so I just kind of ride the wave from project to project.[24]

"I have never really gone, 'This is where I want to go, that is what I had envisioned, this is what I am going to do, and that is what I am going for.' It's more like, 'Oh, here's this thing. I want to explore this thing.' And then I am pleasantly surprised with what comes out of that, and then that makes me think of the next thing. So to me it is not so much following the end goal, but it is more of a process. Does that make sense?"[25] It makes total sense. It's also fascinating to observe how her brain works, both methodically analyzing and organically going with the creative flow. Sense and sensibility.

Proznick has closely watched, and participated in, Tosoff's growth as an artist. Proznick adjudicated a band that included Tosoff when the pianist was about thirteen. Then when Tosoff was in her twenties, they gigged together in Vancouver. After Tosoff's move to Toronto, they weren't in touch as much, but reconnected during the pandemic and forged a strong bond. "She's like a sister to me," said Proznick. "It's just been a treat to watch her grow, and she's still the same Amanda. She's meticulous, professional, kind, humble, and her feel is amazing. It's so easy to play with her, timewise. We just feel time the same. There's never a note out of place." Proznick also believes Tosoff is "one of the best" teachers she's ever seen. "Over the years I've watched her teach and share information, and just like her playing, it's articulate, it's thoughtful, it's well-constructed."

In August 2021, Tosoff announced on Facebook that—at the age of thirty-seven—she had become a full-time music professor at Toronto's Humber College. Her original dream of becoming a band teacher kind of came true. Not for a moment did I think that Tosoff's academic career would prevent her from making music. I'm sure that she'll be able to wholeheartedly do both because it's ingrained in her to share her insights and create.

Six months after the Humber announcement, I saw Tosoff perform at Weeds' Jazz @ The Bolt festival in Burnaby. Tosoff played with a trio, including Proznick and Childs, and the Ostara Project, an all-female group she co-leads with Proznick. Ostara Project, like Artemis, makes an impact that's both mighty and dulcet. With both groups I heard that day, Tosoff's piano playing was equally grounded and elevating. She achieved a fine balance. I couldn't have asked for anything more.

Sense and Sensibility

Amanda Tosoff, February 13, 2022, Shadbolt Centre for the Arts. Photo by Vincent Lim.

24 / LOVE WALKED IN: MIKE ALLEN

One look and I forgot the gloom of the past
One look and I had found my future at last
One look and I had found a world completely new
When love walked in with you

- "Love Walked In" by George and Ira Gershwin

There are tunes that jazz musicians return to again and again. They serve as bellwethers that mark artistic progress. For Vancouver tenor saxophonist Mike Allen, a song in that category is "Love Walked In."

In 1930, George Gershwin composed the music for "Love Walked In." Seven years later, his brother Ira added lyrics so the tune could be used in a movie musical. The song became a timeless jazz standard after great artists interpreted and reinterpreted it. Louis Armstrong, Ella Fitzgerald, Dinah Washington, Oscar Peterson—they all put their own personal stamp on "Love Walked In."

Seventy years after Gershwin wrote the love song, and with that weight of jazz history in his consciousness, Mike Allen kicked off an August 8, 2000, gig with "Love Walked In." It wasn't just any gig—it was opening night at Cory Weeds' Cellar Jazz Club. So the very first notes heard by an audience in Weeds' brand new club, years away from becoming a fabled jazz joint, were Gershwin's as performed by Allen, bassist Darren Radtke, and drummer Julian MacDonough.

Earlier that day, Allen helped Weeds prepare the club for the long-anticipated opening by putting up a curtain behind the bandstand. "I remember being tired because I had spent the afternoon putting up the curtain, drilling holes into the concrete ceiling to put in lead plugs to suspend the hooks to hold the curtain rods up," Allen said. "I had offered to help out, and this was what I ended up doing."[1] Weeds appreciated Allen, for his saxophone playing and handyman help on this monumental occasion. Weeds: "He was there with me hammering the last nail and turning the last screw at the Cellar a mere fifteen minutes before opening [the door] for the first time and sixty minutes before he would take the stage and perform with his trio."[2]

Just as it is impossible to predict which song will become a standard, there's no way to know which jazz club that comes along will endure and become iconic. Allen didn't have any optimistic or prescient thoughts about being in on the beginning of a great run for the Cellar and for himself. "It started out in such a way that it didn't give you that impression that it was going to be really super successful," said Allen. "You know, when you're accepting help from musicians to put up curtains, and you are playing for not great amounts of money."[3]

But it was, in fact, the maiden voyage for what would become a beloved, longstanding venue for Allen and the city's jazz scene. That night, a healthy number of curious and excited jazz fans showed up, Allen and the trio swung hard, and the curtain held.

As for "Love Walked In," Allen continued to be enchanted with the song for years; it was the first track on *Change Is*, a trio album Allen recorded in 1999 with Radtke and drummer Dave Robbins, and he kept turning to it on the bandstand, which he did on the Cellar's final night in February 2014. The evolution of his approach to this one standard serves as a metaphor for his growth as an expressive jazz artist.

There's obviously much more to Allen than the way he plays a Gershwin tune. He's multi-dimensional and complex. Allen solemnly dedicates himself to meeting the challenge of achieving transcendence as a jazz tenor saxophonist and composer. In a completely different vein, he also dreams about getting the opportunity to travel in outer space. After years of absorbing and appreciating his music, I challenged myself to gain insight into Allen's character, motivations, and aspirations.

• • •

Born May 12, 1965, in Toronto, Allen grew up in Kingston, Ontario. He started piano lessons at five and saxophone lessons at thirteen. When not learning how to play music, Allen created futuristic comics and stories about space exploration, inspired by TV shows *UFO* and *Space: 1999*, and NASA's Space Shuttle program.

His father Hugh was a mathematics professor at Queen's University, who played piano, guitar, and flute. "He played music for enjoyment, but he loved good melody and good songs," said Allen.[4] Allen's mother Ginny played piano and violin. So music was a constant in the family home, and his parents supported Allen's decision to study music, which he did initially at Queen's. Going to two Kingston Jazz Society concerts—featuring American tenor saxophonist Zoot Sims at one and Canadian guitarist Sonny Greenwich at the other—inspired Allen,[5] who transferred to McGill University in Montreal. In 1984, McGill became the first major Canadian university to offer a Bachelor of Music program in jazz performance. Three years later, Allen was one of the first graduates from the program. "When I went to McGill, I could barely play," he said. "I could play the horn, but I just had no experience playing with good players. But it provided an environment for me to focus entirely on jazz."[6]

For about a decade, Allen gained extensive experience performing at a high level in Montreal's jazz venues and in local recording sessions. He became one of the city's most noteworthy young players. Then Greenwich—one of Montreal's and Canada's greatest jazz musicians—asked Allen to join the guitarist's band in 1990. Allen was floored by the invitation. Greenwich hadn't included a tenor saxophonist in his band for almost two decades. Years earlier when Allen heard Greenwich for the first time, the performance was astounding. Becoming a member of Greenwich's group was a major milestone in Allen's development. He was part of a three-man horn section in a nonet led by Greenwich that recorded sessions for CBC Radio's *Jazz Beat* program in 1991 and 1992. Greenwich's *Standard Idioms* album features songs from those sessions, and Allen's tenor playing stands out. Allen was also in Greenwich's band for another *Jazz Beat* session in 2001 that came out as *Fragments of a Memory*, and once again he shone.

His time with Greenwich, whom the saxophonist considered his "Miles Davis" for being a primary inspiration,[7] set in motion Allen's career arc.

He steadily advanced his harmonic conception and sound by seeking out mentors, becoming a mentor himself, and looking within for breakthroughs.

Allen followed the path of a number of Canadian jazz musicians and moved to New York City to hone his craft. He studied at New York University, where he earned a Master's Degree in Jazz Performance. Private lessons with sublime players—saxophonists Joe Lovano, Dave Liebman, and Ted Nash, and pianist Jim McNeely—along with Allen's focus on soaking up the city's extraordinary jazz landscape, meaningfully augmented his playing.

After returning to Montreal, Allen recorded his second album as a leader: *Quintet/Quartet*. As the title implied, it consisted of music Allen documented with two groups, including one with two musicians who would become his colleagues in Vancouver's jazz community: pianist Tilden Webb and Dave Robbins. *Quintet/Quartet*, recorded in 1994 and 1995 with seven of nine songs composed by Allen, was my introduction to the saxman. His raw, probing sound on the tenor—influenced by John Coltrane, Greenwich, and others—caught my attention. These were also early days in his development of a distinctive approach to improvisation. On the faster tunes, like the opening track "One Side of a Circle," Allen soloed with a note-heavy approach that didn't leave much breathing space. That approach would change with time and perspective.

In 1995, Allen and his wife Donna Vidas moved "by accident" to Vancouver.[8] The original plan was to move to San Francisco and study with tenor saxophone titan Joe Henderson, but waiting for a green card took months, so they settled in Vancouver. At thirty, Allen found himself in a city and scene on the West Coast that was uncharted for him. He arrived in Vancouver at a time when the city's live jazz scene was uneven, with venues here and there but no central, invigorating hub. As always, Allen found his own way. He taught at Capilano College in North Vancouver and Western Washington University in Bellingham, where he eventually became head of the jazz program. Allen realized the dream of studying with Henderson in 1996 and 1997. "His music was such an influence on my playing and composing—it was hard to not be starstruck while hanging with him," said Allen. "He was always beautifully dressed, ironed pants and shirts and nice leather shoes. He seemed so calm and yet somewhat distant."[9]

I met Allen for the first time in 1997 for an interview in a café on Vancouver's West Side. He gave cerebral and thoughtful answers to my questions. At one point the café's owner noticed a CD sitting on our table. It was the *Standard Idioms* album Allen had recorded with Greenwich. The man offered to play the disc. After hearing a few songs, he came over and remarked about the "beautiful music." Just after making that assessment, sharp, cacophonous sounds came out of the speakers. Timing is everything. Allen smiled nervously and looked across the room to see if the owner was thrown off by the brief but conspicuous free-jazz sounding moments. He wasn't. The music played on.

A few weeks after the interview, I heard Allen perform with a top-notch group. It included American pianist Don Friedman, who had played with a wide range of greats, from Ornette Coleman to Clark Terry, Elvin Jones, and many others. At NYU, Allen studied piano—his second instrument—with Friedman. They forged a strong musical connection and performed together in New York. Part of a mini-tour Allen organized, the Vancouver show also included bassist Chuck Israels—who was in the Bill Evans Trio for about five years—and Robbins. The concert featured robust playing from all. Allen sounded completely comfortable playing alongside the veteran musicians. Seventeen years later, I interviewed Friedman about his brief time with Coleman, and—as an aside—the pianist noted that Allen "is a fine tenor player, and we had a great time on that tour."[10]

By the beginning of the new millennium, Allen had released three more increasingly assured albums. *One Side of a Circle*, released in 1999, remained in memory for me. Encompassing quartet and octet formats, the recording conveys resonant aural textures in the ensemble playing and harmonic substance in the solos by Allen and others.

His next album, *Change Is*, released in 2000, was pivotal for the impression it made on Cellar owner and fellow sax player Cory Weeds. "Mike Allen, quite simply, was a hero of mine," said Weeds about his fellow saxophonist's impact on him at the turn of the century. "That record really spoke to me."[11] As his growing recorded oeuvre demonstrated, Allen had become a leading player in Vancouver's jazz scene. Weeds offered him a weekly gig at the Cellar on Tuesdays, starting with the club's opening night. Allen enjoyed the chance to play regularly at the Cellar with his trio and occasionally with guest artists, such as Americans Gary Bartz, Brian Lynch, and Jim Snidero, as well as François Bourassa from Montreal. But these were early days at the club, when it was struggling to consistently attract a following, and Tuesday nights were a tough sell.

After almost a year of Tuesdays, Allen and Weeds mutually agreed to end the gig. That freed Allen up to play higher-profile nights at the club, with groups like his quartet that included at various times pianists Miles Black and Chris Gestrin, bassists Adam Thomas and Sean Cronin, Julian MacDonough, and others. "It gave my quartet a place to try out all of this new music," said Allen. "I was writing a lot of music in the 2000s, sort of more the spiritual approach to it, more like music that you would associate with Trane's midsixties period. And there weren't a lot of places where you could do that."[12]

The club was also a venue where Allen could lead atypical projects such as the Jazz Ascendants, his little big band that fluctuated between seven and nine musicians. He even proposed playing there with two drummers and two bass players—the musical equivalent of a Tim Hortons "double double." How did Weeds respond to that pitch? "He said, 'Hey, that sounds great. Do it.'"[13]

Mike Allen, the Cellar, April 5, 2006. Photo by Steve Mynett.

The summer of 2009 was another landmark event for Allen and the Cellar. He kicked off the club's portion of the 2009 TD Canada Trust Vancouver

International Jazz Festival with a masterful interpretation of *A Love Supreme*, Coltrane's landmark suite. With Phil Dwyer on piano, bassist Paul Rushka, and MacDonough, Allen played the suite's first three parts and replaced the fourth part with his own composition, "The Man." I wasn't there, but years later I listened to an unreleased recording of the first set. It captures an unrelentingly intense, bravura performance by Allen and the other musicians. "We weren't doing a tribute," said Allen, who improvised fiercely that night. "We were just playing that music our own way."[14] In the second set, they went in a completely different direction, performing "Puttin' On The Ritz" and other tunes with Allen and Dwyer both on tenor sax.

Another highlight: Allen and his quartet playing a pair of nights in a two-tenor frontline with Toronto-born, NYC-based Grant Stewart. On YouTube, there's a five-minute snippet of their April 3, 2010, Cellar show. In it, Allen and Stewart play the melody to Miles Black's "Gold Rush" and solo heartily, while Billie Holiday, with a gardenia blossom in her hair, looks on approvingly from a painting on the Cellar's red wall.

Mike Allen (tenor saxophone), Mike Rud (guitar), and Darren Radtke (bass), the Cellar, August 13, 2011. Photo by Vincent Lim.

In 2012, Allen released his eleventh album, *A Hip Cosmos*. After Allen gave me a CD of the recording, I ignored it for a shallow reason: I thought the cover photo, showing a cluster of galaxies known as "Stephan's Quintet," looked cheesy. Years later, I regretted judging the album by its cover because when actually listening to the music, I heard an urgency and insistent quality in Allen and his quartet's playing that struck me as the group's most fully realized statement. In fact, Allen considers *A Hip Cosmos*, his "tribute to the wonders of the unknown and yet to be discovered,"[15] one of his strongest recordings. In large part it's because the band—including Black, Thomas, and MacDonough—had developed a strong affinity from performing together and teaching alongside each other at Western Washington University, and it was "reaching its artistic peak."[16]

That year, Allen's quartet performed at the final three nights of O'Doul's Restaurant & Bar before the restaurant—which featured live jazz since 1996—ceased to exist. It was apt that Allen played the parting notes at O'Doul's. That's where he hosted the nightly jam at Coastal Jazz & Blues Society's annual international jazz festival for years, plus Allen had a twelve-year run playing weekly solo piano gigs at O'Doul's. These were important contributions to the scene and personally significant for Allen.

By the time the Cellar entered its final days in late 2013 and early 2014, Allen was in a far different creative space from the one he inhabited years earlier, when he was learning his craft in Montreal and New York and making the pivotal move to Vancouver. That evolution continued in the post-Cellar era. He had always focused on sound and rhythm and continued to do so, but now he played fewer notes. "I leave more space. I interact more with the other musicians on the stage." He also experiences his own performances differently. "I hear outwards further. I hear what I played—it rings longer in my imagination—and I hear what's coming up from further in advance . . . You just get better at your relationship with the music, the ability to be in all places at all times."[17]

• • •

On February 26, 2014, the Cellar's bittersweet finale, Allen took on an important role. As the musical director for the night, he lined up some of the bands, provided a few arrangements, and helped organize a send-off jam session. It was a role he was comfortable with, given his lengthy experience hosting the jazz festival jam. To the packed house full of people both mourning and celebrating the club, he also spoke eloquently about the Cellar's vital contribution to the scene.

Alongside the many musicians who turned out to play final choruses at the Cellar, Allen performed a variety of tunes that night with his trio and quartet, as well as with other players. Fittingly, the first song he played was "Love Walked In," which Allen did with the same two musicians he had opened the club with thirteen-and-a-half years earlier: Darren Radtke and Julian MacDonough. What the mourners and celebrants didn't know was that earlier that night, in a back corridor of the Cellar, Allen was intensely practicing the melody to "Love Walked In."

"It must have been weird for the guys that were playing with me . . . to walk in and see me practicing this melody that we had played hundreds of times on hundreds of gigs," said Allen. But there was method to the weirdness. "I had been searching more deeply over the years about how to play the song better, and it wasn't about playing my saxophone louder or faster. It was about knowing this actual song, the lyrics of the song, what the phrases of the lyrics mean, and how to make that work on the saxophone."[18]

"I wanted to cap off my time at the Cellar by feeling good about how I played the music, in a new, deeper way. This was really important to me, that I had learned something over thirteen years about how to play this song better."[19]

In *The Goldwyn Follies*, the 1938 Technicolor film, there's a scene featuring "Love Walked In" that shows what the song is all about. In the scene, Kenny Baker—playing the role of short order cook "Danny Beecher"—sings the tune's lyrics. Two women gaze adoringly at him on the other side of the diner counter as he croons in his tenor voice. One of the women, "Hazel Dawes" played by Andrea Leeds, is especially smitten. Clearly, "Love Walked In" is an ode to love at first sight.

So let me get this straight: Allen, who played hours and hours of original and intricate music at the Cellar, cared deeply about striking the right tone with a tune from the Great American Songbook about instant affection? That was essentially the case, and it was a wonderfully endearing way for

Allen to acknowledge his years at the Cellar and the profound musical and personal growth it had fostered.

The difference between how Allen played "Love Walked In" on *Change Is* in 2000, and how he played it at the Cellar's fond farewell in 2014, was immense. On the former, he raced through the melody; on the latter, Allen took it much slower, savoured every note, and conveyed a warm romanticism. It was the perfect way to celebrate the Cellar's success in fulfilling its quixotic jazz club goals and to quietly acknowledge his own evolution.

Miles Black (piano), Tom Keenlyside (flute), Mike Allen (tenor saxophone), Adam Thomas (bass), and Cory Weeds (tenor saxophone), the Cellar, February 27, 2014. Photo by Steve Mynett.

• • •

On January 5, 2019, Allen stepped inside a sacred space: the Van Gelder Studio in Englewood Cliffs, New Jersey. That day, he recorded an album as a leader for Weeds' Cellar Music label with upper-echelon New York players—bassist Peter Washington and drummer Lewis Nash. It was in the same place where, starting in 1959, hundreds of historic jazz records had been created by exceptional jazz musicians and documented by a gifted recording engineer: Rudy Van Gelder. Among the recordings made there: Coltrane's *A Love Supreme* and all five stellar albums that Joe Henderson recorded for Blue Note Records in the sixties.

Weeds—with his connections to Van Gelder Studio's owner Maureen Sickler and her husband Don Sickler, who operates the studio with her, and to Washington and Nash—had a lot to do with making the session happen for Allen. Weeds more than repaid his debt to Allen for helping put up that bandstand curtain almost two decades before at the Cellar. Allen hugely appreciated Weeds' support.

About twenty years before Allen's Van Gelder session, he recorded *Change Is*, the pianoless trio album that so impressed Weeds. At Van Gelder, Allen chose to use the same tenor-bass-drums format, this time with musicians he had never played with before. They clicked perfectly. The resulting album, *Just Like Magic*, reveals a lot about how far Allen had come in his lifelong pursuance of excellence and meaning in jazz. The distinctive tone of his tenor and the melodic, harmonic, and rhythmic equilibrium he achieves on the originals and standards speak to Allen's progress.

Just Like Magic isn't the name of a tune on his sixteenth album, but it's a fitting title. There's a kind of magic at play here. For Allen, the magic was audible: under the studio's high wooden ceiling, he could hear the echoes of the landmark recordings that had been created in the studio. "It was not at all distracting. Actually, it aided and motivated and inspired." Another effect of being under the Van Gelder spell was attaining such profound focus that his sense of time was transformed. "When the music seems to jell, the song takes on a different feeling in terms of the time. I feel like I'm playing the whole song at one moment. So I'm hearing all the chords in the song happening at that very moment, and everything I'm playing is relating to the whole song, not just to that specific moment in time. There's a kind of a modulation of time, and I think that's what gets captured in that moment."[20]

Peter Washington (bass), Mike Allen (tenor saxophone), and Lewis Nash (drums), Frankie's Jazz Club, October 19, 2019. Photo by Vincent Lim.

In NYC after the session, Allen went by himself to hear Fred Hersch and Miguel Zenón at the Village Vanguard. The Vanguard isn't far from Carmine Street, where Allen and his wife lived about twenty-five years earlier, when he was a student in the city. After the memorable Vanguard show, Allen decided to walk more than forty blocks back to his hotel. As he made his way uptown that Saturday night, listening on his earbuds to Coltrane's *Crescent*—Allen's favourite record, which happened to be recorded at Van Gelder studio—his thoughts went back to the day's recording. "I was just in the moment thinking how much sense all this made. I've dedicated myself to trying to be ready for moments like this my whole life, and when it happened, I felt that I was ready, and I made the most out of it. That was gratifying."[21]

Sometimes questions come to mind about Allen. Given how well he did in the Van Gelder session, and his track record for making impactful music, should he be on the bigger stage of a place like New York? And the corollary: does he get enough opportunities to present his music in Vancouver? About the first question, when Allen lived and studied in NYC, he didn't care for the "hostility" he encountered in the city and its jazz scene. "I don't feel I need that kind of motivation/energy," he said in a 2007 interview. "In fact, it's probably why Vancouver is such a good match for me. Generally, the music environment is relaxed, and the players are very serious."[22]

As for the second question, even someone with his stature in Vancouver's scene can only play at Frankie's and other venues so many times a year. But I don't get the sense that it's about quantity of gigs for him. My impression is that he takes each performing opportunity seriously, preparing thoroughly and always delivering on the bandstand.

In November 2022, I showed up at Frankie's just in time to hear less than half a tune by Allen, leading a band with guitarist Oliver Gannon, Adam Thomas, and drummer Joe Poole. While Allen has played with many internationally renowned jazz artists, this type of band—with excellent local musicians he has shared many bandstands with—is the most meaningful for him. When I walked in, Allen was at the tail end of the night's last solo. The few fleeting moments of hearing him improvise were enough to remind me about his innate ability to both tip his hat to influences and mentors and to express his own, decades-in-the-making tenor sound. As I stood near the club's door, these impressions were evident. I savoured the moments, and looked forward to hearing more personal expression from Allen, sometime soon.

25 / ENDINGS RARELY ARE: NATASHA D'AGOSTINO

IT'S A NIGHT to remember for Natasha D'Agostino. On July 12, 2018, a few hours before she turns twenty-six, D'Agostino stands on the bandstand at a packed Frankie's Jazz Club, brings the mic close to her, and starts singing with her distinctive alto voice. Right away her clarity of intent and wholehearted passion radiate in the room. At the same time, she's immediately in sync with the musicians in her quartet. In front of D'Agostino's family and friends, along with jazz fans who knew it would be a special gig, the key elements of what make a compelling performance come together.

"We didn't even take a second for it to jell," said guitarist David Blake, who played that night with D'Agostino, bassist Paul Rushka, and drummer Bernie Arai. "There was no sort of stumbling to make it into something. It *was* something." It was the CD release show for *Endings Rarely Are*, D'Agostino's first album, which she recorded in August and September 2017 with these same musicians. Her performance represented something tangible and distinct. "A real significant, serious, artistic statement," said Blake. "She just sounded so good."[1]

It went further than that. Blake recognized that he was witness to a young, gifted artist—his best friend—finding her voice. "I remember feeling when we played the CD release that it was even better than the album," he said. "She was just growing so fast. It felt like every time I heard her, she was an order of magnitude better than the last time. So by the time we did the CD release, it just felt like now she really was figuring out what she was doing and how to do it."[2]

No one who was there had any reason to believe the evening's joy was fleeting. Then less than six months later, D'Agostino was gone. In a cruel instant, a car accident ended the beautiful life she crafted as a musician, teacher, daughter, friend, explorer, and humanist. Words can't adequately encapsulate the significance of her presence and the enormity of her loss to loved ones and Vancouver's jazz community. "For so many of us, her death is the deepest grief and a seemingly pointless tragedy," said D'Agostino's friend Tracy Neff. "It is definitely the one event in my life so far that has made me truly question the meaning of all of this. Like, if she's not here, why are we all here? Why her?"[3]

They're profound questions that elude definitive answers. But as the months went by, it became increasingly imperative for me to explore and document D'Agostino's life to ensure her story endures. No one appointed me her biographer. I took it upon myself to chart D'Agostino's course because she embodied the ideal of achieving meaningful artistic expression, not just by drawing from her striking talent, but through determination, curiosity, and fearlessness.

• • •

In 1981, Rocco D'Agostino met Anna Levitsky when they were students at Langara College in Vancouver. That they met at all was somewhat of a miracle. He was born in the small pulp and paper city of Powell River; she started life in Odesa, Ukraine, a port city on the Black Sea in what was then the Soviet Union. Anna's family decided to move from Soviet Ukraine to Canada, and it was challenging to justify why the family should be allowed to leave to the Russian authorities. But when Anna was seventeen, she and her family arrived in Canada. After Rocco met Anna, they fell in love and married in 1986. Their first child was born July 13, 1992, and they christened her Natasha Alexandra D'Agostino. About four years later, her brother Giovanni was born.

The first languages she spoke were Italian and Russian; in kindergarten, D'Agostino was considered ESL because her English was rudimentary. The musical genes in the family lay with Anna, who completed seven years of music school in the Ukraine, studying piano and violin. In Canada, she sang in a church choir. As an eight-year-old, Natasha started piano lessons, which she continued for five years. Growing up in Vancouver and nearby Tsawwassen, there was always music playing in the house, especially ABBA, Elton John, and Neil Diamond. She loved listening to classic seventies pop-rock and picking out the melodies by ear on piano. Her first attempts at vocalizing involved hiding behind a door and singing "O Canada."

At South Delta Secondary School, musical theatre and choir were her core pursuits. D'Agostino performed leading roles in the *Wizard of Oz* (the Scarecrow), *Grease* (Betty Rizzo), *You're a Good Man, Charlie Brown* (Lucy Van Pelt), *Annie* (Miss Hannigan), and *The Taming of the Shrew* (Kate). In real life, D'Agostino didn't have these characters' negative traits. But I can picture her inhabiting the roles, especially the rough, tough, and sarcastic Rizzo and bossy, crabby, and cruel Lucy.

Natasha D'Agostino (far left), playing the Scarecrow in the Wizard of Oz, South Delta Secondary School, 2007. Photo by Greg Hansen, courtesy Greg Hansen and Jalen Saip.

"She just had such a strong and dynamic presence that she was always cast as the meatier and tour de force characters," said Neff, who directed D'Agostino in *Grease* and developed a close friendship with her. "She could capture the entire audience for any length of time." D'Agostino also made "bad guy" roles relatable and lovable because she put her whole self into the characters, Neff explained. "She actually does have an ass-kicking, sassy side," said Neff. "She would often describe her family gatherings to me, and it was pretty clear that they were loud and raucous." Neff also saw a "fiery side" to D'Agostino, who "had no tolerance for people who chose to be small-minded, entitled, or unjust. So she would really clean the clock of anyone who was acting in such a way."[4]

Natasha D'Agostino playing Miss Hanigan in Annie, South Delta Secondary School, 2010. Photo by Greg Hansen, courtesy Greg Hansen and Jalen Saip.

After high school graduation, D'Agostino worked, took non-music classes for a semester at Langara, and thought about going to music school. "She was excited and scared at the prospect of doing it, and I think that deep down she knew she would regret not trying, and that there was something worth exploring," said Neff. "Natasha truly went at life feeling the fear and doing it anyways."[5]

In spring 2011, D'Agostino auditioned for Capilano University's Jazz Studies program. Guitarist Jared Burrows, who was the academic coordinator of the program at the time, said D'Agostino failed the theory test that's an entrance requirement and described the audition itself as "pretty rough."[6] As a result, she was way down the list of applicants vying to enter the program. Then during a discussion about who would get in, Réjean Marois—the man who directed NiteCap, the university's flagship vocal ensemble—pointed out the indisputable factor in her favour: "But the pipes, man!"[7]

"She definitely had the pipes," said Burrows. "Not only that, there was something about her personality, which I would call a genuine humility and a willingness to learn, that was really apparent right from the beginning. And that's something that was very special about her all the way along."[8]

D'Agostino got in, but she wondered why Capilano accepted her. The first year at Cap was hard. "She often reminded me that she was the only first-year student that didn't make it into any vocal ensemble," said Neff. "Not even one."[9] D'Agostino was also well behind with theory.

After that first year, she took an extended break from school and worked as an au pair on a farm in Annecy, France. Photos and videos of her time in France show a happy twenty-year-old, enjoying the detour off her musical path. By the time she returned home after her twenty-first birthday, D'Agostino knew she had to commit to working hard in order to succeed in music. But she also had to hold back from singing in order to rehab a voice condition—vocal nodules. While D'Agostino rested her instrument, she put her downtime to good use. "She spent this time sharpening herself as a musician and learning everything she could to be a step ahead," said Neff. "She was determined not to be seen as just a singer but as an equal member of whatever band or ensemble she played in. She would never even say 'I sang in the band.' She would say, 'I played in the band.'"[10]

One of her first voice teachers at Cap, where D'Agostino resumed studies in 2013, was longtime Vancouver jazz vocalist Kate Hammett-Vaughan. "I picture her so clearly," said Hammett-Vaughan, who remembers the conspicuous pink streaks of hair D'Agostino had at one point, her comfy sweaters, and big voice. The first tune they worked on together was "Moonlight in Vermont." From that point on, D'Agostino was an exemplary student, always open to checking out singers and learning songs Hammett-Vaughan suggested. "She was really something," said Hammett-Vaughan. "I have never seen someone work so hard."[11]

D'Agostino was especially drawn to Carmen McRae and Betty Carter. It's not hard to understand why. McRae and Carter were wondrous song stylists, who made each tune they interpreted their own through distinctive phrasing and vigorous scat singing. D'Agostino focused on these and other elements that would become key to her own vocal style.

The extra work D'Agostino put in paid off. After returning to school, she made it into NiteCap—a big milestone for her—and other Cap ensembles. The university has a long tradition of bringing in prominent jazz artists to deliver workshops and perform with music students. In the summer of 2015, D'Agostino was thrilled to learn that English jazz singer and lyricist Norma Winstone would be among the guest artists to perform with NiteCap and conduct workshops with Cap students in the upcoming school year. D'Agostino deeply admired Winstone, who developed a singular style when she emerged in the sixties and seventies. Hallmarks of that style include an enchanting unadorned tone and emotional, meaning-filled delivery.

The week arrived when Winstone was on campus, and D'Agostino hung on to her every word of wisdom. The brief residency culminated with an extraordinary concert on April 1, 2016. Winstone sang exquisitely and the students shone, including D'Agostino, who delivered a strong solo. Vancouver pianist and singer Jillian Lebeck was in the audience, and she told D'Agostino, "You looked so happy to be singing with Norma!" D'Agostino's response: "Oh man—beyond happy!!"[12] The day after, D'Agostino said: "That is a night I will always remember. So fortunate to have witnessed Norma's beautiful artistry this week."[13]

In 2015, David Blake met D'Agostino when both were part of a NiteCap performance. Right after that, D'Agostino contacted him about playing a duo gig together. When they showed up at the gig, Blake asked D'Agostino what she wanted to play. Her noncommittal reply: "I don't know, what do you want to play?" Blake thought her response was bizarre because he was used to working with singers who were experienced bandleaders, with their music fully organized well ahead of time.[14]

"At first, I was like, 'Oh fuck, this is going to be tedious.'" He asked the question again, and she replied the same way. Then Blake suggested a standard, which D'Agostino said they could try, but she admitted never having sung it before. "Again, I was just like, 'Oh my God, what is she doing?'" The awkward dance continued, with Blake saying they should do something she knows, and D'Agostino insisting that they do the tune he suggested. Which they did. "I think I played a little intro and she started singing, and it was like she had been singing this song for forty years. Like she knew every detail and every little thing. She just sang it like it was her song. And I was in awe the whole time."[15]

The rest of the gig proceeded in the same two-step dance, with Blake proposing a song and D'Agostino saying, "Yeah, I'll try this one," and tune after tune "knocking it out over and over again." For Blake, his emotions during the gig had run the gamut, from curiosity to exasperation, and then incredulity and finally, wonder.[16]

D'Agostino and Blake became romantically involved "in a way that was not good," said Blake. "Basically, what happened was, I was kind of a piece of shit, and she tolerated me." After breaking up, they didn't speak for several months before reconnecting after seeing each other on the Cap campus. Then, like their first gig, the key changed. "We became really, really close to a point where . . . I don't know how to describe it exactly. Our relationship was quite unique. I don't think that I ever went more than half an hour without receiving a text message from her about something or talking to her on the phone."[17]

• • •

At some point, dedicated young jazz musicians can reach a stage where they're ready to pursue gigs as a leader or co-leader playing their own music. There's no formula or set timetable to it. Developing players just innately know it's time to take the initiative and express themselves. During the 2015/2016 school year, D'Agostino had that self-awareness. That year she performed with vibraphonist Saul Alviar and bassist Stephen Edwards in the Satellite Trio at Presentation House Theatre's Anne MacDonald Studio, plus she led a quintet at the Silk Purse. I was at those gigs on Vancouver's North Shore, and D'Agostino's delight in discovering the possibilities of her voice was palpable. Then in the fall and winter of 2016, she led ensembles at Anne MacDonald Studio and the Gold Saucer. The groups performed some of her original tunes, including early versions of songs that would be important in her ephemeral career: "Sorrow Song," "Flutter," and "Field of Green." The pieces—some with lyrics and others that were wordless compositions emphasizing creative improv—were open-ended and texturally engaging works-in-progress. She sang them at an unrushed tempo with beguiling nuances in her tone and phrasing.

I saw and heard firsthand a succession of high points in her final term as a student. In January 2017, she sang "Just a Closer Walk With Thee" with the Capilano A Band, and listening to her achieve gospel fervour with vocal control well beyond her years was astonishing. "She pulled this off with basically no rehearsal and no chart for the tune," said Burrows, who arranged the iconic hymn for the concert.[18]

Two months later D'Agostino aced a duet with Ambrose Akinmusire, when the trumpeter performed with NiteCap. "That was one of the most beautiful nights of music I've ever experienced," she said. "Ambrose Akinmusire not only showed us a beautiful example of being honest and present in the music, but he left behind such powerful wisdom that I will probably spend the rest of my life processing. Such an amazing human and musician."[19]

In June 2017, on a gorgeous sunny day, D'Agostino and her peers graduated from CapU. Beaming, she strode across the convocation stage in cap and gown to receive her degree in jazz studies and the Dean's Award for Academic Achievement. The award meant D'Agostino went from almost flunking the university's entrance audition to being the top student in her graduating class. After the ceremony, while posing for photos, she and her fellow graduates exuded the joy of accomplishment and the nervous excitement of going on to the next phase in their lives.

Natasha D'Agostino, Capilano University graduation, June 5, 2017.
Photo by Chris Wong.

She didn't waste any time. In July 2017, D'Agostino went on a trip to Europe with her mom that included some days in England. D'Agostino went on a solo train trip from London to the Kent coast for a hugely momentous experience she had arranged: taking a lesson and spending time with Winstone. "Today one of my lifelong dreams came true," wrote D'Agostino that night. "I spent the day with Norma Winstone, visiting, listening to music, playing music, and talking about life. Spending a day with my musical hero has brought me so much inspiration, even as early as the train ride home."[20]

Well before graduation day and the European sojourn, she felt ready to move forward as an artist. D'Agostino's conviction in her singing and original repertoire grew, and she started thinking about recording an album. Blake suggested D'Agostino work with older and more experienced musicians. They talked about possible players; bassist Paul Rushka and drummer Bernie Arai emerged as musicians who would be a good fit with her aesthetic. Blake would also be in the quartet. D'Agostino liked where this was going but hesitated. "At that point, when she was going to pick who to hire, she was really, really insecure," said Blake. "She was worried about whether or not these musicians took her seriously, whether or not these people liked working with her."[21]

She had nothing to worry about. Rushka and Arai embraced working with D'Agostino. The musicians already had a strong rapport during their first gig as a band, at Tangent Café in April 2017. "I remember after the gig her expressing to me how perfect she thought it was," said Blake about D'Agostino's belief in the new band. It wasn't, however, always kumbaya when they collaborated. D'Agostino felt some anxiety about working with Rushka, said Blake. "She had a bit of a hard time with Paul because Paul can be very blunt and doesn't really hold back. Especially working with younger people, I find Paul is very likely to be quite critical of everything from how the band sets up to how the charts are presented." D'Agostino ended up appreciating the tough love. "She realized that there was a certain standard of professionalism that she didn't quite have together in terms of being prepared, being organized," said Blake. "She loved working with those guys because she thought they were so good, and they are, and they could make her music sound just the way she wanted."[22]

Natasha D'Agostino, Frankie's Jazz Club, September 24, 2017. Photos by Vincent Lim.

Four months after the Tangent gig they were at Demitone Studio, where Dave Sikula recorded tracks for *Endings Rarely Are*. D'Agostino's singing on the recording—on five songs she composed and four standards—reflected her budding artistry. The originals include tunes she first performed months before when they were embryonic ideas. With a rigorous sonic backdrop from Blake, Rushka, and Arai, she transforms the songs into fully realized personal statements. Highlights of D'Agostino's pieces include her playful improv on "Flutter," powerful delivery of the memorable melody to "Field of Green," and the inviting shape and flow of her scatting on "Home." On the standards, she draws from other elements in her vocal palette to adeptly navigate fast swing ("Angel Eyes") and convincingly portray old school romantic desire ("You Go to My Head").

Four of D'Agostino's compositions on the album feature her lyrics. I never got the chance to ask to what extent the words were autobiographical and metaphorical. But I know this: she had an imaginative storyteller's instinct for crafting engaging scenes, characters, and details. The elements of her lyric craft weren't all in place yet, and that was part of the appeal—the nascent, searching quality of her imagery drew in the listener.

While Sikula (who engineered the recording) mixed and mastered what was captured at the sessions, and D'Agostino assembled the CD's visual components with help from creative friends, she also kept busy with other projects. One was playing in a duo with pianist Sharon Minemoto. They met when D'Agostino took an improv lesson with Minemoto on a bright day, with the sun "shining like a spotlight on Natasha through the living room window," recalled Minemoto. "I remember thinking that she had a great voice and a nice swing feel, but if she could dig deeper into the harmony, she could really be a standout."[23]

D'Agostino was an enthusiastic learner who returned for more lessons and took Minemoto's advice about harmony to heart. As the two women got to know each other, they recognized commonalities. "Natasha very observantly pointed out that maybe we related easily to each other, despite our age difference, because of the way we were raised," said Minemoto. Both were inspired by their parents' experiences of overcoming challenges of displacement and having to adjust to new cultures and languages. "We were not treated like precious little girls, and at no point would our parents be stage parents for us," said Minemoto. "It was made clear that we were going to have to figure out a way to earn the things we wanted."[24] D'Agostino's mother Anna confirmed that's exactly how she and her husband Rocco raised their daughter: "We both wanted to make sure that she would be tough enough and stand on her own two feet. I don't think we had to do much because by nature, her whole character, she was very independent. And if she believed in something, she stood up for it. She wasn't afraid."[25]

Minemoto and D'Agostino had simpatico musical preferences—both embraced recordings Winstone made with pianists John Taylor and Fred Hersch. Minemoto said D'Agostino appreciated how Winstone's lyrics "created an image or conjured a feeling rather than telling a story about heartache in an obvious way." D'Agostino also connected with the unique "intervallic jumps" in melodies on the recordings.[26]

So when D'Agostino and Minemoto performed as a duo, starting in 2016, they did some of the tunes Winstone recorded with the pianists, as well as originals influenced by the harmonies and arrangements on those recordings. "On the gigs, I remember how Natasha would take things up a couple of notches from the rehearsal," said Minemoto. "It was exciting to hear her close her eyes and take that musical jump. I also remember at some point, we were no longer able to look at each other without laughing, so we had to really listen to each other, which I think made for some lovely moments."[27]

That's a sweet image of two pals and collaborators who made each other giggle with just one look. They planned to record a duo album of original material. That would remain an unrealized dream.

Natasha D'Agostino and Sharon Minemoto, Anne MacDonald Studio, March 7, 2018. Photo by Bill Coon.

Beginning in early 2018, D'Agostino and her Cap friends started performing in Otra, a quintet led by guitarist Parker Woods. His ethereal original tunes were perfect vehicles for more melodic splendour from D'Agostino. My son Miles Wong played drums in Otra and in the first jazz groups D'Agostino led, which meant I got to hear more of her singing because many of their rehearsals took place in a small basement music room that was right under my home office. Through the heating vent, I listened as she assuredly found her way through the songs. Aside from practising, they probably spent as much time—if not more—just chatting and laughing like millennials ought to do. D'Agostino had a distinctive hoarse laugh that happily wafted through the house.

Endings Rarely Are

• • •

It was inevitable that D'Agostino would go on a pilgrimage to New York. Her thirst for jazz was getting deeper and more intense, and New York was the ideal place to slake that thirst. Like any jazz artist or aficionado planning a trip there, she made a list of gigs to catch, including many instrumentalists, which reflected her expanding musical interests. As she did in England, D'Agostino lined up a lesson with a vocalist she admired: Kate McGarry. It was an excellent session. McGarry talked a lot about how to maintain vocal health, a topic that was important to D'Agostino because of her history with vocal nodules. "Her ideas on repertoire and having intent with every musical choice and lyric were also great reminders to always seek depth and meaning in creating, retelling, and working on the music," wrote D'Agostino.[28]

A Vancouver friend, visual artist Yuki Aida, was in New York with D'Agostino. Aida is also friends with alto saxophonist Christopher McBride, who lives in Harlem. Aida talked to McBride about D'Agostino, telling him "Natasha is a great singer."[29] McBride hosted a Sunday night series, Singer Meets Saxophonist, where he and an organ trio played with different singers at Minton's Playhouse in Harlem. There happened to be a gig in the series during D'Agostino's trip, so plans were hatched for her and Aida to attend.

Minton's is a hallowed space in jazz history. Charlie Christian, Dizzy Gillespie, Charlie Parker, Thelonious Monk, Kenny Clarke, and other jazz greats pioneered bebop in the 1940s during exciting jam sessions at Minton's. When D'Agostino walked into the modern incarnation of Minton's, still at the original location on West 118th Street, she was likely well aware of the venue's historic significance. D'Agostino listened to the first set by McBride, organist Jonathan Edward Thomas, drummer Curtis Nowosad, and guest trombonist Jeffrey Miller, soaking in the vibe.

In the second set, which functioned more like a jam session, McBride called D'Agostino to the bandstand to sing a tune. Going up cold like that was something she had done many times before at the Pat's Pub weekly jam that Minemoto coordinated and at the Vancouver International Jazz Festival's nightly jam. But this was Minton's. Was she nervous? "If she was nervous, I couldn't see it," said McBride. "The way she sang, the way she counted off, you could tell she had a presence . . . It was a veteran presence on stage. It wasn't like a rookie up there. She was comfortable." McBride can't recall the tune they did, but he clearly remembers D'Agostino sang it well. "She sounded great," McBride said. "She had a very mature sound. A heavy knowledge of how she wanted to approach the tune that she was doing."[30]

The singer and the saxophonist only met and performed together that one time, but that was enough to make a strong mutual impression. They kept in touch and McBride pledged that if D'Agostino returned to New York, he would give her a full Singer Meets Saxophonist gig at Minton's. She told McBride about wanting to someday move to and make a go of it in New York. He believes D'Agostino would have succeeded because of her focus on constant learning. "That's the thing I definitely remember, is that I felt that type of energy of 'I just want to learn and grow,'" McBride said. "If you come to New York with that attitude, there's nowhere to go but up."[31] D'Agostino also talked to Blake about the notion of moving to New York when she was ready. "She was definitely ready, and she could have done anything," Blake said. "She was going to outgrow what was available to her in Vancouver pretty quickly."[32]

While D'Agostino was in New York, copies of the *Endings Rarely Are* CD arrived back home. She was excited about performing the music live, but it would be three months before the CD release at Frankie's. As always, D'Agostino filled that time learning and creating in the East Vancouver house where she lived, when she wasn't seeing friends and family or making, teaching, and listening to music in the community. "Natasha wanted to learn everything," said Blake. "If she wasn't reading, she was painting. If she wasn't painting, she was practicing piano. If she wasn't practicing piano, she was helping one of her many friends. She was cooking, writing, rehearsing, teaching, teaching, teaching, writing lyrics, writing big band music. She contributed so much to this community in such a devastatingly short amount of time."[33]

After the CD release concert, D'Agostino and Blake took the time to acknowledge what they had accomplished. "We talked about how good it felt to create that music that night, how happy with this record we were, how proud of each other we were, and how much we loved making this music together," said Blake. "It's part of the tragedy that this record now is her entire body of work. There was so much more that she was going to do. The music was just going to get better."[34]

As 2018 wound down, D'Agostino kept going. She recorded with Otra at a former church she had performed in many times: Anne MacDonald Studio.

She had one last duo show with Minemoto at Vancouver Community College, where they performed repertoire including Winstone tunes and Jimmy Rowles' ballad "The Peacocks," which D'Agostino sang beautifully.

Her quartet performed a final time at Tangent, December 6, 2018. Plus, she sang with Cory Weeds at Frankie's, five days before Christmas. "I had the great pleasure of having Natasha D'Agostino guest with my quartet last night, and it was phenomenal," wrote Weeds the next day. "She is the real deal, and I'm excited to see what is in store for her."[35] Then there were two nights of duo performances at the Anvil Centre in New Westminster with another friend, bassist Jodi Proznick. The women became very close during a collaborative, mentorship process—pairing an established artist with an emerging one—that culminated with the shows.

Natasha D'Agostino, Frankie's Jazz Club, December 20, 2018. Photo by Vincent Lim.

On New Year's Eve, in a Facebook and Instagram post, D'Agostino looked back at her busy and meaningful year: "2018 was filled with a lot of changes to adjust to and losses to mourn. It was also filled with some of the biggest dreams coming true, and it held the space for some of the best people to enter into my life. 2018 taught me how to see goals all the way through to the finish line, and it also taught me to slow down. It brought me some of my favourite books ever written. It encouraged me to create, and to find new hobbies. It taught me to tell the people in my life that I love them. A lot. It taught me that life is short, and gave me a glimpse of how precious and unpredictable it can be. [Her grandmother—Anna D'Agostino's mother—passed away in 2018, and D'Agostino sang "I'll Be Seeing You" (the last track on *Endings Rarely Are*) at her funeral.] I'm thankful for a year filled with so many opportunities to reflect on what it means to be human, and I'm even more thankful for the wonderful humans that made my year so full. Bring it on, 2019! Happy New Year, friends! Wishing you happiness and health in 2019. I hope all your dreams come true."[36]

The last time I saw her was January 3, 2019, at Tangent. D'Agostino wasn't performing that night but, as always, she was there to hear the music, support her friends who were playing, and hang out with them. The next day, D'Agostino posted about how stoked she was about going to the Banff Centre for Arts and Creativity at the end of the month to spend two weeks with neo-soul band Tiny Havoc. Just over a month earlier, Blake had been to Guilt & Co. in Gastown to hear D'Agostino sing and play keyboards with the same band. "She sounded brilliant singing it [neo-soul]," he said. "She could do that as well as anybody."[37]

• • •

In the early hours of January 6, 2019, after visiting her dear friend Paige Hansen, she drove home in heavy rain on Highway 99. It was a route she had driven many times. According to news stories, a lone female driver died after leaving the roadway.[38] It was twenty-six-year-old Natasha D'Agostino.

Through phone calls, texts, and other means, people received the devastating news. I found out when I came home that Sunday and encountered my son in tears, inconsolable. When I heard the reason for his tears, I couldn't process it. *That can't be true. There must be a mistake.* Those were the pleas, the questions in my mind that couldn't change the heartbreaking finality. That night, her comrades from Cap gathered to remember their friend.

The next night, many more musicians congregated at the Pat's Pub jam. "Thanks to the many, many people who came to the jam last night," Minemoto wrote on Facebook afterwards. "It's not often that so many people in one room are feeling the same way. As sad as we all were, there was something warm, beautiful, and calm about it. I think Natasha would've loved that so many of her friends were connecting with each other in such a real way . . . not through phone screens, but looking at each other in the eye while speaking or hugging a tearful friend. The genuine kindness and concern for others that she was so well-known for came out in all of you, so I am thankful that her magic was not lost when we lost her. Let's keep channelling her as we move forward to make the world a better place."[39]

As part of their grieving, dozens of people who knew and loved D'Agostino did what's done in the digital age—they posted eloquent remembrances on Facebook. The tributes culminated on January 26, 2019, when hundreds of family members, friends, musicians, educators, and others gathered at Capilano University for a celebration of D'Agostino's life. It was fitting that the event revolved around music, with ensembles that honoured her through emotional performances.

Close friends spoke. Like Minemoto, who was the last speaker. She remembered her kindred spirit as "an old soul who always tried to remain grounded in the truth in an age of so many things artificial." Minemoto, who four years later recorded with her quartet the resonant "Alexandra (for Natasha)", addressed the heavy sorrow in the room and suggested a path forward. "I think we would make Natasha proud if we talked less and listened more. If we listened to great storytellers to inspire us to live our lives fully. If we listened to what people's needs are rather than making a big deal about what we want. If we listened to the small nuances in music that make our heart sing."[40]

Rocco and Anna D'Agostino sat not far from the stage where there were spoken and musical tributes to their daughter, and where they saw her perform many times. Their nephew Kevan D'Agostino spoke about how, for his cousin, family was central. "Natasha wasn't just a member of our family—she was the nucleus of our family, and she would remind us of its importance through selfless acts of kindness and support. She would always show up to events no matter how big or small. If it was family, it was important."[41]

After the speeches, as those who were there processed their emotions and feelings, I waited behind some people to offer condolences to Rocco. In this theatre, during the three years when both of our kids were in NiteCap, we had exchanged many warm greetings. I struggled to think of the right words to say. When I got to the front of the line, Rocco took my hand, held on to it, and strongly encouraged my son to pursue his dreams. It was an incredibly generous and beautiful moment.

I consciously let more than two years go by before reaching out to family and friends about telling D'Agostino's story. They needed space and time to heal. David Blake was the first person I connected with to find out what D'Agostino meant—and still means—to the jazz community. Another person I contacted: Proznick. "I really was imagining a lot of collaboration moving forward with her," said Proznick. "She was a very bright light that a lot of us saw as not just being a contributor but being a leader in our community." They talked extensively about being women in jazz. "A lot of the conversation we had was around how to make the scene more welcoming, more inclusive, and more empowering for more women. She was a staunch feminist, and she helped me really think about those questions a lot more . . . I miss her. A lot."[42]

While Blake praised D'Agostino, he also toned down accolades that idealized his friend. "One thing that I experienced when she died, everybody wanted to talk about how wonderful she was. Natasha was a real person with flaws. And she had issues and she had insecurities and she was annoying sometimes, and sometimes I was mad at her and sometimes she was mad at me. She wasn't like this crystal glass that was so wonderful, sparkling from every direction all the time. She was a real, complex person."[43]

After D'Agostino's death, there was an impulse to look back at things she said and titles she chose, in a belated search for meaning. A prime example is the name of her album, *Endings Rarely Are*. The title came about after Blake watched a TV show in which one character recalls the death of her father and says ". . . it wasn't exactly a happy ending." To which another character says wearily: "Endings rarely are." Blake: "I remember hearing this and texting Natasha right away." Blake suggested that she use it for the title, and

Endings Rarely Are

D'Agostino liked the idea. After her death, the title seemed prescient. "There are a lot of ways you could take that title and morph it into some meaning to connect it to Natasha's death," said Blake. "They're all worth thinking about and experiencing."[44]

Natasha D'Agostino, January 14, 2018. Image on the cover of Endings Rarely Are. Photo by Pier-Alexandre Gagné.

One interpretation of the three simple words in the title is that while endings have an unavoidable finality, they are not absolute. In D'Agostino's case, she tragically lost her life. She also, after less than half a decade of being in the scene, left an enduring legacy. "In a certain way, she invigorated and injected the community with this energy that I think kind of still exists," said Blake. "I've certainly had the sense at times, 'Damn, I've got to be working at least half as hard as Natasha was if I want to make anything of my music career.' I think other people felt that way."[45] Blake became one of Vancouver's top jazz guitarists before moving to New York to do his Master's in Jazz Performance at New York University and become part of the preeminent New York scene. The memory of D'Agostino was part of the inspiration that emboldened him to take this path.

In her brief time as a performing artist, D'Agostino struggled with self-doubt, made creative breakthroughs, engaged audiences, and inspired musicians, students, and audiences through hard work, respect for tradition, musical curiosity, and risk-taking. On and off the bandstand, she was a positive and supportive friend to many. I'll always remember Natasha D'Agostino as a rare soul who beautifully expressed, in music and her many other facets, a pure belief and joy in life's possibilities and fulfillments.

IT TAKES A COMMUNITY—AND VISIONARY INDIVIDUALS—TO RAISE A JAZZ SCENE: CODA

I BEGAN *JOURNEYS to the Bandstand* with a focus on the individual in jazz. My rationale for crafting a series of deep-dive portraits of jazz musicians—and a few non-musicians affiliated with Vancouver's jazz scene—was that key moments from each individual's path in music, other disciplines, and life itself, were critical to shaping their unique expression and contributions.

After years of studying and chronicling the thirty jazz lives in the preceding twenty-five chapters, I continue to think it's valid to emphasize individual journeys in jazz. Those passages, with their challenges and triumphs, have engendered extraordinary sounds.

While envisioning, researching, interviewing, writing, rewriting, and reflecting on these portraits, something else emerged. I kept hearing about and witnessing stories that transcended the individual: the camaraderie of playing local gigs and being on the road with unforgettable characters; weekly house jams held, not for audiences, but for the simple pleasure of playing with long-time collaborators and friends; and musicians going to palliative care wards to be there for colleagues in their final days, and gathering at celebrations of life to honour the lives of those who have passed.

They're examples of what's long been at the heart of Vancouver's jazz scene: a supportive community held together by the glue of generous mentorship, shared passion for the music, and deep friendship. While community may be an overused word, its impact is real when manifested through small gestures, as simple as giving someone a gig.

That said, jazz scenes are not conflict-free. Resentment, differences in opinion, and animosity happen in this and other scenes, which reflect society at large where unanimity doesn't exist.

A question preoccupied me. How do a jazz scene's protagonists—the musicians and impresarios—survive and thrive in a place like Vancouver, one of the most expensive Canadian cities to live in, where the number of capable players exceeds the number of gigs, and audiences can hesitate before becoming bums on seats?

Again, the jazz community's pillars of support are key. Crucial to a jazz scene's success are visionary individuals who are hardwired to imagine possibility and take the initiative to make the possible real, which lifts themselves and others up.

So just as there's a balance between the group sound and the soloist's expression, the jazz scenes here and elsewhere depend on both the individual impulse and community sustenance to co-exist. I learned from closely examining the lives of the thirty artists featured on these pages and their collaborators, that when the two forces empathetically come together, creative breakthroughs and fulfilling musical lives are often the result. With some of my subjects, though, the fulfillment never fully arrived.

Among the musicians I studied and chronicled, the person with the most compelling synergy of individual impetus and community connection was the youngest: Natasha D'Agostino. It is my hope that Natasha's story, and the other stories in *Journeys to the Bandstand*, will enduringly remain in the Vancouver jazz scene's collective memory.

SELECTED DISCOGRAPHY

Cannonball Adderley
Swingin' in Seattle, Live at the Penthouse 1966-67
Reel to Real, 2018

Cannonball Adderley Quintet
Mercy, Mercy, Mercy!, Live at "The Club"
Capitol Records, 1967

Mike Allen
Quintet/Quartet
Almus Jazz, 1995

One Side Of A Circle
Almus Jazz, 1999

Change Is
Maximum Jazz, 2000

A Hip Cosmos
Almus Jazz, 2012

Just Like Magic
Cellar Music, 2019

Mike Allen Quartet
Chasin' The Train Radio Podcast #9 – Mike Allen Quartet 'A Love Supreme'
Recorded live at Cory Weeds'
Cellar, 2009

https://www.podomatic.com/podcasts/chasinthetrain/episodes/2011-01-29T15_12_09-08_00
Unreleased

The Anniversary Quartet
You'll See, The Anniversary Quartet Live at the Cellar
Cellar Live, 2005

Peter Bernstein and the Tilden Webb Trio
Peter Bernstein with the Tilden Webb Trio
Cellar Live, 2013

Pat Bianchi, Bill Coon, and Jesse Cahill
Crazy
Cellar Live, 2012

Jim Byrnes
House Of Refuge
Black Hen Music, 2006

Brian Charette
Jackpot
Cellar Music, 2022

Morgan Childs Quintet
Time
Cellar Live, 2008

Seleno Clarke
"Soulful Drop" and "Memphis
Boogaloo" (45 RPM 7")
M.O.C., 1970

"Exploitation of Soul" and "Stimulation"
(45 RPM 7")
Right-On Records, 1970

George Coleman and Tete Montoliu
Meditation
Timeless, 1977

Also released as:
Dynamic Duo
Timeless, 1992

George Coleman
Recorded live at Cory Weeds'
Cellar, 2013
Unreleased

George Coleman Quintet
*The George Coleman Quintet
in Baltimore*
Reel to Real, 2020

Ornette Coleman
Something Else!!!!
Contemporary Records, 1958

Pat Coleman – Bob Murphy Quartet
Come Rain or Come Shine
2001

Coat Cooke Trio
Up Down Down Up
Cellar Live, 2005

Dylan Cramer Quartet
The First One
DSM, 1997

Also released as:
Dylan Cramer
Remembering Sonny Criss
Nagel Heyer Records, 2020

Crash
The Doctor Is In
Cellar Live, 2004

Sonny Criss
Crisscraft
Muse Records, 1975

Saturday Morning
Xanadu Records, 1975

Natasha D'Agostino
Endings Rarely Are
2018

Miles Davis
Birth of the Cool
Capitol Records, 1957

Seven Steps to Heaven
Columbia Records, 1963

Elton Dean's Ninesense
Happy Daze
Ogun, 1977

Kevin Dean/PJ Perry Quintet
Ubiquitous
Cellar Live, 2012

Christine Duncan and Bob Murphy
I Have a Dream
1994

Ella Fitzgerald
*Ella Fitzgerald Sings the Rodgers and Hart
Song Book*
Verve, 1956

Selected Discography

Hugh Fraser Quintet
Looking Up
CBC Records, 1988

Gastown Chronicles
Boathouse Records, 2021

Garbo's Hat
Face The Music
Word of Mouth, 1993

Linton Garner Trio
Quiet Nights
Cellar Live, 2006

Sonny Greenwich
Standard Idioms
Kleo Records, 1992

Fragments of a Memory
Cornerstone Records, 2001

Bobby Hales Big Band
One Of My Bags
Center Line, 1975

Kate Hammett-Vaughan
How My Heart Sings
Maximum Jazz, 1998

Devil May Care
Maximum Jazz, 2001

Eclipse
Maximum Jazz, 2004

Conspiracy: Art Songs for Improvisers
2006

Herbie Hancock
Maiden Voyage
Blue Note Records, 1965

Bruno Hubert Trio
Get Out of Town
Cellar Live, 2002

Live @ THE CELLAR
Cellar Live, 2008

Harold Land Quartet
Jazz at the Cellar 1958
Lone Hill Jazz, 2007

Peggy Lee
Echo Painting
Songlines Recordings, 2018

Joe Lovano and the Brad Turner Quartet
Recorded live at Capilano College Performing Arts Theatre, 2001
Unreleased

The Mangione Brothers Sextet
The Jazz Brothers
Riverside/A Cannonball Adderley Presentation, 1960

Maraca & His Latin Jazz All Stars
Reencuentros
2011

Charles McPherson
Live At The Cellar
Cellar Live, 2002

Metalwood
Metalwood
1997

The Recline
Maximum Music/Universal Music, 2001

Sharon Minemoto
Safe Travels
Pagetown Records, 2016

Montgomery Brothers
The Montgomery Brothers in Canada
Fantasy Records, 1961

Also released as:
Wes Montgomery with Buddy Montgomery and Monk Montgomery
Groove Brothers
Milestone Records, 1979 and 1998

Bob Murphy
Solo piano, recorded live at the Western Front, 1976
Unreleased

Bob Murphy, Torben Oxbol, and Alan Wiertz
Improvisational Communications
1979

Bob Murphy Quartet
Downtown East Side Picnic
Artist Jazz Recordings, 2007

Bob Murphy and Ross Taggart
Mysteries and Tall Tales
Roadhouse Records, 2001

Bob Murphy and Monique Van Dam
Beautiful
2017

Al Neil Quintet
CBC *Jazz Workshop* broadcast, 1956
Unreleased

Al Neil
The Cellar Years – Archival Recordings from 1957
Condition West Recordings, 2017

Al Neil Trio
Retrospective 1965-1968
Blue Minor Records, 2001

The October Trio
Day In
Cellar Live Futures, 2006

The Ostara Project
The Ostara Project
Cellar Music, 2022

Otra
Otra
https://otra.bandcamp.com/releases
2017

Charlie Parker
The Long Lost Bird Live Afro-Cubop Recordings!
S'more Entertainment/Rockbeat Records, 2015

Kenneth Patchen & the Alan Neil Quartet
Kenneth Patchen Reads With Jazz in Canada
Folkways, 1959 and Locust Music, 2004

Art Pepper
Recorded live at the original Cellar, July 23, 1959
Unreleased

PJ Perry
Sessions
Suite Records, 1978

Worth Waiting For
Concord/The Jazz Alliance, 1991

My Ideal
Unity Records, 1992

Selected Discography

PJ Perry/Campbell Ryga Quintet
Joined at the Hip
Cellar Live, 2008

PJ Perry featuring Bill Mays
This Quiet Room
Cellar Music, 2019

Jodi Proznick Quartet
Foundations
Cellar Live, 2006

Sun Songs
Cellar Live, 2017

Dave Quarin Sextet
CBC *Jazz Workshop* broadcast, 1957
Unreleased

Dave Robbins Big Band
Recorded in the early 1960s
Unreleased

Dave Robbins Jazz Orchestra
Recorded live at Seattle World's Fair, 1962
Unreleased

Sonny Rollins and Coleman Hawkins
Sonny Meets Hawk!
RCA Victor, 1963

Sonny Rollins
Now's The Time
RCA Victor, 1964

Bill Runge, Bob Murphy, Buff Allen
B3
2003

Jennifer Scott Trio
Something To Live By
2004

Ray Sikora Big Band
Recorded live at the original Cellar, 1963
Unreleased

Ron Small
Live
Recorded live at the Cotton Club, 1999
Unreleased

Lonnie Smith
Finger-Lickin' Good Soul Organ
Columbia, 1967

Lenox and Seventh
Black & Blue, 1985

Dr. Lonnie Smith
Evolution
Blue Note Records, 2016

Gary Smulyan and Joe Magnarelli with the Tilden Webb Trio
Live at Cory Weeds' Cellar Jazz Club
Cellar Live, 2021

The Sojourners
Hold On
Black Hen Music, 2007

The Sojourners
Black Hen Music, 2009

Fred Stride Jazz Orchestra
Forward Motion
Cellar Live, 2006

Ross Taggart
Ross Taggart & Co
Boathouse Records, 1998

Ross Taggart Quartet
Thankfully
Cellar Live, 2001

533

Ross Taggart Trio
Presenting the Ross Taggart Trio
Cellar Live, 2008

Joani Taylor and Bob Murphy Trio
The Wall Street Sessions
Roadhouse Records, 2002

Joani Taylor and Bob Murphy
The Art of the Jazz Ballad
Roadhouse Records, 2004

Joani Taylor
In My Own Voice
Wet Coast Records, 2008

Amanda Tosoff
Wait and See
Cellar Live, 2008

Looking North
Oceans Beyond Records, 2010

Live at the Cellar
Oceans Beyond Records, 2013

Words
Empress Music Group, 2016

Earth Voices
Empress Music Group, 2021

Amanda Tosoff Quartet
Still Life
Cellar Live Futures, 2006

Jill Townsend Big Band
Legacy, The music of Ross Taggart
Cellar Live, 2015

Brad Turner
Pacific
Cellar Music, 2018

Brad Turner Quartet
Four-song cassette
1993

Long Story Short
1997

Over My Head
Groundhog Recordings, 2015

Brad Turner Quartet featuring Seamus Blake
Live at the Cellar
Maximum Jazz, 2000

Brad Turner Quartet with guest Seamus Blake
Jump Up
Cellar Music, 2019

Brad Turner Quintet
The Magnificent
Cellar Music, 2023

Brad Turner Trio
Here Now
Groundhog Recordings, 2015

Turning Point Ensemble
Seven Scenes From a Childhood, https://soundcloud.com/turningpointensemble/sets/seven-scenes-from-a-childhood
Unreleased

McCoy Tyner
Tender Moments
Blue Note Records, 1968

Fly with the Wind
Milestone Records, 1976

Selected Discography

Vancouver Ensemble of Jazz Improvisation (VEJI)
Recorded live at the Western Front, 1980
Unreleased

VEJI
1981

Classic VEJI
From Bebop To Now Records, 1986

VEJI NOW!
Unity, 1990

Big Works
Boathouse Records, 2002

Canadian Dedication
Boathouse Records, 2021

Tilden Webb Trio with special guest David Fathead Newman
Cellar Groove
Cellar Live, 2005

Also released as:
David Fathead Newman & the Tilden Webb Trio
Cellar Groove
Cellar Live, 2013

Cory Weeds
Big Weeds
Cellar Live, 2008

The Many Deeds of Cory Weeds
Cellar Live, 2010

As of Now
Cellar Live, 2014

Cory Weeds Quintet Featuring Steve Davis
Let's Go!
Cellar Live, 2013

Cory Weeds Little Big Band
Explosion!
Cellar Live, 2018

Cory Weeds with Strings
What Is There To Say?
Cellar Music, 2021

Kenny Wheeler
Music for Large & Small Ensembles
ECM Records, 1990

Various Artists

Dizzy Gillespie, Freddie Hubbard, Clark Terry, Oscar Peterson, Ray Brown, Joe Pass, and Bobby Durham
The Trumpet Summit Meets The Oscar Peterson Big 4
Pablo Today, 1980

Maximum Jazz Presents Live At The Cellar
Maximum Jazz, 2001

Poor Boy: Songs of Nick Drake
Songlines Recordings, 2004

Things About Comin' My Way – A tribute to the music of The Mississippi Sheiks
Black Hen Music, 2009

The Mississippi Sheiks Tribute Concert
Black Hen Music, 2010

BIBLIOGRAPHY

BOOKS

Allen, Mike. *Jazz Anthology: 90 Original Compositions and Recollections.* Tellwell, 2021.

Balliett, Whitney. *American Musicians: 56 Portraits in Jazz.* New York, Oxford: Oxford University Press, 1986.

Best, Christopher. *Hearts, Minds & Souls: The true stories of 23 respected, career B.C. Music Educators who influenced the lives of many young people through music.* Vancouver: Warfleet Press, 2016.

Bowen, Lynne. *Whoever Gives Us Bread: The Story of Italians in British Columbia.* Vancouver/Toronto: Douglas & McIntyre, 2011.

Brown, Adrienne. *The Life and Art of Harry and Jessie Webb.* Salt Spring Island: Mother Tongue Publishing Limited, 2014.

Chapman, Aaron. *Vancouver After Dark: The Wild History of a City's Nightlife.* Vancouver: Arsenal Pulp Press, 2019.

Cramer, Dylan. *Alto Saxophone Mastery.* Dylan Cramer, 2019.

Davis, Chuck, ed. *The Greater Vancouver Book: An Urban Encyclopaedia.* Surrey: Linkman Press, 1997.

Davis, Miles with Troupe, Quincy. *Miles: The Autobiography.* New York, London, Toronto, Sydney, Tokyo, Singapore: Simon & Schuster, 1989.

Gioia, Ted. *West Coast Jazz: Modern Jazz in California.* Berkely, Los Angeles, London: University of California Press, 1998.

Hancock, Herbie with Dickey, Lisa. *Possibilities.* New York: Viking, 2014.

Harvey, Edward B. *Taking Social Research to the Larger World.* Toronto: Canadian Scholars' Press, 2005.

Jago, Marian. *Live at the Cellar: Vancouver's iconic jazz club and the Canadian co-operative jazz scene in the 1950s and '60s.* Vancouver, Toronto: UBC Press, 2018.

Miller, Mark. *Jazz in Canada: Fourteen Lives*. Toronto, Buffalo, London: University of Toronto Press, 1982.

Miller, Mark. *Boogie, Pete & The Senator: Canadian Musicians in Jazz: The Eighties*. Toronto: Nightwood Editions, 1987.

Miller, Mark. *The Miller Companion to Jazz in Canada and Canadians in Jazz*. The Mercury Press, 2001.

Miller, Mark. *Of Stars and Strings*. Tellwell, 2020.

Neil, Al. *Changes*. London, Ontario: Nightwood Editions, 1989.

Neil, Al. *Origins*. Western Front, 1989.

Ratliff, Ben. *The Jazz Ear: Conversations Over Music*. New York: Times Books, Henry Holt and Company, 2008.

Ross, Becki L. *Burlesque West: Showgirls, Sex, and Sin in Postwar Vancouver*. Toronto, Buffalo, London: University of Toronto Press, 2009.

Santoro, Gene. *Myself When I Am Real*. New York: Oxford University Press, 2000.

Smith, Larry. *Kenneth Patchen: Rebel Poet in America*. Bottom Dog Press, 2000.

Varty, Alex. "Al Neil: Music at the Centre." In *The Georgia Straight: What The Hell Happened? The Best of The Georgia Straight*, edited by Naomi Pauls and Charles Campbell. Vancouver/Toronto: Douglas & McIntyre, 1997.

Wallace, Keith, ed. *Whispered Art History: Twenty Years At The Western Front*. Vancouver: Arsenal Pulp Press, 1993.

Williams, Martin. *The Jazz Tradition*. New York: Oxford University Press, 1970.

ARTICLES

See Notes.

FILM

Bloom, Jeffrey, director. *Dogpound Shuffle*. Paramount Pictures. 1975. 98 minutes. https://www.youtube.com/watch?v=c8_nO0MATao.

Forest, Léonard, director. In Search of Innocence. National Film Board of Canada. 1963. 28 minutes.

McDowall, Kerilie, director, writer, producer. *In the Zone: Rick Kilburn*. 2020. 10 minutes, 36 seconds.

Macartney-Filgate, Terence, director. *Fields of Endless Day*. National Film Board of Canada. 1978. 60 minutes. https://www.youtube.com/watch?v=Drt1qvTOZ1U.

Marshall, George, director. *The Goldwyn Follies*. Samuel Goldwyn Productions. 1938, 122 minutes.

Reichman, Thomas, director. *Mingus: Charlie Mingus 1968*. Inlet Films. 1968. 58 minutes. https://www.youtube.com/watch?v=JY_ebWRCPQM.

Rimmer, David, director. *Al Neil / A Portrait*. 1979. 45 minutes. https://vancouverartinthesixties.com/archive/763.

Simard, Michael, director. *Bruno's Blues*. Bruno's Blues Productions Inc., 2011. 80 minutes.

Spring, Sylvia, director. *Madeleine Is*. Spring Releases Ltd., 1971. 90 minutes. https://www.youtube.com/watch?v=fwCegaOCiTk.

TELEVISION

Carney, James, producer. *Mind of Mingus – Jazz One*. January 12, 1961, CBUT and March 28, 1961, *Quest*, CBC-TV.

INTERVIEWS WITH THE AUTHOR

Mike Allen
Bernie Arai
Ross Barrett
Mike Beddoes
Peter Bernstein
Fiona Black
Miles Black
David Blake
Julie Brown
Jesse Cahill
John Capon
James (Jim) Carney
Nikita Carter
Morgan Childs
Bill Clark
Donnie Clark
Seleno Clarke
Terry Clarke
Joanne Clifton
George Coleman
George Colligan
Bill Coon
Dylan Cramer
Anna D'Agostino
Rocco D'Agostino
James Danderfer
Steve Davis
John Dawe
Michael de Courcy
Joey DeFrancesco

Lorae Farrell
Wilmer (Bill) Fawcett
Maurice Foisy
Don Fraser Jr.
Hugh Fraser
John Frederickson
Don Friedman
Jack Fulton
Chris Gestrin
Michael Grunewaldt
Collette Hackl
Bobby Hales
Jeff Hamilton
Kate Hammett-Vaughan
Louis Hayes
Ian Hendrickson-Smith
Terry Hill
Ken Hole
Bruno Hubert
Jim (Jimmy) Johnson
Steve Kaldestad
Tom Keenlyside
Jim Kilburn
Rick Kilburn
John Korsrud
André Lachance
Jenny Larisey
Mike LeDonne
John Le Marquand
Stephano Liapis

Walley Lightbody
Harold Mabern
Katie Malloch
Joan Mariacher
Jon Mayer
Christopher McBride
Roy McCurdy
Ian McDougall
Charles McPherson
Eric Metcalfe
Reece Metcalfe Rehm
Sharon Minemoto
Marcus Mosley
Bob Murphy
Carol Murphy
Margo Murphy
Steve Mynett
Lewis Nash
Brian Nation
Tracy Neff
Karen Newman
Andreas Nothiger
John Orysik
PJ Perry
Ray Piper
Jodi Proznick
Dave Quarin
Jamie Reid
Jack Reynolds
Dave Robbins

Ed Roop	Don Thompson	Cory Weeds
Mike Rud	Amanda Tosoff	Blaine Wikjord
Campbell Ryga	Bob Turner	Tim Williams
Jennifer Scott	Brad Turner	Spike Wilner
Gregg Simpson	George Ursan	Audie Wong
Dick Smith	Monique Van Dam	Rod Wong
Dr. Lonnie Smith	Gavin Walker	Rene Worst
Gary Smulyan	Jan Walters	Doreen Young
Bryan Stovell	Tilden Webb	Henry Young
Joani Taylor	Bill Weeds	

Interviews were also conducted with other musicians and jazz aficionados who were not quoted due to space constraints, but they provided helpful information and context:

Phil Belanger, Warren Chiasson, Jim Chivers, Eleanor Collins, Elaine, Dave Engleman, Oliver Gannon, Brian Guns, Bruce Macdonald, Lynne McNeil, George Robertson, Alice Samworth, Grant Stewart, Bob Wilson, and Norman Young.

NOTES

THE INDIVIDUAL PATH IN JAZZ: PREFACE AND INTRODUCTION

1. Martin Williams, *The Jazz Tradition* (New York: Oxford University Press, 1970), 10.
2. Williams, *The Jazz Tradition*, 11.
3. Ibid.

IN TIME: SELECTED CHRONOLOGY

1. Many of the chapters in this book touch on both the original musician-run Cellar jazz club on Watson Street near Broadway that was open from 1956 to 1964, and Cory Weeds' Cellar on West Broadway that Weeds owned and operated from 2000 to 2014. Weeds' club had multiple variations on its name over the years, but all of them included the word "Cellar." To differentiate the two clubs, in the main text and photo captions, the first Cellar is generally referred to as "the original Cellar" and the second club is simply, "the Cellar."
2. Ibid.

1 / LIVING THE JAZZ LIFE: JOHN DAWE

1. John Dawe, with Gregg Simpson, "The Original Cellar Jazz Club," *The Original Cellar Jazz Club*, December 7, 2010, http://theoriginalcellarjazzclub.blogspot.com/2010/11/story-by-john-dawe.html.
2. Ibid.
3. "John Dawe March 7, 1931 – December 12, 2018," *REMEMBERING.CA, Obituaries*, https://vancouversunandprovince.remembering.ca/obituary/john-dawe-1071861639.
4. Ibid.
5. John Dawe, interview with the author, July 17, 2013.
6. Ibid.

7   Ibid.
8   Ibid.
9   John Dawe, with Gregg Simpson, "The Original Cellar Jazz Club," *The Original Cellar Jazz Club*, December 7, 2010, http://theoriginalcellarjazzclub.blogspot.com/2010/11/story-by-john-dawe.html.
10 Terry Hill, interview with the author, October 15, 2013.
11 Dawe, interview with the author, July 17, 2013.
12 Jim Kilburn, interview with the author, August 13, 2013
13 Wilmer Fawcett, interview with the author, November 22, 2013.
14 Dawe, interview with the author, July 17, 2013.
15 PJ Perry, interview with the author, April 18, 2014.
16 John Frederickson, interview with the author, November 8, 2016.
17 Ed Roop, interview with the author, November 2, 2016.
18 Don Thompson, interview with the author, November 26, 2013.
19 Bobby Hales, interview with the author, October 18, 2013.
20 Ibid.
21 Ibid.
22 Dawe, interview with the author, July 17, 2013.
23 Ibid.
24 Dawe, interview with the author, January 6, 2017.
25 Dawe, interview with the author, July 17, 2013.
26 "John Dawe March 7, 1931 – December 12, 2018," *REMEMBERING.CA, Obituaries*, https://vancouversunandprovince.remembering.ca/obituary/john-dawe-1071861639.
27 Ibid.
28 "John Dawe March 7, 1931 – December 12, 2018," *REMEMBERING.CA, Obituaries*, https://vancouversunandprovince.remembering.ca/obituary/john-dawe-1071861639.
29 Ibid.
30 Tom Keenlyside, interview with the author, October 29, 2016.
31 Ibid.
32 Keenlyside, interview with the author, April 17, 2022.
33 Ibid.
34 Ibid.
35 Ibid.
36 Keenlyside, interview with the author, October 29, 2016.
37 Dawe, interview with the author, July 17, 2013.
38 Dawe, interview with the author, March 9, 2018.
39 Ibid.

40 "John Dawe March 7, 1931 – December 12, 2018," *REMEMBERING.CA, Obituaries*, https://vancouversunandprovince.remembering.ca/obituary/john-dawe-1071861639.

2 / THE ELECTRICAL GUITARIST AND HIS ONLY SON: JIM AND RICK KILBURN

1 Jim Kilburn, interview with the author, August 13, 2013.
2 Jim Kilburn, *1950's—1960's Jazz in Vancouver as recalled by guitarist Jim Kilburn*.
3 Photo caption, *Vancouver News-Herald*, February 23, 1954, 12.
4 Jim Kilburn, interview with the author, August 13, 2013.
5 Photo caption, *Vancouver Sun*, February 24, 1954, 21.
6 "American Jazz Festival Not Kenton at His Best," *Vancouver Sun*, February 24, 1954, 2.
7 Jim Kilburn, interview with the author, August 13, 2013.
8 Western Conservatory Of Music, advertisement, *Vancouver Province*, July 2, 1955, 8.
9 "Fall fatal to popular guitarist," *Province*, December 27, 1958, 5.
10 Don Thompson, interview with the author, November 26, 2013.
11 Jim Kilburn, interview with the author, August 13, 2013.
12 Don Thompson, interview with the author, November 26, 2013.
13 Wilmer Fawcett, interview with the author, November 22, 2013.
14 Ibid.
15 Jim Kilburn, interview with the author, August 13, 2013.
16 Kilburn, *1950's—1960's Jazz in Vancouver as recalled by guitarist Jim Kilburn*.
17 Jim Kilburn, interview with the author, August 13, 2013.
18 Kilburn, *1950's—1960's Jazz in Vancouver as recalled by guitarist Jim Kilburn*.
19 Ibid.
20 Rick Kilburn, interview with the author, January 5, 2019.
21 Ibid.
22 Kilburn, *1950's—1960's Jazz in Vancouver as recalled by guitarist Jim Kilburn*.
23 Orrin Keepnews, Producer's Note for Wes Montgomery, *Groove Brothers*, Milestone Records MCD 47076-2, compact disc.
24 Ibid.
25 Jim Kilburn, interview with the author, August 13, 2013.
26 Ibid
27 Rick Kilburn, interview with the author, January 5, 2019.
28 Ibid.
29 Music Man, "No-alcohol clubs serve music," *Province*, March 16, 1963, 9.
30 Tom Keenlyside, interview with the author, October 29, 2016.
31 Ibid.

[32] Rick Kilburn, interview with the author, January 5, 2019.
[33] Ibid.
[34] Whitney Balliett, "Good, Careful Melody," in *American Musicians: 56 Portraits in Jazz* (New York: Oxford University Press, 1986), 388-391.
[35] Bob Smith, "City bassist moving up," *Vancouver Sun*, February 8, 1980, 10L.
[36] Rick Kilburn, interview with the author, January 5, 2019.
[37] Ibid.
[38] Rick Kilburn, interview with the author, April 11, 2022.
[39] Rick Kilburn, interview with the author, January 5, 2019.
[40] Jim Kilburn, interview with the author, August 13, 2013.
[41] Rick Kilburn, interview with the author, January 5, 2019.
[42] "Joyce Lucille Kilburn," Parksville Qualicum Beach News, Obituaries, https://www.pqbnews.com/obituaries/joyce-lucille-kilburn/.
[43] Rick Kilburn, Facebook, November 20, 2021.
[44] Ibid.

3 / THE MAN WITH THE PLASTIC SAXOPHONE: ORNETTE COLEMAN

[1] Ted Gioia, *West Coast Jazz* (Berkeley, Los Angeles, London: University of California Press, 1998), 351.
[2] Mitch Myers, "Speaking In Tongues With Ornette Coleman," *MAGNET*, March 9, 2022, https://magnetmagazine.com/2022/03/09/speaking-in-tongues-with-ornette-coleman/.
[3] Marc Myers, "Ornette Coleman (1930-2015)," JAZZ.FM91, https://jazz.fm/ornette-coleman-1930-2015-2/.
[4] David Johnson, "Communion: Don Cherry In The 1960s," *Night Lights*, April 26, 2012, https://indianapublicmedia.org/nightlights/communion-don-cherry-1960s.php.
[5] Ralph J. Gleason, "Strictly Ad Lib," *Down Beat*, 24, no. 18 (September 5, 1957): 38.
[6] Al Neil, interview with Jane Gowan, May 22, 2000.
[7] Don Friedman, email to the author, August 12, 2014.
[8] Don Friedman, interview with the author, August 18, 2014.
[9] Jim Banham, "Out goes the junk with a jolt," *Province*, December 8, 1967, 9.
[10] Dave Quarin, interview with the author, December 21, 2022.
[11] Jim Johnson, interview with the author, July 29, 2013.
[12] John Dawe, interview with the author, July 17, 2013.
[13] Al Neil, interview with Jane Gowan, May 22, 2000.
[14] Al Neil, *Origins* (Western Front, 1989), 12.
[15] Friedman, interview with the author, August 18, 2014.
[16] Ken Hole, interview with the author, August 13, 2013.

17. Roger Purves, "L.A. Jazz All-Stars in Review," *The Ubyssey*, November 7, 1957, 4.
18. John Tynan, "Ornette: the first beginning," *Down Beat,* 27, no. 15 (July 21, 1960): 32-33.
19. Ibid.
20. Ibid, 33, 58.
21. John Tynan, "Ornette Coleman, Free Jazz," *Down Beat*, 29, no. 2 (January 18, 1962): 28.
22. Pete Welding, "Ornette Coleman, Free Jazz," *Down Beat*, 29, no. 2 (January 18, 1962): 28.
23. LeRoi Jones, "Don Cherry, Making It The Hard Way," *Down Beat*, 30, no. 24 (November 21, 1963): 17.
24. Bob Smith, "Corrections," *Down Beat*, Chords and Discords (letters), 31, no. 2 (January 16, 1964): 4.
25. Bob Smith, "Music's marrow made to give full flavour," *Vancouver Sun*, September 9, 1970, 32.
26. John Orysik, interview with the author, October 19, 2016.
27. Bob Murphy, interview with the author, December 3, 2013.
28. Gregg Simpson, interview with the author, April 22, 2019.
29. Marke Andrews, "Coming up against a wall of sound," *Vancouver Sun*, June 26, 1986, C6.

4 / FAR OUT: AL NEIL

1. Carole Itter, email to the author, July 8, 2013.
2. Al Neil, *Origins* (Western Front, 1989), 10.
3. "Cambrian Society Eisteddfod Reveals Musical Excellence," *Vancouver Sun*, March 27, 1937, 32.
4. "Young Pianists Praised At B.C. Music Festival," *Vancouver Sun*, May 6, 1937, 9.
5. "Young Piano Players Need Cause No Worry," *Vancouver Daily Province*, May 6, 1937, 7.
6. "Vancouver Gunner Arrives Overseas," *Vancouver Daily Province*, December 18, 1943, 5.
7. "Al Neil Memorial, Jan. 21, 2018," https://www.youtube.com/watch?v=-AyS9Bdp7U0.
8. Jack Reynolds, interview with the author, January 10, 2017.
9. Alan Neil, "a short survey of new jazz," *p m magazine*, 1, no. 3 (February 1952): 45.
10. Ibid, 48.
11. Rod Wong, emails to the author, January 4 and 6, 2022.
12. Kitty Neil, letter to the editor, *Metronome*, 67, no. 6 (June 1951): 19.
13. Sandy Ross, "Al Neil Cuts Freeman; He's Here At Noon," *The Ubyssey*, October 4, 1955, 6.

Notes

14. Phil Matty, "Mail-sorting pianist plays jazz Sunday," *Vancouver Province*, March 10, 1956, 4.
15. Gavin Walker, interview with the author, November 7, 2018.
16. "A different postman---he swings twice," *Province*, March 16, 1957, 31.
17. Al Neil, interview with Jane Gowan, May 22, 2000.
18. Gavin Walker, interview with the author, November 7, 2018.
19. Marian Jago, *Live at the Cellar* (Vancouver, Toronto: UBC Press, 2018), 95.
20. Neil, *Origins*, 11.
21. Larry Smith, *Kenneth Patchen, Rebel Poet in America* (Bottom Dog Press with a Consortium of Small Presses, 2000), 240.
22. Al Neil, interview with Jane Gowan, May 22, 2000.
23. Smith, *Kenneth Patchen, Rebel Poet in America*, 240.
24. Eric Metcalfe, interview with the author, May 9, 2018.
25. Alan Neil, liner notes, *Kenneth Patchen Reads With Jazz In Canada*, Kenneth Patchen With The Alan Neil Quartet, Folkways Records, FL9718, compact disc, 1959.
26. The Cellar, advertisement, *Vancouver Sun*, February 20, 1959, 21.
27. Mac Reynolds, "Jazzy Evening Had By All," *Vancouver Sun*, February 21, 1959, 11.
28. John Dawe, interview with the author, July 17, 2013.
29. Kenneth Patchen, letter to Al Neil, March 5, 1959.
30. Kenneth Patchen, letter to Al Neil, August 14, 1959.
31. "Kenneth Patchen Reads With Jazz In Canada," *The Billboard*, 71, no. 46 (November 16, 1959): 50.
32. Ira Gitler, "Kenneth Patchen Reads With Jazz In Canada," in Gene Lees and Don De Michael, eds., *Down Beat's Jazz Record Reviews Volume V* (Chicago: Maher Publications, 1961), 151-152.
33. Neil, liner notes, *Kenneth Patchen Reads With Jazz In Canada*, Kenneth Patchen With The Alan Neil Quartet.
34. Don Thompson, interview with the author, November 26, 2013.
35. Terry Hill, interview with the author, October 15, 2013.
36. Jack Fulton, interview with the author, September 28, 2017.
37. John Dawe, interview with the author, July 17, 2013.
38. Gavin Walker, interview with the author, November 7, 2018.
39. PJ Perry, interview with the author, April 18, 2014.
40. Bill Smith, "Sacred & Profane, Al Neil Talks to Bill Smith," *Coda*, 9, no. 5 (January/February 1970): 10.
41. "Al Neil / A Portrait," directed by David Rimmer (1979; David Rimmer), https://vancouverartinthesixties.com/archive/763.
42. "Pianist Guilty Of Drug Charge," *Vancouver Sun*, October 14, 1964, 30.
43. Gregg Simpson, interview with the author, April 22, 2019.
44. Ibid.

45 "'We're Nose to Nose in Space,'" *Vancouver Sun*, December 15, 1965, 1.
46 Gregg Simpson, interview with the author, April 22, 2019.
47 Jim Banham, "Armageddon is at hand," *Province*, April 1, 1966, 7.
48 Ibid.
49 Gregg Simpson, interview with the author, April 22, 2019.
50 Ibid.
51 Sandy Lemon, "Vancouver," *Coda*, 7, no. 8 (June/July 1966): 17–18.
52 Sandy Lemon, "Vancouver," Coda 7, no. 11 (December January 1966/67): 19.
53 Al Neil, "what we have to do is devise forms," *The Peak*, October 4, 1967, 11
54 Mark Miller, *The Miller Companion to Jazz in Canada and Canadians in Jazz* (The Mercury Press, 2001), 143.
55 Alexander Varty, "A brief history of the New Orchestra Workshop," *Georgia Straight*, November 15, 2017, https://www.straight.com/music/995451/brief-history-new-orchestra-workshop.
56 Gregg Simpson, interview with the author, April 22, 2019.
57 Michael de Courcy, *michaeldecourcy.com*, introduction, https://www.michaeldecourcy.com/intermedia/intro.htm.
58 Michael de Courcy, interview with the author, September 16, 2013.
59 Alex Varty, "Al Neil: Music at the Centre," in *What The Hell Happened? The Best of The Georgia Straight*, ed. Naomi Pauls and Charles Campbell (Vancouver/Toronto: Douglas & McIntyre, 1997), 103.
60 Ibid.
61 Paul Plimley, interview with Jane Gowan, January 19, 2000.
62 Ibid.
63 Miller, *The Miller Companion to Jazz in Canada and Canadians in Jazz*, 143–144.
64 Gregg Simpson, interview with the author, April 22, 2019.
65 Keith Wallace, ed., Whispered Art History: Twenty Years At The Western Front. (Vancouver: Arsenal Pulp Press, 1993), 26.
66 Brian Nation, email to the author, July 30, 2023.
67 Charles Campbell, "The Remarkable Effort to Save an Artist's Shack," *The Tyee*, https://thetyee.ca/Culture/2019/01/07/Save-Artist-Shack/.

5 / FATHER AND SON: BARRY AND DYLAN CRAMER

1 Allan Levine, "John F. Kennedy's turbulent relationship with Canada," *Maclean's*, January 17, 2016, https://www.macleans.ca/culture/books/john-f-kennedys-turbulent-relationship-with-canada/.
2 Harold Land Quartet, "Cherokee," recorded November 1958, track 1 on Jazz at the Cellar 1958.
3 Ibid.
4 Photo caption, *Vancouver Daily Province*, February 23, 1948, 7.

Notes

5   "Bride Married In Beige," *Daily Province*, June 2, 1951, 29.
6   Birth announcement, *Vancouver Sun*, September 26, 1952, 33.
7   Avon Theatre, advertisement, *Vancouver Province*, May 15, 1954, 8.
8   Photo caption, *Vancouver Sun*, December 30, 1954, 15.
9   John Dawe, with Gregg Simpson, "The Original Cellar Jazz Club," *The Original Cellar Jazz Club*, December 7, 2010, http://theoriginalcellarjazzclub.blogspot.com/2010/11/story-by-john-dawe.html.
10 Gavin Walker, interview with the author, November 7, 2018.
11 John Dawe, with Gregg Simpson, "The Original Cellar Jazz Club," *The Original Cellar Jazz Club*, December 7, 2010, http://theoriginalcellarjazzclub.blogspot.com/2010/11/story-by-john-dawe.html.
12 Ibid.
13 Al Neil, interview with Michael de Courcy, February 28, 2006.
14 Hugh Watson, "the Early Bird," *Province*, November 1, 1958, 3.
15 "Drama and poetry new to the Cellar," *Province*, November 29, 1958, 28.
16 The 711 Shop, advertisement, *Vancouver Sun*, July 16, 1959, 14.
17 Jack Richards, "'Apollo of Bellac' Delightful Satire," *Vancouver Sun*, November 10, 1959, 20
18 Les Wedman, "Play tells old story over again," *Province*, November 12, 1959, 40.
19 "Dialogue Lacking In Off-Beat Play," *Vancouver Sun*, May 27, 1960, 33.
20 Al Neil, interview with Michael de Courcy, February 28, 2006.
21 Barry Cramer, unreleased recording of introduction, Ray Sikora Big Band, June 9, 1963, the Cellar.
22 "Callboard," *Vancouver Sun*, November 13, 1964, 4A.
23 Jack Richards, "Guffaws Greet The Odd Couple," *Vancouver Sun*, November 3, 1967, 32.
24 CHAN-DT, *History of Canadian Broadcasting*," https://broadcasting-history.com/listing_and_histories/television/chan-dt.
25 Dylan Cramer, interview with the author, December 27, 2018.
26 Ibid.
27 Robert Hunter, "How a "filthy" newspaper outmanoeuvred a mayor," *Maclean's*, January 1, 1968, https://archive.macleans.ca/article/1968/1/1/how-a-filthy-newspaper-outmanoeuvred-a-mayor#!&pid=56.
28 Ibid.
29 Jack Wasserman, "Jack Wasserman," *Vancouver Sun*, June 5, 1971, 35.
30 *Georgia Straight*, August 9–22, 1968, 14.
31 "Hippies Acquire Media Minister," *Vancouver Sun*, April 1, 1968, 46.
32 Dylan Cramer, interview with the author, December 27, 2018.
33 Ibid.
34 Joan Lowndes, "Our Joan steps into the pulpit," *Vancouver Sun*, September 18, 1970, 8A-9A.

35 Dylan Cramer, interview with the author, December 27, 2018.
36 "On the media front, a cheeky game with technology's toys," *Maclean's*, January 1, 1971, https://archive.macleans.ca/article/1971/1/1/on-the-media-front-a-cheeky-game-with-technologys-toys.
37 "Friday," *The Montreal Star*, April 3, 1971, 96.
38 "Madeleine Is," directed by Sylvia Spring (1971; Spring Releases Ltd.). https://www.youtube.com/watch?v=fwCegaOCiTk.
39 Peter Hulbert, photo, material republished with the express permission of: Vancouver Sun, a division of Postmedia Network Inc.
40 Eileen Johnson, "And finally it's spring," *Vancouver Sun*, May 14, 1971, 11A.
41 Dylan Cramer, interview with the author, December 27, 2018.
42 Wasserman, "Jack Wasserman," *Vancouver Sun*, June 5, 1971, 35.
43 Ibid.
44 Gavin Walker, interview with the author, November 7, 2018.
45 John Dawe, interview with the author, July 17, 2013.
46 Dylan Cramer, interview with the author, December 27, 2018.
47 Ed Roop, interview with the author, November 2, 2016.
48 Ibid.
49 Mike Beddoes, interview with the author, October 31, 2016.
50 Dylan Cramer, interview with the author, December 27, 2018.
51 Ibid.
52 Ibid.
53 Leonard Feather, "Saxophonist Sonny Criss Found Shot To Death," *The Los Angeles Times*, November 20, 1977, 31.
54 Dylan Cramer, interview with the author, December 27, 2018.
55 Ibid.
56 Ibid.
57 Ibid.
58 Ibid.
59 Ibid.
60 Ibid.
61 Ibid.
62 Alexander Varty, "Tunesmith Cramer passes," *Georgia Straight*, https://www.straight.com/article/tunesmith-cramer-passes.
63 Indio Saravanja Music, Facebook, November 4, 2019.
64 Dylan Cramer, interview with the author, December 27, 2018.
65 Ibid.
66 Ibid.
67 Ibid.
68 Ibid.

6 / MIND OF MINGUS: CHARLES MINGUS

1. Gene Santoro, "Myself When I Am Real – The Life and Music of Charles Mingus (Oxford University Press, 2000), 126-127.
2. Ibid, 172.
3. Russ Wilson, "Charles Mingus Returns to Bay," *Oakland Tribune*, December 16, 1960, 38.
4. The Cellar, advertisement, *Vancouver Sun*, December 9, 1961, 33.
5. The Cellar, advertisement, *Vancouver Sun*, January 6, 1961, 12.
6. Doug Peck, "World's great bass violinist, *Province*, January 7, 1961, 20.
7. The Cellar, handbill, "The Cellar Presents Charles Mingus."
8. James Carney, interview with the author, September 27, 2013.
9. Dave Quarin, accounting records, January 1961.
10. Doug Peck, "Television," *Province*, January 12, 1961, 23.
11. "Best in TV This Week," Province, March 25, 1961, 54.
12. "Mind of Mingus," produced by James Carney (1961; CBC Vancouver).
13. Ibid.
14. Ibid.
15. Ibid.
16. Ibid.
17. Doug Peck, "Television," *Province*, January 14, 1961, 14.
18. Maurice Foisy, interview with the author, January 9, 2017.
19. James Carney, interview with the author, September 27, 2013.
20. Don Thompson, interview with the author, November 26, 2013.
21. Terry Clarke, interview with the author, November 3, 2013.
22. Ibid.
23. Jamie Reid, interview with the author, July 12, 2013.
24. Ibid.
25. "Stephen Dugald COTTER (Steve)," *Vancouver Sun*, February 15, 2022, https://vancouversunandprovince.remembering.ca/obituary/stephen-cotter-1084436361.
26. Gavin Walker, interview with the author, October 24, 2013.
27. Ibid.
28. John Capon, interview with the author, December 6, 2016.
29. Donnie Clark interview with the author, October 8, 2016.
30. Bryan Stovell, interview with the author, September 20, 2016.
31. Blaine Wikjord, interview with the author, October 8, 2013.
32. Don Fraser Jr., interview with the author, December 6, 2016.
33. Jack Wasserman, "Jack Wasserman," *Vancouver Sun*, January 18, 1961, 25.
34. Charles McPherson, interview with the author, October 2, 2013.
35. Ibid.

36. "Matthew 21:12–13," King James Version, *Bible Gateway*, https://www.biblegateway.com/passage/?search=Matthew%2021%3A12-13&version=KJV.
37. McPherson, interview with the author, October 2, 2013.
38. John Clayton, "Vancouver," *Coda*, 3, no. 10 (February 1961): 12.
39. "Tween Classes: Fleming speaks on new Forest Dept.," *The Ubyssey*, January 13, 1961, 8.
40. Clayton, "Vancouver," *Coda*, (February 1961): 12.
41. Edward B. Harvey, *Taking Social Research to the Larger World* (Toronto: Canadian Scholars' Press Inc., 2005),37-38.
42. Ibid, 38–40.
43. Ibid, 41.
44. Les Millin, "Cool 'Cat' in Bag, Couldn't Get Out," *Victoria Daily Times*, January 12, 1961, 13.
45. Harvey, *Taking Social Research to the Larger World*, 41.
46. Charles McPherson, interview with the author, October 2, 2013.
47. Gavin Walker, comment, "Hands Up Those Who Saw Mingus …," *Vancouver Jazz Forum, vancouverjazz.com*, January 17, 2012, http://vancouverjazz.com/forums/archive/index.php/t-4175.html.
48. Bob Smith, "New, economy-size Mingus delivers no-nonsense jazz," *Vancouver Sun*, April 6, 1976, 39.
49. Jeani Read, "Mingus's music moody," *Province*, April 14, 1977, 29.
50. Letter, from Charles Mingus to Ricci Quarin, undated.
51. Ibid.
52. Jim Kilburn, interview with the author, August 13, 2013
53. Rick Kilburn, interview with the author, January 5, 2019.
54. Ibid.
55. Ibid.
56. Ibid.
57. Ibid.

7 / FISHERMAN'S JAZZ: DAVE QUARIN

1. John Dawe, interview with the author, July 17, 2013.
2. Marian Jago, *Live at the Cellar* (Vancouver, Toronto: UBC Press, 2018), 265.
3. George Ursan, interview with the author, November 7, 2013.
4. Dave Quarin, interview with the author, May 11, 2022.
5. Quarin, interview with the author, October 4, 2018.
6. Quarin, interview with the author, October 4, 2018.
7. Bob Smith, "'My Brother Whipped Me Into It …'," *Vancouver Sun*, May 31, 1968, 6A.
8. Quarin, interview with the author, October 4, 2018.

Notes

9. "Capacity Audiences Cheer "Top" Jazz Performances, *Vancouver Daily Province*, October 10, 1946, 5.
10. Rod Wong, email to the author, January 6, 2022.
11. "Gun-Toter Gets Month in Jail," *Vancouver Sun*, October 8, 1948, 21.
12. Ibid.
13. Quarin, interview with the author, October 4, 2018.
14. Quarin, interview with the author, January 9, 2014.
15. Alan Neil, "a short survey of new jazz," *p m magazine*, 1, no. 3 (February 1952): 45–48.
16. Smith, "'My Brother Whipped Me Into It …'," *Vancouver Sun*, May 31, 1968, 6A.
17. Ibid.
18. Quarin, interview with the author, February 15, 2014.
19. Dan Ekman, "Dan Ekman, Walter Mulligan has to miss chief constables annual gathering," *Vancouver Province*, September 22, 1955, 3.
20. Ricci Quarin, interview with Gavin Walker, *JazzStreet*, Coastal Jazz & Blues Society.
21. Ibid.
22. John Dawe, with Gregg Simpson, "The Original Cellar Jazz Club," *The Original Cellar Jazz Club*, December 7, 2010, http://theoriginalcellarjazzclub.blogspot.com/2010/11/story-by-john-dawe.html.
23. John Dawe, interview with the author, April 19, 2014.
24. Yardbird Suite, advertisement, *Edmonton Journal*, November 29, 1957, 51.
25. "City Jazzy Club Brings Artists," *Edmonton Journal*, November 30, 1957, 28.
26. Obituary, Vancouver Sun, October 1, 1957, 26.
27. Quarin, interview with the author, October 4, 2018.
28. Notice of Appointment of Directors, The Cellar Musicians and Artists Society, January 28, 1958.
29. "Dave Quarin," VJNS 1958 Jazz Festival program, 4.
30. Dave Quarin, accounting records, August–September 1960.
31. Quarin, accounting records, January 1961.
32. Don Thompson, interview with the author, November 26, 2013.
33. Don Thompson, interview, *JazzStreet*, Coastal Jazz & Blues Society.
34. Ibid.
35. Thompson, interview with the author, November 26, 2013.
36. Thompson, interview, *JazzStreet*, Coastal Jazz & Blues Society.
37. Gavin Walker, interview with the author, November 7, 2018.
38. Quarin, interview with the author, October 4, 2018.
39. Donnie Clark interview with the author, October 8, 2016.
40. John Capon, interview with the author, December 6, 2016.
41. Quarin, interview with the author, October 4, 2018.
42. Quarin, interview with the author, October 4, 2018.

43 Ricci Quarin, interview, *JazzStreet*, Coastal Jazz & Blues Society.
44 Quarin, interview with the author, October 4, 2018.
45 Bobby Hales, interview with the author, October 18, 2013.
46 Clark, interview with the author, October 8, 2016.
47 John Clayton, "Vancouver," *Coda*, 6, no. 2, September 1963, 11.
48 Bob Smith, "Jazz: Wright Shooting for Revival Of Pioneer Jazz Centre," *Vancouver Sun*, September 20, 1963, 5.
49 "What's About Our Town," *Vancouver Sun*, January 17, 1964, 2.
50 The Cellar, advertisement, *Vancouver Sun*, February 1, 1964, 20.
51 Bob Smith, "Just Jazz . . . .," *Vancouver Sun*, February 14, 1964, 6.
52 Bob Smith, "Just Jazz . . . The Problems of a Fan," *Vancouver Sun*, April 3, 1964, 5.
53 Adrian Tanner, "Vancouver," *Coda*, 6, no. 7, April 1964, 10.
54 Doreen Young, interview with the author, August 8, 2013.
55 "New Night Club In Chinatown," *Vancouver Sun*, November 14, 1964, 35.
56 Kublai Khan, advertisement, *Vancouver Sun*, January 28, 1966, 30.
57 Jack Wasserman, "Jack Wasserman," *Vancouver Sun*, November 7, 1967, 33.
58 Smith, "'My Brother Whipped Me Into It …'," *Vancouver Sun*, September 20, 1963, 5.
59 Ibid.
60 Lorne Parton, "Lorne Parton," *Province*, January 8, 1971, 19.
61 Hales, interview with the author, October 18, 2013.
62 Ibid.
63 Bobby Hales, interview with Gary Barclay.
64 Hugh Fraser, interview with the author, September 17, 2019.
65 Ibid.
66 Campbell Ryga, interview with the author, October 5, 2020.
67 Ibid.
68 John Korsrud, interview with the author, January 9, 2017.
69 Ibid.
70 Walker, interview with the author, November 7, 2018.
71 Quarin, interview with the author, February 15, 2014.
72 Marian Jago, *Live at the Cellar* (Vancouver, Toronto: UBC Press, 2018), 145.
73 Jago, *Live at the Cellar*, 287
74 Quarin, interview with the author, October 4, 2018.
75 Audie Wong, interview with the author, July 22, 2020.
76 Gregg Simpson, interview with the author, April 22, 2019.
77 Walker, interview with the author, November 7, 2018.
78 Ray Piper, interview with the author, November 9, 2013.
79 Quarin, interview with the author, February 15, 2014.
80 Quarin, interview with the author, October 4, 2018.
81 Walker, interview with the author, November 7, 2018.

82 QUARIN — Randy Lee, obituary, *Vancouver Sun*, June 30, 2007, 97.
83 Quarin, interview with the author, October 4, 2018.
84 Quarin, interview with the author, February 15, 2014.
85 Quarin, interview with the author, April 14, 2015.
86 Ibid.
87 Ibid.
88 John Dawe, with Gregg Simpson, "The Original Cellar Jazz Club," *The Original Cellar Jazz Club*, December 7, 2010, http://theoriginalcellarjazzclub.blogspot.com/2010/11/story-by-john-dawe.html.
89 Perry, interview with the author, April 18, 2014.
90 Jack Reynolds, interview with the author, January 10, 2017.

8 / THE ROAD FROM AVONLEA TO THE CELLAR: BOBBY HALES

1 Bobby Hales, interview with the author, October 18, 2013.
2 "Bobby Hales, interview by Guy MacPherson, October 23, 2006," *vancouverjazz.com*, http://vancouverjazz.com/inview/bhales.shtml.
3 Ibid.
4 Interview with Bobby Hales, *JazzStreet*, Coastal Jazz & Blues Society.
5 Ibid.
6 Ibid.
7 Hales, interview with the author, October 18, 2013.
8 George Ursan, interview with the author, November 7, 2013.
9 John Dawe, interview with the author, January 25, 2014.
10 Dave Quarin, interview with the author, October 4, 2018.
11 Hales, interview with the author, October 18, 2013.
12 Ibid.
13 Ibid.
14 Ibid.
15 Ibid.
16 Hales, interview with the author, October 18, 2013.
17 Brian McLeod, "Hales tears apart tunes to add soul, zap and sing," *Province*, August 15, 1970, 39.
18 Marke Andrews, "The supernal Bill Watrous," *Vancouver Sun*, February 17, 1978, B3.
19 Diane Bentley, "Busiest lip in the West," *Weekend Now*, February 7, 1986, 4.
20 Eve Johnson, "No tea, but lots of dancing," *Vancouver Sun*, June 28. 1980, D1.
21 Hales, interview with the author, October 18, 2013.
22 Ibid.
23 Sharman King, interview with Margaret Gallagher, CBC Hot Air, https://www.cbc.ca/player/play/2696960872.

24. Campbell Ryga, interview with the author, October 6, 2020.
25. "Hales, Robert A. "Bob/Bobby"," Obituaries, *Vancouver Sun*, October 26, 2016, N8.
26. Denny Boyd, "Denny Boyd," *Vancouver Sun*, March 10, 1986, B2.
27. Ryga, interview with the author, October 6, 2020.

9 / TOTAL HONESTY: PJ PERRY

1. PJ Perry, interview with the author, April 18, 2014.
2. Ibid.
3. Ibid.
4. Bobby Hales, interview with the author, October 18, 2013.
5. Perry, interview with the author, April 18, 2014.
6. Ibid.
7. PJ Perry, interview with Gavin Walker, *JazzStreet*, Coastal Jazz & Blues Society.
8. Perry, interview with the author, April 18, 2014.
9. Jim Johnson, interview with the author, July 29, 2013.
10. John Dawe, interview with the author, April 19, 2014.
11. Perry, interview with the author, April 18, 2014.
12. John Clayton, "Vancouver, Notes From U.B.C." *Coda*, 4, no. 8 (December 1961): 9.
13. Dawe, interview with the author, April 19, 2014.
14. Don Thompson, interview with the author, November 6, 2013.
15. Perry, interview with the author, April 18, 2014.
16. Nick Lees, "P.J. Perry to graduate cum laude from school of hard knocks," *Edmonton Journal*, May 25, 2007, B3.
17. Graham Hicks, "Music's not the road to riches," *Edmonton Journal*, May 26, 1979, J1.
18. Graham Hicks, "P.J. pays his dues to music world," *Edmonton Journal*, May 26, 1979, J1.
19. Ibid.
20. Lees, "P.J. Perry to graduate cum laude from school of hard knocks," *Edmonton Journal*, May 25, 2007.
21. Perry, interview with the author, April 18, 2014.
22. Lees, "P.J. Perry to graduate cum laude from school of hard knocks," *Edmonton Journal*, May 25, 2007.
23. Cory Weeds, liner notes, *Ubiquitous*, Kevin Dean/PJ Perry Quintet, Cellar Live, CLO5211, compact disc, 2012.
24. Campbell Ryga, interview with the author, October 5, 2020.
25. Perry, interview with the author, April 18, 2014.
26. Ibid.

Notes

[27] Roger Levesque, "The buzz of Broadway gig thrills local sax man Perry," *Edmonton Journal*, June 12, 2010, D1.
[28] Mike Devlin, "Jazz great P.J. Perry no long so self-critical," *Times Colonist*, https://www.timescolonist.com/entertainment/jazz-great-pj-perry-no-longer-so-self-critical-4664777.
[29] Perry, interview with the author, April 18, 2014.
[30] Roger Levesque, "Award-winning saxophonist Perry still prolific at 80," *Edmonton Journal*, January 29, 2022, C3.

10 / JAZZ DREAMER: CAROL FOX

[1] "Steering Wheel The Sport Club," *Vancouver City Directory* (BC Directories, 1965), 296.
[2] "Steering Wheel The Sport Club," *Vancouver City Directory* (BC Directories, 1966), 288.
[3] "Steering Wheel The Sport Club," *Vancouver City Directory* (BC Directories, 1968), 307.
[4] Bob Smith, "Pop Rock Jazz," *Vancouver Sun*, Spring '69 Leisure, March 21, 1969, 3A.
[5] John Dawe, interview with the author, January 25, 2014.
[6] Ross Barrett, interview with the author, November 29, 2016.
[7] Bob Smith, "Pop Rock Jazz," *Vancouver Sun*, May 24, 1968, 6A.
[8] Ibid.
[9] Bob Smith, "Pop Rock Jazz," *Vancouver Sun*, October 11, 1968, 10A.
[10] Brian McLeod, "Music for a 3 a.m. city," *Province*, spotlight, January 10, 1969, 6.
[11] Sandy Lemon, "Vancouver," *Coda*, 8, no. 10 (December 1968), 32.
[12] Barrett, interview with the author, November 29, 2016.
[13] Ibid.
[14] Smith, "Pop Rock Jazz," *Vancouver Sun*, March 21, 1969, 3A.
[15] Nikita Carter, interview with the author, June 9, 2015.
[16] Bob Turner, interview with the author, October 9, 2016.
[17] Barrett, interview with the author, November 29, 2016.
[18] Gavin Walker, interview with the author, November 7, 2018.
[19] Bob Smith, "OUR DAVE IS OFF TO EUROPE, And Shirley revives jazz alley," *Vancouver Sun*, September 4, 1970, 10A.
[20] Henry Young, interview with the author, January 16, 2014.
[21] Turner, interview with the author, October 9, 2016.
[22] Jeani Read, "Still beating drum for jazz here," *Province*, March 7, 1975, 35.
[23] Dick Smith, interview with the author, December 6, 2016.
[24] Barrett, interview with the author, November 29, 2016.
[25] Ibid.

11 / THE VOICE: RON SMALL

1. Collette Hackl, interview with the author, February 5, 2020.
2. October 31, 1958: U.S. Air Force Talent Show, *Metacritic*, https://www.metacritic.com/tv/the-ed-sullivan-show/season-10/episode-49-october-31-1958-us-air-force-talent-show.
3. "Four Pearls: NW Doo-wop 1957-1960," Northwest Music Archives, http://nw-music-archives.blogspot.com/2009/12/four-pearls-northwest-doo-wop-1957-1960.html.
4. Becki L. Ross, *Burlesque West – Showgirls, Sex, and Sin in Postwar Vancouver* (Toronto, Buffalo, London: University of Toronto Press, 2009), 64.
5. Mike Tytherleigh, "Sahl cartoons, lampoons with words," *Province*, April 1, 1961. 68.
6. Ross, *Burlesque West – Showgirls, Sex, and Sin in Postwar Vancouver*, 64.
7. Smilin' Buddha, advertisement, *Vancouver Sun*, October 15, 1966, 18.
8. Ross, *Burlesque West – Showgirls, Sex, and Sin in Postwar Vancouver*, 64.
9. Duke's Cabaret, advertisement, *Vancouver Sun*, March 12, 1965, 16.
10. Ross, *Burlesque West, Showgirls, Sex, and Sin in Postwar Vancouver*, xiii.
11. Bob Smith, "Pop Rock Jazz," *Vancouver Sun*, Leisure, December 20, 1968, 3A.
12. Brian McLeod, "Where jazz has the late night beat on rock," *Province*, November 29, 1968, 14.
13. Gavin Walker, interview with the author, November 7, 2018.
14. Ibid.
15. Hackl, interview with the author, February 5, 2020.
16. Bob Smith, "'The Blues Regenerates a Man'," *Vancouver Sun*, October 8, 1969, 41.
17. "Five facing charges for The Beard," *Province*, November 7, 1969, 2.
18. "Police trim Beard's run," *Province*, November 8, 1969, 33.
19. Bob Smith, "Blind Man's Blazing Music, Let Rahsaan's Sounds Cascade Over You," *Vancouver Sun*, November 12, 1969, 45.
20. Hackl, interview with the author, February 5, 2020.
21. Bob Murphy, interview with the author, December 3, 2013.
22. Robert Rouda, "Vancouver," *Coda*, 9, no. 9 (September/October 1970), 36–37.
23. Herbie Hancock with Lisa Dickey, *Possibilities* (New York: Viking, 2014), 122–123.
24. Bob Smith, "Heady stuff from Herbie," *Vancouver Sun*, September 30, 1970, 34.
25. Hancock with Dickey, *Possibilities*, 123.
26. Murphy, interview with the author, December 3, 2013.
27. Tim Williams, interview with the author, November 6, 2018.
28. Bob Smith, "Chicago Blues pioneer shines in the Cellar," *Vancouver Sun*, November 26, 1970, 47.
29. Bob Smith, "Quintet generates warmth," *Vancouver Sun*, January 13, 1971, 24.
30. Murphy, interview with the author, December 3, 2013.

Notes

31 John Orysik, interview with the author, October 19, 2016.
32 "'Beard' ruled obscene," *Vancouver Sun*, May 28, 1971, 77.
33 The Factory Show Lounge, advertisement, *Vancouver Sun*, May 28, 1971, 77.
34 Williams, interview with the author, November 6, 2018.
35 John Orysik, "Vancouver," *Coda*, 10, no. 6 (March/April 1972), 33.
36 Hackl, interview with the author, February 5, 2020.
37 Ibid.
38 Chris Wong, "Small in name, large on talent," *Vancouver Courier*, September 12, 1999.
39 Murphy, interview with the author, December 3, 2013.
40 Julie Brown, interview with the author, April 8, 2019.
41 Ibid.
42 Monique Van Dam, interview with the author, June 4, 2020.
43 Marcus Mosley, interview with the author, April 20, 2022.
44 Will Sanders, speech, celebration of Ron Small's life, May 26, 2019.
45 Marcus Mosley, speech, celebration of Ron Small's life, May 26, 2019.
46 Mosley, interview with the author, April 20, 2022.
47 Ibid.
48 Ibid.
49 Hackl, interview with the author, February 5, 2020.
50 Mosley, interview with the author, April 20, 2022.
51 Francois Marchand, "Sojourners home for well-earned party," *Vancouver Sun*, June 17, 2010, D9.
52 Hackl, interview with the author, February 5, 2020.
53 Ibid.
54 Mosley, interview with the author, April 20, 2022.
55 Ibid.
56 Will Sanders, interview with the author, October 25, 2018.
57 Steve Dawson, Facebook, November 3, 2018.
58 Mosley, interview with the author, April 20, 2022.
59 Clifton Murray, Facebook, November 3, 2018.
60 Hackl, interview with the author, February 5, 2020.
61 Mosley, interview with the author, April 20, 2022.

12 / DEEP CONNECTION: BOB MURPHY

1 Margo Murphy, interview with the author, January 12, 2021.
2 Tom Keenlyside, interview with the author, April 17, 2022.
3 Brian McLeod, "*Frewer, Murphy: Big names-to-be*," *Province*, April 14, 1969, 31.
4 "*Bluebird On Your Windowsill*," *Canadian Songwriters Hall of Fame*, https://www.cshf.ca/song/bluebird-on-your-windowsill/.

5. "Don Murphy (7) – Bluebird On Your Windowsill / Ma Curly Headed Baby," Discogs, https://www.discogs.com/release/14397230-Don-Murphy-Bluebird-On-Your-Windowsill-Ma-Curly-Headed-Baby.
6. 45 Worlds, 78 RPM, https://www.45worlds.com/78rpm/record/ar155.
7. Clarke, Elizabeth [composer]. New Westminster, Canada: Empire Music Publishers, 1948. There's a bluebird on your windowsill. York University Libraries, Clara Thomas Archives & Special Collections, John Arpin collection, JAC010000. Available at https://yorkspace.library.yorku.ca/xmlui/handle/10315/35647.
8. Murphy, interview with the author, January 12, 2021.
9. Ibid.
10. Bob Murphy website, http://www.bobmurphyjazz.com/bio.htm.
11. Margo Murphy, interview with the author, January 12, 2021.
12. Bob Murphy, interview with the author, December 3, 2013.
13. Bob Turner, interview with the author, October 9, 2016.
14. Murphy, interview with the author, December 3, 2013.
15. Ibid.
16. Joani Taylor, interview with the author, December 1, 2016.
17. Bob Smith, "Classics in a Bag of Jazz," *Vancouver Sun*, March 18, 1969, 31.
18. Murphy, interview with the author, December 3, 2013.
19. Ibid.
20. "For These People, 1968 Was a Very Good Year," *Vancouver Sun*, December 27, 1968, 5A.
21. Turner, interview with the author, October 9, 2016.
22. Murphy, interview with the author, December 3, 2013.
23. Taylor, interview with the author, December 1, 2016.
24. Brian Nation, "How to Open a Jazz Club in Nine Days with No Money," *brian nation: the hot dog palace never closes*," November 15, 2005, http://boppin.com/2005/11/how-to-open-jazz-club-in-nine-days.html.
25. Brian Nation, interview with the author, April 12, 2013.
26. Marke Andrews, "Your basic plywood jazz," *Vancouver Sun*, March 10, 1977, 31.
27. Gavin Walker, email to the author, January 13, 2023.
28. Nation, interview with the author, April 12, 2013.
29. Andreas Nothiger, interview with the author, February 16, 2021.
30. Rene Worst, interview with the author, December 17, 2020.
31. Nothiger, interview with the author, February 16, 2021.
32. Renee Doruyter, "Six players without fame," *Province*, The Magazine, July 6, 1980, 7.
33. Carol Murphy, interview with the author, January 29, 2021.
34. Marke Andrews, "Vancouver jazz pianist Bob Murphy sounded like no one else," *The Globe and Mail*, November 17, 2015, https://www.theglobeandmail.com/

arts/music/vancouver-jazz-pianist-bob-murphy-sounded-like-no-one-else/article27309875/.
35 Carol Murphy, interview with the author, January 29, 2021.
36 Campbell Ryga, interview with the author, September 30, 2020.
37 Ibid.
38 Keenlyside, interview with the author, April 17, 2022.
39 Ibid.
40 Ryga, interview with the author, September 30, 2020.
41 Marke Andrews, "Hot, bothered and no place to jam," *Vancouver Sun*, February 24, 1996, F3.
42 Taylor, interview with the author, December 1, 2016.
43 Ibid.
44 Jennifer Scott, interview with the author, December 17, 2020.
45 Monique Van Dam, interview with the author, January 26, 2021.
46 Margo Murphy, interview with the author, January 12, 2021.
47 Scott, interview with the author, December 17, 2020.
48 Murphy, interview with the author, December 3, 2013.
49 Ibid.
50 Doruyter, "Six players without fame," *Province*, July 6, 1980, 9.
51 Scott, interview with the author, December 17, 2020.
52 Bob Murphy, Facebook, September 26, 2015.
53 Monique Van Dam, liner notes, *Beautiful*, Bob Murphy & Monique Van Dam, BMMVD 0417, compact disc, 2017.
54 Renee Rosnes, Facebook, October 23, 2015.

13 / LET YOUR VOICE BE HEARD: HUGH FRASER

1 Campbell Ryga, interview with the author, September 30, 2020.
2 "Attractive Morning Wedding in Caulfeild Church Thursday," *Vancouver Sun*, November 18, 1939, 11.
3 Hugh Fraser, interview with Margaret Gallagher, *Hot Air*, CBC Radio, June 20, 2020 (broadcast date).
4 Hugh Fraser, interview with the author, September 17, 2019.
5 Ibid.
6 Ibid.
7 Ibid.
8 Marke Andrews, "Serving notice on bigger bands," *Vancouver Sun*, December 14, 1977, C3.
9 Bill Clark, interview with the author, February 10, 2021.
10 Ibid.
11 Fraser, interview with the author, September 17, 2019.

[12] Clark, interview with the author, February 10, 2021.
[13] Ibid.
[14] Fraser, interview with the author, September 17, 2019.
[15] Clark, interview with the author, February 10, 2021.
[16] Ryga, interview with the author, September 30, 2020.
[17] Chris Wong, "Jazz rebels in VEJI chart new ground," *The Ubyssey*, November 25, 1983, 1.
[18] Ibid.
[19] Clark, interview with the author, February 10, 2021.
[20] Chris Wong, "Fraser pursues every avenue in pathway to jazz excellence," *Vancouver Sun*, August 27, 1988, D2.
[21] Ryga, interview with the author, September 30, 2020.
[22] Clark, interview with the author, February 10, 2021.
[23] Fraser, interview with the author, September 17, 2019.
[24] Clark, interview with the author, February 10, 2021.
[25] Ibid.
[26] Wong, "Jazz rebels in VEJI chart new ground," *The Ubyssey*, November 25, 1983, 1.
[27] Hugh Fraser, interview with the author, November 22, 1983.
[28] Jan Walters, interview with the author, February 11, 2023.
[29] "Jazz concert," *Daily News*, June 28, 1985, M1.
[30] Don Thompson, liner notes, *Looking Up*, Hugh Fraser Quintet, CBC Enterprises, JZ 115, vinyl record, 1988.
[31] Wong, "Fraser pursues every avenue in pathway to jazz excellence," *Vancouver Sun*, August 27, 1988, D2.
[32] Walters, interview with the author, February 11, 2023.
[33] Fraser, interview with the author, September 17, 2019.
[34] Ryga, interview with the author, September 30, 2020.
[35] Ibid.
[36] Walters, interview with the author, February 11, 2023.
[37] Ryga, interview with the author, October 5, 2020.
[38] Fraser, interview with the author, September 17, 2019.
[39] Ibid.
[40] Walters, interview with the author, February 11, 2023.
[41] Hugh Fraser, liner notes, *In The Mean Time*, Hugh Fraser Quintet, Jazz Focus Records, JFCD020, compact disc, 1997.
[42] Lorae Farrell, interview with the author, February 6, 2021.
[43] Clark, interview with the author, February 10, 2021.
[44] Ibid.
[45] Farrell, interview with the author, February 6, 2021.

Notes

46. Christine Duncan, interview with Margaret Gallagher, *Hot Air*, CBC Radio, June 20, 2020.
47. Clark, interview with the author, February 10, 2021.
48. Farrell, interview with the author, February 6, 2021.
49. Ibid.
50. Fraser, interview with the author, September 17, 2019.
51. Farrell, interview with the author, February 6, 2021.
52. Fraser, interview with the author, September 17, 2019.
53. Ibid.
54. Ibid.
55. Farrell, interview with the author, February 6, 2021.
56. Ryga, interview with the author, September 30, 2020.
57. Farrell, interview with the author, February 6, 2021.
58. Fraser, interview with the author, September 17, 2019.
59. Farrell, interview with the author, February 6, 2021.
60. Ibid.
61. Ibid.
62. Hugh Fraser, note to Lorae Farrell, December 19, 2018.
63. Farrell, interview with the author, February 6, 2021.
64. Ibid.
65. Lorae Farell, Facebook, May 20, 2019.
66. Ryga, interview with the author, September 30, 2020.
67. Hugh Fraser, VEJI concert, Pyatt Hall, June 23, 2019.
68. Andreas Nothiger, interview with the author, February 16, 2021.
69. Fraser, interview with the author, September 17, 2019.
70. Hugh Fraser, interview with the author, September 20, 2019.
71. Clark, interview with the author, February 10, 2021.
72. Fraser, interview with the author, September 17, 2019.
73. Clark, interview with the author, February 10, 2021.
74. Fraser, interview with the author, September 17, 2019.
75. Clark, interview with the author, February 10, 2021.
76. "An Earful of Vancouver – Hugh Fraser," Hard Rubber Orchestra, June 16, 2020, https://www.youtube.com/watch?feature=youtu.be&v=3_O6qUaf7Dc&app=desktop.
77. Farrell, interview with the author, February 6, 2021.
78. Ibid.
79. Ryga, interview with the author, October 6, 2020.
80. Jan Walters, email to the author, February 13, 2023.
81. Walters, interview with the author, February 11, 2023.
82. Walters, email to the author, February 13, 2023.

83. Will Chernoff, "The Dean Thiessen Big Band debut concert," *Rhythm Changes*, April 19, 2022, https://www.rhythmchanges.ca/dean-thiessen-big-band-brentwood/.
84. Will Chernoff, "Hugh Fraser Canadian Dedication," *Rhythm Changes*, October 14, 2021, https://www.rhythmchanges.ca/hugh-fraser-canadian-dedication/.
85. Clark, interview with the author, February 10, 2021.
86. Fraser, VEJ1 concert, Pyatt Hall, June 23, 2019.

14 / THANKFULLY: ROSS TAGGART

1. "William Reid Taggart, William Taggart Obituary," *Times Colonist*, https://www.legacy.com/ca/obituaries/timescolonist/name/william-taggart-obituary?pid=130960732.
2. "Obituary, Helen F Taggart," *Dignity Memorial*, https://www.dignitymemorial.com/en-ca/obituaries/victoria-bc/helen-taggart-7237182.
3. Reece Metcalfe Rehm, interview with the author, May 15, 2018.
4. Ross Taggart, liner notes, *Presenting The Ross Taggart Trio*, Ross Taggart Trio, Cellar Live, CL110408, compact disc, 2009.
5. Metcalfe Rehm, interview with the author, May 15, 2018.
6. Ibid.
7. Ibid.
8. Taggart, liner notes, *Presenting The Ross Taggart Trio*, Ross Taggart Trio.
9. June Katz, comment, "Ross Taggart 1967-2013," *Vancouver Jazz*, http://vancouverjazz.com/2013/01/ross-taggart.html.
10. Renee Doruyter, "Ross started early," *Province*, September 20, 1991, B24.
11. Campbell Ryga, interview with the author, September 30, 2020.
12. Hugh Fraser, interview with the author, September 17, 2019.
13. Ryga, interview with the author, September 30, 2020.
14. Metcalfe Rehm, interview with the author, May 15, 2018.
15. Sharon Minemoto, interview with the author, December 12, 2016.
16. Ryga, interview with the author, September 30, 2020.
17. John Korsrud, email to the author, June 22, 2022.
18. Monique Van Dam, interview with the author, June 4, 2020.
19. Katie Malloch, interview with the author, December 11, 2016.
20. Ryga, interview with the author, September 30, 2020.
21. Hugh Fraser, interview with the author, September 17, 2019.
22. Peter Hum, ""You can hear a nugget of happiness that is just waiting to explode" – The Sharon Minemoto Interview," *Ottawa Citizen*, March 21, 2018, https://ottawacitizen.com/entertainment/jazzblog/you-can-hear-a-nugget-of-happiness-that-is-just-waiting-to-explode-the-sharon-minemoto-interview.
23. Cory Weeds, interview with the author, March 27, 2018.

Notes

24 Minemoto, interview with the author, December 12, 2016.
25 Chris Wong, "Taggart and his crack band radiate joy on Thankfully," *Vancouver Courier*, February 17, 2002, 30.
26 Jennifer Scott, interview with the author, December 17, 2020.
27 Metcalfe Rehm, interview with the author, May 15, 2018.
28 Wong, "Taggart and his crack band radiate joy on Thankfully," *Vancouver Courier*, February 17, 2002, 30.
29 Cory Weeds, liner notes, *Thankfully*, Ross Taggart Quartet, Cellar Live, CL11201, 2002.
30 Morgan Childs, interview with the author, February 26, 2014.
31 Wong, "Taggart and his crack band radiate joy on Thankfully," *Vancouver Courier*, February 17, 2002, 30.
32 Bob Murphy, interview with the author, December 3, 2013.
33 Mike Rud, interview with the author, February 8, 2014.
34 Bernie Arai, interview with the author, January 26, 2016.
35 Minemoto, interview with the author, December 12, 2016.
36 Cory Weeds, interview with the author, May 17, 2013.
37 Dave Robbins, interview with the author, November 21, 2016.
38 Charles McPherson, interview with the author, October 2, 2013.
39 Minemoto, interview with the author, December 12, 2016.
40 Robbins, interview with the author, November 21, 2016.
41 André Lachance, interview with the author, January 18, 2018.
42 Minemoto, interview with the author, December 12, 2016.
43 Cory Weeds, interview with the author, March 27, 2018.
44 Bill Coon, interview with the author, June 8, 2015.
45 Ian Hendrickson-Smith, interview with the author, June 11, 2013.
46 Minemoto, interview with the author, December 12, 2016.
47 Art Pepper, introduction to blues, unreleased recording, July 23, 1959, the Cellar.
48 Fred Stride, "Ross Taggart (1967-2013)," *Fred Stride Composer and Arranger*, originally posted February 1, 2013, reposted July 11, 2021, https://www.fredstride.com/articles--essays--thoughts/ross-taggart-1967-2013.
49 Cory Weeds, liner notes, *Presenting The Ross Taggart Trio*, Ross Taggart Trio.
50 Taggart, liner notes, *Presenting The Ross Taggart Trio*, Ross Taggart Trio.
51 Metcalfe Rehm, interview with the author, May 15, 2018.
52 Weeds, interview with the author, March 27, 2018.
53 Fraser, interview with the author, September 17, 2019.
54 Ibid.
55 Ryga, interview with the author, September 30, 2020.
56 Metcalfe Rehm, interview with the author, May 15, 2018.
57 Scott, interview with the author, December 17, 2020.
58 George Coleman, interview with the author, July 11, 2013.

[59] Brad Turner, interview with the author, June 6, 2019.
[60] Van Dam, interview with the author, June 4, 2020.
[61] Weeds, interview with the author, March 27, 2018.
[62] Ryga, interview with the author, September 30, 2020.
[63] Coon, interview with the author, June 8, 2015.
[64] Eric Metcalfe, interview with the author, May 9, 2018.
[65] Weeds, interview with the author, March 27, 2018.
[66] Ibid.
[67] "An Interview, Waxwing," *Songlines*, https://songlines.com/interviews/waxwing-2/.

15 / HERE NOW: BRAD TURNER

[1] Brad Turner, interview with the author, August 31, 2019.
[2] Ibid.
[3] Christopher Best, *Hearts, Minds & Souls: The true stories of 23 respected, career B.C. Music Educators who influenced the lives of many young people through music*, (Warfleet Press, 2016), 87-91.
[4] Kerry Turner and John White, In Profile: New Westminster and District Concert Band, https://nwdband.com/wp-content/uploads/2017/08/NWDB-CBA-Article-2011-Published-Version-2-1.pdf.
[5] Turner, interview with the author, June 6, 2019.
[6] *Langley Advance*, March 2, 1977, 10.
[7] Turner, interview with the author, June 6, 2019.
[8] André Lachance, interview with the author, September 3, 2019.
[9] Turner, interview with the author, June 6, 2019.
[10] Ibid.
[11] Chris Wong, "Trumpeter's versatility extends to drums, keyboard," *Vancouver Courier*, January 3, 1998.
[12] Turner, interview with the author, August 31, 2019.
[13] Cory Weeds, liner notes, *Jump Up*, Brad Turner Quartet, Cellar Music, CM123018, 2019.
[14] Turner, interview with the author, June 6, 2019.
[15] Turner, interview with the author, August 31, 2019.
[16] Fiona Black, email to the author, November 16, 2022.
[17] Ibid.
[18] Weeds, liner notes, *Jump Up*, Brad Turner Quartet.
[19] Turner, interview with the author, June 6, 2019.
[20] Ibid.
[21] Turner, interview with the author, June 15, 2015.

Notes

22. Brad Turner, interview with the author, workshop, *Jazz Walk at the Shadbolt*, December 1, 2019.
23. Turner, interview with the author, June 6, 2019.
24. Turner, interview with the author, *Jazz Walk at the Shadbolt*, December 1, 2019.
25. Turner, interview with the author, June 6, 2019.
26. Ibid.
27. Turner, interview with the author, August 31, 2019.
28. Ibid.
29. Turner, interview with the author, June 6, 2019.
30. Turner, interview with the author, August 31, 2019.
31. Lachance, interview with the author, September 3, 2019.
32. Bruno Hubert, interview with the author, August 20, 2019.
33. Turner, interview with the author, August 31, 2019.
34. Ibid.
35. Ibid.
36. Ibid.
37. Ibid.
38. Turner, interview with the author, June 6, 2019.
39. Black, email to the author, November 16, 2022.
40. Ibid.
41. Ibid.
42. Turner, interview with the author, August 31, 2019.
43. Ibid.
44. Cory Weeds, interview with the author, September 3, 2019.
45. Turner, interview with the author, June 6, 2019.
46. Turner, interview with the author, August 31, 2019.
47. Turner, interview with the author, June 6, 2019.
48. Brad Turner, introduction, *Scenes From Childhood*, Rose Gellert Hall, November 23, 2019.
49. Ibid.
50. Turner, interview with the author, *Jazz Walk at the Shadbolt*, December 1, 2019.
51. Brad Turner, email to the author, July 22, 2019.

16 / LIFE OF BRUNO: BRUNO HUBERT

1. "Armand Hubert," *Fédération québécoise des sociétés de généalogie*, https://federationgenealogie.qc.ca/bases-de-donnees/avis-de-deces/fiche?avisID=585762.
2. Bruno Hubert, interview with the author, August 20, 2019.
3. Ibid.
4. Ibid.
5. André Lachance, interview with the author, September 3, 2019.

[6] Ibid.
[7] Hubert, interview with the author, August 20, 2019.
[8] Ibid.
[9] Hubert, interview with the author, May 28, 2022.
[10] Ibid.
[11] Bruno Hubert, interview with Keith MacLachlan, *The Jazz Shed*, https://www.thejazzshed.com/index.php/2016/05/24/bruno-hubert-enigmatic-maestro-marches-to-his-own-beat/.
[12] Ibid.
[13] "Armand Hubert," *Fédération québécoise des sociétés de généalogie*.
[14] Ibid.
[15] Marke Andrews, "Glass Slipper destroyed by fire," *Vancouver Sun*, December 21, 1996, D4.
[16] "HEART OF THE CITY," *Vancouver Sun*, July 5, 1999, B1.
[17] Brad Turner, interview with the author, June 15, 2015.
[18] Turner, interview with the author, August 31, 2019.
[19] Hubert, interview with the author, October 15, 2014.
[20] Cory Weeds, interview with the author, September 3, 2019.
[21] Ross Taggart, liner notes, *Get Out of Town*, Bruno Hubert Trio, Cellar Live, CL011402, compact disc, 2002.
[22] Hubert, interview with the author, August 20, 2019.
[23] Turner, interview with the author, August 31, 2019.
[24] Weeds, interview with the author, September 3, 2019.
[25] Cory Weeds, liner notes, *Live @ The Cellar*, Bruno Hubert Trio, Cellar Live, CL110707, compact disc, 2008.
[26] Weeds, interview with the author, September 3, 2019.
[27] Hubert, interview with the author, August 20, 2019.
[28] Hubert, interview with the author, May 28, 2022.
[29] Ibid.
[30] "WE LOVE BRUNO!," *Do604*, https://do604.com/events/2016/12/13/we-love-bruno.
[31] Weeds, interview with the author, September 3, 2019.
[32] Lachance, interview with the author, September 3, 2019.
[33] Turner, interview with the author, August 31, 2019.
[34] Hubert, interview with the author, August 20, 2019.
[35] Ibid.
[36] Ibid.
[37] Ibid.
[38] Ibid.

17 / HOW MY HEART SINGS: KATE HAMMETT-VAUGHAN

1. Kate Hammett-Vaughan, interview with the author, May 29, 2019.
2. Chris Wong, "Jazz artist makes it in man's world," *The Ubyssey*, March 11, 1983, 6.
3. Ibid.
4. Ibid.
5. Hammett-Vaughan, interview with the author, May 29, 2019.
6. Ibid.
7. Ibid.
8. Hammett-Vaughan, interview with the author, December 14, 2016.
9. Ibid.
10. Marke Andrews, "Good jazz and nice people, *Vancouver Sun*, August 20, 1985, C4.
11. "this WEEK IN VANCOUVER," *TV Week*, 1984.
12. Hammett-Vaughan, interview with the author, May 29, 2019.
13. Hammett-Vaughan, interview with the author, December 14, 2016.
14. Ibid.
15. Hammett-Vaughan, interview with the author, May 29, 2019.
16. Jennifer Scott, interview with the author, December 17, 2020.
17. Kate Hammett-Vaughan, letter to the editor, *Vancouver Sun*, December 12, 1990, A14.
18. Ibid.
19. André Lachance, interview with the author, May 13, 2020.
20. Ibid.
21. Cory Weeds, interview with the author, May 13, 2020
22. Ibid.
23. Hammett-Vaughan, interview with the author, December 14, 2016.
24. Ibid.
25. Hammett-Vaughan, interview with the author, May 29, 2019.
26. Ibid.
27. Ibid.
28. Scott, interview with the author, December 17, 2020.
29. Hammett-Vaughan, interview with the author, May 29, 2019.
30. Ibid.
31. Hammett-Vaughan, Frankie's Jazz Club, October 28, 2021.
32. Hammett-Vaughan, interview with the author, May 29, 2019.

18 / HARDEST WORKING MAN IN JAZZ BUSINESS: CORY WEEDS

PART 1: HOW TO SUCCEED AS A JAZZ CLUB OWNER

1. Cory Weeds, interview with the author, June 14, 2013.
2. Ibid.

3   Joey DeFrancesco, interview with the author, October 10, 2013.
4   Weeds, interview with the author, June 14, 2013.
5   Bill Weeds, interview with the author, March 20, 2014.
6   Ibid.
7   Ibid.
8   Ibid.
9   Cory Weeds, comment, *Vancouver Jazz Forum*, http://vancouverjazz.com/forums/showthread.php?t=1578&page=4.
10 "Auld Lang Syne for dance," *Vancouver Sun*, October 30, 1963, 11.
11 Jack Lindsay, photo, City of Vancouver Archives, Reference code AM1184-: CVA 1184-3635.
12 Brad Turner, interview with the author, June 15, 2015.
13 Chris Gestrin, interview with the author, September 20, 2014.
14 Bill Coon, interview with the author, June 8, 2015.
15 Weeds, interview with the author, May 13, 2013.
16 Ibid.
17 Dave Robbins, interview with the author, November 21, 2016.
18 Morgan Childs, interview with the author, February 26, 2014.
19 Weeds, interview with the author, May 13, 2013.
20 Weeds, interview with the author, May 17, 2013.
21 Classified ad, *Georgia Straight*, 34, no. 1685, April 6-13, 2000, 109.
22 Weeds, interview with the author, May 17, 2013.
23 Ibid.
24 Coon, interview with the author, June 8, 2015.
25 Stephano Liapis, interview with the author, June 8, 2015.
26 Weeds, interview with the author, May 17, 2013.
27 Weeds, interview with the author, May 13, 2013.
28 Mike Allen, interview with the author, September 27, 2016.
29 Coon, interview with the author, June 8, 2015.
30 Allen, interview with the author, September 27, 2016.
31 Weeds, Facebook Live, April 12, 2020.
32 Turner, interview with the author, June 15, 2015.
33 Ibid.
34 Bernie Arai, interview with the author, January 26, 2016.
35 Childs, interview with the author, February 26, 2014.
36 Cory Weeds, "Pic Of The day: Turner/Rosenwinkel," *Cory Weeds – Jazz Impresario*, https://cweeds.wordpress.com/2012/04/28/pic-of-the-day-turnerrosenwinkel/.
37 Weeds, Facebook Live, May 3, 2020.
38 Joan Mariacher, interview with the author, October 15, 2018.
39 Mariacher, interview with the author, August 13, 2018.

Notes

40 Weeds, interview with the author, May 17, 2013.
41 Marke Andrews, "Club owner accepts fear factor," *Vancouver Sun*, February 4, 2022, B7.
42 Jodi Proznick, interview with the author, April 15, 2014.
43 Joanne Clifton, interview with the author, June 2, 2014.
44 Weeds, interview with the author, April 19, 2018.
45 Weeds, Facebook Live, April 5, 2020.
46 Mike LeDonne, interview with the author, March 21, 2014.
47 George Colligan, interview with the author, August 4, 2014.
48 Jeff Hamilton, interview with the author, February 24, 2014.
49 Weeds, interview with the author, May 13, 2013.
50 Dr. Lonnie Smith, interview with the author, December 5, 2015.
51 Karen Newman, interview with the author, July 10, 2013.
52 Weeds, interview with the author, July 9, 2013.
53 Weeds, Facebook Live, April 5, 2020.
54 Ibid.
55 Weeds, Facebook Live, April 12, 2020.
56 Ibid.
57 Michael Grunewaldt, interview with the author, January 20, 2016.
58 Weeds, interview with the author, April 15, 2022.
59 Weeds, interview with the author, May 17, 2013.

PART 2: FIN DE L'AFFAIRE, LIVING THE JAZZ DREAM

60 Jenny Larisey, interview with the author, March 5, 2014.
61 Cory Weeds, interview with the author, April 19, 2018.
62 Ibid.
63 Weeds, interview with the author, June 5, 2014.
64 Nikita Carter, interview with the author, June 9, 2015.
65 Ibid.
66 Weeds, interview with the author, May 17, 2013.
67 Gary Smulyan, interview with the author, January 18, 2014.
68 Joey DeFrancesco, interview with the author, October 10, 2013.
69 Spike Wilner, interview with the author, June 17, 2013.
70 Tom Keenlyside, interview with the author, October 29, 2016.
71 Ian Hendrickson-Smith, interview with the author, June 11, 2013.
72 Cory Weeds, "AN OPEN LETTER TO MUSIC STUDENTS IN VANCOUVER," *Cory Weeds – Jazz Impresario*, https://cweeds.wordpress.com/2012/12/03/an-open-letter-to-music-students-in-vancouver/.

[73] Cory Weeds, "DAY 7 – Village Vanguard Optional," *Cory Weeds – Jazz Impresario*, https://cweeds.wordpress.com/2013/03/23/day-7-village-vanguard-optional/.
[74] Steve Davis, interview with the author, November 23, 2013.
[75] Weeds, interview with the author, October 17, 2013.
[76] Ibid.
[77] Weeds, email to the author and others, November 16, 2013.
[78] Weeds, interview with the author, November 14, 2013.
[79] Smulyan, interview with the author, January 18, 2014.
[80] Weeds, interview with the author, March 21, 2014.
[81] Steve Kaldestad, interview with the author, March 19, 2014.
[82] Coon, interview with the author, June 8, 2015.
[83] Childs, interview with the author, February 26, 2014.
[84] Dr. Lonnie Smith, interview with the author, December 5, 2015.
[85] Louis Hayes, interview with the author, December 6, 2013.
[86] Jon Mayer, interview with the author, December 1, 2013.
[87] Ian McDougall, interview with the author, April 12, 2014.
[88] Weeds, interview with the author, December 31, 2013.
[89] Margaret Gallagher, the Cellar, February, 26, 2014.
[90] Weeds, the Cellar, February, 26, 2014.
[91] Ibid.
[92] Jesse Cahill, interview with the author, April 27, 2014.
[93] Mike Allen, the Cellar, February, 26, 2014.
[94] Weeds, interview with the author, November 14, 2013.
[95] Mike Allen, interview with the author, September 27, 2016.
[96] Weeds, interview with the author, November 15, 2016.
[97] Weeds, interview with the author, March 3, 2014.
[98] Weeds, interview with the author, March 15, 2014.
[99] Weeds, Facebook Live, April 26, 2020.
[100] Katie Malloch, interview with the author, December 11, 2016.
[101] Ibid.
[102] Seleno Clarke, interview with the author, March 16, 2014.
[103] Lewis Nash, interview with the author, March 18, 2014.
[104] Weeds, interview with the author, June 5, 2014.
[105] "Cory Weeds Shares His Story With AnxietyBC," *Anxiety Canada YouTube*, https://www.youtube.com/watch?v=4mAwP6NCvss.
[106] Weeds, interview with the author, June 5, 2014.
[107] Cory Weeds, text message, September 24, 2014.
[108] Cory Weeds, Facebook, September 24, 2014.
[109] Weeds, interview with the author, November 14, 2013.
[110] Malloch, interview with the author, December 11, 2016.

[111] Cory Weeds, email, May 31, 2019.
[112] Weeds, interview with the author, March 17, 2018.
[113] Weeds, Facebook, June 28, 2020.
[114] Weeds, Facebook, September 13, 2020.
[115] Weeds, Facebook, October 6, 2020.

19 / THE DOCTOR AND THE AMBASSADOR: DR. LONNIE SMITH AND SELENO CLARKE

[1] Cory Weeds, interview with the author, May 13, 2013.
[2] Ibid.
[3] Ibid.
[4] Ibid.
[5] Ibid.
[6] Ibid.
[7] Ibid.
[8] Bill Coon, interview with the author, June 8, 2015.
[9] Dr. Lonnie Smith, interview with the author, August 2003.
[10] Dr. Lonnie Smith, interview with the author, December 5, 2015.
[11] Ibid.
[12] Smith, interview with the author, August 2003.
[13] Bill Milkowski, "Dr. Lonnie Smith: The Doctor Is In!," *JazzTimes*, updated September 29, 2021, https://jazztimes.com/features/profiles/dr-lonnie-smith-the-doctor-is-in/.
[14] Greg Bryant, "Dr. Lonnie Smith, Master Of The Hammond Organ, Dies At 79," *NPR*, https://www.npr.org/2021/09/28/1041372956/dr-lonnie-smith-master-of-the-hammond-organ-dies-at-79.
[15] Ibid.
[16] Smith, interview with the author, December 5, 2015.
[17] Seleno Clarke, interview with the author, March 16, 2014.
[18] Ibid.
[19] "Rename 132nd St between 7 & 8 ave in NYC to "Seleno Clarke Way"," *change.org*, https://www.change.org/p/bill-perkins-rename-132nd-st-between-7-8-ave-in-nyc-to-seleno-clarke-way.

20 / BIG G: GEORGE COLEMAN

[1] Miles Black, interview with the author, October 22, 2013.
[2] George Coleman, interview with the author, July 11, 2013.
[3] Gavin Walker, email to the author, September 13, 2016.
[4] Black, interview with the author, October 22, 2013.
[5] Campbell Ryga, interview with the author, September 30, 2020.

6. Cory Weeds, interview with the author, May 23, 2013.
7. Jesse Cahill, interview with the author, April 27, 2014.
8. Jodi Proznick, interview with the author, April 15, 2014.
9. George Coleman, interview with the author, July 11, 2013.
10. Cory Weeds, interview with the author, May 23, 2013.
11. Harold Mabern, interview with the author, September 25, 2013.
12. Steve Kaldestad, interview with the author, March 19, 2014.
13. Coleman, interview with the author, July 11, 2013.
14. Ibid.
15. Miles Davis with Quincy Troupe, *Miles: The Autobiography* (New York, London, Toronto, Sydney, Tokyo, Singapore: Simon & Schuster, 1989), 268-269.
16. Cory Weeds, liner notes, *The George Coleman Quintet in Baltimore*, George Coleman Quintet, Reel to Real, RTRCD005, 2020.

21 / THE RHYTHM SECTION: TILDEN WEBB, JODI PROZNICK, AND JESSE CAHILL

1. Cory Weeds, liner notes, *Cellar Groove*, Tilden Webb Trio, Cellar Live, CL121204, compact disc, 2005.
2. Tilden Webb, interview with the author, October 12, 2018.
3. Webb, interview with the author, April 15, 2014.
4. Jodi Proznick, interview with the author, October 12, 2018.
5. Proznick, interview with the author, April 15, 2014.
6. Cahill, interview with the author, May 2, 2022.
7. Cahill, interview with the author, April 27, 2014.
8. Ibid.
9. Proznick, interview with the author, April 15, 2014.
10. Ibid.
11. Charles McPherson, interview with the author, October 2, 2013.
12. Webb, interview with the author, April 15, 2014.
13. Ibid.
14. Greg Buium, "David (Fathead) Newman blows in to front at the Cellar," *Vancouver Sun*, December 11, 2004, F8.
15. Cory Weeds, interview with the author, June 27, 2013.
16. David "Fathead" Newman, *Cellar Groove*, Tilden Webb Trio, Cellar Live, CL121204, compact disc.
17. Karen Newman, interview with the author, July 10, 2013.
18. Peter Hum, "Tilden Webb remembers David "Fathead" Newman," *Ottawa Citizen*, January 22, 2009, https://ottawacitizen.com/entertainment/jazzblog/tilden-webb-remembers-david-fathead-newman.
19. Webb, interview with the author, April 15, 2014.

[20] Cahill, interview with the author, April 27, 2014.
[21] Ibid.
[22] Jodi Proznick, "DAVID "FATHEAD" NEWMAN AND THE TILDEN WEBB TRIO REISSUE," Jodi Proznick blog, https://jodiproznick.com/david-fathead-newman-and-the-tilden-webb-trio-reissue/.
[23] Proznick, interview with the author, April 15, 2014.
[24] Hum, "Tilden Webb remembers David "Fathead" Newman," *Ottawa Citizen*, January 22, 2009.
[25] Steve Kaldestad, interview with the author, March 19, 2014.
[26] Harold Mabern, interview with the author, September 25, 2013.
[27] Proznick, interview with the author, April 15, 2014.
[28] Ibid.
[29] Webb, interview with the author, April 15, 2014.
[30] Proznick, interview with the author, May 31, 2022.
[31] Webb, Facebook, July 28, 2023.
[32] Kaldestad, interview with the author, March 19, 2014.
[33] Weeds, interview with the author, May 17, 2013.
[34] Proznick, interview with the author, May 31, 2022.
[35] Cahill, interview with the author, April 27, 2014.
[36] Peter Bernstein, interview with the author, June 23, 2013.
[37] Proznick, interview with the author, April 15, 2014.
[38] Proznick, interview with the author, May 31, 2022.
[39] Proznick, interview with the author, October 12, 2018.
[40] Amanda Tosoff, interview with the author, June 13, 2022.
[41] Proznick, Facebook, September 17, 2020.

22 / KEEPING IT REAL: ROY MCCURDY

[1] Roy McCurdy, interview with the author, January 19, 2019.
[2] Ibid.
[3] Ibid.
[4] Ibid.
[5] Ibid.
[6] McCurdy, interview with the author, April 22, 2022.
[7] *Mercy, Mercy, Mercy! Live at "The Club,"* Cannonball Adderley Quintet, Capitol Records, SM-2663.
[8] E. Rodney Jones, liner notes, *Mercy, Mercy, Mercy! Live at "The Club,"* Cannonball Adderley Quintet, Capitol Records, 1967.
[9] McCurdy, interview with the author, June 14, 2013.
[10] McCurdy, interview with the author, January 19, 2019.
[11] Ibid.

12 Ibid.
13 Ibid.
14 Cory Weeds, interview with the author, May 23, 2013.
15 Ibid.
16 André Lachance, interview with the author, January 18, 2018.
17 Weeds, interview with the author, May 23, 2013.
18 Ibid.
19 McCurdy, interview with the author, January 19, 2019.
20 Ibid.
21 McCurdy, interview with the author, January 19, 2019.

23 / SENSE AND SENSIBILITY: AMANDA TOSOFF

1 Amanda Tosoff, interview with the author, December 19, 2016.
2 Ross Taggart, liner notes, *Wait And See*, Amanda Tosoff, Cellar Live, 2008.
3 Morgan Childs, interview with the author, February 26, 2014.
4 Dave Robbins, interview with the author, November 21, 2016.
5 Ibid.
6 André Lachance, interview with the author, January 18, 2018.
7 Tosoff, interview with the author, December 19, 2016.
8 Childs, interview with the author, February 26, 2014.
9 Cory Weeds, interview with the author, March 21, 2014.
10 Cory Weeds, liner notes, *Still Life*, Cellar Live, CLF 001, 2006.
11 Taggart, liner notes, *Wait And See*, Amanda Tosoff.
12 Tosoff, interview with the author, December 19, 2016.
13 Ibid.
14 Weeds, interview with the author, March 21, 2014.
15 Tosoff, interview with the author, October 26, 2020.
16 Tosoff, interview with the author, December 19, 2016.
17 Tosoff, interview with the author, October 26, 2020.
18 "Words," *amandatosoff.com*, https://amandatosoff.com/music/words/bio/.
19 Ibid.
20 Ibid.
21 Ibid.
22 Ibid.
23 Ibid.
24 Ibid.
25 Ibid.

24 / LOVE WALKED IN: MIKE ALLEN

1 Mike Allen, interview with the author, September 27, 2016.

Notes

2. Cory Weeds, liner notes, *Just Like Magic*, Mike Allen, Cellar Music, 2019.
3. Ibid.
4. Allen, interview with the author, November 6, 2019.
5. Mike Allen, *Mike Allen Jazz Anthology: 90 Original Compositions and Recollections* (Telwell Talent, 2021), 7.
6. "A Jazz Hothouse," *McGillNews Alumni Magazine*, https://mcgillnews.mcgill.ca/s/1762/news/interior.aspx?sid=1762&gid=2&pgid=1550.
7. "Canadian jazz's best-kept secret inspires quartet for May 21 show," *The Daily Courier*, https://www.kelownadailycourier.ca/entertainment/article_bb1b7342-7798-11e9-8e21-a3dcf177b78d.html.
8. Allen, interview with the author, September 27, 2016.
9. Brian Nation, "Mike Allen," May 2007, *vancouverJazz.com*, http://vancouverjazz.com/inview/allen.shtml.
10. Don Friedman, interview with the author, August 18, 2014.
11. Cory Weeds, "Mike Allen – Just Like Magic," Cellar Music, *Cory Weeds YouTube*, https://www.youtube.com/watch?v=ZisqdQ_aHqc.
12. Allen, interview with the author, September 27, 2016.
13. Ibid.
14. Ibid.
15. Mike Allen, "Going To Space?," *mikeallenjazz.com*, http://mikeallenjazz.com/index.php/news/going_to_space.
16. Mike Allen, *Mike Allen Jazz Anthology: 90 Original Compositions and Recollections*, 47.
17. Allen, interview with the author, September 27, 2016.
18. Ibid.
19. Ibid.
20. Mike Allen, "Mike Allen – Just Like Magic," Cellar Music, *Cory Weeds YouTube*, https://www.youtube.com/watch?v=ZisqdQ_aHqc.
21. Allen, interview with the author, November 6, 2019.
22. Nation, "Mike Allen," May 2007, *vancouverJazz.com*.

25 / ENDINGS RARELY ARE: NATASHA D'AGOSTINO

1. David Blake, interview with the author, March 21, 2021.
2. Ibid.
3. Tracy Neff, email to the author, May 24, 2021.
4. Ibid.
5. Ibid.
6. Jared Burrows, celebration of Natasha D'Agostino's life, January 26, 2019.
7. Réjean Marois, celebration of Natasha D'Agostino's life, January 26, 2019.
8. Burrows, celebration of Natasha D'Agostino's life, January 26, 2019.

9. Neff, email to the author, May 24, 2021.
10. Ibid.
11. Kate Hammett-Vaughan, interview with the author, May 29, 2019.
12. Natasha D'Agostino and Jillian Lebeck, Facebook, April 1, 2016.
13. Natasha D'Agostino, Facebook, April 2, 2016.
14. Blake, interview with the author, March 21, 2021.
15. Ibid.
16. Ibid.
17. Blake, interview with the author, March 21, 2021.
18. Jared Burrows, Facebook, January 8, 2019.
19. D'Agostino, Facebook, March 31, 2017.
20. D'Agostino, Facebook, July 31, 2017.
21. Blake, interview with the author, March 21, 2021.
22. Ibid.
23. Sharon Minemoto, email to the author, April 21, 2021.
24. Ibid.
25. Anna D'Agostino, interview with the author, April 25, 2022.
26. Ibid.
27. Ibid.
28. D'Agostino, Facebook, March 28, 2018.
29. Christopher McBride, interview with the author, March 25, 2021.
30. Ibid.
31. Ibid.
32. Blake, interview with the author, March 21, 2021.
33. Blake, Facebook, January 8, 2019.
34. Ibid.
35. Cory Weeds, Facebook, December 21, 2018.
36. D'Agostino, Facebook, December 31, 2018.
37. Blake, interview with the author, March 21, 2021.
38. Ian Jacques, "South Delta music instructor killed in Richmond crash," *Delta Optimist*, January 9, 2019, https://www.delta-optimist.com/local-news/south-delta-music-instructor-killed-in-richmond-crash-3091302.
39. Minemoto, Facebook, January 8, 2019.
40. Minemoto, celebration of Natasha D'Agostino's life, January 26, 2019.
41. Kevan D'Agostino, celebration of Natasha D'Agostino's life, January 26, 2019.
42. Jodi Proznick, interview with the author, May 31, 2022.
43. Blake, interview with the author, March 21, 2021.
44. Ibid.
45. Ibid.

INDEX

Page numbers in bold refer to photographs.

A
A&B Sound (Victoria), 271
A Band (Capilano University), 307, 316, 514
Abercrombie, John, 431
Abrams, Lloyd, 219, 482
Abrams, Muhal Richard, 250, 348
Acadia University, 346, 356
Ace Records, 191
Adams, Bryan, 315
Adams, Bucky, 346
Adams, Harvey, 28
Adderley, Cannonball, 195, 228, 319, 406, 416, 471, 473-479, 529, 531
Adderley, Nat, 473
Ad-lib, 324
Advanced School of Contemporary Music (Toronto), 216
Adzenyah, Abraham, 268
Afrocubanismo festival (Banff), 247
Aida, Yuki, 519
Aiello, Raffaele, 414
Akinmusire, Ambrose, 514
Alcan Jazz Competition, 244, 273-274

Alexander, Eric, 4, 6, 285, 368-370, 389, 392, 394, 411, 415, 443, 460
Alexander, Monty, 407
Allen, Buff, 223, 225, 231, 244, 533
Allen, Mike, 5, 301, 331, 373-374, 376, 409, 452, 494-506, **499-500, 503, 505,** 529, 538
[The] Alley (Vancouver), 184-186
Allison, Mose, 36, 40
Alma Academy (Vancouver), 11, **12**, 366, **367**
Alma Street Café (Vancouver), 4, 272, 368, 371
Alma Theatre (Vancouver), 367
Al Neil & His Royal Canadians, 70-71
Al Neil / A Portrait, 68, 537
Al Neil Jazz Probe, 73
Al Neil Jazz Probe Orchestra, 73
Al Neil Jazz Trio (Royal Rascals), 71, **72**
Al Neil Trio, 1, 3, 70, 73, 84, 532
Alviar, Saul, 513
American Legion Post 398 (New York), 413, 433, 435, 437
Anderson, Ernestine, 135, **135**, 137, 142
Anderson, Laurie, 53

577

Andrews, Marke, 221, 348, 389
Anka, Paul, 79, 393
Annapolis Valley Apple Blossom Festival, 346
Annecy, 511
Anne MacDonald Studio (North Vancouver), 513, **518**, 520
Anne of Green Gables, 155
Anstey, Richard, 3, 69-71, 73
Anthony, Stephen, 346
Anvil Centre (New Westminster), 521
AnxietyBC, 414
Apollo Theater (New York), 434
Aragon Records, 214-215
Arai, Bernie, 5, 280-281, 299, 301, 373, 377, 428, 507, 515-516, 538
Arctic Club (Vancouver), 155-156
Argue, Darcy James, 482
Argüelles, Julian, 252
Armanini, Mark, 354
Armoury Studios (Vancouver), 251
Armstrong, Louis, 99, 161, 494
Army & Navy (Vancouver), 238
Arntzen, Evan, 293, 482-483, 485-487
Artaud, Antonin, 68
Artemis, 468, 491-492
Art Ensemble of Chicago, 238
Arts Club Theatre (Vancouver), 86
Asch, Moses, 64
Association for the Advancement of Creative Musicians (AACM, Chicago), vii
[The] Attic (Vancouver), 367
A Tribe Called Quest, 431
Au, Allison, **469**
Austen, Jane, 490
Avonlea, 155-156
Avon Theatre (Vancouver), 81
Axworthy, Lloyd, 249
Ayler, Albert, 71

B

Babin, Tommy, **205**
Bach, Johann Sebastian, 61, 74, 320
Badazjazz, 344, 347
Bad Kreuznach, 173
Bakan, Joel, 92
Baker, Chet, 36, 69
Baker, Kenny, 502
Baker Studios (Victoria), 6,
Balliett, Whitney, 38, 536
Baltimore, 447-448, 530
Banff, 234, 242-243, 245, 247-248, 251, 255, 348-349
Banff Centre for Arts and Creativity, 522
Banff Centre for the Arts, 39, 242, **245**, 348, 453
Banham, Jim, 46, 70
Banks, Tommy, 127, 174
Barclay, Gary, 140
Barker, Don, **240**
Barlow, Emilie-Claire, 481
Bar None (Vancouver), 300
Barnett, Stew, 9, 163, 165, 171
Barrett, Ross, 182-183, 185-187, **188**, 538
Barron, Kenny, 175
Bartók, Béla, 74, 265, 489
Bartz, Gary, 251, 377, 498
Basie, Count, 178, 434
Basin Street (Vancouver), 242
BC Civil Liberties Association, 199
BC Lions, 98, 106, 108
The Beachcombers, 163
[The] Beacon Theatre (Vancouver), 55
The Beard, 3, 194, 198-200
The Beatles, 86, 345, 358
Beck, Glenn, **83**
Becker, Noah, 383
Beckett, Samuel, 65, 84, 92
The Bee Gees, 320
Benjamin, Arthur, 55
Bellingham, viii, 294, 297, 497

Bellow, Saul, 65
Bennett, Tony, 158
Benson, George, 427, 429, 435, 437
Bentley, Jon, 291, 293, 301, 318, 377
Bergonzi, Jerry, **37**, 38
Berglund, Bob, 11, 123
Berklee College of Music (Boston), 36
Berlin, Irving, 269, 312, 358
Bernstein, Peter, 4, 6, 368-369, 389, 395, 407, 415, 433, 449, 464, 468-469, 529, 538
Berry, Chuck, 218
Biali, Laila, 465, 482
Bianchi, Pat, 463, 529
Biddle's Jazz and Ribs (Montreal), 450
Big Brother and the Holding Company, 71
The Billboard, 65
Bill Clark Sextet, 273-274
Billy the Kid, 194
Birdland (New York), 82, 472
Bjornson, Joe, **240**
Black, Fiona, 303, 311, 538
Black History Month, 189
Black, Miles, 6, 325, 327, **407**, 439, **441**, 443, 460, 499-500, **503**, 538
Blackley, Jim, 106, 109
[The] Black Spot (Vancouver), 30, 183, 217
Blackwell, Ed, 3, 51, 195, 219
Blake, David, 507, 512-513, 515-516, 520, 522, 524-526, 538
Blake, Michael, 292, 348
Blake, Seamus, 4, 298, 300, 303, 314-315, **316**, 329, 337, 374, 376, 534
Blaney, Paul, 349
[The] Blarney Stone (Vancouver), 264
Bley, Carla, **126**, 238
Bley, Paul, 71, **126**, 472
Blind Boys of Alabama, 204
Blood, Sweat & Tears, 431, 477

[The] Blue Horn (Vancouver), 2, 70, 113, 183, 367
[The] Blue Monk (Portland), 457
[The] Blue Note (New York), 248
[The] Blue Note Jazz Bistro (Vancouver), 329, 336, 371
Blue Note Records, 397, 416, 430-431, 504, 531, 533-534
[The] Blues Palace (Vancouver), 367
BlueShore Financial Centre for the Performing Arts (North Vancouver), 7
Blue Wave Studios (Vancouver), 95
Boathouse Records, 251, 531, 533, 535
Bobby Hales Big Band, 161, **162**, 163, 531
Bobby Taylor and the Vancouvers, 367
Bogotá, 249
Bollenback, Paul, **397**
Bondo, Sarah, 382
Bonehenge, 257
Booker, Walter, 473
Borrie, Rod, **240**, **245**, 259
Borsos, Jeremy, 77
Borsos, Sus, 77
Boston, 36
Botten, Russ, 278
Boudin, Henry, 329
Bourassa, François, 499
Bowles, Jane, 354
Bowles, Paul, 354
Bowling, Tim, 489
Boyd, Denny, 165, 351
Boyle, Bill, 2, 12-13, 28, 59, **60**, 62, 132, 134
Brackeen, Joanne, 36
Bradley's (New York), 36, 116-118
Brad Turner Quartet, 4-5, 298-304, 312, 314-315, **316**, 317-318, 326, 328-330, 337, 374, 531, 534
Brad Turner Trio, 299-301, 304, 312-313, 534

579

Brain Damage, 91, 96
Braverman, Mike, 354
Braxton, Anthony, 76
Breau, Lenny, 415
Brecker Brothers, 299
Brecker, Michael, 38, 292, 330
Briseno, Modesto, 62
Brochu, Paul, 328
The Bronx (New York), 435
Brooklyn (New York), 53, 243
Brooks, Roy, 420
Brown, Clifford, 16, 44, 60, 170, 365, 447, 486
Brown, Gordy, **12**
Brown, Julie, 202-203, 210, 538
Brown, Ray, 450-451, 535
British Columbia Music Festival, 55
Brubeck, Dan, **37**
Brubeck, Darius, **37**
Brubeck, Dave, 4, 12, 25, 36, **37**, **244**
Bruno Hubert Trio, 5, 321-322, 328-330, 333, 336-337, 342, 381, 531
Bruno's Blues, 6, 334, **335, 336, 340**
Bryant, Greg, 432
Bryant, Jerry, 236
Bublé, Michael, 143
Buckley, Tim, 198
Buffalo, 429
Bukowski's (Vancouver), 333, 336, 341
Bull, Hank, 273
Bullfrog Studios (Vancouver), 242
Bullock's (Los Angeles), 44
Burgess, George, **12**
Burk, Kory, 379
Burnaby, 7, **155**, 217, 296, 318, 417, 467, 492
Burkeview Chapel (Port Coquitlam), 7
Burrows, Jared, 510
Byrne, Derry, **306**
Byrnes, Jim, **201**, 203-205, 209, 529

C

Caballero, David, **422**
Café Deux Soleils (Vancouver), 366
Café New York (Vancouver), 36
Cage, John, 57, 62
Cahill, David, 452, 466
Cahill, Jesse, 5-7, **176**, 285, **306, 369, 391, 397-398**, 409, 439-440, **441**, 443-444, **445**, 449-469, **453, 462-463, 487**, 488, 529, 538
Caird, Patric, 234, 236, **240, 245, 259, 261, 264**
Calgary, 18, 163, 168, 200
California Club (Los Angeles), 43-44
Cambrian Hall (Vancouver), 55
Cameron, Chris, **53**
Campbell, Kathy, 205, 207, **207**
Campbell River, 120-121, 143, 147-149, **150**, 151
Campbell, Tom, 87
Canada Council for the Arts, 275, 304, 327
Canadian Football League, 106
Canadian Stage Band Festival, 233, 259, 324
Cándido, 26, **27**
Candoli, Conte, 131
Cannabis Cellar, 414
Capilano (Cap) College (North Vancouver), 285, 298, 303-304, 325-326, 330, 365, 482-484, 497, 531
Capilano College Performing Arts Theatre, 4, 302, 330, 531
Capilano University (CapU, North Vancouver), 258, 291, 293, 298, 307, 311, 316, 356, 510, **514**, 523
Capilano University A Band, 307, 316, 514
Capitol Records, 474, 529-530
Capon, John, 108, 134, 538
Carello, Joe, 293

Carnegie Hall (New York), 25, 36
Carnegie's (Vancouver), 224-225, 227
Carney, James (Jim), 2, **12**, 12, 101, 104-105, 115, 118, **119**, 538
Caron, Alain, 328
Carter, Benny, 93
Carter, Betty, 347, 355, 472-473, 511
Carter, JP, 9, 482
Carter, Nikita (Coat Cooke), 185, 392-393, 538
Carter, Ron, 442, 473
Carter, Wilf, 214
Cartwright, Sam, 336
Cat's Meow (Vancouver), 366
Caunter, Gerry, 185
The Cave Supper Club (Vancouver), 17, 138, 158, 171, 218
CBC Radio, xv, 14, 29, 33, 85, 127, 164, 235, 278, 408, 412, 496,
CBC Radio Orchestra, 253
CBC-TV, 2, 17, 69, 100, 130, 163, 538
CBUT (CBC-TV), 101, 538
Cégep de Sainte-Foy (Québec City), 324-325
The [original] Cellar jazz club (Vancouver), xvii, 1-2, 7, John Dawe: 10-20, **15**, **17**, 22-23, Jim & Rick Kilburn: 24-25, 28-36, **34**, 40, 42, Ornette Coleman: 43-51, **45-46**, **48**, Al Neil: 54, 59-68, **60**, 71, 73, Barry and Dylan Cramer: 79-86, **83**, 90-92, 94, Charles Mingus: 98-101, **100**, **102**, 103-112, **105**, **111-112**, 115, 117-121, **119**, Dave Quarin: 126-138, **126**, **128**, **130**, **132**, **135**, 144-148, 150-151, 153, Bobby Hales: 154-161, 164, PJ Perry: 171-173, 177, Carol Fox: 181-183, Bob Murphy: 217, 219, Cory Weeds: 367, 373, George Coleman: 442,
[Cory Weeds'] Cellar jazz club (Vancouver), xvii, 5-6, PJ Perry: 176-177, Bob Murphy: 201, **201-202**, 225, **226,** Hugh Fraser: **253**, 255, **256**, 257, Ross Taggart: 269, 278-281, **282**, 283-286, 289, **290**, 293, Brad Turner: 300-304, **301, 305, 306**, Bruno Hubert: 328, 330, 333, 336, **339**, Kate Hammett-Vaughan: 353, **358**, Cory Weeds Part 1: 361-363, **369**, 371-388, **375**, **378**, Cory Weeds Part 2: 389,-417, **391, 395, 396-398, 401-402, 404, 407, 410, 412**, 419, 424, Dr. Lonnie Smith & Seleno Clarke: 426-429, **430**, 432, 435-436, **436-437**, George Coleman: 439-440, **441**, 443-444, **445**, 446, 448, Tilden Webb, Jodi Proznick, and Jesse Cahill: 449-450, **451**, 452, **453**, 454-464, **455**, **459**, **462**, 467-469, Roy McCurdy: 475-479, Amanda Tosoff: 483-486, **485**, **487**, 488-489, Mike Allen: 494-495, 498-504, **499-500**, **503**, Selected Discography: 529-535
Cellar Jazz Café (Vancouver), 4-5, 300-301, 314, 368-369, 372-374
Cellar Jazz Society, 411
Cellar Live, 5-6, 176, 201, 270, 278, 281, 286, 293, 303, 311, 314, 330, 333, 362, 379, 381-382, 392-393, 395, 397, 413, 416-417, 420, 428, 432, 454, 456, 459, 463, 484, 486, 529-531, 533-535
Cellar Live Futures, 484-485, 532, 534
Cellar Music, 8, 314, 417, 420, 423, 432, 468, 503, 529, 532-535
Cellar Music Group, 416, 423, 447
Century, Michael, 242-243
CFUN, 51
Chad Makela Quartet, 394
Chambers, Lionel, 2, 62
Chambers, Paul, 442, 453
Chameleon Urban Lounge (Vancouver), 299
Chan Centre for the Performing Arts (Vancouver), 253
Chaney, Lon Jr., 81

Changuito, 247
CHAN-TV, Channel 8, 86
Chaplin, Charlie, 320
Charles, Ray, 441, 455, 458
Charette, Brian, 420, 529
Chee, Judy, **287**
Cheech & Chong, 367
Chernoff, Will, 267
Cherry, Don, viii, 1, 10, 42, 44-46, **46**, 49-50, 127, 129, **130**
Chicago, vii, 190, 201, 210, 238, 441, 474
Childs, Morgan, 280-281, 370, 377, 405, 482-484, 486-487, **487**, 492, 529, 538
Chilliwack, 42, 155-156
Chilliwack (band), 36
Chivers, Jim, 69
Choboter, Matt, 308
Chong, Tommy, 367
CHQM, 104
Christian, Charlie, 26, 29, 519
Christian, Henry, **240**
Christy, June, 26, **27**
Chycoski, Arnie, 9, **12**, 13, 160, 170, 296
Cinelu, Mino, 302
Citadel Theatre (Edmonton), 233
City Space (Vancouver), 238-239, **240**
Civic Auditorium (Portland), 28
CJOR, 125
CJOR Playhouse (Vancouver), 125
CKNW, 214
Claremont Secondary School, 271
Clark, Bill, 9, 236-242, **240**, 245, 251-252, **256**, 263, 268, 273-274, 538
Clark, Donnie, 9, 108, 134, 538,
Clark, Sonny, 92
Clarke, Elizabeth, 213
Clarke, Kenny, 519
Clarke, Seleno, 6, 413, 433-438, **434**, **436-437**, 530, 538
Clarke, Terry, 106, 113, 167, 176-177, 367, 538

[The] Classical Joint (Vancouver), 187, 222-224, 231, **261**, 261-262, 264, 272, 346
Clay, James, 49
Clayton, Buck, xviii, 123
Clayton, Greg, 452
Clayton, Jay, 348, 354, 356
Clayton, John (bassist), 407, 451
Clayton, John (*Coda* writer), 112, 137, 172
Cleland, Al, 29
Clifton, Joanne, 381-382, **382**, 387, 408, 538
Clitheroe, Tony, **12**, 13, 15, 28-29, 59, 127, 145, 158, 161, 172, 183
Coastal Jazz & Blues Society, 51, 194, 313, 317, 415-416, 501
Cobb, Jimmy, 442, 476
Coda, 68, 71, 73, 112, 137, 172, 176, 183, 195, 198-199
Cole, Josh, 482
Cole, Nat King, 345
Coleman, Denardo, 52
Coleman, George, ix, 6, 275, 285, 290, 385, 394, 401, 411, 413, 434, 439-448, **441**, **445**, **530**, **538**
Coleman, Ornette, viii, 1, 3, 10, 43-53, **45-46**, **48**, **53**, 71, 85, 125, 127, 141, 185, 187, 195, 198, 219, 355, 498, 530
Coleman, Pat, 223, 225, 278, 530
Collier, Graham, 248
Collier, Ron, 173
Colligan, George, 383, **384**, 415, 538
Collins, Eleanor, 33, 367, 539
Collins, Haisla, 210
Colman, Kenny, 351
Coltrane, John, 69, 246, 266, 396, 431, 439, 453, 472, 475, 497, 499-500, 504, 505
Coltrane, Ravi, 426
Commodore Ballroom (Vancouver), 163, 344
Concordia University (Montreal), 452

Concord Jazz, 142
Concours de Jazz Alcan, 4, 244
Connick, Harry Jr., 326
Connors, Stompin' Tom,
Contemporary Records, 44, 46, 530
Cook, Jerry, 5, 427-428
Cooke, Coat (Nikita Carter), 185, 392, 530
Coon, Bill, 284, 292-293, 311, 317, 355, 368, 372, 375, 405, **407**, 415, 429, 452, 463, **518**, 529, 538
Co-op Radio (Vancouver), ix, 272
Copa City (Queens, New York), 114
Copeland, Keith, 248
Coquitlam, 30, 167, 171, 178, **179**
Coquitlam River, **143**
Corea, Chick, 296, 298
Cornista, Alvin, 483
Cory Weeds Little Big Band, 415, 535
Cotter, Steve, 106-107
[The] Cotton Club (Vancouver), 187, 200-201, 279, 371, 533
Coulthard, Jean, 56
Count Rabbit and his Bunnies, 471
Cousin Harley, 464
Cram, Paul, 73
Cramer, Barry, 2, 65, 79-97, **83, 89,**
Cramer, Dylan, 79-97, **95, 530, 536, 538**
Cramer, Gary, 81, 91-92, 96
Cramer, Harry, 83
Cramer, Jack, 83
Cramer, Morris, 80, 83
Cramer, Sofe, 80
Cranshaw, Bob, 472-473
Crash, 5, 366, 374, 384, 427-429, 530
Crawford, Hank, 441
Creative Music Studio (CMS) (Woodstock, New York), 238
Creatures of Habit, 274, **276**
Creed Taylor Appreciation Society (C.T.A.S.), 463

Crippled Children's Hospital (Vancouver), 213
Criss, Sonny, 92-95, **92**, 97, 530
Cronin, Sean, 336, 482-483, 485-487, 499
Crooks, Danny, 26
CTI Records, 463
Cuber, Ronnie, 427
Cultural Olympiad (Vancouver), 206
Cumming, Don, **15, 132**
Curtis, King, 429
C.W. Productions, 4, 368

D

D'Agostino, Anna (Levitsky), 508, 517, 522-523, 538
D'Agostino, Giovanni, 508
D'Agostino, Kevan, 523
D'Agostino, Natasha, ix, 7, 291, 419, 507-526, **509-510, 514, 516, 518, 521, 525,** 528, 530
D'Agostino, Rocco, 508, 517, 523-524, 538
Dameron, Tadd, 305
Danderfer, James, 373, **398**, 399, 538
[The] Dap-Kings, 393
Davis, Chris, 6-7, 9, **256, 362, 477, 484**
Davis, Miles, 16, 49, 52, 60, 68-69, 161, 185, 195, 242, 272, 296, 298-299, 315, 361, 365, 439, 442, 446, 453, 474, 496, 530
Davis, Quincy, 386
Davis, Steve, 402, 406, 535, 538
Davis, Wild Bill, 429
Daw, William, 10
Dawe, John, ix, 9-23, **12-13, 15, 17, 20**, 29, 35, 47, 59, **60**, 64, 67, 81-82, 90, 120, 127, 134, 139, 151, 157-158, 162, 172-173, 182, 502, 538
Dawson, Steve, 204, 206, **207, 209**

Day, Doris, 214
Dean, Elton, 239, 530
Dean, Kevin, 176, **177**, 530
Deardorf, Chuck, 175, 285
Debonair Ballroom (Vancouver), 123
Debut Records, 115
de Courcy, Johnny, 118
de Courcy, Michael, 74, 118, 538
Defrancesco, Joey, ix, 6, 361-363, 390, 396, **397**, 407, 419, 437, 538
DeJohnette, Jack, 238
Del Bucchia, Albert, 124-125
Demitone Studio, 516
Denton, 294, 327
Desmond, Paul, 21, 25, 36, 38, 365
Devlin, Mike, 178
Diefenbaker, John, 79
Diamond, Neil, 509
Dick Grove School of Music, 93
Diggins, Wayne, 365
DiRubbo, Mike, 403
Disterheft, Brandi, 482
Dixie Hummingbirds, 204
DJ Logic, 302
Doggett, Bill, 429
Dogpound Shuffle, 162, 537
Dolphy, Eric, vii, 50
Dolton Records, 191
Donaldson, Lou, 99, 411, **412**, 433, 437
Dootone Records, 191
Doran, Tommy, 219
Douglas, Fred, 66
Down Beat, 44, 49-50, 56, 58, 65
DownBeat, 423, 464
Drake, Nick, 353-354, 535
Drew, Kenny, 331
Drummond, Ray, 251
Dunaway, Blaine, **245**
Duncan, Christine, 225, 252, 257, 530
Duncan, Jack, **256**, 268
Dunfield, El, **312**

Dwyer, Phil, 142, 244, 263, 272-273, 500
Dylan, Bob, 86

E

Eadie, Tom, 236
Eastman School of Music (Rochester), 471
Eastwind, 329
Eckardt, Larry, 198-199
ECM Records, 252, 323, 535
Edmonton, 18, 36, 106, 115, 127, 167-168, 174-175, 178, 180, 222, 233, 242, 259, 352, 415
Edmonton Eskimos, 106
Edmonton Journal, 174-175, 178
The Ed Sullivan Show, 190
Edwards, Stephen, 513
[The] Egress (Vancouver), 414
8east (Vancouver), 317, 319
Eisenman, Mark, 176
Ekman, Dan, 125
Elaschuk, Kevin, 301
Eldridge, Roy, 1, 122, 125, 471, 480
Elevator Head, 377
Eli, Lovie, 204, 344
Ellington, Duke, 60, 99, 141, 200, 290, 327, 331, 352-353, 362, 459
Elliott, Ramblin' Jack, 197
Ellis, Herb, 32
Ellis, Lisle, 73
[The] El Mocambo (Burnaby), 217
Emergency Broadcast System (EBS), 376
Emery, Arnold, **12**
[The] Elvis Cantata, 277
Englewood Cliffs, 503
Eppel, Ralph, 73
Eric Hamber Secondary School, 91
Esler, David, 266
Esquimalt High School,
Espresso Coffee House (Vancouver), 236

Index

Esson, Dennis, **245**, **256**
Ethel, Washington, 371
Evans, Bill, 32, 69, 130, 216, 220, 228, 331, 453, 498,
Evans, Gil, 33
Everyman Repertory Co, 81
Expo 67 (Montreal, 1967), 296
Expo 86 (Vancouver, 1986), 325

F
Fabulous Pearls, 191, 200
Factory Show Lounge (Vancouver), 198
Factory Studios (Vancouver), 286, 485
Fama, Angela, **486, 488**
Famous Ballroom (Baltimore), 447
Farlow, Tal, 30
Farmer, Art, 472
Farnsworth, Joe, 4, 6, **369**, 369-370, 389, 395, 399, 411, 413, 422-423
Farrell, Lorae, 251-255, **256**, 257-260, 262, 264-268, 538
Fat Cat (New York), 394
Faulkner, Beth (Betty), 81
Fawcett, Wilmer (Bill), 14, 18, 30, 538
Feather, Leonard, 93
Feinstein, Sofe, 80
Feldman, Zev, 416, 447, 479
Fences, 200
Ferguson, Bonnie, 347, **347**
Ferguson, Maynard, 243
Ferman, Patricia, xv-xvi
Festival International de Jazz de Montréal, 4, 244, 273
Festival of Modern American Jazz, 1,2, **3**
Fibonacci, Leonardo, 261, 266
Fields, Dave, 183
Fields, Joe, 392
Fields of Endless Day, 200
First Baptist Church Vancouver, 357

Fisk, Simon, 354
Fitzgerald, Ella, 171, 343, 345, 355, 494, 530
[The] Five Spot Café (New York), 49, 472
Flanagan, Tommy, 275
[The] Flat Five (Vancouver), xvii, 2, 11, 35, 69-70, 137, 183, 217, 367
[The] Flatted Fifth (Vancouver), 2, 34-35, 367
Florida Theatre (Jacksonville), 327
Flying Hearts Family, 91
Folkways Records, 2, 64
Foisy, Maurice, 104, 538
Fontana, Carl, 130
Forest, Léonard, 66, 537
Fort Rodd Hill, 235
Foster, Frank, 243
Foster, Tom, 352
Fowles, Mable, 10
Fox, Carol, 3, 20, 181-188, **184**, **188**
Franck, Michel, 324
Francks, Don, **126,**
Frankie's Italian Kitchen & Bar (Vancouver), 415
Frankie's Jazz Club (Vancouver), 7, 96, 263-264, **265**, 267, 312, 315, **316**, 321, **332**, 337-338, 342, 359, 415-418, 421, **422**, 464-465, **476**, **478**, **479-480**, **479**, **505**, **506-507**, **516**, **520-521**, **521,**
Fraser, Don Jr., 109, 183, 538
Fraser, Hugh, ix, 4, 7, 141, 166, 179, 212, 231, 233-268, **237**, **240**, **245**, **249**, **253**, **256**, **261**, **265**, 272-274, 279, 288, 291, 371, 453, 531, 538
Fraser, James (Jimi), 250, 260, 266, 268
Fraser, Kenneth, 234-235, 262
Fraser, Mary, 235
Frederickson, John, 16, 538
Fred Stride Jazz Orchestra, 286, 290, 533
Frewer, Terry, 213
Friedman, Don, 1, 45-49, **46**, 498, 538

Frisell, Bill, 308,
Frogge, Bob, 10, 28, **60**, 126
Froman, Ian, 299,
Fuller, Curtis, 251
Fuller, Jerry, 13, **15**, 15, 170
Fulton, Jack, 67, 372, 538
Fung, Francesca, 466, 490

G

Gage, Chris, 1-2, 33, 61, 136-137, 151, 155-156, 171, 285, 291
Gagné, Pier-Alexandre, **525**
Gallagher, Margaret, 408
Gallimaufry Theatre company, 194
Gannon, Oliver, 163, 271-272, 278, 364, 371, 381, 405, 409, 414, 462, 506, 539
Garbo's Hat, 349, 352, 531
Garner, Erroll, 26, **27**, 278
Garner, Linton, 278, 531
Garrett, Kenny, 382-383,
Gary Cramer and the Works, 96
Gastown (Vancouver), 222, 262, 266, 272, 288, 346, 522
Gastown Players, 86
Gaucher, Dan, 482, 485
Gaudet, Paul "Boogie", 452
Generation Gap Jazz Orchestra, 423
Georgia Auditorium (Vancouver), 1, 26-28, **27**, 59-60, 81, 129
Georgia Straight, 69, 74, 86-87, 90, 371
Gershwin, George, 69, 494-495
Gershwin, Ira, 494-495
Gerussi, Bruno, 81,
Gestrin, Chris, 314, 352, 354, 362, 368, 373-374, 376, 379, 427-428, 456, 499, 538
Gettin' Off Easy, 347, **347**
Getz, Stan, 32, 439
Ghent, 207
Gibson, Austin, 26
Gill, Paul, 4, 368

Gillespie, Dizzy, 1, 11, 26-28, **27**, 57, 124, 156, 247, 271, 457, 519, 535
Gioia, Ted, viii, 536
Giraudoux, Jean, 84
Gittens, John, 154, 158
Gladstone Secondary School (Vancouver), 171
Glasgow, 270
Glasper, Robert, 431
[The] Glass Slipper (Vancouver), 4, 328-329, 371,
G.L. Pop Fine Furs (Vancouver), 114
Glynn, Michael, **476**
[The] Gold Saucer (Vancouver), 513
The Goldwyn Follies, 502, 537
Golson, Benny, 283, 472
Goodman, Benny, 26
Good Noise Vancouver Gospel Choir, 203, 209
Goodwin, Helen, 71
Gordon, Dexter, 271, 280, 292, 439
Gordon, Joe, 130, 148, 150
Gottlieb, Danny, 327
Gould, Jocelyn, **469**
Gowan, Jane, 60
Grammy Awards, 53, 423, 475
Gran Teatro de La Habana (Havana), 254
Grant, Paul, 185
Granz, Norman, 1, 122
[The] Grateful Dead, 71, 91
Great American Jazz Piano Competition (Jacksonville), 326-327
Green, Benny, 387
Greenwich, Sonny, 173, 496, 531
Greta Poontang, 185, 219
Grierson, Ralph, 170
Griffin, Johnny, 439
Griffiths, Clyde, **135**
Grimes, Henry, 472
Grinnell, John, 28, 59, 62

Grolnick, Don, 330
Gross, John, 225, 314
Grossman, Steve, 38
Grove, Dick, 93
Grunewaldt, Michael, 387, 538
[The] Grunt Gallery (Vancouver), 349
Guild, Michael, **346**
Guilt & Co. (Vancouver), 522
Guloien, Jim, 168
Guloien, Kira, 175
Guloien, Nels, 262
Gunn, Shannon, 261, 279
Gurdjieff, George, 227
Guthrie, Woody, 197
Guthro, Don, 279, 372, 380

H

Hackl, Collette, 190, 193, 195, 199-200, 206, 208, 210, 538
Haden, Charlie, 3, 49, 51, 195, 219
Hadley, Ron, 40, **41**
Haerle, Dan, 327
Hair, 161
Hales, Bobby, 7, 9, 17-18, 33, 136, 139-141, 154-166, **155, 160, 162, 166, 170, 182-183, 186, 531, 538**
Hales, Marj, 154, 156-157
Halifax, 344, 346
Hall, Geoff, 168
Hall, Jim, 30, 453
Hambourg, Clement, 12
Hambourg, Ruth, 12
Hamel, Alan, 88
Hamilton, Jeff, 388, 407, 451, 538
Hamilton, Scott, **395**
Hammett-Vaughan, Kate, 4, 343-360, **345, 347, 350, 358-359**, 511, 531, 538
Hampton, Lionel, 218, 451
Hampton, Slide, 243, 257, 288
Hancock, Herbie, 3, 187, 195-197, **196**, 219, 298, 331, 439, 446, 448, 453, 473, 531, 536,
Handy, John, 113, 367
Hansen, Greg, **509-510,**
Hansen, Paige, 522
Hard Rubber New Music Society, 264
Hard Rubber Orchestra, 142, 274, 277, 304
Harlem (New York), 413, 433-437, **434**, 519
[The] Harlem Nocturne (Vancouver), 123, 187
Harlow, Jean, 194
Harrell, Tom, 386-387
Harris, Barry, 244, 275
Harris, Emmylou, 346
Harrison, Lance, 108
Hart, Billy, 3, 195
Hart, Jennifer, 382
Harvey, Edward, 113, 536
Havana International Jazz Festival, 247
Hawkeye, Terry, 18
Hawkins, Coleman, 1, 122-123, 472, 533
Hayes, Louis, 251, 406, 473, 475-476, 538
Haynes, Roy, 476
Hazeltine, David, 7, 411, 415
Heath, Jimmy, 418-419
Heath, Albert "Tootie", 290-291,
Helen's Grill (Vancouver), 426, **426**, 432
Hemphill, Julius, 238
Henderson, Eddie, 3, 195, 437, 444, 459
Henderson, Joe, 243, 255, 439, 497, 504
Hendricks, Charles, **12**
Hendrickson-Smith, Ian, 6, 284, 293, 390, 393, 399, **437, 459, 538**
Hentoff, Nat, viii
Herman, Woody, 149
Hernández, Horacio "El Negro", 254
Herriott, Bobby, 217
Hersch, Fred, 505, 517
Hervey, Pat, 165
Hicks, Graham, 174

Hidalgo, Giovanni, 254
Higgins, Billy, 1, 44-45, **45**, **46**, **48**, 49-50
HighNote Records, 392, 456
Hill, Miles Foxx, 201, 231, **256**
Hill, Terry, 13, 67, 538
Hillary, Dale, 2, 18, 62-63, 65, 69, 173, 176
Hillyer, Lonnie, 2, 99, 102-103, 107, **111**
Hockley, Liam, 41
Hoffman, Jean, 130
Hogan's Alley, 123
Hole, Ken, 11, **12**, 12, 30, 44, 48, 63, 112, 126-128, **126**, 137, 538
Holiday, Billie, 69, 500
Holland, Dave, 243, 252, 348
Hollywood (Los Angeles), 50, 156, 259, 474
Hollywood North (Vancouver), 175
Holy, Steve Bokudo, 452
Hood, Ian, 145
Hood 29 (Vancouver), 358
Hook, Rose, 390
Hooker, John Lee, 194
Hope, Elmo, 2, 31, 80, 85, 130, 144, **144**
Hopson, Jim, **256**
Hornasty, Roy, 154, 156-157
Horne, Lena, 171
Hot Air (CBC Radio), xv-xvi, 164, 408,
Hotel Vancouver, 63, 143
[The] Hot Jazz Club (Vancouver), 142, 165, 236, 371-372
Houle, François, 354
House of Hambourg (Toronto), 12
Hubbard, Freddie, 50, 195, 271, 298, 535
Hubert, Armand, 322, 328
Hubert, Bernadette, 322
Hubert, Bruno, 4-6, 291, 298, 309-310, **316**, 320-342, **321**, **323**, **332**, **335**, **339**, 381, 531, 538
Hubert, Joseph-Olivier, 322
Hubert, Pierre, 323

Hubert, Thérèse, 322
Hugh Fraser Quintet, 4, 7, 244, 246-249, **249**, 251, 254-255, 257-258, 263-264, 267-268, 273-274, 279, 288, 531
Hugh's Room (Toronto), 209
Humber College (Toronto), 356, 492
Hum, Peter, 458
Humeniuk, Mark, 5,, 428
Humes, Helen, 1, 123
Hummingbird Brigade, 399
Humphrey, Paul, 2, 32
Humphries, Graham, 70
Hunter, Robert, 87

I

Igloo Supper Club (Hope), 155
Ike & Tina Turner, 367
Infidels Jazz (Tim Reinert), 8, 421
[The] Inquisition (Vancouver), 137, 161, 442
In Search of Innocence, 66, 537
Intermedia Society, 73, 74, 88
In The Zone: Rick Kilburn, 40, 537
Ionesco, Eugène, 82
Irakere, 247, 254
Iron Maiden, 364
Ironworks (Vancouver), 313
Isy's Supper Club (Vancouver), 2, 3, 136, 138-139, 158, 191, 217-219
Itter, Carole, 54, 76-78, **78**

J

Jackson, Doug, 365
Jackson, Ronald Shannon, 238
Jacksonville Jazz Festival, 326
Jacquet, Illinois, 1, 123
JADA, 346
Jago, Marian, 23, 60, 106, 120, 145, 536
Jamal, Ahmad, 221
James, Harry, 158, 236

Index

Jarrett, Keith, 228, 320, 323, 331
Jarry, Alfred, 68
Java Jazz (Vancouver), 69, 217
Jazz Alley (Seattle), 183
Jazz Alley (Vancouver), 3, 20-21, 161, 182-187, 195, 219
Jazz Alley, Istanbul Restaurant (Vancouver), 183
Jazz @ The Bolt (Burnaby), 8, 420-421, 467, 492
Jazz at the Philharmonic, 1, 122
Jazz Beat (CBC Radio), 278, 412, 496
[The] Jazz Cellar (Los Angeles), 44, 50
Jazz Cultural Theatre (New York), 243-244
Jazz Libre, 73
[The] Jazz Messiahs, 10, 44, 50
The Jazzoids, 238
Jazz Repertory Ensemble (University of North Texas), 365
Jazzsoc (University of British Columbia), 2, 48, 112
The Jazztet, 472-473
JazzTimes, 432
Jazz Workshop (CBC Radio), 14, 29, 59-60, 127, 150, 532-533
Jazz Workshop (CJOR Radio's Playhouse), 125, 127
Jazz Workshop (Banff Centre for the Arts), 242, 247, 348, 453
Jazz Workshop (band led by Charles Mingus), 99
[The] Jazz Workshop (San Francisco), 99
JazzYYC, 490
J.B. Trio, 217
Jefferson, Kelly, 450
Jensen, Christine, 109, 450
Jensen, Ingrid, 298, 491
Jill Townsend Big Band, 7, 293, 311, 425, 431, 534
Joanna's Gallery Café (Vancouver), 368

Jobim, Antonio Carlos, 355
Johnson, Al, 136
Johnson, Jim (Jimmy), **12**, 12, **15, 28**, 47, 59, 134, 172, 538
Johnson, Robert, 197
Johnson, Stan "Cuddles", 2, 151, 156, 285
Johnston, Allan, 262
Johnston, Ron, 95, **95**, 170, 220
J.O. Hubert (Maniwaki), 322
Jolly, Pete, 130, 150
Jones, Etta, 416
Jones, Hank, 251, 275
Jones, LeRoi, 50
Jones, Norah, 337
Jones, Philly Joe, 367, 472
Jones, Sharon, 393
Jones, Thad, 473
Joplin, Janis, 71
Jordan, Clifford, 243, 275
Jordan, Duke, 99
Jordan, Sheila, 354, 356, 462
Judas Priest, 364
Juno Awards, 175, 204, 209, 244, 299, 304, 312

K

Kadota, Diane, 342
Kadoura, Sanah, **469**
Kaizen Sushi Bar (Montreal), 452
Kaldestad, Steve, 404-405, 413, 433, 446, 450, 452, 459-462, 538
Kamloops Symphony, 420
Kane, Daniel Miles, **256**, 262, 336
Kang, Eyvind, 317
Katsuki, Sayaka, 254
Katz, June, 272, 344
Kaye, Maury, 173
Keenlyside, Tom, 20-22, 35-36, 42, 201, 212-213, 224, 227-228, 230, 365, 398, **503**, 538

589

Keens Steakhouse (New York), 290
Keepnews, Orrin, 32
Ken Hole Big Band, 11, **12**
Kenton, Stan, 1, 11, 26-28, **27**, 123, 159, 170, 392
Keremeos, 185
Kerr, Robert, 51
Kerrisdale (Vancouver), 215, 228
Kerrisdale Community Centre (Vancouver), 96
Kessel, Barney, 10, 130, 145, 150, 182
Kilburn, Jim, viii, 13-14, 24-42, **25**, **29**, **31**, **41**, 59, 125-127, 538
Kilburn, Joyce, 30, **31**, 41
Kilburn, Louise, 26
Kilburn, Miles, 25
Kilburn, Rick, viii, 24-42, **37**, **39**, **41**, 116-118, 537-538
King, B.B., 441
King Curtis, 429
King Edward Secondary School (Vancouver), 106
King, Ernie, 123, 187
King, Sharman, 164
Kingston Jazz Society, 496
Kingston, Ontario, 496
Kirk, Rahsaan Roland, 194
Kitsilano (Vancouver), 70, 86, 91, 182, 220, 329, 366
Kitsilano Secondary School (Vancouver), 11
Kiyooka, Roy, 66
Knepper, Jimmy, 114
Knott, Chuck, **132**
Kokoro Dance, 143
Konitz, Lee, 4, 26, **27**, 124, 132-133, 145, 150, 221-222, 238, 252-253, 365, 472
Korsrud, John, 142-143, **245**, 277-278, 538
Kozak, Wayne, 219
Krall, Diana, 109, 234, 302, 368

Krause, Harold, **17**, 29, **132**
Krieger, Milton, viii
Krishnamurti, Jiddu, 227
Kubera, Art, 429
[The] Kublai Khan (Vancouver), 138, **138**,
Kyle, Jack, 125

L
Lachance, André, 4-5, 283-284, 298-300, 303, 309, 315, **316**, 325-326, 300, 333, 338, 352-353, 366, 368, 370, 376, 477, 483, 538
Lackawanna, 429
Lacy, Steve, 76
Ladner, Graham, 199
La Fanfare de Maniwaki, 323, **323**
LaFaro, Scott, 2, 32, 80, 85, 117, 130, 144, **144**
Landham, Byron, 6, 362, **397**
Land, Harold, 2, 31-32 79-80, 82, 85, 92, 117, 130, 144-146, **144**, 420, 531
Langara College (Vancouver), 236, 508, 510
Lang, Curt, 69
Langley, 297, 307, 318
Langley Advance, 297
Langley Community Music School, 296-297, 306, 317
Larisey, Jenny, 293, 390-391, **391**, 410, 538
Lateef, Yusef, 99
[The] Latin Quarter (Vancouver), 352
Law Courts Inn (Vancouver), 40
Lebeck, Jillian, 291, 451, 482, 512
Ledonne, Mike, 383, 389, 395, 399, 406, 538
Leeds, Andrea, 502
Lee, John, 422-423
Lee, Kum-Sing, 74
Lee, Peggy (cellist), 293, 313-314, 319, 531

Index

Lee, Peggy (singer), 171, 352
Lee, Ranee, 450, 461
Lees, Nick, 175
Left Bank Express, 236
Left Bank Jazz Society, 447
Legends of the Bandstand, 251
Legrand, Michel, 178
Le Marquand, John, 217, 538
Lemon, Sandy, 71-73
Lent, Mike, **240**
Leonhart, Jay, 327
Levesque, Roger, 178, 180
Lewis, Frank, 151, **152**, 171
Lewis, George, 348-349
Lewis, Victor, 175
Liapis, Nick, 368
Liapis, Stephanos (Steve), 368, 371-373, 538
[The] Libra Room (Vancouver), 320, 322, 329, 339-341, **341, 483**
Liebman, Dave, 243, 348, 497
Lightbody, Walley, **12**, 30, 63, 112-113, 128-129, 538
Lightfoot, Gordon, 159, 192
The Lighthouse (Los Angeles), 43
Lim, Vincent, **95, 177, 230, 256, 265, 316, 332, 358**, 391, **407, 422, 437, 441, 462, 469, 476, 478-479, 493, 500, 505, 516, 521**,
Lindner, Franz, **102, 135**
Lionel Hampton Jazz Festival (Moscow, Idaho), 451
Lister, Ken, 7, **249**, 249, 263, 286
Little, Booker, 441
Little Daddie and the Bachelors, 367
Little Italy (Vancouver), 121-122, 143
Little Mountain Sound (Vancouver), 140, 165
Living Theatre (New York), 64
Lloyd, Charles, 195, 439, 441, 473
Locarno Beach, 69

Loewen, Kenton, 392
Logan, Chuck, 28, 129, **130**
London, England, 236, 246-248, 251, 279, 405, 459-460, 515
Lone Hill Jazz, 2, 82, 144, 531,
Long Island (New York), 259
Longton, Nield, 183-184
López-Nussa, Harold, 254
Los Angeles, viii, 43, 92, 145, 155, 191, 197, 259, 474, 476
Los Angeles Times, 93
Los Angeles Jazz All-Stars, 45
Louie, Alex, 138
Louie, Harry, 138
Louie, Victor, 138
Lovano, Joe, 5, 53, 302-303, 330, 431, 497, 531
Lovelace, Jimmy, 85
Luscar Recording Studio (Banff), **245**
Lynch, Brian, 366, 376, 498

M

Mabern, Harold, 6, 385, **402**, 402-403, 413, 415, 418-419, 441-442, 446, 460, 462, 472, 538
MacDonough, Julian, 5-6, **256, 437**, 494, 499-502
MacLachlan, Keith, 342
Maclean's, 87-88
MacPherson, Fraser, 33, 158, 161, 163, 171, 271, 278, 364
Madeleine Is, 88, 94, 538
Magee Secondary School (Vancouver), 216
Magnarelli, Joe, 275, 467, 533
Mai, Vince, 9
Majoko, Joanna, **469**
Malaspina College (Nanaimo), 39
Malloch, Katie, 278, 412, 415, 538
Malone, Russell, 387, 437, **462**
Manassas High School (Memphis), 441

591

Mangione, Chuck, 471-473, **471**, 531
Mangione, Gap, 471-473, **471**, 531
Maniwaki, 322-324
Manne, Shelly, 314
Mantrap, 88
[The] Marco Polo (Vancouver), 3, 138-139
Mariacher, Joan, 378, 380, 403, **407**, 407, 418, **419**, 424, 538
Mariano, Charlie, 141
Marois, Réjean, 324-325, 334, 510
Marquette, Pee Wee, 82
Marriott, Thomas, **476**
Marsalis, Wynton, 52, 298
Marsh, Warne, 4, 124, 132, 221-222
Massey, Fred, 16
The Mastersounds, 32
Matheson, Alan, 9
Maupin, Bennie, 3, 195
Maximum Jazz, 5, 300, 374, 379-390, 529, 531, 534-535
Maximum Music, 301, 531
Mayer, John, 475
Mayer, Jon, 406, 475-477, 538
Mays, Bill, 178, 533
McBride, Christian, 400, **401**
McBride, Christopher, 519-520, 538
McBrowne, Lenny, 2, 80, 130, 144, **144**,
McChord Air Force Base (Tacoma), 190
McClelland, Khari Wendell, 207-208
McConnell, Rob, 173
McClure, Michael, 194
McCurdy, Roy, 195, 319, 415, 470-480, **471**, **476**, **478-479**, 538
McDonald, Glenn, 66-67, 159, 442
McDougall, Ian, 160, 235, 251, 406, 538
McDowall, Kerilie, 40, 537
McFetridge, George, 174
McGarry, Kate, 519
McGhee, Brownie, 193-194
McGhee, Howard, 92,

McGill University (Montreal), 450-454, 461, 496
McGowan, Nick, 183
McGriff, Jimmy, 437
McKenzie, Rob, **245**
McLaughlin, John, 361
McLean, Jackie, 475
McLeod, Brian, 161, 183, 193, 213
McLeod, Dan, 86-87, 90
McMurdo, Dave, 183
McNeely, Jim, 497
McPherson, Charles, 2, 5, 99, 102-103, 109-111, **111-112**, 113, 177, 269-270, 283, 381, 444, 454-455, 461-462, 531, 538
McRae, Carmen, 511
Meger, James, 321, 342
Melton, Tommie, 367
Memphis, 92, 441
Méndez, Rafael, 156
Menzies Bay, 121, 143
Metalwood, 299, 301-302, 531
Metcalfe, Eric, 63, 270, 272, **273**, 286, 292, 538
Metcalfe Rehm, Reece, 270-272, **273**, 274, 280, 286, 289, 538
Metheny, Pat, 327, 472
Metronome, 58
Mezzrow (New York), 398
Midnight Special, 373
Mike Allen Trio, 5, 373
Milkowski, Bill, 464
Miller, Bob, 170
Miller, Jeffrey, 519
Miller, Joel, 450
Miller, Mark, viii, 73, 75, **276, 359**
Miller, Mulgrew, 175, 387
Minemoto, Sharon, 274-275, 279, 281, 283-286, 289, 291-293, 301, 308, 310, 381, 516-517, **518**, 519, 521, 523, 531, 538
Mingus, Charles, viii, 2, 10, 28, 64, 85, 98-119, **100, 102, 105, 111-112, 116**, 131,

Index

141, 145, 150, 172, 195, 269, 367, 373, 381, 454, 461, 537
Mingus: Charlie Mingus 1968, 114, 537-538
Minton's (New York), 58, 435, 519-520
Mississippi Sheiks, 205, 535
Mitchell, Blue, 429
Mitchell, Joni, 114, 346, 353, 459
Mobley, Hank, 408, 439
Mock Duck, 185
Mock, Joe, 185
[The] Mojo Room (Vancouver), 300, 328, 372, 483
Monk, Thelonious, 11, 185, 331, 519
Monterey Jazz Festival, 113, 439
Monterose, J.R., 275
Montgomery Brothers, 2, 32, 130-131, 172, 532
Montgomery, Buddy, 2, 32, 130, 177, 378-379, 532
Montgomery, Lucy Maud, 155
Montgomery, Monk, 2, 32, **34**, 130, 532
Montgomery, Wes, viii, 2, 25, 30, 32-33, **34**, 130, 364, 532
Montoliu, Tete, 442, 530
Moore, Michael, 38
Moreton, Mary Jean "Bunny", 378
Morgan, Frank, 283-284, 385-386, 411
Morgan, Lee, 444
Morin, Scott, 393, 421
Moscow, Idaho, 451
Mosley, Marcus, **201**, 203-210, **205**, **207**, 538
Motion Studio (Vancouver), 3, 71, 73
Mötley Crüe, 364
Motown Records, 367
Mount St. Helens, 240
Muirhead, Brad, **240**, **245**, **256**
Mulligan, Gerry, 38, 69, 365-366
Murley, Mike, 299

Murphy, Bob, ix, 4-5, 7, 52, 185, 189, 195, 197-198, 200-203, **201**, 212-232, **218**, **226**, **229-230**, 261, 272, 278, 280-281, 291, 482, 530, 532-534, 538
Murphy, Carol, 222-224, 538
Murphy, Dalton, 213-215
Murphy, Don, 214, **214,**
Murphy, Margaret, 212, 215, 218
Murphy, Margo, 212, 215-216, 227, 538
Murray, Clifton, 209-210
Murray, David, 450-451, 461
Music Arts Collective, 466, 490
Music on Main, 394
Mwandishi band (Herbie Hancock), 197, 219
Mynett, Steve, **202**, **226**, **253**, **256**, **282**, **290**, **301**, **305**, **339**, **363**, 382, **395**, **401-402**, **412**, **430**, **436**, **451**, **453**, **455**, **459**, **485**, **499**, **503**, 538

N

Namedropper, 300
Nash, Lewis, 413, 503-504, **505**, **538**
Nash, Ted, 497
National Film Board of Canada, 66, 537
Nation, Brian, 4, 76, 220-222, 538
Navarro, Fats, 69
NBC Orchestra, 93
Neff, Tracy, 508-511, 538
Neil, Al, viii, 1-3, 12-14, 17, 19, 28, 45, 47, 54-78, **57**, **60**, 82, 84, 90-91, 123-124, 126, 134, 172, 220, 442, 532, 537
Neil, Kitty, 58
Neil, Marguerite, 69, 73
Nelson, Chris, 244, **245**, 291, 298-299, 326
Nelson, Glenn, 55-56
Nelson, Kay, 192
Neruda, Pablo, 489
New Delhi Cabaret (Vancouver), 171, 191, 216

593

Newman, David "Fathead", 5, 384-385, 392, 444, 449, 455-458, 462, **459**, 535
Newman, George, 44
Newman, Karen, 384-385, 457, 538
New Orchestra Workshop (NOW), 73, 185, 349, 352
Newport Jazz Festival, 472
New Westminster and District Concert Band, 296-297
New York Ensemble of Jazz Improvisation, 243
New York, vii, 36, 38-39, 45, 49, 64, 85, 99, 113-114, 124-125, 129, 132, 147, 174, 178, 202, 231, 238, 243-244, 248, 250, 259, 275, 284, 286, 290, 292, 298-299, 302-303, 348, 366, 368-369, 374, 383, 389, 390, 393-395, 400, 402, 411-413, 415, 418, 429, 433-435, **434**, 441, 443, 470-473, 497-498, 501, 503, 505, 519-520, 526, 536-537
The New Yorker, 38, 220
New York Theatre (Vancouver), 52, **53**
New York University (NYU), 433, 497-498, 526
New York With Weeds, 400, 402, 411-413, 433, 435
Nichol, Ray, 14
Nielsen, Bruce, 374
[The] Nightcrawlers, 421, 463
Night Train Revue, 240-241
1988 Winter Olympics (Calgary), 163
NiteCap, 325, 511-512, 514, 524
Nixon, Garry, 113
Noble, Ray, 80
Nogales, 99
Nolan, John, 40, 95, **95**
Norris, Ray, 28-29
North Vancouver, xv, 7, 76, 90, 114, 231, 298, 302, 325, 365, 497, 513
Nothiger, Andreas, 222-223, 262, 538

Notre Dame University of Nelson, 182
Nowosad, Curtis, 519
[The] Nucleus (Vancouver), 415
The Nylons, 202

O

Oakland Tribune, 99
October Trio, 485, 532
O'Day, Anita, 69
Odesa, 508
Odetta, 194
Odin's Eye (Halifax), 346
Odjick, Gino, 322
O'Doul's Restaurant & Bar (Vancouver), 371, 501
Oil Can Harry's (Vancouver), 114, 220-222, 475
Okegwo, Ugonna, 386
[The] Old Cellar, 3-4, 51-52, 92, 182, 186, 195, **196**, 197-200, 219-220
Old Roller Rink (North Vancouver), 114
Old School House Arts Centre (Qualicum Beach), 40, **41**
Old Town Strings, 452
One O'Clock Lab Band (University of North Texas), 297-298, 365
Ord, Graham, **237**, **240**, **261**, 349
Orpheum Annex (Vancouver), 7
Orpheum Theatre (Vancouver), **37**
Otra, 518, 520, 532
Ottawa, 200, 252
Ottawa Citizen, 458
Ottawa Jazz Festival, 252
Orysik, John, 51, 198-199, 347, 538
[The] Ostara Project, 8, 468, **469**, 532
Oxbol, Torben, 174, 221

P

Pacific Coliseum (Vancouver), 162
Pacific Jazz & Blues Festival, 4, 347
Pacific National Exhibition (PNE), 162

Pacific National Exhibition (PNE) Garden Auditorium (Vancouver), 3, 71
Pacific Salt, 95, 174, 235
Page, LaWanda, 192
Pagliacci's (Victoria), 271
Palm Cafe (New York), 435
Panama City, 249
Pantages Theatre (Vancouver), 81
Paris, France, 431
Parker, Charlie, 1, 11, 16, 26, 28, 57, 61, 63, 69, 92, 99, 103, 124-125, 129, 151, 170, 174, 183, 185, 284, 365, 420, 476, 519, 532
Parker, Doug, 59
Parker, Evan, 252
Parker, Maceo, 382
Park Theatre (Vancouver), 58
Parton, Lorne, 139
Pass, Joe, 69, 535
Patchen, Kenneth, 2, 62-66, 532, 537
Pat Metheny Group, 327, 472
Pat's Pub (Vancouver), 231, 258, 358, 519, 523
Patton, Jeb, 290
Paupers Pub (Toronto), 255
Pay, David, 394
Payne, Don, 44, 49-50
Paxton, Tristan, 482
The Peak, **73**
Peggy Lee Band, 313, 319
People Playing Music, 366
Pepper, Art, 1, 2, 10, 60-62, 69, 130, 148, 150-151, 153, 195, 285, 373, 532
Pérez, Danilo, 387
Performance Works (Vancouver), 355
Perkins, Bill, 119, 130
Perry, Paul, 154, 158, 168-169, **169**, 175
Perry, PJ, 13, 15-16, 18-19, 67, 69, 152, 158, 167-180, **176**, **179**, **245**, 262, 271, 462, 530, 532-533, 538
Perry, Sam, 71
Peter Pan Ballroom (Vancouver), 55

Peters, Jim, **12**
Peterson, Margaret, 66
Peterson, Oscar, 32, 216, 270-271, 473, 494, 535
Peterson, Ralph Jr., 463
Petschauer, Rudy, **240**, 293
Pickering, Ken, 51, 194, 198, 347
Pike, Dave, **126**
The Pillar and Post (Vancouver), 217
Pinchin, Jim, 352
[The] Pine Grill (Buffalo), 429
Piper, Ray, 146, 538
Pizzarelli, Bucky, 419, 462
Place des Arts (Montreal), 4, 244, **276**
Plato, Karin, 357, 358, **358**
The Platters, 139
Plimley, Paul, 73-75
p m, 56, 124
Poe, Edgar Allan, 489
Pointe du Bois, 26
Poole, Joe, 314, 321, 342, 506
Poolesville, Maryland, 434
Pop, Iggy, 431
Port Coquitlam, 7, 294, **295**
Portland, Oregon, 28, 291, 294, 327, **384**, 457
Powell, Bud, 11, 66, 68, 99, 178
Powell, Richie, 486
Powell River, 131, 508
Powrie, Don, 236, **240**, **245**
Presentation House Theatre (North Vancouver), 513
Presley, Elvis, 206, 277
Priester, Julian, 3, 195, 243
Prince of Wales Secondary School (Vancouver), 216
Princeton, BC, 121
[The] *Province*, 35, 46, 55, 59-60, 70, 80-81, 84, 100, 123, 125, 130, 139, 147, 161, 183, 186, 193-194, 213, 223
Proznick, David, 451, 482

Proznick, Jodi, 5-6, 8, 270, 285, 290, **375**, 381, 404-405, **407**, 439-440, **441**, 443-444, 449-469, **455**, **462**, **466**, **469**, 488, 490, 492, 521, 524, 533, 538
Proznick, Kelly, 451
Proznick, Tim, 451
Prussin Music, 368, 380
[The] Purple Onion (Vancouver), 328
Pyatt Hall (Vancouver), 7, 260, 262, 268, 411
[The] Pythodd (Rochester), 471

Q

Qualicum Beach, 24, **25**, 35, 39, 40-41, **41**
Quarin (Ceccon), Amabile (Mabel), 121, 123, 127
Quarin, Dave, 14, 29, 44-46, 85, 99-101, 114-115, 120-153, **124**, **126**, **128**, **130**, **132-133**, **143**, **150**, 158, 161, 165, 183, **240**, 533, 538
Quarin, Giovanni (John), 121, 123
Quarin, Kevin, 153
Quarin, Ricci, 114-115, **116**, 125, 134, 138, 139, 143, 150
Queen, Alvin, 431
Queen Elizabeth Theatre (Vancouver), 36, 161
Queens (New York), 114, 394
Queen's University (Kingston), 496
Quest (CBC-TV), 2, 101, 538
[The] Question Mark (Vancouver), 367
Quicksilver Messenger Service, 71
Quinlan, Ted, 261
Quintrell, Bob, 101, 103

R

Radcliffe, Vera, 215
Radtke, Darren, 5, 299, 494-495, **500**, 502
Rae Dene, 138, **138**

Ranger, Claude, 174
Read, Jeani, 186
Rebagliati, Bob, 482
Redd, Freddie, 367
Redman, Dewey, 3, 51, 195, 219, 292
Reed, Clyde, 392
Reel to Real Recordings, 416, 420, 447, 479, 529-530
Reeves, Nat, 413
Regina, 155, 157, 450
Reid, Jamie, 71, 106, 538
Reinert, Tim (Infidels Jazz), 8, 342, 421, 461-462
R.E. Mountain Secondary School (Langley), 297
Reusch, Al, 214
Resonance Records, **416**
[The] Retinal Circus (Vancouver), 87
Reynolds, Jack, 56, 152, 538
Rhythm Changes, 267
Ricci, Vince, 296
Rich, Buddy, 158
Richmond, BC, 10, 12, **20**, 24, 26, 28, 30, 59
Richmond, Dannie, 2, 99, 102-103, 106, 109, **111**, **112**, 113-114, 145
Ridgerunner, 91-92
Ridge Theatre (Vancouver), 90
Rime (Vancouver), 483
Rimmer, David, 68, 537
Ringdahl, Millard, 179
[The] Riverqueen (Vancouver), 3, 192-200, 219, 224, 475
Rivers, Sam, 76
Roach, Kate, 281, 290
Roach, Max, 11, 44, 49, 60, 441, 447, 472, 486
Robbins, Dave (trombonist), 33, 136, 141, 158-159, 161, 236-238, 533

Robbins, Dave (drummer), 4, 249, **249**, **256**, 263, 268, 283-284, 368, 370, 452, 483, 495, 497-498, 538
Roberts, Howard, 30, 130, 314
Roberts, Marcus, 326
Robertson, Gregor, 308
Robeson, Paul, 200, 214
Robinson, Perry, **37**
Robson, Wayne, 194
Rochester, 470-473
Rochester Music Hall of Fame, 480
Rohan's Rockpile (Vancouver), 91
Rollins, Sonny, 44, 69, 170, 439, 472-473, 533
Ronnie Scott's (London, England), 246-247, 250, 254
Roop, Ed, 16, 91, 539
Rose Gellert Hall (Langley), 306, 317
Rosenwinkel, Kurt, 377, **378**, 400
Rosnes, Renee, 167, 231, 272, 297, 303, 413, 482, 491
Ross, Becki L., 191, 537
Ross, Sandy, 58
Rossini's (Vancouver), 288, 371
Ross Taggart Quartet, 5, 225, 377, 379, 533
Rotondi, Jim, 395
Rowles, Jimmy, 36, 116-118, 521
Royal Academy of Music (London, England), 235, 248
Royal Canadian Legion 142 (Vancouver), 414
Royal Theatre (Victoria), 235
Rud, Mike, 5, 280-281, 452, 454, **500**, 539
Ruhland, Paul, 33, 136, 372
Rumi, 489
Runge, Bill, 225, 231, 240, **256**, 274, 293, 533
Rushka, Paul, 500, 507, 515-516
Ruther, Wyatt, 364

Ryga, Campbell, 141-142, 165-166, 176, 212, 224-225, 234, 239, 241, **240**, 244, **245**, 247-249, **249**, 253, **256**, 258, 260, 263-264, **265**, 266-267, 272-275, **277**, 278-279, 288, 291-292, **306**, 365, 371, 374, 443, 533, 539

S

Sam and Dave, 139
Samworth, Ron, 349, 352, 354
Sánchez, David, 254
Sanders, Marguerite, 69
Sanders, Will, **201**, 204, **205**, 207-210, **207**
San Francisco, 16, 71, 99, 248, 447, 497
Sanft, Scott, 377
San Quentin, 284
Santaga, Don Demetrio, 143
Santana, 91
Santos (Vancouver), 298
São Paulo, 249
Satellite Trio, 513
Savage, Colleen, 344, 347, **347**
Savoy Records, 214
The Scene (Victoria), 2, 63, 112-113, 129
Schneider, Maria, 250
Schlossmacher, Bill, **126**
Schoenbeck, Sara, 317
Schoenberg, Arnold, 57
Schreiber, Freddie, **60**
Scofield, John, 302
Scott, Craig, 286
Scott, Jennifer, 226, 228, 230, **256**, 257, 280, 289, 298, 351, 356-357, **358**, 533, 539
Scott, Ronnie, 246-247, 250, 254, 279
Scott, Shirley, 443
Scriabin, Alexander, 141, 237, 260
Seattle, 33, 183, 191, 241, 285, 377, 385, 444, 457, 479, 529, 533
Seattle World's Fair (1962), 33, 533

597

Semiahmoo Secondary School (Surrey), 451, 482, 490
Senensky, Bernie, 272
Sense and Sensibility, 490, 492
711 Shop (Vancouver), 83-84, 87
Seventeen89 (Vancouver), 308, 411
SGaanaGwa, 465
Shadbolt Jazz Walk (Burnaby), 7-8, 318-319, 417-418, 480
Shadbolt Centre for the Arts (Burnaby), 7-8, 318, 417-418, 420, **469**, **493**,
Shadbolt, Jack, 66
[The] Shanghai Junk (Vancouver), 138
Shannon, Del, 296
Shapiro, Nat, viii
Sharman, Rodney, 354
Sharpe, Alan, 52
Shaw, Helen, 270
Shaw, Woody, 298
Sheldon, Jack, 21
Sheldon Williams Collegiate (Regina), 450
Shepp, Archie, 71, 447
Sheraton Landmark Jazzbar (Vancouver), 36, 244, 347
Shier, Robin, **245**
Shiner, Bill, **12**
Shines, Johnny, 197-198
Shorter, Wayne, 298, 439, 453
Show Boat, 200
Showmans (New York), 435
Sickler, Don, 504
Sickler, Maureen, 504
Sid's (Edmonton), 175
Siegel, Annie, 73
Sikora, Ray, 33, 85, 136, 147, 159, 296, 533
Sikula, Dave, 5-6, 373, 377, 428, **437**, 516
Silk Purse Arts Centre (West Vancouver), 230, 513

Silver, Horace, 60, 183, 473
Simard, Michael, 333-334, 538
Simone, Nina, 186
Simon Fraser University (SFU, Burnaby), 55-56, **57**, **73**, **306**
Simpson, Denis, 189, 202
Simpson, Gregg, 3, 56, 69-71, 73, 75, 145, 539
Sims, Zoot, 496
Sinatra, Frank, 86, 122, 148, 162, 178, 351
Sinclaire, Denzal, 336, 452
Sister Jazz Orchestra, 467
Skana (the whale), 219
Skonberg, Bria, 482, 486
Slater, Angela, 194
Small, Ron, 3, 7, 189-211, **192**, **201-202**, **205**, **207**, 226, 533
Small, Shirley, 3, 186-187, 190-191, 193-195, 197-199, 209-210
Smalley, Felix, 29
Smalls (New York), 398
Smilin' Buddha Cabaret (Vancouver), 171, 191-192, **192**, **200**, **215-216**
Smith, Bessie, 189
Smith, Bob, xv-xvii, 38, 50-51, 114, 122, 137-139, 142, 182-184, 186, 193-194, 196-198
Smith, Dick, 183, 185, 187, 222, 539
Smith, Jimmy, 213, 429, 434
Smith, Larry, 62, 537
Smith, Dr. Lonnie, ix, 5, 7, 384-385, 405, 419, 425-438, **426**, **430**, **533**, **539**
Smith, Marvin "Smitty," 431
Smith, Patti, 53
Smoke (New York), 402, 411, 443
Smulyan, Gary, 396, **396**, 404, 407, 467, 533, 539
Sneddon, Carse, 9, 138
Snider, Wally, 125
Snidero, Jim, 498
Sobel, Phil, 93-94, 96-97

[The] Sojourners, 190, 204-209, **205**, **207**, 533
Songlines Recordings, 314, 354, 531, 535
Sonny and Cher, 158
Sopra Sotto (Vancouver), 341-342
Soul, David, 162
Soul Stirrers, 203-204
Soulstream, 300, 352
Soul Train, 241
Sound Gallery (Vancouver), 3, 70-71
South Delta Secondary School, 509, **509-510**
Space: 1999, 496
Sparks, Melvin, 431
Spencer's (Vancouver), 11
Spinning Wheel (Vancouver), 223
Springfield, Dusty, 218
Spring, Sylvia, 88-89, 538
Stafford, Jack, 372
St. Andrew's Wesley Church (Vancouver), 202, 277
Starkey, Judy, 115
Steering Wheel car club (Vancouver), 181
Stephenson, Doug, 227
Steveston, 26
Stewart, Grant, 500, 539
Stewart, Wayne, 262
St. Francis-in-the-Wood church (West Vancouver), 259
St. James Hall (Vancouver), 207
St. John, Daiquiri, 191
St. John's Church Hall (Vancouver), 55
St. Michael's Hospital (Toronto), 190
St. Michaels University School (Victoria), 235
Stone, Alana, 362, **363**, 393-394, 423
Stovell, Bryan, 108-109, 539
St. Paul's Hospital (Vancouver), 77, 266

Strand Theatre (Vancouver), 1, 122
Stranger Friends Orchestra, 267
Strathcona (Vancouver), 54, 76, 121-123
Strayhorn, Billy, 320
Street, William, 470
Stride, Fred, 285-286, 290, 298, 533
[The] Stripes, 171
Strozier, Frank, 441-442
Stryker, Mark, vii
Studio 58, 238
Suderman, Gail, 203
Summerland, 275
Sun Ra and his Arkestra, 241
Sunship Ensemble, 52
Surf Maid (New York), 36
Surrey, BC, 197, 426, 451
Swainson, Neil, 167, 175-176
Swan Silvertones, 204
Sweet Thunder Records (Victoria), 271
Sylvan Lake, 154-156, 160, 168-169, **168-169**
Syme, Bob, 380, 387

T

Taf's Cafe (Vancouver), 187
Taggart, Ross, ix, 4-6, **37**, 143, 176, 200, 212, 225, **245**, 249, **249**, 255, 263-264, 269-293, **273**, **276-277**, **282**, **287**, **290**, 301, 307, 311, 325, 331, 368-370, 371, 374, 377, 379, 395, 397, 401-402, 429, 443-444, 454-455, 460, 482-483, 485, 532-534
Taggart, William, 270
Tallman, Warren, 107
Tangent Café (Vancouver), **230**, 316, 515-516, 521-522
Tanner, Adrian, 137
Tarry, Chris, 299, 374
Taylor, Bobby and the Vancouvers, 367
Taylor, Cecil, 71, 221
Taylor, Creed, 463

Taylor, Joani, 195, 217, 219-220, 225-226, 231, 534, 539
Taylor, John, 517
Taylor, Mike, 193
The Tenors, 209
1067 [Vancouver], 392
Terry, Clark, 271, 498, 535
Terry, Sonny, 193
Tharp, Twyla, 178
Theatre Under The Stars, 81
Therrien, Rachel, **469**
Thiessen, Dean, 267
Thigpen, Ed, 450, 462
Thomas, Adam, **256**, 355, 499, 501, **503**, 506
Thomas, Jonathan Edward, 519
Thomas, Linda Lee, 228
Thompson, Don, 15-16, 18, 30, 66-67, 85, 105-106, 113, 131-132, 159-161, 170, 173, 177, 183, 219, 243-245, 272, 281, 367, 453, 539
Thompson, Don "D.T.", 281
Thrasher, Sibel, 204
The Three Degrees, 139
Tilden Webb Trio, 5-6, 392, 456, 529, 533, 535
Times Colonist, 178
Time Flies festival (Vancouver), 317
Tiny Havoc, 522
Tonic (CBC Radio), 412
Torchinsky, Raymon, 368, 380, 387, 392-393, 420
Tops in Blue, 190
Toren, Cat, 482, 486
Toronto, 6, 12, 18, 29, 73, 94, 173-174, 190, 199-200, 208-209, 216, 223-224, 246, 248, 255, 272, 299, 334, **359**, 466, 471, 486, 492, 496, 500, 536-537
Toronto New Music Ensemble, 73

Torsone, Michael, 437
Toshiko Akiyoshi-Lew Tabackin Big Band, 314
Tosoff, Amanda, 8, 291, 451, 466, 468, **469**, 481-493, **485-486, 488, 493**, 534, 539
Tosoff, Lloyd, 482
Tosoff, Ted, 482
[The] Town Pump (Vancouver), 347
Townsend, Jill, 7, 293, 311, 317, 415, 425, 431, 452, 534
[The] Town Tavern (Toronto), 471
Trail, BC, 182
Tringham, Blaine, 9
Triple Door (Seattle), 285, 444, 457
Trips Festival, 3, 71, **73**
Tristano, Lennie, 57-58, 124-125, 132, 221
Troupe, Quincy, 447
Trussell, Bill, **12**
Trussell, Bud, **12**
Tsakumis, Alex, 371
Tsawwassen, 509
Tucker, Ben, 1, 45, **45-46, 48**
Turnaround, 349
Turner, Bob, 185-186, 216-217, 219, 368, 539
Turner, Brad, 4-5, 9, 269, 286, 290, 294-319, **295, 301, 305-306, 312, 316**, 326-327, 328-330, 332-334, **335**, 337-338, 362, 366, 368, 374, 376, 379, 454, **476**, 477, 482-483, 485, 531, 534, 539
Turner, Evan, 303
Turner, Fred, 296-297
Turner, Gail, 307
Turner, Jeff, 427
Turner, Kerry, 296-297
Turner, Mark, 377, **378**, 423, 450
Turner, Theo, 303
Turner, Tia, 303
Turning Point Ensemble, 306, 317, 534

TV Week, 348
2010 Winter Olympics (Vancouver), 206
Tynan, John, 49-50
Tyner, McCoy, 141, 221, 239, 262, 534
Tyson, Ian, 171

U

UBC Auditorium, 48, 70, 172
The Ubyssey, 49, 58, 343
UCLA Oral History Project, viii
UFO, 496
Ugetsu, 301, 394
Ukrainian Hall (Vancouver), 123
Unitarian Church of Vancouver, 7, 212-213, 228
Unity Center (New York), 413
Universal Music Canada, 301-302, 531
Université Laval (Québec City), 328
University of British Columbia (UBC, Vancouver), 2, 48, 73, 74, 107-108, 112, 161, 216
University of North Texas (UNT, Denton), 294, 297-298, 326-327, 337, 365-366
University of Southern California Thornton School of Music (Los Angeles), 480
University of Toronto, 488, 537
University of Victoria (UVic), 113, 236
Upstairs Jazz Bar & Grill (Montreal), 450
Uptown Saturday Night, 346
Ursan, George, 4, 120-121, 154, 157-158, 160-161, 163, 170, 183, 221, 539
UZEB, 328

V

Valdes, Chucho, 247, 250, 264
Valera, Peter, 433
Valle, Orlando (Maraca), 254, 531
Vancouver Art Gallery, 73-74

Vancouver Canucks, 322
Vancouver Community College (VCC), 39, 236-239, 249, **237**, **287, 356, 521**
Vancouver Courier, 200, 281
Vancouver East Cultural Centre (Cultch), 76, 189, 252, 267, 354
Vancouver Ensemble of Jazz Improvisation (VEJI), 4, 7, 141-142, 166, 179, 233-234, 239-252, **240**, **245**, 254-262, **256**, 267-268, 274, 535
Vancouver General Hospital (VGH), 19, 55, 231, 255, 290
Vancouver International Jazz Festival, 4, 51-52, 143, 194, 260, 313, 347, 355, 377, 402, 415, 500-502, 519
Vancouver Jazz Society, 4, 76, 220, 222
Vancouver Jazz Society Auditorium, 4, 221
Vancouver Lawn Tennis Club, 217
Vancouver Musicians' Association, 164, 208
Vancouver New Jazz Society (VNJS), 59, 125, 129
Vancouver New Jazz Society Jazz Festival, 1, 129
Vancouver Opera Orchestra, 299
Vancouver Sun, xv, xvii, 27-28, **27**, 38, 52, 55, 64, 69-70, 81, **83**, 84, 87-88, 90, 100, **100**, 109, 122-123, 130, 137-138, **138**, 147, 163, 165, 182-183, **184**, 191, **192**, 193, 198, **218**, 219, 221, 236, 348, 351, 380
Vancouver Symphony Orchestra, 30, 228, 234, 236
Vancouver Technical Secondary School, 123, 365
Van Dam, Monique, 203, 227-228, 231, 278, 291, 532, 539
van der Schyff, Dylan, 4-5, 298, 300, 303, 315, **316**, 317, 319, 326, 366
Van Gelder, Rudy, 504

601

Van Gelder Studio (Englewood Cliffs, New Jersey), 420, 503-505
Vannelli, Gino, 327-328
Varsity Hall (Sylvan Lake), 154, 168-169, **168-169**, 170
Varty, Alexander, 74, 537
Vaughan, Muriel, 344-345, **345, 355**
Vaughan, Sarah, 351, 477
Vetta Chamber Music, 465
Victoria, BC, 2, 6, 10, 62-64, 99, 112-114, 129, 235-236, 248, 250-251, 254-255, 270-272, 279, 288, 290, 292, 403, 443, 452, 454
Victoria College, 63, 113
Victoria Daily Times, 113
Vidas, Donna, 497
Village Vanguard (New York), 40, 221, 400, 505
Vinnegar, Leroy, 95
Vinson, Eddie "Cleanhead", 471
Vogue Theatre (Vancouver), 7, 179, 251, 267

W

Wahnapitae, 208-209
[The] Wailhouse (Richmond, BC), viii, 12, 28, 59, 125-126
Walker, Gavin, 59, 61, 67, 82, 90, 107, 112, 118, **119**, 133, 144, 146-147, 186, 193, 195, 221, 442, 539
Walker, Joanne, **83**
Walker, Margaret, 213
Wallace, Kent, **256**
Walters, Jan, 243-244, 246-248, 250, 267, 539
Walton, Cedar, 275, 331
The Warehouse Studio, **256**, 315, 337
Washburn, Jon, 213, 228
Washington, Dinah, 494
Washington, Peter, 413, 503-504, **505**

Wasserman, Jack, 87, 90, 109
Waters, Monty, 85, 133, 147
Watrous, Bill, 163
Watts, Ernie, 304-305
Waxwing, 293
Weather Report, 297, 299
Webb, Harry, 28, 56, 59, 84
Webb, Jessie, 536
Webb, Tilden, 5-6, 392, 449-469, **451, 462, 466**, 497, 529, 533, 535, 539
Webber, John, 6, 399, 413, 422-423
Wedman, Les, 84
Weeds, Betty, 364, 372, 387, 423
Weeds, Bill, 364-365, 372, **375**, 380, 385, **422, 423, 539**
Weeds, Cindy, 364
Weeds, Cory, ix, xvii, 4-8, 11, 23, 175-178, **176**, 201, 225, **256**, 257, 263-264, 269-270, 279-281, 283-286, 288, 291-293, 300-301, 303, 311, 314-315, 318, 328, 330-331, 333, 336, 338, 353-354, 361-424, 363, **375, 378, 395, 404, 410, 419, 422**, 426-429, 432-433, 435-436, **437**, 439, 443-444, 447, 449-450, 454-456, 459-460, 462-464, 466-469, 475-480, **476**, 483-484, 486, 492, 494-495, 498-499, 503-504, **503**, 521, 529, 530, 533, 535, 539
Weeds, Kayley, 423
Weeds, Noah, 362, 423
Weems, Rocky, 21, 183
Wess, Frank, 283
Westcoast Jazz Orchestra, 142
Western Conservatory of Music (Vancouver), 29
[The] Western Front (Vancouver), 4, 56, 76, 141, 220, 240, **273**, 352, 354, 532, 535, 537
Western Music (Vancouver), 83
Western Washington University (Bellingham), 297, 497, 501

Westlake College of Music (Hollywood), 156, 158-160
West Vancouver, 235, 259
We Three Queens, 357, **358**
Wheeler, Kenny, 246, 250, 252-254, 264, 453, 535
Whistler Jazz on the Mountain, 142
White, André, 176, **177**
White, Harold, 448
White, Perry, 234, 238, 240-241, 244, **245, 272**
White Rock, 482
[The] White Spots, 155
White Tower Pizza and Spaghetti House (Vancouver), 368
White, Walter, **245**
Whitehead, Kevin, viii
Whitman, Walt, 489
Wiertz, Al, 193, 213, 220-223, 532
Wightman, Jimmy, 2, 151, 156
Wikjord, Blaine, 5, 109, 221, **245**, 247, 270, **375**, 454, 539
Williams, Buster, 3, 195-196
Williams, David, 411
Williams (Young), Doreen, 28, 137, 391, 539
Williams, Dootsie, 191
Williams, Felicity, 489
Williams, Marcella (Choo Choo), 123, 187
Williams, Martin, xvi-xvii, 537
Williams, Tex, 214
Williams, Tennessee, 65
Williams, Tim, 197, 199, 539
Williams, Tony, 446-447, 453
Willis, Larry, 403
Wilner, Spike, 398, 539
Wilson, August, 200
Wilson, Cam, 354
Wilson, Nancy, 477

Wilson, Tony, 262, 293
Winnipeg, 26, 80, 185, 270
Winstone, Norma, 252, 512, 515, 517, 521
WISE Hall (Vancouver), 279, 483
Witherspoon, Jimmy, 189
WJCT, 327
W.K. Chop Suey (Vancouver), 234
Wold, Al, 325-326
Wolff, Francis, 431
Wonder, Stevie, 158
Wong, Audie, 145, 539
Wong, George, 19
Wong Kee (Vancouver), 280
Wong, Miles, 518
Wong, Rod, 58-59, 122-123, 539
Wood, Bud, 82
Woods, Parker, 518
Woodward's (Vancouver), 11, 364
Wordsworth, William, 489
Worst, Rene, 223, 226, **276**, 539
WOW Jazz Orchestra, 372, 414
Wright, Bill, 137
Wright, Dave, 26
Wright, Donna, 137
Wylie, Wilf, 56

Y
Yardbird Suite (Edmonton), 18, 115, 127
Yeager, Henry, 194
Ye Olde Cellar, 91, 198
Yeo, Margaret, 168
Yogananda, Paramahansa, 227
Yoshi's (San Francisco), 248
Young, Dave, 36
Young (Williams), Doreen, 28, 137, 391, 539
Young, Henry, 185-186, 219, 539
Young, Larry, 314
Young, Lester, 61, 125, 476
Young, Trummy, 1, 123
Yukon Arts Centre (Whitehorse), 336

Z
Zawinul, Joe, 195, 473, 475
Zenón, Miguel, 505
Zorn, John, 53

ABOUT THE AUTHOR

CHRIS WONG is a lifelong music nerd, who is an aficionado of jazz and many other genres. His affinity for writing about music emerged in high school, when Chris received his first byline for a review of the punk band the K-Tels. While writing for the University of British Columbia's *The Ubyssey* student newspaper, he landed an in-person interview with Dizzy Gillespie, which had some tense moments. Chris went on to cover music and other subjects for the *Vancouver Sun, Georgia Straight, Vancouver Courier,* and other publications. He has also written liner notes. It has been an honour for him to write about both international jazz greats and local heroes.

Photo by Amanda Palmer.

Journeys to the Bandstand is a passion project that Chris honed for more than a decade. This is his first book. Born in Regina, Chris lives in Vancouver, Canada with his wife Maria Chu and they have two children, both involved in the arts: Miles Wong and Sarah Wong.

Printed in the USA
CPSIA information can be obtained
at www.ICGtesting.com
LVHW091935230424
778232LV00006B/318